REALITY CHECK

The Distributional Impact

of Privatization

in Developing Countries

CENTER FOR GLOBAL DEVELOPMENT

REALITY CHECK

The Distributional Impact

of Privatization

in Developing Countries

edited by John Nellis

and Nancy Birdsall

Washington, DC

October 2005

9 85 338 1

John Nellis co-directed the Center for Global Development's project to examine the effects of privatization on income and wealth distribution in developing and transitional economies. From 1984 to 2000, he was at the World Bank, where he dealt with privatization, public enterprise reform, transition from a planned to a market system, and governance and public-sector management issues. Nellis worked on these topics in some 50 countries, particularly in sub-Saharan Africa and the transition states in Eastern and Central Europe and the former Soviet Union. While at the Bank, he authored or coauthored four books and 30 other publications on the above topics. His last position at the Bank was director of the private sector development department. Before joining the Bank, Nellis was professor of public administration at the Maxwell School of Syracuse University and professor of international affairs at Carleton University in Ottawa, Canada. He spent six years in Africa with the Ford Foundation—in Tanzania, Kenya, and Tunisia. His recent publications include articles in *World Development, World Bank Research Observer,* and *Privatization Barometer.*

Nancy Birdsall is the founding president of the Center for Global Development. Before launching the center, she served for three years as senior associate and director of the Economic Reform Project at the Carnegie Endowment for International Peace. Her work at Carnegie focused on issues of globalization and inequality, as well as on the reform of the international financial institutions. From 1993 to 1998, Birdsall was executive vice president of the Inter-American Development Bank, where she oversaw a $30 billion public and private loan portfolio. Before joining the Inter-American Development Bank, Birdsall spent 14 years in research, policy, and management positions at the World Bank, including as director of the policy research department. She is the author, coauthor, or editor of more than a dozen books, including *Financing Development: The Power of*

Regionalism (2004) and *Delivering on Debt Relief: From IMF Gold to a New Aid Architecture* (2002).

CENTER FOR GLOBAL DEVELOPMENT
1776 Massachusetts Avenue, NW
Third Floor
Washington, DC 20036
(202) 416-0700   FAX: (202) 416-0750

Nancy Birdsall, *President*

Typesetting by Circle Graphics, Inc.
Printing by Kirby Lithographic Company, Inc.

Printed in the United States of America
07 06 05   5 4 3 2 1

Library of Congress Cataloging-in-Publication Data

Reality check: the distributional impact of privatization in developing countrie / [edited] by Nancy Birdsall and John Nellis.
    p. cm
    Includes bibliographical references and index.
    ISBN 1-933286-00-8
    1. Privatization—Developing countries.
I. Birdsall, Nancy. II. Nellis, John R. III. Title.

HD4420.8.R43 2004
338.9'25'091724—dc22   200458587

The views expressed in this publication are those of the authors. This publication is part of the overall program of the Center, as endorsed by its Board of Directors, but does not necessarily reflect the views of individual members of the Board or the Advisory Committee.

Contents

Preface   **vii**

1   Privatization Reality Check: Distributional Effects on
Developing Countries   1
Nancy Birdsall and John Nellis

I   **Cases from Latin America**

2   Paradox and Perception: Evidence from Four
Latin American Countries   33
David McKenzie and Dilip Mookherjee

3   Inequality and Welfare Changes:
Evidence from Nicaragua   85
Samuel Freije Rodríguez and Luis Rivas

4   Bolivian Capitalization and Privatization:
Approximation to an Evaluation   123
Gover Barja, David McKenzie, and Miguel Urquiola

5   Argentina's Privatization: Effects on Income Distribution   179
Huberto M. Ennis and Santiago M. Pinto

6   Peru after Privatization: Are Telephone Consumers
Better Off?   219
Máximo Torero, Enrique Schroth, and Alberto Pascó-Font

7   Distribution of Assets and Income in Brazil:
New Evidence   253
Roberto Macedo

8   Latin America's Infrastructure Experience:
     Policy Gaps and the Poor   281
     Antonio Estache

II   **Cases from Asia and Transitional Economies**

9   Outcomes of the Russian Model   297
     Svetlana Pavlovna Glinkina

10   Privatization's Effects on Social Welfare in Ukraine:
     The SigmaBleyzer Experience   325
     *Michael Bleyzer, Edilberto Segura, Neal Sigada,
     Diana Smachtina, and Victor Gekker*

11   China's Shareholding Reform: Effects on Enterprise
     Performance   353
     Gary H. Jefferson, Su Jian, Jiang Yuan, and Yu Xinhua

12   Rethinking Privatization in Sri Lanka: Distribution
     and Governance   389
     Malathy Knight-John and P. P. A. Wasantha Athukorala

About the Contributors   **427**

Index   **435**

Preface

Since its beginnings four years ago, the Center for Global Development has put a priority on understanding the effects of market reforms on the well-being of people in developing countries. Among the most controversial of market reforms has been the privatization of state-owned enterprises. The international financial institutions have been consistently and strongly encouraging privatization of inefficient state enterprises, in part because these enterprises were eating up scarce public funds. Throughout the 1990s, privatization was strongly embraced in Eastern Europe and the former Soviet Union as a key part of the transition to a market economy; it was widely adopted in Latin America and throughout Asia and Africa as well. What is surprising is how little attention, before and after the fact, has been paid to the distributional implications of the privatization movement. It is particularly puzzling given the nature of the current backlash in so many settings against further privatization—a backlash nurtured by the widespread view that the effects of privatization have been to enrich the already rich and powerful, and sometimes corrupt, at the expense of the majority.

This book makes a start at rectifying the situation. It brings together a comprehensive set of country studies on the effects of privatization on people—winners and losers in different income, employment, and education groups. The studies are sophisticated and careful; they exploit household-level data on changes in the income of different groups affected by privatization and country data on profits, changes in public tax revenue from privatized enterprises, and shifts in pension and other liabilities. It addresses the big questions: Are the poorest households paying more for water, power, and other basic services? Did those who lost jobs suffer permanent declines in income? Were state assets sold at prices that were too low, and who benefited from the resulting windfalls? Was the process, in laypersons' terms, "fair"?

Some readers will be surprised at the general conclusion: that privatization has, in many cases, been a reasonably good thing, including for the poor. Others will be surprised at its limited effects—for good or for ill— and at the heavy dependence of the results on the setting, the timing, the type of enterprise, and the initial conditions—who was benefiting to start with. Almost all readers will want to understand the potential for future privatizations—which remain on the policy agenda despite public resistance and continuing controversy—to enhance competition and at the same time, be fundamentally more just and fair.

The idea for this book began when I was a senior associate at the Carnegie Endowment for International Peace working on issues of inequality around the world. I was fortunate to be able to persuade John Nellis, then retiring from the World Bank after more than a decade of advising, guiding, and worrying over privatization throughout the developing world, especially in Russia and other countries of the former Soviet Union, to collaborate with me in unbundling the effects of privatization on people. I am enormously grateful to John for his wisdom, his readiness to share his experience, and his overall leadership on the ambitious project, which this book represents.

We are grateful to the Carnegie Endowment for its initial sponsorship and to the Tinker Foundation for its early support of the country studies in Latin America. We thank Nancy Truitt at the Tinker Foundation for her ideas on the proposed scope and approach of the project. We are also indebted to Christine Wallich and her then-colleagues at the Asian Development Bank (ADB), who sponsored several of the Asia country studies, and to Michael Lim of the ADB for his comments on the initial drafts of the studies on China and Sri Lanka. We were fortunate to benefit from the collaboration and contributions of a program on privatization at the Inter-American Development Bank (IADB) developed under the leadership of Nora Lustig (now director of the Center for Studies on Globalization and Development and a Board member of the Center). We also thank Alberto Chong of the IADB for his willingness to have the IADB cohost our February 2003 conference at the Center, where contributors presented draft studies; for his generosity in sharing information and studies he had conducted on related aspects of privatization; and for his comments on several chapters in the study. Among the many who provided critical and constructive comments at the 2003 conference were Navroz Dubash of the World Resources Institute, Carol Graham of the Brookings Institution, Albert Keidel, then at the US Treasury, Minxin Pei of the Carnegie Endowment for International Peace, Louise Shelley of American University, John Williamson of the Institute for International Economics, and Ambassador Kenneth Yalowitz of American University. John and I also thank the two senior scholars who reviewed and commented on the entire manuscript draft: Johannes Linn of the Brookings Institution, who, as former vice president for Eastern Europe and Central Asia at the World Bank, knows the issues well, and William Megginson, holder of the Rainbolt Chair of Finance at the University of Oklahoma's Price College of Business.

The book could not have been completed without the help of Sabeen Hassanali, formerly of the Center, who has been deeply involved in every aspect of the overall project, who helped make the project conference a success, and who has overseen editing and production details with many far-flung authors. I am particularly grateful to our production and publishing team at the Center, especially Noora-Lisa Aberman and Yvonne Siu, as well as to Marla Banov, Madona Devasahayam, and Valerie Norville at the Institute for International Economics.

We thank the scholarly journals *Economia* and *World Development* for permission to use two of these essays, the first versions of which they published in 2003.

In the end of course an edited book relies on the contributions of its contributors. John and I are enormously grateful to our colleagues for their willingness and ability to tackle an issue that is not amenable to simple and clear analysis. Surely one reason for the dearth of earlier work on the distributional implications of privatization programs is that there is no consensus about the methods and the data to address it—and thus no guarantee of success in the narrow research sense. We are grateful to our contributors for their commitment to excellence and the evidence in a controversial area and for their willingness and ability to combine the most advanced theoretical and empirical methods with practical policy insight.

NANCY BIRDSALL
President
September 2005

The Center for Global Development

The Center for Global Development is an independent, nonprofit policy research organization dedicated to reducing global poverty and inequality and to making globalization work for the poor. Through a combination of research and strategic outreach, the Center actively engages policymakers and the public to influence the policies of the United States, other rich countries, and such institutions as the World Bank, the International Monetary Fund (IMF), and the World Trade Organization (WTO) to improve the economic and social development prospects in poor countries. The Center's Board of Directors bears overall responsibility for the Center and includes distinguished leaders of nongovernmental organizations, former officials, business executives, and some of the world's leading scholars of development. The Center receives advice on its research and policy programs from the Board and from an Advisory Committee that comprises respected development specialists and advocates. The Center's president works with the Board, the Advisory Committee, and the Center's senior staff in setting the research and program priorities, and approves all formal publications. The Center is supported by an initial significant financial contribution from Edward W. Scott Jr. and by funding from philanthropic foundations and other organizations.

Privatization Reality Check: Distributional Effects in Developing Countries

NANCY BIRDSALL and JOHN NELLIS

Privatization has not been a popular reform. Economic assessments of its effects on economic welfare and growth in developing and transition economies have generally been positive. At the same time, allegations of political chicanery and corruption in Russia and Malaysia, fiscal mismanagement in Brazil, escalating prices in Argentina, and loss of jobs in numerous countries have sullied privatization's reputation, even among proponents of the liberalization of the last two decades. Thus, Nobel laureate Joseph Stiglitz campaigns for slower and more deliberate privatization, while critics of the larger liberalizing agenda—known as the Washington Consensus—conclude that privatization should be entirely opposed.

At the heart of much of the criticism is the belief that privatization has been unfair—hurting the poor, the disenfranchised, and beleaguered workers, and benefiting the privileged and powerful. Privatization, it is claimed, throws masses of people out of work or forces them to accept jobs with lower pay, less security, and fewer benefits; raises, too far and too fast, the prices of goods and services sold; provides opportunities to enrich the agile and corrupt; and generally makes the rich richer and the poor poorer.[1]

Nancy Birdsall is the president of the Center of Global Development. John Nellis is a senior fellow at the Center for Global Development. The authors are grateful to colleagues William Cline, William Easterly, and John Williamson for their comments on earlier drafts. This chapter draws on Birdsall and Nellis (2003).

1. A more technical critique of privatization attributes perceived efficiency and performance benefits to market reform and the enhancement of competition, not ownership change. For example, Tandon (1995, 229–30) argues: "... there are, of course, many cases where privatization appears to have 'resulted' in efficiency improvement; in most of these cases, however, the privatization appears to have been contemporaneous with deregulation or other types of competition-enhancing measures."

A major complaint is that, even if privatization contributes to improved efficiency and financial performance, as some contest, it negatively affects distribution of wealth, income, and political power. This perception is widespread and growing: 63 percent of people surveyed in the spring of 2001 in 17 countries of Latin America disagreed or strongly disagreed with the statement: "The privatization of State companies has been beneficial. . . ." The extent of disagreement was 6 percent higher than in 2000 and 20 percent higher than in 1998.[2] More than 60 percent of Sri Lankans interviewed in 2000 opposed the privatization of remaining state-owned firms. Similar expressions of popular dissatisfaction with privatization, of equal or greater magnitude, were found in transition countries generally and Russia in particular.

Some popular perceptions and critical assertions are accurate—mistakes have been made; promises have been broken; however, others are inaccurate. One can argue that the concrete outcomes of privatization have, in many cases, been better than people think or that privatization may not be the true cause of the problems people encounter. Nonetheless, perceptions count greatly if they result in political opposition sufficient to slow, halt, or reverse a process that would bring efficiency and growth gains to a society—gains that could, in principle, be fairly shared using tax or other policy instruments.

Moreover, the distributional effects of privatization matter because inequality matters in at least three ways:

- Most societies possess and exercise implicit limits on their tolerance for inequality, independent of its effects on growth and efficiency.

- Mounting evidence suggests that inequality can and does hinder growth, particularly in developing economies where institutions and markets are weak.[3]

---

2. Latinbarometer conducted interviews in April and May (2001), and survey results were presented in August of the same year; see Latinbarometer (2001). Results showed that negative perceptions about privatization had increased greatly in certain countries (e.g., Argentina, Brazil, and Colombia) and slightly in others (e.g., Chile, Ecuador, and Venezuela); however, in all 17 countries surveyed, the percentage had grown. For a general discussion of dissatisfaction with liberalizing economic reform in Latin America, see Lora and Panizza (2002).

3. Aghion, Caroli, and Garcia-Penalosa (1999) discuss the growing theoretical and empirical literature regarding this point. Barro (2000) finds that the inequality effect on growth is negative only in developing countries—a finding consistent with the likelihood that the effect operates where markets and institutions are weak and government policy either reinforces or fails to offset those factors; Easterly (2002) and Birdsall and Londoño (1997) emphasize the relevance of asset distribution.

■ Increasingly, it is evident that inequality can perpetuate itself by affecting the nature and pace of economic policy and locking in unproductive political arrangements.[4]

This book presents a set of country and analytical studies on the distributional effects of privatization programs in developing and transition economies. The cases cover privatization programs in Latin America (Argentina, Bolivia, Brazil, Mexico, Nicaragua, and Peru) and an eclectic set of non-Latin American countries: China, Russia, Sri Lanka, and Ukraine. We examine a relatively understudied issue and derive lessons for minimizing any trade-offs between the efficiency and equity outcomes of the process or (as we hypothesize is also possible) maximizing any complementarities. Reynolds (1985) points out that, as an economist, one cannot pretend to make any value judgment about the right trade-off between efficiency and equity outcomes. However, one can attempt to assess the nature of any trade-off or complementarity to enlighten the public debate about policy and program decisions ultimately made in the political arena.

During the 1980s and 1990s, a wave of privatizations swept across the developing world. Including the many enterprises either partially or fully privatized in the transition economies, the number of divested firms now exceeds 100,000; the total value of assets transferred has been enormous, particularly in Latin America, East Asia, and the transition region (less so in South Asia, the Middle East, and sub-Saharan Africa). Despite the massive shift to private ownership, a surprising number of firms and assets remain in state hands, particularly in China and Vietnam, but also in India, and the African and transition countries, where many large, high-value infrastructure firms have not yet been sold. Thus, information on how to conduct privatization in an appropriate, acceptable manner is still of great value.

Below, we outline a simple framework within which to consider the efficiency and equity gains and losses of privatization. The framework provides a means of thinking about the effects of privatization at the economywide level (of course, it is also possible to assess privatization's effects at the firm and sectoral levels, which many other chapters in this book do). In that context, efficiency refers to the extent to which an economy maximizes output, given inputs of labor and human and physical capital; while equity refers to the extent to which the resulting output is distributed among the population or would be distributed were there equal opportunity (e.g., across households, independent of their income, ethnicity,

---

4. As Hellman, Jones, and Kaufman (2000) documented in the Russian case, initial distribution of resources and property rights to a limited set of actors, in a situation with few institutional impediments to translating economic power into political power, created a group able to block subsequent competition-enhancing and redistributive reforms. Nellis (1999) offers a similar argument.

Figure 1.1 Equity and efficiency: Competitive versus imperfect market

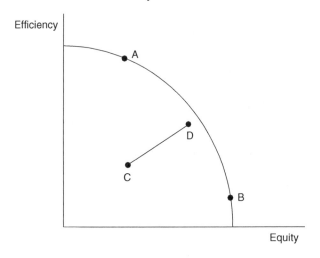

and gender composition).[5] Following their outline of the general framework, we summarize literature on privatization's overall efficiency effects; these are most commonly considered at the firm level, in terms of changes in performance post-sale, gains or losses to aggregate welfare, and competitiveness and prospects for economic growth. The summary of evidence on efficiency effects at the firm level provides useful and necessary background to any assessment of privatization's likely effects on equity at the economywide level. Using the general framework, we then reflect on what is known from theory and existing studies on distributional issues, with special emphasis on this book's case studies and analyses. These findings provide the basis for our conclusions about the distributional effects of the recent wave of privatizations in developing and transition economies.

General Framework

Economists usually frame the question of equity or distribution within the context of a trade-off with efficiency or growth. At the production frontier of a perfectly competitive economy, without any externalities, information asymmetries, or other problems of missing or imperfect markets, such a trade-off is likely (figure 1.1).

---

5. Thus, equity refers not to the distribution of income as an outcome, but to the distribution of opportunity—the latter allowing for differences in motivation, work habits, and other characteristics across individuals that are, in principle, independent of social or economic standing in a society, as well as race, gender, and ethnicity.

At that production frontier, the only efficient means of redistribution is through lump-sum transfers that have no effect on the incentives of economic agents or prices. An efficient economy can be highly inequitable (point A) or equitable (point B), often as a function of some initial allocation of assets (e.g., financial, physical, or human capital) that generate income. Any move along the frontier will lead to either more efficiency and less equity or vice versa, the definition of a trade-off.

In an imperfectly competitive economy, however, such a trade-off is not a necessity. At point C, the economy could potentially move toward both greater efficiency and equity (e.g., to point D).[6] Most developing and transition economies are less efficient than those of industrialized countries. Their low incomes result not only from limited resources; they often fail to use their resources well because of a lack of enforceable property rights, policy failures (e.g., highly distortionary tax systems and labor market rigidities), outright corruption, and protected monopolies that state enterprises often represent.[7] Historical injustices, civil conflict, political instability, crushing levels of disease, and frequent natural disasters may also play their role in keeping economies more or less permanently inside the efficiency frontier.

For any given productive capacity, many of these economies are also highly inequitable—either because of government or policy failures that sustain insider privileges, or corruption or historically driven concentrations of wealth in land, oil, or other assets. Of course, a society could also be inefficient and equitable, such as Cuba, or highly efficient but also relatively inequitable, such as the United States (figure 1.2).

In most developing and transition economies well inside the production frontier, there is no *necessary* trade-off between increased efficiency and resulting economic growth on the one hand, and increasing equity on the other; thus, it should be possible to implement privatization transactions (firm by firm) in ways that promote both equity and efficiency. For example, to the extent that privatization reduces monopoly rents held by the wealthy, it is likely to increase both efficiency and equity in the overall economy.[8]

---

6. Birdsall, Ross, and Sabot (1995) argue that lack of trade-off explains why several East Asian countries, with relatively low inequality, grew rapidly from the 1960s through the 1980s, compared to Latin American countries, with their high inequality; see Alfaro, Bradford, and Briscoe (1998) on privatization's effects on the water sector and James (1998) on partial privatization of pension systems.

7. Thus, as Easterly (2001) notes with compelling examples, using foreign aid to provide additional investment capital or foreign exchange will not necessarily yield additional product or growth.

8. For the theoretical underpinnings of this view, see Aghion, Caroli, and Garcia-Penalosa (1999) and Benabou (1996); for empirical refinements, see Barro (2000) and Birdsall, Ross, and Sabot (1995).

Figure 1.2   Relative efficiency and equity of US and Cuban economies

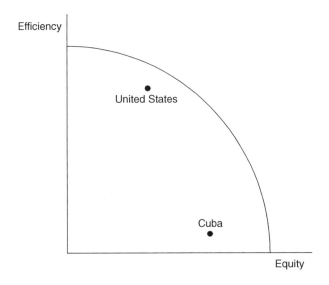

The structure and outcome of each privatization event comprise only one factor in the overall story of privatization's effect on equity (or distribution) at the country level. Conditions before privatization matter—the more inequitable the initial situation, the greater the scope for improvement in equity. The same is true with respect to initial inefficiency (figure 1.3). The environment following privatization—degree of competition and regulatory arrangements—can and often does reinforce or alter the preprivatization path.

Complicating matters further, the one-time privatization event—even if extended over several years—may help determine the postprivatization policy and institutional environment, and thus a society's long-term path. For example, mass privatization efforts in transition economies were justified on the grounds that privatization was necessary—perhaps even sufficient—to create competition and induce increased firm (and overall economic) efficiency. (In figure 1.4, one would move from point A to point B via privatization and then from point B to point C in the competitive environment after privatization). However, the unanticipated outcome in several countries, most notably Russia, was that the event initially increased the economy's inefficiency, but also locked in insider privileges (moving from point A to point D); those insider privileges included competition-eroding corruption, which undermined efficiency (Stiglitz 1999a, b).

Because the postprivatization path of distribution in a society is neither unidirectional nor necessarily fully determined by transfer of ownership, any single snapshot assessment of where a society is, relative to where it

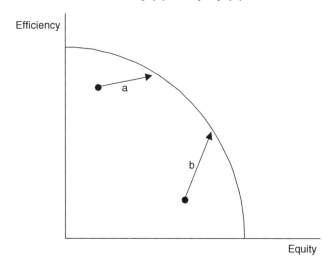

Figure 1.3   Privatization with relatively more efficiency (a) or equity (b)

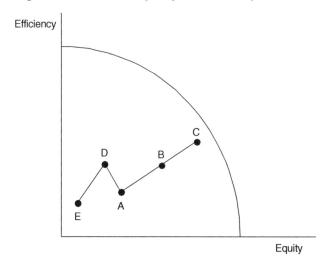

Figure 1.4   Potential postprivatization paths

was, may be a poor indicator of privatization's long-term effects. The outcome will be shaped by the amount of time passed since the process began, the extent to which the process affected the environment following privatization, and a host of independent factors after privatization that can affect the direction of the path (e.g., the efficiency gain at point D was temporary).

We take it for granted that the central objective of privatization in developing and transition economies, as well as in industrialized economies, is to secure efficiency gains for the economy as a whole (although some in the transition region have interpreted privatization as a primarily political act, required to sever links between the state and productive enterprises). Where distributional issues have been considered, they have generally been devised within the context of smoothing out the process to make it politically more palatable (e.g., when employees of enterprises to be privatized are given special deals on obtaining shares in the new firm, or when sellers oblige new owners to accept postprivatization conditions, such as service guarantees for less profitable markets, commit to certain levels of investment, or maintain employee numbers for a specified time). The distinction between a general distributional goal and a technique to obtain support is not always clear. For example, the voucher programs of Eastern Europe and Russia and Bolivia's capitalization program aimed ostensibly at adequate distribution of the "patrimony," although they also were designed to mute political opposition to reform.

Behind the usually paramount goal of improving efficiency has been the implicit assumption that government could and should use more traditional, direct instruments for redistribution, through tax and expenditure policies. Of course, that assumption may not always have been borne out because of political and economic constraints independent of privatization per se. That raises the normative question: Should privatization be exploited as a more direct and less costly opportunity for redistribution or should the likelihood of the process exacerbating inequality at least be minimized?

Some familiar examples illustrate the logic of the framework (we do not claim that these vignettes are absolutely accurate in all details). With its highly planned economy, the former Soviet Union was initially inefficient, though reasonably equitable, because everyone was comparably badly off (figure 1.5, point A). Privatization in Russia may well have made the economy simultaneously more efficient and more inequitable, as some former state assets were acquired by a relatively small group of insiders (path a). The resulting concentration could further worsen equity and stall, or even reverse, efficiency gains as new insiders concentrate on asset stripping rather than productivity-enhancing investments (path b). However, subsequent policy shifts, including a start on controlling corruption, could bring increased equity (by eliminating favors) and efficiency (as the elimination of implicit insider subsidies yields a more competitive environment [path c]).

In Peru, a state-run electricity utility could be inefficient initially, with poor management, high technical losses, poor revenue collection, and irrational pricing. It could also contribute to inequality, providing virtually no services (in effect, services at an infinite price) to poor neighborhoods, while underpricing or failing to charge and collect fees from middle-class and wealthy neighborhoods or large industrial users (figure 1.6, point A). Privatization could increase efficiency dramatically at the enterprise level

Figure 1.5 Efficiency and equity gains and losses: Former Soviet Union and Russia

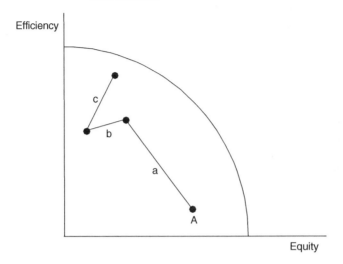

Figure 1.6 Efficiency and equity gains and losses: Peru's electricity sector

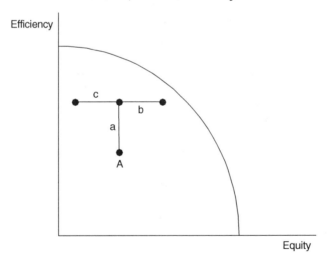

via technical-efficiency gains and, at the economywide level, by stemming the hemorrhage of publicly financed subsidies, thereby promoting responsible fiscal management.

It is easy to imagine offsetting the effects on overall equity (path a); they could result from a combination of higher prices for the previously insulated middle class, with improved access (and a lower than "infinite" price) for the poor. Some of the poor (e.g., those in rural areas) would remain unserved and thus relatively worse off than other poor, though not in any absolute sense. The urban poor—those whose prior access through illegal hookups was eliminated, a common outcome of electricity privatization in Latin America and Asia—might be absolutely worse off as well. In subsequent years, equity gains could be reinforced or reversed, depending on political pressures and regulatory capacity in an institutional and technical sense (paths b and c).

In the United Kingdom, privatization of the electricity sector may provide large efficiency gains initially; however, nonaggressive or incomplete regulation in the years immediately after a sale may mean that the new owners, not consumers, will capture most of the initial gains (figure 1.7, path a). Moreover, if this or any other privatization results in layoffs of relatively low-skilled, low-paid workers, the wage gap between skilled and unskilled workers will likely increase as the supply of the latter in the larger market increases.

In Brazil, privatization of state telecommunications monopolies may bring huge efficiency gains, with greatly increased coverage, access, and quality for consumers and productive sectors for which communications is a critical input. However, underpricing of the firm to ensure successful sale may mean that middle-income taxpayers lose out and that windfall gains to a few new owners increase overall concentration of assets (figure 1.8, path a).[9] If those windfall gains go primarily to foreigners, the domestic distribution of wealth and income may not be affected directly; however, they may spawn a sense of unfairness in the society as a whole. Selling governments could squander the fiscal windfall because it temporarily relieves the budget constraint on acquiring more debt. This could lead to subsequent increases in interest rates or reductions in social and other expenditures that are relatively progressive; these second-stage, indirect effects could exacerbate the initial inequity (path b) (Macedo 2000).

The above framework and simplified examples illustrate that the distributional effects of privatization cannot be easily predicted. The effects on equity depend on at least three factors: initial conditions, sale event, and the postprivatization political and economic environment. The privatization event may reinforce or undermine aspects of the environment that are conducive to equity, may simply reflect that environment, or may be independent of it. Judging those effects may also depend on the point along the path at which one measures the outcome. In the end, the question is empirical, unlikely to yield to any simple generalization across countries and over

---

9. Governments often underprice firms sold through share issues to ensure the sale will go forward. Failure to meet the reserve price is an embarrassment; thus, major purchasers get a bargain. However, another reason for underpricing is to encourage local, first-time small investors to participate. Paradoxically, a mechanism devised with at least some distributional purpose may add to overall inequity.

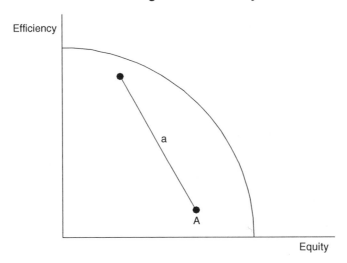

Figure 1.7   Efficiency and equity gains and losses: United Kingdom's electricity sector

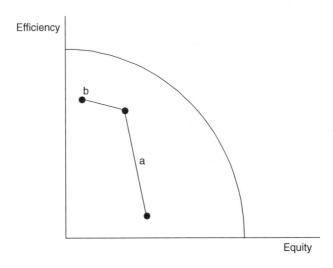

Figure 1.8   Efficiency and equity gains and losses: Brazil's telecommunications sector

time. Thus, understanding the distributional effects of privatization requires assessing real cases and couching those cases in the larger context of their political, economic, and historical environment—precisely the approach undertaken in this book.

At the same time, our framework reflects the view that, in most settings, particularly in nonindustrialized countries, efficiency-enhancing privatization has also left room for equity enhancement. If a trade-off has occurred, it might have been avoided or diminished by an alternative process or earlier, more vigorous attention paid to constructing a different environment after privatization (regarding competition, regulation, and other factors).

Overall Economic Record

On the whole, privatization has proven its economic worth. The shift to private ownership, with few exceptions, has improved firm performance. This finding has held true in most countries, including poor ones and former socialist economies in the transition region. After privatization, profitability has generally increased, often substantially, as have output, dividends, and investment. In their extensive literature review, covering 65 empirical studies at the firm level, and in firms within and across countries, Megginson and Netter (2001, 380) conclude that "privately-owned firms are more efficient and more profitable than otherwise comparable, state-owned firms."[10]

Privatization's economywide effects on the government budget and on growth, employment, and investment are less solidly established. The most elaborate study to date, a review of 18 privatizing countries (Davis et al. 2000), reported substantial gross receipts from privatization, accounting for nearly 2 percent of annual GDP. Governments have generally ended up with about half that amount, reflecting the high costs of clean-ups and sales. Even 1 percent of GDP is substantial; however, the long-run fiscal effects on government revenue generally come not from sales proceeds (resulting from a one-time sale of an asset), but from elimination of preprivatization subsidies to state enterprises and subsequent increased tax revenues from more profitable and productive private enterprises.

Such governments as Ivory Coast, Mexico, and Mozambique received, in the first few years following sales, more from privatized firms in taxes than from direct proceeds of sales. In Bolivia, for example, a flow-of-funds analysis shows a US$429 million return to government in the first four years following sales, despite the fact that the government did not receive any sales proceeds.[11] In addition, Davis et al. (2000) conclude that markets and investors regard privatization as a positive signal of the political likelihood

---

10. The studies range from single-firm case studies to assessments of various privatizations in a single country (e.g., 218 in Mexico) to surveys of all available literature on an entire set of countries (e.g., review of the results of privatization in 26 transition economies).

11. The Bolivians capitalized a group of the largest state firms by selling 50 percent of equity to strategic investors, who committed to investing the total sales price into the firms. For details, see Barja, McKenzie, and Urquiola (chapter 4, this volume).

that a government will stick with its overall reform program, implying somewhat higher investment rates in the economy overall.

This is not to say that privatization always works well everywhere. Studies on the effects of privatization are more numerous in data-rich, industrialized and middle-income economies than in low-income countries. In the latter, privatization has proven more difficult to launch, and less likely to generate quick, positive effects. In certain settings—Armenia and Moldova, for example—privatization has not yielded visible performance improvements. Even in countries where the process has succeeded overall, not every privatization improves firm performance. In three comparable studies examining 204 privatizations in 41 countries, 20 to 33 percent of privatized firms registered slight or no improvement, or, in some cases, worsening situations (Megginson and Netter 2001, 355–56). While a success rate of 66 percent to 80 percent is good, inherited conditions place some firms beyond hope of internal reform even with new owners because markets and policy frameworks are too poor for ownership change alone to turn the tide.

Partly because it is not a panacea, controversy continues about the effects—and thus the desirability—of privatization, particularly in countries where complementary reforms are not in place, competition is limited, and regulatory and supervisory capacity are embryonic. These country conditions are especially relevant for natural monopolies and in such sectors as banking. Nonetheless, evidence shows that privatization has been among the more successful of liberalizing reforms; that is, in many more cases than not, it has yielded good returns to new private owners, freed the state of a heavy administrative and unproductive financial burden, provided governments with a one-time fiscal boost, and helped sustain a larger process of market-enhancing economic reforms.

These results are encouraging—if not surprising—since most developing countries and transition economies are well inside the optimal production frontier. Because of policy distortions and government failures, there is often ample room for increasing efficiency by reducing the state's stranglehold on resources and making room for competition that fosters individual entrepreneurship, motivates workers, and supports overall productivity gains.

We emphasize this broad conclusion about the efficiency effects of privatization, in part, to stress that assessing the distributional question does not imply an attack on privatization per se, even—or especially in—welfare terms. In certain cases, privatization has produced both increased income and wealth for all citizens, while increasing inequitable distribution of that income and wealth. Thus, it usually makes no sense to forgo absolute gains for all because of an increase in relative disparities. We neither deny the need to reform grossly inefficient and financially burdensome public enterprises nor imply that deficiencies of such enterprises could somehow easily be corrected without social pain or economic cost.

Rather, these case studies suggest that, in the process of privatizing, opportunities have been missed for minimizing equity losses or maximizing equity gains. In some cases, lost opportunities have probably reduced the efficiency gains of the privatization process (e.g., by excluding potentially more competitive bidders) or long-term gains to the economy (e.g., where limiting sales to nationals has permanently locked out potential bidders). It may be that privatization's unpopularity is not only a political constraint to sustaining privatization and other efficiency-enhancing reforms, but rooted in a populist view of what is fair. It may be that there is room for a better overall deal—one that is both fairer and more efficient. Determining what has happened regarding distribution and examining the possibility that more equitable outcomes could have been produced are the principal themes of this volume's case studies.

Potential Distributional Shifts

At issue is how privatization affects household consumption and welfare across income groups. Household consumption depends on both income and prices. Income, in turn, depends on assets—labor, human capital, land ownership, and other physical or financial capital—and its return. Areas in which one might encounter distributional shifts resulting from ownership change are discussed below.

Asset Distribution

Privatization usually involves a shift from an asset owned (in theory) by taxpayers as a whole to one owned by private persons or firms. Whether the shift in ownership reduces or increases overall equity in a society depends, in part, on the extent to which the price received by the selling state adequately reflects the asset's underlying value. For example, if the seller underprices the asset to ensure a quick sale, equity will likely decline, at least in the short term. The effects of change in ownership on the long-term income distribution between taxpayers and new owners ultimately depends on both the initial price and postsale stream of value the asset produces. Privatization might be arranged to spread direct (i.e., share) ownership widely among the affected population. It may also confer, or permanently deny, hitherto unrealized pension benefits, creating or eliminating an employee asset.

Return on Assets: Labor

Privatization can change the return on assets, such as labor, in a way that affects income distribution. For example, low-income workers might be more likely to be laid off. These dismissed low-income workers might have a more difficult time finding alternative employment, or the employment they obtain might be less remunerative than the work they left or that generally obtained by higher-income, dismissed workers. Conversely, if privatization is an important element in an overall reform program that leads to higher growth and general job expansion, then previously unemployed or poorly paid workers might gain employment or higher-paying jobs.

Proponents of privatization suggest that poor past performance of public firms requires a period of restructuring, including cuts in employment, a portion of which might occur before sale. However, the job-reduction phase would be temporary; under more dynamic private ownership, total employment numbers would eventually recover and even surpass the number originally employed. On the other hand, critics, particularly union leaders, allege that cost-cutting measures in preparation for sale or by new private owners fall disproportionately—and unfairly—on workers. Labor leaders argue that poor management and government policies are the major causes of the financially troubled state of public firms, while labor is asked to pay the price of reform.

Return on Assets: Physical Capital

Privatization can also change return on the physical capital reallocated. If new private ownership is more efficient than the state, the return on pre-existing capital or profits will rise. This can constitute a legitimate reward for new effort or entrepreneurial skill, with spillover benefits (new jobs at higher wages) from the owners of capital to the economy overall. Conversely, if the new owners further neglect or strip the assets, value can be subtracted and equity could easily suffer, as firms scale back or close, and more jobs are lost.

Pricing and Access

Privatization can affect pricing differentially across income groups. On the one hand, prices could fall. If increased competition is part of or accompanies change of ownership, the private owner might be forced to offer lower prices. If private management is more efficient, savings might be passed on to consumers. Conversely, prices could increase if government action had previously held them below cost-covering levels; new private owners move to end illegal connections to services and collect from previously tolerated, delinquent customers; or bodies regulating privatized infrastructure firms are weak or ineffective. The distributional effects of price shifts will depend on the extent to which consumption of the goods and services in question varies by income group and whether consumption levels or consumer categories face different prices. In the case of infrastructure, it will also depend on the density and competence of regulatory bodies, which, in theory, protect consumers from the abuse of natural monopoly power.

Privatization might improve access to products through business expansion, which the investment-constrained public firm could not carry out. Conversely, the private owner might withdraw from or ignore markets that the public enterprise was obliged to service.

Pricing and access are inextricably linked. The prices citizens and consumers face can be broadly conceived to include whether they have access to a particular good or service (e.g., the price is infinite if they lack access to electric power) and its quality (a lower quality for a given nominal price implies a higher real price). While steep price increases following privatization have been common, they have not been universal in divested network or infrastructure industries, such as electricity, water, and sewerage, and telecommunications.

On the equity side, reformers argue that protecting consumers by keeping prices of essential services artificially low failed, resulting in subsidies to the comparatively wealthy and higher costs elsewhere in the economy, which outweighed the policy's benefits. Better, it was thought, to let the firms operate under private, profit-maximizing ownership, and use other state mechanisms, such as taxes and regulation, to protect consumer welfare and acceptable levels of income distribution.

Nonetheless, one can readily point to situations where rational pricing policies, followed by private profit-maximizing ownership, could impose disproportionate costs onto lower-income groups. Again, infrastructure yields the most obvious examples.[12] Potential price increases in electricity and water—required to cover costs and expand the network—would fall more heavily on poorer consumers, who are more likely to spend a higher percentage of their income on these services than are the wealthy. New private owners' often vigorous moves to collect arrears and end illegal water and electricity connections likely fall most heavily on the poor. Even when a privatized service expands through investment into formerly unserved, and thus probably poorer, neighborhoods, residents might be unable to take advantage of it because of the high upfront costs of equipment that consumers often must provide.

In telecommunications, a common result of reform and privatization has been tariff rebalancing, leading to price increases in formerly subsidized, local fixed-line telephony, while introducing competition—usually producing rapidly falling prices—in international services and mobile phone

---

12. In many countries, the mass of poor are not connected to many infrastructure networks, making moot the issue of gains and losses relative to other income groups; however, recent research shows that a surprisingly high percentage of the developing world's population is connected to the electricity grid. A far smaller fraction has formal water or telephone services. See Komives, Whittington, and Wu (2001).

systems. Since the poor are likely to place most of their calls locally through fixed lines, the price increase could negatively affect distribution.

As with pricing, access or coverage issues most often arise in the context of infrastructure privatization. Because of low tariffs and other investment constraints, many publicly owned infrastructure firms persistently fail to meet demand. Infrastructure sales and concession contracts often give the purchaser exclusive rights of service provision for a period of time in return for commitments to specified levels of investments and expansion targets in order to extend service to formerly unserved clients and regions. In many cases, a disproportionate percentage of new customers is drawn from lower-income groups since they are the only ones not connected. The distributional effects of this expansion are a function of the initial income of the new customers and the relative shifts in expenditure that result from connecting to the network. For example, where the poor were paying vendors for water, network connection could result in lower unit costs if they can afford the often substantial, upfront connection fee. Moreover, they might face a minimal consumption threshold that exceeds the amount they previously consumed, thereby raising their costs and worsening distribution.

Another reason for a period of exclusive monopoly in infrastructure service is the high risk borne by investors. However, if the new private utility uses its exclusivity rights to eliminate less formal—and perhaps less expensive—service providers, then certain consumer groups, including low-income customers, may lose access to an alternative service and become worse off.

Fiscal Effects

Privatization may affect real income net of taxes if its fiscal effects differentially reduce the tax burden across households or differentially increase benefits of such government services as education and health, funded by new tax flows. The fiscal effects of privatization on income distribution—which come through any changes in revenue (including effects on service expansion) and expenditure—are indirect and possibly offsetting. Reduced hemorrhage of tax revenues and increased public expenditures probably benefit the relatively poor. However, the indirect effects are easily offset in countries where broader fiscal problems use up initial sales revenue and invite a prolongation of weak fiscal policy, ultimately with costs to growth and improved equity.

Reality of Distribution: Efficiency over Equity

The empirical work of the last five or six years—some of which was commissioned for this volume—leads one to conclude that, while many, if not most, privatization programs have a stated goal of improving distributional equity and while many have built in specific measures (e.g., vouchers) to achieve this aim, most such programs to date have done more to enhance efficiency than equity. Regarding income distribution, privatization has had slight or no effect in Latin America, the best-studied region. In Russia and Sri Lanka, studies more commonly conclude that privatization has negatively affected income distribution; however, data limitations make these conclusions more speculative. The negative wealth-distribution effect appears to arise primarily from the transfer of assets to the relatively wealthy, not by reducing assets of the relatively poor. Negative income-distribution effects appear to stem primarily from price movements of privatized infrastructure products. As discussed below, the issue is complicated: In most Latin American cases, for example, the equity-enhancing effects of increased access to infrastructure services outweigh the negative effects of increased prices.

Equity consequences have varied greatly by region and country, with certain studies (e.g., Latin America) recording neutral or slightly positive distributional effects and others (e.g., Russia) postulating large negative effects. In terms of this chapter's analytical framework, the average privatization program reviewed in the literature has taken path x (figure 1.9).

Disaggregating this general conclusion is the topic of the sections below.

Ownership

Troubling or disappointing outcomes are particularly common with regard to ownership. In many transition countries, privatization programs and techniques have often resulted in massive, rapid transfer of asset ownership from society at large to a small group of daring, unscrupulous actors. One can argue, as do Åslund (2001) and Shleifer and Treisman (2000), that, despite the admittedly unfair and often illegal manner of asset allocation, the results obtained are superior to the alternative of leaving firms in state hands; the resulting distributional loss is an unavoidable, bearable price that must be paid for the efficiency gains, and, indeed, the transition, to succeed.[13]

Others vigorously dispute this conclusion (Stiglitz 1999a, b). While few would defend the notion that socially- or state-owned enterprises were managed mainly with the public interest in mind during the pretransition period, ownership has become more concentrated, with negative, if perhaps short-term, consequences for asset distribution.

The ownership issue has caused concern in less dramatic, but more empirically determinable, circumstances. In their study on privatizing the United Kingdom's electricity sector, Newbery and Pollitt (1997) show that,

---

13. Åslund (2001, 21) argues that any attempt to avoid or delay privatization in transition economies would only have compounded the pain. Shleifer and Treisman (2000, 38) view the inequities of Russian privatization as troubling but better than the alternative of inaction.

Figure 1.9 Privatization's initial effects: Average-case scenario

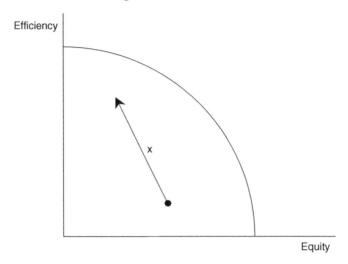

in the first years following the sale, new private shareholders captured the bulk of financial rewards generated by substantial efficiency gains at the expense of taxpayers (caused by both insufficient introduction of competitive forces in initial transactions and weaknesses of the regulatory framework). In this case, both government and consumers reaped some gains; the contrast is not winners to losers, but rather overwhelming winners to small winners. In a subsequent study, Newbery (2001) concluded that, as time passed and electricity regulators gained experience, they became increasingly able to transform efficiency gains into lower consumer prices. As noted, how one assesses privatization outcomes depends partly on when one makes the assessment. Nonetheless, the effect of initial wealth distribution was negative in both the Russian and the British electricity cases.

Mechanisms used to address the ownership issue have included offering the general population vouchers and reserving a tranche of shares in privatized firms for employees (and sometimes retirees), usually offered at a steep discount or with an easy payment arrangement. This has proven useful in reducing employee resistance to privatization. In many cases, sharp increases in share prices post-sale have improved the income position of shareholders—including employees—although the number of people affected by such schemes has usually been too small to influence overall distribution patterns [14]

---

14. Employees often quickly sell shares acquired in this way; even then, however, they tend to benefit since government sellers tend to greatly underprice initial offerings.

In transition economies, vouchers have been widely disseminated; however, the distributional effects have been disappointing, not only in the infamous cases of Russia and the Czech Republic, but also in Kazakhstan, Lithuania, Moldova, Mongolia, and elsewhere. It is disappointing because recipients, who obtained the vouchers for free or at a nominal price, received much less than anticipated or promised on their returns, and much less than the wealth gained by the dishonest few. In some cases, the best companies were not privatized by vouchers but, through nontransparent deals, went to managers and their supporters. In other cases, dispersed minority shareholders (shares obtained by vouchers) found that all assets were "tunneled" out of their firm, which suddenly consisted only of liabilities; the value of minority shares fell overnight to zero (as someone gained a majority stake and had no use for more shares); the company was inexplicably unlisted from the stock exchange; or the privatization fund invested in transformed—without notice, discussion, or appeal—to an unsalable status.[15]

The major distributional problem in transition states may be more psychological than financial: People were told directly or indirectly that the voucher was the means whereby the mass of state property would be equitably shared among citizens. This did not happen—in reality, it probably never could or even should have happened—and the disappointment and resentment engendered by this failure is still discernible and of political import in Russia, the Czech Republic, and most countries of the former Soviet Union.

At the same time, the generally positive distributional outcomes observed in a few cases (see chapter 4, for example) suggest that negative paths are not an automatic or inevitable result of applying privatization. The initial Bolivian program, for example, appears to have promoted both efficiency and equity (figure 1.1, moving from point C to point D) partly because of political foresight and clever program design and partly because the prevailing stable macroeconomic situation—itself a function of wise leadership—allowed the implementers substantial financial latitude. (The Bolivian public's perception of the program, nonetheless, remains negative.) The point, for the moment, is not the extent to or the frequency with which equity-enhancing outcomes occur; it is that they occur at all.

Employment

In terms of returns on assets (other than shares of firms), a pressing question has been the effect of privatization on employment levels and returns

---

15. John Williamson suggests that, in Russia just before price liberalization, an alternative to vouchers might have been converting excess money balances of households into bonds. Households could then have used the bonds to bid for enterprises being sold. This might have avoided the inflation that, inter alia, wiped out the savings of thrifty Russians and transferred enterprises to a group more likely to hold shares and able to take measures to defend their interests. (Personal communication with the authors.)

to labor. Despite the saliency of the employment issue, the matter has only recently been rigorously studied. What is clear is that public enterprises were overstaffed, often severely so. Moreover, in preparing, or as a substitute, for privatization, public enterprise employment numbers have declined, sometimes greatly; these declines have generally continued after privatization. A survey of 308 privatized firms in developing countries shows postsale employment reductions in 78.4 percent of cases, with no change or job gains in the rest (Chong and López-de-Silanes 2002, 43). On the other hand, a review of 81 privatizations in the Ivory Coast (before the recent troubles) found that employment grew faster in privatized firms than it had in state firms before privatization. Many Ivorian firms operated in competitive markets, and their output and overall performance improved with privatization (Jones, Jammal, and Gokgur 1998).

The question of what types of jobs people find after dismissal from public enterprises is just beginning to receive attention; however, fragmentary evidence suggests a lengthening of hours worked and reduced fringe benefits and security of tenure.

Worldwide, more people have lost, rather than have gained, jobs through privatization over the short term. However, calculating the overall distributional effects of these losses is difficult. Few studies provide detailed information about the incidence and size of severance payments or the amount of time required to find alternative employment[16] (or even whether those dismissed derived most of their income from employment, although this is probably a reasonable assumption).

Recently, more rigorous attempts have refined the knowledge of privatization's effects on labor. In Ukraine and Sri Lanka (see chapters 10 and 12, respectively), Mexico (La Porta and López-de-Silanes 1999), and several other countries studied, salary levels have generally risen (sometimes greatly) for those retained by the new private entities. Interestingly, this is not the case in China (see chapter 11).

In summarizing evidence from Latin America, McKenzie and Mookherjee (chapter 2) calculate that the net effects of privatization on overall unemployment in that region were minimal. They argue that the numbers dismissed were small in relation to total work forces and that, during the peak privatization period of the early 1990s, private-sector expansion rapidly absorbed most of those laid off because of divestitures. Similarly, Knight-John and Wasantha Athukorala (chapter 12) shows that the net number of layoffs in eight major privatized firms in Sri Lanka amounted to 5,400, a small fraction of the country's labor force. Large overall increases in

---

16. Galal et al. (1994) attempted to estimate gains and losses to employees for the 12 privatizations they reviewed. They concluded that no worker lost out as a result of privatization because the average severance package received was greater than the average wage lost during the average period of time a worker was unemployed before finding another job.

unemployment in Latin America, Sri Lanka, and other settings are troubling; but they came later and were caused, not by privatization, but by external shocks, labor-market rigidities, and lack of financial discipline. It has even been argued that privatization may have mitigated unemployment; that is, without privatization, unemployment levels would be higher (Behrman, Birdsall, and Szekely 2000).

Despite arguments that privatization has contributed little, if at all, to rising unemployment, the public is persuaded, in Latin America and elsewhere, that the distributional effects of privatization through employment are large and negative.

Prices and Access

A widespread result of utility privatization is network expansion and increased access to services by the population, especially the urban poor (the rural poor remain generally excluded). Expanded access can be seen in Argentina, Bolivia, Mexico, Nicaragua, Peru, and other Latin American countries (see other chapters in this volume, including the summary discussion in chapter 2).[17] Increased access is often large; the rate of increase typically far exceeds that of the predivestiture period, and the Latin America studies mostly conclude that poorer segments of the population have benefited disproportionately from these increases.

Expansion is partly a function of profit-oriented owners moving to expand their markets—easier now that the firm can tap private investment capital—and partly a matter of sales contracts stipulating investment and network expansion targets. In the few cases where access increases significantly and prices do not rise greatly (e.g., Bolivia, except in one water concession where prices jumped), hikes in access rates appear sufficient to increase equity.

Often, however, increased access is accompanied by higher prices. Various studies reveal that the amount and structure of such price increases[18]—caused, in part, by the common need for privatized firms to raise their retail prices to cost-covering levels and, in part, because inexperienced regulators have found it difficult to hold down or reduce tariffs in privatized infrastructure firms—increase short-term inequity (e.g., Argentina, Peru, and Spain [Arocena 2001]).[19] The finding is sufficiently generalized to prompt

---

17. Earlier studies show similar results (e.g., Torero and Pasco-Font 2001, Delfino and Casarin 2001, Paredes 2001, and Barja and Urquiola 2001).

18. This connection appears easy to determine; however, various studies reach different conclusions, depending on the years of comparison and other factors. In the case of Argentina, for example, Delfino and Casarin (2001) assert large price increases after privatization; Ennis and Pinto (chapter 5) state that prices for the privatized utility services declined significantly.

19. As with employment, the counterfactual is imperfectly known; failure to privatize might well have hurt the relatively poor even more through fiscal effects (e.g., regressive overall taxes) or inflation.

Estache, Foster, and Wodon (2002, 9), in their review of infrastructure privatization, to conclude: "One of the most painful lessons is that, unless governments take specific actions, the gains from reform take longer to reach the real poor than the richer segments of the population, and hence worsen income distribution."[20]

An important part of the price effects stems from eliminating illegal connections to electricity and water networks. Delfino and Casarin (2001, 23) note that in Argentina, for example, 436,000 of the first 481,000 additional subscribers to the privatized electricity system were those who formerly had illegal hook-ups. Assuming that most of those subscribers were lower-income people, the result is likely increased inequality in income distribution.

Fiscal Effects

Finally, in studies covering 18 mostly developing and transition countries, the net fiscal effects of privatization amounted to about 1 percent of GDP, a substantial amount for a single year; however, it is a one-time gain that is modest relative to the size of economies or even of government budgets over several years. In certain countries, the critical fiscal benefit of privatization has been to eliminate direct budget transfers (which subsidized commercially unviable enterprises or compensated politically determined underpricing of an enterprise's services or products). That subsidy flow was particularly great for politically visible, public infrastructure services (e.g., energy utilities, railroads, and telecommunications). This usually led to rationing or underpricing of services and penalizing lower-income households that lacked access. Tax-financed subsidies provided benefits primarily to the nonpoor, in the form of employment at above-market wages or underpricing for those with access. Neither helped—and both may have harmed—equity.

Many developing countries have regressive tax systems that rely heavily on indirect trade and value-added (consumption) taxes. To the extent that privatization reduces the hemorrhaging of funds in order to keep losing firms afloat, it produces indirect benefits in terms of increased, retained tax revenues. In addition, more efficiently managed, higher productivity private firms tend to pay more taxes, thus increasing government revenue. All of this could result in increased benefits to the relatively poor; that is, because expenditure patterns in most developing countries are more progressive than income distribution, this might benefit the relatively poor indirectly. The critical question of whether this actually occurs has been neglected. Several cases in this volume examine state spending patterns on health and education during the privatization period; however, the findings are mainly preliminary and speculative.

---

20. This study contains numerous practical suggestions on how to protect the poor during infrastructure reform, in terms of price and access.

In many cases, governments have used revenue from privatization to reduce the stock of public debt, which, prima facie, makes sense. However, the ultimate use of privatization revenue is a function of a government's overall fiscal performance since, even when revenue reduces debt stock, indiscipline on the fiscal side means the revenue indirectly finances the government's current expenditure or increases its space to borrow more. Macedo (see chapter 7, and 2000) indicates the likelihood that privatization revenue in the mid-1990s merely prolonged the period during which Brazil tried to sustain the nominal value of its overvalued currency and put off the day of reckoning, which finally occurred in 1998. Thus, potential fiscal benefits were lost as government used reserves to protect the currency. In the case of Argentina, Mussa (2002) refers to the same failing. Revenue from privatization in the mid-1990s was significant over a period of three or four years. Despite this infusion, the government failed to generate the required fiscal surplus. Both national and subnational governments continued borrowing, and ultimately, privatization revenue was swallowed up in the collapse of the currency and debt default in 2002. In Bolivia, the initial situation seemed better because its government did not accept sales revenue; in effect, it retained one-half the value of the enterprises (as shares held to generate benefits for future pensioners) and exchanged the other half in return for the new owners' commitment to invest an equivalent amount in the enterprises (chapter 4). However, subsequent fiscal problems led the Bolivian government (the successor administration to the one that initiated the program) to reduce benefits to older citizens.

Conclusions

The case studies and analyses presented in this book add substantially to the previously limited knowledge about privatization's effects on wealth and income distribution. Still, these and earlier studies are drawn from a limited set of countries and sectors. Such critical regions as Africa are almost entirely overlooked.[21] While the distribution issue has received great attention in Latin America, most studies of that region, including those in this volume, deal mainly with infrastructure privatization. Little is known about the distributional effects of many privatizations of firms producing tradable or other goods in competitive markets—from large steel mills to small hotels and shops. Our observations on privatization's effects on asset ownership and wealth distribution depend heavily on findings from transition economies of the former Soviet Union and Eastern Europe,

---

21. One exception is the Jones, Jammal, and Gokgur (1998) study mentioned above. For reviews of the economic and performance effects of African privatization, see Appiah-Kubi (2001), Due and Temu (2002), Temu and Due (1998), and Nellis (2003).

especially Russia. These findings arise from initial conditions that, if not sui generis, are thoroughly unlike those encountered in other regions and settings, or even in other transition countries; for example, the outcomes reported in China differ markedly (see chapter 11).

A second limiting factor is that privatization has been, for the most part, a phenomenon of the 1990s. To date, understanding its effects has been based on studies undertaken shortly after its implementation, during a period of general economic boom. Static snapshots, mostly taken within three or four years after the event, cannot tell the whole of what is clearly a dynamic story. It is thus too early to conclude that privatization should be delayed or accelerated across the board—certainly not because of its distributional consequences.

To illustrate, in the mid-1990s, the Czech Republic's early, rapid, and massive privatization program was judged a great success. As more information became available and problems of both performance and fairness surfaced, the consensus interpretation soon shifted sharply toward the negative. In Poland, by contrast, observers were at first critical of the country's hesitant approach to the privatization of large firms, but then switched to greater enthusiasm as the country returned to growth and macroeconomic stability. Indeed, Poland's overall solid performance, in the absence of large-scale privatization (combined with comparatively poor performance in rapidly privatizing Russia and the Czech Republic), led some to question the importance of rapid and massive privatization and others to emphasize that quick privatization in the wrong environment could have deleterious effects altogether. Now the pendulum has once again swung back. The Czech Republic, and to a lesser extent Russia, have returned to stability and growth; Poland's recent fiscal and economic problems are partially attributed to its failure to privatize the set of large lossmakers when it had the chance. One could show similar shifts in interpretation and judgment over time in numerous other countries, including Argentina, Bolivia, and the United Kingdom.

Nearly all these shifts in interpretation have been based on variations over time of financial and operating performance of privatized and state firms, not distributional consequences per se. However, as we have demonstrated, many distributional outcomes depend largely on the efficiency and productivity results of privatization; shifts in interpreting privatization's overall economic consequences also imply changes in the assessment of distributional effects.

Moreover, there is the obvious question: Are observed changes in income distribution associated with privatization or other simultaneously occurring reforms and policies? Pioneering studies (Galal et al. 1994; Newbery and Pollitt 1997; Jones, Jammal, and Gokgur 1998; Domah and Pollitt 2000) construct elaborate counterfactuals that attempt to assign to privatization only those performance shifts clearly caused by ownership change. These studies estimate what performance would have been had the firm not been privatized and attempt to determine the winners and losers from the privatization event. All yield a wealth of insights; however, all the authors in this volume readily admit that counterfactual construction inevitably contains speculative elements. With greatly varying degrees of rigor, led by the Latin American cases, all of the chapters in this volume grapple with this complex issue.

The many other reforms and changes that commonly accompany privatization matter, particularly with regard to distributional effects. Initial conditions, degree of competition, market structure, and level of institutional development all affect firm performance, in some cases as much as or more than ownership type.[22] Thus, more than ownership change is required for most low- and middle-income people to benefit from privatization's efficiency gains.

Despite these limitations and concerns, preliminary conclusions can be drawn. In line with the structure of this volume, we divide them into two parts: Latin America and transition and Asian economies.

Latin America

Privatization has been unfairly criticized in Latin America, in part, because it was the most politically visible, structural reform in that region during the 1990s, a disappointing decade of reform without growth. The studies in this volume confirm that the major privatizations of infrastructure have generally increased access to power, telephone services, and water, particularly for the poor, who, before privatization, often had no services or paid higher prices for private services (particularly in the case of water). Although some privatized firms have raised prices, which has burdened lower-income households, the bottom line is still one of absolute gains in welfare for the poor (though not general improvement in the distribution of monetary income). At the level of transactions, these findings are consistent with evidence that the effect of major structural reforms as a whole was to slightly worsen income distribution in Latin America; however, among other reforms, privatization offset the greater worsening effects of financial-sector reform and opening of capital markets (Behrman, Birdsall, and Szekely 2000). In addition, privatization of what had been loss-making state enterprises has freed up as much as one or two percent of GDP, providing Latin American governments with 5 to 10 percentage points of additional revenue. Though no definitive causal connection can be made, the

---

22. See footnote 1 (Tandon 1995); see also Newbery and Pollitt (1997). Sachs, Zinnes, and Eilat (2000) estimated the relative power of ownership change versus nonownership reforms in explaining privatization outcomes in transition economies. They conclude that both matter; however, in the absence of privatization, the same nonownership changes produce a less positive outcome.

resulting fiscal space probably made it easier for governments to finance their increases in social spending—of 10 to 20 percent in many countries—during the 1990s.

On the other hand, privatization was generally carried out without thought to its potential to reduce the region's high inequality, with the sole exception of Bolivia's capitalization program. The objectives were to reduce the burden of losses on the state and attract new investment. Obviously more remains to be done. Estache discusses the needed next steps in chapter 8.

Transition and Asian Economies

In the early 1990s, expectations were high. Privatization was at the leading edge of what should have been a rapid shift from a centralized economy to an efficient and equitable market economy. In hindsight, the transition was both slower and more uneven than anticipated. During the 1990s, inequality rose rapidly in most transition economies. Across countries, however, there was no particular association between amount of privatization and degree of increase; slow and fast privatizers were found at both ends of the spectrum. More likely explanations were the method of divestiture used; the type of new owner installed; sequencing and intensity of other market reforms; and the nature and density of the prevailing institutional framework in the country before, during, and after privatization events.

In retrospect, while privatization should shoulder a portion of the blame for the problems and corruption that occurred (e.g., in Russia, as argued by Glinkina in chapter 9; Georgia; and many other transition countries), it should also take credit where the shift was more rapid, deep, and successful (e.g., Estonia and Hungary). Moreover, in certain cases, such as Ukraine (see chapter 10), one can argue that, despite serious implementation problems, privatization still offers the best hope for a more efficient and just economy. The distributional outcomes of privatization in the transition economies of the former Soviet Union and elsewhere, including Asian economies (e.g., China and Sri Lanka), are more the result of, rather than a contribution to, a country's concurrent institutional and political setup.

In the case of infrastructure, on which much of the distribution debate is centered, many studies (see chapters 4, 6, and 7) focus on the existence or absence of an independent, accountable regulatory regime, not simply in law but in practice—that is, one that can design and monitor contracts; offer economically reasonable, legally enforceable rulings; lead or cajole government to honor its obligations; and resist capture by private providers. The better the regulatory regime, the better the distributional outcome of the privatization of electric power, water and sanitation, and telephony. A practical implication of this finding is that selling governments and those that assist them should invest more upfront attention and effort into creating and reinforcing regulatory capacity. This means taking the time to lay the institutional foundation on which distributionally positive privatization is based. In the United Kingdom, for example, it took many years for regulators of the privatized electricity industry to master the skills needed to squeeze out benefits for the average consumer (Newbery 2001). If that is the case in an OECD setting, what should one reasonably expect from new regulators in developing and transition countries?

Our advice is to move slowly, at least with regard to infrastructure privatization. That is not a costless prescription. The period between initial construction of a regulatory regime and assessing whether it is in proper working order could, and probably will, be long. In the interim, losses in the affected firms could continue to mount, opposition to reform harden, and reformers grow weary or disillusioned. Nonetheless, the prescription holds. Effective regulation is a double winner: Necessary over the short term to minimize troubling distributional outcomes, it is equally important to maximize efficiency.

Selling governments can and should do more in their privatization programs to maximize potential distributional gains. These cases and studies demonstrate that it is possible for governments to design and implement privatization to obtain gains in efficiency, at least without harming, and perhaps even improving, distribution. It is wrong to dismiss equity problems as the unavoidable, temporary price paid for putting assets back into productive use. As McKenzie and Mookherjee document in chapter 2, efficiency gains do not automatically imply equity losses or increased poverty.

Societies might even reasonably choose a less efficiency-oriented approach first to diminish longer-term risks to efficiency and growth that initial resulting inequities would undermine (e.g., through corruption or rent-seeking). Minimizing the sometimes real inequity in privatization, and—just as important—countering the misperception that it is inevitably unfair is important in order to preserve the political possibility of deepening and extending reform. In the end, a democratic government cannot implement reform when the majority of the people openly protest it, and no government can enact reform if it is not in power.

References

Aghion, P., E. Caroli, and C. García-Peñalosa. 1999. Inequality and Economic Growth: The Perspective of the New Growth Theories. *Journal of Economic Literature* 37, no. 4 (December): 1615–60.

Alfaro, R., R. Bradford, and J. Briscoe. 1998. Reforming Public Monopolies: Water Supply. In *Beyond Trade-offs: Market Reforms and Equitable Growth in Latin America*, ed. N. Birdsall, C. Graham, and R. Sabot. Washington: Brookings Institution Press and Inter-American Development Bank.

Appiah-Kubi, K. 2001. State-Owned Enterprises and Privatization in Ghana. *Journal of Modern African Studies* 39, no. 2: 197–229.

Arocena, P. 2001. *The Reform of the Utilities Sector in Spain*. WIDER Discussion Paper 2001/13. Helsinki: United Nations University/World Institute for Development Economics Research.

Åslund, A. 2001. Think Again: Russia. *Foreign Policy* (July/August), no. 125: 20–25.

Barja, G., and M. Urquiola. 2001. *Capitalization, Regulation and the Poor: Access to Basic Services in Bolivia.* WIDER Discussion Paper 2001/34. Helsinki: United Nations University/World Institute for Development Economics Research.

Barro, R. J. 2000. Inequality and Growth in a Panel of Countries. *Journal of Economic Growth* 5, no. 1: 5–32.

Behrman, J. R., N. Birdsall, and M. Szekely. 2000. *Economic Reform and Wage Differentials in Latin America.* Working Paper 435. Washington: Inter-American Development Bank.

Benabou, R. 1996. *Unequal Societies.* NBER Working Paper 5583. Cambridge, MA: National Bureau of Economic Research.

Birdsall, N., and J. L. Londoño. 1997. Asset Inequality Matters: An Assessment of the World Bank's Approach to Poverty Reduction. *American Economic Review* 87, no. 2: 32–37.

Birdsall, N., and J. Nellis. 2003. Winners and Losers: Assessing the Distributional Impact of Privatization. *World Development* 31, no. 10: 1617–33.

Birdsall, N., D. Ross, and R. Sabot. 1995. Inequality and Growth Reconsidered: Lessons from East Asia. *World Bank Economic Review* 9, no. 3: 477–508.

Birdsall, N., C. Graham, and R. Sabot, eds. 1998. *Beyond Trade-offs: Market Reforms and Equitable Growth in Latin America.* Washington: Brookings Institution Press and Inter-American Development Bank.

Chong, A., and F. López-de-Silanes. 2002. Privatization and Labor Force Restructuring Around the World. Washington: Inter-American Development Bank (November).

Davis, J., R. Ossowski, T. Richardson, and S. Barnett. 2000. *Fiscal and Macroeconomic Impact of Privatization.* Occasional Paper 194. Washington: International Monetary Fund.

Delfino, J. A., and A. A. Casarin. 2001. *The Reform of the Utilities Sector in Argentina.* WIDER Discussion Paper 2001/74. Helsinki: United Nations University/World Institute for Development Economics Research.

Domah, P., and M. G. Pollitt. 2000. *The Restructuring and Privatisation of Electricity Distribution and Supply Businesses in England and Wales: A Social Cost Benefit Analysis.* Working Paper 7. Cambridge, UK: University of Cambridge, Department of Applied Economics.

Due, J. M., and A. Temu. 2002. Changes in Employment by Gender and Business Organization in Newly Privatized Companies in Tanzania. *Canadian Journal of Development Studies* 23, no. 2: 317–33.

Easterly, W. 2001. *The Elusive Quest for Growth: Economists' Adventures and Misadventures in the Tropics.* Cambridge, MA: MIT Press.

Easterly, W. 2002. *Inequality Does Cause Underdevelopment: New Evidence from Commodity Endowments, Middle Class Share, and Other Determinants of Per Capita Income.* Working Paper 1. Washington: Center for Global Development.

Estache, A., V. Foster, and Q. Wodon. 2002. *Accounting for Poverty in Infrastructure Reform.* Washington: World Bank Institute.

Galal, A., L. Jones, P. Tandon, and I. Vogelsang. 1994. *Welfare Consequences of Selling Public Enterprises.* New York: Oxford University Press.

Hellman, J., G. Jones, and D. Kaufman. 2000. *Seize the State, Seize the Day: State Capture, Corruption, and Influence in Transition.* Washington: World Bank.

James, E. 1998. Pension Reforms: An Equity-Efficiency Trade-Off? In *Beyond Trade-offs: Market Reforms and Equitable Growth in Latin America,* ed. N. Birdsall, C. Graham, and R. Sabot. Washington: Brookings Institution Press and Inter-American Development Bank.

Jones, L. P., Y. Jammal, and N. Gokgur. 1998. Impact of Privatization in Côte d'Ivoire. Draft final report. Boston Institute for Developing Economies.

Komives, K., D. Whittington, and X. Wu. 2001. *Access to Utilities by the Poor: A Global Perspective.* WIDER Discussion Paper 2001/15. Helsinki: United Nations University/World Institute for Development Economics Research.

La Porta, R., and F. López-de-Silanes. 1999. Benefits of Privatization—Evidence from Mexico. *Quarterly Journal of Economics* 114, no. 4: 1193–242.

Latinbarometer. 2001. The Latinbarometer Poll. *The Economist* (July 26).

Lora, E., and U. Panizza. 2002. *Structural Reforms in Latin America Under Scrutiny*. Washington: Inter-American Development Bank.

Macedo, R. 2000. *Privatization and the Distribution of Assets in Brazil*. Working Paper 14. Washington: Carnegie Endowment for International Peace. www.carnegieendowment. org/files/14macedo.pdf.

Megginson, W. L., and J. M. Netter. 2001. From State to Market: A Survey of Empirical Studies on Privatization. *Journal of Economic Literature*, 39, no. 2: 321–89.

Mussa, M. 2002. *Argentina and the Fund: From Triumph to Tragedy*. POLICY ANALYSES IN INTERNATIONAL ECONOMICS 67. Washington: Institute for International Economics.

Nellis, J. 1999. *Time To Rethink Privatization in Transition Economies?* Discussion Paper 38. Washington: International Finance Corporation.

Nellis, J. 2003. *Privatization in Africa: What Has Happened? What Is To Be Done?* Working Paper 25. Washington: Center for Global Development.

Newbery, D. M. 2001. Issues and Options for Restructuring the Electricity Sector Industry. Cambridge Institute of Applied Economics. Photocopy.

Newbery, D. M., and M. G. Pollitt. 1997. The Restructuring and Privatisation of Britain's CEGB—Was It Worth It? *Journal of Industrial Economics* 45, no. 3: 269–303.

Paredes, R. 2001. *Redistributive Impact of Privatization and the Regulation of Utilities in Chile*. WIDER Discussion Paper 2001/19. Helsinki: United Nations University/World Institute for Development Economics Research.

Reynolds, Lloyd G. 1985. *Macroeconomics*, 5th ed. Homewood, IL: R. D. Irwin.

Sachs, J., C. Zinnes, and Y. Eilat. 2000. *The Gains from Privatization in Transition Economies: Is 'Change of Ownership' Enough?* CAER II Discussion Paper 63. Cambridge, MA: Harvard Institute for International Development.

Shleifer, A., and D. Treisman. 2000. *Without a Map: Political Tactics and Economic Reform in Russia*. Cambridge, MA: MIT Press.

Stiglitz, J. 1999a. Quis Custodiet Ipsos Custodes? *Corporate Governance Failures in the Transition*. Paris: World Bank.

Stiglitz, J. 1999b. *Whither Reform? Ten Years of the Transition*. Washington: World Bank.

Tandon, P. 1995. Welfare Effects of Privatization: Some Evidence from Mexico. *Boston University International Law Journal* 13, no. 2: 329–49.

Temu, A., and J. M. Due. 1998. The Success of Newly Privatized Companies: New Evidence from Tanzania. *Canadian Journal of Development Studies* 19, no. 2: 315–41.

Torero, M., and A. Pasco-Font. 2001. *The Social Impact of Privatization and the Regulation of Utilities in Peru*. WIDER Discussion Paper 2001/17. Helsinki: United Nations University/World Institute for Development Economics Research.

CASES FROM LATIN AMERICA

2

Paradox and Perception: Evidence from Four Latin American Countries

DAVID MCKENZIE and DILIP MOOKHERJEE

Latin America's supposed privatization failure has recently become a source of street riots, protest demonstrations, and negative news coverage. In June 2002, riots erupted in Arequipa, Peru, following announcement of the proposed privatization of power plants; two years earlier, Cochabamba, Bolivia, witnessed a so-called water war. Ecuador and Paraguay have recently experienced antiprivatization protests, and popular opposition in Lima and Rio de Janeiro have led to cancellation of water privatizations.[1] Street protests by antiglobalization activists have targeted privatization on the grounds that the profit calculus of global capitalism

David McKenzie is an economist in the Development Research Group of the World Bank. Dilip Mookherjee is professor of economics at Boston University. This chapter presents an overview of a research project commissioned by the Poverty and Inequality Unit of the Inter-American Development Bank (IDB) in 2001, sponsored further by the Institute of Public Policy and Development Studies of the Universidad de las Américas, Puebla. The authors are grateful to both these institutions for funding the research and providing logistical support. Research on the four country cases was conducted in 2002 by Huberto Ennis and Santiago Pinto (Argentina); Gover Barja, David McKenzie, and Miguel Urquiola (Bolivia); Luis-Felipe López-Calva and Juan Rosellón (Mexico); and Samuel Freije and Luis Rivas (Nicaragua). This chapter includes the researchers' methodology and summarizes their findings. The authors acknowledge Omar Arias, Nora Lustig, John Nellis, and Máximo Torero for their support and helpful comments, and discussants Gonzalo Castañeda and Jaime Saavedra for their penetrating comments on an earlier chapter draft. This chapter draws largely on McKenzie and Mookherjee (2003).

1. See "Turmoil in Latin America Threatens Decades of Reform," *Boston Globe*, August 18, 2002, A12; William Finnegan, "Letter from Bolivia: Leasing the Rain," *New Yorker*, April 8, 2002; Democracy Center, "Bechtel versus Bolivia: The Water Rate Hikes by Bechtel's Bolivian Company (Aguas del Tunari): The Real Numbers," August 20, 2002, www.democracyctr.org/bechtel/waterbills/waterbills-global.htm.

should not overtake national values. News articles highlight popular objection to private enterprises profiting from such basic services as water; failure of Bolivian water privatization; and problems with quality, price increases, and large-scale employee layoffs.[2] In response to popular opposition, Nicaragua's National Assembly passed a law forbidding privatization of any enterprise related to provision of water services (the country's president subsequently vetoed that law).

Negative sentiment regarding privatization extends beyond protest groups. For example, in the year 2000, Latinobarometer opinion polls showed that a majority disapproved of the privatization process; the pattern was uniform across countries, age, gender, and socioeconomic class. Moreover, the opinions became increasingly negative over time (e.g., disapproval ratings were higher in 2001 than in 2000, and higher in 2000 than in 1998) (see appendix 2A).[3]

Despite negative public opinion, economists tend to view privatization favorably (Megginson and Netter 2001). Evaluation criteria typically include profitability, labor productivity, firm growth, and market valuation. Most empirical studies have focused on the transition countries of Eastern Europe and the former Soviet Union, while public disaffection is more pronounced in Latin America and the Caribbean (LAC). This factor may help to explain the discrepancy between economists' views and public perception. In addition, economists use different evaluation criteria. For example, increased profitability and efficiency may come at the expense of customers, workers, and other social groups (i.e., increased prices may result in lower levels of employment, longer work hours, worsening service conditions, and negative environmental effects).[4] Clearly, a more comprehensive welfare evaluation of privatization must incorporate consumer and worker effects, as well as firm profitability. Particular attention should be devoted to the effects on inequality and poverty, which underlie perceptions of unfairness among privatization's critics and may functionally affect long-term economic efficiency via the effects on human capital investment, entrepreneurship, crime, and governance (Aghion, Caroli, and García-Peñalosa 1999; Bardhan, Bowles, and Gintis 2000).

This chapter presents an overview of the results of a project that evaluated privatization's distributive effect in four Latin American countries. The project aimed specifically to estimate privatization's effects on customers and workers, based on existing household and employment surveys. The

---

2. See "As Multinational Runs the Taps, Anger Rises over Water for Profit," *New York Times*, August 26, 2002.

3. See "An Alarm Call for Latin America's Democrats," *The Economist*, July 26, 2001.

4. La Porta and López-de-Silanes (1999) estimate the fraction of increased profitability of privatized Mexican enterprises attributable to consumer losses at 5 percent and transfers from laid-off workers at 31 percent, with productivity gains accounting for the remainder.

four countries selected—Argentina, Bolivia, Mexico, and Nicaragua—vary in size and per capita income; two are large, middle-income countries (Argentina and Mexico), while two are small, poor countries (Bolivia and Nicaragua). An overview of the methodology, as well as results, is provided for each of the four country studies, which contain details on the privatization process and data sources used.[5]

Since the late 1980s, all four countries have undergone significant privatization, and have similar data sources that permit the application of a common method. The Nicaraguan case, however, differs qualitatively from the other three in that large portions of that country's economy—including agriculture—were privatized as part of its transition from a socialist economy, while state-sector utilities were exposed to greater liberalization throughout the 1990s.

The project's first and most significant component focuses on privatized utilities (primarily electricity, telecommunications, water, and gas); it estimates the effects of price and access changes on household welfare by expenditure categories.[6] Estimated budget shares and price elasticities are used to calculate first- and second-order approximations to consumer surplus changes. Each of the four country assessments address various groups' valuation of access gains.[7]

The project's second component documents privatization's effects on workers, especially accompanying employment changes and potential effects on wage levels and earnings inequality. The four country studies assess employment changes relative to the respective economies' overall levels of employment and unemployment. Employment surveys for Argentina and Mexico are used to calculate upper-bound estimates of the extent to which earnings inequality may have increased as a result of layoffs (Ennis and Pinto 2002, López-Calva and Rosellón 2002). These surveys assume that those who lost their jobs have subsequently failed to secure employment. The rotating panel feature of the Mexican employment surveys permits López-Calva and Rosellón to explore the validity of this assumption by tracking those who lost their jobs for one subsequent year. Finally, effects on wage rates, working conditions, and wage inequality for employed workers are discussed within the context of Argentina and Nicaragua (Ennis and Pinto 2002, Freije and Rivas 2002).

The third project component gathers facts on privatization's fiscal effects. Short of attempting to simulate a structural macroeconomic model, one can

---

5. Argentina: Ennis and Pinto (2002); Bolivia: Barja, McKenzie, and Urquiola (2002); Mexico: López-Calva and Rosellón (2002); and Nicaragua: Freije and Rivas (2002).

6. In Nicaragua's case, this exercise was carried out only for the electricity sector, which, during the 1990s, witnessed the entry of numerous private firms while preparations were under way to privatize major state firms.

7. It should be noted that the available data on quality attributes were not rich enough to incorporate into the welfare calculations.

only speculate about potential implications for public debt, budget deficits, and social spending. Nevertheless, these facts help to put some of privatization's broader implications into perspective.

Severe data limitations make it necessary to qualify inferences that can be drawn from the results. The privatizations were far from constituting a natural experiment; rather, they were part of a broader set of market-oriented reforms including trade liberalization, fiscal reform, macroeconomic stabilization, and changes in regulatory institutions. Certain sectors, such as telecommunications, witnessed significant technological change with the introduction of new products and a reduction in cost of traditional services. Most of these countries underwent significant macroeconomic changes that affected all economic sectors. Attempting to assess privatization's effect per se would have been a futile exercise, in effect, requiring predictions of how the industries would have performed had they not been privatized, while all other changes occurred. Consequently, it was feasible to calculate the effects of observed changes before and after privatization only, while comparing the effects in privatized sectors with other sectors to control for macroeconomic changes in the economy.

Other household survey limitations included lack of information on service quality and household prices paid. Therefore, we were forced to use firm and regulator data on price and quality, assuming that all households were sold the same product at the same price. Because take-up decisions were not recorded directly, we had to estimate access indirectly from availability of the service in the same building or neighborhood, in combination with the households' reported expenditures. In terms of employment, little is known about layoff's effects on income distribution since data is lacking on laid-off workers' subsequent earnings and other forms of transfer (e.g., unemployment assistance or transfers from friends and family) that may have cushioned the income effect. Accordingly, only upper bounds to income losses can be computed by assuming that laid-off workers lost their incomes entirely thereafter.

While one can gauge only the short-term effects of most of these privatizations, experience suggests that the effects three or four years after privatization can differ markedly from the more immediate effects observed one or two years out.[8] In addition, environmental effects are not incorporated. Moreover, the data do not permit any assessment of the distributive

---

8. This observation is evidenced by employment changes. In the case of Bangladesh, for example, Bhaskar, Gupta, and Khan (2002) found that, with regard to privatization of jute mills in the 1980s, the employment effects 15 years later differed markedly from those that occurred in the first few years after privatization. Using the longer time horizon, the employment difference that Bhaskar and Khan (1995) found between privatized and nonprivatized mills during the first six or seven years disappeared entirely.

changes resulting from ownership change (e.g., through changes in firms' value after privatization) or effects on nonprivatized parts of the economy (e.g., through changes in price or competition). Thus, our assessment of the distributive effect must be viewed as a rough approximation to some of privatization's first-order effects on the bottom half of the distribution, assuming that changes in price, access, or employment levels that occurred at the time of the privatization could be attributed to that process.

Privatization Process: An Overview

In the four countries studied, the privatization process began in the 1980s (Argentina and Mexico) and early or mid-1990s (Bolivia and Nicaragua) (table 2.1).

Beginning in 1989 and continuing through the early 1990s, Argentina privatized a wide range of its state-owned enterprises (SOEs). These included major utilities (telecommunications, electricity, water, gas, and air and rail transport); petrochemicals; tankers; natural gas; defense (navigation); and a broad group of services, including insurance and grain control. The method of privatization involved inviting bids from a set of prequalified, international bidders. Over the 1990–97 period, approximately $23 billion was realized from the proceeds, of which $10 billion was used to retire outstanding public debt. The process, whose objectives included macroeconomic stabilization and improved efficiency, was carried out as part of a wider program of fiscal contraction, debt reduction, and trade liberalization. Many privatized firms represented joint ventures between foreign-owned and domestic firms, and were thus subject to equity participation rules for foreigners. The process included a complex system of transferring SOE debt to the new private entities, as well as a voluntary retirement program negotiated with unions in the large privatizations (e.g., the railways), which the World Bank funded. In telecommunications and electricity privatizations, 10 percent of shares were allocated to workers in these enterprises. The total fraction of the economy's labor force in the state sector before privatization was approximately 2 percent.

During 1995–97, Bolivia privatized its major utilities—electricity, telecommunications, transport, and water—as well as oil and gas. The novel feature of the process was the widespread use of capitalization as an alternative to traditional privatization methods. Capitalization involved allocating shares equivalent to 50 percent of the firm's value to the investor with the winning bid, 45 percent to an old-age welfare and pension fund, and the remaining 5 percent to the firm's employees. Investors gained the right to manage the firm, but were required to invest their capital contribution (i.e., what they offered for their 50 percent share) over a six- to eight-year period, in addition to conforming to regulators' expansion and quality

Table 2.1 Main features of privatizations, by country

Country	Period	Sector privatized	Proceeds		Labor force in SOE firms before privatization (percent)	Employment cuts (percent of total labor force)
			Billions of dollars	Percent of GDP[a]		
Argentina	1989–97	Utilities, other manufacturing, services	23	25	1.95	1.46
Bolivia	1995–97	Utilities, oil, gas	2	30	<0.5	0.13
Mexico						
Phase I	1982–88	Manufacturing, services	Negligible	Negligible	2	n.a.
Phase II	1988–94	Manufacturing, services	23	10	2	1.00
Phase III	1994–2000	Utilities	10	3	n.a.	n.a.
Nicaragua						
Phase I	1991–96	All	0.24	14	7–9	n.a.
Phase II	1996–2002[b]	Electricity, telephony, energy	0.17	5	n.a.	n.a.

n.a. = not available
SOE = state-owned enterprise

a. Proceeds are given as percentage of GDP in a midpoint year of the privatization.
b. Electricity sector was liberalized in 1997, and privatization occurred in 2000–02.

Sources: Argentina: Ennis and Pinto (2002); Bolivia: Barja, McKenzie, and Urquiola (2002); Mexico: López-Calva and Rosellón (2002); Nicaragua: Freije and Rivas (2002).

targets. Thus, under this scheme, the government gained no disposable income, with privatization proceeds earmarked mostly for investment and social spending. Of the $2 billion realized from the privatizations—amounting to 30 percent of GDP—approximately $1.6 billion resulted from capitalization and the remainder from traditional privatizations. A second alternative to traditional privatization, used most notably in the case of water, was concessions.

Bolivian officials separated electricity generation and transmission. In 1995, three privatized firms were created in the generation sector, realizing $140 million; these firms were subject to a 35 percent limit on market shares. In 1999, the sector was further liberalized, and two new private firms entered. In 1997, two private firms were created in the transmission sector, realizing $90 million; these firms were subject to tariff regulations and quality controls. That same year, three private firms, valued at $834 million, were capitalized in the oil and gas sector. Between 1997 and 2000, discovery of new reserves multiplied existing ones nearly tenfold, and three more firms were privatized in 2000, realizing $125 million. Because these oil and gas firms were oriented primarily toward exporting to Brazil, sector privatizations were unlikely to affect domestic consumers significantly. In 1995, Bolivia capitalized its monopoly telecommunications firm, ENTEL (Empresa Nacional de Telecomunicaciones), at a value of $610 million, and entry was further liberalized in 2001. In 1996–97, the rail and air transport sectors were capitalized at $90 million. Across all of these sectors, private firms were subject to regulatory controls, and most met their investment targets by mid-2000.

Attempts to privatize water encountered greater difficulties, resulting in the proliferation of concessions for administration of state assets. In 1997, only one municipal firm was transferred to the private sector, and a second attempted transfer failed. The Bolivian government was slow to develop this sector's necessary legal framework (the required legislation was not approved until 2000). In various cities, municipal water firms signed concession contracts that stipulated expansion, internal efficiency, and quality goals. Tariff regulations, designed to permit the firm to comply with its contractual obligations, were established under a rate-of-return mechanism with a five-year regulatory lag.

Mexico undertook large-scale, two-phase privatization of SOEs across a wide range of industries, including mining, manufacturing, and services. The first phase, implemented in 1982–88, was followed by a second, more significant phase in 1988–94 during the Salinas administration. Over the 12-year process (1982–94), the number of SOEs fell from 1,155 to 219. Although more SOEs were privatized during the first phase, most of the larger firms were privatized in the second phase. Of all assets privatized during the two-phase period, about 96 percent was concentrated in the second phase. By 1992, nearly Mexico's entire state-owned sector had been privatized (excluding oil, petrochemicals, gas, water, electricity, highways, railways, and ports). The telephone sector was privatized in 1990. Phase-two proceeds, amounting to $23 billion, were used mainly to repay public debt (table 2.1).

A third phase, started in 1994, saw the privatization of most of Mexico's utilities. During 1993–98, water and natural gas were privatized. The 1990s also witnessed ongoing privatization efforts in civil aviation and banks. In more than 90 percent of cases, the privatization method used involved the sale of control rights or majority stake through a first-price, sealed-bid auction. Third-phase proceeds amounted to $10 billion (table 2.1).

The state-owned sector, which had accounted for 4.4 percent of the labor force in 1982, had shrunk to 2 percent by the 1990s, such that the overall scale of the privatization process amounted to approximately 2.0 to 2.5 percent of the labor force. Privatization's employment implications were largest for railways; after privatization, employment was halved (form 46,000 to 23,000). La Porta and López-de-Silanes (1999) estimate that, during phase two, a maximum of about 30 percent of privatized enterprises' improved profitability resulted from job layoffs.

Unlike privatization in Argentina, Bolivia, and Mexico, Nicaragua's process encompassed the transition from a socialist, war-ravaged economy. The first phase of Nicaraguan privatization, 1991–96, involved divestment of SOEs in many areas (e.g., farming, fisheries, industry, forestry, mining, commerce, trade, transport, construction, and tourism). In 1991, a parallel process was started to allow private participation in banking, and closure or privatization of state-owned banks followed during 1994–2000. The second phase (1996–2002) of Nicaragua's privatization included utilities and involved both entry of private firms and awarding of concessions. Private participation has been allowed in telephony since 1995 and in electricity since 1997. During 1995–98, a comprehensive reform package aimed at full privatization of utilities was implemented, and privatization was slated for electricity distribution (2000), telephony (2001), and energy (2002).[9]

By 1998, divesture of 343 Nicaraguan enterprises had occurred. In addition to liquidation, three reorganization methods were used: mergers with existing firms (mainly other SOEs), restitution to previous owners, and sale or lease. During 1991–96, these methods accounted for 25, 28, and 36 percent of the proceeds, respectively; while shares allocated to workers and war veterans amounts to 13 and 1.5 percent, respectively. Use of proceeds was characterized by a lack of fiscal transparency. Although the proceeds amounted to 2.5 percent of GDP every year during the first phase, they did

---

9. Unfortunately, this study's data did not cover year 2000 or later; thus, our consumer-side analysis is restricted to estimating the effect of liberalization—rather than privatization—on the electricity sector. However, we were able to provide a detailed, economywide analysis of privatization's effect on Nicaragua's wage distribution (analysis in the other three countries is restricted to the utilities sector).

not accrue to the government budget. Portions were used to retire enterprises' outstanding commercial debt and cover the administrative expenses of CORNAP (Corporación Nicaraguense del Sector Público) (the state agency responsible for implementing privatizations). Many sales involved the transfer of credit and liabilities, creating further lack of transparency. By contrast, in 2000–02, electricity privatization proceeds were large (representing about 4.9 percent of GDP in 2000) and relatively transparent (60 percent accrued to the government budget, while the remainder was used to retire debt or settle tax arrears).

Evaluating the Consumer Welfare Effect

Privatization of infrastructure can directly affect consumers by altering network access and service price and quality. In addition, privatization may indirectly affect consumers by causing the prices of substitute goods to change.[10]

Data Description

Household income and expenditure surveys from each of the four countries studied were used to measure the effects of utility privatization on consumers.[11] These surveys enabled measurement of household-level access to electricity, water, and telephone service through questions that asked respondents directly whether their household had a service connection and by observing whether the household had a positive expenditure on the service. The surveys reported total household expenditure on each service; since no specific price information was given, prices were obtained from various other sources. Limited availability of surveys—only two were available for Argentina and Nicaragua and only a few for Mexico[12]—severely restricted the extent to which the country studies could determine whether changes that occurred over the privatization period differed from longer-term trends. In addition, survey coverage was often limited; for example,

---

10. This study does not attempt to measure this indirect effect.

11. The surveys are Argentina: National Household Expenditure Survey (ENGH) (Encuesta Nacional de Gastos de los Hogares) (1985–86, 1996–97); Bolivia: Integrated Household Survey (EIH) (Encuesta Integrada de Hogares) (1992, 1993, and 1994) and Ongoing Household Survey (ECH) (Encuesta Continua de Hogares) (1999); Mexico: National Household Income and Expenditure Survey (ENIGH) (Encuesta Nacional de Ingresos y Gastos de los Hogares) (1984, 1992, 1998, and 2000); and Nicaragua: National Household Living Standards Survey (EMNV) (Encuesta Nacional de Hogares sobre Medición de Niveles de Vida) (1993 and 1998).

12. Bolivia conducted surveys more frequently; however, survey format and design varied somewhat for the years immediately before and after privatization.

while the Mexico and Nicaragua surveys were nationwide, the Argentina surveys covered only the urban area of Greater Buenos Aires and the Bolivia surveys were limited to nine departmental capitals and El Alto.

Access to Services

For several reasons, privatization is expected to improve access to utility services. First, the long waiting periods under public ownership,[13] often associated with unsatisfied demand, would be reduced. Second, many privatization agreements include government-mandated expansion of the network or universal service obligations. For example, Estache, Foster, and Wodon (2002) note that the Bolivian government awarded the La Paz and El Alto water concession based on bids for the number of new connections offered at a predetermined tariff level; in Argentina, awarding of the Greater Buenos Aires concession incorporated connection targets aimed at increasing coverage from 70 to 100 percent by the end of the contract period. Third, private firms may be more apt to innovate and develop new means to reduce the costs of network expansion (Estache, Foster, and Wodon 2002, 40–43).

In all four countries studied, privatization resulted in increased access to infrastructure (table 2.2). While the household surveys provided detail on whether a given household used a particular service, they did not indicate whether the household had the option of connecting to the network. For Bolivia, Mexico, and Nicaragua, water and electricity surveys directly considered physical use of the service; for Argentina, however, access to water and electricity was determined by whether the household had a positive telephone service expenditure. For Bolivia and Mexico, access to telephone service was similarly determined. While Argentina's 1996–97 household expenditure survey provided information on observed physical use, the average take-up rate was reported as 99.88 percent for electricity and 97.39 percent for water.[14] Thus, relying on observed use to determine household access represents a reasonable approximation. A further caveat is that the surveys did not provide information on illegal connections, which may have resulted in overestimating increased access (i.e., certain users merely switched from illegal to legal connections).[15]

---

13. For example, in 1990, the average waiting time for a new phone connection in Mexico was 2.5 years.

14. Take-up rates among the poorest decile were 99.4 percent for electricity and 92.5 percent for water.

15. Nevertheless, the switch from illegal to legal connection can benefit households in other ways. For example, a formal connection can be less hazardous to household members' health; in addition, it provides evidence of an address, making the household eligible for state benefits (see Estache, Foster, and Wodon 2002, 22–23).

Table 2.2 Percentage of households with access to infrastructure services, by decile (percent)

Country and sector	Period	1	2	3	4	5	6	7	8	9	10	Total
Argentina (urban)												
Water and electricity[a]	1985–86	64.8	81.5	87.8	91.2	93.3	93.9	97.4	96.4	97.8	99.3	90.3
	1996–97	82.5	91.6	94.0	94.5	94.9	94.7	95.9	96.1	96.1	96.9	93.7
Telephone[a]	1985–86	18.4	26.5	33.7	43.6	47.0	49.6	61.4	67.2	75.9	82.3	50.6
	1996–97	22.8	39.6	53.5	57.7	68.5	78.2	82.7	86.7	89.8	92.9	67.2
Bolivia (urban)												
Electricity[b]	1994	89.2	93.3	93.2	94.6	96.6	97.7	98.1	98.0	98.8	99.7	96.0
	1999	98.9	95.0	97.9	96.9	100.0	100.0	100.0	100.0	99.9	100.0	98.8
Telephone[a]	1994	2.9	7.2	8.1	9.4	13.4	22.3	27.4	35.6	48.6	69.7	25.5
	1999	7.9	6.9	13.0	22.9	33.4	35.2	36.7	42.6	58.6	62.0	31.0
Water[c]	1994	64.5	68.1	74.7	73.2	76.4	83.0	85.1	91.1	91.5	95.5	80.6
	1999	89.1	82.5	89.1	89.0	87.8	95.7	98.7	97.7	95.7	97.8	92.1
Mexico (all)												
Telephone[a]	1992	2.0	3.3	5.1	5.7	10.1	14.1	19.9	26.4	39.1	60.8	18.6
	1998	3.9	6.0	9.1	12.6	15.9	21.8	28.4	37.9	54.8	72.8	26.3
Water[c]	1992	22.0	30.5	39.1	44.3	48.8	54.1	63.0	66.0	75.0	87.1	53.0
	1998	27.9	35.8	39.3	44.8	49.4	58.5	64.8	72.1	83.3	89.9	56.6
Nicaragua (all)												
Electricity[d]	1993	11.1	25.2	36.2	53.4	64.4	68.5	78.5	81.7	82.0	78.0	57.9
	1998	11.3	29.5	40.3	58.4	72.0	77.2	88.5	91.4	93.2	84.9	64.7

a. Household had infrastructure access if it reported positive expenditure for the infrastructure item.
b. Household had infrastructure access if it had electricity.
c. Household had infrastructure access if the water network reached the building of the household dwelling unit.
d. The 1993 figures were obtained from a 1998 survey using a question regarding whether the household had installed electricity within the past five years.

Sources: Argentina: Ennis and Pinto (2002); Bolivia: Barja, McKenzie, and Urquiola (2002); Mexico: López-Calva and Rosellón (2002) Nicaragua: Freije and Rivas (2002).

The distributional effect of expanded access depends heavily on initial access levels. For example, with the exception of Nicaragua, expansion of water and electricity networks tends to benefit the poor the most since coverage of the richer deciles was already high. In Nicaragua, where initial electricity access was lower than in the other three countries, expanded access benefited the top half of the per capita expenditure distribution more than the poor. In terms of telephone service, the Latin American region has historically had low access levels; thus, expanded access has been directed mainly toward the middle and top of the expenditure distribution. Rapid expansion of cellular service has accounted for some of the increased access to telephony; however, the surveys do not distinguish the two types of service. Introduction of competition in cellular service was particularly important for Bolivian access, because local fixed-line phone cooperatives charge individuals US$1,200–1,500 for a fixed line, more than Bolivia's per capita income. ENTEL-Móvil's entry into cellular service in 1996 prompted a price war with the incumbent firm, Telecel, with cellular access charges falling below US$10. Over the 1996–2000 period, cellular penetration increased from 0.27 to 6.96 subscribers per 100 residents, thereby overtaking fixed-line penetration (ITU 2001).

Current trends make it difficult to determine the precise amount of increased access that resulted from privatization. For Bolivia, increased access was separated from current trends by comparing changes in access to water in La Paz and El Alto, where a private concession was put in place in 1997, with the country's other main cities of Santa Cruz and Cochabamba, which remained public. As table 2.3 shows, access increased in both areas during the 1992–94 and 1994–99 periods. The difference-in-difference estimate, which compares the change in La Paz and El Alto with the change in the nonprivatized areas, is negative over the 1992–94 period, indicating that access was growing faster in the other cities, but was positive after privatization between 1994–99. The resulting triple difference (annual growth in La Paz and El Alto relative to other cities from 1994–99, less the relative annual growth over 1992–94) was positive for all but the bottom quintile, suggesting that privatization increased access to water relative to both the existing trend and nonprivatized areas.[16] For Argentina, Galiani, Gertler, and Schargrodsky (2002) used 1991 and 1997 surveys to calculate the difference-in-difference for access to water between the privatized and nonprivatized areas; they found increased access in privatized municipalities.

Beyond the private benefits of access to water, electricity, and telephony, privatization carries many potential public benefits. For example, telecommunications services benefit from network externalities, whereby the value

---

16. Since 100 percent is the maximum for access, growth rates in access should fall over time as access approaches full coverage. The triple difference should therefore give a lower bound of the privatization effect.

Table 2.3 Increased access to water resulting from Bolivian privatization, by quintile (percent)

Quintile	La Paz and El Alto			Other main cities[a]			Difference-in-difference estimate[b]		Triple difference[c]
	1992	1994	1999	1992	1994	1999	1992–94	1994–99	
1 (lowest)	53.3	66.1	88.8	57.4	66.4	82.5	3.8	6.6	–0.6
2	70.7	73.3	93.3	69.8	74.2	86.9	–1.8	7.4	2.4
3	76.0	77.4	95.6	75.7	80.6	89.4	–3.5	9.5	3.6
4	87.1	89.8	100.0	84.1	87.5	97.3	–0.7	0.4	0.4
5 (highest)	96.2	94.6	100.0	87.8	93.1	95.4	–6.9	3.1	4.1
Overall	78.1	81.7	94.4	75.6	80.3	90.7	–1.0	2.2	1.0

a. Cochabamba and Santa Cruz.
b. The difference-in-difference estimate equals the change in La Paz and El Alto, minus the change in other main cities.
c. The triple difference equals one-fifth the difference-in-difference over 1994–99, minus one-half the difference-in-difference over 1992–94.
Source: Barja, McKenzie, and Urquiola (2002).

of having a telephone depends on how many other people are connected to the system. Expanded access to telephones therefore benefits existing, as well as new, users. Access to telephones can also foster trade networks and enhance remotely located residents' connection with society. With regard to electricity, expanded access implies environmental benefits if new users switch from fuelwood and fossil fuels. In terms of water, expanded access benefits public health by limiting the spread of disease. For example, in Argentina, Galiani, Gertler, and Schargrodsky (2002) found that in areas that privatized water, child mortality fell 5 to 9 percent because of reduced incidence of infectious and parasitic disease. While these public benefits and externalities are difficult to measure and are not included in our valuation of privatization's effect on consumers, they should be acknowledged when assessing the overall benefits of privatizing utility services.

Price Changes

The popular perception is that privatization tends to drive up consumer prices. Since public enterprises were often loss-making and cross-subsidized, subsequent private owners had to raise prices to cover costs. For electricity, Millan, Lora, and Micco (2001) found that industrial users in Latin America subsidized residential customers before privatization, while for telecommunications, high long distance rates often subsidized local calls. In such cases, tariff rebalancing serves to increase the prices paid by residential and poorer customers. However, other reasons lead one to expect that privatization will result in lower prices. In chapter 1, Birdsall and Nellis note that, if private management were more efficient, lower prices may result. The net result often depends on the amount of competition and regulation the

Table 2.4 Price changes after privatization[a]

Sector	Argentina Before	Argentina After	Bolivia Before	Bolivia After	Mexico Before	Mexico After	Nicaragua Before	Nicaragua After
Telephone	100	83.9	100	91.7	100	147.9	n.a.	n.a.
Electricity	100	67.5	100	126.2	n.a.	n.a.	100	124.2
Water	100	84.0			100	109.2	n.a.	n.a.
La Paz and El Alto			100	89.5				
Cochabamba			100	143.0				

n.a. = not applicable or not available (either service was not privatized or data after privatization was not yet available)

a. Real price indices relative to consumer price index (CPI); before privatization = 100.

Sources: Argentina: water data from Galiani, Gertler, and Schargrodsky (2002, table 2.3), electricity prices are residential final prices from FIEL (1999), and telephone based on communications price index from Instituto Nacional de Estadística y Censos (INDEC). Bolivia: telephone prices are the minimum fixed tariff from Instituto Nacional de Estadistica (INE), electricity prices are residential tariff rates from Superintendencia de Electricidad de Bolivia, and water rates in La Paz and El Alto are the tariff for 10 cubic meters from INE, whereas water rates in Cochabamba are R2 category rates (very poor users) from the Democracy Center. Mexico: water prices are from CONAGUA (Comisión Nacional del Agua) and PROFECO (Procuraduría Federa del Consumidor) and telephone prices are residential monthly subscription charges from ITU (2001). Nicaragua: electricity prices are from Banco Central de Nicaragua (Central Bank of Nicaragua).

private firm faces. Price changes will also depend on whether the government awards the privatization contract based on the highest bid (thereby maximizing government revenue) or the lowest tariff bid (which results in lower consumer prices but less government revenue).

Because the household surveys used in this study collected information only on household expenditure for infrastructure services—not the prices the households paid for these services—the four countries had to use aggregate price indices at the city, state, or national level to assess price changes after privatization.[17] As table 2.4 shows, the reported price changes are sensitive to the base year chosen; we used the prevailing prices in the same years as the surveys. The four cases generally avoided basing these price changes on prices from years of high macroeconomic instability, such as 1995 in Mexico (the peso crisis) or 1988–89 in Argentina (hyperinflation). Figures 2.1 to 2.4 provide further context with regard to the price evolution of selected utilities in Argentina, Bolivia, and Mexico.

Of the 10 privatizations studied in the four countries, prices fell in five cases and rose in the other five. Electricity prices increased in two out of the three countries with reforms. The price decrease in Argentina possibly reflected the fact that prior prices were high by international standards and privatization caused increased competition in electricity generation. Delfino

---

17. Unless otherwise noted, price information was provided by national statistics agencies in Argentina (INDEC) and Bolivia (INE) and by the Banco de México in Mexico.

Figure 2.1 Evolution of prices in Argentina, 1982–2000

price relative to CPI (1985 = 100)

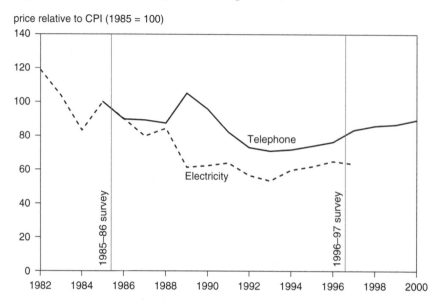

CPI = consumer price index.
Sources: Electricity from FIEL (1999); telephone and CPI from INDEC.

Figure 2.2 Electricity prices in Bolivia, 1992–99

real price index (1994 = 100)

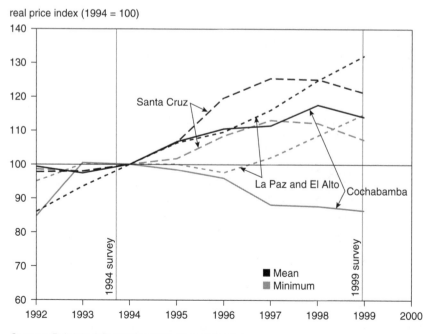

Sources: Bolivia's INE and Electricity Superintendence.

Figure 2.3 Water prices in Bolivia, 1992–99

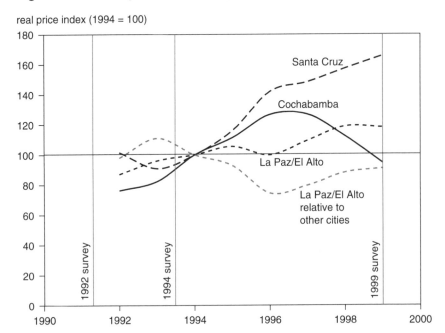

real price index (1994 = 100)

Sources: Water prices for 10 cubic meters from Bolivia's INE.

and Casarin (2001), using only postprivatization price data through 1999, found that electricity prices increased in Argentina. In chapter 5, Ennis and Pinto argue against using 1999 as a comparison point because of the deflation and macroeconomic instability that began in Argentina at that time; instead, they use 1996.[18] Unlike Delfino and Casarin, Ennis and Pinto compare the 1996 price with a preprivatization year, 1986. (We discuss the sensitivity of Ennis and Pinto's results to alternate measures of the price change when we evaluate privatization's overall effects on poverty and inequality.)

Telecommunications prices fell, on average, in Argentina and Bolivia, but rose in Mexico (Galiani, Gertler, and Schargrodsky 2002). Regulatory problems and lack of competition prevented all prices from decreasing in Mexico, although connection charges fell 75 percent between 1991 and 1998 and the prices of long distance and international calls fell more than 20 percent after the introduction of competition in 1995. However, during 1992–98, residential subscription rates increased 48 percent, and local per-unit rates

---

18. Ennis and Pinto justify their choice of comparison years by citing research by Urbiztondo, Artana, and Navajas (1998), which supports their assertion that prices fell.

Figure 2.4   Evolution of telephone prices in Mexico, 1988–2002

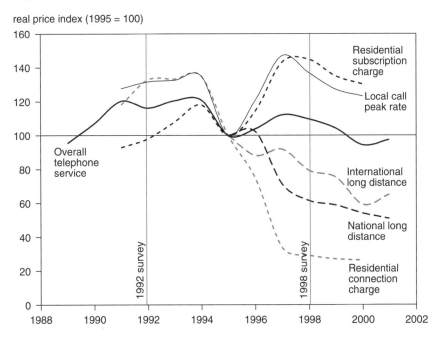

real price index (1995 = 100)

Sources: ITU (2001), Banco de México national consumer price index by expenditure item.

also rose. The increased cost of local calls and decreased cost of long distance calls resulted from Telmex's requirement to eliminate cross subsidies before introducing long distance competition in 1997. In Bolivia, an overall 8 percent decline in telephone prices masked a doubling of the minimum tariff in the city of Santa Cruz, where the local operative moved quickly to raise rates before price regulation was implemented.

In Argentina, the Buenos Aires water concession lowered prices, and addition of a fixed, universal-service fee allowed the concessionaire to reduce access fees to one-tenth of their previous level (Galiani, Gertler, and Schargrodsky 2002). The successful water concession in La Paz and El Alto resulted in lower water price increases in those cities, compared to elsewhere in Bolivia. However, a second concession issued to Aguas de Tunari in 1999 for the city of Cochabamba resulted in tariff increases averaging 43 percent for poor consumers, with some consumers experiencing a more than doubling of their bills.[19] Strikes and demonstrations ensued, followed by the declaration of martial law and eventual expulsion of the private

---

19. See Democracy Center, "Bechtel versus Bolivia: The Water Rate Hikes by Bechtel's Bolivian Company (Aguas del Tunari): The Real Numbers," August 20, 2002, www.democracyctr.org/bechtel/waterbills/waterbills-global.htm.

firm. In Mexico, heavily subsidized water prices resulted in 9 percent price increases in privatized areas, relative to nonprivatized ones. Thus, although prices increased after privatization in some instances, they decreased in many others. While technological advances (particularly in telecommunications) may be partially responsible for these decreases, Mexico's experience suggests that such gains cannot be realized without an appropriate regulatory framework.

Service Quality

Estache, Foster, and Wodon (2002) remark that consumer concern with state-owned utilities' low-quality service, especially in terms of service rationing and supply interruption, is a major justification for privatization, especially in Mexico (figure 2.5). A strong negative correlation of −0.55 is found between public support for privatization or private supply of a service and the perceived quality of that service. A 1991 poll in Buenos Aires, for example, found that 75 percent of respondents expected the quality of telephone service to improve with privatization, although over half thought the improvement would take three to five years to occur.[20]

Improved service quality was not only expected with privatization; in some cases, the government mandated it as part of the conditions for sale of public enterprises. For example, privatization of Bolivian electricity was accompanied by regulations that established a system for measuring quality, including dates by which firms had to comply with quality indicators and financial penalties in cases of noncompliance.

The household expenditure surveys used in this study did not collect information on the quality of infrastructure services used, and information from other sources is scarce. In particular, preprivatization quality indicators are mostly unavailable for the four countries studied. This lack of data made it impossible to formally measure the value of quality changes to consumers.

As table 2.5 shows, privatization is generally followed by improved quality of service (e.g., better quality telephone lines and shorter waiting periods for connection). In Mexico, for example, the waiting time for a telephone connection fell from 2.5 years in 1990—the year of privatization—to 72 days in 1995 and 30 days in 1997. Not all consumers, however, agreed that quality improved; a 1992 GEO (Gabinete de Estudios de Opinion) poll indicated that 36 percent of Mexicans thought telephone service had worsened with privatization,[21] while a 1993 poll found that one in four Mexicans

---

20. The EQUAS Poll (LI034), February 1991, obtained from the Roper Center Latin American Databank.

21. See "Public Opinion in the Valley of Mexico about Public Services," *El Nacional*, January 16–21, 1992 (obtained from the Roper Center Latin American Databank).

Figure 2.5 Support for privatization and perceived service quality—results from a 1992 Mexican poll

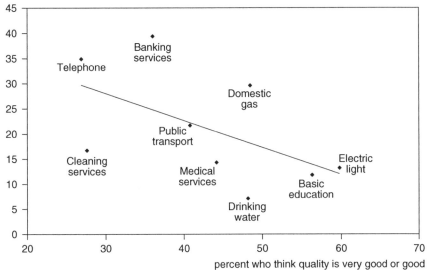

percent who think service should be private

percent who think quality is very good or good

Source: Author's calculations from a 1992 Gabinete de Estudios de Opinion (GEO) poll.

wanted to jail the telephone company management because of poor service.[22] Nevertheless, available data indicate general improvements in quality following privatization.

Methodology

Deaton (1989) shows that the simple, nonparametric estimation of Engel curves can be used to describe the average welfare effects of price changes on consumption. Since essentially all consumers do not privately produce electricity, water, or telephone services, the budget shares of those services provide a first-order approximation of the relative welfare effect of a change in their price. If one lets x_0 equal a household's initial total expenditure per capita, w_{j0} its initial budget share on service j, p_j the price of service j, and U the household's utility, then the first-order approximation to the change in utility is (Banks, Blundell, and Lewbel 1996):

---

22. See "Mexico Phone Monopoly at End of the Line," *Houston Chronicle*, August 13, 1996.

Table 2.5 Selected quality indicators, by country and sector

Country and sector	Quality measure	Baseline value	Postprivatization value (year)		

Argentina

Country and sector	Quality measure	1989–90	1994	1997–98
Telephone	Digitalization (percent)	13	63	100
	Lines in service	3,139,685	4,886,957	6,852,086
	Faults per 100 lines per year	42.4[c]	37.2	17.2
	Average repair waiting time (days)	11	3	n.a.

		1992–93	1994–99	
Water	Spilled water (millions of m³/day)	1.49	1.27	
	Average delay in attending claims (days)	180	32	

Bolivia

Country and sector	Quality measure	Legal limit of goal	1997 or 1999[a]
Electricity	Average response time to users technical complaints (hours)	3	2.26
	Average interruption frequency per user	25	4.7
	Index of commercial complaints	12	1.14
Telephone (percent)			
Long distance	Rural towns connected	25	32.66
	National long distance calls completed	55	69
	Faults corrected within three days	85	88
Fixed line	COTAS digitalization	80	96
	COTEL digitalization	5	5
	COTAS incidence of faults	40	8
	COTEL incidence of faults	60	27

		1993	1999
	Waiting list for main lines (number)	50,000	8,000

Mexico

Country and sector	Quality measure	1990	1995	1997
Telephone	Waiting time for new connection (days)	890	72	30
	Faults per 100 lines per year	6.0[b]	4.6	3.3
	Digitalization (percent)	38.6[c]	88	90.1
	Pending connections (number)	259,875[b]	70,798	91,367

n.a. = not available

a. Electricity results are based on a 1999 average reached by the firms CRE, ELECTROPAZ, ELFEC, ELFEO, and CESSA; telephone results are for 1997.

b. Based on 1993 data (1990 data was unavailable).

c. Based on 1991 data (1990 data was unavailable).

Sources: Argentina: Ennis and Pinto (2002); Bolivia: Galiani, Gertler, and Schargrodsky (2002) (water measures); Barja, McKenzie, and Urquiola (2002); Mexico: López-Calva and Rosellón (2002), ITU (2001).

$$\frac{\Delta U}{x_0} = -\left(\Delta \log p_j\right) w_{j0}. \tag{2.1}$$

A change in service price will have the greatest effect on consumers who devote a larger share of their total budget to that service. The approximation in equation 2.1 provides an upper bound on the loss to consumers of a price rise (or lower bound on the gain from a fall in price), as it assumes that consumers do not adjust their consumption quantity when the price of the service changes.[23] Banks, Blundell, and Lewbel (1996) therefore provide a second-order approximation to the change in welfare, which allows for quantity response to the price change:

$$\frac{\Delta U}{x_0} = -\left(\Delta \log p_j\right) w_{j0} \left(1 + \frac{\Delta \log p_j}{2} \frac{\partial \log w_j}{\partial \log p_j}\right). \tag{2.2}$$

Computation of equation 2.2 requires estimating the elasticity, $\partial \log w_j / \partial \log p_j$. This term is estimated by γ_{jj}/w_{j0}, where the coefficient γ_{jj} is obtained by estimating the Engel equation for household h.

$$w_{hj} = \alpha_j + \sum_{i=1}^{k} \gamma_{ij} \log p_i + \beta_j \log \frac{x_h}{n_h} + \phi_j \left(\log \frac{x_h}{n_h}\right)^2 + \lambda_j' Z_h. \tag{2.3}$$

Here, n_h is the number of members in household h, Z_h contains other demographic control variables, and p_i for $i \neq j$ is the price of good i. In much of this empirical work, the time periods and cross-sectional information are insufficient to allow for including the prices of substitute goods. This lack of sufficient price variation also precludes estimating a complete demand system to calculate welfare changes, as Wolak (1996) does.

These first- and second-order approximations can be used to measure the change in welfare arising from price changes associated with privatization for consumers who had access to the privatized service both before and after privatization.[24] For consumers who lacked access either before or after privatization, change in the price of the privatized good had no direct welfare change; however, if privatization caused a change in the price of substitute goods, this could be valued using first- and second-order approximations.

To value the welfare change for the remaining consumer group—those who gained access to the service after privatization—we used the concept of a virtual price that Neary and Roberts (1980) pioneered to examine

---

23. Waddams, Price, and Hancock (1998), who analyze utility privatizations in the United Kingdom, assume that quantity is fixed.

24. The approach could easily be modified to incorporate welfare gains from quality improvements by using quality-adjusted prices if sufficient data on quality were available.

household behavior under rationing.[25] Within this context, the virtual price of the privatized service is the lowest price at which a household would have chosen to consume zero units of the service before privatization if it had had access to the service in question. Given this virtual price, the welfare change from privatization is then calculated using equations 2.1 and 2.2, with the change in price moving from the virtual price to the postprivatization price and using the postprivatization expenditure share, w_{j1}, and total expenditure, x_1, in place of their preprivatization counterparts as reference points.[26]

The virtual price, p_v, is obtained from the estimated Engel equation 2.3 as the price at which the estimated expenditure share is zero. This virtual price differs across households according to their total expenditure and demographic characteristics—certain households are more able or willing to pay for access to the utility service. One potential concern is that equation 2.3 is only estimated for households that have access to the service; thus, it will result in inconsistent parameter estimates if omitted variables correlated with access also influence demand patterns. Therefore, we carry out Heckman's two-step selection correction, first using a probit to estimate the probability of access and then adding the inverse Mills ratio obtained from this step to equation 2.3 (Heckman 1979).

The method outlined above could be applied directly in the case of Nicaragua to assess welfare changes from privatizing electricity since that country's 1998 EMNV enables one to determine whether a given household had access in both 1993 and 1998.[27] The other three countries studied face the complication that household surveys are repeated cross-sections, rather than a panel. This means that a given household is interviewed only once, either before or after privatization of services; thus, it is only possible to identify whether the household has access in the survey year. Appendix 2.B outlines how the method described thus far is adapted to calculate welfare changes when the surveys contain a different sample of individuals each year.

The budget share allocated to each infrastructure category provides a first-order approximation of the households most affected by price changes. The mean budget shares capture the joint effect of differences in access across groups (those with no access have zero budget share) and income elasticities across those with access (table 2.6). The result is that not all budget shares

---

25. We make the empirically plausible assumption that no consumers lost access to the service as a result of privatization. Prices may have risen sufficiently to enable some users to choose to consume zero quantity; however, the option of paying for the privatized service remained.

26. A change in access has no value if one uses the preprivatization reference point since, in this case, the expenditure share w_{j0} is zero.

27. The 1998 EMNV asked respondents whether electricity service had been installed since 1993.

Table 2.6 Budget shares allotted to infrastructure sector, by decile
(per capita expenditure)

Country and sector	Period	1	2	3	4	5	6	7	8	9	10
Argentina (urban)											
Telecommunications	1985–86	0.3	0.3	0.5	0.8	0.7	0.6	1.0	0.9	1.0	1.1
	1996–97	1.8	2.2	2.3	2.6	2.4	2.7	2.5	2.6	2.3	2.2
Water and electricity	1985–86	2.3	2.6	2.6	2.9	2.3	2.6	2.4	2.3	2.0	1.8
	1996–97	4.7	4.2	3.7	3.6	3.1	2.9	2.7	2.5	2.1	1.5
Bolivia (urban)											
Telecommunications	1994	0.1	0.3	0.4	0.3	0.5	0.9	1.0	1.5	2.0	2.8
	1999	0.3	0.2	0.6	0.9	1.3	1.3	2.2	2.2	4.6	4.4
Water	1994	2.2	1.9	1.6	1.6	1.6	1.9	1.9	1.9	1.8	1.4
	1999	2.1	1.5	1.9	1.8	1.8	2.1	2.0	1.8	1.7	1.7
Electricity	1994	4.8	4.1	3.9	4.0	3.9	4.2	3.9	3.7	3.6	2.9
	1999	4.4	3.6	4.0	3.9	3.4	3.4	3.7	3.6	3.5	2.9
Mexico											
Telecommunications	1992	0.1	0.1	0.4	0.4	0.6	1.0	1.2	1.5	2.0	2.4
	1998	0.1	0.2	0.6	1.0	1.4	1.8	2.4	2.6	2.9	3.1
Water	1992	0.9	1.1	1.1	1.1	1.1	1.0	1.0	1.0	0.8	0.6
	1998	1.2	1.0	1.3	1.2	1.2	1.2	1.2	1.0	0.9	0.6
Nicaragua											
Electricity	1993	2.5	1.9	1.6	2.1	2.3	2.3	3.4	3.5	3.6	3.4
	1998	0.4	0.8	1.1	1.3	1.5	1.9	1.7	2.1	2.1	1.8

Note: Includes all households, including those without access.

Sources: Argentina: Ennis and Pinto (2002); Bolivia: Barja, McKenzie, and Urquiola (2002); Mexico: López-Calva and Rosellón (2002); Nicaragua: Freije and Rivas (2002).

decrease with total expenditure. Taking mean budget shares only across households with access, one finds that water and electricity are necessities—that is, budget shares decline as income increases—in Argentina, Bolivia, and Mexico; while telephone service is a luxury in Bolivia but a necessity in Argentina and Mexico. Price changes in water and electricity therefore tend to have the greatest effect on the poor, except in Nicaragua, where low access to electricity means that fewer poor residents are subject to price changes. By contrast, as telephone service constitutes a higher proportion of richer households' total budget, telephone price changes affect the upper deciles more than the lower ones. In most cases, however, each infrastructure service constitutes only 1 to 3 percent of total household budget; thus, even large price changes should not have dramatic effects.

Tables 2.7, 2.8, and 2.9 present the joint welfare effect of access and price changes obtained by the Nicaragua, Bolivia, and Argentina studies, respectively, using the above-outlined method in equations 2.1 through 2.3. For Nicaraguan electricity reform, Freije and Rivas (chapter 3) distinguish between households that had access before and after privatization and those that gained access after privatization (table 2.7). Clearly, increased

Table 2.7 Nicaragua electricity reforms: Joint effect of price and access change on consumers
(percent of per capita total household expenditure)

Decile[a]	Households with access before and after privatization		Households that gained access after privatization		Overall effect	
	First-order approximation	Second-order approximation	First-order approximation	Second-order approximation	First-order approximation	Second-order approximation
1 (lowest)	−0.78	−0.76	12.99	12.66	−0.09	−0.05
2	−0.55	−0.54	15.98	16.55	−0.16	0.58
3	−0.59	−0.58	15.61	16.25	−0.24	0.47
4	−0.48	−0.46	5.38	6.29	−0.27	0.07
5	−0.43	−0.40	5.38	6.27	−0.32	0.22
6	−0.53	−0.49	3.57	4.30	−0.41	0.04
7	−0.43	−0.39	1.69	2.41	−0.37	−0.07
8	−0.50	−0.43	2.02	2.59	−0.45	−0.10
9	−0.49	−0.39	1.38	1.84	−0.45	−0.11
10 (highest)	−0.49	−0.36	0.74	1.25	−0.40	−0.19

a. Preprivatization.

Source: Freije and Rivas (2002).

Table 2.8 Bolivia privatization reforms: Joint effect of price and access change on consumers
(percent of per capita total household expenditure)

Decile[a]	Electricity (overall effect)		Telephone (overall effect)		Water[b]					
					Scenario 1[c]		Scenario 2[d]		Cochabamba	
	First-order approximation	Second-order approximation	First-order approximation	Second-order approximation	First-order approximation	Second-order approximation	First-order approximation	Second-order approximation	First-order approximation	Second-order approximation
1 (lowest)	11.97	17.36	0.23	0.34	4.12	6.93	0.94	1.48	−0.99	−0.95
2	0.76	1.56	0.13	0.13	0.83	1.58	0.31	0.50	−1.08	−1.04
3	3.48	5.64	0.50	0.70	2.01	2.96	0.46	0.63	−0.55	−0.52
4	1.60	2.65	1.80	2.69	1.30	2.63	0.43	0.77	−0.69	−0.66
5	2.11	3.57	4.06	5.80	1.29	1.94	0.87	1.29	−0.95	−0.92
6	0.97	1.98	4.05	5.65	1.15	1.86	0.47	0.70	−0.76	−0.72
7	0.86	1.62	3.55	4.65	0.85	1.29	0.17	0.17	−0.75	−0.71
8	0.78	1.60	2.62	3.71	0.60	0.83	0.18	0.19	−0.38	−0.34
9	0.02	0.42	8.38	10.51	0.42	0.62	0.26	0.33	−0.50	−0.46
10 (highest)	−0.50	−0.41	−7.44	−9.27	0.42	0.54	0.15	0.16	−0.57	−0.53

a. Preprivatization.
b. Both scenarios 1 and 2 measure the overall effect of water privatization in La Paz and El Alto.
c. Scenario 1 assumes that privatization is the cause for all increased access.
d. Scenario 2 assumes that only increased access above increases in Santa Cruz and Cochabamba is due to privatization.

Source: Barja, McKenzie, and Urquiola (2002).

Table 2.9 Argentina electricity and telecommunications reforms: Joint effect of price and access change on consumers
(percent of per capita total household expenditure)

Decile[a]	Electricity		Telecommunications	
	First-order approximation	Second-order approximation	First-order approximation	Second-order approximation
1	3.05	3.32	0.10	0.14
2	2.22	2.48	0.29	0.37
3	1.79	2.03	0.47	0.61
4	1.71	1.94	0.47	0.59
5	1.19	1.41	0.51	0.67
6	1.29	1.51	0.66	0.86
7	1.11	1.32	0.55	0.72
8	1.08	1.29	0.45	0.63
9	0.88	1.09	0.39	0.57
10	0.81	1.02	0.36	0.52

a. Preprivatization.

Note: Overall effect in urban areas only.

Source: Ennis and Pinto (2002).

price negatively affected households that already had access; because budget shares allocated to electricity are low, however, the welfare loss to these households is less than 1 percent of their per capita expenditure. By contrast, the value of gaining access can be much larger, reaching 16 percent of per capita expenditure for the lowest deciles. Therefore, the overall effect on a decile depends on the number of households who gained access relative to those with existing access. Deciles 2 through 6 experienced small gains in welfare, while the other deciles saw small welfare losses. For Bolivia, Barja, McKenzie, and Urquiola (chapter 4) estimate that the welfare increase from gaining access to electricity exceeded 100 percent for the lowest deciles. Thus, although prices rose, the overall effect was positive for all but the top decile.

Since prices fell in Argentina, Ennis and Pinto (chapter 5) find that the welfare effects were positive for all deciles for both electricity and telephone service (table 2.9). Electricity privatization benefited the poorer deciles relatively more, with an average effect of 2 to 3 percent of per capita expenditure for the lowest three deciles, while telephone privatization benefited the middle class more. As mentioned above, Delfino and Casarin (2001) suggest that privatization caused electricity prices to rise, rather than fall. Using the results of Ennis and Pinto, we estimate that prices would have needed to rise 32 percent to generate a negative welfare effect for decile 1, and more than 60 percent to have an overall negative welfare effect on deciles 2 and 3. Delfino and Casarin report a 38 percent price increase for the poor and a 10 percent decrease for consumers above 150 kWh (which must be viewed as the maximum possible price increase stemming from privatization because of the 1998–99 deflation). Such a price increase would still imply overall positive welfare effects for deciles 2 through 10 and a welfare loss of 0.01 percent of per capita expenditure for decile 1. Thus, the welfare effect is most likely positive, on average.

In Bolivia, the benefits of telephone privatization were highest among the middle class; increased access was greatest for this group, with deciles 5 to 7 receiving overall gains of 5 to 6 percent of per capita expenditure (table 2.8). For the water concession in La Paz and El Alto, we present results under two scenarios: (1) taking privatization as the cause for all increased access and (2) valuing increased access in La Paz and El Alto relative to other major cities. In both cases, the effect was positive, but lower under the second scenario. The benefits of water privatization were relatively larger for Bolivia's poorer deciles since increased access was greatest for them. Decile 1 benefited 7 percent of per capita expenditure, although a gain of only 1.5 percent was attributable to privatization.

The failed concession in Cochabamba, Bolivia resulted in large increases in average water tariffs. Prices for the poorest consumers—for whom water usage consisted of only an indoor toilet and outside water tap—rose 43 percent on average. The middle class and commercial users experienced average price increases of 57 and 59 percent, respectively.[28] The short-lived nature of the privatization meant that agreed-on expansion of the water network under the concession contract was not realized, and consumers had immediate welfare losses from these price increases. Nevertheless, our estimates of the average welfare losses were not nearly as large as press reports suggested. For example, Finnegan reported that "ordinary workers now had water bills that amounted to a quarter of their monthly income."[29] By contrast, our estimated average cost of a 43 percent price rise at a maximum of 1 percent of per capita household expenditure. In the 1999 household survey, the maximum expenditure share on water observed in Cochabamba was 10.5 percent, with an average expenditure share of 1.6 percent and with the 95th percentile at 5.4 percent. For most households, then, expenditure shares were simply too low for even a doubling of price to result in the water bill reaching a quarter of income. The numbers reported in the press represented the maximum possible effect on very few consumers, while the average consumer had smaller welfare losses.

---

28. See Democracy Center, "Bechtel versus Bolivia: The Water Rate Hikes by Bechtel's Bolivian Company (Aguas del Tunari): The Real Numbers," August 20, 2002, www.democracyctr.org/bechtel/waterbills/waterbills-global.htm.

29. William Finnegan, "Letter from Bolivia: Leasing the Rain," *New Yorker*, April 8, 2002.

Poverty and Inequality

Consumer-welfare changes are a household-level money metric of the change in welfare if one assumes no income effects (Banks, Blundell, and Lewbel 1996). To evaluate privatization's effect on inequality, the country studies first calculate the Gini coefficient and Atkinson inequality indices before privatization. They then take each household's per capita expenditures before privatization; add the estimated per capita change in consumer welfare; and recalculate the inequality measures, taking the consumer effect of privatization into account. Use of repeated cross-sectional surveys entails complications associated with not being able to identify the specific households that gained access to the privatized service (appendix 2.C details the adjustments needed with this data).

One popular approach to poverty measurement is unified basic needs measures, based directly on availability of and access to certain essential services (e.g., World Bank 1996). Access to piped water and electricity is often included, in which case the increased access shown in table 2.2 would directly improve poverty measures.

Other poverty measures are based on household income or expenditure; however, the same approach for inequality can be used to evaluate privatization's consumer effect on poverty. The Foster, Greer, and Thorbecke (1984) poverty measures are calculated before privatization and again after adjusting for welfare changes, according to the following formula:

$$P_\alpha = \frac{1}{N} \sum_{i=1}^{N} \left(1 - \frac{x_i}{z} \right)^\alpha 1\left(x_i \leq z \right), \tag{2.4}$$

where z is the poverty line, x_i is household expenditure per capita for household i, N is the total number of households, and the parameter α is 0 for a headcount measure of poverty, 1 for the poverty gap ratio, and 2 for a poverty measure sensitive to distribution among the poor.

Privatization's overall effects on inequality and poverty among consumers in Argentina, Bolivia, and Nicaragua are given in table 2.10. In Argentina, privatization of electricity and telephone service reduced inequality by a small amount and reduced head-count measures of poverty 1.0 to 1.5 percent. That country's poor benefited from both increased access to utilities and reduced prices. In Bolivia, privatization of electricity and water had similar effects, reducing inequality slightly and poverty by 1.0 to 1.5 percent. Cochabamba's failed water privatization is estimated to have increased poverty by 2 percent and to have had little effect on inequality. Privatization of Bolivian telephone services had a larger effect because increased access was largest for the middle deciles. However, privatization is estimated to have resulted in 5 to 6 percent fewer households falling below the poverty line. (Bolivia has a high poverty level; even households in deciles 5 and

Table 2.10 Privatization effects on consumer inequality and poverty

Inequality and poverty measure	Measure before privatization	Estimated measure after privatization								
		Electricity		Telephone		Water[a]				
						La Paz and El Alto		Cochabamba		
		First-order approximation	Second-order approximation	First-order approximation	Second-order approximation	First-order approximation	Second-order approximation	First-order approximation	Second-order approximation	
Argentina (urban)										
Inequality measures										
Gini coefficient	0.400	0.396	0.396	0.396	0.396	n.a.	n.a.	n.a.	n.a.	
Atkinson indices										
A (0.5)	0.130	0.128	0.127	0.129	0.128	n.a.	n.a.	n.a.	n.a.	
A (1.0)	0.241	0.238	0.237	0.237	0.237	n.a.	n.a.	n.a.	n.a.	
A (2.0)	0.424	0.519	0.482	0.417	0.417	n.a.	n.a.	n.a.	n.a.	
Poverty measures										
Head count ($\alpha = 0$)	0.113	0.095	0.095	0.102	0.102	n.a.	n.a.	n.a.	n.a.	
Poverty gap ($\alpha = 1$)	0.032	0.027	0.027	0.029	0.029	n.a.	n.a.	n.a.	n.a.	
Distribution sensitive ($\alpha = 2$)	0.013	0.011	0.011	0.012	0.012	n.a.	n.a.	n.a.	n.a.	
Bolivia (urban)										
Inequality measures										
Gini coefficient	0.442	0.440	0.442	0.455	0.464	0.435	0.430	0.442	0.442	
Atkinson indices										
A (0.5)	0.164	0.162	0.163	0.171	0.176	0.159	0.156	0.164	0.164	
A (1.0)	0.278	0.275	0.278	0.293	0.303	0.270	0.265	0.278	0.279	
A (2.0)	0.660	0.652	0.649	0.641	0.641	0.652	0.647	0.660	0.660	

(table continues next page)

Table 2.10 Privatization effects on consumer inequality and poverty *(continued)*

Inequality and poverty measure	Measure before privatization	Estimated measure after privatization							
		Electricity		Telephone		Water[a]			
						La Paz and El Alto		Cochabamba	
		First-order approximation	Second-order approximation	First-order approximation	Second-order approximation	First-order approximation	Second-order approximation	First-order approximation	Second-order approximation
Poverty measures									
Head count ($\alpha = 0$)	0.625	0.615	0.610	0.572	0.566	0.618	0.612	0.646	0.625
Poverty gap ($\alpha = 1$)	0.259	0.253	0.251	0.240	0.240	0.250	0.245	0.262	0.259
Distribution sensitive ($\alpha = 2$)	0.136	0.132	0.132	0.129	0.128	0.130	0.125	0.138	0.136
Nicaragua									
Inequality measures									
Gini coefficient	0.556	0.557	0.557	n.a.	n.a.	n.a.	n.a.	n.a.	n.a.
Atkinson indices									
A (0.5)	0.265	0.266	0.266	n.a.	n.a.	n.a.	n.a.	n.a.	n.a.
A (1.0)	0.428	0.430	0.430	n.a.	n.a.	n.a.	n.a.	n.a.	n.a.
A (2.0)	0.634	0.636	0.636	n.a.	n.a.	n.a.	n.a.	n.a.	n.a.
Poverty measures									
Head count ($\alpha = 0$)	0.352	0.351	0.352	n.a.	n.a.	n.a.	n.a.	n.a.	n.a.
Poverty gap ($\alpha = 1$)	0.145	0.146	0.146	n.a.	n.a.	n.a.	n.a.	n.a.	n.a.
Distribution sensitive ($\alpha = 2$)	0.081	0.082	0.082	n.a.	n.a.	n.a.	n.a.	n.a.	n.a.

n.a. = not available

a. Water results are reported for Bolivia only and effects of the La Paz and El Alto and Cochabamba privatizations are reported separately; the La Paz and El Alto results assume that privatization is the cause for all increased access (see Barja, McKenzie, and Urquiola [2002] for results under alternate assumptions). In Bolivia, city-level, counterfactual poverty and inequality measures are scaled to be comparable to overall urban levels (first column).

Sources: Argentina: Ennis and Pinto (2002); Bolivia: Barja, McKenzie, and Urquiola (2002); Nicaragua: Freije and Rivas (2002).

6 lie below the poverty line.)[30] In Nicaragua, electricity reforms had essentially no effect on poverty and inequality, with increased price counteracting improved access.

The overall findings that emerge from table 2.10 are that (1) privatization generally has little effect on inequality (change in the Gini coefficient is 0.02 or less), and (2) in three of the four countries studied, privatization either reduced poverty or had no effect on it (that is, the popular perception that privatization is responsible for large increases in inequality and is particularly harsh on the poor is not borne out by the cases considered here).

Evaluating Worker Effects

For a representative worker of any given category (defined by skill, employment sector, age, or gender), the economic rent or surplus depends on the wage rate and employment levels applicable to that category. Therefore, an evaluation of privatization's implications for income distribution must include effects on employment and wage rates. Ideally, employment effects would include job layoffs and changes in hours worked and tenure (i.e., the duration of employment relationships, which would affect level of economic insecurity, search costs, and investment in firm-specific relationships). The distributive effect of privatization requires one to assess effects (1) on average levels of these variables across the entire worker population (insofar as it pertains to the functional distribution of income between labor and capital) and (2) across worker categories to determine the effect on earnings distribution.

The data used for these evaluations are based on either employment or household surveys, which are subject to severe limitations. Therefore, our assessment of wage-employment effects is piecemeal, whereby available data on dimensions are evaluated separately at various levels of precision. In particular, the data do not permit any comprehensive assessment of the distributional effect across categories or income classes comparable to this study's consumer-side analysis.

Employment Layoffs

Job layoffs are typically widely publicized and involve large income changes for the workers affected, at least over the short term. Direct data on layoffs were unavailable for the privatized enterprises examined. The authors of the

---

30. The poverty line is taken from the World Bank (1996), which uses the August 1993, overall urban poverty line of 219.9 Bolivianos per person per month. While city-specific poverty lines are likely to reduce the measured head-count poverty to about 0.52 to 0.54, this change would have little effect on the counterfactual comparisons.

country studies collected data on employment levels directly from most of the privatized utilities in Argentina, Bolivia, and Mexico and supplemented these data with household and employment surveys for selected years at various stages of the privatization process. Therefore, discussion on employment effects excludes Nicaragua, whose many privatized enterprises precluded collecting data on firm-level employment levels.

We assume that all employment reductions corresponded to layoffs, as we were able to observe only net changes in employment and were unable to distinguish resignations or voluntary retirement from layoffs or determine whether larger layoffs were offset by new hires. Thus, this section uses the terms employment reduction and layoff interchangeably. In what follows, we summarize evidence from the country studies on employment reduction after privatization in absolute numbers and relative to preexisting levels of employment in these enterprises. One can also estimate the significance of layoffs relative to the overall labor force in the economy and to changes in unemployment occurring at that time. Upper bounds to the effects of layoffs on inequality and poverty were available for Argentina.

Argentina

Ennis and Pinto report in chapter 5 that, in Argentina, privatized enterprises were subject to a significant number of job losses: Employment fell about 75 percent (from 223,000 jobs to 73,000) between 1987–90 and 1997. Most of these losses were concentrated in Greater Buenos Aires, where the total labor force is approximately 4.2 million. Since the privatized enterprises tended to be capital-intensive, the proportion of the labor force affected was small (no more than 2 percent of the aggregate labor force and 3.5 percent of the labor force in Greater Buenos Aires).

The 1990s were a period of rising unemployment in Argentina; the rate of urban unemployment grew from 7.6 percent in 1989 to 9.6 percent in 1993 and 17.4 percent in 1995, subsequently falling to 14.9 percent in 1997. Between 1987–90 and 1997, the 150,000 jobs that privatized enterprises eliminated in the utilities—electricity, natural gas, water, telecommunications, airlines, and railways—and oil and gas sectors constituted an estimated 13 percent of increased unemployment in the Argentine economy, substantially exceeding the proportion of the economywide labor force originally employed in these sectors (7 percent for private and public enterprises combined in 1987–90). Hence, employment cutbacks in the privatized enterprises were greater than those occurring elsewhere in the economy, suggesting that the privatization process increased unemployment beyond the effect of general macroeconomic shock.

Most of the cutbacks were concentrated in the railway industry, where employment fell from 92,000 jobs in 1987–90 to 17,000 in 1997, accounting for 6.6 percent of increased unemployment in the economy over this period. In other sectors, the cutbacks were far smaller: in the oil sector, cutbacks accounted for only 2.57 percent of increased unemployment and less than 1.5 percent in each of the other sectors. Electricity, telecommunications, water, and gas together generated only 3.6 percent of additional unemployment.

The effect of layoffs on income distribution cannot be estimated without knowing the subsequent job experience of laid-off workers or of the nature of unemployment benefits. Ennis and Pinto use employment surveys to estimate an upper bound to the effect of these job reductions by assuming that all laid-off workers earned zero income. Alternatively, this assumption can be interpreted as the short-term effect if most laid-off workers were unemployed in the year of privatization, with no fiscal assistance in terms of severance packages or unemployment benefits. For 1989—the year before privatization—replacing incomes reported by a randomly selected set of workers in the privatized sectors (whose proportion equals that of job contractions in those sectors) increased the Gini coefficient of earnings distribution from 0.5375 to 0.5545 or about 3 percent. Not surprisingly, the effect on the proportion below the poverty line was somewhat larger, rising from 29.47 to 31.95 percent or about 8 percent.

Some workers who lost jobs in the privatized enterprises might subsequently have been rehired elsewhere in the private sector. Numerous anecdotal reports indicate that many employees in the vertically integrated SOEs who left at the time of privatization joined smaller private companies that became subcontractors of the privatized enterprises. One can estimate a lower bound to the extent of such rehiring by focusing only on employment in the sectors privatized (that is, ignoring laid-off employees who may have found new jobs in other sectors). The employment surveys allowed Ennis and Pinto to estimate the proportion of the Argentine labor force accounted for by the sectors privatized over successive years (aggregating across public and private enterprises). This proportion declined from 7.32 percent in 1989 to 5.14 percent in 1992, owing to contractions in both the SOEs (from 1.95 to 0.58 percent) and the private sector (from 5.37 to 4.56 percent). After 1992, however, private-sector employment grew to nearly 7 percent in 1994, and remained at that level during 1996–97. The share of these sectors in the economywide labor force nearly recovered to its former level (7.06 percent in 1997 versus 7.32 percent in 1989), suggesting that the overall employment contractions in the privatized sectors over a longer time horizon were similar to those occurring in other sectors of the economy. In short, after controlling for macroeconomic changes, expanded private-sector employment eventually absorbed most of the workers laid off in the privatized enterprises.[31] Viewed from this interpretation, the

---

31. The rise in private-sector employment could also have been accounted for employees shifting in from other sectors or new entrants to the labor force, rather than reemployment of workers displaced from the public sector.

income losses resulting from layoffs were temporary, lasting a maximum of three years after privatization. Thus, the inequality effects on long-term income distribution are negligible, as even the 3 percent increase in the Gini coefficient calculated for the year of privatization would largely disappear by 1994.

Analysis of the distribution of employment reductions in the privatized enterprises by skill level reveals that the cutbacks were greater for less skilled employees; however, the extent to which this was so is similar to the changes in skills bias that occurred in other sectors of the economy. Tenure declined disproportionately in the privatized sector, with duration of employment declining almost 70 percent between 1989–95 (from an average of 194 months to 57 months), as opposed to a 27 percent decline (from an average of 96 months to 70 months) for the labor force at large. Average hours worked increased, reflecting the general trend in these sectors for privately employed workers to work more, on average, than employees of SOEs (55 versus 45 hours per week).

Bolivia

The extent of privatization in Bolivia was much narrower than in Argentina. Because information was unavailable on the employment effects of the water concessions, Barja, McKenzie, and Urquiola, in chapter 4, focus on privatizations in the electricity and telecommunications sectors, which represented less than 0.5 percent of the economy's labor force before privatization (about 5,800 jobs of the 1.3 million employed in the capital cities). Thus, these privatizations are unlikely to have exerted a significant effect on economywide employment or wage levels.

Within the privatized Bolivian enterprises, employment levels fell. In electricity generation, the state firm ENDE (Empresa Nacional de Electricidad) split into three privatized enterprises, in addition to leaving an ENDE residual. While data for the residual firm are unavailable, the three privatized enterprises together employed 180 workers, compared with ENDE's 540 employees before privatization. In electricity transmission, data limitations prevented us from obtaining a complete picture; however, we established a 15 to 20 percent upper bound of job losses for 1995–97. In telecommunications, employment in ENTEL's long distance segment rose from 1,745 in 1995 to more than 2,000 in 1997 (likely reflecting growth of the new cellular business), and fell steadily thereafter to about 1,000 by 2000. In the local segment, the number of jobs dropped from about 2,000 in 1995–96 to 1,600 in 2000. The aggregate change in these two sectors was a drop of about 1,700 jobs, implying a job contraction rate of about 30 percent within the privatized enterprises in the five years following privatization.

As a proportion of the total labor force in the capital cities, the job losses in these two sectors are miniscule: about 0.13 percent or 1 out of every 1,000 jobs. Bolivia's ratio stands in sharp contrast to that of Argentina, where job losses in Greater Buenos Aires amounted to 3.5 percent of the labor force or 35 out of every 1,000 jobs.

Data on unemployment rates in the overall Bolivian economy reveal a rise from 3 percent in 1995 to 4.43 percent in 1997, and then to 7.5 percent in 2000. Assuming that unemployment rates in the capital cities were similar to those in the rest of the economy (an assumption borne out for the last year, 1995, for which data on unemployment rates in capital cities are available) and using the estimated size of the labor force in the capital cities (1.3 million in 1995), Barja, McKenzie, and Urquiola estimate 58,000 job losses in the economy as a whole between 1995 and 2000. In the electricity and telecommunications sectors, job losses thus amounted to approximately 3 percent of the aggregate job losses in capital cities. Bolivia's percentage is comparable to the corresponding contributions of these two sectors in Argentina, and is substantially higher than the proportion of the labor force originally accounted for by these sectors. In short, privatization in Bolivia had a contracting effect on employment, even after correcting for overall macroeconomic shocks, but—like the case of Argentina—the effect was small.

No further details are available on the likely effects of these layoffs on income distribution, tenure, hours worked, or skill distribution of the work force. The relatively small scale of the employment cutbacks in these sectors, relative to the rest of the economy, suggests that these effects are unlikely to be significant.

Mexico

Privatization's effect on employment in Mexico falls between Argentina and Bolivia. López-Calva and Rosellón (2002) report that, in 1983, when privatization began, SOEs employed more than 4 percent of the economy's work force; a decade later that percentage had fallen by more than half. The proportion of the labor force involved in enterprises undergoing the first two phases of privatization was thus about 2 percent of Mexico's entire work force. The fraction of the work force—both white- and blue-collar workers— laid off from these enterprises during these two phases was about 50 percent, according to firm-based surveys reported in La Porta and López-de-Silanes (1999). The employment declines started before privatization and were accentuated in the subsequent two or three years. Hence, the fraction of job losses that occurred within a four-year window of privatizations amounted to about 1 percent of the economy's workforce (10 jobs out of every 1,000), compared with 2 percent in Argentina and .13 percent in Bolivia.

Unlike Argentina and Bolivia, however, Mexico witnessed a decline in overall unemployment during the first two phases of privatization. The open (urban) unemployment rate decreased from 5 percent in 1985 to 4 percent in 1994. Applied to the entire economy, this rate is comparable to that of jobs lost in privatized enterprises, suggesting that, without privatization, the drop in the unemployment rate would have doubled.

The rotating panel feature of Mexico's employment surveys permitted López-Calva and Rosellón (2002) to follow the job experience of laid-off SOE workers over one subsequent year. About 45 to 50 percent of those laid off found jobs within the same sector within a year, without loss of social security or health benefits. This data suggests that even the short-term effect of job losses is approximately half the figure given above—that is, about 5 out of every 1,000 workers were unemployed for a full year after privatization. Furthermore, some remaining workers would have shifted into the informal sector or self-employment, sectors whose importance grew within the labor market (together accounting for 49 percent of the labor force in 1980 and 60 percent in 1996).

Summing Up

The proportion of the labor force laid off was small, ranging from a low of 0.13 percent in Bolivia to 2 percent in Argentina; the cutbacks were large within the privatized enterprises, ranging from 30 percent in Bolivia to 75 percent in Argentina; and their effect on unemployment was larger than that of other sectors of the economy. In Argentina and Mexico—the two countries where cutbacks were largest—a significant proportion of laid-off workers was eventually reemployed within the same sector (45 to 50 percent within one year in Mexico and 80 to 90 percent within four years in Argentina).

Wage Rates

Ennis and Pinto find that, in Argentina during 1989–95, average (real) wages rose 50 to 60 percent in both private and public sectors, reflecting recovery resulting from macroeconomic stabilization. The effect of privatization on wages, however, depends on the difference in average wage levels in the two sectors. Public-sector wage rates were higher, on average, by about 10 percent in 1989 and 16 percent in 1995. The labor reallocation created by privatization represented a downward effect on the average wage rate for the work force as a whole. This effect is likely insignificant, however, given that only 2 percent of the workforce was shifted in this manner. Moreover, average hours worked increased by about 25 percent for those workers who shifted sectors, which more than outweighed the drop in the wage rate. Consequently the effect on average wage income was positive for the representative employed worker.

Reallocation's effect on economywide wage inequality is complicated by two counteracting effects. On the one hand, greater wage inequality within the private sector, compared with the public sector, exposed the transferred workers to greater wage dispersion. On the other hand, the deviation between the average public-sector wage rate and the mean wage in the economy was greater than the corresponding deviation between the average private-sector wage and the economywide wage rate, so the transferred workers moved closer to the economywide average.[32] The former effect dominated in Argentina, irrespective of the year chosen as the base. Hence, the labor reallocation increased wage inequality; however, to reiterate, the extent of this effect was insignificant, given the small proportion of workers transferred across sectors.

From 1989 to 1995, the Gini coefficient of the wage rate fell 16 percent, mainly because of a drop in inequality in both the public and private sectors. Based on the above argument, it would have fallen even faster without privatization; however, the extent of the difference caused would probably have been negligible. The fall in inequality within the public and private sectors was similar to the economywide fall: 14 and 17 percent, respectively. Thus, within-group changes are likely to override the effects privatization had on labor reallocation. Unfortunately, analyzing the role that privatization may have played in reducing inequality within each sector requires more detailed data on intrafirm wage distribution than are available for Argentina to date.

No information is available on the wage effects of privatization in Bolivia. In Mexico, La Porta and López-de-Silanes (1999) use intrafirm data to show that wage rates rose in enterprises after privatization, mainly because of rises in worker productivity. The contrast to the general stagnation of wage rates in the economy in 1983–94 is striking. Even more surprising is that the rise in wage rates was significantly higher for blue-collar, than for white-collar, workers (approximately 122 percent versus 77 percent over the same period). This finding suggests that privatization per se reduced wage inequality within the privatized enterprises. The full effect, of course, includes the effect of labor reallocation between public and private sectors (that is, the wage implications for those who lost their jobs in the privatized enterprises and were subsequently hired elsewhere in the private sector). The rotating panel analysis carried out by López-Calva and Rosellón (2002) indicates that those who left the privatized enterprises lost because they were reemployed at a lower wage rate; however, they protected their incomes by working longer hours. On the other hand, most lost access to health care and social security benefits, which must be counterbalanced against the trends in within-sector wage dispersions.

The extent of labor reallocation resulting from the privatization process was substantially larger in Nicaragua than in the other three countries. Over the 1993–98 period, that country's private-sector share in the labor force rose from 77 to 86 percent in urban areas and, during 1993–99 from

---

32. The economywide variance equals the weighted sum of within-group variances, added to the variance of the two group means from the economywide mean, with the employment shares of the two sectors acting as weights. Hence, the effect of a change in the employment shares equals the sum of two effects: the difference in within-group variances and the difference in variance of group means from the economywide mean.

89 to 96 percent in rural areas. Thus, the proportion of the overall labor force reallocated was at least 7 to 9 percent, and probably higher if the entire privatization period were taken into account. This finding reflects the transition from a socialist economy that was under way. Given the country's many privatized enterprises, it was not feasible for Freije and Rivas (chapter 3) to obtain intrafirm data on wages and employment. Therefore, they relied on national household surveys conducted in 1993 and 1998–99.

As is typical, the average public-sector wage was above that of the private sector, such that the labor reallocation lowered the average wage in the economy. In the rural sector, the difference was large and growing: average public-sector wages were 29 percent higher than in the private sector in 1993 and 59 percent higher in 1998. In the urban sector, the differential was negligible in 1993[33] and 20 percent in 1999. Wage rates rose in the urban sector and fell sharply in the rural sector within both private and public employment. Hence, the privatization process is likely to have significantly accentuated the downward drift in the average rural wage.

In Nicaragua's case, the effect on wage inequality is particularly complicated because the choice of sector, base year, and unit matters. Freije and Rivas found that the ordering of variances and means in the public and private sectors depended on whether the urban or rural sector were considered, whether the base or final year were chosen for comparison, and whether the wage or the log of the wage were chosen as the unit. Since the log normal distribution is usually a better approximation than a normal distribution to distributional data, it perhaps makes sense to focus on the log of the wage rate as the relevant unit. In that case, wage dispersion is uniformly higher in private versus public employment, with the difference especially pronounced in the rural sector. This effect contributes to increased inequality stemming from the labor reallocation. On the other hand, the transferred workers moved closer to the economywide average wage, which tended to reduce inequality.

In the rural sector, the balance between the two effects depended on whether base year or final year weights were chosen. Using final year weights, the overall effect on rural wage inequality was negative, but positive if base year weights were chosen. In the urban sector, the effect was positive in both cases, but the magnitude of the effect was sensitive to choice of the base year. Thus, it is difficult to infer the overall effect of labor reallocation on wage inequality.

Within the public sector, wage dispersion rose in both urban and rural areas. It was especially sharp in the urban sector, where the variance of the public-sector log wage rose from 0.501 in 1993 to 0.736 in 1999. This find-

---

33. The arithmetic mean of the wage rate was slightly lower in the public sector, while the geometric mean was slightly higher in 1993.

ing reflects wage-structure convergence of the public and private sectors. Public-sector managers and professionals, in particular, experienced sharp increases in wages, which moved toward parity with private-sector wages for these categories. However, wages for clerical workers, salespersons, and manual workers changed little. Thus, it is plausible that wage structures within the public sector were responding to market pressures at the upper end, causing inequality within the public sector to grow.

Freije and Rivas conducted a decomposition analysis of the wage structure in the two sectors, following Juhn, Murphy, and Pierce (1993); the exercise confirmed the validity of this hypothesis, even after controlling for a range of worker characteristics that affect wages, such as age, gender, schooling, employment sector, and nature of position held. Specifically, the convergence of public-sector wage structures to the private sector at the upper end tended to explain one-third of the rise of the variance of log wages in the urban sector, a proportion reasonably robust across choice of inequality measure (such as generalized entropy measures or Atkinson indices corresponding to differing degrees of inequality aversion). This effect is not related to the privatization process per se, but to increasing market pressures on public-sector wage structures. The dominant source of upward pressure on inequality—far outweighing the effect of changing public-sector wage structures—was the rise in market-wage sensitivity to worker characteristics, which is not surprising in a transition economy.[34] Compared with these changes, the privatization process and changes in public-sector wage structures are modest contributing factors.

Summing up, overall labor reallocation associated with privatization was significant in Nicaragua, but not in Argentina and Mexico.[35] Reallocation tended to lower the average wage since public-sector wages were higher, on average, than private-sector wages. The effect of reallocation on wage inequality was complicated by a set of opposing effects, with no simple pattern emerging across countries. Changes in public- and private-sector wage inequality likely dominated these effects. Over the privatization period, within-sector inequality fell in Argentina (for reasons not yet well understood), within-firm inequality fell in privatized enterprises in Mexico (partly because of the privatization process), and within-sector inequality rose significantly in Nicaragua (probably owing to increased market pressures associated with the political transition).

---

34. Increased sensitivity of wages to worker characteristics typically constitutes 130 to 250 percent of the change in overall wage inequality in the urban sector for 1993–99, in contrast to a 33 to 60 percent contribution from changed public-sector wage structures and 16 to 76 percent of labor reallocation resulting from privatization.

35. Data were not available for Bolivia; the wage employment effect in that country would likely be negligible.

Fiscal Implications

Even though their distributive effect is less visible and difficult to estimate, privatization's fiscal consequences can be just as important as the direct effects on consumers and workers. For example, the often large proceeds from privatization may be used to retire public debt or reduce fiscal deficit, thereby serving as useful accompaniment to macroeconomic stabilization programs aimed at reducing inflation and future debt burdens. The inflation tax often falls disproportionately on the poor, while reductions in debt service burdens can free up resources for social spending programs (e.g., old-age pensions, public schooling, or health clinics). In addition, many SOEs incur operating losses funded by fiscal-budget subsidies. Privatization often leads to elimination of these losses, and profitable private enterprises contribute tax revenues instead of absorbing public subsidies.

Argentina

In Argentina, privatization proceeds were considerable at both the federal ($19 billion) and provincial ($4 billion) levels. Of these amounts, $10 billion was used to reduce public debt ($6.7 billion coming from the 1990 telecommunications privatization and $2.7 billion from the 1992 electricity and natural gas privatizations). This amount equaled about one-eighth of the country's public debt at that time, which fell from $78.9 billion in 1990 to $69.6 billion in 1993. Interest payments on debt fell from 2.98 percent of GDP in 1989 to 1.70 percent in 1993 and 1.61 percent in 1994. Since the early 1980s, social spending programs have tended to be negatively correlated with debt-service payments; following this general pattern, social spending increased by an almost equivalent amount, from 17.63 percent of GDP in 1989 to 19.24 percent in 1994. The fiscal deficit dropped from 3.8 percent of GDP in 1989 to 0.1 percent in 1994 and 0.5 percent in 1995, partly as a result of the additional $13 billion privatization proceeds in the form of cash. Privatization proceeds played a role in the general macroeconomic stabilization that occurred at this time, although it is virtually impossible to disaggregate the specific amount. Concerning annual fiscal transfers between enterprises and government budget, the state-owned sector as a whole received fiscal transfers of 1.92 percent and 1.06 percent of GDP in 1989 and 1990, respectively. Some privatized enterprises were profitable before the privatization; however, data concerning this lost revenue, as well as postprivatization transfers, have not yet been collected.

Bolivia

The Bolivian privatization process was unique insofar as the government treasury did not receive any funds from the capitalizations. The proceeds were earmarked for new investment in the companies, while 45 percent of the shares went to a collective capitalization fund devoted to retirement benefits. Fund dividends amounted to 0.5 percent of GDP in 1997 and 1999, the bulk of which accrued from the telecommunications sector. The fund financed a program called Bonosol, which made cash payments equivalent to $248 per citizen above the age of 65, to approximately 320,000 people. These payments were significant, compared with the country's per capita income of approximately $1,000. Between 1998 and 2000, the payments shrank to about $60, and reached fewer citizens (about 150,000). To date, the total outlay on these cash payments has amounted to approximately $57 million. The collective capitalization fund also supported private pension accounts, through an individual capitalization fund, amounting to $15 million, and paid out another $23 million for funeral expenses.

Mexico

In Mexico, privatization proceeds totaled about $23 billion during 1984–93 and $10 billion in 1994–2000. These were used to retire public debt, reduce fiscal deficit (which fell from more than 15 percent of GDP in 1982–83 to 10 percent in 1984 and near zero during 1993–96), and increase social spending (which rose from 6 percent of GDP in 1990 to 9 percent in 1994 and 9.5 percent in 2000). Many privatized enterprises were converted from loss-making units to profit-making entities, which presumably would have reversed the nature of fiscal transfers.

Nicaragua

Unlike the other three countries, Nicaragua was characterized by a marked lack of transparency in use of first-phase privatization proceeds. These funds, equivalent to about 2.5 percent of annual GDP, had no fiscal (including social spending) implications. More recent phases improved on this dimension, with privatization of electricity distribution raising 5 percent of GDP, 80 percent of which accrued to the government budget "below the line." While these proceeds did not reduce the fiscal deficit, they provided a potential cushion, in the form of reserves, for future crises. Fiscal transfers, on the other hand, were improved on many fronts. Three large companies that had together contributed 1.1 percent of GDP in revenues during the early 1990s increased their contribution to 2 percent in the four years following privatization. In the two fiscal years following the CORNAP privatization, 20 percent of total revenue contributed by large firms came from newly privatized firms. In addition, the Central Bank of Nicaragua reported that, during the 1980s, direct and indirect subsidies to the CORNAP enterprises (later privatized) amounted to 11.2 percent of GDP, the elimination of which has enormous fiscal implications.

Sources of Public Misperception

The statistical evidence presented in this chapter contrasts sharply with popular perceptions of privatization's effects on lower- and middle-income classes in the region. This discrepancy could stem, in part, from limitations in the data, insofar as they overlook key welfare dimensions; it could also reflect biases in the formation of public perceptions.

Data Limitations

As noted above, the data on privatization's distributional effects are limited in key aspects. The most important data qualification involves accurately representing privatization's effect on prices and access. Doing so involves a counterfactual: What would the price path or evolution of access have been without privatization? Answering such a question is intrinsically difficult amid macroeconomic changes, widespread deregulation, and trade liberalization, which affected prices of utility services relative to other goods and services. Moreover, the respective governments may have raised prices before privatization in order to attract private investors, which would artificially exaggerate the fall in prices following privatization. For this reason, as well as to avoid periods of excessive macroeconomic instability, we chose surveys conducted a few years before and after privatization. For example, we chose 1985–86 as the preprivatization year for Argentina. But this decision raises another potential problem: Prices may have fallen after the preprivatization survey but before privatization, in which case, part of the measured price change occurred before privatization. The same problems arise with access data; that is, some access changes attributed to privatization might have occurred without privatization because of technology changes (e.g., the advent of cellular services in the telecommunications industry). Furthermore, a portion of increased access may reflect legalization of previously illegal connections, which resulted in increased expenditure by the poor rather than increased access.

Despite these concerns, no clearly superior method is available for measuring privatization's effect on prices and access. Whenever possible, these country studies attempt to address the above issues. In the case of Bolivia, for example, one could compare price evolution in privatized regions with nonprivatized regions. In both Bolivia and Nicaragua, access to electricity was measured directly rather than by whether households incurred positive expenditures on the service. Certain data problems applied only to particular sectors or countries. For example, the likelihood that measured access improvements masked the legalization of illegal electricity connections was not an issue in Bolivia and Nicaragua, where access is measured directly. Finally, the broad conclusions are similar across most sectors and countries, despite the particularities of each case.

Lack of household-level price data means that the studies had to use a single price for each service in a given region. Consequently, the distributive effects of tariff rebalancing, which usually accompany privatization, could not be incorporated. For example, as Birdsall and Nellis noted in chapter 1, if local telephone rates rise while long distance rates fall, different population groups may be variously affected, depending on their patterns of usage.

Another shortcoming of the analyses is that they ignored privatization's potential environmental effects. For example, private operators might neglect safety and health considerations or inappropriately maintain public facilities.[36] Yet this issue can cut both ways. For example, health hazards may have been reduced if privatization led to the legalization of illegal electricity connections. As noted, Galiani, Gertler, and Schargrodsky (2002) found that Argentina's water privatization had a positive effect on child mortality. The drop was highest (24 percent) for the poorest groups, and it resulted mainly from a reduction in deaths from waterborne parasitic and infectious diseases.

Biases in Popular Perception

While data inadequacies limited inferences, the divergence between study results and popular opinion could also stem from biases in the process through which popular perceptions are formed, as well as use of standards of fairness that differ from those economists customarily apply. Among the many potential sources of bias, lack of adequate information is probably the most important. Popular views are shaped by extreme cases that invite media attention, while widely diffused benefits are rarely noticed. Many benefits accrue to a wide range of customers, each of whom may benefit moderately; their improved welfare is overshadowed, however, by the dramatic losses of a few workers or customers. Fiscal benefits are even more diffuse and invisible. This type of bias reflects the tension between statistical evaluation of economic outcomes and the way that mainstream views emerge on public policy issues, which Tom Schelling eloquently describes as the tension between personal and statistical lives (or, in this case, between a few personal tragedies and the widespread benefits calculated by aggregating the fortunes of diverse individuals within any given income or expenditure class).

Psychological biases also tend to pervade popular opinion. First, the psychological phenomenon of loss aversion causes individuals to react more

---

36. For example, one story reported that the flooding of a Buenos Aires restaurant following water privatization might have been caused by poor maintenance of the water pipes. See "As Multinational Runs the Taps, Anger Rises over Water for Profit," *New York Times*, August 26, 2002.

sharply to losses relative to the status quo than they do to gains. They tend to focus on immediate, short-term implications, such as job layoffs, without following through to the intermediate term (e.g., when laid-off workers may be rehired). Second, the public commonly lumps privatization together with other promarket reforms, such as fiscal contraction and trade liberalization, which collectively constitute the Washington Consensus. Disentangling the distinct roles of these elements of policy reform is a forbidding exercise for academic experts, let alone the common citizen. It is also difficult to isolate privatization's effects from those stemming from macroeconomic shocks or technological changes, which occurred often throughout the 1990s. Such negative associations may cause citizens to overlook the benefits of privatization. Moreover, there is a tension between deeply held ideological principles with regard to basic needs—for example, that water or electricity should not be subject to the profit calculus of multinational corporations—and how SOEs perform with regard to meeting them. That popular discontent is most severe in the case of water privatization, which lends credence to this view. Suspicions that shares in public enterprises were diverted to cronies of political elites or that privatization proceeds have not been used in the public interest likely fueled the discontent. Finally, there is widespread pessimism concerning the ability of market pressure, the media, and regulatory oversight to constrain private enterprises to meet the public interest, which, though realistic in some instances, is exaggerated in many others.

Summary and Conclusions

The country studies summarized in this chapter, and presented in detail in the following three chapters, focus mainly on privatization's effects on consumers, workers, and public finances. The exercises are severely constrained by data limitations; thus, they represent an attempt to extract whatever inferences are possible from available data sources. The analyses ignore effects on ownership, the environment, or other spillover and general equilibrium effects. Ownership changes may conceivably have distributive effects and play a large role in public discussions of the fairness of privatizations, particularly the methods of allocating and pricing shares in the privatized enterprises. However, the absence of data on ownership distribution prevents any assessment of its effect. Moreover, the ownership effects are unlikely to affect the bottom half of the income distribution. To the extent that the latter is of primary interest, consumer and worker effects are more important.

Overall, the studies could not identify, on the basis of their distributive effect, the reasons for popular discontent with the privatization process. Privatization's most widespread effects are on consumers of essential utility services. Much of the public's disenchantment stems from concerns over price increases resulting from privatization. As this chapter shows, however, there is no clear pattern concerning price changes, with prices falling in about half of cases. More important, perhaps, is the finding that, even if prices rose, their effects were outweighed by the corresponding increased access that occurred in the bottom or lower half of the distribution. The only exception was Bolivia's failed water concession in Cochabamba. Most cases displayed no evidence of a significant increase in poverty, and we found evidence of noticeable improvements in service quality following privatization.

In contrast, workers were adversely affected, mainly in the form of lay-offs associated with privatization. Employment contractions were significant within privatized enterprises relative to the rest of the economy, with cutbacks ranging from 30 to 75 percent. As the privatized enterprises were typically capital intensive, however, employment contractions were small in relation to size of the aggregate labor force (2 percent in Argentina, 1 percent in Mexico, and 0.13 percent in Bolivia). The only exception was Nicaragua, which underwent more widespread privatization as part of the transition from a socialist economy. In Argentina and Mexico, a significant proportion of laid-off workers found jobs in other private enterprises in the same sector of activity. Thus, the medium-term effect was much lower than the immediate one. No simple inference could be made about the effects on wage levels and inequality; however, the relatively small scale of labor reallocation in Argentina, Bolivia, and Mexico makes it unlikely that these were significant. The most significant effects arose in Nicaragua, where at least 7 to 9 percent of the labor force was reallocated throughout the urban and rural sectors. This reallocation likely had a modest downward effect on the average wage rate, and raised wage inequality in the urban sector. However, these effects were dwarfed by increasing market pressure on wage structures within both public and private sectors of the economy.

The fiscal effect of reforms were generally favorable. In addition to aiding macroeconomic stabilization, the privatization process supported a shift in public spending away from expensive debt-service obligations and the funding of operating losses in SOEs (which eventually subsidize middle-income workers and consumers) toward increased social spending (which directly targets the poor and elderly).

In sum, the only signs of an adverse distributive effect on the bottom half of the distribution, aside from the failed Cochabamba water concession, involved the small proportion of workers displaced from their SOE jobs, and many of these probably found jobs elsewhere in the economy fairly quickly. This factor must be weighed against the advantages derived from lower prices, widened access for poorer consumers, enhanced service quality, and a changed structure of public finances encompassing a variety of increased benefits for the poor.

Future privatization programs can be designed specifically to minimize the adverse distributive effect. Such design includes three key steps:

(1) establish regulatory institutions for the privatized enterprises (to ensure that prices are kept low; firms operate under competitive pressure and are induced to innovate and keep costs low; and requirements are set for service expansion, quality, and access); (2) fund severance packages, unemployment benefits, retraining, and job search assistance for laid-off employees (to cushion privatization's employment effect); and (3) use privatization proceeds in a transparent way to retire public debt and increase social spending (the earmarking mechanisms featured in Bolivia's capitalization process are notable in this respect).

References

Aghion, P., E. Caroli, and C. García-Peñalosa. 1999. Inequality and Economic Growth: The Perspective of the New Growth Theories. *Journal of Economic Literature* 37, no. 4: 1615–60.

Banks, J., R. Blundell, and A. Lewbel. 1996. Tax Reform and Welfare Measurement: Do We Need Demand System Estimation? *Economic Journal* 106, no. 438: 1227–41.

Bardhan, P., S. Bowles, and H. Gintis. 2000. Wealth Inequality, Wealth Constraints and Economic Performance. *Handbook of Income Distribution*, vol. 1. In *Handbooks in Economics*, vol. 16, ed. Anthony B. Atkinson and Francois Bourguignon, 541–603. Amsterdam: Elsevier Science, North-Holland.

Barja, G., D. McKenzie, and M. Urquiola. 2002. Capitalization and Privatization in Bolivia. Cornell University. Photocopy.

Bhaskar V., and M. Khan. 1995. Privatization and Employment: A Study of the Jute Industry in Bangladesh. *American Economic Review* 85, no. 1: 261–73.

Bhaskar, V., B. Gupta, and M. Khan. 2002. *Partial Privatization and Yardstick Competition: Evidence from Employment Dynamics in Bangladesh*. Discussion Paper 545. Colchester, UK: University of Essex, Department of Economics.

Birdsall, N., and J. Nellis. 2002. *Winners and Losers: Assessing the Distributional Impact of Privatization*. Working Paper 6. Washington: Center for Global Development.

Deaton, A. 1989. Rice Prices and Income Distribution in Thailand: A Non-Parametric Approach. *Economic Journal* 99, no. 395: 1–37.

Delfino, J., and A. Casarin. 2001. *The Reform of the Utilities Sector in Argentina*. WIDER Discussion Paper 2001/74. Helsinki: United Nations University/World Institute for Development Economics Research.

Ennis, H., and S. Pinto. 2002. Privatization and Income Distribution in Argentina. West Virginia University. Photocopy.

Estache, A., V. Foster, and Q. Wodon. 2002. *Accounting for Poverty in Infrastructure Reform: Learning from Latin America's Experience*. WBI Development Studies. Washington: World Bank.

FIEL (Foundation for Latin American Economic Research). 1999. *La regulación de la competencia y de los servicios públicos: teoría y experiencia argentina reciente*. Buenos Aires: Foundation for Latin American Economic Research.

Foster, J., J. Greer, and E. Thorbecke. 1984. A Class of Decomposable Poverty Measures. *Econometrica* 52, no. 3: 761–65.

Freije, S., and L. Rivas. 2002. Privatization, Inequality, and Welfare: Evidence from Nicaragua. Caracas, Center for Human Development and Organization, Institute of Advanced Studies in Administration (IESA). Photocopy.

Galiani, S., P. Gertler, and E. Schargrodsky. 2002. Water for Life: The Impact of the Privatization of Water Services on Child Mortality. Universidad Torcuato Di Tella. Photocopy.

GEO (Gabinete de Estudios de Opinion) for *El Nacional*. 1992. Opinion in the Valley of Mexico about Public Services, January 16–21. Obtained from the Roper Center Latin American Databank.

Heckman, J. 1979. Sample Selection Bias as a Specification Error. *Econometrica* 47, no. 1: 153–61.

ITU (International Telecommunications Union). 2001. *Yearbook of Statistics: Telecommunication Services, 1991–2000*. Geneva: International Telecommunications Union.

Juhn, C., K. Murphy, and B. Pierce. 1993. Wage Inequality and the Rise in Returns to Skill. *Journal of Political Economy* 101, no. 3: 410–42.

La Porta, R., and F. López-de-Silanes. 1999. The Benefits of Privatization: Evidence from Mexico. *Quarterly Journal of Economics* 114, no. 4: 1193–242.

López-Calva, L. F., and J. Rosellón. 2002. Privatization and Inequality: The Mexican Case. Universidad de las Américas, Puebla. Photocopy.

Megginson, W., and J. M. Netter. 2001. From State to Market: A Survey of Empirical Studies of Privatization. *Journal of Economic Literature* 39, no. 2: 321–89.

Millan, J., E. Lora, and A. Micco. 2001. Sustainability of the Electricity Sector Reforms in Latin America. Washington: Inter-American Development Bank. Photocopy.

Neary, J. P., and K. W. S. Roberts. 1980. The Theory of Household Behaviour Under Rationing. *European Economic Review* 13, no. 1: 25–42.

Urbiztondo, S., D. Artana, and F. Navajas. 1998. *La Autonomía de los Entes Reguladores Argentinos*. Working Paper R-340. Washington: Inter-American Development Bank.

Waddams Price, C., and R. Hancock. 1998. Distributional Effects of Liberalising UK Residential Utility Markets. *Fiscal Studies* 19, no. 3: 295–319.

Wolak, F. 1996. Can Universal Service Survive in a Competitive Telecommunications Environment? Evidence from the United States Consumer Expenditure Survey. Stanford University. Photocopy.

World Bank. 1996. *Bolivia: Poverty, Equity and Income, Selected Policies for Expanding Earnings Opportunities for the Poor*. Report 15272-BO, vol. 2. Washington: World Bank.

Appendix 2A
Public Perception of Privatization

Through the LAC region, a common belief among the general populace is that privatization of public utilities has not resulted in welfare improvements. Results from the Latinbarometer polls of 1998 and 2000 identify the percentage of country populations that disagrees or strongly disagrees with the following statement: "Privatization of state companies has been beneficial to the country." Table 2.A1 presents results from seven countries, four of which were summarily assessed in this chapter.

Table 2A.1 Citizens who disagree that privatization has been beneficial, by country (percent) 1998 and 2000

Country and year of poll	Total	Gender		Age in 2000			Educational level			Socioeconomic class[a]		
		Male	Female	20–24	40–44	60–64	Illiterate	Primary	Tertiary	Upper	Middle	Lower
Argentina												
1998	49	49	50	47	47	51	50[b]	49	47	42	48	50[b]
2000	68	68	68	66	69	70	65[b]	67	61	71	68	62[b]
Bolivia												
1998	40	38	42	43	31	44[b]	36	46	30	26	44	
2000	59	58	59	50	59	59	53	54	52	67[b]	57	50[b]
Brazil												
1998	45	46	43	45	41	31	43	49	40	39	50	29[b]
2000	62	59	64	67	61	58	47	71	50	54	62	20[b]
Chile												
1998	41	44	38	37	54	39	24[b]	45	37	35	43	30[b]
2000	58	60	56	58	61	56	46[b]	66	56	39	60	59[b]
Mexico												
1998	39	41	38	38	37	29	40	46	39	34	39	40
2000	56	57	55	54	65	59	52	60	60	56[b]	55	53
Nicaragua												
1998	47	47	47	48	45	63	50[b]	42[b]	37[b]	34	50	55
2000	52	54	50	51	62	55	40	49	55	53	48	46[b]
Peru												
1998	50	50	50	51	56	52	35[b]	57	45	36	53	62
2000	57	54	61	54	63	61	77[b]	68	52	43[b]	62	41[b]

a. Socioeconomic class is self-reported; "upper," "middle," and "lower" correspond to the respondent answering whether his or her socioeconomic class was "very good," "average," or "very bad," respectively.
b. Fewer than 30 observations were available.

Source: Authors' calculations from Latinbarometer data.

Appendix 2B
Welfare Changes with Repeated Cross-Sections

The household surveys for Argentina, Bolivia, and Mexico only provide access information for the survey years. Since different households were surveyed each year, it is not possible to determine which households experienced a change in access to privatized services. Evaluation of the welfare change from privatization therefore requires further approximating assumptions.

One can divide the sample into deciles, where N_t^d represents the total number of households sampled from decile d in time t, where $t = 0$ denotes the preprivatization period and $t = 1$ denotes the postprivatization period. $A_{h,t}$ can then indicate whether household h has access ($A_{h,t} = 1$) or not ($A_{h,t} = 0$) at time t. At time t, F_t^d households in decile d have access to the service, while I_t^d households in decile d lack access. Thus, the expected welfare change to household h in decile d from privatization would be

$$EAU_h^d = P\left(A_{h,0} = 1, A_{h,1} = 1\right) \Delta U\left(A_{h,0} = 1, A_{h,1} = 1\right)$$
$$+ P\left(A_{h,0} = 0, A_{h,1} = 1\right) \Delta U\left(A_{h,0} = 0, A_{h,1} = 1\right)$$
$$+ P\left(A_{h,0} = 0, A_{h,1} = 0\right) \Delta U\left(A_{h,0} = 0, A_{h,1} = 0\right). \tag{2B.1}$$

Here $P(.\,,.)$ is the probability distribution function for household h. The last term in equation 2B.1 will be 0 unless the prices of substitutes change. If one assumes that households with access in period 0 do not lose access in period 1, then taking means of equation 2.B1 across all households in decile d in time 0 gives the mean expected change in welfare in decile d:

$$EAU^d = \frac{F_0^d}{N_0^d} \frac{1}{F_0^d} \sum_{h:A_{h,0}=1} \Delta U\left(A_{h,0}=1\right) + \frac{1}{N_0^d} \sum P\left(A_{h,0}=0, A_{h,1}=1\right)$$
$$\Delta U\left(A_{h,0}=0, A_{h,1}=1\right). \tag{2B.2}$$

In equation 2B.2, the first term is the proportion of households with access in period 0, multiplied by the mean change in welfare for those without access. One must estimate the second term using the period 1 survey data. We make the simplifying assumption that, within a given decile, all households with access in period 1 had equal probability of having lacked access in period 0.[37] For households with access in period 1,

---

37. One could compare the observable characteristics of those households within a decile that have access in period 0 to the characteristics of households with access in period 1 to identify dimensions along which increased access has occurred. This information could then be used to allow the probability of moving from no access to access to differ across households within a

$$P(A_{h,0} = 0 \mid A_{h,1} = 1) = \left(\frac{F_1^d}{N_1^d} - \frac{F_0^d}{N_0^d} \right). \qquad (2B.3)$$

Plugging equation 2B.3 into equation 2B.2, replacing the second term of equation 2B.2 with period 1 reference values, and rearranging the order results in

$$E\Delta U^d = \frac{F_0^d}{N_0^d} \frac{1}{F_0^d} \sum_{h:A_{h,0}=1} \Delta U \left(A_{h,0} = 1 \right) + \left(\frac{F_1^d}{N_1^d} - \frac{F_0^d}{N_0^d} \right)$$

$$\frac{F_1^d}{N_1^d} \frac{1}{F_1^d} \sum_{h:A_{h,0}=1} \Delta U \left(A_{h,0} = 1, A_{h,1} = 1 \right). \qquad (2B.4)$$

In equation 2B.4, the second term is the conditional probability of having no access in period 0 given access in period 1, multiplied by the probability of access in period 1, multiplied by the mean value of gaining access for households with access in period 1. The first-order approximation of the mean decile change in welfare is therefore

$$E\Delta U^d = \frac{F_0^d}{N_0^d} \frac{1}{F_0^d} \sum_{h:A_{h,0}=1} \left(\Delta \log p_j \right) w_{h,j0} x_{h,0}$$

$$+ \left(\frac{F_1^d}{N_1^d} - \frac{F_0^d}{N_0^d} \right) \frac{F_1^d}{N_1^d} \frac{1}{F_1^d} \sum_{h:A_{h,1}=1} \left(\log p_{j1} - \log p_{h,vj} \right) w_{h,j1} x_{h,1}, \qquad (2B.5)$$

and the second-order approximation to mean decile welfare change is similarly

$$E\Delta U^d = \frac{F_0^d}{N_0^d} \frac{1}{F_0^d} \sum_{h:A_{h,0}=1} \left(\Delta \log p_j \right) w_{h,j0} x_{h,0} \left(1 + \frac{\Delta \log p_j}{2} \frac{\partial \log w_{h,j0}}{\partial \log p_j} \right)$$

$$- \left(\frac{F_1^d}{N_1^d} - \frac{F_0^d}{N_0^d} \right) \frac{F_1^d}{N_1^d} \frac{1}{F_1^d} \sum_{h:A_{h,1}=1} \left(\log p_{j1} - \log p_{h,vj} \right) w_{h,j1} x_{h,1}$$

$$\left(1 + \frac{\left(\log p_{j1} - \log p_{h,vj} \right)}{2} \frac{\partial \log w_{h,j1}}{\partial \log p_j} \right). \qquad (2B.6)$$

decile that have access in period 1. (This extension is not pursued here.) The various political, strategic, geographic, and economic reasons that determine where increased access occurred can counterbalance one another to make our assumption a reasonable approximation.

Appendix 2C
Poverty and Inequality with (Repeated) Cross-Sections

For households with access prior to privatization, one can use the first- and second-order approximations to estimate the change in utility resulting from the price changes after privatization. One can take the preprivatization, per capita expenditure for these households, and add the estimated change in welfare divided by household size to obtain the household per capita welfare after privatization. However, one cannot determine which households that lacked access before privatization gained access after privatization. Instead, as above, we use the postprivatization households with access, and calculate their mean welfare change if they gained access. The first- and second-order approximations of this mean welfare change are

$$E\left(\Delta U_h^d \mid A_{h,0}=0, A_{h,1}=1\right)=-\frac{1}{F_1^d}\sum_{h,A_{h,1}=1}\left(\log p_{j1}-\log p_{h,vj}\right)w_{h,j1}x_{h,1}, \text{ and}$$

$$E\left(\Delta U_h^d \mid A_{h,0}=0, A_{h,1}=1\right)=-\frac{1}{F_1^d}\sum_{h,A_{h,1}=1}\left(\log p_{j1}-\log p_{h,vj}\right)$$

$$w_{h,j1}x_{h,1}\left(1+\frac{\log p_{j1}-\log p_{h,vj}}{2}\frac{\partial \log w_{h,j1}}{\partial \log p_j}\right) \qquad (2C.1)$$

We make the simplifying assumption that all households without access in period 0 had equal chance of gaining access in period 1. We then randomly choose households without access from the preprivatization survey and add the expected welfare change from access in equation 2C.1 divided by their household size to their preprivatization per capita expenditure. The fraction of households without access for which this is done, τ, is the conditional probability of having access in period 1, given no access in period 0, and is given by

$$\tau=\frac{\left(\dfrac{F_1^d}{N_1^d}-\dfrac{F_0^d}{N_0^d}\right)}{\left(1-\dfrac{F_0^d}{N_0^d}\right)}.$$

The remaining fraction, $1-\tau$, of households without access before privatization will only have a welfare change if the prices of substitutes change. Otherwise, this fraction is assigned zero welfare change.

3

Inequality and Welfare Changes: Evidence from Nicaragua

SAMUEL FREIJE RODRÍGUEZ and LUIS RIVAS

In countries that have implemented mass privatization programs, such as the transition economies of Eastern Europe, it seems reasonable to think that the divestment process affected the overall economy, rather than a single firm, group of firms, or economic activity. The large flow of workers from the public to the private sector alone might have affected economywide inequality. To the extent that it also affected labor-market institutions, privatization could have significantly affected private-sector, as well as public-sector, inequality through changes in employment, productivity, and wages.[1] Privatization of public utilities, in turn, might have affected consumer welfare through changes in access, pricing, and service quality.[2]

Nicaragua's privatization occurred under conditions that were nearly identical to those that the transition economies of Eastern Europe faced: Nicaragua had undergone a socialist period, and authorities had conducted extensive

Samuel Freije is assistant professor of economics at the Universidad de Las Américas in Puebla, Mexico, and Luis Rivas is chief economic advisor at the Ministry of Finance and Central Bank of Nicaragua. At the time of this writing, Rivas was a visiting professor at the Department of Economics, Vanderbilt University. The authors are grateful to Huberto Ennis, Luis Felipe López-Calva, David McKenzie, Dilip Mookherjee, Santiago Pinto, Miguel Urquiola, and Network on Inequality and Poverty (NIP)/Inter-American Development Bank (IDB) participants at the Latin American and Caribbean Economic Association (LACEA) 2001 and 2002 conferences for their helpful suggestions. Special thanks go to André Portela Souza, who provided insightful comments on an earlier draft. The authors also thank José J. Rojas and Horacio Martínez, both at the Central Bank of Nicaragua, for providing the data.

1. Newbery (1995), for example, shows that such reforms as privatization might increase income inequality through price changes.

2. See McKenzie and Mookherjee (chapter 2) and references therein.

transfer of ownership to the public sector through nationalization and expropriation of private enterprises (De Franco 1996; Buitelaar 1996). In 1989, two years before initiating the privatization effort, most of the country's productive capacity was in public hands. Excluding the banking sector, public utilities, and state-held infrastructure services, including airports and ports, state owned enterprises (SOEs) produced approximately 30 percent of GDP.[3]

Unlike the former socialist countries of Eastern Europe, however, Nicaragua was under a planned economy for only a decade (1980–90), during which time the country experienced civil war. When the socialist regime lost the 1990 elections, the newly elected government initiated a large-scale, economic liberalization program aimed at stabilizing the economy, including the divestment of SOEs (CORNAP 1993). In addition to the political constraints that transition economies typically face (e.g., pressure to move swiftly from a command to a market system, low financial savings, and strong union power), Nicaraguan authorities faced an unusually large demand for firms whose main asset was cultivable land, especially from war veterans and demobilized army soldiers. In addition, immigration pressures were strong, as the former elite and professional middle and upper-middle classes returned from abroad.

We divide Nicaragua's privatization process into two overlapping phases: 1991–96 and 1995–99. The first phase was characterized by the divestment of SOEs under the control of the National Corporation of the Public Sector, known by its Spanish acronym, CORNAP. Created in 1990 to privatize some 350 SOEs that operated in various sectors (e.g., farming, fishery, industry, forestry, mining, commerce, trade, transportation, construction, and tourism), CORNAP assumed direct control of the SOEs, 22 of which it clustered into shareholding companies labeled as corporations. The second phase of privatization began in 1995 and continued through at least 1999, the last year for which data are available. During 1995–98, a comprehensive reform package was launched, aimed at the eventual full privatization of public utilities. In certain areas, however, private-sector participation was immediately allowed, and some SOEs were given in concession to the private sector (e.g., in telecommunications and electricity, where private participation had been allowed since 1995 and 1997, respectively). Despite severe data constraints, this chapter attempts to capture the welfare effects of reform, with regard to changes in access, pricing, and service quality.

Data and Methodology

The data used were obtained, for the most part, from three surveys: Living Standard Measurement Surveys for 1993 and 1998 (LSMS-93 and LSMS-98,

---

3. Value added comprised 45 percent of manufacturing, 70 percent of mining, and 26 percent of agriculture. For a full account, see CORNAP (1993).

respectively), conducted by the Nicaraguan Instituto de Estadísticas y Censos, and the Household Income and Expenditure Survey for 1999 (HIES-99), conducted by the Central Bank of Nicaragua.

The LSMS-93 and LSMS-98 were nationwide surveys based on methods the World Bank used in its Living Standards Measurement Study. LSMS-93 included information on household characteristics, including education, health, employment, migration, and household expenditures. LSMS-98 added an extended questionnaire, which included questions on anthropometric data, fertility, time allocation, independent businesses, and household savings. Both surveys had a complex design that used population weights, two-stage sampling, and stratification; both interviewed some 25,000 individuals in approximately 4,500 households.

The HIES-99 was a nationwide urban survey that collected information on housing, household characteristics, and household income and expenditure. Like the two LSMSs, the HIES-99 also had a complex design using population weights, two-stage sampling, and stratification; some 5,900 households in approximately 4,800 dwellings were interviewed.

For employment and earnings data, we use those portions of the survey that list the principal job of all individuals aged 15 and older. Given the differences at the individual level in hours worked per day and days per week, as well as frequency of payment, earnings were computed in hourly terms to facilitate comparisons. In the case of consumption expenditures, data was gathered on weekly household consumption of food products, monthly household consumption expenditures, and biannual expenditures on clothing and home appliances. Again, the various measures were homogenized into a single frequency unit. All expenditure data were transformed into monthly real data using the consumer price index reported by the Central Bank of Nicaragua.

For selected descriptive statistics, establishment-level data generated by the Ministry of Labor was used to calculate national labor-market aggregates. Administrative data from public utilities, regulatory agencies, CORNAP, and the Central Bank of Nicaragua were used to calculate performance of CORNAP divestment, including number of privatized firms, beneficiaries of the privatization process, divestment methods, and fiscal effects of the divestment process.

Privatization Process

Divestment of CORNAP Enterprises

CORNAP's divestment of commercial enterprises occurred almost entirely between 1991 and 1998 (De Franco 1996). At the beginning of the period, most enterprises under CORNAP had large debts, and a large portion of their assets were subject to restitution claims from previous owners whose property had been confiscated in the 1980s. The capital stock of most SOEs under CORNAP was highly depreciated or obsolete. Many SOEs presented negative cash flows, and their revenue contribution to the government was less than the large quasi-fiscal deficits that they generated.

The above constraints forced CORNAP to divest enterprises through various methods: liquidation, merger and acquisition, restitution, and sale or lease. Liquidation consisted of dissolving the enterprise, usually justified on grounds of financial nonviability, lack of investor interest, or other reasons rendering the firm inoperable. Merger or acquisition consisted of fusing an SOE to an existing firm, or incorporating it into a state institution, such as a ministry or government facility (whenever it was believed that the state should continue providing the good or service in question). Restitution involved returning firms, assets, or shares to their previous owners or their relatives or heirs. Finally, firms could be divested through a sale of the firm, assets, or shares, or through a lease, which gave temporary rights to the assets of a firm and/or the management thereof. This arrangement also gave the leasing party the option to buy the firm. Certain enterprises used only one method, while others used various ones (Central Bank of Nicaragua 1996). As table 3.1 shows, by 1998, nearly 98 percent of the 351 enterprises under CORNAP—with the exception of a few manufacturing and construction firms—had been divested (De Franco 1996).

Table 3.2, which summarizes the results of CORNAP divestment, shows that, for the 1991–96 period, acquisitions and restitutions corresponded to approximately 25 percent and 28 percent, respectively, of total divested assets. The remainder was divested through sales or leases. In terms of beneficiaries, more than 47 percent of total assets divested through CORNAP ended up in the hands of entrepreneurs, roughly 28 percent remained in the public sector through acquisitions by other government institutions, and the remainder went to workers and war veterans. As table 3.2 shows, all restitutions went to entrepreneurs, while all acquisitions went to other government institutions. Distribution of divested assets among beneficiaries and the structure and incentives that emerged from the divestment process suggest that privatization might have consequently affected income distribution. For example, Buitelaar (1996) explains that 47 percent of divested manufacturing firms became conventional firms, 15 percent co-managed firms, 8 percent worker-owned firms, and the remainder liquidated. Buitelaar also shows that 68 percent of conventional firms were returned to the original owners, who had been expropriated during the 1980s. These firms were the only ones with access to new capital investment and the only ones that increased efficiency and profitability. Comanaged firms also increased productivity to a lesser extent, while worker-owned firms were unable to do so. Worker-owned firms tended to underinvest, which eventually led to their failure, with most workers turning to agricultural activities.

Table 3.1   Nicaragua: Privatization under CORNAP, 1993 and 1998

Corporation or enterprise	Number of enterprises	Year privatized 1993	Year privatized 1998
Corporations and enterprises under CORNAP	351	289	343
Farming public-sector corporations	80	76	80
Agroindustry (CONAZUCAR)	9	8	9
Banana production (BANANIC)	2	2	2
Coffee (CAFENIC)	14	13	14
Livestock (HATONIC)	16	16	16
Milk (CONILAC)	3	3	3
Poultry (CAN)	5	5	5
Promotion of agroexport products (AGROEXCO)	7	7	7
Rice (NICARROZ)	8	8	8
Tobacco (TABANIC)	5	5	5
People's industry corporations (COIP)	89	57	83
Primary sector of economy linked	30	23	30
Fishery (INPESCA)	7	7	7
Forestry (CORFOP)	13	10	13
Mining (INMINE)	10	6	10
Internal and external trade linked	83	73	81
Commerce (CORCOP)	34	33	34
Construction supply (CATCO)	21	14	19
Foreign trade enterprises (CONIECE)	7	7	7
Imports and farming services (IMSA)	11	9	11
Pharmaceuticals (COFARMA)	10	10	10
Transportation and construction linked	28	23	28
Construction enterprises (COENCO)	6	6	6
Transportation (COTRAP)	22	17	22
Nicaraguan tourism corporation (COTUR)	30	27	30
Autonomous enterprises[a]	11	10	11
Agroindustrial enterprise of Sébaco	1	1	1
Agroindustry (IFRUGALASA)	2	2	2
Agroindustry (YUCASA)	1	1	1
Construction (SOVIPE-ENFARA)	1	1	1
ENDEPARA African palm El Castillo	1	1	1
ENDEPARA African palm Kucra Hill	1	1	1
Engineers (PROA)	1	1	1
Enterprise Arlen Siu	1	1	1
Grains (ENABAS)	1	0	1
SOVIPE Investments	1	1	1

a. Enterprises whose shares corporations under CORNAP did not hold.

Source: Central Bank of Nicaragua.

Table 3.2 Nicaragua: CORNAP and beneficiary divestment procedures, 1991–96 and 1997–2000

Period and procedure	As percent of total asset value				
	Entre-preneurs	Workers	War veterans	Other government institutions[a]	Total
1991–96	47.4	12.9	1.5	27.9	89.7
Acquisitions	0.0	0.0	0.0	25.0	25.0
Restitution	28.4	0.0	0.0	0.0	28.4
Sales and leases	19.0	12.9	1.5	2.9	36.3
Cash and credit sales	12.1	6.1	0.5	0.0	18.7
Lease with option to buy	0.0	4.9	1.0	0.0	5.9
Transferred liabilities[b]	6.9	1.9	0.0	2.9	11.7
1997–2000	7.7	1.4	0.2	1.0	10.3
Total	55.1	14.3	1.7	28.9	100.0

a. Composed mainly of government institutions.
b. Refers to transfers of outstanding debts.

Source: Central Bank of Nicaragua.

Reform and Privatization of Public Utilities

During 1995–99, utilities remained in public hands. However, with enactment of the telecommunications law of 1995,[4] the legal framework required to privatize utilities began to take shape and continued with passage of two other laws intended to prepare energy and water to be fully privatized and sewage to be given in concession to the private sector.[5] Privatization of electricity distribution did not occur until 2000. Telephone service followed a year later, as did a portion of energy generation in 2002. Private participation (less than full ownership) was allowed in telecommunications in 1995 and in electricity generation in 1997.

Telecommunications

Before 1995, the state-owned Telecomunicaciones y Correos de Nicaragua (TELCOR) was the telecommunications monopoly. In 1995, the National Assembly passed a law creating a new enterprise, Empresa Nicaragüense de Telefonía (ENITEL),[6] by exchanging TELCOR assets for shares accruing

---

4. See Ley 210: Incorporación de Particulares en la Operación y Ampliación de los Servicios Públicos de Telecomunicaciones (1995), and its later reform, Ley de Reformas a la Ley 210: Ley de Incorporación de Particulares en la Operación y Ampliación de los Servicios Públicos de Telecomunicaciones (1998).

5. For energy and water, see Ley de la Industria Eléctrica (1998) and Ley General de Servicios de Agua Potable y Alcantarillado Sanitario (1998), respectively.

6. The law also created another enterprise, Correos de Nicaragua, to provide postal service.

to the government. The law authorized the government to sell up to 40 percent of ENITEL shares to a firm or group of firms, which would also be awarded a management contract. The law committed the government to donate and sell 1 and 10 percent of shares, respectively, to employees, and to gradually sell remaining shares through public offerings (or bids), starting six months after the initial sale. Finally, the law entitled the government to a single control share, which it needed for any substantial sale of the company's assets, change in its social objectives, or to allow new owners to take steps to dissolve or merge the company.

Initial sale of 40 percent of company shares occurred in 2001 through a two-stage process: (1) preselection of potential buyers and (2) public bidding among selected candidates. Delays in the sales process were attributed to the burden of preselection criteria and required investment/expansion plans to which the buyer would be contractually bound.[7] Equally important delaying factors were the difficulty of obtaining audited financial statements and large outstanding debt with providers.

One key provision of the reform was that TELCOR would remain the regulatory agency. The main regulatory mechanism would be the signing of concession contracts between TELCOR and ENITEL. Such contracts were required to state how services should be provided, service quality, coverage area, system charges, and expansion plans.

Electricity

Before reforms, the state-owned Instituto Nicaragüense de Energía (INE) was engaged in electricity generation, transmission, and distribution. In 1997, private-sector participation was allowed in generation, and some state-owned generating plants were given to the private sector in concession. In accord with emerging best practices in the sector, the 1998 law vertically separated generation, transmission, and distribution, by unbundling INE into six companies: three generation plants, one transmission company (Empresa Nicaragüense de Transmisión de Energía, S.A., or ENTRENSA), and two distribution companies.

In addition to INE's unbundling, the law created a national energy commission to design policies and strategies regarding the energy sector, while INE remained the regulatory agency. INE, therefore, is in charge of carrying out three major tasks: promoting competition by guarding against collusion among providers, keeping firms from taking dominant market positions, and setting system charges according to efficiency considerations. The objective is that final prices remain close to competitive prices and financial viability, and that sufficient revenue is allowed to recover investment, operation, and maintenance costs and service expansion-related

---

7. Preselection criteria included lower bounds on the potential experience of the buyer, billing volume, minimum number of active subscribers, and minimum capital size.

expenditure. In an attempt to set prices right, distribution companies must submit system charges to INE. The latter would review the proposal and allow changes to approved charges only in cases where the general price level or energy costs change. In addition, the law authorizes INE to grant tax exemptions to the importing of machines, equipment, and other materials used in electricity generation, transmission, distribution, and commercialization, as long as these exemptions do not conflict with general tax laws.

In 2001, electricity distribution was privatized; the following year, two generation plants were sold to the private sector. The transmission company, on the other hand, remained state-owned.[8] It should be noted that electricity is provided under a national interconnected system and other independent systems. Before reforms, INE distributed most, but not all, electricity. The coexistence of the national interconnected system and independent networks continued even after reforms and could be a source of future vertical integration. For example, the law states that economic agents engaged in generation cannot engage in transmission through the national interconnected system; however, they are allowed to engage in secondary transmission. In addition, generation companies are allowed to sign contracts directly with distributors and large users. In distribution, some integration is allowed, since the law allows agents to engage in generation, transmission, and commercialization outside the national interconnected system.

Water and Sewage

Although the water and sewage law of 1998 and subsequent reform in 2001 have paved the way for a concession system, the industry has encountered difficulties implementing it, mostly because the system is obsolete or destroyed.[9] The 1998 law created a new enterprise to provide water services, Empresa Nicaragüense de Acueductos y Alcantarillados (ENACAL); while the Instituto Nicaragüense de Acueductos y Alcantarillados (INAA), the previously state-held company, was left as the regulatory agency. A concession system has been designed, consisting of production and distribution of potable water and collection and disposal of serviced water. INAA proposes candidates for concession. In the case of private firms, the National Assembly must ratify any concession. Concessions to public firms can be granted directly. In all cases, concessions last 25 years.

---

8. Generation plants were sold to Coastal Power, while Unión Fenosa, a Spanish company, acquired the two distribution enterprises.

9. In 1998, Hurricane Mitch seriously damaged the water and sewage systems; no estimates to assess the extent of the damage were found.

INAA will undertake public bids for concessions, determine the limits of geographic areas to be given in concession, and set system charges. However, limits to the area of expansion after concession are fixed at the outset.[10] Prices are to be set so that economic, operative, and financial efficiency are attained and users assume the corresponding total cost.[11] The law does not immediately eliminate cross-subsidies; temporary cross-subsidization may be allowed for system and basic service users.

The 2001 reform makes clear the authorities' objective: segmenting ENACAL into independent regional enterprises. With this division, investment in obsolete or destroyed systems can be prioritized to minimize the time needed to have enterprises ready for concession. Thus far, this scheme remains at the concept stage.

Fiscal Effects of Privatization

Privatization of SOEs can variously affect a country's fiscal stance.[12] Davis et al. (2000) argue that immediate, direct effects of privatization on fiscal balance depend on the share of privatization proceeds that accrue to the budget. In addition, how proceeds are used and how the privatization process affects macroeconomic aggregates may, in turn, have further fiscal consequences. The relative importance of these factors depends on the actions authorities take before privatization, the sales process, and the regime after privatization (McKenzie 1998).

The fiscal consequences of privatization in Nicaragua, estimated below, are based on major data limitations. We concentrate on the contemporaneous effect of privatization, as well as its effect over time, by studying whether privatization proceeds were accounted for in the na-tional budget, how they were used, and how fiscal and quasi-fiscal variables evolved over the active privatization period.

As table 3.3 shows, the privatization proceeds from CORNAP divestment averaged 2.5 percent of GDP per year during the years of active privatization. Strikingly, the proceeds did not accrue to the budget, nor was there any regulation enacted for proceeds oversight. Presumably, authorities thought that keeping the proceeds off the budget would reduce the possibility of misuse, notwithstanding the lack of transparency in subsequent use of these funds.

---

10. The limit established by law is no more than 30 percent expansion of the initial concession.

11. In the law, economic efficiency means equality in prices of additional units of the service; financial efficiency means that enough financial resources should be generated to cover operations, management, maintenance, and expansion.

12. For discussion of fiscal and macroeconomic issues related to SOE privatization, see Davis et al. (2000); Gupta, Schiller, and Ma (1999); McKenzie (1998); and Heller and Schiller (1989).

Table 3.3 Nicaragua: Gross and net proceeds of privatization that accrue to the budget[a]

Entity	Years of active privatization	Gross proceeds		Net proceeds	
		Millions of US dollars[d]	Percent of GDP[e]	Millions of US dollars[d]	Percent of GDP[e]
CORNAP enterprises[b]	1991–96	242.9	2.5	0.0	0.0
Public utilities	1995–ongoing	167.9	7.2	108.4	4.6
Electricity		167.9	7.2	108.4	4.6
Generation	2002	52.9	2.3	19.4	0.8
Distribution[c]	2000	115.0	4.9	89.0	3.8

a. Proceeds from CORNAP privatization were not registered in the fiscal balances. Electricity generation and distribution were accounted below the line as privatization proceeded. Although telephone services were privatized in 2001, this study did not include these proceeds because of the potential for reversal of the privatization process (due to corruption claims). In 2001, gross proceeds totaled $83.9 million and net proceeds totaled $33.9 million.
b. Proceeds from CORNAP privatization were never registered in the fiscal balance.
c. Net proceeds from privatization of electricity distribution equals gross proceeds minus ENEL's commercial debt (US$26 million).
d. Annual data in national currency converted into US dollars, using annual average exchange rates.
e. Average of annual ratios of privatization proceeds to GDP during active privatization for CORNAP; percent of GDP for public utilities in the year 2000.
Source: Central Bank of Nicaragua.

Since cash proceeds amounted to a yearly average of only 0.6 percent of GDP, gross receipts underestimate the extent of asset divestment under CORNAP. Most CORNAP privatization occurred through credit and liability transfers. Table 3.4 shows that nearly 90 percent of transactions consisted of sales or lease, while the remainder constituted capital increments from restituted assets. No acquisitions or liquidations were recorded.

In the case of electricity distribution, privatization receipts represented close to 5 percent of GDP, of which 80 percent accrued to the budget (table 3.3).[13] Since, at the time of privatization, Nicaragua was under an adjustment program sponsored by the International Monetary Fund (IMF), the authorities were advised to register the proceeds "below the line," meaning that the receipts obtained from privatizing public utilities were not deficit determining. The argument for this practice is that, since privatization is an exchange of assets, the proceeds should be differentiated from other government revenue in the design of fiscal policy (McKenzie 1998). A second argument follows that privatization proceeds should not be used

---

13. Proceeds from telephone privatization were excluded because of the potential, at the time of this writing, for the process to be reversed, resulting from allegations of corruption. If telephone privatization proceeds had been included, gross receipts of public utilities privatization would have amounted to about 7 percent of GDP.

**Table 3.4 Nicaragua: CORNAP divestiture procedures and form
of payment until 1996** (percent share of total)

Procedure	Cash	Form of payment Credit	Liability transfer	Total
Liquidation	0.0	0.0	0.0	0.0
Merger or acquisition	0.0	0.0	0.0	0.0
Restitution	0.1	2.1	8.2	10.5
Sale or lease	22.3	38.3	28.9	89.5
Total	22.4	40.5	37.1	100.0

Source: CORNAP.

to support the fiscal position permanently, since they may present a misleading view of the deficit.[14]

In sum, privatization proceeds did not affect the overall balance of government operations and, therefore, the government's net worth. Contrary to privatization of electricity distribution, the proceeds from divestiture of CORNAP enterprises did not even affect the government's liquidity position.

The lack of transparency and oversight that characterized the privatization of CORNAP enterprises have made it difficult to pin down the use of sales proceeds. A large portion was presumably used to support the bureaucracy in charge of CORNAP. Proceeds from the privatization of electricity distribution and generation were used as a financial cushion (although a significant fraction was used to finance short-term gaps).

Since privatization in Nicaragua occurred as part of a larger set of reforms, it is difficult to assess privatization's fiscal and macroeconomic effects, other than how proceeds were accounted for and used. To this end, we present evidence on the evolution of tax revenue and gross government transfers to SOEs and information on the quasi-fiscal balances of public utilities.

There is evidence that, at least in the case of large divested firms, tax revenues increased in the period after privatization. For example, three large companies, which together contributed to a yearly average of 1.1 percent of GDP during the 1990s, increased their contribution to an annual average of 2 percent of GDP in the four years following privatization.[15] The same report shows that, in the two fiscal years after CORNAP privatization started, 20 percent of the total revenue large firms contributed came from

---

14. See Davis et al. (2000) and the references therein.

15. These companies were two bottling enterprises (ENSA and MILKA) and the beer producer Compañía Cervezera Nicaragüense. For details, see Central Bank of Nicaragua (1996).

Table 3.5 Nicaragua: Fiscal balances and net transfers to public utilities (percent of GDP)

Utility	Period 1991–95	Period 1996–2000
Electricity (ENEL)		
Fiscal balance[a]	−0.99	−0.78
Net transfers[b]	−0.16	0.00
External and domestic financing[c]	0.58	0.57
Telephone services (ENITEL)		
Fiscal balance[a]	1.55	1.23
Net transfers[b]	0.43	0.21
External and domestic financing[c]	0.47	−0.20
Water and sewage (ENACAL)		
Fiscal balance[a]	−0.41	−1.35
Net transfers[b]	−0.14	−0.17
External and domestic financing[c]	0.20	0.23

a. Average overall deficit before net transfers to the government.
b. Average net transfers to the government.
c. Includes external loans net of payments and net financing from the central bank, financial system, and providers.

Source: Central Bank of Nicaragua.

newly privatized firms. This finding is consistent with Galal et al. (1994), Shaikh and Abdala (1996), and La Porta and López-de-Silanes (1999), who found that privatized firms became significant tax contributors after privatization. In addition, using panel data analysis, Davis et al. (2000) provided evidence that privatization leads to a positive, ongoing increase in tax revenue as a share of GDP in nontransition economies.

In addition, the Central Bank of Nicaragua (1996) reported that, during the 1980s, direct and indirect subsidies to CORNAP enterprises amounted to an average of 11.2 percent of GDP per year. A fraction of this amount corresponded to an implicit subsidy, since CORNAP enterprises enjoyed nonindexed credit from the then state-owned banks (an estimated 7.5 percent of GDP per year during the period). The other fraction was calculated by annualizing the outstanding unpaid debt that CORNAP enterprises acquired during the 1980s from state-owned banks and the Central Bank, which the government absorbed in 1990 before divestment. This amount corresponds to an annualized 3.7 percent of GDP. Elimination of these subsidies suggests a significant lessening of the fiscal burden from these enterprises.

With regard to public utilities, it is difficult to assess the full fiscal effect of reform because their privatization process has not yet ended.

At the firm level, Nicaragua's electricity utility, ENEL (Empresa Nicaraguense de Electricidad), which still controls part of electricity generation and transmission, and ENITEL, the telecommunications company, have improved their fiscal balance positions since reforms started in 1995. Table 3.5 shows that, in the case of ENEL, net transfers to the government

Table 3.6 Nicaragua: Comparison of inequality indexes for real monthly wages (excluding zero-earnings workers), 1993 and 1998

	Year		Change	
Inequality index	1993	1998	Amount	Percent
Gini coefficient	0.5165	0.5418	0.0253	4.9
Generalized entropy	1.0837	1.3645	0.2808	25.9
Between	0.0587	0.0518	−0.0069	−11.8
Within	1.0250	1.3127	0.2877	28.1
By industry				
Agriculture, hunting, forestry, and fishing	1.4484	1.8423	0.3939	27.2
Community, social, and personal services	1.0026	1.4138	0.4112	41.0
Construction	0.4908	1.4542	0.9634	196.3
Electricity, gas, and water	0.3269	0.4621	0.1351	41.3
Financing, insurance, real estate, and business services	0.5545	0.5456	−0.0089	−1.6
Manufacturing	0.6725	0.6725	−0.1992	−29.6
Mining and quarrying	0.8297	0.6350	−0.1946	−23.5
Transportation, storage, and communication	0.6481	1.2021	0.5540	85.5
Wholesale and retail trade, restaurants, and hotels	1.1041	1.0175	−0.0866	−7.8

Source: Authors' calculations, using EMNV-93, EMNV-98, and EIGH-99.

were negative during 1991–95, and neutral during 1996–2000. ENITEL has reduced average external and internal financing, which reflects increased efficiency, presumably stemming from preparation for privatization. In the case of ENACAL, which will not be privatized, the fiscal balance worsened slightly on average, and average net transfers from the government increased after 1995.

Employment and Wage Inequality

We believe that changes in public and private ownership patterns influenced shifts in employment patterns and other labor-market aggregates. Taken alone, however, this factor does not constitute conclusive evidence of a relationship between privatization and inequality. Table 3.6 shows that, after privatization, inequality in Nicaragua increased in certain economic activities, such as agriculture, which had a large share of privatized enterprises. However, inequality also increased in other activities, such as social services, which had little or no privatization. Moreover, inequality decreased in certain activities that had a high proportion of privatized assets, such as mining and quarrying; manufacturing; and financing, insurance, real estate, and business services.

Clearly, overall wage inequality in Nicaragua increased during 1993–98. To determine the extent to which privatization contributed to the rise, we start with this hypothesis: If CORNAP privatization directly affected inequality, then changes in the fraction of workers employed in the public sector should account for most of the changes in overall wage inequality. However, the CORNAP divestment process may have also affected inequality indirectly, to the extent that it affected collective bargaining practices (e.g., coverage or scope) and government labor-market policy. If so, one must distinguish between sources of inequality arising from changes in worker characteristics (e.g., education, occupation, and gender) and the observed rewards to such characteristics from unobservable changes that might be attributed to the privatization process.

First-Order Assessment: Variance Decomposition

To assess privatization's distributional effect, one must first determine the sources of change in inequality. We begin with a decomposition of Nicaragua's overall wage dispersion, which yields a first-order approximation of how privatization affected private- and public-sector inequality. This decomposition is used to study privatization's role in producing inequality differences among rural and urban workers during 1993–98 and 1993–99, respectively.

The decomposition was carried out as follows: At any date t, $Var(y_t)$ and $Var(y_t^j)$ denote the economywide variance of wages and the variance of wages in sector $j = p, s$, respectively; α_t^s stands for the fraction of individuals working in the public sector; $Var(y_t^j)$ and $\bar{y}_t^j$ are the variance and mean of wages of sector j; and $\bar{y}_t$ is the overall or economywide average of wage.[16]

For any two years, t and t-l, the change in overall wage dispersion is:

$$Var(y_t) - Var(y_{t-l}) = (\alpha_t^s - \alpha_{t-l}^s)\left[Var(y_t^s) - Var(y_t^p) + (\bar{y}_t^s - \bar{y}_t)^2 - (\bar{y}_t^p - \bar{y}_t)^2\right]$$

$$+ (1 - \alpha_{t-l}^s)\left[Var(y_t^p) - Var(y_{t-l}^p)\right]$$

$$+ \alpha_{t-l}^s\left[Var(y_t^s) - Var(y_{t-l}^s)\right]$$

$$+ \alpha_{t-l}^s\left[(\bar{y}_t^s - \bar{y}_t)^2 - (\bar{y}_{t-l}^s - \bar{y}_{t-l})^2\right]$$

$$+ (1 - \alpha_{t-l}^s)\left[(\bar{y}_t^p - \bar{y}_t)^2 - (\bar{y}_{t-l}^p - \bar{y}_{t-l})^2\right] \qquad (3.1)$$

That is, equation 3.1 decomposes the overall change in earnings dispersion between dates t and $t-l$ into five sources: how the change in the fraction of people working in the public sector contributes to the change in overall inequality (the first term on the right-hand side of the equation); how the change in the relative wage dispersion in the public and private

---

16. Blau and Kahn (1996) use a similar decomposition to assess the role of unionism on US wages and for international comparisons, respectively. Juhn, Murphy, and Pierce (1993) use a similar approach to assess industry's effect on wage inequality.

sectors contributes to the change in overall inequality (the second and third terms, respectively, on the right-hand side of the equation); and how the mean earnings gap in each sector affects the change in total inequality (the fourth and fifth terms on the right-hand side of the equation).

The decomposition in equation 3.1 is not unique; alternative decompositions can be calculated in which the weights in equation 3.1 may differ. However, it is clear from equation 3.1 that the dispersion of wages may have been affected through various channels. Privatization could have caused a reduction in the share of individuals working in the public sector. The effect of this reduction on inequality would depend on these workers' situation in the absence of SOEs. However, the relative earnings gap in both public and private sectors, as well as initial inequality within each sector, also affected total inequality significantly.

In computing the decomposition, we were forced to make an identifying assumption (Freije and Rivas 2003). The LSMS-93 allowed one to identify individuals by geographical location (urban or rural) and work sector (public or private), whereas the LSMS-98 allowed one to identify individuals by geographical location (urban or rural) but not by work sector. Conversely, the HIES-99 allows one to disaggregate individuals by sector (public or private); however, since it is an urban survey, no rural-urban sorting is possible.

Thus, we first estimated equation 3.1 for individuals in urban areas, using the LSMS-93 and the HIES-99. We then estimated decomposition using the LSMS-93 and the LSMS-98 for individuals who worked in rural areas, assuming that, by 1998, public-sector employment in rural areas was negligible. This assumption was not restrictive in light of evidence from establishment-level data mentioned earlier. The Survey for Establishments, used by the Ministry of Labor to construct labor-market statistics, indicates that 1993 shares of SOEs in agriculture, fishery, and mining (32.8, 100, and 100 percent, respectively) dropped to 0 percent by 1998. The share of SOEs, including all economic activities, dropped from 60 to 25.4 percent (Freije and Rivas 2003).

Table 3.7 shows that, in the rural areas, the mean log real wage declined in both the public and the private sectors. However, inequality, as measured by the variance, increased only slightly in rural areas. On the other hand, increase in the average log real wage in urban areas—in both public and private sectors—was accompanied by a considerable increase in inequality in the public sector only. In both the rural and urban sectors, the unconditional average log real wage was higher for public-sector workers in 1993, and the difference continued in 1998.[17]

---

17. As shown below, when one controls for worker characteristics, private-sector workers earn higher wages than their public-sector counterparts.

Table 3.7 Nicaragua: Variance decomposition

Factor/sector	Urban sector 1999	Rural sector 1998
Employment share (percent)		
Public	13.6	4.1
Private	86.4	95.9
Variances (real hourly wage)		
Public	618.9	16.4
Private	417.8	38.1
Total	446.5	37.3
Means (real hourly wage)		
Public	16.8	5.4
Private	13.4	3.4
Total	13.9	3.5

	1993	
Employment share (percent)		
Public	22.9	11.0
Private	77.1	89.0
Variances (real hourly wage)		
Public	117.1	80.2
Private	380.5	74.7
Total	318.9	75.7
Means (real hourly wage)		
Public	11.2	8.1
Private	13.3	6.3
Total	12.8	6.5

	Real hourly wage	Percent	Real hourly wage	Percent
Change in total variance	127.6	100	−38.4	100
Decomposition I				
Public-sector employment share	−19.5	−15	1.2	−3
Public-sector variance	115.0	90	−7.0	18
Private-sector variance	28.7	23	−32.7	85
Public-sector mean gap	1.4	1	0.1	0
Private-sector mean gap	0.0	0	0.0	0
Decomposition II				
Public-sector employment share	24.3	19	−0.5	1
Public-sector variance	68.2	53	−2.6	7
Private-sector variance	32.2	25	−35.2	92
Public-sector mean gap	0.8	1	0.1	0
Private-sector mean gap	0.0	0	0.0	0

Sources: Freije and Rivas (2003, appendix 3.1). The appendix provides a formal explanation of decomposition. Authors' calculations, using LSMS-93, LSMS-98, and HIES-99.

Decomposition of the change in total inequality shows that, for two decomposition methods, the change in public-sector inequality and the mean income gap account for a large share of the change in overall inequality. On the other hand, the change in private-sector inequality caused a decline, instead of a rise, in total inequality. The size of the effect caused by change of employment sector share is not robust to the decomposition method. In some cases, it has little negative effect, while in others, it has a large positive effect.[18]

The data in table 3.7 imply that factors other than reduction in α^s are responsible for increased wage dispersion. Ownership patterns, however, might have affected overall inequality indirectly by affecting inequality within particular sectors. One could argue that state ownership contained wage dispersion in the public sector through wage standardization because of uniform rates among comparable workers across SOEs and ranges of rates for occupational categories within SOEs. After all, unions were more prevalent before privatization; their bargaining power declined considerably during and after privatization. Collective bargaining became more decentralized, with single-firm agreements prevailing over industry or economywide arrangements (Freeman 1980, Blau and Kahn 1996). In addition, government policies that aimed at equalizing pay among similarly skilled workers within establishments could have also contained public-sector wage dispersion.[19] The importance of within private-sector dispersion at the national level could be explained, in part, by the extension of collective bargaining agreements for public-sector workers to the private sector.[20]

Thus, one must further examine wage dispersion within the public and private sectors. The main problem in comparing public- and private-sector wage dispersion is differentiating the effect of other factors correlated with privatization. One must thus distinguish between (1) the portion of the change in inequality that can be attributed to changes in worker characteristics, (2) the fraction attributable to the market values of such personal characteristics, and (3) the fraction attributable to privatization (to the extent it can be delinked from other reforms).

Changing Attributes and Market Values

The next step in this exercise is to decompose the change in overall wage inequality in three components: (1) changes in distribution of observed characteristics (e.g., education, occupation, and gender); (2) changes in the

---

18. Freije and Rivas (2003) show the same decomposition exercise using real hourly wages (instead of its logarithm). Again, changes in public-sector inequality is the main positive factor explaining the change in overall inequality, whereas changes in public-sector employment have no consistent effect across sectors and decomposition methods.

19. These policies were undertaken on the basis of perceived inequality before "statization," when individuals were paid wages based on management-perceived worker characteristics, rather than position characteristics.

20. This phenomenon is common in socialist countries, where most workers belong to unions and where the state controls wages. See also Rezler (1973).

Figure 3.1 Average rural wage by employment sector and occupation level, 1993 and 1998

real hourly wages (in 1999 córdobas)

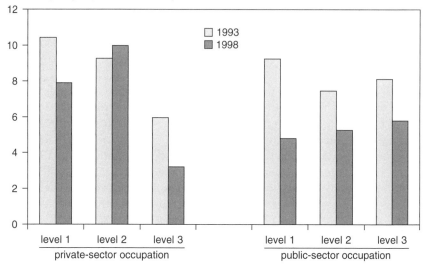

Note: Occupations are managers and professionals (level 1); clerical and salespersons (level 2); and craftspersons, operatives, laborers, and service workers (level 3).

Source: Author's calculations using LSMS-93 and LSMS-98.

market value of such characteristics; and (3) changes in unobservable attributes and market values, along with any remaining measurement error. In doing so, one follows Juhn, Murphy, and Pierce (1993); we refer to these respective effects as (1) observable characteristics effect, (2) observable market value effect, and (3) residual effect. This technique allows one to decompose the overall change in inequality in four additive components: (1) changes in observable quantities, (2) changes in observable prices, (3) changes in observable prices related to public-sector employment, and (4) changes in distribution of unobservable prices.[21]

From this exercise, one can conclude that occupational categories did not significantly contribute to individual earnings in the rural sector in 1993 or 1998. However, in the urban sector, managers and professionals earned significantly higher wages than workers in any other occupation (including clerks, salespersons, craftspersons, operatives, and service workers). In addition, the wage premia for managers and professionals increased between 1993 and 1999. Public-sector managers and professionals earned

21. For a thorough exposition of the methodology used and the general results, see Freije and Rivas (2003).

Figure 3.2 Average urban wage by employment sector and occupation level, 1993 and 1999

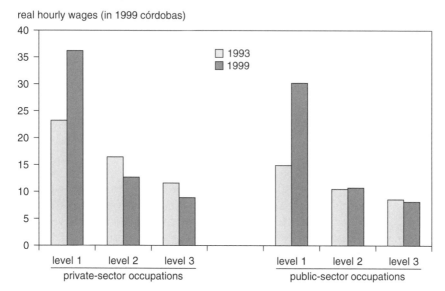

real hourly wages (in 1999 córdobas)

Note: Occupations are managers and professionals (level 1); clerical and salespersons (level 2); and craftspersons, operatives, laborers, and service workers (level 3).
Source: Authors' calculations using LSMS-93 and HIES-99.

significantly more than their private-sector counterparts, with the premium declining over time. Moreover, other occupational categories had a narrower differential with managers and professionals if they worked in the public, rather than private sector, and this differential increased over the period.

Figures 3.1 and 3.2 illustrate the argument, showing the average hourly wages for various occupations in public and private sectors for urban and rural areas. In the public sector, the difference in hourly wages between levels 1 and 3 remained at about 1 córdoba in the rural area but increased to more than 20 córdobas in the urban area. A similar pattern was found in the private sector. This finding is consistent with the story of increasing inequality in the urban public and private sectors and the declining or stagnant inequality in the rural public sector.

Clearly, the demand for skilled labor increased in the urban formal sector, particularly for individuals skilled in operating in the market-oriented economy that emerged from privatization and deregulation, especially in such areas as finance, marketing, and management.

Another key finding is that the rural-sector education premia declined for all education categories. Subsistence-level agriculture probably expanded as cultivable land was given to demobilized soldiers, retired army members, and landless organized peasants. These groups, who by 1993 had benefited from privatization in manufacturing by forming workers-owned firms, opted for agricultural activities by 1998. At the same time, demand for laborers without formal education may have increased in such labor-intensive activities as coffee gathering (Freije and Rivas 2003). Another possibility is that reversed migration (from the urban to the rural sector) occurred during the period; as the former elite and middle and upper-middle classes returned from abroad, skilled urban-sector labor became relatively more abundant.[22]

Finally, the premium that urban public-utilities workers earned decreased (the premium of both urban and rural public-utilities workers was high, at 73.3 percent and 48.8 percent, respectively). It became statistically insignificant over the period—a pattern consistent with the streamlining of public utilities.

As tables 3.8 and 3.9 show, for the urban and rural sectors respectively, inequality in Nicaragua has increased, except for the variance in real hourly wages in rural areas, which has decreased (apparently because of a decline in the fifth to first decile ratio). Inequality increased in all other percentile differentials in both rural and urban sectors. The increase in inequality is robust to the index choice. The Gini coefficient and various generalized entropy and Atkinson indexes also indicate that inequality increased across the board.

We find greater widening at the top of the distribution in both rural and urban sectors. Despite the relatively short time span, one can see that changes in observable characteristics can explain most of the increased inequality in the rural sector, while the market value of such characteristics accounts for greater inequality in the urban sector. We interpret this distinction as the consequence of changes in the composition or rural labor. In fact, the share of agricultural activities rose dramatically in rural Nicaragua, while agricultural wages stagnated over the period (Freije and Rivas 2003). We hypothesize that demographic pressures stemming from the return of refugees, demobilization of war veterans, and internal population growth resulted in a flooded labor supply, which the rural sector could not absorb.[23]

In the urban sector, price changes of observable characteristics are key to explaining inequality changes. Over the last decade, resurgence of private banking and telecommunications in urban Nicaragua may have contributed

---

22. Migration of unskilled labor from the rural sector to neighboring countries also occurred during this period.

23. One datum that hints in this direction is that about 55 percent of the total new employment generated in the rural sector was composed of individuals between the ages of 15 and 19. By contrast, over the same period, only 26 percent of new urban employment was in that age group.

Table 3.8 Nicaragua: John-Murphy-Pierce decomposition for various inequality indices, urban sector
(in 1999 real hourly wages)

Inequality index	1993 (1)	1999 (2)	Difference (3)	Effect			
				Measured characteristics[a] (4)	Wage equation all coefficients[a] (5)	Public-sector coefficients[b,c] (6)	Wage equation residuals[a] (7)
Variance of logarithms	.817	.867	.050	.00 / 3	.13 / 251	.04 / 33	−.08 / −153
Variance	318.880	446.510	127.620	248.45 / 195	145.41 / 114	−70.66 / −49	−266.24 / −209
Decile ratio							
Ninth to first	9.61	10.27	.66	−.51 / −77	.23 / 337	.74 / 33	−1.06 / −160
Ninth to fifth	3.33	3.82	.49	.04 / 8	.67 / 137	.30 / 45	−.22 / −45
Fifth to first	2.89	2.69	−.20	−.19 / 93	.10 / −49	−.03 / −32	−.11 / 56
Generalized entropy							
(−1)	.72	.84	.12	−.04 / −30	.16 / 136	.06 / 38	−.01 / −6
(0)	.46	.52	.05	.02 / 45	.09 / 175	.03 / 37	−.06 / −120
(1)	.52	.59	.07	.07 / 96	.11 / 157	.05 / 42	−.11 / −153
(2)	.98	1.16	.18	.36 / 194	.28 / 151	.16 / 58	−.45 / −245
Gini coefficient	.51	.54	.03	.02 / 54	.05 / 151	.02 / 36	−.03 / −105
Atkinson indices							
A(0.5)	.22	.24	.02	.02 / 68	.04 / 161	.02 / 38	−.03 / −129
A(1.0)	.37	.40	.03	.01 / 46	.05 / 168	.02 / 36	−.04 / −113
A(2.0)	.59	.63	.04	−.01 / −34	.05 / 140	.02 / 35	.00 / −5

a. Percentage of total difference.
b. Refers to the effect due only to changes in the coefficient of public-sector employment (as well as its interaction with occupation) in the wage equation. See Freije and Rivas (2003, appendix 3.1).
c. Percent of all coefficients effect.

Source: Calculated by the authors.

Table 3.9 Nicaragua: Juhn-Murphy-Pierce decomposition for various inequality indices, rural sector
(in 1999 real hourly wages)

Inequality index	1993 (1)	1999 (2)	Difference (3)	Measured characteristics[a] (4)	Effect Wage equation all coefficients[a] (5)	Effect Public-sector coefficients[b,c] (6)	Effect Wage equation residuals[a] (7)
Variance of logarithms	.773	.786	.013	.15 / 1,142	.04 / 280	.05 / 145	−.18 / 1,323
Variance	75.700	37.300	−38.400	35.01 / −91	−71.40 / 186	−12.65 / 18	−2.02 / 5
Decile ratio							
Ninth to first	10.29	10.79	.50	.98 / 194	.08 / 15	.90 / 1,199	−.55 / −109
Ninth to fifth	30.04	3.42	.38	2.40 / 627	−.17 / −45	.19 / −111	−1.85 / −482
Fifth to first	3.39	3.15	.24	−1.32 / 561	.08 / −36	.10 / 115	1.00 / −425
Generalized entropy							
(−1)	1.15	3.08	1.93	−.37 / −19	.01 / 0	.05 / 855	2.29 / 119
(0)	.49	.53	.05	.09 / 189	.01 / 11	.02 / 289	−.05 / −100
(1)	.50	.54	.04	.17 / 437	−.02 / −62	−.01 / 24	−.11 / −275
(2)	.90	.97	.07	.43 / 634	−.16 / −229	−.08 / 53	−.21 / −305
Gini coefficient	.51	.52	.02	.07 / 399	.00 / 5	.00 / 558	−.05 / −304
Atkinson indices							
A(0.5)	.22	.23	.02	.06 / 354	.00 / −14	.00 / −117	−.04 / −239
A(1.0)	.38	.41	.03	.06 / 184	.00 / 10	.01 / 290	−.03 / −94
A(2.0)	.70	.86	.16	−.09 / −55	.00 / 1	.01 / 882	.25 / 154

a. Percentage of total difference.
b. Refers to the effect due only to changes in the coefficient of public-sector employment (as well as its interaction with occupation) in the wage equation. See Freije and Rivas (2003, appendix 3.1).
c. Percentage of all coefficients effect.

Source: Authors' calculations.

to the widening gap at the top of urban distribution. Price differentials related directly to having a public-sector job also contribute significantly to the explanation. These findings are consistent with our previous argument that privatization brings about a new set of industrial relations in both the public and private sectors, where wages will be more in line with productivity patterns and competitive forces than with political conventions, government coordination, or union pressures.

Despite these observations, we conclude that unobservable characteristics and prices, as well as measurement error, contributed to increased inequality to a much lesser degree. Indeed, most of the values in the far-right columns of tables 3.8 and 3.9 are negative; that is, they contributed to a reduction in inequality, indicating that privatization was not the only factor explaining inequality. In the urban sector, privatization may have been the largest contributing factor one can single out; however, in the rural sector, one can argue that demobilization of war veterans, together with the small redistribution of land held by CORNAP, indirectly influenced the widening of inequality.

Welfare Effects of Utilities: Prices, Access, and Quality

To assess the welfare effects of reforms and participation of private firms in providing electricity and telecommunications, one must examine the reforms' effects on these services' pricing, access, and quality. By observing expenditure decisions, one can infer the underlying changes in indirect utility functions, which can then be used to estimate the welfare effects. Because of data limitations, the focus of our analysis, described below, is electricity.[24]

Distributional Effect of Price Changes

The first step is to examine the effect of electricity prices on the distribution of real incomes across different households, using simple nonparametric techniques to uncover the shape of the Engel curves and estimate kernel densities.[25] These methods describe the average welfare effects of price

---

24. Although the telecommunications sector allowed private participation earlier than did electricity, private provision consisted exclusively of cellular services, and household surveys lacked information on their share of expenditure.

25. Deaton (1989) provides both a theoretical motivation for the use of nonparametric techniques for assessing the welfare effect of small price changes, as well as the nonparametric analysis adapted by us. See also McKenzie and Mookherjee (2003).

Figure 3.3 Electricity bill within total expenditures, 1993

electricity bill share (ratio)   density function

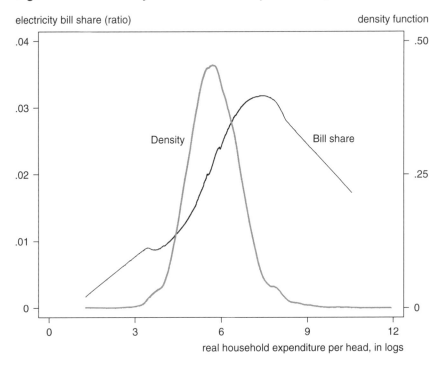

real household expenditure per head, in logs

Source: Authors' calculations.

changes that operate through consumption. The next step focuses on alternative analyses of welfare, estimating consumer surpluses and accounting for changes in access to electricity.

During 1993–98, the price of electricity increased 24.2 percent.[26] Most of the increase was concentrated during 1995–98, the years of active reform. How does one account for the distributional consequences of such price increases? Since nearly all surveyed households did not produce electricity services, one alternative is to describe consumption patterns for electricity in relation to consumers' living standards. These data provide an estimate of the first-order welfare effect of the price increase (Deaton 1989). This procedure is done by taking expenditure shares of electricity services at various points along the total expenditure, per capita distribution. The logic is simple: A price increase has the greatest effect on consumers who devote a larger share of their budget to electricity.

---

26. In constant Nicaraguan córdobas, electricity increased from 0.95 per kWh in 1993 to 1.18 per kWh in 1998; these prices are reported according to the consumer price index elaborated by the Central Bank of Nicaragua.

Figure 3.4   Electricity bill within total expenditures, 1998

electricity bill share (ratio)   density function

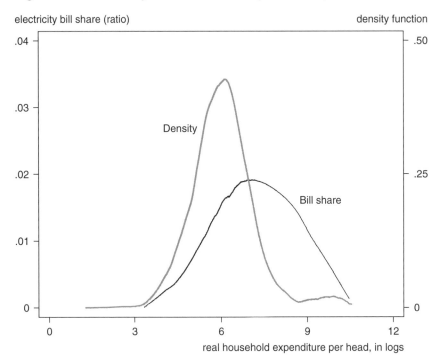

Source: Authors' calculations.

Implicitly, we take total expenditure per capita as their measure of household living standard. Per capita monthly expenditure is calculated by taking the total monthly expenditure on all items that the household consumes (reported in the surveys), and dividing this amount by the number of household members.[27]

Figures 3.3 and 3.4 present nonparametric regressions of the electricity expenditure share on the logarithm of total expenditure per capita for years 1993 and 1998, respectively. The estimation is performed with kernel smoothing.[28] At any given value of total expenditure per capita, excluding the extreme 5 percent of observations (2.5 at each extreme of the distribution), the graphs show the values of electricity expenditure share for observations nearby (within the kernel). In addition, they show the density function.

The Engel curves are nonmonotonic. In 1993, the budget share spent on electricity declined as living standards rose for the wealthiest; however, it

---

27. In the surveys, frequency of expenditure for certain goods varied from weekly to annually; thus, we homogenized all expenditure to the monthly frequency.

28. For a detailed explanation of the technique, see Deaton (1989) and the references therein.

Figure 3.5 Electricity bill share, rural and urban, 1993

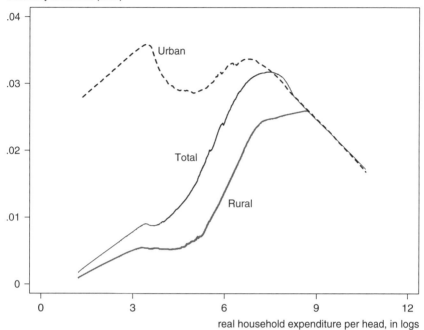

electricity bill share (ratio)

Source: Authors' calculations.

increased for the middle range of the distribution, where most households were concentrated (greater mass). In 1998, households with expenditure below 2 in logarithmic scale spent nothing on electricity, suggesting that the poorest households may have been priced out. Consumers spent less on electricity in 1998 than in 1993, even when controlling for budget size. Clearly, in both 1993 and 1998, for a large range of expenditure distribution, the budget share spent on electricity increased. Moreover, at all expenditure levels, households spent less on electricity in 1998 than in 1993.

Figures 3.5 and 3.6 show the same regressions of the electricity expenditure share, separating rural from urban areas. The increasing section of the curve stems mainly from rural-sector behavior. Electricity bill shares strongly increase for rural households with expenditures below 7 (in logarithms), while shares are less sloped for the urban sector.

Clearly, the nonparametric approach described above has its limitations. Nonetheless, it provides considerable information on the evolution of access to electricity between 1993 and 1998. The approach also helps to set a boundary on the distributional effect of the price increase.

Figure 3.6   Electricity bill share, rural and urban, 1998

electricity bill share (ratio)

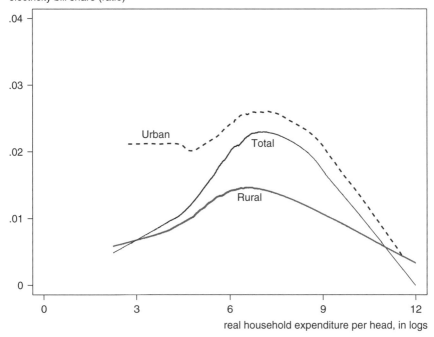

real household expenditure per head, in logs

Source: Authors' calculations using LSMS-93 and LSMS-98.

First- and Second-Order Approximations to Consumer Surplus

The approach that Deaton (1989) outlines is best suited for small price changes, and does not account for quantity adjustment. Banks, Blundell, and Lewbel (1996) suggest that first-order approximations, like the one described above, may display systematic bias and that second-order approximations work better; however, second-order approximations require more information, meaning that first-order approximations to welfare measures do not require knowledge of substitution effects, as do second-order approximations. In fact, second-order approximations depend on distribution of substitution elasticities and therefore require estimates of derivatives of the demand functions (McKenzie and Mookherjee 2003).[29]

---

29. A more standard approach to examining the distributional effect of price changes is to construct cost-of-living indexes and observe whether the living costs of poor households are disproportionately affected. See Levinsohn, Berry, and Friedman (1995).

One can assume that each household receives an equal social weight, temporarily ignoring access issues. Under this assumption, the first-order approximation of the change in utility for an individual between any two dates, t and t-l, $\Delta u = (u_t - u_{t-1})$, is given by:[30]

$$\Delta u = -(q_{t-1}\Delta p) \qquad (3.2)$$

where q denotes the quantity of electricity consumed and $\Delta p = (p_t - p_{t-1})$ represents the change in electricity price.

Clearly, equation 3.2 overestimates the welfare effect of the price increase since it does not allow consumers to change the quantity consumed in response to the price change. Banks, Blundell, and Lewbel (1996) show that it is better to use the second-order approach:

$$\Delta u = -q_{t-1}\Delta p \left(1 + \frac{\Delta p}{2p_{t-1}} \frac{\partial \log q}{\partial \log p} \right) \qquad (3.3)$$

where the partial derivative is evaluated at 1993 prices. Equation 3.3 shows that the second-order correction depends on the own price elasticity. Since the own price elasticity is generally negative, the second-order approximation allows for some quantity response to the price change.

To estimate the first- and second-order approximations empirically, it is convenient to work with log prices and budget shares, w, instead of level prices and quantities. In this case, equation 3.3 becomes

$$\Delta u = -(\Delta \log p)w_{t-1} \qquad (3.4)$$

and equation 3.4 becomes

$$\Delta u = -w_{t-1}(\Delta \log p) \left(1 + \frac{\Delta \log p}{2} \frac{\partial \log w}{\partial \log q} \right) \qquad (3.5)$$

Assuming that households only consume, and do not produce, electricity (a relatively nonrestrictive assumption), total income does not change with variations in electricity price. Once the first- and second-order approximations are cast in terms of log prices and expenditure shares, the electricity share regressions of the previous subsection provide an estimation of the distributional effect of the price change that is equivalent to the first-order approximation in equation 3.5.

---

30. Banks, Blundell, and Lewbel (1996) show that, with no income effects, the change in utility equals a money metric measure of the change in welfare.

In order to compute equation 3.6, one must first estimate the elasticity $\frac{\delta \log w}{\delta \log q}$. We estimated the Engel equation parametrically, using the Almost Ideal Demand System (AIDS) model (Deaton and Mullbauer 1980) for household h and good j, as follows:

$$w_{hj} = \alpha_j + \sum_{i=1}^{k} \gamma_{ij} \log p_i + \beta_j \left(\log \frac{x_h}{n_h} \right) + \phi_j \left(\log \frac{x_h}{n_h} \right)^2 + \lambda_j' Z_h \quad (3.6)$$

where n_h equals the number of households with h members, x_h is total real expenditure of household h, and Z_h contains other household characteristics. For robustness, we estimated the equation by ordinary least squares, including all data and excluding extreme observations and households with zero electricity expenditure. Moreover, we fit a model correcting for electricity access; therefore, we reestimated the Engel equation using a two-stage auto-selection correction. We did not include the price of kerosene, the only approximate substitute, because it was not significant in every case. Data on quality were unavailable and were therefore not included.[31] On the other hand, an interaction between electricity price and having a refrigerator was included. Because the coefficients for electricity price are robust across estimation methods, only the results for the second procedure are presented (table 3.10).[32]

The average coefficient is about −0.03 in the urban sector, ranging from -0.01 for those without a refrigerator to −0.08 for those with one. The coefficient for the rural sector is −0.01, ranging from 0.0 to −0.06. These coefficients allow one to estimate the expected elasticity for every household, which, in turn, makes it possible to compute welfare changes as expressed in equation 3.6. Thus, as expected, households with electrical appliances are more price elastic than households without them. Table 3.11 shows the average price elasticity by expenditure deciles in Nicaragua. Elasticity is increasing in expenditure so that households up to the sixth deciles are inelastic to price changes, whereas households in the top three deciles have elastic demand for electricity.

Table 3.12 presents the welfare effect of the change in electricity prices between 1993 and 1998, using equations 3.4 and 3.5, once equation 3.6 was estimated. The top panel presents the first- and second-order approximations in constant córdobas, while the bottom panel presents the approximations as a percentage of real household expenditure per capita. One computes the mean change in utility by expenditure deciles, assuming equal social utility weights within groups, and distinguishing total rural

---

31. Data on service quality (i.e., number, duration, and source of blackouts) is available only after 1998, when the regulatory agency began operations.

32. For a thorough explanation of the procedure and results for both estimations, see Freije and Rivas (2003).

Table 3.10 Nicaragua: Engel equation estimations with Heckman's selection correction, 1993–98

Factor	Urban sector All observations		Urban sector Excluding households[a]		Rural sector All observations		Rural sector Excluding households[a]	
	Coefficient	Standard error	Coefficient	Standard error	Coefficient	Standard error	Coefficient	Standard error
Total observations	4,702		4,539		3,709		3,471	
Censored	541		972		2,536		2,545	
Uncensored	4,161		3,567		1,173		926	
Pseudo R-squared	.039		.053		.111		.154	
Wald × 2	603.700		587.870		150.530		111.520	
Dependent variable								
Electricity budget share								
Electricity price	-.032c	.005	-.011b	.006	-.021c	.008	.000	.010
Real household expenditure per head	-.011c	.004	-.032c	.008	-.009	.006	-.018	.012
Real household expenditure per head, squared	.000	.000	.002c	.001	.000	.000	.001	.001
Refrigerator	.025c	.001	.028c	.001	.026c	.002	.028c	.003
Refrigerator × electricity price			-.070c	.011			-.058c	.023
Constant	.085c	.014	.158c	.025	.070c	.019	.104c	.038
Access to electricity service								
Real household expenditure per head	.352c	.033	.321c	.030	.231c	.022	.409c	.034
Shanty dwelling	-.690c	.115	-1.013c	.109	-.815c	.079	-.870c	.094
Access to piped water	1.244c	.056	.790c	.050	1.207c	.056	1.047c	.057
Constant	-1.710c	.201	-1.715c	.180	-1.940c	.126	-3.076c	.190
Rho	-.164c	.045	-.160c	.047	-.115c	.062	-.078c	.080
Mills ratio	-.005c	.001	-.005c	.002	-.003c	.002	-.002c	.002

a. Excludes households without access and households with access but electricity bill equal to zero; also excludes households in the top and bottom 2.5 percent household expenditure per head.
b. Significantly differs from zero with 90 percent confidence.
c. Significantly differs from zero with 95 percent confidence.

Source: Calculated by the authors.

Table 3.11 Nicaragua: Elasticity and virtual price for approximations to consumer surplus

Decile	Price elasticity (of elasticity budget share)	Virtual price (in real córdobas)
1 (lowest)	−.013	2163.0
2	−.042	480.4
3	−.102	104.4
4	−.237	35.3
5	−.475	11.3
6	−.601	9.1
7	−.831	4.3
8	−1.400	4.4
9	−2.726	3.1
10 (highest)	−3.921	3.4

Source: Authors' data.

and urban areas. The results in table 3.12 ignore any change in access to electricity services, an issue incorporated below.

Although the first-order approximation shows that the increase in electricity price reduced welfare at all expenditure deciles, the estimation shows that the effect was stronger at the top of the distribution. This finding suggests that the price effect was at least nonregressive. Both in monetary and percentage terms, the loss is smaller in the bottom deciles than in the top deciles (with the exception of the bottom decile in percentage terms). When adjustments in the quantity of electricity are allowed (second-order approximations), the negative welfare effect is slightly less severe; the nonregressiveness is still present in monetary terms, but less so in percentage terms.

Incorporating Changes in Access

The calculations of welfare changes in table 3.12 exclude the fact that certain households who lacked access to electricity before the reforms might have obtained access by 1998. One can modify the approach used in the previous subsection to incorporate changes in access in calculating the welfare effects that resulted from increased electricity price. A necessary assumption is that those households who had access in 1993 continued to have it in 1998. Such an assumption does not preclude the possibility that some households who had access in 1993 were priced out by 1998. Conceivably, extremely poor households with access to electricity who demanded electricity services in 1993 demanded zero electricity by 1998 because of price increases.

In computing welfare changes, we divided households into three groups: (1) those with access in 1993 and 1998, (2) those without access in 1993 and 1998, and (3) those without access in 1993 but with access in

Table 3.12 Nicaragua: Effect of change in electricity price on welfare (not accounting for change in access), 1993–98/99

Decile	First-order approximation			Second-order approximation		
	Total	Urban	Rural	Total	Urban	Rural
In real (1998 = 100) córdobas						
1 (lowest)	–.079	–.041	–.375	–.077	–.040	–.368
2	–.260	–.178	–.537	–.254	–.176	–.519
3	–.532	–.469	–.658	–.521	–.467	–.627
4	–.793	–.468	–1.192	–.759	–.463	–1.120
5	–1.190	–.678	–1.618	–1.112	–.664	–1.486
6	–1.909	–1.216	–2.395	–1.772	–1.156	–2.203
7	–2.207	–1.290	–2.635	–1.994	–1.225	–2.353
8	–3.530	–1.533	–4.132	–3.050	–1.332	–3.568
9	–5.234	–3.789	–5.526	–4.223	–3.437	–4.382
10 (highest)	–13.935	–4.706	–16.323	–7.332	–2.069	–8.694
As a percent of real household expenditure, per capita						
1 (lowest)	–.090	–.040	–.430	–.080	–.040	–.420
2	–.160	–.110	–.330	–.160	–.110	–.320
3	–.240	–.210	–.300	–.230	–.210	–.280
4	–.270	.160	–.410	–.260	–.160	–.380
5	–.320	–.180	–.430	–.300	–.180	–.390
6	–.410	–.260	–.510	–.380	–.250	–.470
7	–.370	–.220	–.440	–.330	–.210	–.390
8	–.450	–.190	–.530	–.390	–.170	–.460
9	–.450	–.300	–.480	–.360	–.270	–.380
10 (highest)	–.400	–.190	–.460	–.290	–.160	–.330

Source: Calculated by the authors.

1998.[33] For the first group, one can proceed as in the previous subsection. For the second group, for whom welfare changes could have arisen only through induced variations in the price of electricity substitutes, one can also use the methods outlined in the previous subsection. The third group cannot be handled in the same manner as the first two groups. The problem involves how one handles the price of electricity that this group faced in 1993. For these consumers, the 1993 price can be thought of as the lowest price, such that consumers demand zero electricity if it were offered to them at that price. This virtual price is calculated as the lowest price, such that the expenditure share on electricity is zero. In practice, one recovers this price from the estimated Engel equation 3.6, by finding the price, such that the estimated expenditure share, w_h, is zero.[34]

---

33. Certain complications with the first group may have been ignored because the surveys (1) provided information on individual use of electricity, but not on whether consumers had the option of access in 1993, and (2) did not ask consumers how long they had had access.

34. This virtual price differs by household, according to total expenditure and demographic information. See McKenzie and Mookherjee (chapter 2).

Households with access in both 1993 and in 1998 experienced a loss in welfare across all deciles. In monetary terms, the losses were monotonically increasing from bottom to top deciles; however, in contrast to the results obtained, when the issue of access was ignored, the welfare losses in percentage terms were nearly monotonically decreasing in the urban area and U-shaped in the rural area. That is, percentage welfare losses were larger for poorer households than wealthier ones because poorer households are less elastic to electricity price changes and must allocate a larger share of household expenditure to electricity (particularly those in urban areas).

As expected, households without access in 1993 and 1998 obtained welfare gains, but they were negligible. In effect, these households' welfare remained unchanged.

At the same time, households without access in 1993 who obtained access by 1998 experienced substantial gains in welfare. Among these households, the poorest obtained the largest welfare gains in percentage terms. For these same households, quantity adjustments (second-order approximations) enhanced the welfare gains obtained from gaining access. Again, households at the bottom of the expenditure distribution benefited most as a result of two opposing factors. On the one hand, households in the poorer deciles had a lower expansion of electricity access, compared to wealthier households. Growth in electricity access was higher in urban, rather than rural, areas and faster in the top five, as opposed to the bottom five, deciles. On the other hand, virtual prices were higher in the poorer, rather than wealthier, deciles (table 3.11). Therefore, poorer households had larger gains in welfare not only because they gained access to electricity, but also because they valued that access more than did other households.[35]

The final step is to sum all households and compute the total welfare effect. As table 3.13 shows, the welfare effect was negative in monetary terms for most deciles in urban areas but positive for the bottom six deciles in rural areas. In both rural and urban areas, as well as the country overall, welfare changes were progressive; that is, poorer deciles had either welfare gains or smaller losses than those experienced by wealthier deciles. When considering welfare changes in percentage terms, no gains were registered for first-order approximation in rural areas.

The conclusions from monetary and percentage welfare calculations are the same: The welfare changes of electricity reforms in Nicaragua were progressive. That is, positive welfare changes were larger for the bottom than for the top deciles.

To estimate the effect of these welfare changes on total welfare in Nicaragua, we used the money-metric welfare changes reported above and assumed a class of social welfare functions (Freije and Rivas 2003, appendix

---

35. For a full account of the welfare gain of these groups, see Freije and Rivas (2003).

Table 3.13 Nicaragua: Effect of electricity price change on welfare (accounting for access change for all households)

Decile	First-order approximation			Second-order approximation		
	Total	Urban	Rural	Total	Urban	Rural
In real (1998 = 100) córdobas						
1 (lowest)	−.038	.004	−.371	−.037	.004	−.364
2	.804	1.027	.050	.844	1.014	.269
3	.925	1.517	−.248	.998	1.506	−.009
4	−.008	.482	−.608	.160	.476	−.228
5	.483	.915	.122	.805	.915	.713
6	−.179	.631	−.747	.258	.698	−.051
7	−.972	−.933	−.990	−.345	−.858	−.106
8	−1.693	−.550	−2.038	−.837	−.376	−.976
9	−2.870	−2.366	−2.972	−1.372	−2.013	−1.243
10 (highest)	−12.199	−4.124	−14.288	−3.405	−2.209	−3.715
As a percent of real household expenditure, per head						
1 (lowest)	−.09	−.04	−.43	−.05	.00	−.42
2	−.16	−.11	−.33	.58	.69	.22
3	−.24	−.21	−.30	.47	.71	−.01
4	−.27	−.16	−.41	.07	.19	−.08
5	−.32	−.18	−.43	.22	.27	.18
6	−.41	−.26	−.51	.04	.13	−.02
7	−.37	−.22	−.44	−.07	−.15	−.03
8	−.45	−.19	−.53	−.10	−.05	−.12
9	−.45	−.30	−.48	−.11	−.14	−.11
10 (highest)	−.40	−.19	−.46	−.19	−.15	−.20

Source: Calculated by the authors.

3.3). Table 3.14 shows the results for various areas, databases, and approximation methods. In nearly all cases, a small loss in total welfare was reported. The estimates range from a maximum welfare gain of 0.01 percent to a welfare loss of 0.07 percent in rural areas.

To determine the effect of these welfare changes on inequality and poverty in Nicaragua, we used the estimated money-metric welfare changes, added them to the 1998 household expenditure data, and computed poverty and inequality indexes with and without the welfare change to evaluate changes in expenditure distribution. Table 3.15 shows the results of these simulations for various areas, databases, and approximation methods. That no effect on poverty or inequality was found is not surprising, given the small size of the monetary changes reported above and the limited scope of the privatization considered (i.e., partial privatization of electricity generation).

Conclusion and Comments

Privatization in Nicaragua differs from most Latin American countries because it did not merely transfer ownership or management of several

Table 3.14 Percent change in welfare due to changes in electricity price (including access changes)

Value	First-order approximation			Second-order approximation		
	Total	Urban	Rural	Total	Urban	Rural
$\sigma = 0.5$	−.04	−.05	.01	−.01	−.03	.01
$\sigma = 1.0$	.00	−.01	.01	.00	−.01	.01
$\sigma = 2.0$[a]	−.04	.02	−.07	−.06	.01	−.07

a. A negative percentage change for this social-welfare function means a less negative social welfare; that is, the society is better off.

Source: Freije and Rivas (2003, appendix 3).

Table 3.15 Nicaragua: Poverty and inequality with and without welfare effect (including access changes), 1998

Index	Sector			First-order approximation[a]			Second-order approximation[b]		
	Total	Urban	Rural	Total	Urban	Rural	Total	Urban	Rural
Poverty									
FGT									
(0)	.359	.193	.578	.358	.192	.578	.352	.193	.578
(1)	.148	.060	.263	.149	.060	.265	.146	.061	.265
(2)	.085	.028	.155	.083	.028	.156	.082	.028	.156
Inequality									
Gini coefficient	.556	.496	.589	.557	.496	.590	.557	.497	.590
Atkinson indices									
A(0.5)	.265	.203	.320	.266	.208	.321	.266	.208	.321
A(1)	.428	.346	.470	.430	.346	.471	.430	.347	.471
A(2)	.634	.531	.537	.636	.532	.539	.636	.532	.539

FGT = Foster-Greer-Thorbecke poverty index

a. Indices computed using 1998 consumption minus first-order approximation of welfare change.
b. Indices computed using 1998 consumption, minus second-order approximation of welfare change.

Source: Calculated by the authors.

SOEs to the private sector. Rather, Nicaraguan privatization was a transition from a socialist to a market economy. In assessing the consequences of privatization on distribution—through its effects on fiscal balance, labor markets, and consumer prices—we identified two phases: 1993–98 (privatization of SOEs under CORNAP) and 1998–present (privatization of public utilities). The first stage was characterized by lack of transparency. Because allocation of proceeds from privatization was not fully recorded in fiscal records, it is difficult to ascertain the distributional effect of this process. Nonetheless, its visible characteristics (i.e., large asset restitutions and a few transfers to workers and war veterans) suggest nonprogressive distributive effects. The second stage has a more complete public record of procedures and proceeds, and evidence shows that utilities have improved their balance positions since the reforms begun in 1995.

In the case of Nicaraguan labor markets, a large reallocation of labor occurred as a consequence of transition, accounting for nearly 15 percent of the labor force. This process was accompanied by increased wage dispersion within the public sector, stable wage dispersion in the private sector, and an unchanged mean wage gap between public and private sectors. Consequently, wage dispersion in Nicaragua increased for the period under study. Increasing dispersion in public-sector wages cannot be attributable solely to a simple transfer of assets; however, it appears to result from the increased market pressures that a transition economy faces. We thus acknowledge that privatization was a large, but not the sole, cause of increasing inequality in Nicaragua. Depending on the inequality measure used, changes in the compensated wage differential between public- and private-sector occupations can account for up to one-third of total inequality change.

Finally, the welfare effect of privatization is measured through estimates of first- and second-order approximations to changes in indirect utility functions. We found that the change in electricity prices, observed during 1993–98, produced welfare losses for all households across all deciles of expenditure distribution. However, losses were larger for wealthier households. When accounting for changes in access to electricity, household gains were concentrated in deciles 2 through 6. Summing up all of the effects (i.e., prices and access), the welfare effect of reforms in the Nicaraguan electricity sector was slightly progressive over the period studied. However, simulations of the monetary effect of this welfare effect on indexes of poverty and inequality were negligible.

Several limitations must be overcome in future research. First, privatization of public utilities is still ongoing, and the data available for this chapter do not register the ultimate consequences of the process. Privatization of telecommunications and electricity distribution and generation in 2001 and 2002, as well as the eventual divestment of water and sewage, will undoubtedly have effects in subsequent years. Evaluating this process will require additional household data that will eventually be available. Second, the effect on ownership has been mentioned only cursorily. Privatization is mainly a process about ownership changes. No formal evaluation of asset and wealth distribution has been conducted. Such a study will require data on distribution of agricultural land, housing, and corporate assets. Third, intergenerational distributive issues—mainly related to privatization's effects on the environment—have not been addressed. Such a study will require evaluating changes in farming methods, public expenditure on conservation, and regulation of polluting industries.

References

Banks, J., R. Blundell, and A. Lewbel. 1996. Tax Reform and Welfare Measurement: Do We Need Demand System Estimation? *The Economic Journal* 106, no. 438: 1227–41.

Blau, F., and L. Kahn. 1996. International Differences in Male Wage Inequality: Institutions Versus Market Forces. *Journal of Political Economy* 104, no. 4: 791–837.

Buitelaar, R. 1996. *La privatización de la industria manufacturera en Nicaragua: Evidencia de estudios de caso para evaluar el impacto en la eficiencia y equidad.* Serie de Reformas de Política Pública 42. Santiago: Economic Commission for Latin America and the Caribbean.

Central Bank of Nicaragua. 1996. Privatización de la CORNAP. Resultados, Reunión de Finanzas Públicas, Honduras.

CORNAP. 1993. *Reporte de progreso del proceso de privatización en Nicaragua.* Managua: National Corporation of the Public Sector.

Davis, J., R. Ossowski, T. Richardson, and S. Barnett. 2000. *Fiscal and Macroeconomic Impact of Privatization.* Occasional Paper 194. Washington: International Monetary Fund.

Deaton, A. 1989. Rice Prices and Income Distribution in Thailand: A Non-Parametric Approach. *The Economic Journal* 99: 1–37.

Deaton, A., and J. Mullbauer. 1980. An Almost Ideal Demand System. *American Economic Reveiw:* 312–26.

De Franco, M. 1996. *La economía política de la privatización en Nicaragua.* Serie de Reformas de Política Pública 44. Santiago: Economic Commission for Latin America and the Caribbean.

Duryea, S., and M. Szekely. 1998. *Labor Markets in Latin America: A Supply Side Story.* Working Paper 374. Washington: Inter-American Development Bank.

Freije, S., and L. Rivas. 2003. *Privatization, Inequality and Welfare: Evidence from Nicaragua.* Institute for Public Policy and Development Studies Working Paper 2003-03. Puebla, Mexico: Universidad de las Américas.

Galal, A., L. Jones, P. Tandon, and I. Vogelsang. 1994. *Welfare Consequences of Selling Public Enterprises: An Empirical Analysis.* New York: Oxford University Press.

Gupta, S., C. Schiller, and H. Ma. 1999. *Privatization, Social Impact, and Social Safety Nets.* IMF Working Paper 99/68. Washington: International Monetary Fund.

Heller, P., and C. Schiller. 1989. The Fiscal Impact of Privatization, with Some Examples from Arab Countries. *World Development* 17, no. 2: 757–67.

Juhn, C., K. Murphy, and B. Pierce. 1993. Wage Inequality and the Rise in Returns to Skill. *Journal of Political Economy* 101, no. 3: 410–42.

La Porta, R., and F. López-de-Silanes. 1999. The Benefits of Privatization: Evidence from Mexico. *The Quarterly Journal of Economics* 4: 1193–242.

Levinsohn, J., S. Berry, and J. Friedman. 1995. *Impacts of the Indonesian Economic Crisis: Price Changes and the Poor.* NBER Working Paper 7194. Cambridge, MA: National Bureau of Economic Research.

McKenzie, G. A. 1998. The Macroeconomic Impact of Privatization. *IMF Staff Papers* 42, no. 2: 363–73.

McKenzie, D., and D. Mookherjee. 2003. Distributive Impact of Privatization in Latin America: An Overview of Evidence from Four Countries. *Economía* 3, no. 2: 161–218.

Newbery, D. 1995. The Distributional Impact of Price Changes in Hungary and the United Kingdom. *The Economic Journal* 105, no. 431: 847–63.

Rezler, J. 1973. *The Industrial Relations System in Hungary after the Economic Reform, In Annaire de L'URSS et des Pays Socialistes Européens, 1972–73.* Paris: Libraire ISTRA, Centre National de la Recherche Scientifique.

Shaikh, H., and M. A. Abdala. 1996. *Argentina Privatization Program: A Review of Five Cases.* Washington: World Bank.

4

Bolivian Capitalization and Privatization: Approximation to an Evaluation

GOVER BARJA, DAVID MCKENZIE,
and MIGUEL URQUIOLA

The wave of privatizations Latin America experienced during the 1990s was integral to stabilization programs and a general reordering of states' roles in the regional economy. Over the past few years, however, these privatizations have come under increasing fire. Their purported adverse effects range from higher utility prices to aggravating—or even causing—the current regional recession. In short, privatization shares in the criticism directed at the entire liberalization process.

Within this context, accurate knowledge of privatization's real consequences can be of considerable value. While research has been conducted on certain economic effects, less is known about privatization's broader social consequences. This chapter attempts to fill some of those gaps as they concern Bolivia.

We first describe Bolivia's privatization process, emphasizing the particularities of the capitalization mechanism used and the regulatory framework introduced as its essential complement.[1] We then detail the changes in industrial organization and ownership patterns in the electricity, oil and gas, telecommunications, transportation, and water industries. Our concern is mainly with large infrastructure privatizations because of their

---

Gover Barja is the public policy program director at Bolivian Catholic University, La Paz. David McKenzie is assistant professor of economics at Stanford University. Miguel Urquiola is assistant professor at the School of International and Public Affairs and the Department of Economics at Columbia University. The authors thank Dilip Mookherjee, John Nellis, and participants at World Institute for Development Economics Research (WIDER) and Inter-American Development Bank (IDB) seminars.

1. In terms of the amount of assets transferred, capitalization was clearly more important than privatization. As a result, this chapter's discussion often uses the two terms interchangeably.

economic size and the data and methods available to estimate the social and distributional effects of these transactions.

The discussion then turns to these processes' economic and social outcomes. The key economic issues are which agents benefit from assets transfer and the effects on such firm-level variables as investment, profitability, and transfers to the state. The main social issues are the effects on employees in the sectors involved and consumer welfare, including access, prices, and service quality of privatized utilities.

This chapter also highlights the Bolivian population's changing assessments of the entire capitalization and privatization process. Although data limitations make full treatment impossible, the information that is available leads to the following broad conclusions:

- By design, capitalization and privatization have generated significant asset transfers to foreign firms. However, the Bolivian population was not excluded from this benefit since it collectively received a 45 percent share in most of the transferred enterprises. Dividends from this ownership have been used to pay old-age benefits.

- These processes, combined with introduction of a regulatory framework, have met their core stated goal: to substantially increase investment—and competition, in some cases—in the sectors affected.

- These investments have been associated with significant increases in capacity and output—from improvements in utility access rates to a tenfold rise in proven gas and oil reserves within five years of reform.

- Productivity increased significantly across all sectors, in part, because of employment reductions; however, these reductions were small relative to the overall economy. Unless the indirect effects are large, privatization cannot account for the increasing unemployment observed in recent years.

- Tax receipts from regulated firms increased after reform. In the current recession, however, there is pressure—particularly from the oil and gas sector—for further increases.

- While most capitalized firms report positive profits, their returns on equity have declined in recent years, particularly during the ongoing recession.

- In urban areas, capitalization is associated with increased household access to utility services; these expansions—especially in electricity and water—have not bypassed the poor. On the contrary, in many cases, the lower-income deciles have benefited the most. For telephone services, improvements have been greater further up the income distribution ladder. Several of these findings persist when the effects resulting from privatization are isolated.

- There are large gaps in available pricing information. On balance, price increases have not been large, with the exception of those involving the Cochabamba water concession.

- Taken together, improved access outweighs increased prices, resulting in welfare gains for many households. Lower-income deciles gained significantly in access to electricity. For phone services, improved access was observed nearly across the board. For water, the La Paz and El Alto concession also produced welfare gains. In the case of the failed Cochabamba concession, we found that—had the concession continued—the welfare effects would have been negative unless substantially improved access had accompanied the proposed tariff increases.

- While the regulatory framework has strengthened the rule of law and promoted competition and transparency in certain sectors, it is still necessary to improve this regulatory and broader institutional framework.

- In Bolivia, as elsewhere, privatization, capitalization, and regulation are part and parcel of a broader economic restructuring. While privatization lagged stabilization significantly, it was still crucial in the state's shift of focus from productive to social-sector activities. Nevertheless, after seven or eight years of reform and four of recession, private investment slowed and a reemerging consensus now calls for greater state involvement.

These findings provide a brief—and admittedly incomplete—evaluation of privatization in Bolivia. Further, it should be emphasized that the combination of privatization and capitalization on the one hand and regulation on the other was substituted for state ownership, although for conciseness, we often refer to these processes collectively as privatization. Moreover, it is impossible to fully disentangle the effects of these processes from those of associated events, such as introduction of new technologies.

Despite the overall success of reforms, they are unpopular, judging by polls and politicians' pronouncements. The final section of this chapter offers hypotheses to explain this phenomenon. One popular suspicion highlighted is that, even if output and productivity have improved, the capitalized enterprises have only the best interests of the majority (foreign) owners in mind, and the regulatory system has been unable to adequately restrain this tendency. The recent worldwide focus on corporate malfeasance has helped bring these concerns to the forefront. This standard issue has gained salience in Bolivia since its population collectively owns a 45 percent share in capitalized firms. Another issue emphasized is that the government oversold reforms, promising more than it could reasonably deliver. Finally, the reforms' reputation has been hurt by two high-profile failures: the national airline and the Cochabamba water concession.

In a healthy economic environment, none of these issues might have mattered. However, within the context of Bolivia's economic slowdown since 1999, they have contributed significantly to privatization's negative reputation. Moreover, the fiscal rigidities introduced by other reforms, such as decentralization and pension reform, have prolonged the slowdown. For example, the fiscal deficit created by the transition away from the pay-as-you-go pension system reached 5 percent of GDP by 2002, and is not expected to decrease for at least a decade. This deficit, in turn, has generated pressure for economywide tax increases, thereby contributing to further questions about structural reform as a whole.

Capitalization/Privatization and Regulation: An Overview

In 1985, Bolivia initiated significant economic liberalizations in order to tame hyperinflation and emerge from a deep recession. Despite success with early market-friendly initiatives, the country did not engage in sustained privatization until about a decade later. When it finally embarked on this process, the government used traditional privatization in certain cases, but mainly relied on capitalization as a mechanism for the transfer of state-owned firms.

Under traditional privatization, the government transfers a majority of ownership in a state firm to the private sector, receives the sale proceeds, and has freedom over how to spend it. Under Bolivian capitalization, the state transferred shares (mainly in infrastructure firms) equivalent to 50 percent of the firm to the investor with the winning bid. It also yielded 45 to 50 percent to private pension-fund administrators who represent the general citizenry and use the funds to pay old-age benefits complementary to individual retirement accounts. The remainder (about 4 percent, on average) accrued to the company's employees.

By its payment, the investor gains the right to manage the firm, and commits to investing its capital contribution—the total amount it offered for its 50 percent share—in the firm's development. It must carry this out within a specified period (typically six to eight years), agree to fulfill obligations that encompass expansion and quality goals, and operate under regulation and a long-term (typically 40 year) contract.[2]

Thus, this option assigns investment a high priority, and the government gains no disposable income. Capitalization, introduced relatively late in Bolivia's liberalization process, was not viewed as a means to cover deficits but as a way to attract foreign investment and improve management in key areas of the economy. Together, privatization and capitalization raised

---

2. The investor made a bank deposit with this payment and was instructed to keep records on its use. Government audits of investment, firm management, and performance took a long time to be initiated and are only currently under way.

significant amounts of capital. Total commitments amounted to about $2 billion (about 30 percent of GDP), $1.7 billion of which was from capitalization.[3]

Capitalization was complemented by reforms to each sector's industrial organization and a regulatory framework, whose stated goal was to promote competition and efficiency.[4] The key legislation was the 1994 SIRESE (Sistema de Regulación Sectorial) Law, which created a regulatory system for the infrastructure sector. It defined the institutional structure, including the role of five regulatory agencies (*Superintendencias*) for the electricity, telecommunications, hydrocarbons (oil and gas), potable water, and transportation industries. In addition, it set up an oversight agency responsible for systemwide coordination and second instance appeals and evaluation. SIRESE also introduced market competition as a guiding principle for the sector.

Four specific laws round out the legal framework: Electricity (1994), Telecommunications (1995), Hydrocarbons (1996), and Potable Water (2000). These introduced changes in each sector's industrial organization and govern aspects related to tariff regulation, entry, service quality, and sanctions. The sector-specific regulatory agencies created as part of SIRESE administer each law.

Changes in Industrial Organization and Regulatory Arrangements

The following sections briefly describe the more important changes implemented in the electricity, hydrocarbons (oil and gas), telecommunications, transportation, and water and sewage sectors.

Electricity

Before reform, the electricity industry was divided into the National Interconnected System (NIS) and other independent networks.[5] The NIS covers the largest cities, while the other independent networks service other urban and selected rural areas.[6] This chapter focuses on the NIS, where the state-owned National Electricity Company (ENDE) (Empresa Nacional de

---

3. While privatization started in 1992 with about 50 percent of its proceeds concentrated in 1999, capitalization occurred during the 1994–97 period.

4. For more details on Bolivian regulation and regulatory institutions, see Barja (2000) and SIRESE (2000).

5. The NIS accounts for nearly 90 percent of electricity consumption.

6. In Bolivia, the main cities are departmental capitals. The three largest have populations of nearly 1 million and form the so-called central axis: Cochabamba, La Paz and El Alto, and Santa Cruz. These central-axis cities reflect the fact that Bolivia has no single dominant urban center and has one of the lowest urban concentration ratios in the region.

Electricidad) had been active in generation and transmission activities, as well as distribution, mainly through the Cochabamba Light and Electric Company (ELFEC) (Empresa de Luz y Fuerza Eléctrica Cochabamba). The Bolivian Electricity Company (COBEE) (Compañía Boliviana de Energía Eléctrica), long a private company, participated in generation and distribution in La Paz and Oruro. Other distribution firms or cooperatives were the Rural Electric Cooperative (CRE) (Cooperativa Rural Eléctrica) in Santa Cruz, Potosí Electricity Services (SEPSA) (Servicios Eléctricos de Potosí), and Sucre Electric Company (CESSA) (Compañía Eléctrica Sucre). Competition between ENDE and COBEE was limited to the direct provision of electricity to a few mining and industrial concerns.

The 1994 Electricity Law vertically separated generation, transmission, and distribution, with certain firms privatized in each. In generation, capitalization created three firms—Corani, Guaracachi, and Valle Hermoso—valued at about $140 million. Each received part of ENDE's generation activities, with the Law limiting market share to 35 percent of the NIS. Exclusive rights were initially granted to these three companies; however, by 1999, entry was liberalized and some smaller firms began operations.

In transmission, network operations passed from ENDE to the private electricity transport company (Transportadora de Electricidad) without exclusive rights. The Electricity Law did not allow transmission firms to participate in purchase or sale activities, but it did establish open access and tariff regulations. The privatization transfer was valued at about $40 million.

Several types of distribution firms remained after reform, all of which operate under tariff regulation and are subject to quality controls. CRE, a former distribution cooperative, remains as an independent regional monopoly. CESSA and SEPSA, formerly municipal distribution firms, also retain their monopolies. ELFEC, a municipal company before reform, now operates as a private firm (the privatization transfer was valued at about $50 million). COBEE's distribution divestiture produced two local private distributors: ELECTROPAZ (La Paz) and ELFEO (Oruro). For all of these distribution firms, tariff regulation consists of several average cost caps, with productivity factors set using a four-year lag. Tariffs are updated twice yearly to allow for pass-through of energy cost increases.

These reforms, together with introduction of a load dispatch coordination office, have created a wholesale electricity market that seeks to simulate competitive conditions. Partially as a result, the NIS has experienced excess capacity since 1999.

Oil and Gas

Before reform, virtually all of the hydrocarbons (oil and gas) industry was under control of the state-owned YPFB (Yacimientos Petrolíferos Fiscales Bolivianos), a vertically integrated monopoly. Limited private participation in exploration, as well as in crude oil and natural gas production, occurred through joint ventures with YPFB.

With capitalization and introduction of the 1996 Hydrocarbons Law, the priority became removing YPFB from production and promoting a natural-gas export industry aimed at southern Brazil. The state intended this industry to support (through taxes and royalties) development of other economic sectors; with this goal in mind, reforms and foreign investment focused on exploration and infrastructure. Inauguration of the Bolivia-Brazil pipeline in 1999 turned this vision into a reality.

These reforms were also associated with a substantial increase in natural gas reserves. Proven and probable reserves increased from about 5.7 trillion cubic feet (ft^3) in 1997 to 52.3 trillion ft^3 in 2002, making Bolivia Latin America's leader in free reserves. With reserves now exceeding served Brazilian and domestic market demand, the Bolivian government is considering new projects, including liquefied natural gas (LNG) exports to the United States and Mexico;[7] petrochemical and thermoelectric plants; and export pipelines to Argentina, Brazil, Chile, and Paraguay.[8] With regard to the domestic market, a general policy of private control was adopted for all phases up to retail commercialization.

To implement these objectives, the Hydrocarbons Law required that exploration, production, and commercialization (upstream) be executed only by private firms in joint ventures with YPFB—which remains the upstream regulator—while placing few restrictions on the export and import of petroleum products. Based on 2001 data, the most important upstream operators, in terms of reserves, are Petrobrás (34.8 percent), Maxus (29 percent), Total Exploration (19.8 percent), Andina (5.9 percent), and Chaco (4.6 percent). Capitalization resulted in the creation of two upstream-sector firms: Chaco (valued at $306 million) and Andina (valued at $265 million).

The Hydrocarbons Law stipulates that the government is entitled to a share of the production value—50 percent from fields before capitalization (at the wellhead) and 18 percent from those discovered after capitalization.[9] In both cases, firms are also required to pay a 25 percent profit tax, a 25 percent surtax,[10] and a 12.5 percent remittance tax.

In the downstream area, oil and gas pipelines owned by YPFB were transferred to the capitalized Transredes, without exclusive rights and a total

---

7. Given that Bolivia is a landlocked country, one major debated issue is whether the export port should be in Chile or Peru.

8. A regional distributional issue has emerged because most new reserves are in the Tarija Department, which stands to receive significant royalty revenues.

9. The old 1990 Hydrocarbons Law required that all fields pay 50 percent in royalties, plus a profit tax.

10. The surtax base is equal to the profit tax base minus 33 percent of accumulated investment and 45 percent of the value of production at each field, up to a maximum of $40 million per year.

value of $264 million.[11] The administration of other pipelines (*poliductos*) was entrusted to the private Oil Tanking, with the remainder still under YPFB control. Most YPFB refinery units were transferred to the private Bolivian Refinery Company (EBR) (Empresa Boliviana de Refinación).

With regard to commercialization, most YPFB storage terminals were transferred to the Bolivian Hydrocarbons Logistics Company (CLHB) (Compañía Logística de Hidrocarburos Boliviana) of Oil Tanking, but other private firms are also active. All distribution plants of bottled liquefied gas are private; about 19 percent of bottling capacity continues under YPFB, but all are expected to become privatized. All compressed natural gas (CNG) service stations are private, and about 15 percent of service stations for liquids continue under the state firm. Nationwide, airport service stations were transferred to the private sector. Except for Transredes, all other downstream transfers were privatizations that reached a total of $125 million.

Mixed ownership continues in network-based natural gas distribution: Santa Cruz Gas Services Company (SERGAS) (Empresa de Servicios de Gas Santa Cruz S.A.M.), Cochabamba Gas Company (EMCOGAS) (Empresa Cochabambina de Gas S.A.M.), Sucre Gas Distribution Company (EMDIGAS) (Empresa Distribuidora de Gas Sucre S.A.M.), and Tarija Gas Company (EMTAGAS) (Empresa Tarijeña de Gas). YPFB operates in La Paz, Potosi, and Oruro. The expectation is that these companies will eventually become privatized.[12] Despite this activity, the network-based natural gas industry is still underdeveloped; by 2001, it included only 14,435 connections. Nevertheless, current policy is to increase connections to 250,000 over the next five years as part of an effort to direct energy consumption toward natural gas.

Except for vertical-integration restrictions imposed on pipeline transport firms, the industry structure is flexible and determined by export market needs, although mergers and acquisitions are subject to approval. This flexibility has permitted Petrobrás, in association with others, to integrate several phases directed at natural gas exports to Brazil and simultaneously participate, through EBR, in domestic-market refinement.

Rate-of-return regulation (with a four-year lag) is used for pipeline transportation, with a tariff structure that differentiates between domestic and export transportation. In natural gas network distribution, tariff regulation has not been implemented thus far. Initially, consumer prices for all petroleum derivatives were calculated starting with an international reference price and then adding the costs of processing, transportation, and commercialization, plus an oil derivatives tax. In response to price volatility, liquefied gas, diesel oil, and gasoline have been subsidized since 2000. Further, by decree (January 2003), the government froze all consumer prices, eliminated the

---

11. Other operators are Gas Transboliviano (GTB), Gas Oriente Boliviano (GOB), Transierra, and Petrobrás.

12. The first privatization attempt in April 2002 failed.

refining margin, and increased the oil derivatives tax—with the effect of lowering prices for upstream firms. However, due to fiscal pressures generated by subsidies, the government, by recent decree (February 2004), is promoting the gradual return to market-determined consumer prices.

Telecommunications

Before reform, the telecommunications industry was divided between the National Telecommunications Company (ENTEL) (Empresa Nacional de Telecomunicaciones), the state monopoly covering national and international long distance services; 15 cooperatives, with monopolies in fixed local telephone services; and Telecel, a private monopoly in the cellular market. Capitalization created the private ENTEL, valued at $610 million, and the 1995 Telecommunications Law maintained these separations until entry was liberalized at the end of 2001. Until then, ENTEL and the cooperatives retained exclusive rights; however, the mobile market was opened gradually by allowing entry of ENTEL-Movil (1996)[13] and Nuevatel-Viva (2000).[14]

Before entry liberalization, legislation mandated tariff regulation for firms that controlled more than 60 percent of a given market. This scheme had a similar structure in all areas, establishing an initial price cap for baskets of services, adjusted for inflation, and a productivity factor with a three-year lag. In addition, the Telecommunications Law stipulated annual expansion, quality, and technological goals.

November 2001 marked the end of exclusive rights in all markets.[15] Entry occurred in the long distance market through AES Corporation (in association with COTEL), Teledata (a division of COTAS), Boliviatel (a division of COMTECO), Telecel, Nuevatel, and ITS. In addition, Nuevatel and COTAS-Movil entered the mobile market, while ENTEL expanded its local network to business clients. Most of these companies are also expanding in the data transmission and Internet markets. Until the end of 2002, registers showed 16 firms providing public phone services, 42 offering cable television, 48 value-added services, 288 television, 612 radio, 18 data transmission, and 557 private networks.

Moreover, market liberalization was accompanied by a four-year restriction on mergers, acquisitions, and stock swaps accounting for 40 percent or more of total local fixed lines in service by one firm or a group of related firms. Tariff regulation continues where a firm controls more than 60 percent of a given market (this regulation is expected to change with introduction

---

13. A division of capitalized ENTEL.

14. A joint venture between COMTECO (Cochabamba cooperative) and Western Wireless International.

15. A year earlier, the government approved the so-called Opening Decrees (Decretos de la Apertura).

of dominant-firm regulation rules), and new rules are being implemented to facilitate interconnection agreements. A proposed Universal Access and Service Fund, financed by foreign aid and operators' contributions, would have the broad aim of reaching rural areas and the urban poor.

Transportation

Bolivia's transportation industry is divided into air, rail, road, and water segments. To date, capitalization and regulation have affected only air and rail, and the long awaited Transportation Law has not yet been approved.

Before air-market reform, the state-owned Bolivian Air Lloyd (LAB) (Lloyd Aéreo Boliviano) and the Private Bolivian Air Transport Company (AEROSUR) (Compañía Boliviana de Transporte Aéreo Privado) competed in the main domestic-market route. LAB also participated in the international market, and the Airport and Auxiliary Navigation Services Administration (AASANA) (Administración de Aeropuertos y Servicios Auxiliares a la Navegacion Aérea), the state monopoly, administered the national airport system. Capitalization of LAB created a new private firm (also known as LAB), with a capital contribution of $47 million; and the three main air terminals—Santa Cruz, La Paz and El Alto, and Cochabamba—were transferred to the Bolivian Airport Services (SABSA) (Servicios Aeroportuarios Bolivianos), a private firm, as concessions. AASANA retains administrative control of 34 small airports, while AEROSUR has entered the international market.

Before reform, the National Railway Company (Empresa Nacional de Ferrocarriles) (ENFE), a state monopoly that administered passenger and freight services in Andean and eastern regions, dominated Bolivia's rail sector. Reform created two separate regional firms, Andina Rail Company (FCA) (Empresa Ferroviaria Andina) and East Rail Company (FCO) (Empresa Ferroviaria Oriental), which where then capitalized, generating two firms that received a total capital contribution of $87 million.

Lack of a sector law has limited regulatory activities of the Transportation Superintendence. Nevertheless, it advanced actions based on existing norms and several government decrees. In air transportation, a tariff band was set for the regular domestic market, with the stated objective of discouraging anticompetitive practices. Some airport terminal tariffs are also regulated. Rail transport regulations involve economic, technical, and security aspects of service.

Water and Sewage

While the above-mentioned sectors underwent capitalization and the introduction of regulation, the water industry has witnessed limited changes and significant difficulties. Only one municipal firm, SAMAPA (La Paz and

El Alto), was transferred as a concession to Aguas del Illimani (in 1997).[16] Under the new model, the concession seeks to improve internal efficiency, coverage, and quality. The Aguas del Illimani contract reflects these aims; for example, the objectives set for 1997–2001 included (1) 100 percent access to potable water or sewage (excluding public fountains) in the Achachicala and Pampahasi areas of La Paz; (2) 82 percent access to potable water in El Alto by 2001, of which 50 percent should be expansion connections and 41 percent access to sewage; and (3) compliance with long-term expansion goals. Quality norms cover aspects related to water source, quality, abundance, and pressure as well as continuity of service, infrastructure efficiency, customer service, and emergency preparedness. Tariff regulation was established under a rate-of-return mechanism with a five-year regulatory lag and no productivity factors. In addition, tariffs were set in dollar terms, payable in bolivianos.[17]

The expectation was that, within a short period, legislation would be in place to incorporate the remaining firms into a similar model. However, the long awaited Potable Water and Sewerage Law—finally approved in 2000—together with significant failure in a second transfer of a municipal firm (SEMAPA) to Aguas del Tunari in Cochabamba,[18] significantly slowed sector change.

Nevertheless, until 2002, the Water Superintendence was able to incorporate the new regulatory regime and sign concessions with the other 25 existing municipal water firms and cooperatives. The new law makes municipal governments responsible for providing water and sewage services, which they can perform through private or municipal firms, cooperatives, civil organizations, or any existing rural community organization. The Bolivian population is divided according to whether areas are subject to concession (which depends on financial viability). Concessions are subject to rate-of-return regulation, with a five-year regulatory lag, while universal access in nonconcession areas should be achieved with government investment.

Other Regulatory Characteristics

SIRESE, the regulatory system, consists of five sector-specific offices—electricity, hydrocarbons, telecommunications, transportation, and water and sewage—and one General Superintendence. By design, the system is financially and administratively independent, and Superintendents are appointed by congress for five-year periods.[19] The functions of each Superintendence

---

16. The main shareholder is Lyonnaise des Eaux, with 35 percent.

17. This feature has generated wide protest among El Alto residents.

18. The main shareholder is a private firm with British International Water (with 55 percent).

19. Seven years in the case of the General Superintendent.

vary by sector, although they generally include: granting rights, regulating tariffs, promoting competition, monitoring operator obligations, resolving controversies among firms, imposing sanctions, hearing first in-stance appeals, and receiving consumer claims. It should be noted that the regulatory system administers the law, while its design is left to the corresponding government ministries (although SIRESE can propose legislation).

The General Superintendence evaluates each sector Superintendence once a year, considering such factors as compliance with general functions, internal organization, and sector performance relative to regulatory objectives. Aside from its effect on specific regulatory activities, SIRESE has succeeded in improving availability of transparent information and strengthening the rule of law.

In terms of appeals, the system has a first instance, whereby any operator can appeal a decision made by its sector Superintendence. If the decision is upheld, the operator has a second chance to appeal before the General Superintendence. Even after these stages, the operator retains recourse to the judiciary system. Until 2003, there had been 456 first instance and 351 second instance appeals and 54 cases in the judiciary system.

With regard to consumer protection, the system sets up a first reclamation instance directly with the operator. If the dispute is not settled, the consumer has a second chance before the sector Superintendence. This set-up has revealed numerous consumer complaints in certain sectors, particularly telecommunications and electricity.

In 2001, cost of the overall regulatory system was estimated at 0.2 percent of GDP; it is fully financed by operators from a levy on gross income (usually less than 1 percent). While this investment has brought significant advances, various factors have hampered its effectiveness; these include lack of continuity of Superintendents caused by political pressures, lack of a sectoral law for water (until 2000) and transportation (to date), and slow approval of detailed regulations across sectors. Operators have often lobbied the executive and legislative branches successfully in order to bypass the regulatory system; meanwhile, consumers believe they are underrepresented. Certain Superintendencies have been slow to produce transparent information or have lacked specialized human resources in their earlier stages. In recent years, the system has had to reduce costs in response to similar initiatives in the rest of government.

Pension Reform and Further Ownership Effects

Capitalization transferred 50 percent of state enterprises (and their control) to foreign firms. Moreover, 45 to 50 percent of shares in capitalized firms were given to the Collective Capitalization Fund (CCF), to be held for the benefit of the population at large. Table 4.1 lists the enterprises capitalized in the utilities and hydrocarbons sectors, the number of shares issued, and

Table 4.1 Distribution of share ownership for the capitalized firms (December 31, 1999)

Sector/firm	Total number of shares	Ownership (percent)		
		Capitalizing firm	CCF (represented by fund administrators)	Firm workers
Electricity				
Corani	3,144,486	50	47.23	2.77
Guaracachi	3,358,284	50	49.83	0.17
Valle Hermoso	2,927,322	50	49.87	0.13
Oil and gas				
Petrolera Andina	13,439,520	50	47.86	2.14
Petrolera Chaco	16,099,320	50	47.31	2.69
Transredes	10,048,120	50	33.43	16.57
Telecommunications				
ENTEL	12,808,993	50	47.47	2.57
Transportation				
Ferroviaria Andina	1,322,448	50	49.93	0.07
Ferroviaria Oriental	2,296,982	50	49.91	0.09
LAB	2,293,764	50	48.64	1.36
Mean		**50**	**46.80**	**4.20**

CCF = Collective Capitalization Fund

Source: Pension Bulletin (1999), Pension Superintendence.

their distribution among the capitalizing firm (50 percent), CCF (46.4 percent, on average), and employees of each enterprise (3.6 percent, on average). To reiterate, in the second case, shares are made out to the CCF and are represented by private pension-fund administrators; they are not owned by administrators, the state, or individual citizens.

The CCF receives dividends due from its shares in capitalized firms. During 1997–2000, these shares represented 0.39 to 0.55 percent of GDP per year, with the telecommunications sector contributing the most. In 2001, dividends grew to 0.65 percent of GDP, with the energy sector providing the most; however, in 2002, its contribution dropped to 0.45 percent of GDP.

The CCF has a significant social effect as a source of transfers to private citizens. These include an old-age benefit, known as the Bonosol; funeral expenses; and investment in the Individual Capitalization Fund (ICF) (pension plan that individual citizens own), and, subsequently, the Bolivida.

The Bonosol was a cash payment (equivalent to $248 in 1997) directed at all citizens 65 years and older. This amount was a substantial transfer, given that Bolivia's GDP per capita is about 1,000 dollars.[20] A total of $56.5 million was paid to some 320,000 people.

---

20. By December 31, 1999, the CCF had also been used to acquire shares of the ICF for approximately $14.7 million and funeral expenses worth $2.3 million.

The Bonosol was paid only once before the administration that implemented the capitalization process left office. A debate immediately ensued over whether the CCF had sufficient funds to continue payments at that pace. The next administration did not make payments for a period and then switched to the Bolivida, which it began disbursing in December 2000. The Bolivida was a cash payment of $60 for every citizen over age 65. Retroactive payments for 1998 and 1999 ($60 per year) were made; by March 2001, 150,000 individuals had benefited.

The year 2002 witnessed the return of the administration that had originally implemented capitalization and, hence, a desire to return to the Bonosol. Because of further reductions in the dividend flow, however, the CCF now lacked sufficient funds to make payments at this level.

Reforms' Effects on Firm Performance

Capitalization and privatization have involved major changes in the industrial organization of the sectors affected and the conditions within which the firms in each sector operate.

Investment

In any evaluation of the capitalization process, investment is a key parameter since increasing it was an explicit objective. Table 4.2 summarizes the sector-specific information presented earlier, and complements it with the investment activity observed in each case.

As table 4.2 illustrates, most firms have exceeded their investment commitments; thus, from this perspective, the process appears to have met its goal. Firms under concession agreements—Aguas del Illimani and SABSA—have also invested to comply with contractual goals not shown in table 4.2.

Employment and Labor Productivity

One frequent criticism of privatization is that it leads to unemployment. After 1997, Bolivia witnessed economywide unemployment, which reached about 8 percent by 2002. To what extent did privatization and capitalization account for this rise in unemployment? Because of data restrictions, we can arrive at only a partial answer in this chapter. It involves information on the evolution of labor productivity and sector analysis (Barja, McKenzie, and Urquiola 2004).

Electricity

During 1995–98, the number of employees in each electricity generation firm remained relatively constant, with some decline by 1999. Associated with

Table 4.2 Resources and investment generated by privatization and capitalization

Firm created by reform, by sector	Year created	Privatization value (millions of US dollars)	Capitalization value (millions of US dollars)	Investment (percent of commitment, as of 2002)[a]	Company or institution in charge of investment
Electricity					
Corani, S.A.	1995	n.a.	58.79	74.7	Corani, S.A.
Elfec, S.A.	1995	50.30	n.a.	n.a.	TGN-Investment
Guaracachi, S.A.	1995	n.a.	47.13	150.0	Guaracachi, S.A.
TDE, S.A.	1997	n.a.	n.a.	n.a.	ENDE Residual
Valle Hermoso, S.A.	1995	39.90	33.92	111.9	Valle Hermoso, S.A.
Oil and gas					
Airport Service Stations	2000	11.10	n.a.	n.a.	TGN-Investment
Andina, S.A.	1997	n.a.	264.77	108.9	Andina, S.A.
Chaco, S.A.	1997	n.a.	306.66	89.2	Chaco, S.A.
CLHB, S.A.	2000	12.05	n.a.	n.a.	TGN-Investment
EBRS, S.A.	2000	102.00	n.a.	n.a.	TGN-Investment
Transredes, S.A.	1997	n.a.	263.50	102.5	Transredes, S.A.
Telecommunications					
ENTEL, S.A.	1995	n.a.	610.00	21.4	ENTEL, S.A.
Transportation					
FCA, S.A.	1996	n.a.	13.25	167.6	FCA, S.A.
FCO, S.A.	1996	n.a.	25.85	241.6	FCO, S.A.
LAB, S.A.	1997	n.a.	47.47	100.0	LAB, S.A.
Total		**215.35**	**1,671.34**		

n.a. = not available

a. Based only on the amounts the regulatory system designated for capitalization.

Source: Fiscal Action Unit.

increased output, these trends have resulted in increased labor productivity, which, for the 1995–99 period, ranged between 14 and 100 percent.

Distribution enterprises can be split into two groups: (1) ELECTROPAZ, CRE, and ELFEC (which respectively operate in the three largest cities of La Paz and El Alto, Santa Cruz, and Cochabamba), and (2) CESSA, SEPSA, and ELFEO (which operate in smaller markets). Employment in distribution enterprises experienced a downward trend, while labor productivity grew somewhat consistently. In La Paz and El Alto, for example, ELECTROPAZ consistently reduced its employment level during 1996–99 and increased productivity by 59 percent over the same period. In Santa Cruz, CRE reduced personnel until 1997 and raised productivity 43 percent (it increased employment in 1998, but this failed to reverse productivity increases). In Cochabamba, ELFEC reduced employment until 1998, and increased productivity by 105 percent over the same period. Two firms, CRE and SEPSA, increased their employment levels between 1995 and 1999.

To summarize, both generation and distribution firms have experienced, on average, relatively moderate decreases in employment levels, particularly two or three years after they initiated operations (in the case of capitalized firms), while enjoying significant, consistent increases in labor productivity.

Telecommunications

ENTEL-Movil initiated its operations in 1996 and possibly completed hiring in 1997, which may have accounted for more workers during 1996–97. After employment peaked in 1997, a continuous, increasing decline began (15 percent in 1998, 19 percent in 1999, and 30 percent in 2000). Labor productivity, as measured by long distance minutes per employee, continued to grow until 1998; a decline followed in 1999, despite falling employment levels, reflecting weakening demand for long distance services, induced by the recession and perhaps growing Internet use.

In the case of cellular services, the data record is incomplete; nonetheless, one might venture that the Telecel experience reflects that of both operators. Telecel increased its employment continuously until 1996, but then reduced it in 1997, partially in reaction to ENTEL-Movil's entry and the onset of price competition. Increased labor productivity also displayed an upward trend during this period, reaching 152 percent by 1996. After 1997, Telecel resumed its employment increases, and its personnel count in 2000 was nearly double that of 1996. Despite this success, labor productivity continued to increase (57 percent in 1997 and 172 percent in 1998). These positive results reflect expansion resulting from price competition and quality-related improvements.

For local telephony, growth in labor productivity is consistent in all cases, reflecting increased number of connections. Nevertheless, some operators reduced personnel in certain years (e.g., COTEL in 1995, COTAS in 1993–96 and 1998–99, and COMTECO in 1998–99).

Oil and Gas

YPFB had employment decreases after the 1997 reforms; however, one should distinguish between upstream (exploration and production) and downstream (transportation and commercialization) activities. Before reforms, the number of upstream-sector employees fluctuated around 25 percent of the total. These were substituted by the capitalized Andina and Chaco, which, in 1998, operated with about 40 percent of the total upstream personnel YPFB had in 1996. The continuing decrease in YPFB employment extended beyond 1999 as downstream-sector activities were privatized.

Although the number of employees in oil and gas transportation (which Transredes represents) is known, no information is available on the rest of downstream activities (industrialization, storage, distribution, and commercialization).

Summary

Since employment in the electricity and telecommunications sectors peaked around 1997, one cannot rule out that capitalization might have caused personnel reductions. However, the employment level in these sectors is small, accounting for fewer than 6,000 jobs of the more than 1.3 million workers in the capital cities alone. Nonetheless, job losses in these sectors account for about 3 percent of aggregate job losses in capital cities during 1995–2000; thus, while small, the effect is not negligible.

Taken together, the evidence on employment levels suggests that capitalization was indeed associated with employment reductions, amid increasing output and labor productivity. Within the broader context of Bolivian employment, however, incomplete data indicate that direct employment losses have accounted for no more than a small proportion of the unemployment increases that started in 1998.

Profitability and Fund Flows

Financial results are another relevant firm-level outcome. In reviewing the descriptive statistics shown in table 4.3, one must recall that part of YPFB was capitalized in 1997, ENDE and ENTEL in 1995, and ENFE in 1996. With the exceptions of ENTEL and LAB, residuals of these firms remained, and privatizations (or portions of them) occurred later. If one considers current expenditures over revenues until the year of capitalization, the data show that, except for ENDE and ENFE in 1995, these firms covered their operating expenses and were capable of making short-term transfers to the state, although certain ones (e.g., ENDE and ENTEL) were positioned more comfortably. When one considers total—including capital—expenditures over revenues, state firms were in deficit (except for YPFB in 1995–97, ENDE

Table 4.3 Cash flow statistics of government firms, 1990–2001 (percent)

Firm	1990	1991	1992	1993	1994	1995	1996	1997	1998	1999	2000	2001
YPFB												
C. Exp./C. Rev.	0.90	0.89	0.90	0.95	0.90	0.88	0.90	0.95	1.05	0.97	0.95	0.97
T. Exp./T. Rev.	1.08	1.05	1.06	1.08	1.07	0.99	0.97	0.96	1.06	0.98	0.95	0.97
I/GDP	2.17	2.16	1.86	1.65	1.67	0.98	0.63	0.10	0.05	0.08	0.00	0.01
T/GDP	7.92	8.85	7.21	6.47	5.93	5.52	5.79	3.34	3.41	3.09	-0.18	-0.30
ENDE												
C. Exp./C. Rev.	0.65	0.63	0.63	0.58	0.62	1.31	0.87	0.55	1.12	1.02	2.05	2.15
T. Exp./T. Rev.	0.94	1.14	1.43	0.95	0.82	1.16	1.64	0.82	1.35	0.69	1.39	1.54
I/GDP	0.32	0.55	1.01	0.53	0.33	0.52	0.32	0.09	0.03	0.01	0.00	0.01
T/GDP	0.06	0.07	0.02	0.15	0.19	0.73	0.16	0.04	0.00	-0.02	0.00	-0.01
ENTEL[a]												
C. Exp./C. Rev.	0.72	0.70	0.72	0.84	0.88	0.87						
T. Exp./T. Rev.	1.23	1.04	0.89	1.15	0.98	0.93						
I/GDP	0.57	0.40	0.24	0.45	0.14	0.09						
T/GDP	0.41	0.49	0.44	0.63	0.80	0.71						
ENFE												
C. Exp./C. Rev.	0.97	0.84	0.77	0.95	0.88	1.03	0.97	2.68	2.33	6.91	1.88	4.26
T. Exp./T. Rev.	1.44	1.05	1.07	1.12	1.05	1.11	0.86	1.33	1.39	1.42	1.33	1.49
I/GDP	0.39	0.28	0.32	0.24	0.18	0.09	0.00	0.01	0.00	0.00	0.00	0.00
T/GDP	0.06	-0.10	0.12	-0.09	0.07	0.06	-0.20	-0.02	-0.01	0.00	0.00	0.00
All												
I/GDP	3.87	3.75	4.08	3.29	2.63	2.15	1.69	0.66	0.33	0.22	0.17	0.17
T/GDP	8.65	9.50	8.00	7.44	6.57	7.75	6.14	3.46	3.34	3.13	-0.22	-0.33

C. Exp. = current expenditures, including current transfers
C. Rev. = current revenues, including current transfers and operational revenues
T. Exp. = total expenditures, including current and capital expenditures
T. Rev. = total revenues, including current and capital revenues
I = investment
T = taxes, royalties, and net transfers to government.
GDP = gross domestic product
a. Data for ENTEL not available for all years.
Source: Fiscal Action Unit.

in 1991 and 1993–94, and ENTEL in 1992 and 1994–95). Thus, most of the time, state firms had to finance their investments through debt,[21] and many years witnessed investment shortfalls.

The magnitude of these firms' investment can be observed as a percentage of GDP and in relation to all state enterprise investment.[22] In both of these areas, YPFB stands out in terms of size.

During the postcapitalization period, the outlook for residual firms changed substantially in terms of investment and net contributions. However, other indicators worsened dramatically, particularly for ENDE and ENFE residuals.

During 1997–2002, electricity generation companies Corani and COBEE (hydroelectric firms) performed better than did Guaracachi and Valle Hermoso (thermoelectric firms) for the criteria considered (table 4.4). In terms of distribution, in the year 2000, ELECTROPAZ had the lowest expenditure-to-revenue ratio and the highest return on equity, followed by ELFEC and ELFEO. The remaining firms were cooperatives (CRE) or had municipal participation.

For hydrocarbons (oil and gas), information is available only on Andina, Chaco, and Transredes. In upstream activities, both Andina and Chaco have increasingly improved their internal efficiency and return on equity. Transredes, the main firm in pipeline transport, has managed to generate annual surpluses, except in 2000, when an oil spill resulted in a capital loss.

Telecommunications data show that internal efficiency in ENTEL and COMTECO deteriorated in 1999; the measure of profitability fell from 8.9 in 1998 to 5.3 percent and from 5.2 in 1998 to 2.8 percent, respectively. For COTEL and COTAS, the efficiency indicator remained stable; however, COTEL generated loses each year while COTAS had weak profits. During 1998–2000, TELECEL improved its profitability; however, it experienced substantial losses during 2001–02.

In the airline sector, LAB managed to break even in 1999, but incurred significant losses during 2000–02. VASP, the company that capitalized LAB, departed in 2002 under allegations of asset stripping. At that point, Bolivian investors took over LAB, allegedly paying a gift price for it. AEROSUR, which participated in the domestic market only, produced better results during the years considered. Since 1997, SABSA, the airport terminal operator, has had deteriorating performance and, in 2000, experienced a dramatic loss; however, it bounced back by 2001–02.

The rail sector has experienced a more positive outlook. In 1997, FCA made a 13.6 percent return on equity; although, by 2000, it had fallen to

---

21. In general, state firms could not obtain commercial credit, and their debt consisted mainly of concessionary credit from bilateral or multilateral agencies, with government guarantees.

22. Infrastructure, hydrocarbons, minerals, and industrial sectors.

Table 4.4 Performance indicators of main firms in regulated sectors, 1997–2001

Sector and company	Operational costs and revenues					After tax profit or equity				
	1997	1998	1999	2000	2001	1997	1998	1999	2000	2001
Electricity generation										
Corani	0.38	0.40	0.38	0.48	0.6	12.2	7.2	9.3	8.0	5.2
COBEE	0.65	0.69	0.59	0.63	0.5	11.1	7.2	11.6	9.8	14.3
Guaracachi	0.99	0.94	0.94	0.82	0.8	3.6	5.6	4.4	5.3	2.7
TDE-Transmission	n.a.	n.a.	0.66	0.65	0.65	n.a.	n.a.	5.2	6.2	6.6
Valle Hermoso	1.02	0.90	1.02	1.01	2.5	2.6	4.8	4.7	3.7	-0.9
Electricity distribution										
CESSA	0.93	0.90	0.77	0.97	0.97	4.6	8.4	0.6	7.5	5.7
CRE	0.90	0.89	0.89	0.93	0.94	6.0	6.8	3.0	2.8	2.3
ELECTROPAZ	0.81	0.78	0.77	0.84	0.86	11.1	10.9	14.2	14.4	6.9
ELFEC	0.82	0.83	0.83	0.92	0.95	10.1	9.1	10.3	14.2	7.2
ELFEO	0.81	0.77	0.82	0.91	0.87	12.4	16.9	12.4	8.2	4.6
SEPSA	0.98	0.92	0.92	0.90	0.94	6.8	6.5	6.3	4.4	4.2
Oil and gas										
Andina[a]	n.a.	0.92	0.91	0.75	0.00	n.a.	0.7	1.3	6.1	0.0
Chaco[a]	n.a.	0.76	0.54	0.38	0.37	n.a.	-2.1	6.1	9.6	8.5
Transredes[b]	0.58[c]	0.57	0.61	1.60	0.87	7.3	6.0	8.3	-4.0	2.5

Telecommunications										
COMTECO	0.85	0.73	0.98	n.a.	n.a.	3.3	5.2	2.8	n.a.	n.a.
COTAS	0.89	0.89	0.88	n.a.	n.a.	1.7	0.5	0.6	n.a.	n.a.
COTEL	1.32	1.29	1.30	n.a.	n.a.	−30.5	−9.4	−11.0	n.a.	n.a.
ENTEL	0.80	0.83	0.94	n.a.	n.a.	6.2	8.9	5.3	n.a.	n.a.
TELECEL	0.95	0.84	n.a.	n.a.	n.a.	−24.3	33.4	n.a.	n.a.	n.a.
Transportation										
Airlines and airports										
AEROSUR	1.18	0.98	1.04	0.83	n.a.	−19.3	1.6	−9.4	0.0	n.a.
LAB	0.97	1.00	0.99	1.03	n.a.	2.5	−5.8	0.4	−14.0	n.a.
SABSA	0.93	0.97	1.10	1.16	n.a.	33.3	12.0	−15.7	−83.9	n.a.
Rail										
FCA	0.85	0.85	0.93	0.86	n.a.	13.6	7.3	8.7	8.2	n.a.
FCO	0.57	0.59	0.71	0.68	n.a.	27.0	28.5	15.5	15.2	n.a.
Water										
Aguas del Illimani	0.86	0.85	0.84	0.64	0.65	0.9	15.0	18.4	4.9	−4.9

n.a. = not available

a. For years ending in March.
b. Includes deferred-account revenues.
c. Seven months of operation.

Source: General Superintendence.

8.2 percent and to 2 percent by 2002. For FCO, the 1997–98 profit rate fluctuated around 28 percent, falling to 15 percent by 1999–2000 and to 10.6 percent by 2002. Nonetheless, FCO is considered the most profitable firm among those capitalized. This may partially reflect its monopolization of the Santa Cruz–Puerto Suarez route, where it faces no trucking competition.

In terms of the water industry, Aguas del Illimani is the only privately administered firm. Indicators for the 1997–99 period show a consistent tendency toward improvement; however, its profitability fell significantly during 2000–01.

Utilities Access and Price Changes: Effects on Consumer Welfare

Privatization may affect consumers of utilities services in three main ways:

- If privatization results in expanded utilities networks, then unserved households might become consumers of the services.

- For consumers with access, privatization may bring about price changes.

- Privatization may affect the quality of the services provided.

We focus on the utilities sectors for which direct consumer expenditure data is available (i.e., electricity, telecommunications, and water). Data on transport is unavailable by type,[23] while hydrocarbons (oil and gas) privatization is likely to have affected consumers indirectly because of its export-intensive nature.[25]

Increasing consumer access to infrastructure, especially water and electricity, has long been regarded as an essential component of poverty reduction strategies. Poverty measures of unmet basic needs are based directly on access to such services. Electricity helps to generate income for the poor; for example, 78 percent of all municipal workshops in Bolivia's rural areas identified rural electrification as the most important action in combating poverty (Government of Bolivia, or GOB 2001).

Changes in Access

The fifth (1992) and seventh (1994) rounds of the Integrated Household Survey (Encuesta Integrada de Hogares, or EIH) and the first round (1999)

---

23. This is unfortunate because transportation tends to account for a larger portion of poor household budgets.

24. Although the price volatility introduced by liberalization could have important welfare consequences.

of the Ongoing Household Survey (Encuesta Continua de Hogares, or ECH) can be used to examine changes in access to utilities services before and after the capitalization reforms of 1995 and 1996 (see appendices 4A and 4B).

The surveys determined household access to telephone and electricity services by directly asking whether the household had service. Calculations for communications, which included telephone and mail, were based on whether the household reported positive expenditure on this item during the past month. A household was considered to have access to water if it had a pipe connection to the dwelling unit's building (table 4.5).

During Latin America's rapid urbanization of 1994–99, Bolivian consumers' access to all services increased as low-income, rural residents migrated to urban areas, putting pressure on urban infrastructure. Without such significant investment, coverage rates would, in all likelihood, have declined.

Access changes by per capita, household-expenditure decile were also reported (table 4.6). Coverage for electricity was the highest before privatization (in 1994, more than 98 percent of the top half of the distribution had access). As a result, improvements concentrated mainly on the poor (during 1994–99, an additional 9.6 percent of the poorest decile gained access).

Access to water was initially high among the richer deciles, but lower than access to electricity among the poor. During 1994–99, each of the bottom seven deciles increased access of more than 10 percent; remarkably, an additional 24.6 percent of the poorest decile gained access to water. By contrast, access to telephone service was less common, and increased access occurred mainly for middle and upper portions of the overall distribution.

While access increased after privatization, it also increased before privatization (table 4.6). To estimate whether privatization changed the rate of increase, one can consider the difference between the annual growth rate in access before (1992–94) and after (1994–99) privatization.

This simple counterfactual will tend to bias downward any effect of privatization since access rates cannot grow beyond 100 percent; hence, one would expect growth rates to fall as coverage grows. Nevertheless, as table 4.6 shows, rates doubled for communications (for most deciles) and water (for middle deciles). The growth rate in electricity access has slowed, which is to be expected, given that access now stands at 97 percent or above for all but the second decile.

Another way to determine whether privatization increased access is to compare changes in access to water in La Paz and El Alto—the only city with a sustained concession—to changes in other major cities. This comparison is particularly relevant because the government chose to award the La Paz and El Alto concession on the basis of bids for the number of new connections to be offered at a predetermined tariff level, suggesting that increased access was a goal of this process.

As table 4.6 shows, for the top four quintiles, access to water during 1992–94 increased faster in the other cities than in La Paz and El Alto.

Table 4.5 Evolution of Bolivian capitals' access to basic services, for selected years (percent of households)

Income decile (household, per capita)	Telephone[a]		Communications			Electricity			Water		
	1994	1999	1992	1994	1999	1992	1994	1999	1992	1994	1999
1	0.9	8.3	1.2	2.9	13.5	85.4	89.2	98.9	52.2	64.5	89.1
2	4.5	15.8	2.7	7.2	18.0	88.5	93.3	95.0	59.8	68.1	82.5
3	4.5	20.4	6.6	8.1	27.4	90.3	93.2	97.9	67.4	74.7	89.1
4	6.4	30.7	8.1	9.4	45.0	90.9	94.6	96.9	72.5	73.2	89.0
5	8.8	38.6	13.9	13.4	57.4	94.1	96.6	100.0	71.9	76.4	87.8
6	16.1	51.1	18.5	22.3	62.5	94.8	97.7	100.0	79.4	83.0	95.7
7	20.8	60.4	21.7	27.4	69.4	96.0	98.1	100.0	85.0	85.1	98.7
8	28.6	62.1	29.6	35.6	75.7	97.3	98.0	100.0	84.9	91.1	97.7
9	41.5	72.2	45.0	48.6	86.0	98.5	98.8	99.9	88.4	91.5	95.7
10	60.3	77.4	53.5	69.7	85.1	97.6	99.7	100.0	92.0	95.5	97.8
Total	20.0	42.5	21.1	25.5	52.7	93.6	96.0	98.8	76.3	80.6	92.1

a. Access on telephone access was not available for 1992.

Notes: Access to telephone, electricity, and water is based on direct survey questions on household ownership of phone, electricity services (including lighting), and water network services (whether water is connected to the building that houses the dwelling unit). The household is considered to have access to communications (telephone and mail) if it had positive expenditure on these items within the last month.

Sources: Authors' calculations from fifth (1992) and seventh (1994) rounds of EIH and first (1999) round of ECH.

Table 4.6 Access changes resulting from privatization

1994–99 annual change minus 1992–94 annual change (difference-in-difference)

Decile	Communications	Electricity	Water
1	1.3	0.0	-1.2
2	-0.1	-2.1	-1.3
3	3.1	-0.5	-0.8
4	6.5	-1.4	2.8
5	9.0	-0.5	0.1
6	6.1	-1.0	0.7
7	5.5	-0.7	2.6
8	5.0	0.0	-1.7
9	5.7	0.1	-0.7
10	-5.0	-1.0	-1.3
Total	3.2	-0.6	0.1

Access to water, by expenditure quintile and region

Quintile	La Paz and El Alto			Other main cities			Difference-in-difference[a]		Triple difference[b]
	1992	1994	1999	1992	1994	1999	1992–94	1994–99	
1	53.3	66.1	88.8	57.4	66.4	82.5	3.8	6.6	-0.6
2	70.7	73.3	93.3	69.8	74.2	86.9	-1.8	7.4	2.4
3	76.0	77.4	95.6	75.7	80.6	89.4	-3.5	9.5	3.6
4	87.1	89.8	100.0	84.1	87.5	97.3	-0.7	0.4	0.4
5	96.2	94.6	100.0	87.8	93.1	95.4	-6.9	3.1	4.1
Overall	78.1	81.7	94.4	75.6	80.3	90.7	-1.0	2.2	1.0

a. The difference-in-difference is the change in La Paz and El Alto minus the change in other main cities (Cochabamba and Santa Cruz).
b. Triple difference is the difference between one-fifth the double difference over 1994–99 and one-half the double difference over 1992–94.

Sources: Authors' calculations from fifth (1992), sixth (1993), and seventh (1994) rounds of EIH and first (1999) round of ECH.

However, after the water concession, access during 1994–99 increased more in La Paz and El Alto. The resulting threefold change is positive overall for the richer four quintiles, suggesting that privatization increased access. By contrast, access by the poorest quintile increased at a faster rate in La Paz and El Alto than it did in other main cities, both before and after privatization; thus, the overall triple difference is small.

Penetration rates for telephone service in Bolivia overall—not only the largest cities—reveal increased access. Until 1996, the growth rate was fairly stagnant, after which cellular and Internet growth was rapid, and both fixed-line and public phone services grew. Cellular subscribers (per 100 inhabitants) grew from 0.27 in 1996 to 6.96 in 2000, surpassing the number of residential main lines per inhabitant in this period (International Telecommunication Union, or ITU 2001). Over the years, Bolivia has made an effort to extend rural telephone coverage; the capitalization contract with ENTEL, in fact, contained clauses in this regard. Rural lines grew from 0.65 lines (per 1,000 rural inhabitants) in 1997 to 2.03 lines (per 1,000 rural inhabitants) in 2000.[25] While the number of connections is low, these new connections can mean substantial welfare gains for rural residents.

Although technology improvements are responsible for a portion of the increases, it is likely that rapid growth rates would not have been achieved without liberalization in general and introduction of competition in cellular services in particular. In Bolivia, cellular access gains have been critical because local cooperatives charged $1,200 to $1,500 for access to local lines (an amount that entitles the buyer to one share of the cooperative).[26] In 1996, the GDP per capita was only about $1,000, putting the cost of a local fixed line beyond the reach of many consumers; thus, cellular competition dramatically reduced these access costs.

Price Changes

Despite the popular perception that privatization causes price increases, its effect is uncertain; much depends on the process itself, as the government can award the contract on the basis of the highest bid or lowest tariff offer. In addition, the existing amount of direct government subsidies will determine whether the private firm needs to raise prices to cover losses. If cross-subsidization occurs before privatization, rebalancing can contribute to price changes. Moreover, private firms may act to reduce illegal connections, resulting in de facto price increases for consumers who obtained the service illegally before privatization. Competition and regulation are also important factors; for example, if private management is more efficient and

---

25. Rural lines from the Telecommunications Superintendent, SITTEL. See www.sittel.gov.bo.

26. See Fernando Cossio Muñoz, "Bolivia: Telecommunications Sector," 1999, www.tradeport. org/ts/countries/bolivia/isa/isar0001.html.

the private firm faces competition or regulation, prices can fall (Estache, Foster, and Wodon 2002).

Several reasons suggest that Bolivian prices should not have increased dramatically after privatization. First, because the government did not use capitalization proceeds to cover deficits, there were fewer incentives to build high tariffs into the contracts. Second, promoting competition and implementing regulation may have helped reduce the pressure for price increases. Third, as existing firms were often cooperatives or private companies (e.g., COBEE in the electricity sector), the government's distributional goals were not always implemented through utility prices. Moreover, the autonomous nature of existing firms likely lessened the problem of illegal connections, although the household surveys do not enable one to examine such changes. Finally, in telecommunications, ENTEL, the state-owned long distance provider, was always separate from local cooperatives; thus, the typical cross-subsidization of long distance and local rates was not an issue.

The household surveys used for this chapter collected data only on household expenditure, not the prices individual households paid for infrastructure services. As a result, we had to use aggregate price indices at either the city or national level with which to assess price changes after privatization.

As figure 4.1 shows,[27] water prices rose in La Paz and El Alto before the 1997 concession and continued to rise until 1998. Prices rose faster in Santa Cruz, where reforms did not occur; thus, privatization resulted in slower increases in La Paz and El Alto relative to other cities. Using the weighted average price in Cochabamba and Santa Cruz to predict what price increases would have been in La Paz and El Alto without privatization, one finds that privatization lowered prices 10.5 percent, relative to the average in other cities (Barja, McKenzie, and Urquiola 2004).

Price increases for water are especially interesting because they led to a spectacular failure in the privatization process. In 1999, Aguas de Tunari, a subsidiary of Bechtel Enterprises, was the sole bidder in an auction for a water concession in Cochabamba. The city faced a chronic water shortage, with many poor households unconnected to the network, while state subsidies went mainly to the middle class and industry.[28]

When the first monthly bills arrived in January 2000, consumer price increases averaged 51 percent (some household increases were more than 90 percent because of small increases in usage, coupled with large rise in price).[29] Because water prices had fallen during 1997–99 (figure 4.1), the price rise was an even greater shock to consumers. The poorest consumers—for

---

27. Data supplied by the Instituto Nacional de Estadística (INE).

28. See William Finnegan, "Letter from Bolivia: Leasing the Rain," *The New Yorker*, April 8, 2002.

29. See www.democracyctr.org/bechtel/waterbills/waterbills-global.htm.

Figure 4.1 Evolution of water prices in Bolivia, 1992–99 (for 10 m³)

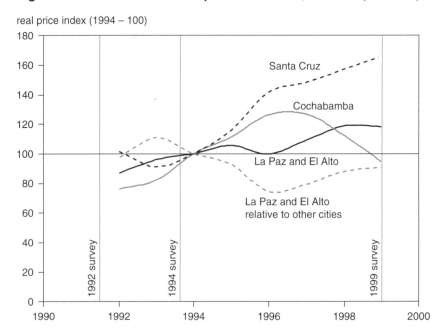

real price index (1994 – 100)

Source: Bolivia's INE.

whom water usage consisted of only an indoor toilet and outside water tap—had an average price rise of 43 percent, with some consumers reporting a doubling of their bill.[30] Prices rose even more for richer consumers; the middle class had average increases of 57 percent, while commercial-user prices rose 59 percent.

The exclusive rights granted the concessionaire affected local investors' interest in private wells and distribution systems. In addition, Aguas del Tunari agreed to invest $200 million in the popular Misicuni water provision project (30 percent of which had to come from equity and the rest from debt). The tariff increase occurred before the company had complied with the equity commitment and the debt financing had been lined up. The perception was that the firm was attempting to finance its equity share of the tariff increases.

Within this context, the so-called "water war" occurred, involving local labor strikes, demonstrations, and violent confrontations that ended with cancellation of the concession and expulsion of Aguas del Tunari from

---

32. See SEMAPA analysis in the Democracy Center, "Bechtel versus Bolivia: The Water Rate Hikes by Bechtel's Bolivian Company (Aguas del Tunari): The Real Numbers," August 20, 2002, www.democracyctr.org/bechtel/waterbills/waterbills-global.htm.

Cochabamba. Control of the water network reverted to SEMAPA, the municipal utility.

Figure 2.2 in this volume which shows the evolution of electricity prices during 1992–99, plots price indices relative to the overall CPI for the mean residential tariff and the minimum electricity tariff (0–20 kWh per month), the amount most relevant to poorer households.

Since the 1994–95 reforms, prices have generally risen, except for the minimum tariff in Cochabamba, which decreased 14 percent during 1994–99; since 1998, some price decreases have been realized. On average, however, prices increased 26.2 percent over the five-year period. Because prices were increasing before privatization, we extrapolated the trend of price increases before privatization (during 1992–94) to predict 1999 prices. Comparing the predicted 1999 prices to the actual ones enables one to approximate the privatization effect. Overall, privatization raised prices 5.6 percent in 1994–99, with prices increasing in La Paz and El Alto and decreasing relative to trend in Cochabamba and Santa Cruz (Barja, McKenzie, and Urquiola 2004).

With regard to telecommunications during 1994–99, local cooperatives reacted differently (figure 4.2 and 4.3). COTAS, the Santa Cruz cooperative, raised both its minimum tariff and the price of a public phone call by more than 250 percent. By contrast, prices fell in La Paz and El Alto (which is related to COTEL, the La Paz cooperative, later falling into financial distress). Across cities and weighting for population, the average drop in the minimum tariff was 8.3 percent, while the cost of national long distance calls increased 83 percent.

Allowing the entry of ENTEL-Movil in 1996 opened the mobile market to competition. From the early 1990s to October 1996, incumbent Telecel charged a fixed monthly tariff of $29.90 (which did not include free minutes), a per-minute tariff of $0.41 (for both incoming and outgoing calls), and $417 for initial connection. An aggressive marketing campaign accompanying ENTEL-Movil's entry dramatically lowered the cost of cellular services. Under ENTEL's Family Plan and Telecel's Economy Plan, connection fees for digital lines were free, the fixed monthly tariff without free minutes dropped to $1.93 in November 1996, and the per-minute tariff increased to $0.45. Before competition, tariffs were set in dollars; after competition, they were set in bolivianos and thus subject to depreciation. By December 1999, the dollar value of the fixed tariff dropped to $1.67 and the per-minute tariff dropped to $0.39. Both ENTEL and Telecel simultaneously introduced various plans and prepayment mechanisms, with the latter contributing to further penetration. Competition was so effective that, although the regulator set a price cap of $180 for access and $51 for use, both firms began charging average rates roughly 5 percent of this level.

These reductions, combined with availability of low-cost cellular phones, dramatically lowered access prices (particularly compared with the historical performance of local telephone cooperatives, which charged fees in excess of

Figure 4.2 Evolution of telephone prices in Bolivia, 1992–99

real price index (1994 – 100) (log scale)

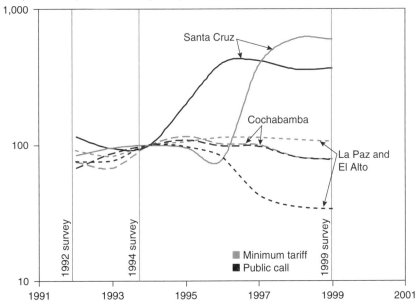

Source: Bolivia's INE.

$1,000 for a fixed connection/share). Because a new operator entered the market in late 2000 and all of these markets were liberalized in 2001, these trends are expected to continue.

Service Quality

In addition to access and price changes, service quality is a major concern for consumers. With regard to electricity, the 1994 sector law introduced regulations on distribution quality,[31] establishing four stages of implementation. During the first stage (January 1996–October 1997), distribution firms helped establish the method for measurement and control of quality indicators. In the second stage (November 1997–April 1998), the distributor tested the method. During the third stage or transition period (May 1998 to April 2001), the firms had to comply with the quality indicators established by the rules, subject to monetary penalties. In the current fourth stage (May 2001–ongoing), the distribution firms must comply with more demanding

---

31. Rules for the Quality of Distribution (1995).

**Figure 4.3 Change in minimum per-minute tariff
in cellular telephony, 1992–99**

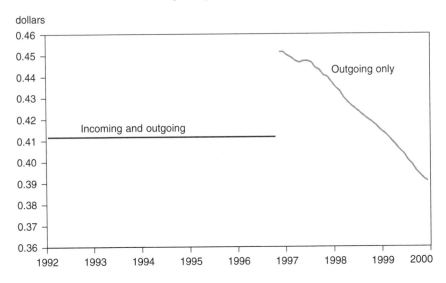

levels of the quality indicators established by the rules, with similar financial penalties for noncompliance.

This information can only establish that the electricity sector has made recent efforts to improve quality; it does not indicate whether these levels are better than those one would have observed before privatization, especially since the firms helped to draft the quality guidelines under which they now operate. Anecdotal evidence indicates that, since capitalization, distribution problems—particularly blackouts, which may have originated in the generation sector—are down, and consumers are generally more satisfied.

With regard to telecommunications, the sector had goals for expansion, quality, modernization, and operators' fulfillment of long distance, local, and cellular services (Barja, McKenzie, and Urquiola 2004). In long distance services, ENTEL was in full compliance until 1998. In local services, the three largest cooperatives achieved the 1998 goals. In certain cases, these goals were easily attained (e.g., COTAS and COTEL percentage of digitalization achieved or COTEL and COMTECO percentage of completed calls attained). In other cases, the objectives were barely met (e.g., COTAS percentage of completed calls). Only COTEL had unmet goals by 1999. In cellular services, operators ENTEL-Movil and Telecel achieved 1998 expansion and quality goals in all cases. In fact, most goals were achieved by 1997, reflecting, in part, this sector's competitive pressures. Indeed, available data cannot account for the substantial welfare improvements that may have come about thanks to new services or such substitutes as cellular telephony.

To the extent that capitalization facilitated their arrival, one can credit this process with welfare consequences in this area.

Welfare Effects of Price and Access Change

Privatization is associated with increased access and a mix of price increase and decrease. As most consumers do not produce water, electricity, or telephone services, Deaton (1989) notes that the nonparametric estimation of Engel curves will approximate the average consumer welfare changes resulting from price changes. Disregarding access changes, household expenditure shares allocated to each infrastructure service will allow one to determine which consumers price changes affected most.

Examining expenditure shares by household expenditure decile, one finds that electricity is a necessity, with expenditure shares falling with total expenditure.[32] With access rates high across all deciles, changes in electricity price will have the greatest effect on the poor. Water expenditure shares fall slightly with expenditure levels; with greater access to water, price changes will affect the poor most. Given that access to telephones is higher among richer deciles, price changes will clearly affect the rich most.

Expenditure share details the effect of price change on consumers, provided they do not adjust the quantity of the service consumed. Banks, Blundell, and Lewbel (1996) refer to this expenditure share as the first-order approximation of welfare change. If x_0 represents a household's initial total expenditure per capita, w_{j0} the initial budget share for service j, p_j the price of service j, and U the household's utility; then the first-order approximation of the relative change in utility for a price change of service j is:

$$\frac{\Delta U}{x_0} = -\left(\Delta \log p_j\right) w_{j0}. \tag{4.1}$$

Intuitively, a change in the price of service will have the greatest affect on consumers who devote a larger share of their total budget to that service. In practice, consumers often adjust the quantity consumed when prices change; thus, Banks, Blundell, and Lewbel (1996) provide a second-order approximation to welfare change, which allows for quantity response:

$$\frac{\Delta U}{x_0} = -\left(\Delta \log p_j\right) w_{j0} \left[1 + \frac{\Delta \log p_j}{2} \frac{\partial \log w_j}{\partial \log p_j}\right] \tag{4.2}$$

The elasticity $\partial \log w_j / \partial \log p_j$ is estimated by γ_{jj} / w_{j0}, where the coefficient γ_{jj} is obtained from estimating the Engel equation for household h

---

32. Barja, McKenzie, and Urquiola (2004, table 23), provides a detailed breakdown of budget shares, by expenditure decile.

$$w_{hj} = \alpha_j + \sum_{i=1}^{k} \gamma_{ij} \log p_i + \beta_j \log \frac{x_h}{n_h} + \phi_j \left(\log \frac{x_h}{n_h} \right)^2 + \lambda'_j Z_h \qquad (4.3)$$

where n_h is the household size for household h, Z_h contains other demographic control variables, and p_i for $i \neq j$ is the price of good i. Because detailed information on the price of substitute goods was unavailable, we did not include other prices in estimating equation 4.3.

Equations 4.1 and 4.2 would allow for estimating the first- and second-order approximations of the welfare effects of price changes for households with access to the infrastructure service both before and after privatization. To value consumers' welfare benefit of gaining access to a service, McKenzie and Mookherjee (in chapter 2) suggest using the virtual price of the service for those who gain access. The virtual price, obtained from the Engel equation 4.3, is the price at which the household would have chosen to consume zero units of the service prior to privatization if it had had access to the service in question. For a household that gains access, the effective price change is the fall from the virtual to the postprivatization price.

Two additional issues must be resolved to estimate access value. The first is that equation 4.3 is estimated only for households with access, leading to inconsistent estimates if omitted variables correlated with access also influence demand. Therefore, a Heckman two-step selection correction is used to estimate equation 4.3.

The second issue is that, because the Bolivian household surveys are repeated cross-sections, it is impossible to identify which households gained access during 1994–99 since the 1999 survey contains households not included in the 1994 survey. In chapter 2, McKenzie and Mookherjee provide a method for estimating the average change in welfare for a decile, incorporating changes in access with repeated cross-sections, which we use here.

As table 4.7 shows, access is greater for richer households, those with larger houses, those with more household members, those who rent, and those with fewer children. These probits can be used to correct for selection in the Engel equation 4.3.

Table 4.8 presents the results estimating the Engel equation by ordinary least squares (OLS) for households with positive expenditure shares and after the Heckman two-step correction. In the case of communications services, more than 12,000 households have zero expenditure shares, compared with 2,500 with positive shares; the resulting price elasticity under the two-step method is positive and differs insignificantly from zero. In this case, we use the elasticity estimated under the OLS.

Because the surveys do not report the prices individual households pay for each service, one must use aggregate indices when estimating the welfare effects in equations 4.1 and 4.2. Only city-specific price indices are available for the central-axis cities of La Paz and El Alto, Cochabamba, and Santa Cruz; thus, this analysis is limited to these cities.

Table 4.7 Probit regressions for access to infrastructure services, 1992–99

Household variable	Water		Electricity		Communications	
	Coefficient	Standard error	Coefficient	Standard error	Coefficient	Standard error
Household head						
Age	0.0023	0.0053	-0.0024	0.0076	0.0094	0.0054*
Age squared	0.0000	0.0001	0.0000	0.0001	-0.0001	0.0001
Male	-0.2005	0.0321***	-0.0291	0.0466	-0.0397	0.0309
Household size	0.0408	0.0107***	0.0690	0.0170***	0.0458	0.0102***
Per-capita expenditure decile	0.1052	0.0049***	0.0950	0.0075***	0.2107	0.0053***
Number of rooms	0.1549	0.0100***	0.2924	0.0188***	0.2455	0.0083***
Dummy, if rented house	0.3787	0.0292***	0.3644	0.0440***	0.1395	0.0295***
Household members (number)						
Under 15 years old	-0.0740	0.0134***	-0.1194	0.0210***	-0.0469	0.0137***
Over 65 years old	0.0501	0.0437	-0.0728	0.0653	0.0792	0.0383**
Constant	-0.0621	0.1145	0.6178	0.1636***	-3.0524	0.1226***
Number of observations	17,581		17,581		17,581	
Pseudo-R2	0.0964		0.1281		0.2565	

* = significant at the 10 percent level
** = significant at the 5 percent level
*** = significant at the 1 percent level

Sources: Authors' calculations from fifth (1992), sixth (1993), and seventh (1994) rounds of EIH and first (1999) round of ECH.

Table 4.8 Engel equation estimations[a]

Variable	Water		Electricity		Communications	
	Coefficient	Standard error	Coefficient	Standard error	Coefficient	Standard error
OLS regression results						
Log price	0.175	0.146	−0.118	0.320	−0.156	0.178
Log expenditure per capita	−1.512	0.244***	−2.749	0.398***	−1.286	1.061
Log expenditure per capita squared	0.077	0.021***	0.122	0.035***	0.092	0.086
Log household size	−0.427	0.041***	−0.741	0.067***	−0.491	0.131***
Heckman two-step results						
Log price	−0.582	0.260**	−0.162	0.319	0.289	0.280
Log expenditure per capita	−4.726	0.512***	−0.844	0.408**	−4.624	1.851**
Log expenditure per capita squared	0.305	0.042***	−0.013	0.036	0.335	0.146**
Log household size	−1.027	0.089***	−0.527	0.080***	−1.369	0.245***
Lambda	−2.016	0.275***	3.364	0.025***	−0.660	0.197***

** = significant at the 5 percent level
*** = significant at the 1 percent level
OLS = ordinary least squares

a. Dependent variable equals expenditure share for specified infrastructure service.

Note: Regressions also include dummy for male head, city dummies, and proportion of the household aged 0–4, 5–9, 10–14, and 65 and older.

Sources: Authors' calculations from fifth (1992), sixth (1993), and seventh (1994) rounds of EIH and first (1999) round of ECH.

For telecommunications, we use the city-specific change in the minimum tariff during 1994–99 as the price change for households with access. For electricity, we present results under two scenarios: (1) using actual change in the city-specific mean tariff rate during 1994–99, and (2) using only the increase in tariff rates relative to that predicted by the 1992–94 trend. For the water concession in La Paz and El Alto, we use the price change relative to the average price in Santa Cruz and Cochabamba; for the second water concession in Cochabamba in 2000, we use the average 43 percent price change reported for poorer households.

Table 4.9 presents the estimated joint welfare effects of communications and electricity price and access changes. The estimated value of gaining access to telephones is 80 percent of per capita monthly expenditure (PCME) for the poorest deciles and up to 180 percent of PCME for the richest deciles. By contrast, price increases in Santa Cruz and decreases elsewhere had a welfare effect of less than 2 percent of PCME since budget shares allocated to telecommunications are small. The overall effect of price and access changes in communications is positive for all but the top decile, for which access increase was insufficient to offset price increases in Santa Cruz. Deciles 5 through 9 benefited the most from expanded access and price changes, and their average welfare effect was about 5 percent of one month's per capita expenditure.

During 1994–99, the average price of electricity increased in all three cities, which negatively affected consumers with access. Consumers in the poorer deciles were hit hardest, with an average cost of 1.4 percent of PCME for the bottom decile. If one allows for only part of the price increase to have resulted from privatization (scenario 1), then the direct privatization effect on consumers with access is, at most, a welfare loss of 0.5 percent of PCME. Poorer deciles value gaining access to electricity more, with the welfare gain estimated at 150 to 200 percent of PCME for the poorest deciles. Because increased access concentrated more on the poor, the overall effect of privatization is viewed as positive and largest for the poorest deciles. During 1994–99, these groups had an average welfare gain of 17 percent from electricity access and price changes, whereas the richest decile, for which access was already above 99 percent, had an overall welfare loss of 0.4 percent of PCME.

Table 4.10 presents results for welfare changes from the water concessions in La Paz and El Alto and Cochabamba. For the La Paz and El Alto concession, two scenarios are offered. The first assumes that privatization is responsible for all increased access that occurred, while the second only values increased access relative to access increases in Santa Cruz and Cochabamba. Gaining access to water is valued at 11 to 25 percent of PCME for the poorest five deciles, while the relative price decrease has only minor welfare effects. Overall, privatization is viewed as having benefited the poor most, particularly if one ascribes all increases in access to it.

By contrast, Cochabamba's failed privatization was a welfare loss for consumers. Prices increased, and the short-lived nature of the privatization

Table 4.9 First- and second-order approximations to welfare change
(as percent of per capita household expenditure)

1994 expenditure decile	Households with access (both periods)		Households who gain access		Overall mean effect	
	First-order approximations	Second-order approximations	First-order approximations	Second-order approximations	First-order approximations	Second-order approximations
Communications						
1	0.59	0.62	53.10	80.64	0.23	0.34
2	1.81	1.88	20.87	39.55	0.13	0.13
3	1.73	1.79	56.88	88.25	0.50	0.70
4	1.35	1.41	54.03	82.77	1.80	2.69
5	1.79	1.86	57.25	83.17	4.06	5.80
6	0.77	0.84	85.41	120.17	4.05	5.65
7	0.47	0.55	99.98	131.57	3.55	4.65
8	−0.09	−0.02	88.97	124.42	2.62	3.71
9	−0.40	−0.31	146.99	182.68	8.38	10.51
10	−0.86	−0.77	142.51	181.82	−7.44	−9.27
Electricity Results based on part of price change attributable to privatization						
1	−0.50	−0.50	139.04	195.54	12.80	18.19
2	−0.27	−0.27	102.95	151.32	1.46	2.26
3	−0.23	−0.23	96.95	144.58	4.19	6.35
4	−0.21	−0.21	115.29	163.85	2.30	3.36
5	−0.23	−0.23	88.68	130.94	2.83	4.29
6	−0.20	−0.20	84.54	128.42	1.75	2.76
7	−0.18	−0.18	93.21	133.31	1.59	2.34
8	−0.15	−0.15	83.37	124.34	1.51	2.33
9	−0.19	−0.18	78.16	113.02	0.71	1.12
10	−0.15	−0.15	61.51	91.99	0.04	0.13
Results assuming all price change attributable to privatization						
1	−1.44	−1.43	139.04	195.54	11.97	17.36
2	−1.02	−1.02	102.95	151.32	0.76	1.56
3	−0.99	−0.99	96.95	144.58	3.48	5.64
4	−0.96	−0.95	115.29	163.85	1.60	2.65
5	−0.99	−0.98	88.68	130.94	2.11	3.57
6	−1.00	−1.00	84.54	128.42	0.97	1.98
7	−0.92	−0.92	93.21	133.31	0.86	1.62
8	−0.89	−0.89	83.37	124.34	0.78	1.60
9	−0.89	−0.89	78.16	113.02	0.02	0.42
10	−0.69	−0.68	61.51	91.99	−0.50	−0.41

Sources: Authors' calculations from fifth (1992), sixth (1993), and seventh (1994) rounds of EIH and first (1999) round of ECH.

Table 4.10 Welfare changes from water privatizations (as percent of per capita household expenditure)

Results for La Paz and El Alto

1994 expenditure decile	Households with access (both periods)		Households who gain access		Overall mean effect		Overall mean effect	
	First-order approximations	Second-order approximations	First-order approximations	Second-order approximations	First-order approximations	Second-order approximations	First-order approximations	Second-order approximations
1	0.290	0.293	14.48	24.83	4.12	6.93	0.94	1.48
2	0.218	0.222	5.48	11.48	0.83	1.58	0.31	0.50
3	0.193	0.196	11.60	17.49	2.01	2.96	0.46	0.63
4	0.170	0.174	5.08	10.81	1.30	2.63	0.43	0.77
5	0.181	0.185	8.19	12.82	1.29	1.94	0.87	1.29
6	0.194	0.198	5.31	9.09	1.15	1.86	0.47	0.70
7	0.202	0.206	4.52	7.39	0.85	1.29	0.17	0.17
8	0.196	0.200	6.52	10.12	0.60	0.83	0.18	0.19
9	0.195	0.199	2.53	4.65	0.42	0.62	0.26	0.33
10	0.159	0.163	6.18	8.89	0.42	0.54	0.15	0.16

Results for Cochabamba

1999 expenditure decile	Mean effect		Maximum effect	
	First-order approximations	Second-order approximations	First-order approximations	Second-order approximations
1	-0.99	-0.95	-3.69	-3.65
2	-1.08	-1.04	-3.52	-3.49
3	-0.55	-0.52	-2.30	-2.26
4	-0.69	-0.66	-2.72	-2.68
5	-0.95	-0.92	-3.04	-3.00
6	-0.76	-0.72	-1.98	-1.95
7	-0.75	-0.71	-3.77	-3.73
8	-0.38	-0.34	-1.03	-0.99
9	-0.50	-0.46	-1.01	-0.97
10	-0.57	-0.53	-2.12	-2.08

Sources: Authors' calculations from fifth (1992), sixth (1993), and seventh (1994) rounds of EIH and first (1999) round of ECH.

Table 4.11 Inequality and poverty measures of privatization

Measure	Gini coefficient	Inequality — Atkinson indices A (0.5)	A (1)	A (2)	Poverty: Foster-Greer-Thorbecke index a = 0	a = 1	a = 2
1994 measure (in four main cities)	0.442	0.164	0.278	0.660	0.625	0.259	0.136
After telecommunications privatization:							
First-order approximation	0.455	0.171	0.293	0.641	0.572	0.240	0.129
Second-order approximation	0.464	0.176	0.303	0.641	0.566	0.240	0.128
After electricity privatization:							
Based on price change attributable to privatization							
First-order approximation	0.439	0.161	0.275	0.650	0.612	0.250	0.130
Second-order approximation	0.442	0.163	0.277	0.648	0.607	0.249	0.130
Based on entire price change							
First-order approximation	0.440	0.162	0.275	0.652	0.615	0.253	0.132
Second-order approximation	0.442	0.163	0.278	0.649	0.610	0.251	0.132
1994 measure (in La Paz and El Alto)	0.434	0.158	0.269	0.633	0.691	0.305	0.168
After water privatization:							
Assuming all access increase attributable to privatization							
First-order approximation	0.427	0.153	0.260	0.626	0.683	0.295	0.160
Second-order approximation	0.422	0.150	0.255	0.621	0.677	0.289	0.155
Assuming only increased assess in Santa Cruz and Cochabamba is attributable to privatization							
First-order approximation	0.432	0.156	0.266	0.631	0.691	0.302	0.165
Second-order approximation	0.431	0.156	0.265	0.629	0.688	0.299	0.164
1999 measure (in Cochabamba)	0.378	0.116	0.210	0.437	0.290	0.086	0.036
After water privatization:							
First-order approximation	0.378	0.116	0.210	0.437	0.300	0.088	0.037
Second-order approximation	0.378	0.116	0.210	0.437	0.300	0.088	0.037

Sources: Authors' calculations from fifth (1992), sixth (1993), and seventh (1994) rounds of EIH and first (1999) round of ECH.

meant that the water-network expansions agreed to under the concession contract were not realized. Nevertheless, our estimates of the average welfare losses are not as large as some press reports have suggested.[33]

Table 4.10 shows that the estimated average cost of a 43 percent price rise is, at most, 1 percent of PCME. For the 1999 household survey, the maximum expenditure share for water observed in Cochabamba was 10.5 percent, with an average expenditure share of 1.6 percent and the 95th percentile at 5.4 percent. Table 4.11 reports the maximum welfare losses in each decile, which is the welfare loss for households with largest water expenditure shares in each decile. The maximum welfare loss of a 43 percent price rise for the households sampled is 3.8 percent of PCME. Although some households had larger price increases, most households' expenditure shares were too low for even

---

33. See, for example, William Finnegan, "Letter from Bolivia: Leasing the Rain," *The New Yorker*, April 8, 2002.

a doubling of price to result in the water bill reaching one quarter of income. Thus, the numbers reported in the press represent the potential maximum effect on a limited number of consumers, while the average consumer had much smaller welfare losses.

Poverty and Inequality

The consumer welfare changes estimated here are household-level money metric measures of welfare change if one assumes no income effects (Banks, Blundell, and Lewbel 1996). McKenzie and Mookherjee (chapter 2) therefore suggest that these estimated changes can be used to evaluate the effect of privatization on inequality and poverty.

The approach first calculates the preprivatization Gini coefficient; Atkinson inequality indices; and Foster, Greer, and Thorbecke (1984) measures of poverty, using preprivatization household per capita expenditures. It then estimates counterfactual inequality and poverty measures by adding the estimated per capita change in consumer welfare to preprivatization household expenditure and recalculating the Gini coefficient and other measures. Use of repeated cross-sections means that one is unable to identify the specific households that gained access to the privatized service; thus, in this case, McKenzie and Mookherjee provide a method for calculating the counterfactual inequality and poverty measures.

Table 4.11 uses this method to present the overall effect of each privatization on inequality and poverty. Privatization of electricity, for example, reduced inequality slightly and poverty 1 to 1.5 percent—mainly because of the poor's increased access. Privatization of telephone services had larger effects; while it increased inequality, it reduced headcount poverty 5 to 6 percent.

The explanation for increased inequality and decreased poverty is that access increased mainly for Bolivia's middle deciles, which increased inequality; however, because the country has a high level of poverty—even households in deciles 5 and 6 lie below the poverty line—gain in access reduced poverty. As a result, the distribution-sensitive poverty measure of Foster, Greer, and Thorbecke ($\alpha = 2$) shows a lesser reduction in poverty.

The successful water concession in La Paz and El Alto is also viewed as having reduced inequality and poverty. Increased access to water benefited the poor primarily, while water prices decreased slightly, relative to those in nonconcession cities. Despite media attention and widespread protest, water privatization in Cochabamba apparently had little effect on inequality; as a result, only an additional 1 percent of households fell below the poverty line. As with estimated welfare effects, the water expenditure shares of most households were too small for price changes to have dramatically affected household poverty levels.

Macroeconomic Consequences

Since 1999, the Bolivian economy has been in recession. It began with external shocks that hit the export and construction sectors, further aggravated by reduced investment and aggregate demand. This macroeconomic environment created two distinct periods in which to analyze capitalization reforms' performance. In turn, capitalization significantly affected macroeconomic variables and was part of a broader economic transformation. The most visible consequence was increased foreign direct investment (FDI); observed since 1994, it can be explained, in part, by capitalized firms' activities. Capitalization-related FDI reached 7.5 percent of GDP by 1998, and total FDI peaked at 11.9 percent in 1999. This increase helped to raise total investment from 14.9 percent of GDP in 1994 to a maximum of 23.2 in 1998. This investment focused mainly on energy and infrastructure sectors, which gained importance relative to such traditional activities as mining. Moreover, FDI resilience to the downturn helps to explain why Bolivia's recession has, by some measures, been less severe than those in neighboring countries.

Since 1995, FDI has been greater than domestic private investment and contributed to total private investment, surpassing government investment during 1995–2000.[34] This is an important factor, considering the vision of private sector–led growth that has accompanied the capitalization process and the traditionally greater importance of government investment. In addition, FDI strengthened the balance of payments accounts and enhanced their sustainability.

However, this process ran out of steam with the recession and end of capitalization-related investment commitments. By 2001, total investment dropped to 13.9 percent of GDP, with a tendency for total government investment to decrease slower than private-sector investment, implying a return to foreign debt financing. Although FDI has remained strong, private domestic investment has fallen rapidly, providing evidence of capital flight.

In addition to seeking to stimulate investment, the decision to capitalize was considered a second-generation reform, with the usual aim of leaving the private sector in charge of productive activities in an environment of open markets and competition. The state retained responsibility for regulation, legal administration, ensuring macroeconomic stability, and social-sector investment—all within an environment of decentralization and greater local participation.

Gradually, the composition of government investment came to reflect these priorities. Although total investment decreased as percent of GDP, the social sectors' participation rose from 2.2 percent in 1994 to 3.7 percent in 2001. Investment in production increased from 0.7 to 1.4 percent of GDP, largely reflecting greater support of the agricultural sector. However, in-

---

34. See Barja, McKenzie, and Urquiola (2004, table 29), for a detailed breakdown of the source and structure of investment over the 1990–2001 period.

vestment in extractives production fell from 1.8 percent in 1994 to about 0 percent in 1999, mainly because of withdrawal from hydrocarbons production. Decline in infrastructure (from 3.9 to 2.9 percent of GDP) partially reflects withdrawal from the electricity, telecommunications, and transportation sectors. However, one cannot attribute these changes exclusively to capitalization, given the restrictions foreign lenders and heavily indebted poor country (HIPC) obligations imposed on government investment. Capitalization also affected state revenue. Government income increased through tax collection (taxes and royalties on hydrocarbons were added after 1996). By contrast, since 1995, income from the sale of hydrocarbons decreased substantially.

The net effect of these changes was a substantial lowering of Bolivia's fiscal deficit, particularly if considered separate from pension reform (which came about the same time as capitalization). By 1996, the deficit was low, and the government even attained a modest surplus (excluding pension consideration) in 1999–2000.[35] With the recession, the situation deteriorated severely; by 2002, the deficit (including pension costs) had reached 9 percent of GDP.

To summarize, capitalization reforms were part of a broader economic restructuring that indirectly affected households in multiple ways. This process underscores the increased importance of social components in public expenditure.

Political Economy and Capitalization

Implementation of capitalization had significant effects on Bolivia's political economy, four of which we highlight below. We also hypothesize why this reform has proven unpopular, despite technical standards that would suggest success.

The Promise of Capitalization

Bolivia's transition from a state-led to a market-driven economy, initiated in 1985, focused initially on liberalization of key prices and promotion of market allocation mechanisms, with the goals of ending hyperinflation and returning to macroeconomic stability.

During 1985–89, the Paz Estenssoro administration focused on achieving and defending stability; strict fiscal discipline; and structural reforms, including tax reform and a move toward independent monetary authorities. These measures achieved some intended results; for example, negative GDP growth in 1985 recovered to 3.8 percent in 1989, with an investment level of 11 percent of GDP.

---

35. See Barja, McKenzie, and Urquiola (2004, figure 11), for details on evolution of the fiscal deficit.

The Paz Zamora administration (1989–93) emphasized change (at least in principle) from stability to growth, within the general outlines of the economic model introduced in 1985. This administration's key initiatives were an Investment Law (to promote domestic and foreign investment), Hydrocarbons Law and Mining Code (to attract foreign investment via joint ventures with YPFB and COMIBOL), and Privatization Law (which provided a framework for initiating privatizations with small state firms generally owned by public regional development corporations). To this end, the government organized an office devoted to reordering state enterprises, establishing their number and characteristics in preparation for eventual privatization. By 1993, growth reached 4.3 percent, with a 15.7 investment rate.

The consensus remained that, despite having achieved stability, Bolivia needed significantly higher growth to reduce poverty substantially. In the free-market setting adopted, this need implied further promotion of FDI and technological change. Since 1985 stabilization, domestic private investment had advanced slowly; domestic firms generally had not yet developed the capacity to compete in global markets.

Moreover, macroeconomic stability was repeatedly questioned, given that various levels of government were heavily involved in production and public investment remained the principal growth engine. In addition, this investment had to meet multiple needs in electricity, water, sewage, telecommunications, transportation, and oil exploration as well as growing priorities in health and education. This situation, coupled with international pressure (e.g., World Bank), made it clear that privatization was the path to follow.

During 1993–97, the Sanchez de Lozada administration was more aggressive in structural reform. Capitalization was only a part of overall changes that included greater local participation and pension reform. Emphases were twofold: (1) transfer of productive activities to the private sector, and (2) sharing of social responsibilities with local jurisdictions. The first required sector-by-sector reform to establish the conditions under which the private sector would participate, and the second required government reform. While the first was mostly efficiency oriented, the second was directed to distributional issues. This plan responded to a vision of economic development in which the private sector would lead investment and growth, and the state would regulate markets and increase efficiency in providing public and quasi-public goods.

Initially, the capitalization mechanism promised that a 51 percent share of each firm would remain in Bolivian hands. This would accomplish the dual objectives of democratizing business ownership and stimulating investment and broad-based growth. Along with regulation, the promise was one of growth and efficiency under private-sector leadership, coupled with social equity embodied in an effort to avoid further wealth concentration.

At the time of implementation, the promise of majority control by Bolivians at large had to be abandoned. Foreign enterprises demanded at least a 50 percent share and control of each company; without this concession, it would have been difficult to allay their fear of politically based interference and intervention. Majority private control, the argument went, guaranteed managerial and technological improvements. In addition, that foreign firms' payments would be invested (rather than fill government coffers) would relieve long-standing capital constraints and promote increased coverage rates, quality, and employment.

This argument was directed toward reducing the fear that the government, awash in newfound money, would immediately spend it on social or infrastructure projects that, however well-intentioned, would fail to have an enduring positive effect on growth and responsible financial management.

Conflicts of the Process

Approval of the Capitalization Law in March 1994 authorized the executive power to contribute state firms' assets to create mixed enterprises, known as SAMs (*Sociedades Anónimas Mixtas*). The law authorized transfer of portions of these firms to their workers and the population at large. In addition, it allowed the government to sell capital increasing shares at international auctions.

The law's approval was feasible because the governing party enjoyed a congressional majority through a coalition with smaller parties.[36] This majority was key to approving all other relevant laws mentioned above, which enabled the executive to specify their application through extensive detailed regulatory decrees (*decretos reglamentarios*). The opposition parties later claimed that the laws the government promoted, including capitalization law, were prepared and approved without regard to any opposition or debate.[37]

One critical issue was the position of organized labor. On the one hand, Central Obrera Boliviana (COB), the broadest labor organization, expressed opposition to the entire process. On the other, the government decided to turn workers into partial owners to gain their support.

From the outset, COB, much weakened since the 1980s, rejected the idea of capitalization, arguing instead for strengthening state firms' finances and management. Despite its unwavering position, it could not prevent direct contact between the government and worker and employee unions

---

36. The Nationalist Revolutionary Movement (MNR) (Movimiento Nacionalista Revolucionario), the main political party in government, acted in coalition with the Civic Solidarity Union (UCS) (Unión Cívica Solidaridad), Free Bolivia Movement (MBL) (Movimiento Bolivia Libre), and Tupaj Katari Revolutionary Movement (MRTK) (Movimiento Revolucionario Tupaj Katari).

37. Mainly the Leftist Revolutionary Movement (MIR) (Movimiento de Izquierda Revolucionaria) and Nationalist Democratic Action (ADN) (Acción Democrática Nacionalista).

in firms to be capitalized. While these initially remained loyal to COB, their leaders initiated direct contact with the government, seeking to achieve the best deal for their members.

Capitalization began with ENDE, perhaps in part because its workers were not as organized as those in other state firms. In any event, they were the first to agree to partial ownership in exchange for supporting (at least not actively opposing) the process. ENTEL workers were the second group to fall in line, after negotiating an agreement that guaranteed benefits and job security. Similarly, YPFB capitalization was made viable, and workers obtained a significant share in Transredes.

In the case of ENFE, the government guaranteed job security for a seven-month period, but workers obtained a relatively small ownership share. The firm's sale price was well below book value, an outcome that workers perhaps foresaw. The LAB union posed the strongest opposition to capitalization but supported it once job security was guaranteed.

Industry-specific conflicts arose in the telecommunications sector when the government sought to transfer ENTEL (with a period of exclusivity) in the long distance market and introduce local-sector competition. Independent cooperatives that provided local phone services strongly opposed abandoning their monopolies. In response, the government asked that they transform into fully private firms in order to attract private investment and compete in open markets. The cooperatives rejected the request, continuing to demand a period of exclusivity in local service. The government complied, but imposed price-cap regulation, together with expansion and quality goals.

Criticisms

Not surprisingly, the capitalization process spawned considerable criticism. Four much debated issues were that:

- The state enterprises to be capitalized had been run to benefit only a small group of bureaucrats and politicians and that, even before capitalization, these firms had been a source of corruption and rent-seeking behavior. State-enterprise workers rejected this notion, arguing that earlier corruption and inefficiency had been introduced or aggravated by the free-market reforms the government now wanted to implement further.

- Bolivians would always have a majority stake in new enterprises (i.e., never less than 51 percent). The government eventually settled for retaining 50 percent of equity, divided between workers and private pension funds. Since management's 50 percent was concentrated while the remainder was dispersed, management effectively controlled the firms. This upset some citizens, who claimed the promise of domestic control had been broken. The government objected to this characterization, arguing that investors wanted 51 percent, but that, thanks to its negotiation, they settled for less.

- Foreign management would allow the transfer of technological and managerial skills, which would reduce corruption. This affirmation caused strong reaction among workers since state firms (some more than others) had historically propelled modernization in different sectors. Union leaders claimed that factors exogenous to the firms, such as the 1980s debt crisis, accounted for why their sources of funding had dried up. Indeed, lack of investment capital and foreign funding was the key justification for capitalization.

- State enterprises might be transferred hastily. Several observers noted that the government may have created the conditions for a "fire sale" by publicizing the poor state of certain firms. People suspected the government would have to absorb substantial debt and that, in the case of oil and gas, investors would be rewarded with risk-free reserves.

Change of Government

The Banzer-Quiroga administration (1997–2000)[38] campaigned on the promise to undo the capitalization process. After taking office, it proposed changes in contracts and functioning of the regulatory system, which created unease in the affected sectors and among potential investors. The World Bank recommended that contracts not be altered, and the American Embassy advocated on behalf of US firms holding contracts.

Thus, the Banzer-Quiroga government coexisted with capitalization, but constantly criticized the arrangement; key officials complained that government firms had been given away and that their transfer limited government income and reduced expenditure and social investment. It alleged that capitalization was the main cause of the recession that started in 1998–99, accounting for the government's inability to spend its way out of it.

MNR, the ruling party during capitalization and the then current opposition party, retorted that capitalization had not met all expectations, in part, because it lacked the necessary continuity. The MNR argued that reform was left in the hands of those who did not understand or support capitalization. It also made the case that external factors caused the recession, which would have been worse had capitalization not occurred.

---

38. President Hugo Banzer served four years out of his five-year term. He resigned due to ill health amid significant opposition; after his death, Vice President Jorge Quiroga assumed office for the remaining year.

Nevertheless, the MNR admitted that the reforms might require adjustments, particularly the strengthening of laws and regulation. For example, while capitalization and regulation may have led to increased natural gas reserves (from 5 to 53 trillion m^3), adjustments were necessary to improve the government's revenue share and prevent the emergence of vertical monopolies.

Why Was Capitalization Unpopular?

The conceptualization and implementation of capitalization involved controversy and acrimony, and constant public carping between proponents and opponents may well have been a major source of the program's unpopularity. Additional hypotheses can be grouped into (1) unfulfilled expectations; (2) high-profile failures; (3) ownership and corporate governance issues; and (4) problems induced by associated structural reforms, particularly pension reform.

First, the administration that implemented capitalization may have oversold it, having made excessive claims about the employment growth that would be generated and the financial dividends that would eventually accrue to the population at large. Performance on these fronts, while perhaps not poor, proved disappointing compared to the government's stated expectations.

For example, intuition leads one to expect employment declines with privatization, to the extent that state firms have too many workers to operate efficiently. Our analysis shows that declines were modest, given the size of the country's labor force. An economist's conclusion, therefore, might be that employment outcomes were not poor, especially since these firms' investment focused on capital-intensive nontradables.

The general population was led to believe that capitalization would generate large, rapid improvements in the quantity and quality of available jobs. In fact, the rate of employment growth during postcapitalization (even before the current recession) did not differ qualitatively from rates during earlier periods of stability, which may have disappointed the average voter.

Similarly, citizens may have been led to expect that foreign and domestic private investment would boom with capitalization. While investment increased, it declined significantly with the recession and the end of foreign investment commitments under capitalization—to the extent that the state's role is again becoming larger than that of the private sector (especially if investment in oil and gas is not considered), implying the need for greater public indebtedness.

Second, high-profile failures among foreign firms have increased public suspicion about the entire privatization and capitalization process. This was the case for VASP, the Brazilian airline that failed in its administration of LAB. VASP departed amid allegations of asset stripping and accounting fraud. The case of the Aguas del Tunari consortium led to the "water war" described above and the end to water-related concessions.

The third issue concerns corporate governance. Despite improvement in output, productivity, and consumer welfare, the Bolivian population suspects that capitalized enterprises are run mainly with the interests of the majority (foreign) owners in mind and that the regulatory system has been unable to adequately restrain this tendency. Of course, news of the deluge of US corporate scandals has accorded these problems further salience.

With respect to ownership, the Bolivian population expected that, through its share in capitalized enterprises (about 45 percent), it would rapidly come to share again in profit flows. Firms have not paid dividends as large as those predicted, which have directly affected the elderly. People suspect—fed by political opponents' assertions—that the firms have found ways to transfer profits to their home countries rather than pay them out in Bolivia.

Negative popular perception was a particular headache for the Sanchez de Lozada administration, whose party initiated implementation of capitalization. This administration's return to power occurred after an acrimonious election in which the MNR captured only about 20 percent of the vote, but, by gaining first place, nonetheless put together a coalition in parliament; in short, the administration was vulnerable. Like the preceding Banzer-Quiroga government, it was buffeted by periodic waves of protest, particularly from rural unions, including those tied to coca-growing regions.

A key campaign promise was to return the Bonosol (the old-age payment described above) to its initial level of about $240. Because of the low flow of dividends, however, the Common Capitalization Fund (FCC), which pays this benefit, could not afford it. As a short-term solution, the government forced individuals, through individual retirement accounts (FCI), to buy FCC commitments. This arbitrary measure was much debated (it could be viewed as a confiscation and forceful redistribution of private property by the very administration that had earlier been its staunch defender).

More generally, the recession and a large budget deficit severely constrained the administration's ability to spend and stimulate the economy. The deficit was tied to the pension reform that the original Sanchez de Lozada administration had introduced, along with capitalization.

Before reform, Bolivia's social security system consisted of a basic pension fund and several complementary funds, all of which were pay-as-you-go. Coverage (about 12 percent of the economically active population) and the worker-to-retiree ratio (3:1) were low. Moreover, financial transparency was lacking, investments were subject to political interference, and hyperinflation of the 1980s had substantially eroded reserves. Management costs—about 17 percent of contributions—were high, as were evasion and debt. By 1995, the system had become insolvent. The National Pension Secretariat estimated that the government would have to absorb a pension system deficit, which, by 2016, would reach 0.6 percent of GDP, and reaching 4.3 percent by 2060.

In 1996, the Pension Law introduced the ICF and CCF system, both administered by private administrators. The Pension Law also created a transition regime characterized as follows:

- The national treasury finances the benefits of current pensioners and those who fulfill requirements under the previous system.

- Persons, who contributed to the former system but who do not yet qualify for retirement, switch to the new system with pension adjustments.

- Agreements with strategic sectors (e.g., military, police, judiciary, and universities) require treasury financing.

- The later Caracollo and Patacamaya agreements, in response to social unrest, resulted in a substantial increase in the average pension, which also require treasury financing.

By 2002, the new system had nearly doubled coverage (still low by international standards), mobilized savings to more than $1 billion, and introduced greater transparency in fund management. However, transition costs have been substantially higher than expected. In 2002, the direct financial cost of reform represented 5 percent of GDP, an amount not expected to decrease for another decade. Transition costs, in turn, put the government under substantial fiscal pressure. The administration attempted to raise taxes in February 2003 but after substantial violence, was forced to withdraw the initiative.

A national discussion ensued on whether Bolivia should sell natural gas to the United States, Mexico, and possibly other countries and, if it did, whether to run the pipeline through Peru or Chile.[39] For many Bolivians, this commercial deal added insult to injury, with respect to the perceived damage caused by capitalization. At issue was the belief that Bolivians should be the first to benefit from the country's natural resources (in this case, through the installation of domestic natural gas networks; conversion of vehicles to natural gas; and installation of industrial plants, thereby adding local value). Another issue was the belief that petroleum-related rents from capitalization should effectively reach the Bolivian people through investments in education, health, and infrastructure. In both cases, the widespread perception was that the government represented corporate and political, rather than popular, interests. A third, shorter-term issue was pressure for more oil and gas rents to help the government reduce its fiscal deficit.

---

39. Bolivia lost its coastal territories to Chile in the 1879 war. For this reason, many Bolivians strongly opposed pipeline construction through Chile, even though technical studies suggested that it was the optimal commercial option. In the end, clear information on the precise cost differential was never provided.

In the end, these issues helped catalyze and unify all opposition to the Sanchez de Lozada government, which, in October 2003, began to lose control of the country in the face of widespread protests, strikes, and road blockages. Attempts to reassert authority backfired, resulting in dozens of deaths, increased opposition, and finally the resignation of Sanchez de Lozada (who was replaced by his vice president, Carlos Mesa). These conflicts were both complex and multifaceted;[40] thus, it is impossible to pinpoint the exact role the opposition to capitalization—or even the natural gas export controversy—played in the eventual collapse of the government.

One of the new government's first actions was to declare that any decision on natural gas exports would be made only after a referendum. In addition, the government promised a new Constitutional Convention (*Asamblea Constituyente*) to redefine the Bolivian state to make it more representative of people's interests. Other short-term goals included increased taxes on private oil-sector firms and a stronger role for YPFB, the original state-run oil company.

With regard to the gas industry, the public was told that the enormous expansion in Bolivia's proven and expected reserves since capitalization would generate great wealth for the country. On closer examination, however, citizens might wonder how this wealth would ever reach them; for example, the companies in which the Bolivian population owns shares—mainly Chaco, Andina, and Transredes—are arguably no longer central industry players; thus, the touted windfall gains may, in fact, accrue to firms in which they have no stake.

The Bolivian population has gained from relatively high royalties on gas production and an ex-post high price on the gas sold to Brazil (this price was negotiated before); as in the 1990 legislation, royalties were set equal to 50 percent of wellhead value. However, the 1996 law reduced the royalty rate on new wells to 18 percent. Thus, in the future, royalties will become a less important income source.

In principle, profit taxes and introduction of a surtax are to compensate for these drops; however, in practice, these revenue sources have not—and are not expected to—fully make up for the shortfall. For that, the country will need substantially greater export volumes.

In addition, the Bolivian public perceives that capitalized firms are adept at tax evasion. Recently, for example, a prominent politician made the charge (which was, to our knowledge, left uncontested and unexplained by the capitalized firms) that the Bolivian Catholic University pays more taxes than any capitalized oil enterprise.

The gas industry has provided the concerned public with other examples of alleged corporate malfeasance in collusion with government officials.

---

40. Many other issues played a role, including land tenure and interregional and ethnic conflicts.

For example, in the negotiations with Brazil, the giant San Alberto and San Antonio fields were classified as new (hence paying substantially lower royalties); however, YPFB workers insisted these fields had long been discovered. While the fields' status was never clarified entirely, a large portion of the Bolivian public had the impression that excessive concessions had been made.

Summary and Conclusions

Bolivia's response to its 1982–85 recession and instability was initiating a transition from a state-led to a market-driven economy. By 1989, it had liberated key prices in the economy, and by 1993, it had a privatization law in place. However, the state continued as the main investor in the economy, and remained dependent on foreign debt. Although growth resumed, it did so at rates that would not significantly reduce poverty.

The 1993–97 period—the most aggressive in terms of structural reform—concentrated on two redefinitions: (1) the state-market frontier, as privatization and regulation replaced government firms, and (2) central-local frontiers within the state, as local jurisdictions were given greater funding and responsibilities. These redefinitions implied that the private sector (particularly the foreign one) would lead investment and growth, while the state would regulate markets and increase efficiency in providing public and quasi-public goods.

In addition to the capitalization mechanism used to attract foreign investment, FDI replaced government foreign debt as the engine of growth. Growth increased somewhat, reaching 5.3 percent by the end of 1998. At that time, a series of external shocks hit, beginning with the Asian crisis and continuing with the Brazilian and Argentine crises. Although the domestic response to these external events remains a matter of debate, the economy was pulled into a recession that persists to date. By the end of 2002, private investment had fallen substantially, forcing a return to government (debt-financed) investment as the main source of growth—this time within an environment where limited resources can only be directed toward production of public and quasi-public goods.

This bit of history demonstrates that any evaluation of capitalization must consider the mechanism as part of a structural reform aimed at broader objectives. It also highlights two periods under which capitalization and regulation had to perform. The first period, 1994–98, featured reform implementation and initial positive results within an environment of stability and economic growth. The second period, 1999–present, is characterized by reform consolidation in an environment of economic recession and increasing political difficulties.

A complete evaluation of capitalization and privatization is difficult; admittedly, this chapter provides only initial insights into the issue. At the simplest level, the key goal of capitalization was to attract foreign investment into the affected sectors, and evidence suggests the process met with success at this level.

Combined with regulation, additional positive outcomes were increased access to utilities services and significant expansions in proven gas reserves. The benefits of both outcomes did not bypass the poorer segments of Bolivian society. In fact, welfare improvements for households were, in certain cases, greatest in lower-income quintiles. In addition, productivity increased nearly across the board, and most firms have remained moderately profitable.

On the negative side, employment decreased (although decreases were the partial flipside of productivity increases and were small relative to the economy overall). In addition, prices for certain utilities increased; with the exception of the Cochabamba water concession, price increases were overwhelmed by increased access in the welfare calculations.

The reader should note several caveats to these conclusions:

- It is difficult to disentangle the effects of privatization and capitalization from introduction of regulation.

- It is impossible to fully isolate the effects of these processes from those of concurrent events, such as introduction of new technologies and enhanced competitive forces. Moreover, the economic slowdown that started in 1999 introduced substantially strained performance of the capitalized sector. Without this event, our assessments of these reforms might have differed notably.

- Many of these results, particularly those regarding consumer welfare, refer only to the population in the department capitals. Access and welfare in general remain significantly lower in the rest of the country.

Despite these concerns, our assessment suggests that the reforms were fairly successful. That popular opinion does not agree with this conclusion may have resulted from the government's having oversold reforms, and promising more (e.g., in terms of job creation) than it could reasonably deliver. Moreover, the reputation of reform has been hurt by high-profile failures and a perceived weakness in Bolivia's regulatory and corporate governance frameworks.

We speculate that a key lesson from the Bolivian experience is that private ownership should be kept as a credible threat and a real option to any other firm organization and in any activity. This threat allows privatization to generate spillovers; for example, several cooperatives have improved their management and become more competitive. Finally, Bolivian experience reaffirms the adage: In many sectors, introducing private participation and market forces is no panacea; the specifics under which privatization is implemented matter greatly.

References

Banks, J., R. Blundell, and A. Lewbel. 1996. Tax Reform and Welfare Measurement: Do We Need Demand System Estimation? *Economic Journal* 106, no. 438: 1227–41.

Barja, G. 2000. Las Leyes Sectorales y el Sistema de Regulación Sectorial. In Fundación Milenio, Las Reformas Estructurales en Bolivia. Tomo II. La Paz: Fundación Milenio.

Barja, G., D. McKenzie, and M. Urquiola. 2004. Capitalization and Privatization in Bolivia: An Approximation to an Evaluation. Photocopy. Center for Global Development, Washington.

Deaton, A. 1989. Rice Prices and Income Distribution in Thailand: A Non-Parametric Approach. *The Economic Journal* 99: 1–37.

Ennis, H., and S. Pinto. 2002. Privatization and Income Distribution in Argentina. West Virginia University. Photocopy.

Estache, A., V. Foster, and Q. Wodon. 2002. *Accounting for Poverty in Infrastructure Reform: Learning from Latin America's Experience*. WBI Development Studies. Washington: World Bank Institute.

Foster, J., J. Greer, and E. Thorbecke. 1984. A Class of Decomposable Poverty Measures. *Econometrica* 52: 761–65.

GOB (Government of Bolivia). 2001. Bolivia: Poverty Reduction Strategy Paper. Government of Bolivia. Photocopy.

ITU (International Telecommunication Union). 2001. *Yearbook of Statistics: Telecommunication Services 1991–2000*. Geneva: International Telecommunication Union.

McKenzie, D., and D. Mookherjee. 2003. The Distributive Impact of Privatization in Latin America: An Overview of Evidence from Four Countries. *Economía* 3 (no. 2): 161–218.

Pension Superintendence, Bolivia. 2000. *Pensions Bulletin*, Year 4, no. 13 (April–June): 91.

SIRESE (Sistema de Regulación Sectorial). 2000. *La Regulación Sectorial en Bolivia, 1999*. Annual Report. La Paz: Superintendencia General.

Appendix 4A
Household Surveys

For household and individual-level data, including socioeconomic characterizations, we used three rounds (fifth, sixth, and seventh in 1992, 1993, and 1994, respectively) of the Integrated Household Survey (EIH) (Encuesta Integrada de Hogares) and one round (first in 1999) of the Ongoing Household Survey (ECH) (Encuesta Continua de Hogares). The EIH was collected in department capitals and had a sample size of 5,829 households in 1992, 4,270 households in 1993, and 6,128 households in 1994. Although the ECH has national coverage, for comparability, we used only the 1,324 households, which corresponded to the same department capitals as the EIH.

These surveys contain essential access and consumption information. Earlier rounds of the EIH contained certain information on utility access and expenditures, but lacked comparable questions on other expenditure items (meaning that these surveys cannot be used in consumer welfare calculations that require expenditure shares).

Because the telecommunications, telephone, and water reforms occurred in 1995 and 1996, the 1994 survey is considered "before" and the 1999 survey an "after" observation. We also focus on the 1992 survey and use annualized changes over the 1992–94 period to control for annualized changes over the 1994–99 privatization period. This comparison is aided by the country's having had a similar economic performance and relatively stable political structure during both periods. The 1993 wave of the EIH was used only in the Engel curve regressions to provide more points of temporal and spatial price variation over which to estimate price elasticities.

For employment and wage information, firms in the privatized sectors considered (i.e., water, electricity, and telecommunications) are relatively small employers in Bolivia; thus, the household surveys offer only small samples of workers in these industries. The 1999 survey asked respondents to state both the sector and the firm they worked for. In the electricity sector, no respondent declared that s/he worked for the electricity firms mentioned in the survey section. Indeed, many respondents worked in the electricity sector as electricians or electric appliance vendors. In light of this reality, administrative information on employment and wage levels were collected from firms and regulatory agencies, providing the basis for our analysis of privatization's labor-market effects. Additional administrative information on quality-related issues was collected directly.

Appendix 4B
Access Definitions and Utilities Expenditure

The household surveys included various questions with regard to utilities access. In all cases, access must be measured based on whether households have the utility in question, rather than their having the option to connect. In Argentina, Ennis and Pinto (2002) found average take-up rates for electricity and water were 99.9 and 97.4 percent, respectively; thus, determining access based on what households are using should be a reasonable approximation. Based on the household survey questions, we define measures of access that are fully consistent across the surveys listed in appendix 4A (unless otherwise noted).

Access to Water. A household is considered connected to the water network and therefore has access if it declares it has a water connection either inside its dwelling or otherwise within the building the dwelling is a part of. Households obtaining water from a public faucet, well, delivery truck, river, lake, or other sources are not considered to have access to the water network.

Expenditure on Water. The surveys directly ask for total monthly expenditure on water from all sources.

Access to Electricity. The 1992 and 1994 EIH directly ask whether the dwelling has electricity, while the 1999 ECH asks whether the household uses electricity for lighting. A household is therefore defined as having access if it has electricity or uses electricity for lighting. Most use it for lighting, and given the 1999 access rates of nearly 100 percent, we do not believe the 1999 measure is much understated compared to earlier measures.

Expenditure on Electricity. The surveys directly ask for total monthly expenditure on electricity service.

Access to Telephone. The 1994 EIH directly asks whether a household has a telephone, while the 1999 ECH asks whether the household has a fixed-line or cellular telephone service. A household with a telephone or telephone service is defined as having access. The 1992 and 1993 EIH do not contain a comparable question; thus, telephone access is available only for 1994 and 1999. Only the 1999 survey asks for expenditure on telecommunications separately; therefore, we used expenditure on communications.

Access to and Expenditure on Communications. All surveys asked consumers for expenditure on communications, including telephone and mail expenses. Households reporting positive communications expenditure were defined as having access to communications, which was a proxy for telephone access. Although using communications expenditure is likely to overstate telephone access somewhat, the change in access to communications between 1994 and 1999 has a 0.945 correlation at the decile level with changes in access to telephones over the same period. This measure should therefore be a good proxy.

5

Argentina's Privatization:
Effects on Income Distribution

HUBERTO M. ENNIS and SANTIAGO M. PINTO

Until the 1990s, Argentina's government directly administered a substantial portion of the country's economy. Telephone and electricity, fuel production and distribution, railways, banks, and a range of other services—from hotels to television stations—were all part of the public sector. In August 1989, the Public Sector Reform Law (No. 23696) was signed. The law stated a set of general rules to be used in privatizing most of Argentina's publicly owned enterprises (POEs). In 1997, the first major privatization—the national telephone company—occurred and, by 1997, most of the privatization plan had been completed.

This chapter evaluates this reform's distributive effects by estimating privatization's effects on Argentina's consumers, workers, and fiscal condition. We use survey data where available and estimate the change in standard measures of income distribution and poverty attributable to privatization. We restrict our analysis to the 1989–97 period. More recently, Argentina has experienced pronounced macroeconomic instability. The

Huberto M. Ennis is a senior economist at the Federal Reserve Bank of Richmond. Santiago M. Pinto is assistant professor at West Virginia University. The original version of this chapter was part of the project Effects of Privatization on Income Distribution in Latin America, supported by the Inter-American Development Bank (IDB) and Universidad de las Americas (UDLA), Mexico. The authors wish to thank the project coordinator, Luis Felipe López-Calva, and other project participants for their comments on earlier drafts. The authors also thank John Nellis, Nora Lustig, Sabeen Hassanali, and seminar participants at the National University of La Plata, Argentina, for their comments. In addition, they acknowledge Leonardo Gasparini, Fernando Navajas, and Sebastian Galiani for their help in data collection. The views expressed here are those of the authors and do not reflect the views of the Federal Reserve Bank of Richmond or the Board of Governors.

role that privatized firms have played in this crisis is a critical issue requiring careful study; however, the issue is beyond the scope of this chapter.

Two factors limited our ability to obtain definitive results. First, the available data were of poor quality, thereby restricting their analysis to the household sample in the Greater Buenos Aires area. Second, during the period that privatization occurred, Argentina's economy underwent significant transformation, including substantial trade liberalization and long-term macroeconomic stabilization. Thus, concurrent changes in economic organization made it more difficult to identify the specific effects of each reform.

Reform Period (1989–97): An Overview

During privatization, Argentina's economy underwent significant macroeconomic changes (table 5.1). In early 1991, a strict stabilization program was implemented, bringing an end to hyperinflation, which had started in 1989. The 1994 collapse of the Mexican economy also affected Argentina's macroeconomic aggregates.

As table 5.1 shows, the government deficits of the 1980s were a key factor in increasing pressure toward privatization. In several cases, privatization was organized to maximize the immediate revenue accrued to the government. In addition, the level of investment in most public utilities was inadequate. Total gross fixed investment fell from 23 percent of GDP in the early 1980s to about 15 a decade later. Lack of investment was part of a more general phenomenon with 20 years of no aggregate economic growth. After 1992, investment levels gradually recovered, reaching 24 percent of GDP by 1997–98.

Per capita income bottomed out after the hyperinflation of 1989–90. From 1991 to 1998, per capita income grew steadily, with only a short slowdown in 1995 in reaction to the Tequila crisis. Beginning in 1992, income inequality also increased, partly affected by the plan for structural reform. Table 5.1 shows that the Gini coefficient dropped 10 percent immediately after stabilization; subsequently, it rose steadily, reaching levels that in 1997 were 7 percent higher than the average for the 1985–90 period. However, the economic conditions that determined the evolution of income inequality during the 1990s inherently differed from those of the 1980s. While annual inflation averaged 50 percent during the 1980s, the decade of the 1990s was characterized by sustained price stability.[1]

Poverty indicators show an important decline immediately after hyperinflation ended. After 1993, however, the percentage of households below the poverty line increased significantly and never recovered to these low

---

1. Canavese, Escudero, and Alvaredo (1999) have shown that the 1980s inflation was especially harmful to low-income households.

Table 5.1   Argentina's macroeconomic indicators, 1985–97 (percent)

Year	Inflation rate	Urban unemployment rate	Fiscal surplus (percent GDP)	GDP growth rate	Gini coefficient
1985	672.2	6.1	–4.0	–6.7	40.9
1986	90.1	5.5	–3.1	7.1	41.7
1987	131.3	5.8	–5.0	3.0	44.4
1988	387.7	6.3	–6.0	–2.1	44.9
1989	4,923.6	7.6	–3.8	–6.9	51.5
1990	1,343.9	7.4	–1.5	–2.3	46.1
Average, 1985–90	1,258.1	6.5	–3.9	–1.3	44.9
1991	84.0	6.4	–0.5	11.8	46.1
1992	17.3	7.0	0.6	11.0	44.2
1993	7.4	9.6	1.2	6.4	44.3
1994	3.8	11.5	–0.1	5.8	45.7
1995	1.6	17.4	–0.5	–2.8	48.4
1996	0.1	17.2	–1.9	5.5	48.4
1997	0.3	14.9	–1.5	8.1	48.0
Average, 1991–97	16.4	12.0	–0.4	6.5	46.4

Sources: Bebczuk and Gasparini (2001); Gasparini and Escudero (1999).

levels. During 1991–96, the proportion of households with unsatisfied basic needs decreased from 10.1 percent to 6.1 percent. This decline may, in fact, be directly associated with increased access to public services related to privatization.

Structural reforms—government rationalization, privatization, and trade liberalization—brought increased unemployment. The high, sustained rate of unemployment may explain, in part, the evolution of inequality and poverty.

Privatization Process

Argentina's privatization program was large relative to the size of the country's economy: 154 privatization contracts were signed during the 1990s. The federal revenue collected from privatization in the 1990s reached $19.44 billion.[2] During 1991–92, these revenues represented more than 1 percent of GDP and about 10 percent of public revenues. Table 5.2 shows the sectors subject to privatization, total revenue from sale, and dates of privatization. (The list includes only companies privatized or given in concession by the federal government; some firms were sold by subnational governments.)

---

2. This figure understates the true amount of revenue obtained from privatization, since it excludes revenue from royalties received from POEs that were privatized as concessions and revenues from privatization of provincial and local POEs.

Table 5.2 Privatization of federal publicly owned enterprises, 1990–99

Sector privatized	Total revenue (millions of US dollars)	Dates of privatization
Oil and gas production	7,594	1990–99
Electricity	3,908	1992–98
Communications	2,982	1990–92
Gas transport and distribution	2,950	1992–98
Transportation (airlines, rail, ships)	756	1990–94
Petrochemical and oil derivatives	554	1991–95
Banks and finance	394	1994–99
Steel	158	1992–92
Other	126	1991–99
Railways	Concession	1991–95
Highways	Concession	1990–93
Ports	Concession	1990–94
Airports	Concession	1998
Radio and television	Concession	1990–91
Water and sewerage	Concession	1993
Mail service	Concession	1997
Total revenue	**19,422**	

Source: Argentina Ministry of the Economy.

The main revenue sources were the oil and gas sectors; together with electricity, they accounted for 60 percent of sales proceeds.

The selling mechanism most frequently used was international, competitive tenders with open bidding. Public utilities were tendered by price after a prequalification stage. In the case of utility concessions, exclusivity of service provision was usually granted for a fixed period. Whenever possible, competition was favored (i.e., in the wholesale energy market). In addition, several features of the sale contract were used to please special interest groups and, hence, find political support. For example, in most cases, employment stability was guaranteed to certain personnel of companies, and sometimes this extended to tenure and level of unionization.

Effects on Public Utilities

Privatization had significant effects on Argentina's public utilities. We focus on the effects of the privatization process on the telecommunications, electricity, water, and natural gas sectors.

Telecommunications

Until 1990, Argentina's national public telephone company, ENTEL (Empresa Nacional de Telecomunicaciones), controlled most of the country's service. In November 1990, the government transferred the company to the private sector as part of Argentina's first public-service concession.

ENTEL was thus divided into the north market (Telecom) and the south market (Telefónica de Argentina). These two companies became the exclusive providers of basic telephone and international services (in their respective areas) for seven years; a two-year extension followed, based on satisfactory performance. The companies' 51 percent control of shares was sold in a competitive, international public biding. Tariffs were regulated, using a British-style retail price index (RPI), minus a factor for innovation (RPI − x) mechanism adjusted every five years.[3] Certain service and quality obligations were imposed in the concession contract. Of the total number of shares, 10 percent were reserved for employees and 5 percent for cooperatives. French (32.5 percent), Italian (32.5 percent), US (10 percent), and Argentinean (25 percent) shareholders acquired the Telecom shares. Telefónica de Argentina's major shareholders were the United States (20 percent), Argentina (14.56 percent), and Spain (10 percent). Public bonds were used to cover a large proportion of the initial payment.

At the time of privatization, Argentina's regulatory entity, National Communication Commission (CNC), established a tariff discount of up to 25 percent for pensioners collecting the minimum payment. After privatization, regulatory changes were introduced that were expected to have distributive effect. For example, low-consumption customers were favored through increasing tariff blocks. Before January 1997, interurban calls cross-subsidized urban services; hence, the rest of the country subsidized the Greater Buenos Aires area (Chisari and Estache 1997).[4] In 1997, consumers were divided into four tariff groups (households, commercial consumers, professionals, and government), and within-group charges became uniform across country regions. At the time of privatization, regulation mandated that the supplier could suspend service if a bill had not been paid 30 days after the due date. Because of high reconnection charges, this policy tended to increase the cost for users with credit constraints and highly variable income. New postsale, regulatory changes limited this suspension of service only to outgoing calls for the first 60 days (after that the full service could be discontinued). In addition, in 1997–98, both companies were mandated to install 1,000 semipublic phones for receiving calls located in schools, aid centers, and other intermediate associations without charging connection or fixed monthly fees.

After privatization, quality and productivity improved. For example, the average annual growth rate of lines installed increased from 5.2 percent in 1980–89 to 12.2 percent in 1991–97, while the rate for public telephones

---

3. The RPI − x mechanism adjusts prices according to variations in the retail price index minus a factor, x, estimating the degree of technological progress and productivity.

4. In October–November 1999, competition was introduced in the long distance market; the new companies were allowed to operate and offer services in each other's previously exclusive areas.

grew from 7.6 to 25.3 percent over the same period. Lines available and lines installed per employee increased considerably; other key quality measures also improved (e.g., pending repair orders, repair waiting time, and network digitalization) (Ennis and Pinto 2003).

Electricity

Before reform, POEs provided electricity generation, transmission, and distribution. Provincial governments controlled distribution. In the case of the Greater Buenos Aires area, SEGBA, a public company, was the only provider. Restructuring began in 1991. Each of the three stages of production was subject to a different regulatory framework. Competition was allowed at the generation level. Transmission and distribution, when privatized, became regulated private monopolies (concessions). The regulatory mechanism for these monopolies was basically an RPI-x system, with the productivity gains x adjusted every five years. Private companies in the distribution segment hold roughly 70 percent of the market (covering more than 60 percent of the country's total population). Furthermore, the three largest companies control about 50 percent of the market.

Private firms that trade daily in the wholesale market or MEM (Mercado Eléctrico Mayorista) hold about 60 percent of Argentina's electricity generation. This industry is less concentrated, with the three largest firms providing about 30 percent of total supply (Millan, Lora, and Micco 2001). MEM's CAMMESA (Compañía Administradora) determines the spot price every day according to estimated demand and cost-quantities schedules that the generation firms submit. Distribution companies and large users represent wholesale-market demand; they submit their expected demands to CAMMESA, which uses this information to determine the spot price. Bosch, de Gimbatti, and Giovagnoli (1999) provide a careful description of this system. Other large users can also sign contracts directly with firms in the generation stage.

Transmission is done through two systems: STEEAT (Sistema de Transporte de Energía Eléctrica de Alta Tensión) and STEEDT (Distribución Troncal). Transener obtained a 95-year concession of STEEAT, a system that connects every region in the country to the same electricity network. STEEDT distributes electricity within a specific region from the generators to the distribution companies. The entire transmission system is subject to the principle of open access, which allows indiscriminate network access when committed capacity is not compromised.

As of 2000, 70 percent of distribution had been privatized. EDENOR, EDESUR, and EDELAP are the main private distribution companies, created after SEGBA's privatization. The Law established that pricing should be in accordance with cost and, hence, rules out cross-subsidization. Subsidies are available for pensioners, charities, and government-financed nonprofit organizations. (ANSES, the social security agency, reimburses companies for pensioners collecting minimum pension.)[5] In addition, the National Electricity Fund finances broader regional subsidies. In 1994, Edenor and Edesur signed an agreement with the government to provide electricity to "very poor" neighborhoods in special ways, such as use of collective meters. The agreement affected 650,000 users who previously had been illegally connected, with attendant inefficiencies and safety issues. The program succeeded: Companies' collection rate reached 85 percent in 1997 and quality of service improved significantly.

At the national level, privatization considered two concession areas: (1) the concentrated market, connected to the national or provincial distribution system, and (2) the scattered market, with no electricity supply. Users in scattered areas are serviced by alternative systems (e.g., diesel-run), and have special tariffs, with provinces paying any associated subsidy.

Privatization of SEGBA. In 1992, energy generation, transmission, and distribution facilities in the Greater Buenos Aires were sold. Three companies were created to handle the distribution stage: Edenor, Edesur, and Edelap. Edenor has a 95-year concession with the exclusive franchise to distribute electricity in the northern section of Greater Buenos Aires. The concession area comprises a territory of about 4,650 square kilometers (km²), with a total population of more than 7 million and 2.2 million customers. During its first two years, Edenor suffered losses. Over the 1992–95 period, its owners invested $400 million and reduced energy losses from 30 percent to 16 percent—mainly through improved metering, invoicing, and collection of charges for electricity delivered but not previously paid for. Edesur distributes electricity in the southern section of Greater Buenos Aires. The company started operations in September 1992 (at the same time as Edenor), and has some 2 million customers. Edelap, which started operation in December 1992, is the electricity distributor for Greater La Plata, with 270,000 customers.

Water and Sewage

In many areas of Argentina, water and sewage services have been privatized. A national water and sanitation organization (Ente Nacional de Obras Hídricas de Saneamiento) finances water and sewage projects across the country and strengthens regulatory capacity at the provincial level. The two main markets are the city and province of Buenos Aires. Water service in the city of Buenos Aires was privatized in the early 1990s, while privatization in the province occurred in 1998.[6]

---

5. Pensioners subject to these benefits are given a 50 percent discount on the fixed charge and the first 210 kilowatt hours (kWh) of electricity used in the last two months; all consumption above 210 kWh is billed at the normal tariffs, and users with bimonthly consumption above 430 kWh receive no discount.

6. The effect of this privatization is not part of this study's analysis.

Privatization of water and sewage services affected low-income households in several ways. The main advantage was opportunity for increased access; however, not everyone benefited from the extended network. Some households, for example, cannot afford to take on the new obligations.

City of Buenos Aires. Aguas Argentinas, S.A. is the sole provider of potable water and services for the city of Buenos Aires. In April 1993, the company obtained an exclusive, 30-year concession; as of June 30, 1998, it supplied potable water to some 7.8 million residents and sewage services to about 5.9 million. Tariff adjustments are based on a cost-plus rule. The concession contract stipulated service obligations, investment requirements, and quality standards. At the time of privatization, metering of water consumption was limited to only 15 percent of connections. After privatization, some users were allowed to switch to the metering option. If meters were unavailable or the household chose not to switch, a fixed charge was billed. If the customer chose metering, fixed charges were reduced 50 percent (Chisari and Estache 1997, Abdala 1996). The licensee can charge interest if bills are not paid on time and cut off the service 180 days after the due date (low-income users and hospitals may be exempt after government evaluation). In general, residents in the serviced area are required to enter the network. If they prefer to have their own water well and not connect to the network, they must obtain permission from the licensee, who will accept the request upon verifying that water from the alternative source meets established quality standards.

Province of Buenos Aires. In 1998, the provincial government of Buenos Aires decided to privatize AGOSBA, provider of water and sewage services in 50 of the province's 134 municipalities. AGOSBA's territory was divided into six concession areas, and potential private operators were invited to bid on any combination of the six. The privatization process consisted of two parts: (1) a technical offer presenting the credentials of prospective concession operators, demonstrating their ability to meet legal, technical, and financial requirements, and (2) an economic offer, which was a one-time payment to the province. The rules allowed for bidding on more than one area, but a single bidder could not be awarded all areas. In the end, five concession areas went to one operator, ABA (Agua de Buenos Aires), while the remaining one went to the consortium AGBA (Aguas del Gran Buenos Aires). ABA began operations in July 1999 and AGBA in January 2000. The two concessions have exclusive rights to service these areas for 30 years.

Natural Gas

Prior to privatization, the natural gas industry consisted of two companies: GE (Gas del Estado) and YPF (Yacimientos Petrofíleros Fiscales). In 1992,

GE was privatized and awarded a 35-year concession. A new regulatory institution, ENARGAS (Ente Nacional Regulador del Gas) was created, and a new set of sector regulations was established. The industry was divided into three segments: production, transportation, and distribution. Sector reform also entailed creation of wholesale and retail markets. In the wholesale market, producers, distributors, customers, and wholesalers determined prices and volumes. In the retail market, the regulator ENARGAS set the ceiling price. Sector competition was encouraged. For example, access to transportation and distribution was open to third parties, and transportation capacity could be resold. Producers and transmission companies could not hold stock in distribution companies; producers, consumers, and distribution companies could not hold stock in transportation companies; and transportation companies could not trade natural gas.

Following privatization, efficiency improved. Capacity utilization increased, while consumption restrictions and leakage decreased. Since 1992, the number of consumers of network-provided natural gas increased an average of 3 percent annually, although Abdala (1998) suggests that this percentage differs little from the penetration rate GE achieved a decade earlier. Sector investment rose from an annual average of $84 million (under public ownership) to $348 million (under private control).

Data Limitations

The data useful for empirically evaluating privatization's effects on Argentina's firms and citizens are of low quality. To assess the social effects, we use systematic data from two sources: Household Expenditure Surveys (HES 1985–86 and 1996–97) and Permanent Household Surveys (PHS).[7] These surveys consider household expenditure and income variables, in addition to occupational, demographic, and educational ones. The 1985–86 HES was relatively limited with regard to reporting monetary variables. For the year surveyed, inflation was 41.3 percent; however, because the interviews were spread over a long period, comparing nominal values from interviews can be problematic. Moreover, this survey was directed only at households in the Federal Capital and Greater Buenos Aires area. The 1985–86 HES survey did not include several key questions introduced in the 1996–97 survey concerning availability of telephone and other services. While the 1996–97 HES survey covers urban households at a national level, for the purpose of comparison, we use only that portion of the survey corresponding to Greater Buenos Aires.

---

7. In August 1997, the INDEC, Argentina's statistical agency, conducted a national Social Development Survey that provided data on household quality of life and access to social services across the country. Since no comparable survey was conducted before privatization, before and after comparisons are not possible.

Biannual PHSs, available for 1980 through 1999, are conducted in May and October in Greater Buenos Aires (after 1980, other metropolitan areas were incorporated). These data are the main source for tracking employment information in Argentina's economy. Labor force participation, income, educational composition, and other household characteristics are the main components.

Consumption Effect

Utility sectors—telecommunications, natural gas, electricity, and water and sewerage—have properties that make them suitable for studying the elusive consumption effect of privatization on income distribution. First, these are the privatized sectors that most directly affect household consumption. Second, the goods and services they produce are less easily substituted by other privately produced goods.[8]

To study privatization's effects on consumption, two key factors should be considered: (1) change in relative prices, and (2) change in access to public services. To estimate changes in consumer welfare resulting from privatization, we first examine changes in expenditure in selected public services and the corresponding budget shares per income deciles. Next, we report the evolution of prices, provide potential measures of the changes in access, and estimate the change in consumer welfare. Finally, using these results, we examine the change in inequality and poverty attributable to privatization of various public services.[9]

Household Budget Shares

During 1985–86 and 1996–97, household budget shares for telecommunications, natural gas, water, and electricity experienced a remarkable boost for all deciles and public services (with the sole exception of electricity in decile 10) (table 5.3). These pronounced changes might reflect the binding quantity constraints that existed before privatization.

Telecommunications and natural gas witnessed the largest increases (lower deciles had greater increases). Generally, budget shares do not decline with income; only shares in natural gas, water, and electricity for 1996–97 followed this pattern. The substantial increase in telephone budget shares for middle deciles may indicate the significant quantity restric-

---

8. The case of natural gas still presents a significant problem; the alternative of bottled gas is readily available and used throughout Argentina.

9. Navajas (1999) provides an alternative approach to analyzing the welfare effects of price changes stemming from privatization in Argentina.

Table 5.3   Budget shares, by decile, 1985–86 and 1996–97

	1985–86			1996–97		
Decile	Telecom	Natural gas	Water and electricity	Telecom	Natural gas	Water and electricity
1	0.30	0.50	2.25	1.82	2.91	4.69
2	0.33	0.73	2.64	2.19	2.64	4.20
3	0.46	0.94	2.63	2.32	2.47	3.73
4	0.75	0.94	2.93	2.57	2.49	3.62
5	0.68	0.94	2.29	2.35	2.18	3.10
6	0.63	0.96	2.61	2.65	2.05	2.94
7	0.99	0.99	2.44	2.53	1.94	2.74
8	0.87	0.95	2.32	2.56	1.65	2.48
9	0.95	0.74	2.00	2.27	1.38	2.10
10	1.08	0.54	1.78	2.15	0.94	1.45
Average	**0.80**	**0.81**	**2.28**	**2.33**	**1.74**	**2.61**

Sources: 1985–86 HES, 1996–97 HES, INDEC.

tions and rationing in place before sector reforms. Similarly, that budget shares were increasing in income in 1985–86 likely reflects limitations in access and high-income groups' ability to circumvent restrictions by paying special fees or bribes. Furthermore, the quality of telecommunication services was low before privatization, which presumably lowered desired budget shares. For example, before privatization, the waiting time for repairing telephone lines was very long.

Price Evolution

Several previous studies evaluated price performance following privatization; however, the outcomes varied depending on the choice of baseline and final years. To estimate privatization's effects on prices of the affected services, we first discuss the evolution of prices over the period and fix preprivatization and postprivatization dates. We then evaluate the effects of price change on consumer welfare between these two dates.[10]

In general, when the government administered the firms, they used tariffs as macroeconomic instruments to control inflation. In most cases, those prices included a distributional component (Navajas and Porto 1990). Immediately before privatization, the evolution of real tariffs in most sectors reflected an explicit government policy aimed at making a POE sale more attractive. Thus, while hyperinflation caused real tariffs to decline significantly in 1989, prices started to increase in real terms in 1990–91.

---

10. Consumption data are available for only two points in time: 1) before the privatization (1985–86), and 2) after privatization (1996–97); thus, one can identify only one overall change in price elicited from any type of dynamic price behavior over the period.

Telecommunications

Before privatization, the real tariff decreased during high inflation in 1989 and then increased after 1990, fully recovering before change in ownership. This pattern is consistent with the price behavior in other sectors. After privatization, the value of each pulse went from $0.0484 in November 1990 to $0.0455 in December 1997. However, this comparison is not straightforward, as time per pulse changed according to type of call, beginning in 1990. After privatization, connection charges decreased dramatically. For residential users, connection charges fell 88 percent, while commercial and professional users saw even greater decreases (96 percent and 94 percent, respectively). In 1997, fixed charges and tariffs for local calls increased, while the price of long distance calls decreased.

The Latin American Foundation for Economic Research, known as FIEL, provides information on price evolution in the commercial and residential sectors (FIEL 1999). The foundation's index uses the basket of calls and services corresponding to 1996. It does not incorporate connection costs, but takes into account changes that occurred in the time-per-pulse for various calls. Deflated by the wholesale price index (WPI), the index of residential tariffs in constant pesos decreased nearly 18 percent from 1990 to 1998. The decrease in the index of commercial tariffs is even greater (55 percent). For the residential sector, the behavior of real tariffs after privatization has not been uniform, with tariffs declining until 1996 and rising thereafter.

Because of data limitations, the FIEL index cannot be constructed for the period before privatization. INDEC offers an alternative index, using a basket based on the 1985–86 HES. Figure 5.1 presents the annual averages of this price index between 1985 and 2000, relative to the consumer price index (CPI). In the welfare calculation that follows, we use these numbers to determine the change in telecommunication prices associated with privatization.

In 1998, connection charges in Argentina were above the international average. Fixed charges were also relatively high; even after the tariff rebalancing of 1997, long distance tariffs remained above international standards. High connection and fixed charges made telecommunication services more expensive for low-income households, who generally use it less intensively (and hence at a higher unitary price). The 1997 rebalancing decreased variable charges in long distance calls, making the tariff structure even more regressive.

Electricity

Figure 5.2 shows the evolution of electricity tariffs (including taxes) for various consumption segments.[11] In residential and commercial segments,

---

11. Residential tariffs are deflated using the CPI. Residential tariffs with taxes include value-added tax (VAT) and national taxes. Commercial and industrial tariffs are deflated by the RPI, and tariffs with taxes for these sectors only incorporate national taxes. Moreover, all tariffs include fixed and variable charges. See Ennis and Pinto (2003).

Figure 5.1   Consumer price index, 1985–2000 (annual averages)

Index (1985 = 100)

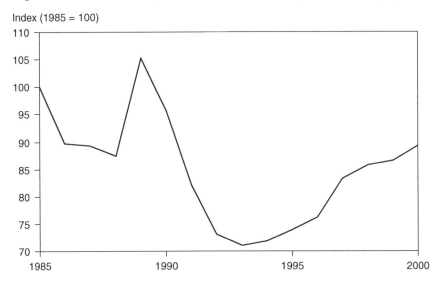

Source: INDEC.

prices tended to decline. On the other hand, industrial electricity prices remained relatively constant. In general, a declining tendency should be the rule as technological improvements lower generation and distribution costs. In Argentina's case, however, extensive organizational changes in the country's electricity sector and the fact that pricing before privatization was used for political and distributional objectives can make the technological trend less important.

Taxes significantly affect final consumer electricity prices in Argentina. For example, residential tariffs, including taxes, decreased from 1986 to 1996 (from $0.172 to $0.124); over the same decade, tariffs before taxes increased (from $0.095 to $0.097). This observation is important because the demand elasticity of electricity tends to be low, and taxes were a significant component of prices during the period before privatization.[12]

Natural Gas

In the natural gas sector, residential consumer prices, when deflated by the CPI, showed a decreasing trend from 1980 to 1998 (figure 5.3). However, price behavior was not uniform during the period: prices decreased in real values until 1989, rose from 1990 to 1992, and stabilized thereafter.

---

12. To complete the analysis, Ennis and Pinto compared electricity prices in Argentina with those in other selected countries. They found that the tariffs charged in Argentina in 1996 were relatively competitive and even below international averages in all segments. See Ennis and Pinto (2003).

Figure 5.2   Evolution of electricity-sector tariffs with taxes, 1970–97
(dollars/kWh, 1997 constant prices)

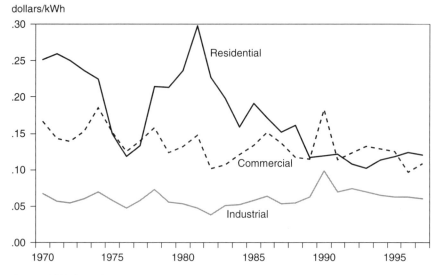

Source: FIEL (1999).

Commercial and industrial tariffs were relatively stable during the 1980s. While commercial tariffs tended to increase somewhat after 1993, industrial tariffs tended to decrease. Tariffs in Argentina's natural gas sector are generally below international averages for all user types.

Access to Public Utilities

This study used HES data to analyze privatization's effects on access to selected public services. For 1985–86, "households with access" are those households that report a positive expenditure for the corresponding public utility.[13] For 1996–97, the study measures access in two ways. The first way is a direct measure based on the following questions from the 1996–97 HES: "In the block where your house is located, is there: a water network, an electricity network, a gas network?" and "Does your house have a telephone?" Unfortunately, these questions were not asked in the 1985–86 HES. We present the estimates obtained using this first alternative in table 5.4. Clearly, after privatization, the degree of access to public utilities changed notably. Access to water services increased significantly,

---

13. In the cases of natural gas and water, Ennis and Pinto considered only the expenditure on the service provided through the network.

Figure 5.3 Evolution of natural gas sector tariff, 1980–98
(final prices, dollars/m³, 1997 constant prices, various
deflators)

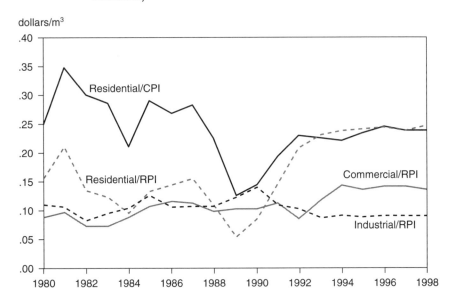

CPI = consumer price index
RPI = retail price index

Source: Ennis and Pinto (2003).

as did access to telephone, natural gas, and electricity (with respective
increases of 33, 32, and 11 percent, respectively).

The second way to evaluate the changes in access is to define "households
with access" in 1996–97 as those households with a positive expenditure
on the services. This method is most consistent with the 1985–86 HES measures, except that, in 1996–97, the expenditure reported was not restricted
to network provision, as it was in 1985–86. Measuring access using positive
expenditure, however, is not without problems. First, illegal connections
tend to be reported as zero expenditure, even though for welfare calculations households with illegal connections should be counted as having
access to the service (this is especially relevant in the case of electricity).
Second, in the case of water and natural gas, private substitutes (e.g., wells
and bottled gas, respectively) were common in Argentina. The observed
changes in this study's measure of access during the reform period might
simply reflect the household's decision to switch from alternatives to formal provision through the network. Finally, one additional limitation arises
for the 1996–97 HES using the number of households that report a positive
expenditure. During that period, information on water and electricity
expenditure is reported as a single category. To maintain consistency, we
aggregated 1985–86 data on water and electricity into a single category.

Table 5.4 Access by income group (direct measure) (percent)

Decile	1985–86[a]				1996–97[b]				Percent change			
	Natural gas	Water	Electricity	Telephone	Natural gas	Water	Electricity	Telephone	Natural gas	Water	Electricity	Telephone
1	21.98	10.26	65.20	18.32	46.44	46.44	98.98	22.81	111.28	352.75	51.81	24.55
2	41.11	25.44	80.49	26.48	62.78	61.37	99.60	39.64	52.69	141.27	23.74	49.68
3	50.20	28.63	87.45	33.73	77.48	68.39	99.79	53.51	54.35	138.89	14.11	58.67
4	54.95	38.83	90.48	43.59	83.13	75.81	100.00	57.72	51.30	95.25	10.53	32.42
5	65.56	34.07	92.96	47.04	86.50	75.05	99.59	68.51	31.95	120.26	7.13	45.65
6	68.35	43.53	93.53	49.64	91.24	79.84	100.00	78.21	33.50	83.43	6.92	57.55
7	78.65	47.19	97.00	61.42	93.69	84.32	99.80	82.69	19.12	78.67	2.88	34.62
8	77.74	55.84	95.99	67.15	96.33	87.14	100.00	86.73	23.91	56.06	4.18	29.16
9	85.04	58.03	97.45	75.91	97.96	91.22	100.00	89.80	15.20	57.20	2.62	18.29
10	90.94	63.02	99.25	82.26	99.18	96.33	100.00	92.86	9.06	52.85	0.76	12.88
Average	63.29	40.43	89.91	50.41	83.45	76.57	99.78	67.22	31.77	89.41	10.97	33.26

a. For 1985–86, households that reported expenditures greater than zero were considered to have access to the corresponding public utility.
b. Access to public utilities for 1996–97 was based on the household survey questions: "In the block where your house is located, is there: water network, electricity network, gas network?" and "Does your house have a telephone?"

Sources: 1985–86 HES and 1996–97 HES, INDEC.

Increased access was generally higher when measured using this second method, except in the case of telephones. The proportion of households with a positive expenditure on natural gas was substantially higher than the proportion of households that reported having a gas network in the block where they live. Based on this finding, it is evident that network substitutes for natural gas were relatively popular in Argentina (especially for low-income households). The direct measure is the most appropriate for across-time comparisons of natural gas because, while 1985–86 expenditures account only for natural gas obtained through the network, 1996–97 data include expenditures on natural-gas substitutes, which likely constituted a significant share (table 5.4).

Take-Up Decision

If a high proportion of consumers with potential access choose not to use a service—that is, if take-up is low—then the benefits of increasing access by privatizing the service are smaller. The 1996–97 HES allows one to consider take-up decisions by decile. This variable is constructed by determining the number of households connected to the corresponding public service when the service is made available to them. On average, take-up decisions are high: 99.88 percent for electricity, 97.39 percent for water, and 87.49 percent for natural gas. For all deciles, electricity and water show a high percentage of household adoption; for natural gas, the take-up percentage increases with income, starting with 45.61 percent for the poorest households. These numbers are consistent with the fact that poor households mainly use bottled gas. It is noteworthy that Argentina's electricity, natural gas, and telecommunication connections are not mandatory for consumers. While connection to the water network is not mandatory either, proof of an alternative source of potable water is required (and private wells are relatively popular).

Change in Consumer Surplus

In general, a change in the price of a good or service will have a greater effect on consumers who devote a larger share of their budget to purchasing such goods or services. Thus, in order to estimate the changes in welfare, we start by estimating the average budget for the relevant services.

Engel Curves: Nonparametric Estimation

To approximate the welfare effects brought about by a price change in telephone, natural gas, and electricity services, this section uses a nonparametric method to estimate both Engel curves for the various services and distribution of consumers across expenditure levels. Given a change in price,

Figure 5.4 Engel curves for selected public services, 1985–86 and 1996–97

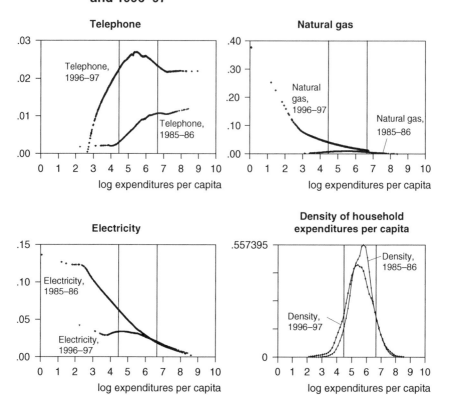

knowing the budget share for each income level and distribution of agents across income allows one to better determine the main winners and losers and their importance in number.

In the 1996–97 HES data, expenditure on electricity is pooled with that on water and sewage. For this reason, to compute the Engel curve for electricity, we also pooled the expenditure data for 1985–86 HES. Then, for the electricity sector, we use the change in prices and access corresponding to that service but use the price elasticity corresponding to the pooled expenditure data. Unfortunately, no results were obtained for water services.[14]

Figure 5.4 presents the budget share for public services (telephone, water and electricity, and natural gas) across levels of total expenditure per capita

---

14. In 1985–86 on average, expenditure on water was less than half that on electricity; there is some evidence that the proportion of total expenditure corresponding to water remained relatively stable during the decade under study (FLACSO 1998), while that for electricity clearly increased.

(expressed in logarithms). It also compares consumer density by level of income/expenditure for 1985–86 and 1996–97. For all four graphs, the vertical lines indicate the cutoff expenditure levels for deciles 1 and 9. In constructing these figures, the agents reporting zero shares were included in the sample, assuming they represented consumers without access (in this regard, these estimates are comparable to the budget shares reported in table 5.3). Considering households with zero shares as not having access represents an upper bound in the number of households with no access. Some households report a zero share even if they do have access because they consume a minimum amount of service (that they deem not worth reporting) or because they wish to hide their consumption.

For 1996–97, natural gas and electricity show monotonically decreasing budget share curves. For 1985–86, the telephone curve increases monotonically; in all other cases, the curves increase, peak, and then decrease (suggesting that the corresponding public service is a normal good for low-expenditure households and becomes an inferior good for higher-income ones).

We performed the same calculations without including consumers with zero-share expenditure in the corresponding service. Although the figures are not shown, all Engel curves sloped downward—that is, conditional on spending a positive amount. Thus, the budget share spent on each corresponding public service decreased systematically with rise in living standards.

First- and Second-Order Approximations to Consumer Surplus

To estimate the change in agents' utility resulting from the observed price change for public services after privatization, we calculated two possible approximations: (1) a first-order approximation (FOA), and (2) a second-order approximation (SOA). The FOA of the change in utility stemming from the price change was calculated using the following formula:

$$\Delta_1 U_j^h = -\left(\Delta \log p_j\right) x_0^h w_{j0}^h,$$

where p_j represents the price of service j, w_{j0}^h the expenditure share of household h on public service j before privatization, and x_0^h the total household expenditure per capita. The FOA is the weighted average of the log change in prices, where the weights are given by the amount that each household h spends on each particular public service before price change.

The SOA of the change in utility resulting from price change allows for some quantity response. In terms of w_j^h, the expenditure share in public service j of household h, the SOA can be expressed as:

$$\Delta_2 U_j^h = -\left(\Delta \log p_j\right) x_0^h w_{j0}^h \left[1 + \frac{\Delta \log p_j}{2} \frac{\partial \log w_j^h}{\partial \log p_j}\right].$$

We use these numbers, $\Delta_i U_j^h$, in calculating the change in inequality and poverty reported in tables 5.8 and 5.9.

Finally, we incorporate into our calculations the change in utility caused by access changes. As the privatization process may have variously affected household access, we divide the total number of households into four groups: households with access before and after privatization, households that gained access after privatization, households that no longer had access after privatization, and households with no access in both periods. The first group was affected through the price change in privatized services; thus, the change in their consumer surplus is simply $\Delta_i U_j^h$. For households that gained access, the change in consumer surplus can be approximated using the difference of the virtual price (the price that would make their expenditure in the service equal zero) and the price after privatization.[15] The last two groups are affected through the price changes of goods and services that substitute for those that have been privatized. Given the information available, one cannot assess the effect on these last two groups, although it will likely be less important.

To compute the FOA and SOA, it is necessary to estimate price change during the reform period and the virtual prices for each service and household. In addition, calculating the SOA requires estimating the elasticity of demand (i.e., $\partial \log w_j^h / \partial \log p_j$). Based on the information presented earlier (figures 5.1 to 5.3), we concluded that the best estimates with regard to price change are those provided in table 5.5.

Determining the change in prices attributable to the privatization of public utilities is a controversial issue. Various studies reach different conclusions. For example, Delfino and Casarin (2001) suggest that privatization produced price increases. On the other hand, Urbiztondo, Artana, and Navajas (1998) conclude that prices decreased in percentages similar to those presented in table 5.5. Our estimated price changes were computed using an index of final prices and deflating them by the RPI. We chose the years of the available expenditure surveys, 1985–86 HES and 1996–97 HES, for the comparison. While the results are sensitive to the years used, we believe they are reasonable years upon which to base our comparisons. The 1988–89 period was one of high inflation, with significant devaluation of prices for public services. Thus, choosing the initial prices during the years that prevailed just before privatization would have distorted the results. The period starting in 1991 proved relatively stable. By 1996, prices in privatized firms

---

15. The authors also estimated the premium associated with having access to public services, using a hedonic rental regression. Ennis and Pinto used household rent payments or imputed rents as the dependent variable and indicators of access to the various public services (in addition to a set of control variables) as explanatory variables. For lack of data, however, it was not possible to include potentially important neighborhood characteristics in the regression (e.g., neighborhood amenities or crime levels) or estimate this hedonic rental regression for any year other than 1996–97. In general, they found positive premiums associated with access, but the relationships were not highly significant. See Ennis and Pinto (2003).

Table 5.5   Change in relative utility prices (percent)

Utility	1985–86	1996–97
Electricity	100.00	67.49
Natural gas	100.00	86.56
Telephone	100.00	83.94

Sources: FIEL (1999), INDEC (www.indec. menoc.ar).

had probably adjusted to what one can consider normal levels. Hence, 1996 is a reasonable year for measuring prices after privatization. Choosing a later year would imply smaller price decreases—or even increases, as shown in Delfino and Casarin (2001), where 1999 prices are used.

We believe Argentina's economy entered another abnormal path in 1998, with overall deflation that did not translate into the prices of public services for regulatory reasons (their prices were dollar indexed). By 1999, the prices of public services were again misaligned because of macroeconomic instability. Thus, we exclude these periods from our calculations. An important lesson from the price increases of the late 1990s is that the regulatory framework of an unstable country, such as Argentina, should be adapted to handle extreme macroeconomic situations. Estache, Carbajo, and de Rus (1999) evaluate the potential gains that could be obtained from improving the regulation of Argentina's privatized public utilities.

To estimate the virtual prices and the expression $(\partial \log w_j^h / \partial \log p_j)$, we use the results of the following Engel equation:

$$w_{hj} = \alpha_j + \beta_j \log p_j + \gamma_j \log x_h + \delta_j \left(\log x_h \right)^2,$$

so that

$$\frac{\partial \log w_j^h}{\partial \log p_j} = \frac{\hat{\beta}_j}{w_j^h}.$$

This estimation uses the subsample of households with access to each public service.[16] We use a Heckman two-step correction method to account for potential bias.[17]

Using the price elasticities computed in table 5.6, we obtain the prices that would make those shares equal zero, even under unrestricted access. These virtual prices are used to calculate the welfare change associated with consumers who had no access before privatization and gained access

---

16. It should be noted that the estimation is based on weak data and only two data points. For electricity, the authors use the expenditure share on water and electricity and the corresponding electricity prices for 1985–86 and 1996–97.

17. The additional step is required because estimates could be inconsistent if omitted variables correlated with access also affected the services demand.

Table 5.6 Heckman two-step correction

Variable	Telephone (tsh) tacc = 1 Coefficient	Telephone (tsh) tacc = 1 Standard error	Natural gas (gsh) gacc = 1 Coefficient	Natural gas (gsh) gacc = 1 Standard error	Electricity (wesh) eacc = 1 Coefficient	Electricity (wesh) eacc = 1 Standard error
Lp	-0.0997	0.0063*	-0.0342	0.0043*	0.0033	0.0021
lexppc	-0.0673	0.0070*	-0.0739	0.0029*	-0.0408	0.0033*
lexppc2	0.0047	0.0006*	0.0051	0.0003*	0.0017	0.0003*
lambda	0.0005	0.0011	-0.0067	0.0008*	-0.0156	0.0010*
_cons	0.7047	0.0324*	0.4323	0.0198*	0.2063	0.0120*
Number of observations	4,666		5,812		7,335	
R-squared	0.14		0.31		0.22	
Adjusted R-squared	0.14		0.31		0.22	

tsh = telephone expenditure share; tacc = households with access to telephone; gsh = natural gas expenditure share; gacc = households with access to natural gas; wesh = water and electricity expenditure share; eacc = households with access to electricity; Lp = log of prices; lexppc = log of expenditures per capita; lexppc2 = log of expenditures per capita squared; lambda = inverse Mills ratio; cons = constant; * = significantly different from zero, with 90 and 95 percent confidence.

Note: The variable lambda in the regression is the inverse Mills ratio constructed using the estimates of a standard logit regression. See Ennis and Pinto (2003). For natural gas and electricity, this variable differs significantly from zero.

Source: Authors' calculations, based on 1985–86 and 1996–97 HES (INDEC).

after privatization. The virtual prices (per decile), p_v, are shown in the last column of table 5.7; they are, in general, decreasing in income.

We then compute the change in consumer surplus, using the prices reported in table 5.5 and the elasticities and virtual prices obtained from table 5.6. We calculate the FOA and SOA of the mean decile change in welfare resulting from privatization of service j, incorporating both changes in price and access. Throughout our computations, we assume that consumers who initially had access did not lose it after privatization.

Table 5.7 reports the percentage change in expected utility (i.e., the expected change in utility as a percentage of initial total expenditure).[18] The second and third columns show the results of calculating the expected change in utility for households with access before and after privatization. The fourth and fifth columns show the corresponding values for households that gained access after privatization. The sixth and seventh columns present the total expected change in utility (the sum of the corresponding previous columns). Since the price elasticity for electricity does not differ significantly from zero (and with the wrong sign) (table 5.6), we use the elasticity without the Heckman adjustment (also showing an inelastic demand).

Figures 5.5, 5.6, and 5.7 show that the increase in consumer surplus for households with access to telephones in both periods is higher for those households in the middle and upper declines of the income distribution. For natural gas and electricity, the benefits are relatively uniform across income distribution. In telephone and natural gas, the change in utility

---

18. See appendix 5A for the formulas used in the calculations reflected in table 5.7.

Table 5.7 Mean change in consumer surplus across deciles

Decile	Household access for both periods		Household access after privatization		Total		Virtual price (p_v)
	FOA	SOA	FOA	SOA	FOA	SOA	
Telephone sector							
1	0.0354	0.0626	0.0622	0.0763	0.0975	0.1389	164.7599
2	0.0653	0.1054	0.2230	0.2653	0.2883	0.3707	152.7779
3	0.0873	0.1385	0.3792	0.4673	0.4666	0.6058	146.8454
4	0.1826	0.2487	0.2906	0.3442	0.4732	0.5930	147.1503
5	0.1293	0.2007	0.3823	0.4708	0.5116	0.6715	138.4307
6	0.1237	0.1990	0.5401	0.6615	0.6639	0.8605	136.1053
7	0.1818	0.2750	0.3646	0.4486	0.5464	0.7236	134.0514
8	0.1727	0.2746	0.2782	0.3561	0.4510	0.6307	129.4471
9	0.1978	0.3129	0.1970	0.2521	0.3948	0.5650	128.1028
10	0.2215	0.3463	0.1361	0.1746	0.3576	0.5209	124.9354
Average	0.1609	0.2495	0.2978	0.3685	0.4588	0.6181	136.3856
Natural gas sector							
1	0.0788	0.0885	0.7015	0.7933	0.7804	0.8818	229.8922
2	0.1247	0.1431	0.5583	0.6203	0.6829	0.7633	210.1655
3	0.1661	0.1885	0.7291	0.8226	0.8952	1.0111	198.1320
4	0.1534	0.1780	0.8125	0.8940	0.9660	1.0720	198.1804
5	0.1527	0.1820	0.5506	0.6167	0.7033	0.7987	188.9667
6	0.1572	0.1878	0.4899	0.5591	0.6471	0.7469	175.2390
7	0.1600	0.1951	0.2818	0.3221	0.4418	0.5172	168.8682
8	0.1409	0.1756	0.2668	0.3115	0.4077	0.4871	156.0288
9	0.1270	0.1650	0.1334	0.1590	0.2604	0.3240	145.1724
10	0.0964	0.1370	0.0568	0.0693	0.1531	0.2063	133.0477
Average	0.1378	0.1690	0.4250	0.4801	0.5628	0.6491	175.2874
Electricity sector							
1	1.0284	1.1743	2.0229	2.1496	3.0513	3.3239	350.6822
2	1.2616	1.4450	0.9598	1.0355	2.2214	2.4804	310.8645
3	1.3235	1.5211	0.4617	0.5056	1.7852	2.0266	273.4237
4	1.4561	1.6613	0.2566	0.2802	1.7128	1.9415	275.2321
5	1.0901	1.3000	0.1009	0.1115	1.1910	1.4115	255.8005
6	1.2465	1.4577	0.0430	0.0483	1.2895	1.5060	235.3945
7	1.1716	1.3907	−0.0652	−0.0743	1.1064	1.3164	221.0698
8	1.0869	1.3036	−0.0087	−0.0100	1.0782	1.2936	205.8540
9	0.9321	1.1521	−0.0495	−0.0586	0.8826	1.0935	188.3328
10	0.8490	1.0722	−0.0397	−0.0506	0.8093	1.0217	161.9198
Average	1.1423	1.3478	0.3427	0.3665	1.4850	1.7144	245.9665

FOA = first-order approximation
SOA = second-order approximation

Source: Authors' calculations, based on HES (INDEC).

resulting from increased access is more important than the change stemming from decreased price. However, this is not the case for electricity, where access was relatively high before privatization. An important finding is that the access effect was significant for low-income households who gained access to electricity. For telephone and natural gas, households in the middle deciles of income distribution benefited the most. The values of changes in consumer surplus associated with electricity are considerably higher than those associated with the other services.

Figure 5.5 Telephone first- and second-order approximations

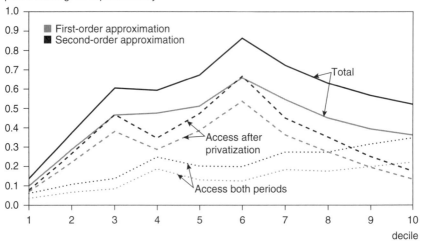

Source: Authors' calculations based on 1985–86 and 1996–97 HES (INDEC).

Figure 5.6 Natural gas first- and second-order approximations

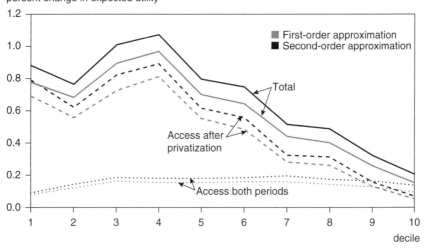

Source: Authors' calculations based on 1985–86 and 1996–97 HES (INDEC).

Inequality and Poverty

One can use the estimates of change in consumer surplus to assess privatization's effect on inequality and poverty. In terms of inequality, we calculate Gini coefficients and Atkinson inequality measures under various assumptions that consider the effects of price and access changes on utility.

We assume that the expected change in utility (explained in the previous section) is the only change to initial household expenditure. For households with access before privatization, we add preprivatization household expenditure per capita and the change in utility (per capita) resulting from the change in the previously calculated price ($\Delta_i U_j^h$, i = 1, 2). For households that gained access after privatization, the procedure to compute postprivatization utility is less straightforward; one needs to compute various inequality indicators (table 5.8). In general, the effect of privatization on income inequality is small. In all cases, the Gini coefficients decrease. However, the Atkinson measure shows that, as the index of inequality rises— that is, as the importance of households with lower income increases—the privatization of natural gas, and electricity and water have significantly increased inequality.[19]

We also compare the change in the inequality measures attributable to privatization of the public services with the total changes that occurred from 1985–86 to 1996–97. The first-order effects of privatization on inequality are small; the largest change in the Gini coefficient is only –1.2 percent (the case of the SOA for electricity and water). Clearly, however, Argentina experienced a significant increase in overall inequality indicators during that period (the Gini coefficient increased about 16 percent). We conclude that, while inequality increased, privatization was not a principal contributor.

To evaluate poverty, we used the Foster, Greer, and Thorbecke measures.[20] We calculated consumers' utility after privatization by adding the corresponding estimated change in utility to the per capita expenditure before privatization. Table 5.9 reports our estimates of the change in the poverty measures attributable to privatization. The values in the first and last columns are obtained using the observed household total expenditure per capita for 1985–86 and 1996–97, while the middle columns show the effect on poverty attributable to privatization of the public services

---

19. The purpose of the exercise is to show the effects of each sector's privatization on income distribution. Calculating an aggregate effect, including all these sectors, would involve making arbitrary assumptions on the patterns of access across the privatized sectors and the joint probability of changes in access to public services after privatization. The authors chose not to pursue that route.

20. The Foster, Greer, and Thorbecke poverty index is given by the formula:

$$P_\alpha = \frac{1}{N} \sum_{i=1}^{N} \left(1 - \frac{x_i}{z} \right)^\alpha 1(x_i \leq z),$$

where z denotes the poverty line, x_i total expenditure per capita in household i, N the total number of households, and 1(.) an indicator function. Different values of the parameter α describe various poverty measures. For α = 0, 1, and 2; P_0 is the headcount ratio; P_1 is the poverty gap; and P_2 considers the distribution of the poor, respectively.

Figure 5.7   Electricity first- and second-order approximations

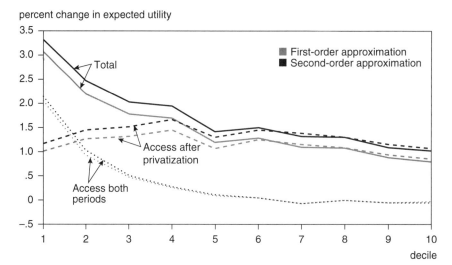

considered. All poverty indicators decline; the reductions are more important for electricity. We conclude that privatization's effects on the standard measures of inequality and poverty are not significant.[21]

Employment Effect

To estimate privatization's effect on employment, we examine the evolution of employment and wages in privatized sectors, using both firm-level and PHS data. We also use the PHS data to analyze qualitative changes in the labor market during the reform period. We then estimate the change in inequality attributable to privatization. Specifically, we calculate an upper bound to the change in inequality resulting from layoffs in the privatized sectors and then examine the changes in wage inequality.

The large employers subjected to privatization were railways (FFAA), the oil company (YPF), and electricity and telephone companies. Table 5.10 shows firm-level data for the main (and largest) individual firms in these sectors and the changes in employment they experienced. On average, the number of jobs in those firms decreased by a striking 67 percent. FFAA had the largest absolute reduction in workforce—75,000 jobs, representing an 82 percent decrease; however, YPF had the largest relative change, with an

---

21. These results do not consider privatization's effects on changes in service quality. For example, Galiani, Gertler, and Schargrodsky (2002) find that Argentina's privatization of water and sewerage had a significant negative effect on child mortality; that is, child mortality caused by waterborne diseases declined in areas where water services had been privatized.

Table 5.8 Inequality indicators

Index	1985–86	Telephone FOA	Telephone SOA	Natural gas FOA	Natural gas SOA	Electricity and water FOA	Electricity and water SOA	1996–97
Gini coefficient	0.4003	0.3964	0.3963	0.3994	0.3993	0.3961	0.3955	0.4637
Atkinson indices A (0.5)	0.1304	0.1285	0.1284	0.1311	0.1310	0.1278	0.1274	0.1746
A (1.0)	0.2406	0.2371	0.2371	0.2429	0.2426	0.2375	0.2366	0.3213
A (2.0)	0.4235	0.4172	0.4173	0.7785	0.6925	0.5190	0.4821	0.5930

FOA = first-order approximation
SOA = second-order approximation

Source: Authors' calculations, based on HES (INDEC).

83 percent reduction in jobs. Although employment variations are large in specific sectors, relative importance in terms of the country's aggregate employment is not that significant. Before privatization, employment in the relevant firms was 2.3 percent of the total national workforce (table 5.10). Yet, privatization's effect on the rate of unemployment was probably important. Job losses stemming from privatization equal about 13 percent of the change in unemployment from 1987–90 to 1997 (table 5.10).[22]

Changes in employment were relatively abrupt and concentrated within a short period of time. In addition, the overall economy underwent widespread restructuring during this period, making reemployment of laid-off workers difficult (Galiani, Gertler, Schargrodsky, and Sturzenegger 2001). Many workers in POEs were dismissed in preparation for privatization. The government produced an estimate of the optimal workforce size for each POE; however, this estimate significantly underestimated the reduction in workforce that finally occurred.

Estache, Carbajo, and de Rus (1999) report that employment in the railways company, FFAA, was reduced by 72,000 in the first three years after privatization, constituting 90 percent of that company's total reduction in employment. Before privatization, the federal government—under a World Bank-sponsored plan—had arranged a portion of this sector's employment reduction (Ramamurti 1997). From a total of 92,000 railway employees at the time of privatization, 30 percent accepted voluntary retirement. The petroleum company also implemented an aggressive program of voluntary retirement: 64 percent of the 37,000 workers in that company joined the voluntary retirement program at the time of the privatization.

---

22. These numbers are calculated using Argentina's total urban employment and unemployment. If one only considers the corresponding numbers for Greater Buenos Aires (GBA), the percentage of change in unemployment rises to 25 percent.

Table 5.9 Household poverty changes for selected public services

| 1985–86 | Telephone | | Natural gas | | Electricity | | 1996–97 |
	FOA	SOA	FOA	SOA	FOA	SOA	
0.1127	0.1016	0.1016	0.0994	0.0994	0.0954	0.0950	0.1965
0.0316	0.0285	0.0285	0.0287	0.0286	0.0270	0.0266	0.0681
0.0133	0.0118	0.0118	0.0123	0.0123	0.0110	0.0108	0.0346

FOA = first-order approximation
SOA = second-order approximation

Source: Authors' calculations, based on HES (INDEC).

Thus, firm-level data indicates that job loss associated with privatization was important. However, the analysis of PHS employment data reveals a somewhat different picture. These data show no clear evidence of a significant change in privatized sectors' total participation on aggregate employment. Rather, while these sectors' public side shrank, the private side gained participation and largely compensated for reduced public employment.

The PHS does not allow one to distinguish those individuals working in a privatized company from all other workers performing activities in that sector. However, it is possible to distinguish public from private employment levels in the affected sectors. Table 5.11 shows the evolution of these numbers for 1989–97. Public employment in the privatized sectors decreased from about 2 percent to nearly 0 percent, while private-sector employment increased from 5.37 to 6.97 percent. Total private and public employment in those sectors directly affected by privatization was 7.32 percent of total employment in the economy in 1989. Even though this percentage decreased immediately after privatization began, it then recovered to 7.06 percent as employment in the private side of the privatized sectors increased by 1997.

In the sectors studied, public employment decreased from an average of 0.8 percent in the years before privatization (1989–91) to nearly 0 percent in 1997. By 1993, most of the reduction in public employment had occurred. Private employment in these sectors, however, grew over most of the decade. The process of adjustment first reduced the total labor force employed in the privatized sectors; however, levels slowly recovered as the new private organizations normalized services provision. Even though the behavior of public and private employment during this period shows an inverse relationship, the expansion of the latter did not fully compensate the reduction in former. As a result, the participation of privatized sectors in total employment experienced some decline.

Qualitative Changes in Employment

Argentina's public sector tends to employ workers with more education than the private sector. Nearly half of private-sector workers are low-skilled

Table 5.10 Employment in privatized firms as a proportion of total employment and change in total unemployment

Company	E 1987–90	E 1997	E/TE (percent) 1987–90	E/TE (percent) 1997	Layoffs	Layoffs/ΔTU (percent)
AA (airline)	10,283	4,840	0.11	0.04	5,443	0.48
ENTEL (telecommunications)	45,882	29,690	0.48	0.27	16,192	1.43
FFAA (railway)	92,000	17,000	0.96	0.15	75,000	6.61
GE (natural gas)	9,251	3,462	0.10	0.03	5,789	0.51
OSN (water)	9,448	4,251	0.10	0.04	5,197	0.46
SEGBA (electricity)	21,535	7,945	0.22	0.07	13,590	1.20
YPF (oil)	34,870	5,700	0.36	0.05	29,170	2.57
Total	**223,269**	**72,888**	**2.32**	**0.66**	**150,381**	**13.24**

E = employment in each company
TE = total employment
TU = total unemployment

AA = Aerolíneas Argentinas
ENTEL = Empresa Nacional de Telecomunicaciones
FFAA = Ferrocarriles Argentinos
GE = Gas del Estado
OSN = Obras Sanitarias de la Nación
SEGBA = Servicios Eléctricos del Gas Buenos Aires
YPF = Yacimientos Petrolíferos Fiscales.

Sources: CNC; ENARGAS; ENRE; SIGEP; Estache, Carbajo, and de Rus (1999).

individuals, while public-sector employees tend to have secondary or post-secondary qualifications. During privatization, a significant shift occurred in employment composition by education level.[23] The electricity, gas, and water sectors have transitioned toward a more qualified labor force (especially through changes in extreme groups of the distribution of education levels, reducing the relative participation of workers with primary education and increasing workers with higher education). In telecommunications and transportation—the other major privatized sectors—the participation of workers with secondary education has increased. Before privatization, the percentage of employees in these two sectors who had completed secondary studies was 41 percent for those working on the public side and 45.5 percent for those on the private side. After privatization, this percentage increased to nearly 50 percent (by that time, virtually all employees were working on the private side).

Workers with higher levels of education increased their participation in the private side of all sectors. Since privatization reduced public employment significantly, these changes partly account for better-educated workers' increased participation in the private sector after privatization (qualified

---

23. Analysis of the qualitative characteristics of the labor force employed during privatization is based on detailed discussions not provided due to limited space. See Ennis and Pinto (2003).

Table 5.11 Privatized-sector employment as a percentage of all sector employment, 1989–97

Year	Public sector E, NG, and W	T & T	Total	Private sector E, NG, and W	T & T	Total	Total E, NG, and W	T & T	Total
1989	0.51	1.44	1.95	0.05	5.32	5.37	0.56	6.76	7.32
1990	0.83	0.83	1.66	0.10	3.92	4.03	0.93	4.75	5.69
1991	1.00	0.68	1.68	0.02	4.17	4.19	1.02	4.85	5.87
1992	0.14	0.43	0.58	0.48	4.08	4.56	0.62	4.51	5.14
1993	0.00	0.11	0.11	0.41	4.97	5.38	0.41	5.08	5.49
1994	0.02	0.24	0.27	0.61	6.32	6.93	0.63	6.56	7.19
1995	0.07	0.12	0.19	0.53	5.72	6.25	0.60	5.84	6.44
1996	0.05	0.00	0.05	0.73	6.47	7.20	0.78	6.47	7.25
1997	0.05	0.05	0.09	0.53	6.44	6.97	0.58	6.49	7.06

E = electricity
NG = natural gas
W = water
T & T = telecommunications and transportation

Sources: PHS data (INDEC).

employees who lost their public-sector jobs were, in part, rehired by private firms). For all sectors considered, the percentage of workers with primary schooling has declined, on average; while the percentage of workers with secondary or higher education has increased.

On average, individuals employed in the private sector work more hours than those in the public sector. Moreover, during the 1990s, the average number of hours worked per week in the public sector decreased from 42 to 36, while that in the private sector decreased slightly from 45 to 44. The variability of hours worked in the private sector is higher than in the public sector, and this variability increased after 1991. The latter might be an indication of greater flexibility in labor-market rules during the 1990s, which allowed firms to offer a broader set of labor contracts (the frequency of part-time jobs increased significantly). Similar conclusions hold for all privatized sectors (electricity, natural gas, water, telecommunication, and transportation). The private portion of these sectors tended to employ workers for a longer time and with a higher dispersion of the number of hours worked. By 1997, most workers in these sectors became subject to the regime of private employment, which contributed to increased income heterogeneity among those workers. The average number of hours worked on the public side of the privatized sectors was higher, and the standard deviation smaller than in the public sector overall.

During 1989–95, job security decreased across all sectors; however, the decrease was more significant in those sectors directly subject to privatization (in 1995, average tenure declined from nearly 15 years to only 5).

This change suggests that employees with long careers in the POEs might have suffered the consequences of layoffs in that sector. Moreover, these individuals had a reduced likelihood of regaining employment, as they tended to be older and their skills more specialized.

Data quality and coverage were problematic with regard to privatization's effect on wages. For example, to identify wage changes associated with privatization, we considered 1991 as the preprivatization period even though the process started in 1989. Because the PHS did not distinguish between public and private organizations before 1989, it was not possible to differentiate between public and private employment in the privatized sectors before that year. Moreover, the hyperinflation of 1989–90 affected the quality of the data for those years and introduced noise in the wage structure. For these reasons, we compare the postprivatization wage structure of 1997 with that of 1991.[24] Three changes are noteworthy:

- The skill premium that workers with higher education earned significantly increased after privatization.

- The wage profile became steeper with increased tenure (i.e., wages rose as tenure did).

- No significant wage differential was found between public and private workers, either before or after privatization.

In general, the public sector tended to employ more middle- and high-income workers. The income composition of employment did not change much after privatization. In the privatized sectors, private-sector income distribution was relatively uniform before privatization (compared to the public sector), and changed toward a higher concentration of workers in the third- and fourth-income quintiles. Public-sector income distribution before privatization was bimodal (with modes in the second and fourth quintiles), and this pattern was more pronounced in the privatized sectors.

Income distribution of the labor force employed in other parts of the private sector—that is, private but not directly subject to privatization—is similar to that of the privatized sectors. The changes in the distribution were also similar, except that the proportion of agents in the fourth quintile decreased. It is possible that, after privatization, the private side may have rehired many workers employed on the public side before privatization, particularly those in the fourth quintile. This explanation is consistent with the increased proportion of fourth-quintile workers in the private side of the privatized sectors. In sum, privatization does not appear to influence greatly the evolution of worker income distribution in each of the sectors.

---

24. It is possible to think that, as it would take time for relative wages to fully adjust to the postprivatization equilibrium, the 1991 wage structure would better represent the structure before privatization (compared with 1989 and 1990, when Argentina underwent hyperinflation).

Table 5.12 Gini coefficient

Year	$G^{91}(1)$	$G^{91}(2)$	Change (percent)	Year (t)	$G^t(1)$	$[G^{91}(2) - G^{91}(1)]/[G^t(1) - G^{91}(1)]$ (percent)
1991	0.4390	0.4554	3.75	1995	0.5405	16.16
				1996	0.5484	14.99
				1997	0.5151	21.55

Note: $G^{91}(1)$ and $G^t(1)$ are the Gini coefficients for 1991; t = 1995, 1996, and 1997 when all unemployed individuals are imputed an income equal to zero. $G^{91}(2)$ is the authors' constructed measure.

Source: Authors' calculations, based on PHS data (INDEC).

Inequality and Poverty

To estimate the extent to which privatization's effects on workers affected income inequality and poverty, we considered the two main aspects of the problem. First, we investigated the effect on employment and unemployment. We provided upper-bound estimates, assuming that all workers who lost their jobs during privatization failed to find new ones after the period. Second, we computed various wage inequality measures to approximate the change in inequality that occurred among those who remained employed.

Changes in Employment Level

What is the upper bound—the maximum amount possible—for the change in income inequality attributable to the changes in employment associated with privatization? To estimate this effect, we used 1991 as their reference year and computed two Gini coefficients constructed under different assumptions. The first Gini, $G^{91}(1)$ in table 5.12, included all individuals in the 1991 survey.[25] To calculate the second Gini, $G^{91}(2)$, we assumed that all workers laid off because of privatization during 1989–95 switched to permanent unemployment. Accordingly, we then randomly selected individuals from the pool of workers employed on the public side of the privatized sectors in 1991, imputed their income as equal to zero, and recalculated the Gini coefficient with these new imputed incomes. The proportion of individuals chosen is given by the change in public employment from 1989 to 1995 in the privatized firms (table 5.11).[26] We also calculated Gini coefficients for 1995, 1996, and 1997, assigning zero income to those individuals who reported unemployment for the corresponding years.

---

25. Unemployed individuals were imputed an income equal to zero.

26. Given that some individuals have an income equal to zero, Atkinson inequality measures cannot be computed for certain values of the parameter v; thus, only the Gini coefficient is reported.

Table 5.13 Poverty indicators, individuals

Year	α	$P^{91}(1)$	$P^{91}(2)$	Change (percent)	Year	$P^t(1)$	$[P^{91}(2) - P^{91}(1)]/$ $[P^t(1) - P^{91}(1)]$ (percent)
	0	0.0914	0.1154	26.25	1995	0.2475	15.37
					1996	0.2732	13.20
					1997	0.2260	17.83
1991	1	0.0772	0.1014	31.31	1995	0.2122	17.92
					1996	0.2342	10.32
					1997	0.1852	13.06
	2	0.0724	0.0966	33.53	1995	0.2033	18.54
					1996	0.2234	10.86
					1997	0.1733	14.00

Note: $P^{91}(1)$ and $P^t(1)$ are the corresponding measures for 1991; $t = 1995$, 1996, and 1997. $P^{91}(2)$ is the authors' constructed measure.

Source: Authors' calculations, based on PHS data (INDEC).

Table 5.12 shows that the Gini coefficient would have been 3.75 percent higher if all dismissed workers had remained permanently unemployed. The Ginis for 1995, 1996, and 1997 show an inequality increase of at least 17 percent over the Gini of 1991, $G^{91}(1)$, implying that privatization's unemployment effect explains, at most, 16 to 22 percent of the change in inequality (depending on the final year under consideration). The remainder may be attributable to other changes affecting the performance of Argentina's economy during that period.

Table 5.13 shows the change in the Foster, Greer, and Thorbecke poverty measure from 1991 to 1995, 1996, and 1997. $P^{91}(2)$ is calculated using the same approach as the one used to compute $G^{91}(2)$ above. The number of poor (corresponding to the poverty measure when $\alpha = 0$) would have increased 26.25 percent (from 9.14 to 11.54 percent) if all workers in privatized firms who lost their jobs had remained unemployed. One should note that the number of poor effectively increased by nearly 16 percent during 1991–95 ($[P^{95}(1) - P^{91}(1)]$), while this percentage increased between 1991 and 1996 and decreased between 1991 and 1997. The last column estimates the change in poverty resulting from privatization. The values correspond to the difference between $P^{91}(1)$ and $P^{91}(2)$ as a proportion of the effective change in the poverty indicator. These results differ, depending on the final year considered; on average, however, the change in unemployment stemming from privatization can explain only 15 percent of the total change in the number of poor individuals. The measure of poverty with $\alpha = 1$ indicates that a large proportion of poor individuals in 1995, 1996, and 1997 had income further away from the poverty line, compared to 1991.

Changes in Relative Wages

To assess privatization's effect on inequality, it is also important to evaluate the changes on wage distribution among employed agents. Table 5.14 shows

Table 5.14   Wage inequality among employed

Gini coefficient	1989	1991	1995	Change (percent) 1989–95	1991–95
Total	0.49	0.39	0.41	–15.9	6.2
Public	0.40	0.33	0.34	–14.2	3.7
Private	0.50	0.40	0.42	–16.6	5.5
Privatized	0.44	0.34	0.40	–5.8	16.0

Source: PHS data (INDEC).

that wage inequality across Argentina's economy substantially decreased from 1989 to 1995. However, if one compares 1991 and 1995, the previous conclusion does not hold. Wage inequality increased between those two years, and this effect is even more important in the privatized sector.[27]

Fiscal Effect

In 1989, the main POEs received fiscal transfers from the federal government equal to 1.92 percent of GDP. This number fell to 1.06 percent of GDP in 1990 (FIEL 1992). Even after these transfers, when capital expenditure is included, the POEs had a negative balance that had to be financed with private and public loans. The federal transfers imply that funds were insufficient to finance capital expenditures. The resulting limitations on investment help explain the evident obsolescence of the infrastructure and the low quality of the services provided before privatization.

In aggregate, the POEs had an operative surplus for several years before privatization began; however, certain firms were notorious for their large deficits. Ramamurti (1997), for example, documents that, before privatization, FFAA (the railways company) was receiving $829 million per year to cover its operating deficit and $298 million per year to finance capital projects—a subsidy of more than $3 million per day.

In 1990–91, just before privatization reform, government deficits were historically low, owing to the financial restrictions on the government during the hyperinflation of the late 1980s. Supporting this hypothesis is the fact that total public expenditure, as a percentage of GDP, decreased from 34 to 29 percent over this period.

Both cash and government bonds were used to pay for the privatized companies. Privatizations at all levels of government from 1990 to 1999 produced total revenue of $23.9 billion. Federal sales generated $19.4 billion (72 percent in cash and the rest in bonds, valued at market price). Additional

---

27. We also computed the Atkinson coefficient of inequality for various parameter values and obtained similar results. See Ennis and Pinto (2003).

cash revenue was later generated through sale of oil and telecommunications companies' shares that the government had initially retained at the time of ownership change.[28] Provincial governments, on the other hand, collected $4.4 billion (paid in cash) from privatizations that started in 1993.

During 1990–93, as a result of privatization, the government recovered $10 billion of public debt, equivalent to one-third the total amount of public bonds outstanding in 1990 and 13 percent of the total public debt in 1990 (about $79 billion). However, during the 1990s, the government consistently created new debt, more than offsetting the reductions brought about by privatization; thus, the total outstanding debt in the form of public bonds grew steadily over this period.

It is difficult to determine privatization's effects on social expenditure. Argentina undertook broad public-sector reform during the 1990s. As the number of public employees decreased—stemming not only from privatization—total public expenditures decreased from 33 percent of GDP during the 1980s to 27 percent during the 1990s. However, social expenditure, as a percent of GDP, increased over the same period.[29] The main reduction in overall public expenditure, excluding the decline in government operational costs, came from the rollback of state involvement in directly productive, economic activities. For example, energy, gas, and communications were important categories of public expenditures that experienced major reductions stemming from the privatization process.

After 1980, social expenditure (as a proportion of public expenditure) increased, peaking during the mid-1990s. While the percentage of total expenditures devoted to interest payments of the public debt decreased during the first years of privatization, it increased thereafter. There is a strong negative correlation (–0.7) between the percentage of total expenditure dedicated to social aims and the corresponding percentage used to pay interest on public debt. This correlation can indicate a crowding-out effect on social expenditures. To the extent that privatization reduced the amount of outstanding public debt, and, hence, the amount of annual interest payments, social expenditure may have increased as a result of less fiscal pressure.

Summary and Conclusions

We assessed privatization's redistributive effects in Argentina, particularly its consequences for consumption, employment, and fiscal conditions. To reiterate, the analysis was limited by the scarcity and poor quality of empirical data.

---

28. Delfino and Casarin (2001) estimate that about $2 billion for these extra cash revenues originated in telecommunications privatizations.

29. Social-public expenditure includes expenditures on education, social security, health services, housing, assistance to poor households, and other urban services.

On the consumption side, we calculated the change in welfare caused by price changes and changes in access to privatized public utilities. We concentrated on privatization in the telecommunications, natural gas, and electricity sectors, but also reviewed preliminary evidence related to the water and sewerage sector. In terms of household expenditure, the electricity sector was the most important before and after privatization. The other sectors were relatively small before privatization but increased their participation notably (in terms of expenditure) as a result of reforms. With regard to access, many more households have connected to telephone, natural gas, and water networks after privatization, particularly lower-income households. However, the case of electricity is unique: The change in access was not as significant, given that connection to the electricity network was common before privatization.

Following privatization, relative prices changed; however, it is unclear how much of this change is attributable to privatization. We argue that relative prices of public services decreased because of privatization, although this conclusion is sensitive to the choice of reference periods. Even if prices have not decreased, the quality of the services provided have increased markedly in quality after privatization.

To measure privatization's effect on consumption, we computed the change in consumer surplus attributable to privatization and distinguished the effects on households with access for every period and households that gained access. The combination of these two effects revealed that the change in welfare is mostly driven by the electricity sector. For both the telecommunications and natural-gas sectors, the access effect is more important than the effect associated with price change. In general, however, these effects are relatively small. Finally, we found that the limited evidence suggests that the effects of privatizations on consumers have not produced large changes in the traditional measures of inequality and poverty.

With respect to employment, notable qualitative changes were observed after privatization; nonetheless, the quantitative effects were small. In sectors subject to privatization, the public-employment level declined by about 150,000 jobs; while the private-employment level expanded, partially compensating for the losses. In terms of working conditions, the privatized sectors have moved toward the labor organization and work terms that predominate in those sectors primarily controlled by the private sector. As our calculations show, employment changes caused by privatization have not significantly influenced the usual measures of inequality and poverty.

Finally, in terms of privatization's effects on fiscal conditions, available evidence suggests that Argentina's privatization allowed for a significant initial reduction in interest payments on the public debt. Moreover, this reduction in fiscal need might have contributed to reducing the crowding out of social public expenditures in the early 1990s.

References

Abdala, M. A. 1996. *Welfare Effects of Buenos Aires' Water and Sewerage Service Privatization.* Bahia Blanca, Argentina: Asociación Argentina de Economía Política (AAEP).

Abdala, M. A. 1998. Instituciones, Contratos y Regulación de Infraestructura en Argentina. Documento 15. Buenos Aires: Fundación Gobierno y Sociedad.

Bebczuk, R., and L. Gasparini. 2001. *Globalization and Inequality: The Case of Argentina.* Working Paper No. 32. Buenos Aires: National University of La Plata (UNLP).

Bosch, E., A. N. de Gimbatti, and Paula Giovagnoli. 1999. *Eficiencia técnica y asignativa en la distribución de energía eléctrica: El caso de EPE SF.* Rosario, Argentina: Asociación Argentina de Economía Política (AAEP).

Canavese, A., W. S. Escudero, and F. Gonzales Alvaredo. 1999. El Impacto de la Inflación sobre la Distribución del Ingreso: El Impuesto Inflacionario en la Argentina en la Década del Ochenta. In *La distribución del ingreso en la Argentina.* Buenos Aires: Latin American Foundation for Economic Research (FIEL).

Chisari, O., and A. Estache. 1997. *Universal Service Obligations in Utility Concession Contracts and the Needs of the Poor in Argentina's Privatizations.* Buenos Aires: World Bank and UADE.

Delfino, J., and A. Casarin. 2001. *The Reform of the Utilities Sector in Argentina.* WIDER Discussion Paper No. 2001/74. Helsinki: UNU/WIDER Publications.

Ennis, H. M., and S. M. Pinto. 2003. *Privatization and Income Distribution in Argentina.* Working Paper No. 2003-02. Puebla, Mexico: Public Policy and Development Studies Institute, University of the Americas.

Estache, A., J. C. Carbajo, and G. de Rus. 1999. *Argentina's Transport Privatization and Re-Regulation: Ups and Downs of a Daring Decade-Long Experience.* Washington: World Bank.

FIEL (Latin American Foundation for Economic Research). 1992. *Capital de infraestructura en la Argentina: Gestión pública, privatización y productividad 1970–2000.* Buenos Aires: Latin American Foundation for Economic Research.

FIEL (Latin American Foundation for Economic Research). 1999. *La regulación de la competencia y de los servicios públicos: Teoría y experiencia Argentina reciente.* Buenos Aires: Ed. Manantial.

FLACSO (Facultad Latinoamericana de Ciencias Sociales). 1998. *Privatización en la Argentina: Marcos regulatorios tarifarios y evolución de precios relativos durante la convertibilidad.* Buenos Aires: Facultad Latinoamericana de Ciencias Sociales.

Galiani, S., P. Gertler, and E. Schargrodsky. 2002. Water for Life: The Impact of Water Supply Privatization on Child Mortality. UDESA, Buenos Aires. Photocopy.

Galiani, S., P. Gertler, E. Schargrodsky, and F. Sturzenegger. 2001. *The Benefits and Cost of Privatization in Argentina: A Microeconomic Analysis.* Washington: Inter-American Development Bank.

Gasparini, L., and W. S. Escudero. 1999. *Bienestar y distribución del ingreso en la Argentina, 1980–1998.* Rosario, Argentina: Asociación Argentina de Economía Política (AAEP).

Millan, J., E. Lora, and A. Micco. 2001. *Sustainability of the Electricity Sector Reforms in Latin America.* Washington: Inter-American Development Bank.

Navajas, F. 1999. *Structural Reforms and the Distributional Effects of Price Changes in Argentina.* Buenos Aires: Latin American Foundation for Economic Research (FIEL) and National University of La Plata (UNLP).

Navajas, F., and A. Porto. 1990. Aspectos de Equidad en el Diseño y Evaluación de Tarifas Públicas No Uniformes. In *Economía de las empresas públicas: Funcionamiento, desregulación y privatización,* ed. A. Porto. Buenos Aires: Instituto Torcuato Di Tella.

Ramamurti, R. 1997. Testing the Limits of Privatization: Argentine Railroads. *World Development* 25, no. 12: 1973–93.

Urbiztondo, S., D. Artana, and F. Navajas. 1998. *La autonomía de los entes reguladores Argentinos.* Working Paper R-340. Washington: Inter-American Development Bank.

Appendix 5A
First- and Second-Order Approximations of Mean Decile Change in Welfare

One can let N_t^d equal the total number of households sampled from decile d in period t, F_{jt}^d the number of households in decile d at time t with access to the formal sector j, and I_{jt}^d those households with informal connection (or no access), so that $N_t^d = F_{jt}^d + I_{jt}^d$. If one considers 1985–86 the preprivatization period $(t = 0)$, and 1996–97 the postprivatization period $(t = 1)$, it then follows that (F_{j0}^d/N_0^d) represents the proportion of households with formal access in both periods, and $[(F_{j1}^d/N_1^d) - (F_{j0}^d/N_0^d)]$ is the proportion with no access (or informal connection) that later gained access to a formal connection. To compute the change in welfare for those households that gained access after privatization, we use the postprivatization period as the reference period and, for each household h and service j, we compute a virtual price $(p_{h,jv})$ using the estimates reported in table 5.6. Therefore, the FOA of the mean decile change in welfare resulting from privatization of public service j is

$$
E\Delta U_j^d = \frac{F_{j0}^d}{N_0^d} \frac{1}{F_{j0}^d} \sum_{h \in d: A_{j0}^h = 1} \Delta_1 U_j^h - \left(\frac{F_{j1}^d}{N_1^d} - \frac{F_{j0}^d}{N_0^d} \right) \frac{1}{F_{j1}^d}
$$

$$
\sum_{h \in d: A_{j0}^h = 1} (\log p_{jv}^h - \log p_{j1}) w_{j1}^h x_{j1}
$$

where A_{jt}^h is an indicator variable of whether household h has access $(A_{jt}^h = 1)$ or not $(A_{jt}^h = 0)$ to service j at time t. For the SOA, we adjust the previous calculations by allowing some quantity response; thus, the formulas for the changes in utility become

$$
E\Delta U_j^d = -\frac{F_{j0}^d}{N_0^d} \frac{1}{F_{j0}^d} \sum_{h \in d: A_{j0}^h = 1} \Delta_1 U_j^h \left[1 + \frac{\Delta \log p_j}{2} \frac{\partial \log w_{j0}^h}{\partial \log p_j} \right]
$$

$$
- \left(\frac{F_{j1}^d}{N_1^d} - \frac{F_{j0}^d}{N_{j0}^d} \right) \frac{1}{F_{j1}^d} \sum_{h \in d: A_{j0}^h = 1} (\log p_{jv}^h - \log p_{j1}) w_{j1}^h x_{j1}
$$

$$
\left[1 + \frac{(\log p_{jv}^h - \log p_{j1})}{2} \frac{\partial \log w_{j0}^h}{\partial \log p_j} \right].
$$

Expected Welfare Change

First, we assume that the change in utility of households that gained access in decile d after the privatization of public service j is given by the following FOA and SOA:

$$E\left(\Delta U_j^d \middle| A_{j0}^h = 0, A_{j1}^h = 1\right) = \frac{1}{F_{j1}^d} \sum_{h \in d: A_{j1}^h = 1} \left(\log p_{jv}^h - \log p_{j1}\right) w_{j1}^h x_{j1},$$

and

$$E\left(\Delta U_j^d \middle| A_{j0}^h = 0, A_{j1}^h = 1\right) = \frac{1}{F_{j1}^d} \sum_{h \in d: A_{j1}^h = 1} \left(\log p_{jv}^h - \log p_{j1}\right)$$
$$w_{j1}^h x_{j1}\left[1 + \frac{\left(\log p_{jv}^h - \log p_{j1}\right)}{2} \frac{\partial \log w_{j1}^h}{\partial \log p_j}\right].$$

The previous equations represent the expected change in welfare attributed to the change in access for decile d, and consist of the average difference between the virtual price and the price after privatization weighed by the amount spent on public service j. Note that the expressions are estimated using survey data after privatization.

Because we cannot determine which households in the period before privatization (1985–86) gained access, we randomly select households from decile d without access before privatization and add the expected change in utility from access shown above. Assuming that all households in 1985–86 (period 0) had the same probability of gaining access after the privatization (period 1), the fraction of households chosen from decile d is given by

$$\tau = \frac{\left(F_{j1}^d / N_1^d\right) - \left(F_{j0}^d / N_0^d\right)}{1 - \left(F_{j0}^d / N_0^d\right)},$$

where τ is the conditional probability of having access in period 1, given that the household lacked access in period 0. The proportion of households without access in period 1, given that they did not have access in the previous period, $(1 - \tau)$, will only be affected by the privatization process if the price of substitutes changed. In this exercise, we do not consider this effect.

6

Peru after Privatization: Are Telephone Consumers Better Off?

MÁXIMO TORERO, ENRIQUE SCHROTH, and ALBERTO PASCÓ-FONT

Over the last decade, Peru's telecommunications market has undergone fundamental changes resulting from market liberalization, privatization, technical progress, and changes in consumer demand. These forces have had direct, long-term effects on consumers and providers. To evaluate this process and assess the effects of these changes, this chapter focuses on one of the greatest forces that has changed Peru's telecommunications industry: privatization of the Peruvian Telephone Company (CPT) and the National Telecommunications Company (ENTEL), which Telefónica de España purchased in 1994.

Today, a decade after privatizing Peru's telecommunications market, its overall effect is still puzzling. More people, mainly at the lower socioeconomic levels (SELs), have access to a telephone. On the other hand, many potential consumers do not take advantage of this option, presumably because they cannot afford the flat monthly charge.

In this chapter, we estimate the effects that various changes in telephone services resulting from privatization have had on consumer welfare at different SELs. We analyze the benefits to consumers of having greater access to telephone lines, along with the cost of the simultaneous increase in monthly telephone tariffs. We measure changes in consumer welfare to

Máximo Torero is a research fellow at the International Food Policy Research Institute. Alberto Pascó-Font was the director of the Group of Analysis for Development (GRADE). Enrique Schroth is assistant professor at the University of Lausanne, Switzerland. This research was supported by a research grant from the Tinker Foundation. The authors are indebted to the comments of Sebastian Galiani, Miguel Urquiola, Paul Gertler, John Nellis, and a remarkably talented team of research assistants: Virgilio Galdo, Eduardo Maruyama, and Gisselle Gajate.

determine whether the gains (i.e., more people with access to a telephone line) offset the higher tariffs, particularly the increased, flat monthly charge.

Sector Overview: The Road to Privatization

Before 1994, the Peruvian telecommunications sector was state-owned. The sector was characterized by a high, unmet demand for access to basic telephone services. Lack of investment and the political control of policies within the firm were responsible for much of this great imbalance. It was assumed that privatization would close the demand gap by boosting efficiency and relaxing the investment constraint, while encouraging development of a competitive market. Indeed, given its degree of development in the mid-1900s, as measured by GDP per capita, Peru should have had a 6 percent ratio of penetration (i.e., 6 out of every 100 households should have had a telephone). Until 1993, the ratio of penetration was 2 percent. The distribution of telephone lines was concentrated in Lima and in wealthier households.

Peru's telecommunications sector was also characterized by distorted tariffs. Installation costs were high (close to $1,000 per residential telephone line in 1993), compared to the international average; however, the flat monthly charge was relatively low. By contrast, tariffs for long distance and additional local calls were high. Like many other countries, Peru assumed that only wealthier consumers used international long distance service; thus, the privatized Telefónica del Perú (TdP) provided a cross subsidy between that service and local telephony. Parallel to the decision to privatize the sector, the Peruvian government decided to rebalance tariffs to reflect the marginal costs of providing the service. The plan was to phase in the adjustment over five years since a full, immediate adjustment was considered too harsh for the welfare of consumers (indeed, the monthly charge for basic service would have increased from $1 to $17). During the five-year adjustment period (1994–98), TdP was permitted to reduce the cross subsidies gradually and finally eliminate them.

Privatization Strategy

The economic reforms implemented in early 1990 by the administration of Alberto Fujimori included privatization of companies in which the state had held a sizeable share. Between November 1991 and February 1992, the Peruvian government put into effect a comprehensive privatization strategy; it defined the methods and prioritized sectors according to their economic significance, potential ease of privatization, and degree of crisis faced. It created Special Privatization Committees or CEPRIs to promote and facilitate this process.

Until 1994, two state-owned companies—CPT and ENTEL—provided telecommunications services. CPT provided local telephony service in metropolitan Lima, while ENTEL served the rest of the country and handled national and international long distance services. The government had organized the sector in this way through the 1970 Telecommunications Act, which considered the sector strategic and therefore kept domestic and foreign private businesses from participating in it.

Under this scheme, all infrastructure investment was undertaken by the public sector. However, because of low tariffs and limited management capacity, the sector experienced little growth, inadequate coverage, and low-quality service.

To manage privatization of the sector, the Fujimori administration passed the Telecommunication Law in 1991 and formed the Telecommunications CEPRI, which issued an international call for bids and set the base price at $546 million. Three consortia responded to the call for bids:

- Telefónica de España, Graña y Montero, Backus, and Banco Wiese;

- Southwestern Bell, Korea Telecom, Daewo Telecom, Condumex-Carso, and Banco de Crédito; and

- GTE, Compañía Portuguesa, and Empresa Brasilera de Telecomunicaciones.

The winning consortium, headed by Telefónica de España, offered $2.002 billion, almost four times the base price, for a 35 percent share in CPT and ENTEL. Of the remaining 65 percent of shares, minority shareholders held 36 percent and the Peruvian state retained 29 percent. Consequently, the privatization process did not conclude in 1994. In July 1996, the state sold off 26.6 percent of its shares through a diversified operation to small and individual shareholders.

Toward a Competitive Sector

The privatization agreements called for a merger of CPT and ENTEL. However, the two entities were required to keep separate accounts. The agreements also established a five-year period of limited competition, during which new competitors could not provide basic telephony services. Remaining telecommunications services (value-added services, mobile telephony, data transmission, e-mail, and cable television) were open to immediate competition.

In exchange for granting this partial natural monopoly, the government required the operator (the winning bidder) to meet goals for expanding service and improving quality. Consequently, expansion and modernization goals in the concession contract called for a total of 1,197,600 lines.

Table 6.1   Maximum rebalancing tariffs, 1994–98
(in 1994 Peruvian soles)

Service tariff	1994	1995	1996	1997	1998
Basic residential	12.970	14.600	18.640	25.290	31.930
Basic commercial	21.800	25.990	29.430	30.520	31.930
Local call (three minutes)	0.144	0.140	0.135	0.128	0.120
Domestic long distance call					
(one minute)	0.575	0.519	0.458	0.416	0.371
International long distance call					
(one minute)	3,532	3,205	2,834	2,398	2,035
Residential installation	924	798	672	546	420
Commercial installation	1,848	1,428	1,092	756	420

Note: Exchange tariff in 1994 was 1.6 Peruvian soles per US dollar.

Source: OSIPTEL, CPT, and ENTEL concession contract.

The privatization process also established a tariff-rebalancing period in which to gradually reduce existing tariff distortions. The goal was to increase monthly service charges considerably, while reducing the cost of local calls (table 6.1). For reasons discussed below, this period of limited competition ended in August 1998, one year before the date established under the contract.

In July 1993, the government created the Supervisory Agency for Private Investment in Telecommunications or OSIPTEL to replace the Telecommunications Regulatory Commission and regulate and oversee development of the telecommunications market. The 1991 Telecommunication Law, which established a competitive sector framework, gave OSIPTEL technical, economic, financial, functional, and administrative autonomy.

End of Limited Competition

The period of limited competition for TdP was to have ended in August 1999. However, as noted above, TdP and OSIPTEL mutually agreed to end it one year earlier (August 1998). OSIPTEL decided that TdP had met most of the goals set forth in the 1994 concession contract. The agreement between the two entities called for a series of changes. Two of the most important were

■ setting maximum tariffs for the service, applicable until 2001 (this delayed what the contract established—i.e., that the new calculation of prices, including the productivity factor, would enter into effect in 1999); and

■ reducing the installation charges from $270 to $150.

With the end of the limited competition period, the government opened the market to new operators willing to provide local, national, and international long distance telephony services. To do so, new operators had to

Table 6.2 Telephone density of selected countries, 1993

Country	Telephone density[a]	Telephone penetration[b]	GDP per capita (US dollars)
Argentina	12.3	27.9	6,910
Bolivia	3.0	11.0	700
Brazil	7.5	21.0	2,550
Chile	11.0	39.1	3,035
Colombia	11.3	33.9	1,305
Ecuador	5.3	19.7	1,150
Mexico	8.8	25.3	3,880
Peru	2.9	10.1	1,450

a. Lines per 100 inhabitants.
b. Lines per 100 households.

Source: World Telecommunications Indicators, International Telecommunications Union (ITU 1993).

pay TdP an interconnection fee, [1] i.e., a charge for using TdP-owned infrastructure. As has been the case in other countries with liberalized telecommunications sectors, new entrants have not, to date, been able to reach agreement on the fee TdP should charge new competitors.

Supply-Side Changes

The major supply-side changes that resulted from privatization can be summarized in terms of five indicators: coverage, service quality, tariffs, the company's earnings structure, and its economic efficiency and results.

Coverage

In 1992 and 1993, Peru's penetration was a mere 2.6 lines and 2.9 lines, respectively. This was a low density compared with other countries in the region (table 6.2).

Declining fiscal revenues, the debt crisis, and subsidized tariffs that did not reflect the cost structure limited network expansion. These, in turn, resulted in low levels of telephone density and growing unsatisfied demand. In 1993, Peru's customers had to wait an average of 118 months for line installation, compared with 17 months for customers in Colombia and 11 months for those in Mexico.

In response, one of the first actions of the privatized TdP was to expand the telecommunications network to satisfy unmet demand. Figure 6.1 clearly

---

1. The maximum fee for daytime interconnection was first set at $0.029 per minute, which was much higher than fees charged in Chile ($0.017) or Mexico ($0.022).

Figure 6.1 Evolution of the number of lines installed and in service, 1993–98

number of lines (millions)

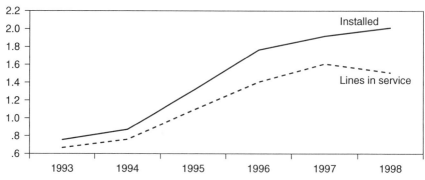

Source: OSIPTEL (1998b).

shows the process of network expansion between 1993 and 1998 and the overall increase of approximately 167 percent in the number of lines installed.

In terms of coverage, TdP amply met the goals set forth in the concession contract (table 6.3). By 1998, TdP had already covered the entire market for basic telephony, which may explain why it decided to advance the date for ending the limited competition period. Decreasing growth in the number of lines in service, which occurred around 1998, could have indicated over-coverage in the sector (figure 6.1).

Service Quality

Before privatization, service quality was well below international standards. In 1992, only 35 to 40 percent of all phone calls were successfully completed. Such low efficiency was caused, in part, by the network's small size and obsolete technology. In addition, inadequate maintenance of telephone cables affected quality of communications (cables have a useful life of 15 years; by 1993, some had been in use for more than 60 years). In 1993, only 33 percent of the network had been digitized. By 1998, 90 percent had been digitized, and 99 percent of international long distance and local calls were successfully completed.

Tariffs

The low level of investment by CPT and ENTEL can be partially attributed to the companies' low earnings as, over time, telephone-service charges fell increasingly behind costs. This kept these state-owned companies from generating the funds needed to finance network expansion or quality improvements. In effect, sociopolitical, rather than technical, criteria guided tariff administration. The government subsidized local telephony services by charging well above the cost of tariffs for international long distance and other services. As a result, approximately 5 percent of ENTEL clients provided 29 percent of its earnings, and 6 percent of CPT clients provided 28 percent of its earnings.

Though many other countries in the region had this type of cross subsidy, Peru differed substantially in its telephone-service tariff. For example, in 1993, the price of installing a telephone line in Peru was $1,500 (well above the average for Latin American countries), while it had a low basic monthly tariff of $2; for those who used more than the minimum service, the excess tariff was extremely low. Conversely, the tariff for international long distance service was extremely high.

The contract established the average maximum rebalancing tariffs, which increased basic monthly tariffs and lowered costs of local, national, and international long distance calls. Figure 6.2 shows the evolution of the index of the basic tariff and cost of a local call. Table 6.4 shows the evolution in real terms of the tariffs for local, national, and international long distance calls.

TdP markedly raised the price of monthly service, almost doubling it in nominal terms, and raised the charge for a local call by changing the unit of measurement, in 1998, from a three-minute to a one-minute pulse.

Earnings Structure

During the period of state ownership, the amount of international traffic each company handled was markedly disproportionate to its assigned sector. CPT generated 86 percent of outgoing and 90 percent of incoming international traffic, while ENTEL generated the remaining 14 percent and 10 percent, respectively. This situation, along with ENTEL's exclusive concession to outgoing, international long distance service and lack of an interconnection policy, resulted in conflicts between the two companies over interconnection charges. As a consequence, they stopped making transfers for interconnection services.

Following privatization, important changes have occurred in earnings composition. Local telephony has become the most important service category, while earnings for national and international long distance services have fallen proportionately. These results were foreseen in the tariff-rebalancing scheme. Furthermore, an observable increase in earnings has occurred in mobile telephony, business communications, and publicity.

Efficiency and Economic Results

CPT and ENTEL had an excessive number of employees proportionate to their scale of activities and low productivity. For example, at one time,

Table 6.3 Compliance with the program to expand and modernize the sector, 1994–98 (thousands)

Item	1994	1995	1996	1997	1998
Additional lines to be installed	104.00	140.00	216.00	259.30	259.30
Additional lines installed	116.68	439.24	445.71	203.92	n.a.
Lines to be replaced	20.00	30.00	50.00	50.00	50.00
Lines replaced	63.49	111.78	45.10	n.a.	n.a.
Public telephones to be installed	2.10	3.50	4.40	4.50	4.50
Public telephones installed	5.17	15.54	14.64	3.64	n.a.

n.a. = not available

Source: Telefónica del Perú, annual reports (1994–98).

ENTEL's Lima office had 3,700 employees, an extremely high figure, considering that the company's scope of operations did not include Lima. Another indicator of the inefficiencies within both CPT and ENTEL was their structure of operating costs. In 1992, CPT allocated 40 percent of its costs to wages and salaries, in contrast to ENTEL, which allocated 20 percent (Coopers & Lybrand, Morgan Grenfell, and ProInversión 1993). The results were high operating costs per telephone line and low profits.

Table 6.5 presents the results achieved by TdP in terms of efficiency and profits. The gains in efficiency are obvious (measured by the number of lines per employee). Accordingly, profitability is also high.

Methodology for Measuring Consumer Welfare

To determine whether privatization was regressive and which types of households (classified by their observable characteristics) bear a greater portion of the burden or enjoy a greater portion of the benefits of the price changes resulting from privatization, this study used an approach that differs from previous efforts (e.g., Galal et al. 1994; Martin and Parker 1997).

Unlike the cited studies, we did not build welfare measurements for each interest group involved in the privatization to obtain indicators of aggregate welfare.[2] Although we used certain concepts developed by the cited works, we devised a different model to put a value on consumer welfare before and after privatization and to measure the net effects on consumers: We estimated a partial demand equation for access to and use of the various telecommunications services. This allowed us to evaluate the effects of privatization of all services offered by TdP on consumer welfare. We used a specific panel of households surveyed by GRADE, a Peruvian research institute, in 1997, concerning household use and consumption of

---

2. Jones, Tandon, and Vogelsang (1990, 21–51) discuss in detail the construction of these indicators.

Figure 6.2 Evolution of the basic local-tariff index, 1991–97

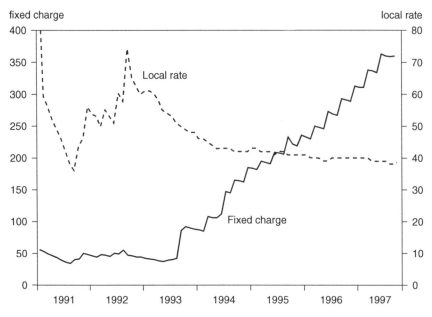

Source: Central Bank of Peru Weekly Notes.

telecommunications services for which monthly consumption for each service had been collected over the previous year.

Two prior GRADE studies conducted at OSIPTEL's request (Escobal, Fry, and Schroth 1996; Gallardo and Galdo 1998b) and a third study by OSIPTEL (1995b) provided data that allowed us to estimate key parameters.[3] The GRADE studies estimate functions of residential demand for access to and use of local and long distance services, using a household survey. The OSIPTEL study reports average costs of each service provided by TdP (e.g., residential access, local calls, long distance calls, mobile calls, and value-added services).

Market Models

The next step was to model the market for each product under the preprivatization and postprivatization scenarios. The model envisioned the demand for specific telecommunications services as a two-stage decision rule. In deciding whether to request a telephone line, and given the price

---

3. Using studies from other countries is often arbitrary because the characteristics of these experiences differ from the Peruvian context.

Table 6.4   Evolution of telephone tariffs, 1993–98
(in 1995 Peruvian soles)

Year	IPC	Nominal				Real			
		Rent	Local	DLD	ILD	Rent	Local	DLD	ILD
1993	0.820	5.000	0.170	0.484	4.860	1.000	0.034	0.097	0.972
1994	0.946	11.990	0.180	0.628	3.860	1.000	0.015	0.052	0.322
1995	1.000	14.166	0.185	0.629	3.871	14.136	0.185	0.629	3.874
1996	1.166	25.150	0.207	0.618	3.824	1.000	0.008	0.025	0.152
1997	1.241	36.670	0.213	0.603	3.477	1.000	0.006	0.016	0.095
1998	1.316	43.220	0.234	0.444	3.360	1.000	0.005	0.010	2.547

DLD = domestic long distance
ILD = international long distance
IPC = indice de precios al consumidor

Note: 1995 average, otherwise end of the period.

Source: OSIPTEL (1998b).

for use of the telephone service, consumers compare their surplus to the service charges they would have to pay. Using this framework, we estimated functions of demand from private households and businesses for access to and use of a range of services. Using these estimations, we compared the situations before and after privatization.

The estimated demand functions identified all relevant factors for determining the position on the demand curve, given observed price, quantity, and, in the case of access, statistics of waiting lists. Because the demand functions were estimated from a panel of households that evidenced variations in prices, income, and demographic characteristics, we could directly calibrate the position of each curve at different points of time without needing additional assumptions for unobserved variables.

Furthermore, the calibration could be less arbitrary than those used in previous studies since it was unnecessary to assume linearity for the demand curves. In fact, we chose the functional form of the demand curves in order to obtain the best fit rather than achieve algebraic simplicity (Escobal, Fry, and Schroth 1996).

In this study, we associated access to the main telephone services with each of their corresponding services. We identified the following access services that TdP has provided for residential lines:[4]

■ local calls,

■ domestic long distance calls, and

■ international long distance calls.

---

4. This study covers only the cities of Arequipa, Chiclayo, Cuzco, and Trujillo and will be complemented by a similar study financed by the Tinker Foundation for the city of Lima.

Table 6.5 Performance indicators, 1994–98

Indicator	1994	1995	1996	1997	1998
Lines installed (per employee)	98.0	155.0	281.0	329.0	355.0
Lines in service (per employee)	87.0	132.0	228.0	282.0	275.0
Lines in service (per 100 inhabitants)	3.8	3.8	3.8	3.8	3.8
Waiting time (months)	33.0	5.0	2.0	2.0	1.5
Net profits (in millions of US dollars)	35.5	305.1	348.3	400.5	213.0
Net profits/earnings (percent)	5.0	29.4	28.8	24.9	16.9
Net profits/equity (percent)	2.9	21.1	28.8	24.9	15.7

Source: Telefónica del Perú, annual reports (1994–98).

Changes in Access and Use

The next step aimed to discover changes in welfare caused by privatization only, not by other changes that may have occurred had the telecommunications sector remained under state ownership and control. For this purpose, we assumed that the magnitude and levels of price increases would not have occurred in the absence of privatization.

After calibrating the demand functions to approximate the result observed using the information on lines of access, changes for basic service and installation, and number of potential subscribers on a waiting list, we then measured consumer welfare five years before and five years after privatization. It became clear that the reduction in installation costs and the progressive reduction in the waiting time for installation would significantly raise consumer welfare above its preprivatization levels.

Figure 6.3 illustrates how simultaneously increasing the number of lines installed and reducing access charges affect consumer welfare. In this particular case, the average charge for monthly service (the sum of the charge for basic service and the one-time, installation payment divided into monthly installments) falls from rp_0 to rp_1. The demand function, $q^{da} = q^{da}(p, y, x)$, in which p is a vector of all relevant prices (average charge for basic monthly service, complementary and substitute goods), y is the income, and x is a vector of other causal variables, can also be expressed inversely, $rp^{da} = rp^{da}(q, y, x)$, to reflect the maximum price that a home defined by the pair (y, x) is willing to pay for access to a telephone line. Given these charges and a restriction on supply, expressed as q_0, a waiting list is given by the difference of $q^{da}(rp_0, y_0, x_0) - q_0$. Given that the number of lines installed increased to a level of q_1, the new waiting list time is then $q^{da}(rp_1, y_1, x_1) - q_1$.

According to figure 6.3, the components to be estimated would be the areas $ACFrp_1$ and $ABDrp_0$. The difference between them (the shaded area) would yield the increase in consumer surplus resulting from more households having access to residential lines.[5] Once the demand function was

---

5. The method of estimation would be the same for commercial users.

Figure 6.3 Welfare effects of relaxed supply restrictions and the change in regulated prices on telephone-line access market

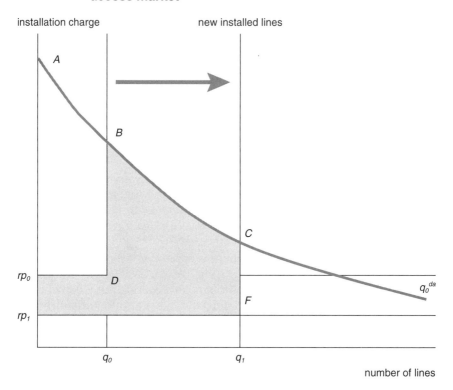

installation charge   new installed lines

A

B

C

rp_0 *D*

F

rp_1

q_0^{da}

q_0 q_1

number of lines

Source:

known and its position calibrated, one could directly register this increase, as follows:

$$\int_{q_0}^{q_1} p(q, x_0, y_0) + rp_0 \cdot q_0 - rp_1 \cdot q_1 \qquad (6.1)$$

As mentioned above, one also needed to estimate the welfare effects of using a specific service (i.e., a telephone line) on consumer surplus. During the first five years of the concession, cross subsidies were eliminated, charges for access and international long distance service were reduced, and tariffs for local services were increased. Consequently, a complete measurement of the change in consumer surplus for basic telephony services requires adding the welfare gains resulting from access to the potential reductions derived from increased local-service tariffs.

Once the demand functions and the observed quantities and prices were known, registering the consumer surplus would become a straightforward

Figure 6.4 Welfare effects of changes in regulated prices and increase in number of users on market for telephone-line services

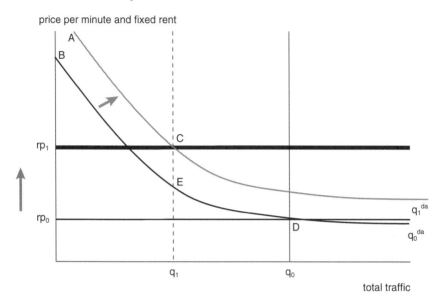

price per minute and fixed rent

task, given that consumers no longer have to be on a waiting list for service. The demand functions estimated for the use of local and long distance services (i.e., demand for calls) include the effects of a new equilibrium on the access market, which is reflected by a displacement of the demand function from q_0^d to q_1^d. The specifications include the number of lines in service, as an explanatory variable, as a way to incorporate network externality effects (Taylor and Kridel 1990).

Figure 6.4 provides an example of the effects of simultaneous increases in access lines and charges per minute for any type of call available to residential lines (local, national, and international long distance calls). The increase in number of access lines is caused by the reduction in cost of access (from rp_0 to rp_1) and is represented by the displacement of the demand curve to q_1^{da}. Furthermore, the increase in the charge per minute for calls is represented by the change in price (from p_0 to p_1).[6]

Thus, to register the change in consumer welfare, we simply evaluated the following:

$$\int_0^{q_1} p(q, x_1, y_1)dq - \int_0^{q_0} p(q, x_0, y_0)dq + p_0 \cdot q_0 - p_1 \cdot q_1 \qquad (6.2)$$

---

6. Based on the tariff-rebalancing program shown in table 6.1.

This equation is equivalent to the difference between the areas ACp_1 and BDp_0.

Clearly, there was no reason to infer an increase or reduction in consumer surplus as a result of the simultaneous changes. Furthermore, in some markets, regulated charges per call had increased (local exchange), while charges for other services had decreased (international long distance). Consequently, to evaluate the consumer-welfare implications of privatizing CPT and ENTEL precisely, we had to compare the gains arising from relaxing supply restrictions on the access market with changes in welfare arising from all associated consumer services.

We next estimated and then evaluated the income-distribution effects of price increases, and determined which types of households shouldered a greater portion of the burden or enjoyed more benefits of these price changes. This allowed us to estimate the effects of privatization and delineate whether these changes in price scenarios were a net gain or loss to the welfare of Peruvian households.

Estimating Demand

We started from the premise that household preferences are represented by a utility function:

$$u = u(x_{local}, x_{ldn}, x_{ldi}, z) \tag{6.3}$$

in which x_l is the total amount that a residential customer consumes of each service available (local, national, and international long distance calls), and z is an index of the consumption of other goods. Solving the optimization problem, we derived the indirect utility function, $V(p,y)$, in which y is the income of each household and p is a vector with the prices of the three basic services and a general index of prices for the remaining goods.

A household chooses the services it will use on the basis of access to lines. In making its decision, it compares the value of using the services $V(p,y)$, given the prices, with the cost of access attributable to that period. In this case, having access to a line allowed a customer to make any of the three types of calls mentioned. In households for which we were able to obtain a telephone bill, we observed that some made only local calls while others made local and long distance calls. This characteristic allowed us to order the households based on their consumption decisions. However, data restrictions prevented our demand estimations from capturing changes in quality of telephone services.

Econometrically, we modeled the demand for a specific telecommunications service as a two-stage decision rule. First, we modeled the decision to access the network using a probit model. From this equation, we obtained the Mills inverse ratio to correct for the access problem. This ratio was included in demand estimations to obtain price elasticities and consumer surpluses for the three services under study, correcting for the bias for lack of access.

Measuring Consumer Surplus

Using the estimations of demand at the residential level, we obtained a functional form for the demand for use of local, national, and long distance services. This demand curve represents households that, at that point in time, had access to a telephone line.

According to the Living Standards Measurement Survey (LSMS), the functional form that yielded the best fit—for all of Lima's SELs, those surveyed in four other major Peruvian cities, and later for the whole of urban Peru—was

$$q_{it}^n = \exp(x_{it}\beta^n + p_{it}\alpha^n + \varepsilon_{it}) \tag{6.4}$$

The superscript n indicates the SEL, i equals the household, and t equals time. The relevant prices are p_{it}; thus, the elasticities are recovered from the estimators of the parameters, α, for each SEL. Lastly, q_{it} is the traffic measured for each of the three services considered in this study.

The basic idea is to measure consumer surplus as the difference between the surplus for making a certain number of calls at a specific point in time and the fixed amount paid for access to the line.[7] Thus, for a given SEL, we define

$$S_{it}^j(p_{it}, .) = \int_{P_t}^{P_{max}} q_{it}^j(p, .)dp, \forall j \in \{Local, DLD, ILD\} \tag{6.5}$$

as the consumer surplus for using the line for any of the three services and r_{it} as the annual installment made on the flat installation charge. Then

$$\tilde{S}_{it}(p_{it}, r_{it}) = \sum_j S_{it}^j(p_t) - r_{it} \tag{6.6}$$

measures the total net surplus of all services.

Replacing the functional form given in equation 6.6, and solving the equation, one obtains the surplus as

$$\tilde{S}_{it}(p_{it}, r_{it}) = -\frac{1}{\alpha^j}\exp(x_{it}\beta^n + p_{it}\alpha^n + \varepsilon_{it})\Big|_{p_{it}}^{p\,max} - r_{it}$$

$$\tilde{S}_{it}(p_{it}, r_{it}) = -\frac{1}{\alpha^j}\exp(x_{it}\beta^n + p'\alpha^n + \varepsilon_{it}) - r_{it} \tag{6.7}$$

in which α^j is the elasticity of the price itself.

---

7. The value of the flat installation charge converted into a perpetuity (e.g., annualized) value.

Household Survey

For Peru's urban population, we used a household panel surveyed especially for this study. We applied the survey to 7.6 million residents, who accounted for more than 50 percent of the country's urban population and more than 80 percent of its fixed telephone installations. The total sample size of 1,708 urban households, selected during the 1996–97 period, was constructed to be representative of residential demand for telephony services in metropolitan Lima and Peru's principal provincial cities. In metropolitan Lima, the 907 households selected were grouped into high, middle, low, and very low SELs. In the four other cities—Cuzco, Arequipa, Chiclayo, and Trujillo—801 households were chosen and grouped into the four SEL categories (Pasco-Font, Gallardo, and Fry 1999).

The survey questionnaire consisted of five sections:

■ present use and quality of telecommunications services,

■ household's potential use of services,

■ household characteristics,

■ household-member characteristics, and

■ information from the household telephone bill.

The study also required information, by SEL, on the number of families and the telephone penetration tariff. For metropolitan Lima, the data source was the SEL report prepared by Apoyo S. A. The penetration tariffs reported in the tables were weighted by size of households in each SEL. No similar information was available for the provincial cities for the period studied.[8] Consequently, we estimated the number of households and used the penetration tariff of the middle SEL of metropolitan Lima. As input for estimating the number of households, we used the final results of the 1993 National Census.

Results Using Household Surveys for Lima and Four Major Cities

Based on estimates of demand for basic telephony services, we computed household welfare changes for the four SEL categories (A, B, C, and D).[9] We also used Torero's results for households in SELs A and B in Cuzco, Arequipa, Chiclayo, and Trujillo (Torero and Pasco-Font 2000).

---

8. Information was available only for 1996 for the cities of Arequipa, Chiclayo, and Trujillo.

9. SELs were grouped according to income and other characteristics, with category A comprising the wealthiest households and category D the poorest.

Tables 6.6 and 6.7 provide details of the results obtained and the demand estimates for the cities studied. Each table presents three models. The first corrects for the selection bias resulting from (1) whether consumers had a telephone, and (2) households for which telephone bill information could not be obtained. The second model corrects only for the first selection bias. The third model includes a dummy variable identifying whether the household has a cellular phone.[10] Although all three models are correct, the third is more econometrically sound because it incorporates both types of selection (i.e., by access and charges billed).

Results for the cities studied exhibited the expected signs and coefficients. Thus, the tariff for the respective service is significant and has the expected negative sign. Furthermore, the price of international long distance service is significant (and has a positive sign) in explaining the use of local service and national long distance service, indicating a degree of substitution between the two products. Lastly, household demographic characteristics (education and income) are significant and have the expected signs. We also included fixed-district effects for the Lima estimates and those of the cities included on the panel for the rest of Peru. In both cases, the F statistical test demonstrated that the fixed effects were significant overall.

Based on these estimates and deriving equation 6.4 with regard to price, we recovered the price elasticities of use demand for each of the three services studied. As table 6.8 shows, demand for local and domestic long distance services was inelastic in the cities studied. This result is consistent with many other studies,[11] including those of Pasco-Font, Gallardo, and Fry (1999);[12] Doherty (1984); Zona and Jacob (1990); Gatto et. al. (1988); Duncan and Perry (1994); and Levy (1996).

Using the demand elasticities obtained from these estimates, the next step was to measure the welfare effects for local, national, and international long distance calls. We also included the effect of increases in the flat, monthly service charge on each household's surplus, in terms of having the fixed residential service, following the methodology set forth in the preceding section.

---

10. Accounting for access to cellular phones is crucial, especially since 1997, when intensity of use increased substantially. From 1993 to 1998, the density of cellular phones jumped from 0.2 to 3; however, as this study's results show, cellular phones complement, rather than substitute for, possession of a fixed-line phone, thereby increasing expenditures resulting from calls from fixed-line phones to cellular ones.

11. Elasticities in these studies ranged from –0.21 to –0.475. See Pasco-Font, Gallardo, and Fry (1999) for further details.

12. Although this study used the same data that Pasco-Font, Gallardo, and Fry (1999) used, it estimated demand using a different method that incorporated people who did not provide information from their telephone bills into the correction for selection bias. In addition, this study included the difference in price, based on the time calls were made, into the calculation of implicit prices.

Table 6.6 Estimate of local telephone demand in metropolitan Lima

Variable	Local calls			National long distance calls			International long distance calls		
	Model 1	Model 2	Model 3	Model 1	Model 2	Model 3	Model 1	Model 2	Model 3
Local rate	-2.50** (1.08)	-2.44** (1.065)	-2.70** (1.145)	-3.62 (2.388)	-3.45 (2.366)	-3.61 (2.386)	3.28 (2.069)	3.27 (2.067)	3.63* (2.017)
International long distance rate	0.47*** (.145)	0.47*** (.145)	0.57** (.229)	0.23** (.101)	0.22** (.1)	0.23** (.101)	-0.30** (.133)	-0.30** (.133)	-0.30** (.129)
Domestic long distance rate	-0.03 (.026)	-0.03 (.026)	-0.07 (.069)	-0.76** (.375)	-0.77** (.375)	-0.76** (.375)	0.47** (.257)	0.47** (.258)	0.17 (.312)
Rate of penetration in Lima (network externality)	1.55*** (.481)	1.50** (.479)	1.68*** (.478)						
Relatives in provinces				0.80*** (.101)	0.80*** (.101)	0.80*** (.101)			
Relatives abroad							0.42*** (.08)	0.42*** (.079)	0.44*** (.08)
Household with cellular phone			0.25* (.13)			-0.06 (.203)			0.82*** (.212)

Constant	4.33*** (.378)	4.27*** (.37)	4.41*** (.447)	0.33 (.729)	0.46 (.715)	0.33 (.73)	-0.31 (.697)	-0.21 (.691)	-0.25 (.687)
Mills inverse ratio (reported bill)	-0.35*** (.075)		-0.36*** (.075)	-0.16 (.115)		0.16 (.115)	0.16* (.091)		0.15* (.091)
Mills inverse ratio (has telephone)		-0.48*** (.102)			-0.34** (.156)			0.16 (.126)	
Observations	2021	2021	2021	1993	1993	1993	1940	1940	1940
F-test	39.18	39.27	37.71	14.94	14.89	14.47	8.63	8.61	8.72
Prob > F-test	0.0000	0.0000	0.0000	0.000	0.000	0.000	0.000	0.000	0.000
R-squared	0.4472	0.4471	0.4489	0.1802	0.1813	0.1802	0.107	0.106	0.129

* = significant at 90 percent
** = significant at 95 percent
*** = significant at 99 percent

Note: First three regressions correspond to the demand for local calls (minutes), the second three for the demand of national long distance calls, and the last three for the demand of international long distance calls. Within each dependent variable, three models are presented. The first model corrects not only for the selection bias resulting from whether consumers have a telephone but also for the selection bias caused by households for which telephone bill information could not be obtained. The second model, on the other hand, corrects only for the selection bias for consumers having a telephone. Finally, the third model includes a dummy variable identifying whether the household possesses cellular phones. Standard errors are in parentheses. Robust standard errors account for sample clustering and stratification. Demographic controls include: household income, household income squared, percentage of young people in the household (13–24 years old), percentage of young females in the household (13–24 years old), household size, and education-degree level of household head. Additionally all regressions include district fixed effects, and the F-test was significant, with p < 0.001.

237

Table 6.7   Estimate of local telephone use demand outside metropolitan Lima

Variable	Local calls			National long distance calls			International long distance calls		
	Model 1	Model 2	Model 3	Model 1	Model 2	Model 3	Model 1	Model 2	Model 3
Local rate	-2.52** (1.09)	-2.50** (1.086)	-2.74** (1.026)	-4.12*** (1.613)	-4.12*** (1.612)	-4.44*** (1.469)	-0.02 (.393)	-0.02 (.395)	-0.07 (.406)
International long distance rate	0.13 (.174)	0.14 (.175)	0.09 (.174)	-0.13 (.155)	-0.12 (.155)	-0.17 (.162)	-0.43** (.197)	-0.43** (.195)	-0.43** (.194)
Domestic long distance rate	-0.17** (.085)	-0.16** (.083)	-0.20** (.08)	-0.89*** (.267)	-0.88*** (.267)	-0.93*** (.266)	0.04 (.147)	0.04 (.145)	0.03 (.148)
Relatives in provinces				0.65*** (.248)	0.65*** (.248)	0.61** (.246)			
Relatives abroad							0.23*** (.032)	0.22*** (.032)	0.22*** (.033)
Household with cellular phone			0.49*** (.105)			0.67*** (.191)			0.13 (.138)
Constant	5.03*** (.605)	4.99*** (.513)	5.33*** (.594)	2.72*** (.98)	2.51** (.885)	3.05*** (.987)	1.49** (.762)	1.68** (.738)	1.55** (.753)
Mills inverse ratio (reported bill)	-0.22* (.126)		-0.23* (.125)	-0.11 (.197)		-0.11 (.197)	-0.06 (.101)		-0.06 (.102)
Mills inverse ratio (has telephone)		-0.48*** (.153)			-0.06 (.264)			-0.30 (.119)	
Obs.	1367	1367	1367	1348	1348	1348	1356	1356	1356
F-test	18.84	19.99	20.70	9.04	8.89	9.31	5.56	5.7	5.25
Prob > F-test	0.000	0.000	0.000	0.000	0.000	0.000	0.000	0.000	0.000
R-squared	0.143	0.147	0.154	0.094	0.094	0.103	0.094	0.098	0.096

* = significant at 90 percent
** = significant at 95 percent
*** = significant at 99 percent

Note: See table 6.6.

Table 6.8   Price elasticities of use demand

City	Service	Elasticity
Lima[a]	Local	−0.494
	Domestic long distance	−0.478
	International long distance	−1.095
Province cities[b]	Local	−0.689
	Domestic long distance	−0.548
	International long distance	−1.585

a. Metropolitan Lima (SELs A, B, C, and D).
b. Arequipa, Chiclayo, Cuzco, and Trujillo (SELs A and B).

Given the functional form of our directly estimated demand functions, when the percentage of change in the tariffs is the same, the percentage of change in a household's welfare is also the same—i.e., the latter does not depend on total consumption, but on the parameters of the demand function. However, the measure of change in consumer surplus varies by household because the flat, monthly service charge represents a different proportion of each household's spending on telephony services. Obviously, this variance is less within the respective SELs because each level comprises households with similar spending patterns for basic telephony services.[13]

---

13. Appendix table 6A.1 presents detailed results obtained for the four SELs of metropolitan Lima. It first shows the percentage change in the average welfare of the households surveyed—i.e., the changes projected for the years outside of the survey period are representative of the average household in SELs A, B, C, and D that had a telephone at the time the survey was conducted. This part does not incorporate the welfare gains for households that obtained a connection to the fixed network after privatization. By 1995, all households in SEL A had a telephone; thus, the dynamics of joining the network did not affect this calculation. However, for SELs B, C, and D, one would expect the average change in consumer surplus to be underestimated if the dynamics of new entrants joining the fixed network were not considered. Thus, the second half of the table attempts to incorporate the gains in household welfare that resulted from obtaining a connection to the fixed network after privatization. We quantified the number of new households that obtained a telephone line in the following period ($t + 1$). Also, because households that had just obtained a line were not expected to place as much value on the service (because they had not spent a long time on the waiting list), we assigned them the minimum welfare for households in their SEL and pertinent year. Lastly, we again weighted the surplus per home and obtained the change in surplus weighted by access (last column). It should be noted that they performed various simulations assigning different surplus values to the last households that acquired telephone lines, and the percentages of change were not substantially affected. Finally, the table reports the average change in consumer surplus, weighting the change of each component by its relative importance in the total surplus.

Results for other cities are presented in appendix table 6A.2. Although the results are similar to those for metropolitan Lima, the degree of change is smaller because of lower consumption by SELs A and B and a lower penetration ratio. Thus, Chiclayo has practically no drop in percentage of change, while Cuzco experienced the largest drop.

Tables 6.9 and 6.10 summarize this study's main results (appendix tables 6A.1 and 6A.2). Since privatization in 1994, consumer surplus has seen an absolute gain, both by service and SEL, with only a small reduction in growth rate since 1997. However, this analysis of per-household consumer surplus shows that results have not been uniform across SELs.

As tables 6.11 and 6.12 illustrate, while high and medium SELs (A and B, respectively) have experienced a clear gain in welfare, that of SELs C and D has decreased since 1996. For the lowest-income consumers (SEL D), welfare is lower than preprivatization levels, and low-income consumers (SEL C) have received increasing gains per household only since 1996. Moreover, the per-household consumer surplus has a relatively regressive distribution.

The main explanation for the decline in consumer surplus is the permanent increase in the fixed monthly payment (figure 6.2). This price increase had a greater effect on lower SELs because these households use the service less (i.e., they make fewer calls). As a result, a greater proportion of their spending goes to pay the flat monthly charge. There is also a cross-price impact with local calls since the proportionately larger reduction of long distance tariffs has led to a substitution of local calls for long distance ones.

To make matters worse, in 1997, OSIPTEL reduced the unit of measurement for local calls from a three-minute to a one-minute pulse (at a higher equivalent tariff) and expanded the definition of the geographic area. These measures, which translated into an increase in the price of a local call, help to explain the reduction of growth in total consumer surplus since 1997. When Peru's prices for local calls and fixed monthly fees are compared with those of Argentina and Chile—two countries that have also undergone privatization—it is clear that Peru still has room for tariff reduction (figure 6.5).

Thus, although gains have accrued from privatization in terms of increased efficiency, productivity, access, and consumer welfare, further tariff rebalancing is needed to avoid disruption of the benefits of privatization. The steep rise in the fixed monthly tariff, together with higher charges for local calls, has had a direct, negative effect on consumers.

Summing Up

In the early 1990s, Peru's telecommunications service was characterized by long waiting times, outdated technology, poor service, artificially low prices that failed to cover costs and provide for capital investment, and the capture of firms by workers and unions. As the country became mired in recession, inflation, budget deficits, and balance of payments crises, the situation worsened. However, by the end of the decade, the situation was much improved, mainly as a result of privatizing Peru's two national telecommunications companies, CPT and ENTEL, by Telefónica de España.

Table 6.9 Estimated total welfare gains in metropolitan Lima, 1993–98

Service	1993	1994	1995	1996	1997	1998
With direct and cross effect in prices						
Local	11,771,097	20,085,738	25,000,310	29,356,177	35,349,003	28,826,896
Domestic long distance	1,409,310	1,991,975	2,852,576	4,496,533	5,862,459	7,534,980
International long distance	817,119	1,755,544	2,432,837	3,750,699	5,148,160	6,061,222
Total	13,997,525	23,833,262	30,285,719	37,603,409	46,359,621	42,423,095
Total-fixed charge	11,322,804	17,449,544	21,763,703	23,703,544	27,104,010	18,700,779
Without cross effect in prices						
Local	13,002,981	19,516,369	25,000,310	31,807,954	39,417,483	40,193,995
Domestic long distance	1,997,683	2,183,086	2,852,576	4,074,443	5,008,968	7,106,803
International long distance	1,503,654	1,966,274	2,432,837	3,188,643	3,976,477	4,882,022
Total	16,504,318	23,665,729	30,285,723	39,071,040	48,402,929	52,182,820
Total-fixed charge	13,829,596	17,282,011	21,763,707	25,171,175	29,147,318	28,460,504

Table 6.10 Estimated total welfare gains in rest of Peru, 1993–98

Service	1993	1994	1995	1996	1997	1998
With direct and cross effect in prices						
Local	573,530	1,334,367	1,792,757	2,207,613	2,594,140	2,576,037
Domestic long distance	194,091	444,578	782,187	1,143,480	1,430,908	2,031,302
International long distance	75,795	121,203	142,409	170,852	195,439	219,337
Total	843,415	1,900,147	2,717,353	3,521,946	4,220,487	4,826,676
Total-fixed charge	638,937	1,178,908	1,522,214	1,664,320	1,884,881	1,793,080
Without cross effect in prices						
Local	749,316	1,401,535	1,845,421	2,234,657	2,594,140	2,575,566
Domestic long distance	674,745	753,934	952,687	1,235,154	1,430,908	2,093,021
International long distance	76,722	121,108	142,178	170,907	195,439	221,892
Total	1,500,783	2,276,577	2,940,286	3,640,719	4,220,487	4,890,479
Total-fixed charge	1,296,305	1,555,337	1,745,147	1,783,093	1,884,881	1,856,884

Table 6.11 Estimated average per-household welfare gains in metropolitan Lima, 1993–98

Service	1993	1994	1995	1996	1997	1998
With direct and cross effect in prices						
Local	40.5	57.1	59.9	54.2	55.3	37.9
Domestic long distance	4.6	5.3	6.3	8.1	8.7	9.7
International long distance	2.7	4.9	5.6	6.7	7.6	7.9
Total	47.8	67.3	71.8	69.0	71.7	55.4
Total-fixed charge	39.1	50.2	52.9	44.4	43.6	24.8
Without cross effect in prices						
Local	44.7	55.5	59.9	58.7	61.7	52.8
Domestic long distance	6.5	5.8	6.3	7.3	7.5	9.1
International long distance	5.1	5.4	5.6	5.7	5.9	6.4
Total	56.3	66.8	71.8	71.7	75.0	68.3
Total-fixed charge	47.6	49.6	52.9	47.2	47.0	37.7

Table 6.12 Estimated average per-household welfare gains in rest of Peru, 1993–98

Service	1993	1994	1995	1996	1997	1998
With direct and cross effect in prices						
Local	12.4	25.8	30.5	34.5	37.7	36.9
Domestic long distance	4.2	8.6	13.3	17.6	20.9	29.2
International long distance	1.6	2.3	2.4	2.6	2.9	3.1
Total	18.2	36.7	46.2	54.7	61.4	69.2
Total-fixed charge	13.8	22.8	25.9	26.0	27.4	25.7
Without cross effect in prices						
Local	16.2	27.1	31.4	34.9	37.7	36.9
Domestic long distance	14.6	14.6	16.2	19.0	20.9	30.1
International long distance	1.7	2.3	2.4	2.6	2.9	3.2
Total	32.5	44.0	50.0	56.6	61.4	70.1
Total-fixed charge	28.0	30.1	29.7	27.8	27.4	26.6

From 1993 to 1998, the Peruvian telecommunication sectors dramatically expanded their network by approximately 167 percent. Moreover, in the early 1990s, telephone density per 100 residents rose from 2.9 to 7.8 lines. Improvement in coverage, quality, and technology was dramatic. By 1998, TdP amply met the expansion and quality goals set forth in the concession contract and covered virtually the entire market for basic telephony. Apparently, this explains why Telefónica and OSIPTEL decided to shorten by one year the limited competition period established under the contract.

With the end of limited competition, the government opened the market to new operators willing to provide local, national, and international long distance telephony services. It also established that new operators could provide these services using TdP infrastructure by paying an interconnection fee.

The privatization process established a tariff-rebalancing period in which to gradually reduce existing tariff distortions. Tariff rebalancing increased monthly service charges considerably, while reducing the cost of local, national, and international long distance calls. This rebalancing schedule affected consumers directly through shifts in prices and access to telephone services.

Compared with other utility sectors, such as water and electricity (Torero and Pasco-Font 2000), Peru's telephony sector has improved dramatically since privatization. While the coverage and quality improvements registered since privatization have been welcome and positive, there is still room for substantial improvement in terms of the distributional impact of privatization. This is largely because more competition is required to reduce tariffs to international standards.

During 1997–98, following three years of postprivatization growth, a significant reduction in household consumer surplus occurred. For Lima, the growth rate of total consumer surplus, compared to the previous period, was −2.4 percent and −3.1 percent when the cross-price effects of this study's equation are included.[14] Outside Lima, the decrease was less important because of the significant increase in access. The negative growth in consumer surplus was even larger, both within and outside Lima, when viewed in terms of average, per capita consumer surplus.[15] Explanations for this reduction in consumer surplus include an increase in the price of local calls, a permanent increase in the price of fixed rent, and the cross-price effect of local calls because of the proportionately greater reduction in prices of long distance calls.[16]

Conclusions and Recommendations

Although privatization is associated with increased efficiency, productivity, access, and total consumer welfare, a further rebalancing of tariffs is needed to maintain and consolidate its benefits. The steep rise in the fixed monthly tariff, together with the increase in charges for local calls—by reducing the unit of measurement from a three-minute to a one-minute pulse at a higher equivalent tariff—has had a direct, negative effect on consumers.

The principal remaining problem is that sector competition is insufficient. Newbery (2000) once mentioned that it should be easy to introduce competition into long distance telephony via entry of new fiber-optic

---

14. In both cases, we took the fixed tariff into account.

15. For Lima, the decline in consumer surplus was −19.83 when only the direct price effect is included, and −43 percent when the cross-price effect is also included. Outside Lima, the decrease was −2.9 percent and −6.2 percent, respectively.

16. This result implies that local calls are relatively inferior to long distance ones.

Figure 6.5 Comparing fixed tariff and local call prices with Chile and Argentina

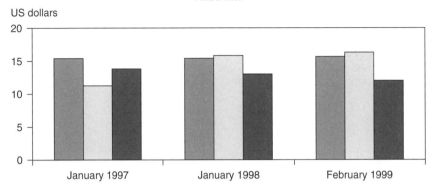

Fixed rate

US dollars

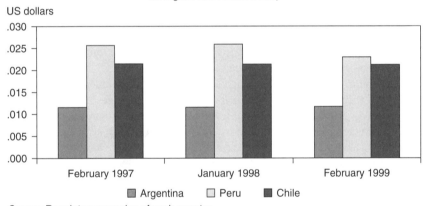

Local tariff per minute
(weighted average by number of hours available
for regular and reduced rate)

US dollars

■ Argentina ☐ Peru ■ Chile

Source: Regulatory agencies of each country.

backbones.[17] However, Peru's market for long distance is not yet competitive, and prices remain higher than in many other South American countries. To date, contrary to expectations, no substantial increase in consumer gains has accrued from the privatization of long distance national and international calls.[18]

---

17. These will likely be needed for Internet and data traffic.

18. In Chile, the average tariff of its major international long distance providers (BellSouth and Manquehue) is significantly lower than that of Peru; for example, a one-minute call from Lima to the United States is 71 percent more expensive in terms of the regular tariff and 55 percent more expensive in terms of the reduced tariff than is a one-minute call from Santiago to the United States, even though BellSouth also operates in Peru.

Figure 6.6   The three stages of Peru's telecommunications reform

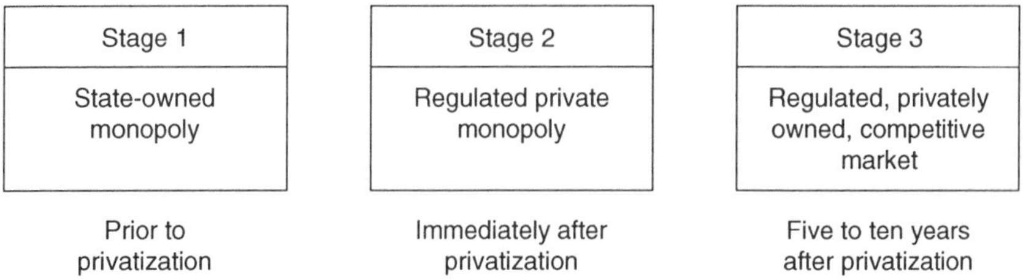

Stage 1	Stage 2	Stage 3
State-owned monopoly	Regulated private monopoly	Regulated, privately owned, competitive market

Prior to privatization	Immediately after privatization	Five to ten years after privatization

Source: Ramamurti (1996).

We expect that the entry of new firms—hindered to date by disputes concerning interconnection fees—will generate more competition for the dominant provider and exert downward pressure on prices in the future. This will require strengthening OSIPTEL, the telecommunications regulatory agency, allowing it to create and enforce the conditions needed to encourage new entry.

All observers agree that the greatest difficulty in liberalizing telecommunications is creating a competitive choice at the local level (Newbery 2000). Partly because of the technology involved, competitive markets are more easily introduced for long distance than for local services. Local companies can offer a bundle of local and long distance services, whereas long distance firms find it difficult to offer the full range of local services unless they can secure access to all local facilities. In the case of the Peruvian telecommunications market, lack of adequate interconnection policy and fees prevent other companies from using the incumbent infrastructure to compete in the local market. For more complete and larger welfare and distributional benefits to accrue, the obstacles to competition and new entry must be resolved.

Peru's privatization of telecommunications has involved a three-step process, as shown in figure 6.6. The government did not transform the telecommunications sector from a state monopoly (stage 1) into a competitive, privately owned sector (stage 3) in one swift step. Instead, it opted for a more gradual achievement of its aims, via an intermediate stage of regulated, private monopoly (stage 2). This decision was understandable and had much to do with the critical lack of infrastructure inherited from the state monopoly. The major risk with this intermediate step, however, was that the incumbent firm might become entrenched during stage 2, making it difficult even for industry giants, such as AT&T Latin America (FirstCom) or BellSouth to dislodge it in stage 3. New entrants might be expected to contest the incumbent firm's grip. To do so, however, the regulatory agency OSIPTEL must ensure in stage 3 that new entrants can readily interconnect with the monopolist's network on reasonable terms and compete with it fairly. Regulation is key.

Initially, OSIPTEL recommended an interconnection tariff of 2.9 cents, which gave TdP, the incumbent firm, excessive protection.[19] Then, in late August 2000, OSIPTEL reduced the interconnection fee, proposing that the average charge should fall to 1.68 cents by June 2001. OSIPTEL claimed that this fee was close to the average mid-2000 interconnection fee of 1.67 cents charged by a sample of 25 countries.[20] However, when one compares this fee with that of the three South American countries with the lowest interconnection costs—Brazil, Chile, and Colombia—one finds that their average interconnection cost by mid-2000 was 1.24 cents, significantly lower than the converging tariff proposed by OSIPTEL. We conclude that Peru's interconnection fee is still too high.

Increasing competition is a medium-term measure. To increase consumer surplus and more equitable distribution in the short run, we recommend two other measures. The validity of both requires that our estimated-demand calculations accurately describe the observed household-level consumption patterns.

First, we recommend reducing the unit of measurement for local calls from minutes to seconds (already done in many countries), which would indirectly reduce the local charge and therefore benefit consumers. Because most of the network is digitized, the costs of this switch would be negligible—although not necessarily neutral for the private provider.

Second, we recommend even more strongly the use of optional calling plans, in which volume discounts are given to large users (second-degree price discrimination). Conceptually, and as mentioned in Pasco-Font, Gallardo, and Fry (1999), introduction of differentiated prices can simultaneously generate a greater benefit for the company and larger consumer surplus for families. This is possible when consumer heterogeneity exists, allowing an increase in aggregate welfare of consumers on the regulatory side and the potential to discriminate prices from the company perspective.

For example, decreases in long distance prices have little benefit to low-income households, who purchase little or none of this good, either at the original, higher price or the new, lower one.[21] Therefore, balancing local-service price reductions with increases in long distance access charges would likely result in net welfare gains for many households.

---

19. The European Economic Commission's recommended range of interconnection cost was 1.10 to 2.11 cents, which it derived by taking the average of the three lowest charges of member countries. OSIPTEL adjusted these numbers to the Peruvian reality, taking into account the higher cost of capital and tax difference (see OSIPTEL 1999).

20. The 25 countries were Argentina, Austria, Belgium, Bolivia, Brazil, Canada, Chile, Colombia, Denmark, Finland, France, Germany, Greece, Holland, Ireland, Italy, Mexico, Norway, Portugal, Spain, Sweden, Switzerland, the United Kingdom, the United States, and Venezuela.

21. As more low-income people migrate to other areas and countries in search of work, they and their families will likely use more long distance services.

Moreover, it is reasonable to think that households from the lowest SEL use their phones primarily for receiving calls; therefore, their major burden is the fixed monthly rent. A calling plan with a low, fixed monthly tariff and a higher charge for local calls could also improve the welfare of low-income households. The opposite is true for wealthier households, whose major welfare gain is through intensive use of the phone. Their welfare would increase if local and long distance tariffs were reduced and the fixed monthly tariff increased. In either case, the central objective of not breaking the equilibrium in tariffs must be maintained to avoid entry of inefficient competitors.

From this discussion, it appears that Peru could have done better by moving directly from stage 1 to stage 3, without spending several years in stage 2. Admittedly, doing so might have robbed the government of the chance to solve fiscal problems through privatization or signal their commitment to market-oriented policies. Moreover, in the absence of those incentives, the sector might not have been reformed at all. The adage, better late than never, may well apply here. Nonetheless, while the overall results of telecommunications privatization have been good, we believe they could have been—and still could be—better.

References

Coopers & Lybrand, Morgan Grenfell, and ProInversión. 1993. Telecommunications Sector Restructuring in Peru. Lima: OSPITEL.

Doherty, A. 1984. Empirical Estimates of Demand and Cost Elasticities of Local Telephone Service. In *Changing Patterns in Regulated Markets and Technology: The Effect of Public Utility Pricing*. Lansing, MI: Institute of Public Utility Pricing, Institute of Public Utilities, Michigan State University.

Duncan, G., and D. Perry. 1994. IntaLATA Toll Demand Modeling: A Dynamic Analysis of Revenue and Usage Data. *Information Economics and Policy* 6: 163–78.

Escobal, J., V. Fry, and E. Schroth. 1996. *Estudio de Demanda de Servicios Telefónicos*. Lima: GRADE.

Galal, A., L. Jones, P. Tandon, and I. Vogelsang. 1994. *Welfare Consequences of Selling Public Enterprises: An Empirical Analysis*. Oxford: Oxford University Press.

Gallardo, J., and V. Galdo. 1998. *Estudio de Demanda Comercial de Servicios Telefónicos*. Lima: GRADE.

Gatto, J., J. Langin-Hooper, P. Robinson, and H. Tyan. 1988. Interstate Switched Access Demand Analysis. *Information Economics and Policy* 3, no. 4 (November): 333–58.

Jones, L., P. Tandon, and I. Vogelsang. 1990. *Selling Public Enterprises. A Cost-Benefit Methodology*. Cambridge, MA: MIT Press.

Levy, A. 1996. Semi-Parametric Estimation of Telecommunications Demands. Ph.D. Dissertation. University of California, Berkeley.

Martin, S., and D. Parker. 1997. *The Impact of Privatization: Ownership and Corporate Performance in the UK*. London: Routledge.

Newbery, David M. 2000. *Privatization, Restructuring, and Regulation of Network Utilities*. The Walras-Pareto Lectures, 1995. Cambridge, MA: MIT Press.

OSIPTEL. 1994. Marco Legal de las Telecomunicaciones: Contratos de Concesión de Telefónica del Perú. *Temas de Telecomunicaciones*, no. 1.

OSIPTEL. 1995a. Marco Conceptual para la Implementación del Sistema de Contabilidad Separada. Lima.

OSIPTEL. 1995b. La Transformación de las Telecomunicaciones: Memoria 1994. Lima.

OSIPTEL. 1996. Regulación y Mercado de las Telecomunicaciones: Memoria 1995. Lima.

OSIPTEL. 1997. Apertura del Mercado de las Telecomunicaciones: Memoria 1996. Lima.

OSIPTEL. 1998a. Los Usuarios y las Telecomunicaciones: Memoria 1997. Lima.

OSIPTEL. 1998b. Cinco Años en el Mercado de las Telecomunicaciones: Memoria 1998. Lima.

OSIPTEL. 1999. *Estudio de Comparación Internacional de Cargos de Interconexión.* Gerencia de Políticas Regulatorias y Planeamiento Estratégico. Working Paper. Lima.

Pasco-Font, A., J. Gallardo, and V. Fry. 1999. La Demanda Residencial de Telefonía Básica en el Perú. In *Estudio en Telecomunicaciones,* no. 4. Lima: OSIPTEL.

Ramamurti, R. 1996. *Privatizing Monopolies: Lessons from the Telecommunications and Transport Sectors in Latin America.* Baltimore: John Hopkins University Press.

Taylor, L., and D. J. Kridel. 1990. Residential Demand for Access to the Telephone Network. In *Telecommunications Demand Modeling,* ed. A. de Frotenay, M. H. Shugard, and D. S. Sibley. Amsterdam: North Holland Publishing Co.

Torero, M., and A. Pasco-Font. 2000. *The Social Impact of Privatization and Regulation of Utilities in Urban Peru.* Helsinki: UNU/Wider.

Zona, J., and R. Jacob. 1990. The Total Bill Concept: Defining and Testing Alternative Views. Paper presented at Telecommunications Demand Analysis with Dynamic Regulation, Bellcore and Bell Canada Industry Forum, Hilton Head, South Carolina (April 22–25).

Appendix 6A Tables

Table 6A.1 Estimation of change in total welfare, discounting the fixed charge, for metropolitan Lima, 1993–98

Socio-economic level	Year	OLS estimations using Mills inverse ratio (reported bills)—discounted fixed charge		Minimum welfare	Total households	Households with telephone	Penetration ratio	New households with telephone in t+1	Welfare per household (weighted for access) (W: 0 ->Min)	Welfare changes (weighted for access) (W: 0 ->Min)
		Average welfare	Welfare changes							
High (A)	1993	86.10		44.54	55,400	50,968	0.92	732	86.10	
	1994	124.46	0.446	60.87	51,700	51,700	1.00	0	122.70	0.425
	1995	131.01	0.053	64.12	56,800	56,800	1.00	0	131.01	0.068
	1996	133.20	0.017	63.45	56,400	56,800	1.00	0	133.20	0.017
	1997	138.87	0.043	65.02	62,100	62,100	1.00	0	138.87	0.043
	1998	99.86	-0.281	44.03	62,100	62,100	1.00	0	99.86	-0.281
Medium (B)	1993	38.68		10.46	240,900	153,754	0.64	21,878	38.68	
	1994	52.90	0.368	9.80	252,000	175,632	0.70	31,868	48.09	0.243
	1995	55.87	0.056	10.23	273,700	207,500	0.76	9,922	47.78	-0.006
	1996	55.01	-0.015	6.84	259,200	217,422	0.84	25,134	53.29	0.115
	1997	56.23	0.022	4.92	278,800	234,192	0.84	5,954	50.32	-0.056
	1998	37.03	-0.342	2.54	278,800	248,510	0.89	13,562	36.28	-0.279
Low (C)	1993	18.44		2.50	494,700	50,693	0.10	24,632	18.44	
	1994	22.22	0.205	3.45	471,700	75,325	0.16	37,049	16.65	-0.097
	1995	23.88	0.075	2.75	528,300	112,374	0.21	67,938	17.67	0.061
	1996	22.28	-0.067	1.87	491,500	180,312	0.37	26,708	14.16	-0.198
	1997	21.92	-0.016	2.12	470,500	207,020	0.44	48,915	19.59	0.383
	1998	12.05	-0.450	2.05	470,500	255,935	0.54	35,775	10.04	-0.488
Very low (D)	1993	9.53		2.45	562,900	5,629	0.01	316	9.53	
	1994	8.45	-0.113	1.25	594,500	5,945	0.01	-765	7.84	-0.177
	1995	8.90	0.052	0.57	518,000	5,180	0.01	32,326	13.77	0.755
	1996	5.66	-0.364	1.20	535,800	37,506	0.07	41,664	2.11	-0.846
	1997	3.83	-0.323	1.11	609,000	79,170	0.13	73,080	2.84	0.342
	1998	1.40	-0.634	1.32	609,000	152,250	0.25	6,090	0.78	-0.725

OLS = ordinary least squares

Table 6A.2 Estimation of the change in total welfare, discounting the fixed charge, for principal cities outside Lima, 1993–98

City	Socio-economic level	Year	OLS estimations using Mills inverse ratio (reported bills)—discounted fixed charge								
			Average welfare	Welfare changes	Minimum welfare	Total households	Households with telephone	Penetration ratio	New households with telephone in t+1	Welfare per household (weighted for access) (W: 0 ->Min)	Welfare changes (weighted for access) (W: 0 ->Min)
Arequipa	High/medium (A/B)	1993	22.99		10.06	24,815	13,400	0.54	3,861	22.99	
		1994	34.59	0.504	11.37	25,383	17,261	0.68	2,005	28.17	0.225
		1995	40.35	0.167	11.25	25,687	19,265	0.75	2,647	37.70	0.338
		1996	40.15	-0.005	7.51	26,401	21,913	0.83	664	35.52	-0.058
		1997	41.99	0.046	6.60	26,877	22,576	0.84	1,517	41.20	0.160
		1998	38.16	-0.091	1.64	27,379	24,093	0.88	821	35.82	-0.131
Cuzco	High/medium (A/B)	1993	9.90		3.79	9,280	5,011	0.54	1,357	9.90	
		1994	11.12	0.123	0.14	9,365	6,368	0.68	795	8.77	-0.114
		1995	11.57	0.041	-3.63	9,550	7,163	0.75	815	9.88	0.126
		1996	8.39	-0.276	-9.83	9,611	7,977	0.83	191	7.29	-0.262
		1997	7.73	-0.078	-12.41	9,724	8,168	0.84	496	6.79	-0.069
		1998	4.23	-0.453	-19.75	9,846	8,665	0.88	295	3.31	-0.512
Trujillo	High/medium (A/B)	1993	15.18		4.69	22,223	12,000	0.54	3,437	15.18	
		1994	21.14	0.393	2.39	22,702	15,437	0.68	1,826	16.72	0.101
		1995	24.28	0.148	-0.64	23,017	17,263	0.75	2,550	21.62	0.293
		1996	22.82	-0.060	-6.27	23,587	19,813	0.84	4,206	18.55	-0.142
		1997	23.41	0.026	-8.53	24,019	24,019	1.00	432	19.16	0.033
		1998	21.17	-0.096	-14.96	24,451	24,451	1.00	0	20.79	0.085
Chiclayo	High/medium (A/B)	1993	17.77		6.71	10,324	5,575	0.54	1,575	17.77	
		1994	25.83	0.454	5.92	10,515	7,150	0.68	927	20.91	0.177
		1995	30.05	0.163	4.92	10,769	8,077	0.75	1,015	27.22	0.302
		1996	29.20	-0.028	0.91	10,954	9,092	0.83	1,186	26.06	-0.043
		1997	30.30	0.038	-0.43	11,171	10,277	0.92	1,122	26.76	0.027
		1998	28.02	-0.075	-3.96	11,399	11,399	1.00	0	25.27	-0.056

OLS = ordinary least squares

7

Distribution of Assets and Income in Brazil: New Evidence

ROBERTO MACEDO

This chapter revisits the effects of Brazil's privatization program on asset and income distribution, in light of updated program information. After summarizing the current status of the program, I review and extend an earlier analysis of privatization's effects on asset distribution. Core arguments, drawn from that study, focus on a particular form of privatization—public offerings, with special conditions that allow and encourage workers to participate—which was advocated in the earlier study but adopted only after its publication.

The chapter then shifts its focus to privatization's more direct effects on income distribution, resulting from the higher prices that the former state-owned enterprises (SOEs) charged for services, following SOE auction to private entrepreneurs. The analysis relies heavily on Macedo (2003), which examined the socioeconomic policies of President Cardoso's administration (1995–2002) and made a first reference to the effects of higher prices resulting from that program on consumers. This section is followed by a discussion on the pricing policies of three industries: telecommunications, which has been totally privatized; electricity, which has been partially privatized; and oil—specifically, bottled cooking gas—which, at the wholesale stage, remains dominated by Petrobrás, a state company.

Roberto Macedo is professor of economics at the University of São Paulo and Presbyterian Mackenzie University, São Paulo. He was a research associate at the Foundation Institute of Economic Research (FIPE). The author wishes to thank John Nellis for his helpful comments and suggestions. He gratefully acknowledges the assistance of Sabeen Hassanali, Noora-Lisa Aberman, Patricia Guedes, and Gisela Macedo. Thanks also go to Heron do Carmo, Luiz Afonso F. de Lima, Francisco Anuatti-Neto, and Ethevaldo Siqueira for their valuable information.

Program Overview: Recent Developments

By international standards, Brazil's privatization program has been major in scale and scope.[1] Over the decade ending July 2001, the state auctioned off control of 119 firms and minority stakes in various other companies. The auctions produced $67.9 billion in revenue, plus the transfer of $18.1 billion in debt. The government also sold $6 billion in shares of firms that remained as SOEs, obtained $10 billion from new concessions of public services to the private sector, and sold $1.1 billion in scattered noncontrol stakes owned by the National Social and Economic Development Bank (BNDES)—the government agency in charge of the program—in various private companies.

The program has three parts: (1) the federal National Program of "Desestatization" (NPD), initiated in 1991; (2) similar programs at the state level, which began in 1996; and (3) a special telecommunications program (referred to as the Telecom Program).[2] Initiated in 1997 and completed the following year, the Telecom Program is a separate federal program parallel to the NPD. Its auctions, heavily concentrated in 1997 and 1998, produced $28.8 billion in revenues, plus $2.1 billion in debt transfers. The NPD produced $28.2 billion in revenues, plus $9.2 billion in debt transfers; while state-level programs produced revenues of $27.9 billion, and $6.8 billion in debt transfers.[3]

After 1998, the privatization program virtually stalled. According to BNDES, proceeds from the auctions, including new concessions of public services, which had risen from $26.3 billion in 1997 and peaked at $35.7 billion in 1998, subsequently fell to $4.2 billion in 1999. Proceeds then climbed to $10.2 billion in 2000 (sale of a major state bank, Banespa, long in the pipeline, accounted for $3.6 billion of that total), fell to $2.8 billion in 2001, and declined further to $2.2 billion in 2002.

Earlier studies of Brazilian privatization focused primarily on efficiency changes in companies that underwent the process. Two major studies concluded that performance of the former SOEs, as measured by various indicators, improved after privatization. Pinheiro (1996), then at the BNDES, analyzed the performance of 50 firms before and after privatization, using data until 1994; he concluded that "in general, the obtained results confirm that privatization brings a significant improvement . . . of the performance of the firms." Anuatti-Neto et al. (2003) analyzed a data set covering 66 privatization contracts, corresponding to 102 firms and 94 percent of the total value of the auctions until July 2001. Performance of these firms was

---

1. This section draws heavily on my contribution to Annuati-Neto et al. (2003).

2. Until July 2001, program composition (total value of the auctions), by industry, was: electricity (31 percent), telecommunications (31 percent), steel (8 percent), mining (8 percent), oil and gas (7 percent), petrochemicals (7 percent), financials (6 percent), and others (2 percent).

3. These values exclude concessions of public services.

reviewed before and after privatization until 2000, comparing performance of the privatized firms to those observed in the private sector over the years.

In addition to the improved-efficiency finding, Anuatti-Neto et al. (2003) identified sources of the gains privatized firms made, in the form of reduced direct employment and more rewarding prices. Moreover, drawing from Macedo (2000), they showed macroeconomic costs; that is, the benefits of privatization could have been higher had the government not used the money to sustain its misguided policy of enlarging fiscal deficits and adding to them by adopting high interest rates to defend the currency, the Brazilian real, from 1995 to 1999. Macedo pointed out that resources from privatization made the government's budget constraint softer, making room for additional debt. Moreover, the foreign investment that privatization attracted and the high interest rates helped to postpone devaluation by softening the external debt constraint. High interest rates, large public deficits, and an overvalued currency had the combined effect of seriously enlarging both the public and external debt. This effect, in turn, severely increased the vulnerability—both domestic and external—of the Brazilian economy and aggravated problems that became entrenched by the late 1990s.

Regarding capital markets, Anuatti-Neto et al. (2003) pointed out that privatization also entailed the cost of reducing minority-shareholder rights, thereby hampering the development of such markets. Drawing from Macedo (2000), Anuatti-Neto et al. showed that the benefits of privatization could have been higher had the government not neglected the opportunity to democratize capital ownership.

Accounting for Public Opposition

Privatization is unpopular in Brazil. A Latinbarometer public-opinion survey conducted in 2001 in 16 Latin American countries reported that 53 percent of respondents in Brazil believed that privatization had not benefited the country (Lora and Panizza 2002). Nonetheless, the Brazilian public's attitude toward privatization is more favorable than that of populations in neighboring countries: On average, 63 percent of respondents in all the countries surveyed believed that privatization had not benefited their nations. The only other countries whose public opinion of privatization was less negative than Brazil were Chile (47 percent) and Venezuela (46 percent). For all other surveyed countries, the percentage of negative opinions was higher.[4]

Various reasons account for weak popular support of reform in Brazil. First, the average citizen is rarely in a position to calculate and fully identify the benefits of privatization, as described by Pinheiro (1996) and Anuatti-Neto et al. (2003). Since the end of the Second World War, when

---

4. The other countries surveyed were Argentina, Bolivia, Colombia, Costa Rica, Ecuador, El Salvador, Guatemala, Honduras, Mexico, Nicaragua, Paraguay, Peru, and Uruguay.

nonbanking SOEs were created, the belief has been that the state should play a major role in large strategic industries, such as steel and mining. The detailed functioning of such industries is far from the pressing concerns of most people; thus, it is unreasonable to expect the average citizen to be concerned with the outcome or be positioned to evaluate the technicalities of privatizing such industries.

Second, developments following total privatization of the telecommunications industry and partial divestiture of the electricity SOEs contributed to a negative popular attitude. Higher tariffs partially blurred the favorable effects of a major expansion of telecommunications services. A further negative effect emerged in 2001, when the country was forced to ration electricity due to drought (which resulted in lower reservoir levels at hydroelectric plants), coupled with remaining SOEs' mishandling of planned investments in generation capacity and transmission lines to consumption centers. Opponents of privatization were eager to blame privatization for the crisis, overlooking that the shortage came at the generation stage, which remains largely under government control.

Third, privatization coincided with sluggish overall economic growth, particularly after the program peaked in 1997–98. Therefore, dissatisfaction with lower economic gains or even losses, such as those that emerged with higher rates of unemployment, were likely to have promoted criticism of government policies generally and privatization in particular.

Fourth, as highlighted above, the government failed to use the privatization program to democratize capital ownership. Only recently has it resorted to successful public offerings, in which workers are entitled and empowered to participate. Thus, as a rule, the average citizen has been distanced from the privatization process and its benefits (rewards to controllers and shareholders of privatized firms).

A fifth reason for opposing the program was its unfavorable portrayal by the media, whose coverage of court battles disrupted auctions, sometimes necessitating police intervention. Press coverage of telecommunications privatization was particularly negative, as it was accompanied by news that certain government authorities had coerced groups to participate in the auctions. Recorded tapes of government authorities' conversations with each other and interested parties reached the press and subsequently raised suspicions. Even though the legal battles decided in favor of privatization, the public uproar was serious enough to cause the minister of communications to resign in late 1998.

Other Viewpoints and Factors

Despite the program's unpopularity, a study by Lamounier and De Souza (2002) depicts another view, focusing only on the opinions of a group called the Brazilian elites. This group is composed of 500 businesspeople (including leaders of associations of small- and medium-sized firms), union leaders, congress members, high-echelon members of the executive and judiciary branches of government, journalists, religious leaders, directors of non-governmental organizations, and intellectuals. On average, 62 percent responded that they approved or tended to approve of privatization. The rates varied from a high of 87 percent for members of the executive branch of government to a low of 13 percent for union leaders (the only rate below 45 percent). Another question concerned company performance after privatization. In this case, the approval rating showed large variations by industry.[5]

Several other factors explain the current status of privatization. First, advancing it further will affect those SOEs that have stronger political support than the ones privatized thus far. For example, the remaining SOEs in the banking sector includes the nearly two-century-old Banco do Brasil, a commercial bank of which the federal government is the controlling shareholder. This bank holds the government's accounts and is the major actor in federally subsidized, agricultural credit. It has built a major constituency, as private banks have long refrained from extending agricultural credit. Staff of the Banco do Brasil, traditionally selected by public examination, is a source of high-level government officers. Some have reached ministerial level or have become congress members; they are influential and tend to disapprove of changes in the bank's status. Moreover, the bank is not entirely an SOE, as it has private shareholders who also act as a group to maintain its privileged status.

Petrobrás, the oil industry giant, remains in state hands. Established in 1954, following a strong nationalist stand against foreign oil companies, the company has been effective in finding oil. In the 1980s, it began offshore drilling and has set worldwide records in deepwater exploitation. Domestic production currently meets about 90 percent of the country's needs, which is viewed as a sign of success. Until 1995, Petrobrás had a monopoly of the upstream market in prospecting, production, and importing. Despite a theoretical opening of the market in 1995, the company effectively continues to have a virtual monopoly on these activities, as well as refining. As oil is associated with national security issues, the military views keeping Petrobrás under government control as crucial. Again, the company has private shareholders who strongly support its present profitable and protected status.

In the electricity industry, privatization occurred mainly in distribution, while the generation segment remains mostly under federal control. After

---

5. The highest industry ratings went to aviation (80 percent), in which Embraer, the former SOE, has been successful; steel (65 percent); and telecommunications (58 percent). The lowest ratings went to railroads (9 percent), airlines (11 percent) (in this case, a single, small company owned by the state of São Paulo was individually privatized in the mid-1980s); and electricity (13 percent).

the 2001 rationing, the process of restructuring stalled. Rationing stimulated industry and households to adopt energy-saving measures; in the aftermath, demand has not recovered to its previous levels. Both rationing and demand reduction brought losses to the industry, worsening the situation of heavily indebted—largely in dollars, which have appreciated since 1999—privatized companies. With both distribution and generation companies currently suffering enormous losses, the federal government, which regulates the entire industry, is presently preparing a new sector arrangement. A pressing concern is that BNDES must find a way to manage the sector's enormous debts, some of which are on their way to default. Thus, electricity is an industry in disarray, presently unattractive to private investors; before any discussion of a new round of privatization can occur, policy and financial reorganization are required.

Despite these shortcomings, reversing privatization is highly unlikely in the foreseeable future. The Workers' Party, whose leader was inaugurated as president in 2003, fought privatization in congress and the courts during the 1990s; however, after moving into government, it has adopted conservative fiscal and monetary policies and has avoided condemning privatization. Given Brazil's financial realities, I see no room for a privatization reversal (the government has not suggested a reversal, even in theory). The government is likely to keep the program stalled—that is, no renationalizations or reversals will occur, but no further advances will be made.[6]

Asset Distribution

Studies on income distribution in Brazil abound, as the country represents one of the world's worst cases of inequality.[7] According to 1999 data from the Brazilian Census Bureau (IBGE), the income share of the poorest 50 percent was only 13 percent, while the wealthiest 10 percent took a hefty 48 percent of total income, a picture that has changed little over time.[8] Since measurement began in the 1960s, the Gini coefficient of income inequality has remained almost constant, fluctuating close to 0.60. (Most analyses of income inequality in Brazil focus on such measures as the Gini coefficient.) After examining minor changes in measurement over time, analysts proceed to investigate the causes in terms of flow variables, such as wage policies in the 1960s or recent increases in cash transfers from the government

---

6. Some reversal, however, might occur, not as a result of policy change, but because of certain privatized firms having defaulted debts owed to BNDES who risk takeover by a state-owned creditor (as happened in Chile in the early 1980s).

7. This section draws on Macedo (2000) and updates of that analysis.

8. For historical data, see www.ipeadata.gov.br.

to the poorest groups. Most studies ignore or take for granted stock or wealth variables, such as asset distribution, which contribute to the high degree of income inequality.

Against this background, together with a few other Brazilian economists (particularly Paulo Rabello de Castro of the Getúlio Vargas Foundation, Rio de Janeiro), I view privatization in Brazil as an opportunity for democratizing capital ownership, changing the heavily concentrated nature of capitalism, and opening room for improving income distribution at its roots.

Change of Direction: Public Offerings

For the reasons explained below, the government long neglected this course of action. Only after the privatization program had made major advances did the government decide to move in this direction. Thus, in 2000 and 2001, instead of auctioning major blocks of equity capital in the former SOEs through tenders, the government resorted to public offering of minority stakes of shares it had kept of Companhia Vale do Rio do Doce (CVRD), privatized in 1997, and of Petrobrás (which remains under federal control but with minority private shareholders). In these public offerings, workers in the formal labor markets were also entitled and empowered to participate, using the money they had accumulated in their Workers' Tenure Guarantee Fund (FGTS), a compulsory savings program (an individual account adds one month's salary each year).[9]

In this way, any worker with a positive FGTS account balance was entitled to participate in public offerings by converting a portion of his or her money into quotas of stock funds created specifically for this purpose and managed by banks the worker chose. In the case of Petrobrás, the maximum exchange allowed was 50 percent of the FGTS account balance. In the case of CVRD, this percentage was reduced in practice, as there was excess demand for the shares. For offers made by FGTS participants, funds were exchanged on a pro-rata basis.

Advocates of democratic capital ownership had long suggested this process. Use of FGTS deposits to purchase shares being privatized was exceptional since, as a rule, the money could be withdrawn only if the labor contract was broken, the money was used to buy a house, or upon retirement. In essence, FGTS is a funded form of unemployment compensation or social security, organized as personal accounts in the name of the beneficiaries. The accounts are kept by the National Savings Bank (CEF), a major banking-sector SOE.

---

9. Workers in the informal labor market do not participate in the FGTS program, as they do not have a formal labor contract. A major segment of government's civil service and military personnel are also not enrolled in FGTS, as they are subject to statutory regimes that generally guarantee job tenure.

Why Didn't the Government Democratize Capital Ownership Earlier?

To understand why the government previously neglected the option of democratizing capital ownership, it is necessary to understand certain aspects of the Brazilian privatization program's legal framework.

Legal Framework

Law 8031, of April 12, 1990, established the legal framework of the Brazilian privatization program.[10] The first article set forth six objectives: (1) reestablish the state's strategic position in the economy by transferring to the private sector activities unduly undertaken by the public sector; (2) contribute to the reduction of public debt, thereby helping to adjust public-sector finances; (3) make room for increased investment in companies and activities transferred to the private sector; (4) contribute to modernization of the country's industrial sector by improving its competitiveness and strengthening entrepreneurial skills in various sectors of the economy; (5) allow public administration to concentrate its efforts on activities in which presence of the state is fundamental to accomplishing national priorities; and (6) contribute to strengthening capital markets by increasing the supply of securities and democratizing capital ownership of the SOEs included in the program.

Thus, although not explicitly concerned with income distribution, the program formally adopted the idea of democratizing capital ownership. However, in putting the process into practice, the Brazilian government (like many other governments around the world) opted to emphasize the financial resources and revenues it could generate from sales. Thus, the government decided to auction its shares of the SOEs to obtain the highest value after establishing minimum prices as evaluated by outside consultants. In this way, until the aforementioned moved into public offering in 2000, the auctions attracted only large businesses and investors, both national and foreign.

Macedo (2000) argued that privatization is not merely an exchange of assets. A major aspect of its relation to asset and income distribution is that buyers of previously state-owned firms believe they will be better able to manage the companies and that their superior effort, skills, and incentives will allow them to obtain a higher return than that of less competent or motivated government managers. They believe they can overcome or avoid the effects of past government policies, such as wage and price policies, which precluded government managers from performing well. Experience in Brazil and elsewhere generally indicates that these expectations are correct.

---

10. Law 9491, of September 9, 1997, is the most recent version.

Thus, with the sale of an SOE comes the opportunity to improve efficiency and profitability. By having relied exclusively on auctions of controlling blocks of its former SOEs, the government had generally excluded small investors from participating in the process. In my view, shifting to public offerings, along with the entitlement and empowerment of specific groups of small, often first-time, investors, better facilitates the democratization of capital and creates a more positive income-distribution effect.

Asset Ownership: Rewards and Risks

The proponents of broadening asset ownership have also suggested a more daring course of action—that is, using pension liabilities that the government owes present and future pensioners to purchase shares. In this scheme, citizens could use all or part of the present value of their future payments to participate in public offerings. Underlying this idea is the fact that the government-sponsored social security systems are largely deficient, with no solution in sight. Thus, this scheme would be tantamount to reducing public deficits and debt, while, at the same time, handing over a potentially valuable asset to citizens. It might also serve to help capitalize a new public-pension system (as did Bolivian privatization). Certainly, the present pension system is in great need of reform, as it has adopted the traditional pay-as-you-go model, together with such indigenous schemes as receive-more-than-you-pay and receive even-if-you-don't-pay.

The concept of broadening asset ownership, however, has not yet gained a wide audience in the country. Thus far, it has neither major political nor public support, except in the recent, limited cases of CVRD and Petrobrás. The chief concern of the economic teams of administrations (Collor, Franco, and Cardoso) that have pushed the privatization process consistently has been to raise local and foreign money from privatization to alleviate the fiscal crisis and finance the balance of payments.

In the past, the Workers' Party preferred to fight privatization in congress and the courts and by various other public means. Now in power, the Workers' Party has revised its previous beliefs, moving ideologically closer to the social-democratic mainstream. Democratizing capital ownership is typically a social-democratic idea. Indeed, during the Cardoso administration (1995–2002), when the privatization program was at its height, the social democrats in power could have used the law stating this objective. As noted, the law was not put into practice until 2000, when it was applied in two minor cases; nevertheless, these could have set a new pattern for future privatizations.

Clearly, taking this alternative course of action would bring its own difficulties. In particular, one could not guarantee that workers would adhere en masse to schemes that might be more financially rewarding than the FGTS deposits or the assurance of a public pension; it could also lead to losses: Definite risks are involved, and poorer people tend to be more risk averse. In this respect, the government was wise to allow only a partial exchange of FGTS deposits for shares, which encourages a more balanced portfolio of financial assets in terms of risk.[11] It has also been suggested that the equity received from the government should go into private funds to gain from efficient management, a procedure that was followed in the CVRD and Petrobrás cases, with FGTS monies going into specific funds created for this purpose. Further, there is the question of program scale: Some have recommended joint ventures of funds, with foreign and local traditional investors sharing in the companies and their management.

That the privatization program has stalled should not discourage those in favor of broadening asset ownership, because the case for this type of privatization is defensible. I am convinced that, unless bold actions are taken with respect to asset distribution in Brazil, the country's highly concentrated income distribution will not move in a favorable direction. Thus, this alternative course of action should be assigned a larger role in future privatizations. At some point, this form of privatization might become attractive to the Workers' Party, making it willing to enter into a new round of public offerings with strong participation of its major constituency, labor.

In this respect, it is important to review the experiences of cases in which privatization has been adopted on a small scale: Petrobrás (2001) and CVRD (2002). The funds that emerged from those public offerings are known as CVRD-FGTS and Petrobrás-FGTS, and their prices shift on a daily basis, like any other stock market fund. A daily newspaper that follows the Bovespa (São Paulo Stock Exchange), list 36 CVRD-FGTS and 52 Petrobras-FGTS funds.[12]

As the results in table 7.1 show, the two cases added hundreds of thousands of new shareholders to the companies. Success of the first case increased the demand for the second, which was almost twice as high. When one compares the return (to date) on investment made in those companies' shares with the one that would have been received had the money remained in the traditional FGTS account, the difference in favor of the former is enormous.

Effects on Pricing

Privatization also affects income distribution through its effect on the pricing of goods and services that privatized companies offer. Charging real-

---

11. Workers were advised of the higher risks of their investment in stocks, including lack of government guarantees, unlike their FGTS accounts. It should be noted that workers have been losing money in traditional FGTS accounts, after accounting for inflation. Renato Fragelli of the Getúlio Vargas Foundation, who calculated the returns of FGTS deposits from January 1999 to July 2003, found they lagged a national cost-of-living index for the same period, according to *O Estado de S. Paulo* (September 11, 2003).

12. *Valor Económico*, September 19, 2003, C4.

Table 7.1   Brazil: Results of public offerings, with participation of FGTS depositors

Company	Percent capital share	Transaction date	Number of FGTS depositors	Percent return on investment (until stated date)	Percent return of FGTS (over the same period)
Petrobrás	n.a.	August 2000	312,194	76 (until May 2003)	28[a] or 18[b]
CVRD	4.6	March 2002	584,588	89 (until December 2002)	7[a] or 5[b,c]
				114 (until September 2003)[c]	16[a] or 11[b,c]

n.a. = not available
FGTS = Spanish acronym for Workers' Tenure Guarantee Fund.

a. For participants enrolled until September 1971.
b. For participants enrolled thereafter.
c. Author's estimates.

Sources: Petrobrás em Ações (2003, 4); *CVRD 2002 Report*, www.cvrd.com.br (for returns until December 2002 and author's estimates thereafter).

istic prices is part of privatization's rationale, as it seeks to make companies more efficient and overcome past effects of government's unrealistic pricing. Realistic prices can, however, create an additional burden for consumers, particularly low-income ones, pointing to the need for public policies to alleviate this burden. Another key issue is defining the term *realistic price* because regulatory agencies can err when establishing criteria for initial prices and their adjustments. The latter are particularly relevant in an economy such as Brazil's, where inflation rates are still higher than those observed in developed countries.

Macedo (2003) made a first incursion into this issue, showing that, after privatization, several public-service tariffs had increased more than a general index of the cost of living during the Cardoso administration (1995–2002), when the privatization program made great strides.

In the three industries examined—telecommunications (totally privatized), electricity (partially privatized) and oil, specifically bottled cooking gas (dominated by Petrobrás through the refining stage)—I found distortions whereby consumers pay higher prices for goods and services for no justifiable economic reason. Moreover, even without such distortions, the new price reality imposes an additional burden on consumers, which specific strategies aimed at alleviating its effect on the poor should address.

That price distortions were found in totally privatized, partially privatized, and state-controlled sectors suggests that price distortions do not result from privatization per se, but from pricing policies that Brazilian regulatory agencies have adopted. Moreover, tax rates in these three industries are high; only in such exceptional cases as electricity are taxes lower for the poorest groups, although with distortions in their targeting. Thus,

Table 7.2 Brazil: Cost of living changes in city of São Paulo, by expenditure type, July 1994 to August 2003 (percent)

Expenditure type	Total change	January 2000–August 2003	September 2002–August 2003
Telephone services			
Access to fixed line	–98	–84	13
Services: fixed lines	592	67	15
Services: mobile phones	n.a.	36	13
Electricity	209	76	16
Cooking gas[a]	468	97	16
Total cost of living	133	30	13

n.a. = not available, as services were just starting in 1994 and included in the index only later.

a. Bottles of liquefied petroleum gas (LPG).

Source: Consumer price index as published monthly by Brazilian Portugues Fundação Instituto de Pequisas Econômicas (São Paulo).

there is room for additional tax cuts along the same lines, as well as improvement in the targeting mechanisms.

Table 7.2, which provides an overview of the changes in costs of telephone services, electricity, and cooking gas, shows the increase in the cost-of-living index for São Paulo during 1994–2003. The total change in cost of living is presented, together with changes for the three reviewed items in household budgets. In addition, more recent changes (from January 2000 to August 2003 and September 2002 to August 2003) are isolated.

Except for access to fixed phone lines, whose price decreases are explained below, the other items increased more than the general cost of living (although not for the last 12 months in which the various rates show only minor differences). However, in relation to this last period, cooking gas prices had already increased sharply, causing protests from consumers and politicians. In the case of telephones, a tariff adjustment is due, pending a court ruling. A new annual readjustment became effective for electricity in January 2004.

In addition to the poverty faced by a great portion of the population, difficulties to consumers generally, brought about by cost-of-living increases (table 7.2), are compounded by a decline in real earnings, which have shrunk family budgets. Starting in the 1980s, the economy grew slowly, at approximately 2 percent annually. More recently, after the exceptional growth of 4.4 percent in 2000, the growth rate declined to 1.5 percent in 2001 and 2002 and to 0.5 percent in 2003.

Weak economic growth brought increased unemployment. Under such conditions, workers faced mounting pressures to preserve the purchasing power of their earnings when negotiating annual wage readjustments due to cost-of-living increases, as shown in table 7.3 (São Paulo is used because it is the most important state in terms of population and GDP).

Table 7.3 Brazil, state of São Paulo: Survey of collective readjustments obtained by unions compared with cost of living measured by INPC (percent)

Nature of readjustment	Year (first semester)[a] 2002	2003
Above INPC	32.2	12.5
Equal to INPC	26.6	22.5
Below INPC	41.2	65.0

INPC = Brazil's consumer price index

a. a semester represents 6 months.

Source: Interunion Department for Statistics and Socio-economic Studies (DIEESE) (2003); *Valor Econômico*, July 16, A1-2.

This issue raises further concern for the damaging effects of increased costs revealed by table 7.2. While I acknowledge that certain prices before privatization were set at unrealistically low levels, I am also convinced that part of the postprivatization increases were not based on reasonable calculations—rather, they arose from distortions that government policymakers should address, particularly in the areas of regulation and social policy.

Following the total privatization of telephone services and partial privatization of electricity services, and even earlier, as state companies were being prepared for sale, more realistic tariffs were adopted, and regulatory agencies were created in these industries. Deregulation of the oil sector legally eliminated Petrobrás monopolies and, in principle, opened the door for industry competition. However, the company still retains a virtual monopoly of the market, as strong competitors have not yet come into action.

With the memory of inflation still prevalent, most public tariffs have been linked to price indices to avoid private-investor uncertainty, which could discourage participation in privatization auctions. In the process, a major distortion in telephone and electricity tariffs has arisen, as a result of contaminating the price indices adopted in these cases by dollar-linked prices, such as those of tradable commodities. These are applied to index tariffs of services whose costs are not necessarily determined by dollar-pegged prices, making the distortion particularly relevant after 1999 because of the various devaluations of the Brazilian currency (real) since then.

Telephone Services

The telephone industry, considered the most successful example of service expansion following privatization, had suffered from chronic shortage of

Table 7.4   Brazil: Telephone services, 1998 and 2002 (millions of units)

| | Fixed lines in service | | | |
Year	Home	Business	Mobile	Public
1998	14.5	4.8	5.2	0.6
2002	29.4	8.4	33.4	1.3

Source: National Telecommunications Agency (ANATEL), courtesy of Ethevald Siqueira.

supply before its sale. Phone lines had been offered through a limited self-financing system, in which future customers registered by buying stocks for about R$1,200 (roughly US$400). A secondary market for phone lines also had existed, with transactions that sometimes reached more than US$3,000 or more per line. Before privatization, state-owned companies also had begun to offer mobile phones, but in limited quantities due to scarce resources to expand supply.

Table 7.4 shows that the number of fixed personal lines roughly doubled from 1998 to 2002 period, as did the number of public phones. The number of mobile phones skyrocketed, as a result of large private-sector investments. The National Telecommunications Agency (ANATEL), the regulatory agency, estimates that investments between 1998 and 2002 totaled R$73 billion (about US$24 billion).[13]

In addition, the expansion virtually eliminated the cost of buying a fixed line through acquisition of company stocks or resorting to the parallel market (table 7.2).[14] Expansion also reached lower-income families to a greater extent. However, as table 7.5 shows, distribution of fixed telephone lines remains unequal among income classes, as lower-income groups still have relatively limited access, compared to higher-income groups.

The relation between phone service providers and consumers involves issues of access and phone line use. Table 7.3 shows the larger number of installed fixed lines; however, other data demonstrate that an impressive number of lines have been disconnected due to nonpayment of bills. According to ANATEL, by December 2002, disconnected phone lines totaled 5.97 million, with 5.4 million available for installation.

Several factors explain the large number of disconnected lines. The first is low levels of household income and the difficulties families face in maintaining purchasing power of earnings (table 7.3). The second is high ser-

---

13. According to *O Estado de S. Paulo*, August 18, 2003, B5.

14. The 98 percent reduction from July 1994 to August 2003 represents close to total elimination; as a result, the increase shown in the last column (13 percent) of table 7.2 was on top of minor installation charges.

Table 7.5 Brazil: Fixed and mobile telephone services by family income groups, 1998 and 2002[a]

Income class in minimum wages per month	Percent of families, 2002	Percent with fixed lines		Percent distribution of mobile telephones	
		1998	2002	1998	2002
Up to 2	n.a.	0	9	0	3
4 to 6	45[b]	1	51	1	10
6 to 15	31	25	87	6	19
15 to 30	19	77	99	31	31
30 and up	5	91	99	62	37

n.a. = Data not available for this income class alone.

a. As of July 29, 1998 and December 31, 2002.
b. Includes previous class.

Source: National Telecommunications Agency (ANATEL).

vice tariffs, particularly for fixed lines. For a household, these tariffs have two components: a fixed subscription cost and a variable cost, which depends on telephone use. In addition, the private provider has an incentive to cut off service to nonpayers. In the past, this was not a serious issue, as services were more limited, particularly in their coverage of poorest groups.

Postprivatization tariffs increased to levels viewed as realistic to attract investors. The regulatory regime allows for periodic adjustments as warranted by the General Price Index-Internal Availability Criterion, known as the IGP-DI, calculated by the Fundacao Getulio Vargas. (An IGP variant is the IGPM, which was adopted as a standard for variations in certain electricity contracts.) These IGP variants differ according to the period in which the index is calculated, but they use the same price changes as their basis. In any case, I argue that this index presents a series of detrimental distortions for consumers.

Created in 1947, the IGP has never changed its structure. Wholesale prices represent 60 percent of the calculation, consumer prices 30 percent, and civil construction costs 10 percent. When it was created, the IGP had a pragmatic objective: to estimate the overall rate of inflation before calculating the nominal GDP deflator based on the national accounts.

Focusing now only on recent developments, since the adoption of a floating exchange rate system in 1999, the Brazilian real underwent three major rounds of devaluation, which led to sharp increases in wholesale prices, particularly for tradable commodities, such as soybeans and steel. As a result, the IGP became detached from consumer price indices, thereby revealing its bias toward dollar-linked prices. For example, over the 12-month period ending December 2002, the IGP-DI increased by 26.4 percent, while IPCA, a national consumer price index produced by IBGE, increased 12.5 percent, less than half as much.

The IGP is also subject to other criticisms, including that certain wholesale prices are collected from price lists, which are not used in transactions. Another criticism is that a general price index should have a formula based on the structural composition of the economy's GDP, in which the industry represents 36 percent, agriculture 8 percent, and services 56 percent. These would be only technicalities if not for the fact that the IGP used to index the telephone and other tariffs for public services, thus contributing to the picture revealed in table 7.2.

Many in Brazil perceive the need to adjust the IGP or remove its distortions; however, since the 1973 inflation episode, it has been taboo to criticize price indices in the country. At that time, under a military regime, the anti-inflationary policy also controlled the price indices, and the government pressured institutions that produced them to underestimate rates. Thus, some continue to view criticisms of the IGP as smacking of this older attitude, even when they aim to point out clear distortions in its measurement.

In short, the resulting dilemma is that legislation imposes use of a distorted index. The institution that produces it does not fix it, and the government, afraid of being misinterpreted, is paralyzed. In turn, the consumer ends up paying the bill.

These distortions became more evident with the last tariff adjustment that ANATEL authorized in July 2003, with rate increases ranging from 24.6 percent to 41.74 percent, depending on the service. For example, the minimal commercial tariff had the higher rate, while the residential tariff had the lowest.[15] Given the difference in relation to the consumer price indices, public opinion, consumer protection agencies, and many politicians (including the Minister of Communications) strongly opposed the rise in tariffs. Some entities filed lawsuits, which led to court decisions to suspend the increase temporarily, only authorizing a variation following the IPCA of IBGE. A final court ruling is pending.

One idea gaining ground within government circles is the adoption of indices that specifically measure the evolution of costs by industry, after 2006, when the contract rules will be reexamined. However, no proposal has been made to compensate consumers for the distortions that are leading to excessively high rates (although there may be a court ruling or a renegotiation of contracts induced by the uproar caused by the higher tariffs).

Another issue is the comparatively high price of fixed telephone services, which (along with convenience of usage) has led to a strong increase in mobile phone use (table 7.4). The fixed-telephone subscription tariff, the basic tariff for services, is high, particularly for poorer families. At R$32 (about US$10) per month, in the case of residential service, it represents approximately 13 percent of a minimum monthly wage. Thus, many consumers have begun to opt for the mobile phone, particularly in its prepaid

---

15. According to *O Estado de S. Paulo*, July 12, 2003, B1.

calling card form, which has no minimum tariff and eases consumer management of cost. Mobile phones of this sort are often sold at reduced prices (R$200 or US$66, in 10 monthly installments, for example). Many consumers also content themselves with using the mobile phone to receive calls only, as no tariffs are charged in this case.

This alternative facilitates phone access and use, but raises the overall cost of service because tariffs for mobile calls are more expensive on a used-time basis. An additional dilemma is that fixed phone companies do not want to reduce the basic subscription tariff on fixed lines to facilitate access, while mobile phone companies facilitate access, as well as use, but charge higher tariffs. The convenience and the status of owning a mobile phone also influences individual choice, but does not necessarily take the family's interest into account. This issue remains unresolved.

A parallel issue is that Internet access in Brazil, available almost entirely through fixed telephone lines, excludes many poor families. The price of a computer is also an obstacle; however, a large second-hand market has affordable prices (sometimes only US$100–$150). More affordable prices increase access to the machine, but not to Internet use, which is precluded by the need for affordable access to telephone lines.

Electricity Services

Electricity tariffs are set according to more complex criteria than those used in the telecommunications sector because the electricity sector's structure includes both generators—95 percent of which are hydroelectric power plants—and distributors.[16] Thus, the sector requires rules to guide relations between these two components, and between distributors and consumers. Privatization occurred mainly among distributors and some generators, although the largest ones (Furnas, Chesf, Eletronorte, and Itaipu) remain in federal hands. Moreover, a considerable portion of energy is imported from a joint venture with Paraguay, through the Itaipu hydroelectric plant.[17] There is also a short-term exchange market, Wholesale Electricity Market, known as the MAE.

Regarding generation, the cost of electricity is roughly determined by combining the following supply sources: Itaipu (30 percent), with the dollar as the reference; contracts between generators and distributors (30 percent), with the IGPM (30 percent) as the reference; bilateral contracts using MAE prices as the reference (15 percent); and the distributors' own generating

---

16. I thank Francisco Anuatti-Neto for his guidance in this chapter section.

17. Itaipu is the world's largest hydroelectric plant (although it will lose its title to China's Three Gorges, currently under construction). Itaipu produces 30 percent of all energy consumed in Brazil (a minor portion comes from Argentina).

Table 7.6 Brazil, state of São Paulo: Low-income urban electricity consumption compared with standard rate, 2003 (Brazilian real)

Standard rate	Low-income rate[a]	Consumption level (kWh)
0.027521	0.009362	Up to 30
Flat rate	0.016047	31 to 100
	0.024073	101 to 200
	0.026745	201 and above

a. Mandated by ANEL by range of residential monthly consumption.

Source: ANEL and Bandeirantes Electricity Company.

power (25 percent). Except for MAE, all contracts are long term in order to limit the short-term market to 15 percent of supply. Distribution prices have as a basis an initial value, adjusted according to generation plus distribution changes in costs. As in the case of telephones, the readjustment is linked to the IGP, this time in its variant IGPM. Under such conditions, electricity tariffs in Brazil have been largely influenced by the US dollar and amount of rainfall. The US dollar acts directly, through supply from Itaipu, and indirectly, through its important role in determining the IGPM.[18] In recent years, devaluations of the Brazilian real, along with low reservoir levels, have pressured tariffs.

Given all of these factors, which affect absolute energy prices and their increase over time, it is not surprising that the effect on consumers is considerable (table 7.2), especially considering that earnings are not keeping pace with rise in the cost of living. ANEL, the government agency in charge of the industry, provides some relief by setting lower rates for less consumption in a scheme designed to protect low-income groups. Rates for a major distributor in the state of São Paulo are presented in table 7.6; other states and regions have adopted similar schemes.

The low-income rates listed in table 7.6 show a progression of roughly 1 to 3, which seems reasonable. To qualify for low-income rates, a family must either have maintained monthly consumption, over the past 12-month period, at or below 79 kWh or have kept it at 80 to 280 kWh over the same period and presented proof of low-income status by enrolling in the roster of one of two locally administered, federal-income support programs: Child in School (Bolsa-Escola) and Food Money (Bolsa-Alimentação). Child in School benefits children between the ages of 6 and 15 years in families living on up to one-half the minimum monthly wage per capita. The monthly benefit, paid to the mother, is R$15 (roughly US$5). At the end of 2002,

---

18. A press article illustrated the seriousness of the burden of the dollar-indexed supply from Itaipu, showing that the average residential tariff in five partially supplied areas is roughly 50 percent above the average in five areas not supplied by the same plant. See *Folha de S. Paulo,* September 8, 2003, B-3.

the number of beneficiaries was 10.2 million. Food Money is provided to children between 0 and 6 years of age and pregnant and nursing women living in families under the same income condition. The allowance is the same, to a maximum of three children. The number of beneficiaries is about 1.6 million.[19]

Many families are enrolled in these federal programs. The Cardoso government developed the programs to illustrate the administration's social concern and action. The Money in School program has received international recognition, including that of the World Bank. With regard to the roster of entitled families, major concerns involve its level of completeness and the degree to which it is affected by local-level, political patronage. The press has denounced individual cases of mismanagement, but these have not tainted the programs' good image, particularly Money in School. It should be noted that, following privatization, distributors became responsible for the selection of beneficiary families for lower electricity tariffs. It appears that distributors' compliance with the existing rules have not been evaluated, although consumer interests are an obvious force in this direction.

In any case, the tariffs described in table 7.6, combined with federally established criteria for targeting income groups, is a move in the right direction. Like any such initiative, it requires evaluation and improvement. The Brazilian tradition of establishing lower tariffs for lower consumption only has benefited many middle-class and wealthy families who have second homes that remain vacant for long periods and thus have low consumption. (This problem extends electricity taxes; telephone services are subject to a flat tax rate.)

An insufficiently understood issue is that of service interruption due to payment default by low-income consumers. Distributors have difficulty adopting this measure, which requires that a company representative visit the consumer's household to cut off service. In poorer urban and other low-quality housing areas, the cutting off of service is not always done because of community protests and threats, often supported by politicians. Moreover, the customer whose service is to be cut may live in a high-crime area, which company agents prefer to avoid. In many poorer areas of Brazil, clandestine or illegal wiring, directly hooked onto the distribution cables, with no access to meters, is common. Although this study failed to obtain the number of payment defaults or an estimate of illegal wiring, its practice presents a serious problem for distribution companies.

I conclude that electricity tariffs overall have been designed to cushion the effects of needed price increases on the poorest households. They have also moved toward improved targeting. However, a comprehensive evaluation is needed to determine effective coverage of these mechanisms nationwide.

---

19. See Macedo (2003) for a description of these and other federal-income transfer programs. I have not been able to determine the number of families (in São Paulo or nationally) covered by the program described in table 7.6.

At the same time, moves to correct distortions in the indexation of tariffs are badly needed, given the problems in constructing the index used in the process. To reiterate, both private and state companies must contend with this issue; clearly, the problem is not privatization per se, but rather a regulatory system that sets distorted readjustments of tariffs and overlooks their effects on consumers.

Issues of access and consumption differ from those of telephone services. In general, electricity access comes with use, given that use has a high benefit-cost ratio—that is, electricity has many uses, no effective substitutes, and the poorest households have access to lower rates. According to data from the 2001 National Household Survey, only 0.8 percent (311,000) of urban Brazilian households had no access to electricity. Two-thirds of these households were poor families, half of which resided in the northeast, the country's poorest region. As expected, access is a more serious issue in rural areas, where 1.49 million households—22 percent of the total rural population—are without electricity. Sixty-five percent of the rural nonconnected are poor families, and 73 percent reside in the northeast.[20] For these poor segments, both access and use need improvement. However, even the relatively small problem of urban access is worthy of attention because minor investments could potentially solve the problem immediately.

Bottled Cooking Gas

Among the Petrobrás-supplied consumer products, cooking gas is used by more than 90 percent of Brazilian households. It reaches consumers after being bottled by distributors (gas pipelines for residential use have a limited scope in Brazil). Cooking gas can be considered a type of public service that private bottlers who receive Petrobrás supplies provide. It is an important source of energy and a major item in poor families' household budgets. As a rule, the average consumption is one bottle of 13 kilograms (kg) per month per family, at a present cost of R$30 (about US$10) per bottle filling, or 13 percent of the minimum monthly wage.

For decades, the refinery subsidized the cooking gas price, and the government set its prices to the consumer. This process favored all consumers, including the wealthy and businesses. Price-setting was first eliminated in regions with a higher average income—the southeast (in 1997) and the south (in 1998). Starting in 2001, the government eliminated the subsidy, as well as price controls, in all other Brazilian regions. To compensate for higher prices, it opted for another income transfer to the poorest households, at the rate of R$7.5 per family per month, as long as the family is

---

20. These numbers do not include the northern or Amazon states, where population density of population is low.

enrolled in the rosters of the federal income programs mentioned above. No proof of acquisition is required. As the transfer is provided to consumers, cooking-gas price changes since 1997 reflect the end of the old subsidy, but not the effect of the new one. Moreover, given that price increases have been high, the government requires Petrobrás to charge lower prices when the product is sold to distributors to be bottled in 13-kg cylinders, the standard size used by most households.

Like telephone and electricity services, there is also room for challenging the way cooking gas prices are set (table 7.2). The cooking gas price is linked to the international market and has risen fast in the wake of recent increases in the price of oil and the exchange rate. Moreover, Petrobrás supplies nearly all gas at the refineries. Although the company has formally lost its monopoly, it has not been exposed to significant competition, as private investors are still reluctant to face this giant. Thus, Petrobrás continues to act as a monopoly. In the case of cooking gas, like other fuels, its policy aims to set domestic wholesale prices to cost, insurance, and freight (CIF) international prices, even though the product comes mostly from Brazilian oil (or from imported oil that is refined in-country). Moreover, its import prices are set by long-term contracts and specific deals at prices below international rates. Thus, the CIF international price criterion makes no sense for local production, and there is room to dispute these monopolistic practices to reduce the price of cooking gas. Thus far, Petrobrás remains virtually unchallenged.

The distribution chain is too long, with one or more intermediaries between bottlers and consumers. The former have their own distribution networks; however, discouraged by past government price-setting, they have withdrawn from activities. The distribution chain also includes informal firms and individuals who deliver bottles to consumers living in the most remote areas, increasing the margins charged on prices and the burden on the poorest groups, who reside in these areas. In this case, I suggest pushing the bottlers into expanding their distribution network again. As they are only about a dozen, it would be easier to monitor their margins and put pressure on them if excesses were found. Moreover, this move is likely to increase competition along the final stages of the supply chain. It would also serve bottlers' interests, since they are often blamed for the high price of the product and then argue, unconvincingly, that they cannot interfere with the price that final distributors charge.

Total Effect of TEG Services on Cost of Living

Figures 7.1 and 7.2 measure the total effect of the prices of telephone, electricity, and cooking gas (TEG) services on a national consumer price index, the IPCA (National Consumer Price Index). The IPCA covers family incomes, ranging from 1 to 40 minimum monthly wages. The Central Bank uses the IPCA in its inflation targeting policy.

Figure 7.1 Brazil: Percent share of utility expenditures, in monthly changes of IPCA index,[a] 1991–99 annual averages

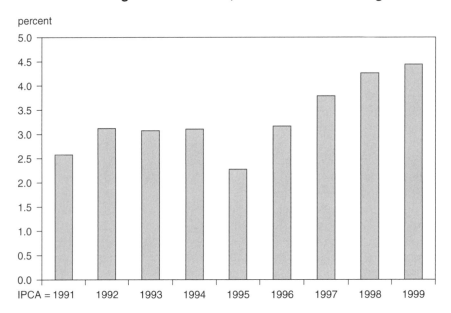

percent

a. Following weights provided by 1987–88 Household Budget Survey.

Note: Utilities include telephone, electricity, and liquified petroleum gas expenditures.

Source: IBGE, courtesy of Luiz A. F. de Lima, Bradesco Bank.

These two figures show that monthly price variations were calculated based on their weights in two household surveys conducted by IBGE, the governmental agency responsible for this index. The first survey, conducted in 1987–88, produced the TEG set of services weights used to aggregate the price variations shown in figure 7.1, in their participation over total IPCA variations. The second survey, conducted in 1995–96, served as the basis for figure 7.2.

As figure 7.1 shows, the share of the TEG set of services prices in the IPCA changes remained around 2.5 and 3 percent from 1991 to 1996. From 1997 through 1999, the increase was clear, linked in part to the privatization effect, because companies were being prepared for sale before privatization and the process included more realistic prices. One should recall that, until 1994, Brazil was close to hyperinflation. Even with an ample indexing system, public service tariffs had often lagged inflation. In the new household survey, shown in figure 7.2, the TEG set of services weight started from a higher value than the one shown at the end of figure 7.1 (close to 4.5 percent). Thus, the initial value in figure 7.2 is about 7.7 percent, which reflects higher prices, as well as the expansion of services to

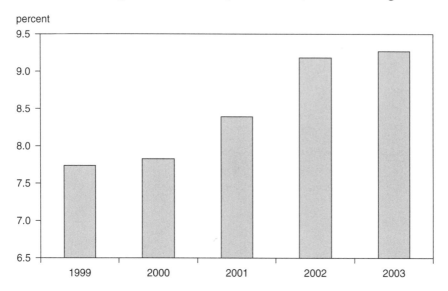

a. Following weights provided by the 1995–96 Household Budget Survey.
Note: Utilities include telephone, electricity, and liquified petroleum gas expenditures.
Source: IBGE, courtesy of Luiz A. F. de Lima, Bradesco Bank.

consumers, particularly in the case of telephone lines. (Note that the house-hold survey on which figure 7.1 is based did not include the use of mobile phones, which was identified as relevant in the subsequent survey.)

Thus, both figures 7.1 and 7.2 indicate, in aggregate, the expansion of telephone services and price increases above the index average. An additional result is the major increase in the share of household budgets spent on the TEG set of services, strengthening the notion that the pricing issue of these services concerns low-income groups.

Until now, discussion has centered mainly on the distortions in the index used to adjust telephone and electricity tariffs, the IGP, and Petrobrás price policies. An additional problem, as mentioned above, is the high taxes charged on the TEG set of services.

Taxes on TEG Services

In discussing the taxes charged on the TEG set of services, only service-specific taxes charged by the various levels of government are included; while general taxes, such as corporate income tax and others, are excluded.

Table 7.7   Brazil: Taxes on TEG set of services for residential use, 2003 (percent of price minus tax)

Service	ICMS	Range of consumption, kWh per month	CIDE[a]
Telephone	33.3		
Electricity	0	Up to 50	
	13.6	51 to 200	
	33.3	201 and above	
Bottled cooking gas	33.1		18.8

TEG = telephone, electricity, and cooking gas (LPG)
ICMS = tax on value added by trade and services
CIDE = economic dominance intervention contribution

a. The CIDE tax applies to oil derivatives only.

Sources: Telephone and electricity bills and National Association of LPG Distributors (SINDIGÁS).

Table 7.7 shows the tax on the turnover of goods and services (ICMS), which states charge and share with municipalities, and the economic dominance intervention contribution (CIDE), a federal tax on imports and commerce of oil and its derivatives.

The tax burden on the TEG set of services is high and provides leeway, if not for a subsidy, at least for a lower tax rate for low-income classes. This is not a new idea for the three services analyzed. For example, in the case of electricity, a lower tax rate is already in place for monthly consumption that remains below 200 kWh. However, as has often been the case in Brazil, its targeting is defective—that is, the second homes of middle-class and wealthy families have low consumption, on average. In the case of bottled cooking gas, the two taxes total what seems a high rate of 51.9 percent of the price of gas at the Petrobrás refineries. The ICMS is charged on the basis of an estimate of its final price to the consumer.

It has been mentioned that a cash subsidy for bottled cooking gas is supposedly available to low-income families enrolled in the roster of the federal government's income transfer programs for the poorest households. As the price of gas has risen, however, this subsidy has decreased, when measured in relation to the bottle price. It stands at R$7.50 per family per month, or about 25 percent of the cost of a 13-kg bottle, the usual monthly consumption. However, it is not an authentic subsidy because it is estimated that the price of a bottle includes R$5.90 of ICMS and CIDE taxes, thus reducing the net subsidy to only R$1.60 per bottle.

Finally, as the discount is not given directly on the price, the price increases generate a substitution effect, stimulating the use of other environmentally harmful fuels, particularly wood. The press has published articles showing poor urban consumers already following this course. In rural areas, the substitution effect is likely to be stronger.

Concluding Remarks

This chapter has argued that the Brazilian privatization program begun in 1990 missed a major opportunity to democratize capital property, which would have allowed for better income distribution. To reach the goal of enhancing efficiency and equity, the program should have opted earlier and more extensively for a scheme of public offering of stock, after entitling and empowering common citizens to participate. Even when lacking voluntary savings, Brazilian workers in the formal sector participate in a mandatory savings scheme, known as FGTS, whereby workers accumulate the equivalent of one month's salary in an individual account every year, which the employer pays.

Viewing the FGTS within the context of privatization, some Brazilian economists, including myself, have defended the idea of allowing workers to use the money in their FGTS accounts to buy stocks in the companies being privatized. Active and retired workers in general could also exchange the present value of their social security pensions by stocks.

The government administrations that managed the privatization program over the past decade (1990–2000) neglected these alternatives. Since then, in 2000 and 2002, partial use of FGTS funds was allowed in public offerings of Petrobrás and CVRD stocks, respectively, but in a limited way and only after the privatization program had already made major advances. Yet, this small initiative attracted great interest from hundreds of thousands of workers, who became shareholders of those two companies, demonstrating that the idea could have been implemented in the past and can still be extended. Moreover, in both companies, the stocks that workers have bought, to date, have yielded gains that far surpass traditional returns of their FGTS accounts. However, these are two highly profitable companies; their positive share performance cannot be taken as the general rule. Even so, the idea deserves further consideration and adoption, as other companies, including Petrobrás, could be privatized using this voluntary scheme.

This chapter has also identified that, after privatization, certain public-service tariffs or prices—particularly telephone, electricity, and cooking gas—together forming what is called the TEG set of services, have been increasing well above cost-of-living indices. These prices are regulated by agencies created as part of the total privatization of telephone services, the partial privatization of electricity, and the liberalization of the oil industry. The latter is still largely dominated by Petrobrás, a state company, which has been given more leeway than ever to determine its prices, despite a formal removal of its monopoly position.

One goal of privatization was to allow for realistic (or scarcity) prices. However, I found distortions in the indexing of telephone and electricity tariffs, as they have been linked to price indices biased toward an appreciated US dollar. It is true that dollar-linked costs, as in the case of imported electricity and oil, have also played a role in pushing prices of public services, but not to the point of justifying indexation of costs in general by indices largely affected by the appreciated dollar. For this and other reasons, the cost of the TEG set of services to consumers has accounted for an increased share in the total cost-of-living increases. Moreover, workers' earnings have lagged behind these increases.

In the case of Petrobrás, I argue that the company abuses its monopoly power when setting the price for cooking gas at its refineries, while the distribution chain, which also includes bottlers and other distributors, also shows distortions, such as compounding margins of various intermediaries (which is also worth the regulating authorities' attention). Moreover, as part of oil industry liberalization, cooking gas prices are no longer directly subsidized, for which reason, among others, their prices have sharply risen, thus aggravating the consumer's burden. The government has created a new cash subsidy to offset increased gas prices for low-income households (no proof of gas consumption required); however, the allowance has been falling in relation to the price per gas bottle, which is also aggravated by taxes that erode the subsidy's effect. Therefore, I conclude that the government should take steps to correct the various sources of price distortions of the TEG set of services, by resorting to appropriate regulatory and other measures.

It is not surprising that more realistic tariffs, regardless of their distortions, ended up creating a greater burden for consumers, especially low-income families. They face two problems: access to services, such as fixed phone lines, and their use. In the case of fixed telephone lines, both access and calling tariffs are obstacles to further extending the impressive expansion of services that came with privatization, as now millions of available lines are not in use. The high cost of access to fixed telephone lines has created a boom in the demand for mobile phones, whose access is cheaper but with more expensive calling rates. Electricity access in urban areas, on the other hand, is more universal. However, its higher cost is leading to default among poorer consumers. Still, their services, due to security and sociopolitical reasons, are not always disconnected. The rising cost of cooking gas has not only gradually eroded the existing subsidy, it has even induced poor consumers to revert to using wood.

Given these conditions, the case for alleviating the plight of the poorest Brazilian groups becomes stronger. Without excluding the role of tariffs, it has been shown that the TEG set of services has such high taxes that its reduction could provide the poorest households considerable relief. Certain states, including São Paulo, already do this with electricity, placing smaller taxes for household consumption under 200 kWh per month. However, this program has targeting problems, as even the wealthiest families benefit from it, as noted above.

To improve the targeting of smaller taxes, a registration process, similar to the one adopted by federal regulations in the case of lower electricity tariffs, should be created to allow only families enrolled in federal income transfer programs, which are designed to reach low-income groups, to benefit. This targeting scheme has been considered an improvement over former ones, in which access was determined only by low consumption. In any case, the overall effectiveness of the current targeting scheme needs to be evaluated, and it is likely that the findings will offer room for further improvements.

Taxes are also high on telephone use and cooking gas. The latter is close to a basic need. Cooking gas dominates the Brazilian market, as electric stoves are expensive and microwave ovens still have a low penetration rate in households. High taxes on cooking gas are nearly equivalent to the subsidy provided to low-income families, thereby eliminating its effect. Telephone services in Brazil have not yet reached the status of a basic need; in my opinion, this view is misguided, based on the fact that supply was extremely scarce before privatization, when access was mostly a privilege of the middle class and wealthy. Considering that telephone services save people's time and facilitate their access to such basic services as health care and police, it would seem reasonable to regard them as a basic need, a view that should guide the implementation of tariffs, taxes, and even subsidies for the poorest households.[21]

It is important to stress that this price analysis of the TEG set of services demonstrates that the current problems do not result from privatization per se. Indeed, as the chapter's findings have shown, problems can occur in a totally privatized industry, such as telecommunications; a partially privatized industry, such as electricity; and a state-controlled industry, such as oil.

Therefore, privatization cannot be blamed for these problems. The difficulties faced in the TEG set of services is essentially the result of more realistic prices after privatization or liberalization from state intervention, combined with regulatory weaknesses and mistakes of agencies that emerged only in the late 1990s. Regulators are still engaged in an on-the-job training phase and have not managed to work effectively and efficiently in harmonizing the interests of regulated companies with those of consumers.

Finally, the aggravating fact remains: Policymakers and society at large have yet to fully acknowledge or understand the consequences of increased costs in the TEG set of services to consumers, thereby precluding emergence of a strong concern about its effects on low-income families.

References

Annuati-Neto, F, M. Barossi-Filho, A. Gledson de Carvalho, and R. Macedo. 2003. *Costs and Benefits of Privatization: Evidence from Brazil.* Working Paper R-455. Washington: Inter-American Development Bank.

21. One example of lower telephone tariffs for the poorest groups is the United States, where those who qualify for Medicaid, Supplemental Security Income, or food stamps can obtain a discount of up to $12 on their monthly bill. On the basis of the same targeting criterion, another program provides a 50 percent discount on the cost of a line installation (according to columnist Marshall Loeb, CBS.MarketWatch.com, July 3, 2003).

Estache, Antonio, and Marianne Fay. 1995. Regional Growth in Argentina and Brazil: Determinants and Policy Options. World Bank, Washington. Photocopy.

Lamounier, B., and A. De Souza. 2002. As elites brasileiras e o desenvolvimento nacional: Fatores de consenso e dissenso. *Relatório de pesquisa.* São Paulo: Instituto de Estudos Econômicos, Sociais e Políticos (IDESP).

Lora, E., and U. Panizza. 2002. Structural Reforms in Latin America Under Scrutiny. Paper prepared at the seminar Reforming Reforms, held at the annual meeting of the Board of Governors, Inter-American Development Bank, Fortaleza, Brazil.

Macedo, R. 2000. *Privatization and the Distribution of Assets and Income in Brazil.* Working Paper 14. Washington: Carnegie Endowment for International Peace.

Macedo, R. 2003. *Macroeconomic Volatility and Social Vulnerability in Brazil: The Cardoso Government (1995–2002) and Perspectives.* Financiamento del Desarollo Series 132 (June). Santiago: Economic Commission for Latin America and the Caribbean.

Pinheiro, A. C. 1996. Impactos Microeconômicos da Privatização no Brasil. *Pesquisa e planejamento econômico.* 26, no. 3: 357–98.

8

Latin America's Infrastructure Experience: Policy Gaps and the Poor

ANTONIO ESTACHE

A central conclusion of studies on infrastructure privatization in Latin America is that the poor will eventually gain via increased access.[1] However, when infrastructure services are turned over to private owners, the poor can lose in many ways over the short term. Reforms can result in losses for the poor, as opposed to the nonpoor. Reducing the major policy gaps that can create such losses, while maintaining the economic gains from privatization, is the main topic of this chapter. The gaps discussed include

- lack of care in documenting the initial conditions of public services before their reform, including the degree of regressivity that previously characterized the financing of service delivery;

- lack of a much needed distinction between access and affordability;

- failure to account for the weakness of safety nets during the difficult transitions associated with reform;

- failure to recognize the distortions caused by all levels of government in using these sectors as tax handles;

Antonio Estache is a senior economic adviser at the Infrastructure Vice-Presidency of the World Bank. This chapter is based on comments made at the conference, The Distributional Consequences of Privatization, held at the Center for Global Development, Washington, DC, February 24–25, 2003. The author wishes to acknowledge his discussions with Nancy Birdsall, Omar Chisari, Alberto Devoto, Marianne Fay, Vivien Foster, Andres Gomez-Lobo, Dany Leipziger, Martin Rodriguez-Pardina, Lourdes Trujillo, Tito Yepes, and Quentin Wodon. Special thanks go to John Nellis for his contributions over several months.

1. See McKenzie and Mookherjee (chapter 2), as well as other chapters in this volume.

- failure to recognize that effective regulation is needed to achieve fair outcomes that benefit the poorest; and

- insufficient appreciation of the political commitment required to ensure that reforms benefit all segments of the population.

Any complete assessment of the effects of the 1990s privatization experience on income distribution, as well as any restructuring of policies and practices to minimize risks of negative social effects, should include the above-mentioned points.

Current Knowledge Base

The current state of knowledge on linkages between infrastructure reform and the poor is a combination of results from three empirical research areas:[2]

- establishing linkages between infrastructure and growth,

- studying the effects of infrastructure on welfare of the poor,[3] and

- documenting the linkage between infrastructure reform and improved access to infrastructure—from safe water and sanitation, to transportation, telecommunications, and electricity.[4]

The combined message from these three research fields is that infrastructure is good for growth; since growth is good for poverty reduction, infrastructure is good for poverty reduction. Moreover, the literature shows that policy changes that improve the level and quality of infrastructure in developing countries positively affect health and education indicators.[5] The literature also shows that these improvements matter most to the poorest; hence, the importance of measuring the effects of the 1990s infrastructure-privatization experience across income groups. The explicit linkages between infrastructure reforms and changes in poverty rates and income distribution, however, have not yet been systematically analyzed. Only recently—mainly in Latin America—have studies attempted to assess

---

2. Certain theoretical areas provide important insights into the efficiency-equity trade-offs of policy options for such instruments as regulatory mechanisms design, including the design of universal service obligations. However, this discussion is beyond the scope of this chapter. For a survey, see Laffont (2003).

3. The most often quoted, and still relevant, resource on this is the World Bank's 1994 *World Development Report*.

4. This third area, the most recent, includes several studies presented at the 2003 conference, The Distributional Consequences of Privatization.

5. See Brenneman (2002) for a recent survey.

and measure these linkages.[6] This section reviews major results emerging from these various research areas and concludes with an initial assessment of the policy gaps.

Empirical literature on infrastructure and growth in Latin America shows the extent to which infrastructure promotes growth in this region.[7] For example, Baffes and Shah (1998) show that the elasticity of output to infrastructure is about 0.14–0.16 in Bolivia, Colombia, Mexico, and Venezuela— that is, a 1 percent increase in the stock of infrastructure is associated with an additional 0.14 to 0.16 percentage points increase in the growth rate. For Brazil, Ferreira (1996) finds an elasticity between 0.34 and 1.12, depending on the discount rate used. Research also shows the role infrastructure plays in facilitating the growth convergence of regions, allowing the poorest to catch up with the wealthiest. For example, evidence from Argentina and Brazil shows that improved access to sanitation and roads is a significant determinant of convergence for the poorest regions (Estache and Fay 1995).

Linkages between access to infrastructure and well-being of the poorest have been less covered. The work undertaken on health and educational achievements has been based largely on event studies or anecdotes. In recent years, the rapidly growing body of literature increasingly indicates that improved access to all types of infrastructure can have positive social effects among the poorest, including reduced child mortality and higher educational achievements. Leipziger, Fay, and Yepes (2002) suggest, based on a sample of 73 countries, that a 10 percent improvement in a country's infrastructure index can lead to a 5 percent reduction in child mortality, a 3.7 percent reduction in infant mortality, and a 7.8 percent reduction in the maternal mortality ratio, controlling by income effect and differentials in access to health services. For an extremely poor country, such as the Central African Republic, a general expansion of infrastructure of 10 percent could annually help to save nine children under five years of age (who currently die for each 1,000 live births) and nearly 100 mothers (per each 100,000 live births).[8]

From the viewpoint of social analysts, the drawback of many of these studies is that they focus on the effects of infrastructure investments (or stock levels) on growth in general, and only rarely on income levels or

---

6. Two recent exceptions (in addition to McKenzie and Mookherjee [chapter 2] and other chapters in this volume) are Estache, Foster, and Wodon (2002) and Ugaz and Waddoms Price (2003).

7. Disagreements among academics are based on technical, econometrics grounds (de la Fuente 2000).

8. The effectiveness of this intervention would have to be compared with the cost of an equivalent intervention in the health or education sector. Leipziger, Fay, and Yepes' point, however, is that this type of calculation is needed in order to understand which sector can deliver the "biggest bang for the buck."

income level per income class. The effects on income level per income class are needed to assess quantitatively the income distribution effects of reform.[9] Galiani, Gertler, and Schargrodsky (2002) provide an alternative, effective bridge linking changes in access resulting from reform and social effects on the poorest. Because of the simplicity and strength of its message, their study has quickly become one of the most often quoted in the privatization literature. Galiani, Gertler, and Schargrodsky show, for example, that child mortality caused by waterborne diseases fell 5 to 9 percent in the 30 Argentine localities where water services were privatized, with the strongest benefit—more than a 25 percent decline—occurring in the poorest neighborhoods.

Considered collectively, these studies are insufficient to settle the too often ideological debate over the full social effects of privatization. Partial and sometimes anecdotal assessments of specific experiences are important; however, they should be complemented by a more systematic, cross-country approach to assessing the winners and losers of reform and privatization, and, hence, their distributional consequences. Despite the solid contributions of the other chapters in this volume, they contain gaps in terms of identifying ways in which the poor can lose from reform. Offering suggestions on how to identify and, more importantly, close these gaps is the main goal of the sections that follow.

Importance of Initial Conditions

History textbooks currently used in the high schools of major cities in Brazil, Argentina, Bolivia, and Chile provide interesting insights into the emotional biases of the privatization debate.[10] An informal review of these textbooks suggests that, in all of these countries, the collective memory—approximated by what the educational systems want to teach the next generation—largely ignores many of the dimensions of the basic living conditions of the 1970–80s. The texts focus on the dramatic political changes that occurred in the region, but provide little coverage of the economic history, and even less of the poor quality of public services that previously prevailed. Yet, when they were introduced at the end of the 1980s, infrastructure reforms were relatively easy to sell politically because the majority of voters were fed up with the poor quality and rationed nature of most public services. Most of these countries could no longer afford investment and maintenance costs for their infrastructure networks, which explains why service quality was poor to begin with and was expected to further deteriorate.

---

9. Until recently, Chisari, Estache, and Romero (1999) and Navajas (2000) were the only studies that addressed this issue quantitatively.

10. For a larger survey, see Birdsall and Nellis (chapter 1).

While effective tariff levels (taking into account large shares of unpaid bills) appeared low, power outages and water shortages were the expected norm in many regions of these countries. Few today recall the 5- to 10-year waiting period to acquire a residential, and sometimes a commercial, telephone, interminable delays in obtaining repairs and services, and the high costs of bribes paid to utility officials to jump the line and obtain—and maintain—connections. In many of these countries, lack of safe, reliable public transportation strongly contributed to increased use of private modes of transport. It was within this context that many reforms were initially welcomed—except by public-sector workers (and their families), who lost jobs and associated privileges, financed by taxes paid by the contemporary population, or bonds currently being repaid by the subsequent generation. The key point is that the standards applied today to assess the effects of reform are significantly higher than those used to gauge the delivery systems under which people were living in the early 1990s.

Today's critics also tend to forget that, to a certain extent, the regressivity of the current financing schemes was inherited from the prereform area. Consider the case of Colombia (Velez 1995). In 1992, 38 percent of all public-sector subsidies (including health, education, housing, and other public services) were, in fact, spent on utility services, representing 1.4 percent of GNP. Of these, 80 percent were spent in the electricity sector; the study found that these subsidies benefited mostly middle-income households. Indeed, many direct or cross-subsidy schemes typically used in Latin America were so poorly designed that they failed to reach the poor. Various studies have shown that as much as 60 to 80 percent of cross-subsidies were aimed at households well above the poverty threshold, while as much as 80 percent of poor households failed to benefit (Estache, Foster, and Wodon 2002).

The regressivity of the previous financing system reflected the reality that the poorest of the poor were often unconnected to utility services and, hence, were not positioned to benefit from direct or cross-subsidies. Before reform, the supply systems were already regressive. Indeed, middle- and upper-income groups had significantly greater chances of getting connected than did the poor. That regressivity is an inherited problem does not justify inertia in correcting it. However, because initial conditions matter, any assessment of privatization should carefully distinguish between inherited and additional regressivity caused by reforms, just as it should apply comparable standards to assess performance before and after reforms.

Finally, one should remember that context matters. In nearly all countries, privatization and infrastructure reforms are part of a wider reform agenda. Benitez, Chisari, and Estache (2003), for example, provide a test of the relative effects of privatization and credit-market restrictions as a reason for the increased unemployment observed in Argentina. The test suggests that most of the increase in unemployment can be attributed to credit rationing, thereby calling into question a standard myth associated with privatization. To reiterate, it is important to differentiate the causes of observed events to assign credit and blame, thereby moving beyond emotional debates on the effects of reform.

Private-Sector Participation

Just as important as the need to recognize the initial conditions is the need to bear in mind basic figures when attempting to assess the social effect of infrastructure privatization in Latin America. One frequently overlooked datum is the volume of foreign direct investment (FDI) brought in by new operators of many of these services.

Latin America recorded a massive $361 billion in private infrastructure investment in 1990–2001 (with FDI peaking in 1998). Although this is the largest volume recorded for any region, it covered only about 25 to 33 percent of the region's annual investment needs. Despite their enormity, these figures show that the private sector never assumed full responsibility for the financing requirements of the sector, even during the glory days of privatization. This sector has been and will remain one in which the public and private sectors must work together.

A crucial difference between the two forms of provision is that the state has the option to finance delivery through taxes, while private providers usually must recover their investments directly through user fees. Even rough calculations of what this cost recovery means from the perspective of the poorest may help provide a sense of where the social problem lies in any proposed reform.

On a per capita basis, the large FDI volume represents roughly 15 cents per person per year, which the operators want to recover.[11] One should recall that, during the 1990s, 15 to 20 percent of Latin Americans lived on less than a dollar a day. Asking them to allocate 15 percent of their meager daily income to the amortization of private investment (and probably they would have been required to pay more in order to finance the operational cost) would have been unreasonable. It should have been evident that this was a social issue deserving of policymakers' attention through sector-specific regulatory design. Any failure of the regulatory regime or government to identify and finance the needs of the poorest would and did have a strong effect on the poor. However, these were, and still are, public-sector, not private-sector, failures.

Asking users to allocate more than 20 percent of their income for public services, with little tolerance for nonpayment of bills (which state-owned firms tended to tolerate) largely accounts for the negative perception among

---

11. This figure, calculated by dividing the annual FDI volume by the population, roughly approximates what cost recovery will entail in the near future.

the poorest of the private sector. The question is this: Why was this outcome not perceived and predicted during the first half of the 1990s, when the reform process was launched? Part of the answer is that the negative reaction began to spread widely only after the Asian crisis, when unemployment increased significantly, along with a corresponding increase in the number of people living below the poverty line. These factors were combined with the return of increasingly binding fiscal constraints, which limited the public sector's ability to subsidize, and the failure of many family or neighborhood social networks that assisted the poorest. In such circumstances, the tension among private providers, the public sector, and users was bound to increase.

Needs of the Poor: Getting the Facts Right

A prime political and financial challenge of liberalizing reform and privatization is to aim to ensure that, after privatization, access to infrastructure services improves, while affordability of services continues at least at preprivatization levels. Since needed increases in service quality and coverage often necessitate raising the average tariff level, affordability of privatized services for the poor is a core policy concern.[12] This is why the main regulatory challenge is to develop the technology and mode of service delivery that ensure affordability for low-income groups, while giving operators reasonable assurance of cost recovery.[13]

The Latin American experience suggests that policymakers have been less effective in addressing affordability than access. Many looked at overall affordability but focused on tariffs, ignoring the often prohibitively high connection costs for both electricity and water/sanitation. While ambitious targets for extending services to unserved populations were laudable, virtually all were predicated on full cost recovery. Early on, it was not sufficiently recognized that the often exorbitant connection charges were beyond the ability of the poor to pay. Thus, although services are now available in many more neighborhoods, the poorest segments of society often cannot afford to become connected. It is now known that access often entails substantial upfront, fixed costs, which are problematic for poor households that lack savings and ready access to credit. Future schemes must take this fact into account.

Most practitioners have their own horror stories from the 1990s illustrating that, from the perspective of poor households, affordability can pose a greater barrier than access to using services. For the Buenos Aires

---

12. For example, on average, cost recovery in water and sanitation in the public sector was about 25 percent, according to the 1994 *World Development Report*.

13. For a full treatment of this question with illustrations, see Estache, Foster, and Wodon (2002).

water concession, for example, the connection charges initially allowed by the contract were up to $600 for water and $800 for sewerage, to be recovered over a 24-month period from households with monthly incomes of little more than $200. For many, this meant allocating nearly 30 percent of their income to these charges, which was clearly unsustainable. To the government's credit, the fee was later incorporated into a more socially viable tariff structure, which entailed cross-subsidies from families with existing connections to newly connected families.

Impeding access forces poor, unconnected households to pay for inferior substitutes, such as tankered water or kerosene lamps, the per-unit energy cost of which is much higher than that paid by middle- and upper-income groups for use of formal utility services. Estimates for Guatemala and Honduras, for example, suggest that families with access to the formal network of electricity services can meet their basic energy needs 20 to 30 percent more cheaply than can households who lack access (Estache, Foster, and Wodon 2002). These observations suggest that resources channeled into subsidizing service tariffs could be better used by subsidizing connection charges.

Ultimately, this discussion points to the need to make better poverty diagnoses. The starting point in preparing a strategy or action plan aimed at addressing distributional issues within the context of privatization is to establish whether poor households genuinely cannot afford connection costs or a subsistence level of consumption once connected. Relatively straightforward indicators, using readily available sector statistics in combination with household survey data, can be applied to identify the relative importance of access and affordability.

Policymakers attempting to address the needs of the poor in infrastructure reform must answer three broad questions regarding the state of access:

- What is the level of service coverage among poor households?
- Is the problem of access caused primarily by demand- or supply-side factors?
- Can the poor afford the initial costs associated with connecting to the network?

A diagnostic of the state of affordability must answer the following questions:

- How much are the poor able to pay for utilities services?
- How much are the poor willing to pay for utilities services?
- Are the poor's utilities payment cycles synchronized with their income cycle?[14]

---

14. Foster and Tre (2003) and Wodon and Ajwad (2002) provide good examples.

Assuming that the diagnostic reveals that the policymaker faces both access and affordability problems, but (as is nearly always the case) only limited fiscal resources are available to finance subsidies, the main question then becomes: How does one choose between access and consumption subsidies? The problem is solvable, but the optimal solution requires serious analytical work that few governments (or their advisors) have taken the time to undertake; few governments have made the effort to obtain good knowledge of the expenditure patterns of the poorest.[15] The simple starting point is that governments should subsidize goods that are consumed in larger proportion by the poor.

Household consumption surveys or living standard measurement surveys often fail to collect the relevant data, and do not adequately disaggregate even the limited good data they obtain. Many collect information only in urban areas, while the majority of poor people reside in rural areas. Subsidies end up being either overgenerous (because they benefit many nonpoor) or too harsh (because they exclude those most deserving of support). For example, recent surveys in Central and South America show that subsidies for water and urban transportation tend to have greater poverty-reduction potential than those for electricity and telephone services simply because the poor's share of total expenditures for water and urban transportation is larger than for electricity and telephone services.[16] Yet, as noted, relevant data on transportation are seldom collected.

The Case for Infrastructure-Specific Safety Nets

Certain social problems associated with infrastructure reform, often pointed out by critics, are relatively predictable for policymakers who have done their homework. These include transition costs associated with formalization of illegal users (common with electricity and water reform) and inclusion of poor users in the customer basis of the profit-oriented private operators. If the effect of a reform process on the poor is a major source of concern, the first recommendation an economic advisor will usually give is to rely on the general welfare system—that is, stop burdening a supposedly productive enterprise with what are, ideally, the functions of general economic policy or a specialized government body or agency. This solution works when policy is sound and where a functioning welfare system is in place. However, this is usually not the case. Most social welfare systems in Latin America are procyclical in nature,

---

15. For a more technical discussion, see Estache, Foster, and Wodon (2002).

16. See, for example, Siaens and Wodon (2003) for Bolivia and Makdissi and Wodon (2002) for Mexico.

which impedes their effectiveness during transitions. Moreover, most social safety nets fail to consider the costs of commercializing infrastructure.[17]

Since the welfare system is often unable to accomplish its expected role, it may make sense to consider a special program for the infrastructure poor. Indeed, one main lesson of the 1990s may be that introducing distributive considerations into an infrastructure reform process, perhaps by designing a special welfare program, is not only necessary for equity reasons, but may also be imperative for political reasons. The acceptability and long-term success of an infrastructure reform may depend on such a policy, even when strict welfare considerations may not justify it. The need for an infrastructure-specific social policy does not necessarily mean that a utility regulator designs or even administers the welfare program. On the contrary, such programs should be integrated into a government's general welfare and poverty alleviation policies, thereby maintaining coherence with complementary poverty-reduction efforts. Chile and Colombia have achieved this goal with their water subsidy scheme and residential utility subsidy, respectively.

A special-welfare infrastructure program can be used for multiple purposes; however, credible, sustained funding is critical in all cases. This can come from a variety of sources. First, governments can provide funds from general tax revenues. This is often the case of urban transportation and "negative concessions," such as those awarded for toll roads. Second, funding can come from charging certain customers or sets of customers a higher price than the cost of service, using the resources to cover the lower fee paid by the poor. While historically, this type of cross-subsidy was regressive, many ways have since been discovered for bolstering transparency and progressivity. Moreover, private utilities are likely to continue applying such cross-subsidies, since many governments cannot make credible commitments to finance subsidies from public funds. Third, a fund can be established whereby all companies must contribute according to a proportional rule (e.g., number of customers that each company serves or proportional to each company's revenue). Companies still charge customers a price/cost markup in order to pay for this contribution. Various Central American countries have adopted this approach for their telecommunications sectors. Deciding which type of funding is best depends, in part, on the efficiency, equity, and administrative costs associated with the distortions created by the general tax system (the cost of public funds).

In sum, effectiveness of designing the transition from public to private supply drives the distributional effects of the full reform package. The challenge is to avoid dogmatism (e.g., cross-subsidy versus the need to undergo the general welfare-system debate) and to be transparent and accountable about targeting and financing decisions made to mitigate the risks of undesirable social effects of reform.

---

17. For more details, see Estache, Gomez-Lobo, and Leipziger (2001).

Legacy of Regressive Taxation

An underestimated source of unfair distributional outcomes from reform is the transformation of the public-service sector into a major source of tax revenue for all government levels. When operated by the public sector, infrastructure services sometimes generated large revenue volumes for the level of government responsible for operating the service (even though this was often insufficient to cover all costs). Since privatization—at least in the case of utilities, but not always in the case of transportation—these sectors have increasingly become net cash cows for all government levels. In Argentina, for example, utilities generate about 1 percent of tax revenue for all levels of government, mostly from a 35 percent income tax and a 21 percent value-added tax (VAT) passed on to consumers. However, the effective tax rate that users pay is typically significantly higher than 21 percent because of municipal and provincial taxes. Indirect taxes on telecommunications and electricity can total more than 55 percent of the cost of service in certain large municipalities.

When assessing the effects of reform on tariffs, it is important to examine the evolution of tariffs with and without taxes. (This is also important when undertaking international tariff comparisons for similar services since tax burdens vary across countries.) The failure to make this distinction can hide the gains from reform. More importantly, the general complexity of the information processed by regulators may create situations in which private operators effectively share achieved efficiency gains with the government rather than users. This may be appropriate, but not when done through a regressive tax system. Moreover, the major tax instruments available to most subnational governments are indirect taxes, which tend to be regressive. Thus, the odds of having an enormous tax burden financed disproportionately by the poor are relatively high.

Importance of Regulation

A principal reason for infrastructure privatization's lack of popularity is a perception that the quality-adjusted efficiency gains have not been distributed fairly. When this is the case, the remedy is, to a large extent, the responsibility of regulators—either as part of the ordinary or extraordinary reforms or within the context of tariff-structure design. The major distributional mandate of regulators is to assess the cost reductions achieved by operators and pass on a fair proportion of those gains to consumers as part of the scheduled tariff-revisions processes. In too many developing countries, and even in certain industrialized ones, the regulator may be too weak (that is, influenced by politicians and/or operators), or may simply be incompetent in delivering on this mandate. The basic efficiency gains that should be eventually shared are typically not measured and, hence, seldom redistributed.[18] In sum, regulators are the crucial players in determining the perception of the equity of privatization because they largely determine the extent to which the poor get their fair share of the gains from reform (if they are working with appropriate legislation).

Chisari, Estache, and Romero (1999) support this conclusion in their review of privatization and regulation of Argentina's energy, telecommunications, and water sectors. Their analysis separates the benefits of privatization per se from those of effective regulation. Their findings shows that privatization yielded operational gains in the infrastructure sectors equivalent to 0.90 percent of GDP or 41 percent of the average expenditure on utility services. Effective regulation added gains amounting to 0.35 percent of GDP (16 percent of the average expenditure on utility services). Higher-income households gained more in absolute terms than did lower-income households; however, the benefits of effective regulation, as a proportion of existing expenditures on utility services, were highest for the lowest-income quintiles. The reason is that regulation acts as a mechanism for transferring rents from owners of capital to consumers of the service. Overall, according to the simulations, the Gini coefficient of income inequality drops significantly if regulation is effective.

Estache, Manacorda, and Valletti (2002) provide additional support by analyzing determinants of growth in Internet hosts and use in Latin America during the 1990s. Their study tested whether there was a diffusion of growth in Internet access and use and, if so, its main determinants. Given the concern that recent technological innovations are creating a digital divide between rich and poor countries and between rich and poor regions within countries, analysis of this phenomenon is clearly relevant to this discussion. As expected, Estache, Manacorda, and Valletti found that regulation aimed at facilitating sector entry boosted Internet diffusion. Interestingly, from an equity perspective, initial income distribution has been a determinant of the effectiveness of reform and the speed at which the poorest regions catch up with the richest. In terms of growth in Internet hosts, they found that a 10 percent fall in the Gini coefficient (that is, a 10 percent improvement in a standard measure of income distribution) led to a doubling of Internet diffusion—a dramatic result. Moreover, they found that a 10 percent deterioration in the Gini coefficient halved Internet diffusion. The key point is that linkages between reform and income distribution may be a two-way street, a fact often ignored in policy debates on reform.

---

18. More precisely, the efficiency gains are distributed from the government, politicians, and managers of public enterprises to a new combination that includes these three groups, along with shareholders of the privatized regulated services. As a group, consumers get only a share of the cost savings in the form of tariff reductions if the regulators are fair.

Conclusion

Macroeconomic context often matters more than infrastructure reforms, and it matters most to the poor. Employing the poor, replacing regressive tax systems with progressive ones, designing more effective welfare systems, and promoting local capital markets to reduce credit rationing and local sensitivities to international crises are all effective ways of ensuring that the poor enjoy access to the basic services they need and are often willing to pay for. In isolation, infrastructure reform can do little to fully offset macro-policy failures.

In addition, because macro policies take time to implement, transitional safety nets may be necessary to mitigate the adjustment costs imposed by infrastructure reforms. While decentralization may complicate the challenges of transition and reform, national governments cannot accomplish them alone. Jurisdiction of national reformers over certain tax decisions is limited, and subnational governments' choice of tax levels is a crucial determinant of rents distribution resulting from reform.

Regulating the remaining natural monopoly elements of an infrastructure sector is the main engine of the distributional effects of infrastructure reform. The specific design of regulation and the competence, independence, and skills of its implementation agency determine the extent to which the efficiency gains achieved by reform can be passed on to users.

Moreover, it is critical that regulators, tax reformers, and welfare-program designers carefully analyze the facts and assess the preexisting situation not only to explain the distributional effects of reform but, more importantly, to enable the design of new reforms. Current reformers must be more knowledgeable about the poor they seek to help. Once they know who the poor are and the specific ways in which they are poor, there is broader scope for win-win decisions in infrastructure reform and many beneficial ways in which both the public and private sectors can cooperate.

Finally, Latin America's experience underscores that all of these decisions are intensely and invariably political. Politicians must decide to "get the facts right," prioritize choices, and take action. If political support is lacking in any node of the decision tree, the reforms will, at best, leave income distribution unaltered or, at worst, make it more unfair, leaving the poor even worse off. The less transparent the reform process—the less accountable decision makers and other actors intervening in and interfering with the decision process are—the more likely reforms and marginal players, rather the actors guilty of the failures, will be blamed.

References

Baffes, J., and A. Shah. 1998. Productivity of Public Spending, Sectoral Allocation Choices and Economic Growth. *Economic Development and Cultural Change* 48, no. 2: 291–303.

Benitez, D., O. Chisari, and A. Estache. 2003. Can the Gains from Argentina's Utilities Reform Offset Credit Shocks? In *Utility Privatization and Regulation: A Fair Deal for Consumers?* ed. C. Ugaz and C. Waddams Price. Northampton, MA: Edward Elgar.

Birdsall, N., and J. Nellis. 2002. *Winners and Losers: Assessing the Distributional Impact of Privatization.* CGD Working Paper 6. Washington: Center for Global Development.

Booth, D., L. Hanmer, and E. Lovell. 2000. *Poverty and Transport.* London: Overseas Development Institute.

Brenneman, A. 2002. Infrastructure and Poverty Linkages: A Literature Review. The World Bank, Washington. Photocopy.

Chisari, O., A. Estache, and C. Romero. 1999. Winners and Losers from the Privatization and Regulation of Utilities: Lessons from a General Equilibrium Model of Argentina. *The World Bank Economic Review* 13, no. 2: 357–78.

de la Fuente, A. 2000. Growth and Infrastructure: A Survey. World Bank, Washington. Photocopy.

Estache, A., A. Gomez-Lobo, and D. Leipziger. 2001. Utilities Privatization and the Poor: Lessons and Evidence from Latin America. *World Development* 29, no. 7: 1179–98.

Estache, A., V. Foster, and Q. Wodon. 2002. *Accounting for Poverty in Infrastructure Reform: Learning from Latin America's Experience.* Studies in Development Series. Washington: World Bank Institute.

Estache, A., M. Manacorda, and T. Valletti. 2002. Telecommunications Reform, Access Regulation and Internet Adoption in Latin America. *Economia* 2, no. 2 (Spring): 153–217.

Ferreira, P. C. 1996. Investimento em infraestrutura no Brasil: fatos estilizados e relacoes de longo prazo. *Pesquisa e Planejamento Economico* 26, no. 2: 231–52.

Foster, V., and J. P. Tre. 2003. Measuring the Impact of Energy Interventions on the Poor: An illustration from Guatemala. In *Infrastructure for Development: Private Solutions and the Poor,* ed. P. Brooke and T. Irwin. London: Private Provision of Infrastructure Advisory Facility (PPIAF), Department for International Development (DIFD), and World Bank.

Galiani, S., P. Gertler, and E. Schargrodsky. 2002. Water for Life: The Impact of the Privatization of Water Services on Child Mortality. Universidad Torcuato di Tella, Argentina. Photocopy.

Laffont, J. J. 2003. Regulation and Development. IDEI, Toulouse. Photocopy.

Leipziger, D., M. Fay, and T. Yepes. 2002. The Importance of Infrastructure in Meeting MDGs. World Bank, Washington. Photocopy.

Makdissi, P., and Q. Wodon. 2002. Consumption Dominance Curves: Testing for the Impact of Indirect Tax Reform on Poverty. *Economic Letters* 75: 227–35.

Navajas. 2000. El impacto distributivo de los cambios en los precios relativos en la Argentina entre 1988–1998 y los efectos de las privatizaciones y la desregulacion economica. In *La Distribucion del Ingreso en la Argentina.* Buenos Aires: Fundación de Investigaciones Económicas Latinoamericanas.

Siaens, C., and Q. Wodon. 2003. Food Subsidies and Consumption Inequality in Mexico. *Statistics/Estadíistica* 55: 164–65.

Ugaz, C., and C. Waddams Price, eds. 2003. *Utility Privatization and Regulation: A Fair Deal for Consumers?* Northampton, MA: Edward Elgar.

Velez, C. E. 1995. Gasto Social y Desigualdad: Logros y Extavios. Santa Fe de Bogota: Social Mission, National Planning Department.

Wodon, Q., and I. Ajwad. 2002. Infrastructure Services and the Poor: Providing Connection or Consumption Subsidies? World Bank, Washington. Photocopy.

World Bank. 1994. *World Development Report: Infrastructure for Development.* London: Oxford University Press.

II

CASES FROM ASIA
AND TRANSITIONAL ECONOMIES

9

Outcomes of the Russian Model

SVETLANA PAVLOVNA GLINKINA

To date, little research has been conducted on the effects of privatization on Russia's employment and income distribution. What has been achieved considers the problem from a regional or branch level, or through case studies of particularly affected groups. However, this research always works within a narrow privatization framework predominant in Russia, which implies simple transfer of existing state assets to private possession. Existing studies tend to exaggerate or underplay privatization's role in the making of Russia's emerging social structure. Assessing the distributional effects of privatization requires at least a cursory analysis of the Russian privatization model as it has shaped current property structure. I argue that privatization has substantially affected income distribution throughout the Russian workforce and society.

This chapter broadly defines *privatization* as the process of creating an environment for the emergence of private capital and for extending the private-sector share in aggregate assets and the national product of the country by all possible means, official or unofficial. My concept of privatization encompasses:

- transfer of existing state-run enterprises to private ownership (privatization in its narrow sense),

- relocation of financial flows from the state to the private sector (deliberate de-capitalization of the state sector), and

Svetlana Pavlovna Glinkina is the deputy director for research at the Institute for International Economic and Political Studies, Russian Academy of Sciences.

- establishment of private enterprises (sometimes called "greenfield" investments).

This chapter provides an overview of this broader privatization process and analyzes the outcomes of mass privatization; resulting ownership and income structure; effects on the labor market, including the emergence of oligarchs and growing shadow employment; and the distributional model that emerged after the 1998 financial crisis.

Privatization Process and Outcomes of Mass Privatization

The final days of the former Soviet Union witnessed unofficial "spontaneous privatization," as well as leasing and cooperative arrangements. The first official, purely Russian phase of privatization, which occurred during 1992–94, was mass privatization. During this phase, all Russian citizens above the age of 18 received, for a minimal charge, property certificates with a 10,000 ruble nominal value. Citizens were granted the right to exchange their vouchers for shares of enterprises and use them to buy property within the framework of small-size privatization or invest in newly created, privatization investment funds.

The launch of mass privatization coincided with the Russian people's exposure to the consequences of price-shock liberalization and spreading hyperinflation, which had led to the loss of virtually all savings. About 34 percent of all Russian voucher holders, finding themselves in serious economic difficulty, sold their vouchers without hesitation. According to the time and place of sale, the voucher price fluctuated in the range of $5 to $20. For this amount, one could buy a toy car[1] or a couple of bottles of vodka. Even less fortunate were the 25 percent of Russians who invested their property certificates in unregulated privatization or voucher investment funds, which sprang up spontaneously. Nearly all such investors lost everything within a short time. Many voucher investment funds failed after only several weeks. Those that managed to survive on the market usually offered poor dividends.

A surprisingly high percentage (11 percent) of the population gave away their vouchers as presents; about 5 percent of vouchers were held beyond their expiration date and never invested (suggesting that a sizeable segment of the population neither understood nor believed in the process). Some people may have lost their vouchers, while others may have decided to hold them until better times returned, perhaps not realizing that, after a certain date, vouchers would be worthless.

---

1. In 2002, Anatoly Chubais (2002), an architect of Russian privatization, claimed: "Reasonably used, the voucher's initial value (10,000 rubles) may have been increased 100 and even 1,000 times, which would have been more than enough to buy two Russian-made cars."

Surveys show that only 15 percent of citizens invested their vouchers directly in enterprises, thereby becoming minority shareholders. A few such investors were lucky, choosing one of those few enterprises that, under the new economic conditions, eventually became profitable. Buying stocks of solid companies was not easy, even in the rare cases where information was available, because directors of high-potential firms were reluctant to admit outsiders as shareholders. As a result, most citizens, after holding onto their vouchers for a period of time and then getting little or nothing for them, ended up feeling betrayed.

The official starting and end dates of the voucher phase of Russian privatization were December 1992 and June 1994, respectively. During this relatively short period, shares of more than 12,000 enterprises, with an overall charter capital of more than 800 billion rubles (balance sheet value as of July 1, 1992), and with more than 13 million workers (nearly 50 percent of employees of Russian industry overall), were slated for voucher auctions. For each enterprise, 35 to 70 percent of the stock was placed on sale for vouchers (no more than 80 percent was allowed by law). This included the amount reserved on "closed subscription"—i.e., for members of the work collective (Deryabina 1996, 35).

About 41 percent of all medium and large state firms were privatized during this mass-privatization stage. A parallel program for small-sized privatization succeeded in divesting more than 50 percent of available assets of this type. Combined with leased enterprises bought out, small-privatized enterprises, by the end of 1994, amounted to nearly 80 percent of the total stock of such small business units (Deryabina 1996, 36).

Workers and Managers

Workers and managers, who became known as insiders in enterprises selected for mass privatization, could choose between several variants of privatization:

- **Variant 1** stipulated that 25 percent of shares of "A" (nonvoting) category would be distributed free of charge among employees; 10 percent of ordinary shares, the "B" (voting) category, would be sold to workers at a 30 percent discount. Five percent of ordinary shares would be sold to management at face value, and 60 percent for cash to other investors.

- **Variant 2** envisaged the sale of 51 percent of stock against privatization vouchers or for cash, under a subscription limited to workers and management. The remaining 49 percent would be offered for sale at auctions (usually not all at once), both against privatization vouchers and for cash to other investors.

- **Variant 3** applied only to medium-sized enterprises. The idea was to form a management group of enterprise employees who would take responsibility for devising and implementing a privatization plan and preventing the enterprise from going bankrupt.

All employees in the work collective would approve the privatization plan. The management group would then sign a contract with the local division of the state Committee for Property Management (the privatization authority), accepting material responsibility secured on its personal property (by way of mortgage). The group would post a deposit of not less than the amount of 200 minimum wages. The contract would be signed to cover a one-year period. Once the contract expired and its conditions had been met, the management group would have the option to buy 20 percent of ordinary shares of the enterprise at face value, with a two-year payment deferral. If the group failed to meet the conditions stipulated by the contract, it would forfeit the option.

In addition, all employees of a given enterprise (including members of the controlling management group) were entitled to buy 20 percent of ordinary shares representing its own capital, provided that the total sum did not exceed $30 per employee, after taking the 30 percent deduction from the face value. Payment for shares could be made over three years, with the first installment not exceeding 20 percent of the face value of the shares.

Of the three privatization variants, variant 2 proved by far the most popular. The government's failure to re-value assets to account for the high rate of inflation made this option attractive to insiders. Variant 1 was applied in a few larger firms where insiders could not afford the purchase price. variant 3, which was hopelessly complex, was hardly applied.

Under variant 2, the bulk of property transferred to private ownership went to the workers and management—the insiders—of the enterprise concerned. In up to 80 percent of firms privatized by vouchers, the work collectives held a controlling amount of stock. Voucher privatization thus produced a typical capital structure of 60 to 65 percent of shares in insiders' possession. Outside investors succeeded in obtaining 18 to 22 percent, and the state retained an average of 17 percent of stock of privatized enterprises. Until the August 1998 crisis, the portion of inside shareholders tended to decrease; however, insiders' property was still dominant. Moreover, from 1999 on, a reinforced insider position emerged.

By the end of 1994, 40 million Russian citizens had formally become shareholders through voucher exchanges and share purchases. In theory, privatization had transformed millions of ordinary Russians into shareholding capitalists overnight. However, as this chapter will show, voucher distribution minimally affected incomes and employment of the broader population. In short, the Russian voucher variant, unprecedented in world practice, was applied behind the smoke screen of allowing popular privatization in the shortest time possible to expropriate a significant portion of common property to benefit a small group (Nekipelov 1996, 281).

Substantiating this assertion requires an analysis of property relations emerging in enterprises privatized to insiders. One objective of such privatization is to motivate firms to improve performance. To date, Russian research suggests the absence of any positive effect of privatization on enterprise workers' motivation and behavior. The greatest interest in privatization among the workers interviewed was expected dividends. However, even this interest faded rapidly since, in many Russian enterprises, opportunities for shareholders to obtain any cash dividend or benefit were limited.[2]

New shareholder interest in participating in an enterprise development strategy and decision making proved far weaker than initially presumed. Blasi and Shleifer (1996) concluded that rank-and-file workers were not represented on the advisory boards of privatized companies and behaved passively at shareholder meetings, even though they had the legal right to participate. This was often the outcome of management manipulation on the eve of such meetings and Russian workers' traditional apathy and distrust in their ability to influence events. Their assessment was realistic, as members of work collectives had insubstantial control of their managers' activities. Gurkov and Maital (1995) stated that more than 40 percent of workers in privatized Russian enterprises claimed a marked contraction of their chances to influence the decision-making process after becoming shareholders (38 percent of those polled held that privatization brought about no changes in this respect). Moreover, they reported that 46 percent of ordinary shareholders perceived that their access to information about company performance diminished after privatization. It is often claimed that, when workers displayed the slightest initiative about ownership rights, management launched all conceivable mechanisms to block it; even active workers rarely succeeded in passing any decisions that contradicted those proposed by management. Alliances between rank-and-file workers and outside investors aimed at supporting ordinary shareholders—enterprise workers—in their opposition to established management occurred in only 12 to 13 percent of firms (Bim 1996, 12). Similar conclusions can be reached based on press reports.

In conflicts between management and potential outsider investors, workers—convinced that their own management would be less radical and more likely to guarantee employment than any external investor—frequently sided with enterprise management. The idea of concentrating stock in the hands of managers, although unpopular among workers, was, nevertheless, more acceptable than having outsiders—who might lay off workers—assume a controlling stake.

Therefore, it is not surprising that privatization did not immediately motivate enterprise workers (Bim 1996, 13). Of the enterprise directors polled, 100 percent claimed that only in exceptional cases were ordinary

---

2. Economic results of 1994 showed that only one-third of privatized enterprises declared their intention to pay dividends.

workers interested in practicing their ownership rights. In 1993–94, from 10 or 12 percent to 15 or 18 percent of rank-and-file workers had no interest in owning stock and were willing to immediately sell their shares on financial markets or to enterprise management (Bim 1996, 12). The remainder was unsure of what to do with their shares and saw no opportunities to influence enterprise development strategy. Thus, in many cases, one byproduct of privatization was that enterprise control became increasingly concentrated in the hands of only a few managers.

Bim (1996, 5–8) showed that 82 percent (in 1993) and 80 percent (in 1994) of enterprises privatized according to variant 2 fell under management control—that is, as time passed, managers took effective steps to concentrate their control of share ownership. For example, in 1993, management held 3 to 5 percent of the stocks of 20.8 percent of privatized firms, 5 to 10 percent of another 20.8 percent, 10 to 20 percent of 12.5 percent, and 20 to 30 percent of 8.3 percent. Nonetheless, in most enterprises controlled by insiders, managers were dissatisfied with their controlling power and generally initiated measures to obtain even larger portions of equity. Indeed, by early 2001, top management's block of shares approached that of workers (21.0 percent and 27.2 percent, respectively). Russian Economic Barometer respondents predicted that managers, on average, tended to become owners of the largest package of group shares within two years of privatization (Kapelyushnikov 2002).

To concentrate property, managers of many privatized Russian enterprises pressured workers into selling management their shares at par or a discounted price. Managers offered workers the chance to either exchange their shares for consumer goods upon retirement or dismissal or sell management shares in lieu of disciplinary action. Heads of enterprises managed to impose self-serving conditions for closed subscription shares in the second issue, which further secured their privileged position. They also concentrated property by buying shares at the first money auctions, at which events (following the voucher auctions) residual state holdings were sold for cash.

Success in the money auctions required access to both vouchers and money with which to buy them. The task was easily accomplished by top enterprise managers through voucher funds, set up under their control using personal savings or other monies accumulated during 1988–91, the initial and highly fluid stages of liberalizing the Soviet economy. Ownership accumulation also occurred through spontaneous (*nomenklatura*) privatization, whereby managers became asset owners through lease and cooperative arrangements. In this way, and without any state regulation or supervision, a large amount of assets formally held by the state was transferred to managerial ownership. Even more dubious methods aimed at property concentration were widely used to (1) create private affiliated structures—private subsidiary firms or investment funds—aimed at concentrating shares in the hands of top managers; and (2) allow private persons, formally not associated with the given enterprise but in collusion with management, to purchase shares at auctions or on the secondary market and to turn them over to the control of managers.

It is not possible to cite reliable quantitative data on the scale of these processes. Informative data might be gathered if registers of shareholders could be analyzed. An indication of Russia's deficient state of corporate governance in Russia is that share registers, as a rule, are usually inaccessible for both independent researchers and shareholders. Exceptionally, Bim managed to gain access to a set of registers of Russian joint-stock companies; he found that, in 67 percent of cases, 10 to 12 percent of outside shareholders of the company have the same postal address as the headquarters of the relevant enterprise (Bim 1996, 13). This finding indicates that these shareholders were "satellite" or "affiliated" structures under control of enterprise leadership.[3] In 58 percent of enterprises, the number of outside shareholders whose family names were the same as those of the top leaders was as high as 19 percent (Bim 1996, 18).

Emergence of the Russian Oligarchs

Russian research literature uses the term *money privatization* to refer to the period following initial formation of private property, first allocation in voucher auctions, and subsequent redistribution and concentration in the hands of enterprises' bank directorates and favored private investors. However, the term is not justified for several reasons. First, the price of a privatization transaction was rarely the main factor determining a sale. Far more decisive was the political component of the privatization process— that is, the degree of influence enterprise managers had with high-ranking political authorities. This component was often decided by blatantly corrupt means. The term applies not only to the main privatization transactions of the federal government, but also to many—if not most—transactions at the regional and municipal levels. In short, the voucher privatization stage (1992–94) was followed by a quasi money or market stage of privatization, with two substages: 1995–98 and 1999–present.

During these years, typical forms of property redistribution or acquisitions involved

- lobbying by privileged participants to obtain, from desired firms, substantial blocks of shares remaining in the hands of federal and regional authorities;

- voluntary or administratively forced absorption of firms into holdings or financial-industrial groups, often with unclear ownership;

---

3. In 1993, 25 percent to 33 percent of all Russian enterprises had satellite companies (Dolgopyatova and Yevseeva [Boeva] 1994, 28).

- loans-for-shares schemes; and

- legalized dilution of state-owned shares through conversion of debt into equity, sale of receivables, trust schemes, buying up of promissory notes, manipulation of dividends on privileged shares, and unannounced capital increases.

All of this was in addition to managers' aggressive, but legal, purchase of shares on the secondary market from workers, investment institutions, brokers, individuals, and banks. The largest, high-potential Russian companies in which one could verify and locate the government's holding were the main objectives of this privatization phase.

The loans-for-shares scheme that followed largely affected wealth distribution in Russia. Under this scheme, a private Russian bank would lend a sum to the state budget against a collateral pledge of federally retained blocks of shares in a valuable company, usually a firm in the natural-resources sectors. In theory, a transparent tender, open to all lenders—both domestic and foreign—was held on the pledged shares. The winner was chosen according to the size of the loan pledged.

The nature of the firms and size of the equity involved might lead one to think that competition to offer loans would be great and the sums pledged would be large. In reality, all foreign banks and many domestic ones were excluded from tender. A few private Russian banks, politically well-positioned, colluded to determine which one would make the sole offer and receive collateral shares. Thus, the blocks of shares were pledged for low sums. For example, a near-controlling equity stake in the giant Norilsk Nickel company was provided as collateral for a loan of $179 million, compared to an expert's evaluation of $2 billion. Moreover, the government never made any effort to repay any of the money. These tenders and loans were, in effect, indirect sales at a low price to a buyer known in advance, without any bidding or competition. In this way, ownership stakes in the best natural-resources firms fell to Russian oligarchs at low prices. In sum, a vast amount of highest-potential equity was transferred to only a few people, while the state and the Russian people received little.

Another example of wrongdoing in the loans-for-shares scheme was the Menatep St. Petersburg Bank (SPB) acquisition of shares in Yukos oil company. In this case, collusion among the participating banks broke down. Heads of three other Russian banks—Rossiyskiy Kredit, Alfa-bank, and Inkombank—later charged the State Committee for Property Management (Russian Federation Privatization Ministry, headed by Anatoly Chubais) and Menatep SPB with mercenary collusion during preparations for auction of Yukos shares, arguing that Menatep designed and organized the auction. Losing bankers alleged that the government funds officials of the State Committee for Property Management had deposited in Menatep were used to make a loan to the government (in effect, to buy Yukos). Before the auction, a leading Menatep official reportedly claimed: "Two opinions are impossible; Yukos will be ours" (Pelekhova 2000).

A similar rigged scheme was applied in the loans-for-shares arrangement for 51 percent of shares of Sibneft oil company (founded in mid-1995) by means that bypassed government-approved sales procedures. On December 28, 1995, the commission overseeing the sales tender announced that SBS joint-stock bank and Oil Financial Company closed joint-stock company had won the competition for Sibneft. An investigation carried out by the Russian Federation (RF) Audit Chamber alleged that, before the tender, the RF Ministry of Finance deposited $137.1 million with SBS joint-stock bank; the bank then "lent" the government these funds following its winning of the tender.[4] This made a mockery of the notion that the scheme was imposed on a cash-short government, and lent weight to the allegation that, from the outset, the idea had been to transfer ownership of valuable property to a well-connected few.

Before the 1998 financial crisis, the key conflict in property redistribution was the clash of interests: old-line natural monopolies—with a new corporate façade—and major industrial and mining structures led by still-powerful Soviet-era managers versus younger entrepreneurs in new financial-industrial groupings. The expansionist and acquisitive interests of these two groups clashed over distribution of former state property. To reiterate, behind the largest transactions of 1995–98, including those in the loans-for-shares schemes, property redistribution outcomes were determined, not by economic factors or fair distribution of assets, but by the political power and interests of enterprise managers, emerging oligarchs in the banking sector, and representatives of state authorities.

---

4. The agreement (paragraph 3.1) stipulated that the loan would be extended until one of two dates expired: 1) January 1, 1996, when the borrower (Ministry of Finance) would pay the date liabilities using 1995 federal budget funds; or 2) the date determined by adding five calendar days to the date when revenues from selling shares transferred as security of the loan (stipulated by paragraph 2 of the agreement) were deposited.

In signing the loan agreement, paragraph 6 of "Mandatory Conditions of a Loan Agreement" (approved by Decree No. 889, August 31, 1995, by the RF President) was bypassed, which absolutely ruled out the right of the borrower (Ministry of Finance) to redeem liabilities on the account of the federal budget, since the 1995–96 budgets did not provide for assigning funds to redeem the loan. The Ministry of Finance was given only one working day (December 29, 1995) to locate resources with which to pay off the loan. According to the report of the Audit Chamber, on December 29, 1995, the SBS joint-stock bank transferred $97.3 million of the loan value ($100.3 million offered as loan, minus $3 million as security) to the currency account of the RF Ministry of Finance, No. 704000011420, with Menatep SPB; however, the federal budget did not receive the monies until a month later because they were continuously transferred from one account to another until January 31, 1996. Menatep SPB, the second auction bidder, was virtually granted a month loan of $97.3 million. In this way, it was rewarded for participating in the auction.

The 1998 financial crisis and the changeover in political leadership a year later had little effect on the privatization process; however, it led to substantial regrouping of the main players on the privatization stage, reevaluation of their role in economic management, and an occasional shift in their political power.

By 2002, redistribution of property to benefit outside investors—which began to emerge in the 1995–98 period—came to a virtual standstill. A second surge of rapid growth of managers' equity share and stagnation in the increase of outside investors' property are correlated with the 1998 financial crisis and subsequent economic recovery. The August 1998 shock undermined the positions of many financial institutions owned by oligarchs, thereby limiting—at least temporarily—their opportunities for expanding further into the real sector of the economy. General economic revival of many enterprises in 1999–2002 allowed enterprise managers to sharply promote the process of obtaining additional shares, mainly from workers.

Today, the battle for control continues; in 1996, it was estimated that not more than 30 percent of enterprises had been completely privatized (Radygin 1996). Surprisingly, despite a decade of giveaways and sales, property valued at roughly $90 billion (equal to nearly 30 percent of GDP) remains in state hands. In the gas industry alone, assets still available for privatization equal about 8 percent of GDP. Privatization reform in the railway industry might also yield 8 percent of GDP (already one can witness oligarchs seeking to "occupy the lower floor" of the industry by buying depots and repairing facilities and other assets). An increasing number of large-capital owners have shifted their focus to the agro-industrial sector (7.5 percent of GDP). The financial-services market, representing 4 percent of GDP, is another new field of activity since the Russian government aims to eventually end Sberbank's exclusive right in offering deposit insurance. Forthcoming pension reform will allow private financial structures to accept and manage pension monies. Both investors and oligarchs await the persistently rumored privatization of the electricity sector (2.5 percent of GDP).

Evolution of Employment Patterns

Under privatization, a new employment pattern rapidly emerged. The labor market influenced distributive relations in modern Russia, which resulted in

- narrowing of the scale and impact of the state-owned sector,

- major employment shift from the production to the services sector, and

- change in the social structure of employment and worker status.

Figure 9.1 Employment in enterprises by property types, selected years (percent of end result)

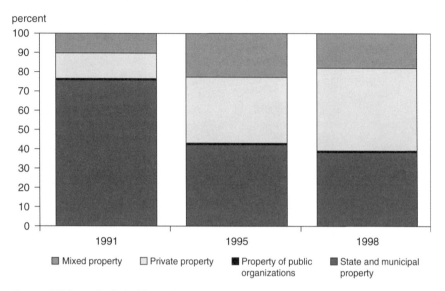

Source: RF State Statistical Committee.

As figure 9.1 demonstrates, the public sector has lost the principal-employer status. Figure 9.2 illustrates, employment declined most sharply in the leading branches of the real economy (industry, construction, and—to a lesser degree—transportation) and in science. Trading and middleman activities and financial, administrative, and social spheres (e.g., education and healthcare) have attracted labor resources. Moreover, as table 9.1 shows, a clear-cut differentiation between hired and nonhired workers has occurred.

However, the data do not allow one to assess the absolute numbers of hired and nonhired workers. Until 1996, official statistics stated with certitude the ever-increasing proportion of nonsalaried workers (6 percent in 1992 and 11.2 percent in 1996). Surprisingly, this category then decreased sharply (from 12.5 percent in 1994 to 4.8 percent in 1997 and 4.6 percent in 1998) (Civil Society European Academy 1998). In 1997, employment surveys showed that the criteria for identifying nonhired labor had changed, resulting in lower figures for the share of self-employed. With this in mind, evolution of the ratio of hired to nonhired labor in the late 1990s appears less volatile (table 9.1). Moreover, Moskovskaya and Moskovskaya (1999) correctly state that numerous divisions of large- and medium-sized enterprises began converting rapidly into independent economic agents during the first stage of reforms. However, numerous enterprises—many of which

Figure 9.2 Employment in individual branches, 1991 and 1998

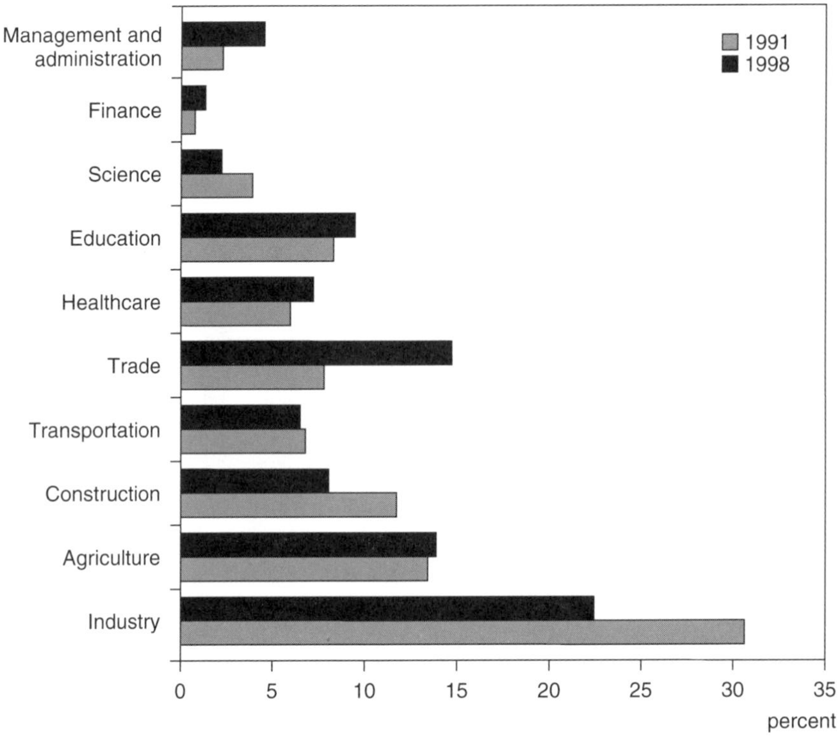

Source: Civil Society European Academy (1998).

started as production cooperatives[5]—could not compete and folded, resulting in fewer nonhired workers. In addition, the share of nonhired workers fell gradually as a result of property concentration—that is, large enterprises' acquisition of small businesses.

The category of salaried workers is heterogeneous in composition, including both managers of large enterprises and nonskilled workers. Among

---

5. Cooperatives were the first and, for a period of time, the only officially allowed form of private entrepreneurship in prereform Russia. Each member of the cooperative (consisting of at least three people) was responsible for contributing materially to set up and develop production, working on the enterprise they founded, and voting in decision making, irrespective of the amount of material contribution, which ultimately determined the income share obtained. Inevitably, this organizational pattern suffered from permanent, sharp conflicts among cooperative members. As soon as an opportunity emerged, most cooperatives changed their legal status and chose one of the two possible variants: limited partnership or open/closed joint-stock company, where relations among business partners are based on the amount of the founding contribution shares (in financial terms) or the stock acquired.

Table 9.1 Russia: Worker differentiation by employment status, for selected years

Worker type	1994	1995	1997
Hired	85.60	86.00	95.20
Nonhired	14.40	14.00	4.80
Employer	0.35	.37	1.30
Self-employed	1.40	1.80	2.90
Member of production cooperative	12.50	11.60	.60
Unpaid worker of family enterprise	0.10	.15	.10

Source: Moskovskaya and Moskovskaya (1999).

those who ventured to start their own businesses, most were self-employed and only 25 percent became employers.

Unemployment: The New Russian Phenomenon

Over the last decade, Russia has faced previously unheard of phenomena: unemployment and underemployment. While these came about slowly, and on a considerably lesser scale than reformers anticipated, they were accompanied by large and troubling wage arrears—one of the principal methods the Russian labor market used to adjust to the shocks of transition. Enterprises of all sizes, branches, and property forms have used the arrears mechanism. Because of workers' difficulty in seeking other employment, most tolerated wage arrears or partial payments at first. The overwhelming majority passively waited for the situation to improve. The typical reaction to wage delays was declining labor discipline and productivity. Low labor productivity, rooted in Soviet times, persisted throughout the transition.

Many other postsocialist European countries, including Poland and Hungary, more rapidly restricted subsidies and soft budgets to enterprises, which inevitably accelerated growth in open unemployment.

According to the official definition of the RF State Statistical Committee, the unemployment rate of a certain age category is the proportion (in percent) of jobless to the economically active population of the same age category. The State Employment Service considers an individual jobless if he or she is an able-bodied RF resident, is without a job or earnings from labor, is registered by employment agencies, is seeking a job, and is willing to start work.

During 1992–2000, both general and registered unemployment grew moderately (figure 9.3). General unemployment increased from 5.2 percent in 1992 to 13.2 percent in 1998, then fell to 9.8 percent in 2000. Registered unemployment rose from 0.8 percent in 1992, peaking at 3.6 percent in 1996, and falling to 1.8 percent in 2000. Only in the sixth year of market reforms did general unemployment pass the 10 percent level, reaching a level more typical of most transition countries. Kapelyushnikov (2001) points to the atypical behavior of the Russian labor market in the 1990s: a

Figure 9.3 General and registered unemployment rates, 1992–2000

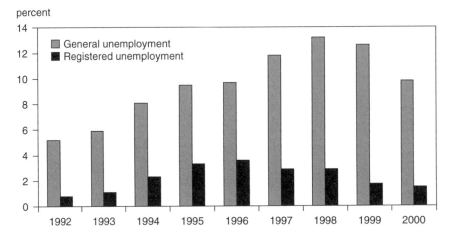

Note: The RF Ministry of Labor and Social Development reports registered unemployment at the end of each year.

Source: Russian Statistical Yearbook 2001.

much weaker, less explosive unemployment crisis than what occurred in other countries of Eastern and Central Europe.

Contrary to the declared shock-therapy policy aimed at the instantaneous development of genuine market relations, unemployment resulting from privatization was mitigated by artificially maintaining surplus employment in many privatized enterprises. To illustrate: In 1992–97, GDP fell by 36 percent, while, remarkably, the number of hired workers fell by only 17 percent, less than half. In the mid-1990s, 60 percent of surveyed industrial enterprises—both state and privatized—had a worker surplus, which, in certain cases, amounted to 50 percent of the total number of employed (according to the Russian Economic Barometer). The Institute of Employment Problems at the Russian Academy of Sciences concluded that 50 percent of the enterprises surveyed had a surplus work force. According to this study, in half of the excess labor at firms, the surplus was not more than 10 percent of the total number of employed; in 42 percent of such enterprises, the surplus ranged from 10 to 30 percent; and in 5.6 percent, it was 30 to 50 percent (Federation of Independent Trade Unions of Russia 2002).

Surplus employment is found in enterprises of various property forms (table 9.2); however, in privatized enterprises, one can detect specific features of the problem, which vary according to the privatization method used. For example, excess labor is less typical of enterprises privatized according to nonstandard schemes (e.g., leased and bought out). As expected, privatization that transfers a controlling share of stock to the work collective is associated with preservation of surplus labor. These variants are most frequently chosen by enterprises in which the initial workforce overhang

Table 9.2 Russia: Share of enterprises with surplus work force, 1995–99 (percent)

Status or variant	1995	1996	1997	1998	1999	Special poll, 1997
Enterprise group status[a]						
State-run	61	68	62	65	46	53
Nonstate-run	58	61	60	61	48	55
Intermediate	63	60	61	62	50	65
Variants of benefits offered to the work collective during privatization						
First	55	66	58	75	65	54
Second	73	68	65	58	52	69
Third	100	100	50	60	23	100
Nonstandard schemes	42	59	62	64	40	38

a. As reported by enterprise managers.

Source: Kapelyushnikov (2001).

is large, while more dynamic, better performing enterprises tend to select nonstandard ways.

According to Kapelyushnikov (2001, 111, 222), the causes of surplus-labor retention involve the high costs of laying off surplus workers as well as Russian management's expectations and inherited paternalistic orientation. He demonstrates that the costs of severance payments to enterprises are 5 to 10 times that of maintaining the same quantity of surplus workers over the same period. However, while a policy of maintaining as much employment as possible may have been positive in distributional terms, it was highly inefficient and costly over the long run, delaying needed enterprise restructuring. Since one observes the same policy applied in state and private firms, it cannot be said that privatization was a serious obstacle to gradually eliminating surplus labor; over time, it may have helped.

The high costs mentioned above consist of severance payments and paying off wage arrears, which, under widespread nonpayment conditions, are difficult to tackle. Apart from purely financial costs, enterprises must also consider transaction costs linked to a range of legal and administrative procedures, which must be completed before dismissal is allowed. Moreover, at the outset of property-relations reform, there were many legislative barriers to job reduction. For example, national-privatization legislation guaranteed workers' rights and jobs: The State Privatization Program of State-Owned and Municipal Enterprises in the Russian Federation (Article 20, paragraph 12) prohibited layoffs of more than 10 percent in an enterprise wholly owned by the state or municipalities in the six months before the date of its transformation into an open joint-stock company and until the time of its official registration by state bodies.[6] Difficult conditions were

---

6. State Privatization Program of State-Owned and Municipal Enterprises in the RF approved by the Decree of the RF President no. 2284, December 24, 1993.

imposed on enterprises sold through a tender that employed half or more of a locality's population: retaining the jobs of not less than 70 percent of those employed in the enterprise at the time of sale and professionally retraining any dismissed workers or placing them in new jobs (Law on Insolvency [Bankruptcy],[7] Article 137).

Thus, large-scale reductions in workforce of privatized enterprises began only in mid-1994, after mass privatization ended.[8] By the end of 1995, official unemployment increased almost five times compared to 1992, according to the RF State Statistical Committee. From 1995 until 1998, when the financial crisis broke, observed employment trends included relatively high employment, with strong dynamics toward reduction; relatively low, open unemployment that tended to become chronic; and large-scale latent or hidden unemployment or underemployment, which was chronic for certain categories of workers. Hidden unemployment grew as ever-increasing numbers of employees failed to receive wages. In 1992, the average period of back-wages payments was 1.6 months; by 1997, the period had increased to 5.7 months, with massive growth in informal and secondary employment for all groups.

Coping with the New Reality

By the end of 2001, officials estimated the unemployment rate at 18 to 20 percent of the economically active population. (This estimate included part-time workers in the informal sector, workers with long-standing wage arrears, and those receiving wages significantly below the minimum subsistence level.) An even larger percentage of the economically active population was classed in a marginal situation—neither employed nor officially recognized as unemployed. Thus, from 1992 to 1998, employment in the overall economy decreased from 71 million to 58 million workers; registered jobless grew from 0.6 million in 1992 to 2.5 million in 1996, falling to 0.6 million by late 1998. The distributional effect of such enormous increases in unemployment and underemployment was negative; however, the question was whether privatization or the general process of economic transformation was to blame for increased inequality.

As the transition deepened, informal-sector activity became an important survival mechanism for many Russian people. For a period of time, incomes from second jobs or sources amounted to half or more of major work-place earnings. Popularity of secondary employment peaked in 1994 and then faded until the crisis year of 1998 (table 9.3).

---

7. Federal Law on Insolvency (Bankruptcy) No. 6-FZ, January 8, 1998.

8. Massive layoffs before completing privatization might have caused problems for managers, who needed the work collective's support to achieve a controlling portion of equity.

Table 9.3 Russia: Share of employed with secondary job, selected years (percent)

Share of employed	1994	1995	1996	1998
Without secondary job	87.8	89.7	89.8	90.5
With secondary job	12.2	10.3	10.2	9.5
With permanent secondary job	4.7	4.5	4.4	4.5
With extra earnings	8.2	6.3	6.2	5.7

Source: Razumova and Roshin (2001).

In 1994–95, 11 to 13 percent of the working population held at least two jobs,[9] mainly ones in the same firm or agency (34 to 44 percent of additional employment). Repair, construction, and tailoring services accounted for 19 to 23 percent of additional employment. The main source of secondary work has been the new private sector. In most cases, the labor force has been hired informally, a profitable situation for both employers and workers. For employers, workers constitute cheap, readily available labor. Workers, in turn, can earn additional income without having to learn specialized professional skills; secondary employment has been a vital source of financial support for many families during the period of radical market transformation.

It is estimated that the informal labor market employed 7.5 million Russian citizens (11.6 percent of overall employment).[10] More than half (56.6 percent) provided services in construction, maintenance repair, and tailoring; 11.8 percent were engaged in street trade, while another 8.4 percent owned private enterprises (shops, cafés, and stalls). Many of the informally employed held several part-time jobs. By the mid-1990s, informally arranged work was widespread, involving about 20 percent of private-sector workers (though not more than 1 percent of public-sector workers).

Labor intensity is higher in the sphere of unregistered employment. The average work week for those informally employed is an estimated 50 hours, or 8 hours more than that of the officially employed, and 60 percent of the informally employed work more than 40 hours a week. Despite the informally employed work week often exceeding the legally established norm, only 4 percent of workers reported that they were remunerated for overtime. In the informal sector, piecework payment affects more than 50 percent of employees, 30 percent more than in the formal sector. Labor rights of those employed in the informal sector are not protected. Nearly two-thirds of

---

9. According to the Russian Monitoring of the Population's Economic Situation and Health (RMES).

10. Federal Target Program of Providing Employment of the RF Population 1998–2000 approved by the RF Government Resolution, July 24, 1998.

those with unregistered employment state that they can be fired without legitimate cause; half claim to have been unjustifiably punished materially. Registered employees make such statements more seldom (23 to 25 percent of cases). In short, workers in the informal employment sector are vulnerable.

Although one cannot directly link the above trends with privatization, I believe that privatization affected the move toward additional secondary and informal employment. In most state-run enterprises, in contrast to private ones, the mentality of workers and managers still approximates the socialist game rules. However, labor and social guarantees stipulated by the Labor Code are reportedly often ignored, even in legal private business. Private-sector workers may accept less security of tenure and rights (than in state-run firms) as a form of payment for their substantially higher remuneration.

Higher Private-Sector Wages

By 2000, public-sector wages averaged only 60 percent of those in the private sector. The share of income wages for a family with all its members engaged in the public sector accounted for only 24.5 percent, compared with 41 percent for families engaged in the private sector.

If one considers hidden wages from informal and secondary employment, the difference between these proportions is even more striking. In 2000, wages averaged 61.3 percent in total per capita income of the population. If one assumes that the hidden wage is derived largely from the private sector, then the wage proportion (hidden wages included) of a family's monetary income—with all members engaged in the private sector—amounts to 74 percent. For example, in October 1999, the average wage in the public healthcare system was only 66 percent of the average wage in nonstate, healthcare institutions (not including hidden wages). Proportions in other branches of the social sphere were: 51 percent (education), 76 percent (science), and 24 percent (culture and art). Workers in state-run sectors of economy, including healthcare, education (mostly high-school level), and culture and art did their best to find professional jobs in the nonstate sector (table 9.4).[11]

Table 9.4 shows that the share of enterprises admitting breaches of labor legislation is significantly higher in the private, than public, sector of the economy. Though private-sector workers have fewer legal rights, they are, indisputably, in a privileged financial position, compared to state-sector workers—an important factor in modern Russia's income, property, and social differentiation. The transition period, with its not yet fully established game rules, has largely justified the situation.

---

11. See Main Directions and Priorities of State Social Policy in Improving Incomes and the Living Standard of the Population, www.nasledie.ru.

Table 9.4 Russia: Guarantees to labor stipulated by legislation and labor contracts in enterprises of various property forms (percent of workers who answered positively)

Share of workers	State-owned enterprises	Privatized enterprises	Private enterprises
Regularly paid wage			
Twice monthly	51.7	61.6	65.6
Regular leave	1.6	2.3	22.6
Unpaid or paid lower than what legislation stipulates, including workers whose pay is additionally guaranteed by contract	1.1	1.4	8.4
Temporary disablement	8.0	8.8	37.8
Unpaid or paid lower than what legislation stipulates, including workers whose pay is additionally guaranteed by contract	5.9	6.5	16.1
Overtime	29.6	47.3	50.1
Unpaid or paid lower than what legislation stipulates, including workers whose pay is additionally guaranteed by contract	6.6	10.1	6.1
Total number polled	558.0	771.0	884.0

Source: Chetvernina and Lomonosova (2001).

To sum up, the main findings are that privatization results in a decline in employment; however, those fortunate enough to be retained generally earn higher salaries, with less likelihood of suffering arrears. Even so, the terms of service and rights of private-sector workers are more vulnerable.

Privatization, Income, and Property Differentiation

Privatization has contributed significantly to the new economic pattern, characterized by considerable differentiation in income and property. Indeed, by the end of 2001, the degree of inequality (as measured by the Gini coefficient) reached 40.9 percent, a dramatic increase from the estimated 1990 figure of 25 percent (table 9.5).

Privatization and Societal Inequality

To what extent did privatization contribute to increased income inequality in society, especially with regard to the large decline in shares of the two

Table 9.5 Russia: Overall income distribution, by population quintile, 1991–2001 (percent)

Factor	1991	1992	1993	1994	1995	1996	1997	1998	1999	2000	2001
Quintile											
1 (poorest)	11.9	6.0	5.8	5.3	5.5	6.2	6.0	6.1	6.1	6.1	5.9
2	15.8	11.6	11.1	10.2	10.2	10.7	10.2	10.4	10.5	10.6	10.4
3	18.8	17.6	16.7	15.2	15.0	15.2	14.8	14.8	14.8	14.9	15.0
4	22.8	26.5	24.8	23.0	22.4	21.5	21.6	21.1	20.8	21.2	21.7
5 (wealthiest)	30.7	38.3	41.6	46.3	46.9	46.4	47.4	47.6	47.8	47.2	47.0
Gini coefficient	0.26	0.289	0.398	0.409	0.381	0.375	0.381	0.398	0.399	0.394	0.396[a]

a. The 2001 Gini coefficient, provided by the RF Ministry of Labor and Social Development, differs from that in the text, provided by the RF State Statistical Committee.

Source: RF Ministry of Labor and Social Development (2002).

poorest quintiles and the equally large increase in the share of the wealthiest quintile (table 9.5)? I believe that privatization contributed to increased inequality; the single most important factor was concentration of business income and property revenue with a limited cadre—a phenomenon heavily influenced by the Russian privatization model. A second factor, stemming partly from privatization, was the rapid differentiation in wages, the major income source for most people.

At the end of 1991, the government abolished wage limits.[12] The new, more flexible Labor Code contributed to the sharp differentiation in people's incomes. Reduced state regulation of citizens' incomes (e.g., outside the public sector, this role is reduced to fixing a minimum wage) led to large differences in pay between those deriving their incomes from labor and those engaged in business activity. Large income differences appeared between regions and sectors of activity, and between enterprises of differing property forms.

Pay-scale differentiation between the highest and lowest income deciles reached 34 points in 2000.[13] Obviously, income and property differentiation is not unfair; what is inequitable in Russia is its rapid increase and large scale compared to other transition countries. For example, in 1997–99, the average Gini coefficient for Central and Eastern Europe was 0.30, compared to 0.40 for Russia. Also noteworthy is that, in 1999, the decile coefficients (ratio of rich to poor income) for Hungary and Poland were 3.0 and 4.0, respectively, compared to 8.8 for Russia (RF Ministry of Labor and Social Development, 2002). This finding suggests that, in post-transition Russia, sensible regulatory or taxation limits to preserve social cohesion were exceeded. Ever-increasing numbers of marginalized citizens on the one hand and the super-rich—even by world standards—on the other pulled the social pyramid in opposing directions, threatening those in the middle.

The current situation is fraught with increasing social tension. Inter-branch differentiation in pay is high, amounting to 8.5 times in 2000.[14] The highest wages are concentrated in the country's fuel and energy complex, nonferrous metallurgy, and financial sectors, while the lowest are in agriculture and forestry, light industry, and remaining public-sector branches of the economy.

Enormous regional differences in pay do not compensate sufficiently for the labor conditions of climatically harsh areas, which results in labor-force migration to the western and southern regions of the country (table 9.6).

---

12. RSFSR Government Resolution No. 195 (On the Abolition of Wage Limits), December 26, 1991.

13. See Main Directions and Priorities of State Social Policy in Improving Incomes and the Living Standard of the Population, www.nasledie.ru/fin/6_7-1/1.html.

14. See Main Directions and Priorities of State Social Policy in Improving Incomes and the Living Standard of the Population, www.nasledie.ru.

Table 9.6 Russia: Monthly professional wages, by region, 2002 (in US dollars)

Region	Department chief, mid-size bank	Department chief, Gazprom or Mezhregion-gaz structure	Department chief, regional energy system	Worker, private fuel station	Taxi driver	Therapist, state-run hospital	Therapist, private medical institution	Programmer, provider firm	Regional-administration department chief
Chelyabinsk	.25–.30	.50–.60	.45–.55	.12–.17	.20–.25	.07–.12	.20–.25	.30–.50	.40–.50
Kaliningrad	.60–.70	.75	.70	.20–.30	.18–.20	.07–.09	.12–.20	.25–.35	.40–.45
Kemerovo	.50	.40–.50	.25–.50	.07–.15	.12–.20	.07–.12	.13–.20	.20–.30	.60
Kirov	.35–.50	.40–.70	.30–.60	.15–.20	.20–.24	.05–.10	.13–.15	.18–.20	.25–.40
Krasnoyarsk	2.00–2.50	1.00	1.00	.13–.16	.70–1.00	.07–.10	.16–.18	.33–.70	.27–.40
Kursk	.50–.80	.40–.60	.40–.50	.20	.30–.50	.025–.050	.20–.25	.15–.40	.30–.40
Nizhni Novgorod	2.00–3.00	2.00–3.00	2.00–3.00	.10–.20	.15–.20	.05–.10	.15–.20	.15–.50	.15–.20
Novosibirsk	.60–.80	n.a.	n.a.	.10–.20	n.a.	.05–.10	.10–.30	.10–.30	.20–.50
Orenburg	1.50	2.00	3.00–4.50	.05–.80	.09–.13	.10	.15–.20	.115–.270	.40
Perm	.26–.40	.40–.50	1.00–1.50	.16–.20	.15–.20	.05	.10	.15–.20	.10–.20
Rostov	1.00	1.00–1.50	1.00–1.50	.10	.30–.45	.10	.30	.30–.50	.50–.70
Samara	.50–.70	.30–.50	.25–.50	.15–.20	.15–.30	.05–.10	.20–.25	.15–.35	.30
St. Petersburg	2.00–2.50	n.a.	n.a.	.12–.15	.10–.12	.080–.105	.20–.25	.40–.50	.15–.30
Stavropol	.50–.70	2.50–2.80	2.30–2.50	.20	.20–.40	.10	n.a.	.20–.50	.30
Tomsk	.50	2.00	1.00	.065	.160–.225	.08–.10	.16–.30	.10–.30	.13–.65
Tula	.50–.80	.40–.50[a]	.40–.60[b]	.12–.17	.30–.40	.05–.17	.20–.25	.15–.20	.20–.35
Ulyanovsk	.50–.70	.30–.40	.32–.35	.065–.100	.12–.14	.042–.068	.08–.09	.16–.19	.20–.25
Yekaterinburg	1.00–1.30	2.50–2.80	3.20–3.50	.30	.20–.30	.03–.05	.20–.30	.20–.30	.18–.30

n.a. = not available

a. Data are for Tularegion-gaz.
b. Data are for Tul-energo.

Source: Mikeli (2001).

Another factor responsible for increased inequality was, paradoxically, preservation of the system of social transfers to the population. Attempting to maintain the existing system with considerably reduced financial means produced a dispersion of transfers and weakened their connection with real need. According to the RF Ministry of Labor and Social Development, the country currently has some 1,000 social benefits, allowances, subsidies, and compensation payments; these are introduced for more than 200 categories of citizens: veterans, invalids, children, the unemployed, and students. Nearly 100 million people or about 70 percent of the Russian population receive various types of payments or benefits, while those in real need represent less than 30 percent. Consequently, as of the late 1990s, about 70 percent of property revenue, 62 percent of other incomes (including business incomes), 38 percent of the aggregate wages fund, and a disproportionate 27 percent of social transfers accrued to the fifth population quintile (those in the top 20 percent of Russia's citizenry, who received 47 percent of all income) (Ovcharova 2001). Only in 2004 did the Putin administration start addressing these issues.

Population Patterns: Adapting to the New Environment

Increasing property and income differentiation also involves the ways in which people choose to adapt to new living conditions. One can observe two major adaptation strategies:

- **Active.** Workers interrelate with the changing labor-market environment, thereby ensuring an acceptable income level through self-employment, entrepreneurship, work in a high-wage sector, or secondary employment.

- **Passive.** Workers aim to preserve an acceptable level of income; adaptation occurs by providing the family foodstuffs from one's plot of land,[15] leasing one's property, and obtaining social assistance.

Within the framework of the passive adaptation strategy, intra-family redistribution of income—getting help from other family members'

---

15. During the transition, a barter economy—exchanging self-made production without cash—emerged. In 1991–95, 1.5 to 2 times more potatoes, vegetables, meat, and milk were produced on personal plots of land than during the 1980–90 decade. In 1992, the ratio of consumed foodstuffs that were bartered versus purchased was about 7 percent; by 1995–97, it had grown to 15 to 16 percent. As a rule, the share of self-made foodstuffs delivered outside (for sale or further processing) was insignificant, but revenues from sales were a marked addition to rural residents' monetary incomes (by the end of the period, they represented more than 10 percent of rural cash incomes). On balance, production of foodstuffs (i.e., meat, milk, potatoes, eggs, and vegetables) on personal plots of land helped preserve the consumption level and, thus, in many ways, compensated for failing cash incomes.

incomes—is widespread. One can see a relationship between the unemployment level in a particular region and business-income shares in aggregate incomes. For example, in the Evenk Autonomous Region, where unemployment was 3.2 percent in 2000, the business-income share accounted for only 1.2 percent; however, in the North Ossetian-Alaniya Republic, the unemployment rate in 2000 was 28.5 percent and the business-income share was 34.8 percent of citizens' overall income. One may observe a similar regularity when analyzing corresponding overall statistical data by region (Goskomstat Rossii 2001). Real unemployment drives people to start a private business, which helps them provide an adequate living standard for their families. Thus, during market transition, privatization and private business development play key roles in an alternative survival strategy for the most flexible, enterprising segment of the population, which is more willing to run economic risk.[16]

Sociological surveys show a relationship between successful adaptation to the new conditions and employment type; probability of the former is higher among workers engaged in the private sector and business managers and owners—that is, groups that emerged as a result of privatization.

Under influence of the above factors, a deep stratification of Russian society occurred (table 9.7).[17] Experts from the Institute for Social-Economic Problems of Population in the Russian Academy of Sciences find that 8 to 12 percent of Russian citizens occupy the well-off category, according to Russian standards. The lower-income margin of this category is about $5,000 per month, while the upper tier is $10,000 per month. Those above $10,000 are considered the rich and super rich.

Two-thirds of the wealthy polled hold that they necessarily need strong patrons in state administrative bodies, which reflects precisely the shift in

---

16. Undoubtedly, such factors as local authorities' policy toward small- and medium-sized businesses may disrupt this relationship. In regions where favorable administrative, legal, credit, and financial conditions have been created to harness the population's business potential and effective demand exists for goods and services produced by this economic sector, the proportion of business income is high, irrespective of the unemployment rate. Typical cases include the city of Moscow and the regions of Belgorod, Nizhny Novgorod, Novgorod, Ulyanovsk, and Chelyabinsk, where the unemployment rate is 3 to 6 percentage points lower than the average for Russia (10.5 percent in 2000), and the proportion of business income equals or is 1 to 4 percentage points higher than the country average (15.9 percent in 2000). At the same time, several regions have an extremely unfavorable relationship of the above indicators. For example, the unemployment rate is high in Kalmyk Republic (20.1 percent), Tyva Republic (22.9 percent), and Buryat Autonomous Region (15.6 percent) and is not compensated by developing business activities. In fact, business income is 1 to 5 percentage points lower than the average Russian indicator.

17. Stratification is considerably less equitable in Russia than in such transition countries as Slovakia, Czech Republic, or Hungary. In Russia, 6.2 percent and 47.4 percent of incomes go to the poorest and wealthiest quintiles, respectively. The respective figures are 12 and 31 percent in Slovakia; 10 and 37 percent in the Czech Republic; and 9 and 37 percent in Hungary. See Savchenko, Fedorova, and Shelkova (2000).

**Table 9.7 Russia: Distribution of employed,
by income characteristic, 1998** (percent)

Employed classification	Incomes exceeding twice subsistence minimum	Incomes below twice subsistence minimum
Private enterprise	24.6	75.4
State-owned enterprise	13.2	86.8
Activity type		
Manager	30.6	69.4
Worker	14.1	85.9
Additionally employed		
Yes	26.8	73.2
No	17.2	82.8
Business-owner status		
Yes	40.5	59.5
No	15.6	84.4
Work-day duration		
Eight hours or less	15.2	84.8
More than eight hours	23.1	76.9

Note: Selection value is 4,249 persons.

Source: Popova (2002).

perception and ethos in postprivatization Russia. Half of those polled think that connections with the criminal world are extremely important, and 84 percent of those polled believe that the largest fortunes in Russia have been and are being built by criminal or illegal means.[18]

Conclusions

Privatization's effect on the overall Russian economy—and on distribution in particular—is multifaceted (figure 9.4).

Income distribution in Russia is the outcome of various interconnected factors associated with radical systemic transformations of the economy and society, of which privatization is one factor. Nonetheless, the Russian privatization model has helped to evolve an ownership structure similar to that of countries in developing regions (e.g., Latin America). Such countries are typified by high concentration of property within oligarchic structures, low levels of transparency in important transactions, nonexistence of a broad class of petty owners, and failure to protect minority shareholders. Small business is not integrated into the national economic network— rather, in most cases, it is driven into the shadow economy and represents the sphere of survival for the majority of its agents.

---

18. See *Argumenty i fakty*, December 13, 2000.

Figure 9.4   Privatization's effect on Russian economy and distribution

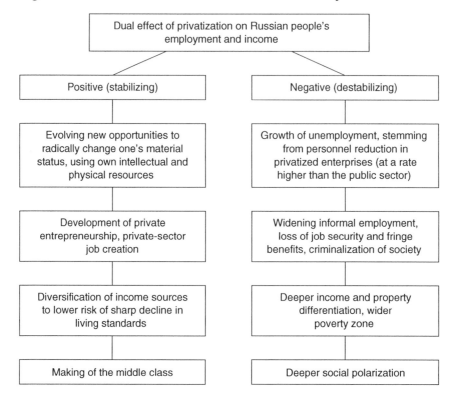

In Russia, the scale of capital flight is unprecedented, even in the post-socialist world. Much of the wealth placed offshore has grown out of privatization processes. Only recently has privatization begun to exert great influence on the labor market. Dismissal of inefficient or redundant workers has proceeded slowly because of the high price to employers and because managers and owners have discovered mechanisms—mainly wage nonpayments—whereby they can avoid overt unemployment. Low wages and low minimum wage help to keep workers in line.

References

Bim, A. S. 1996. *Ownership Control Over the Enterprises and Strategies of Stockholders.* Vienna: IIASA.

Blasi, J., and A. Shleifer. 1996. Corporate Governance in Russia: An Initial Look. In *Corporate Governance in Central Europe and Russia*, ed. R. Frydman , C. Gray, and A. Rapaczynski. London: Central European University Press.

Chetvernina, T., and S. Lomonosova. 2001. Social Protection of Workers of the New Private Sector: Myths and Reality. *Voprosy ekonomiki*, no. 9.

Chubais, A. 2002. Has the Voucher Ever Existed? *Mir Novostev*, 20 August.

Civil Society European Academy. 1998. Analytical Report of the Civil Society Academy. www.academy-go.ru.

Deryabina, M. A. 1996. Reforming Property Relations (Privatization) in Russia (1992–1996 Experience). In *Problems of Market Transformation in Transition Countries (Vestnik nauchnoy informatsii)*, no. 12. Moscow: IIEPS RAS.

Dolgopyatova, T., and I. Yevseeva (Boeva). 1994. *The Survival Strategy of State-owned and Privatized Enterprises under Transformation Conditions*. Moscow.

Federation of Independent Trade Unions of Russia. 2002. On the Employment Policy. Analytical Report. www.fnpr.ru.

Goskomstat Rossii. 2001. *The Social Situation and the Living Standard of Russian Population*. Moscow: Goskomstat Rossii.

Gurkov, I., and S. Maital. 1995. Perceived Control and Performance in Russian Privatized Enterprises: Western Implications. *European Management Journal* 14, no. 2: 160–66.

Kapelyushnikov, R. I. 2001. *The Russian Labor Market: Adjustment Without Restructuring*. Moscow: GU-High School of Economics.

Kapelyushnikov, R. I. 2002. The Kingdom of Insiders. Property and Control in Russian Industry: Some Results of Polling Russian Enterprises.

Mikeli, M. 2001. Where Wages Are Growing. *Profil*, 17.

Moskovskaya, A., and V. Moskovskaya. 1999. Qualitative and Quantitative Shifts in Employment. *Voprosy ekonomiki* 11: 18.

Nekipelov, A. D. 1996. *Essays on Post-Communist Economics*. Moscow: TsISN Minnauki Rossii.

Ovcharova, L. 2001. Inequality in Income Distribution. *Demoscope Weekly:* 11–12.

Pelekhova, Y. 2000. Russian Oligarchs. *Versiya* (July 1).

Popova, D. 2002. Adaptation Strategy of Russian Workers to Market Reforms. *Russian Economic Review* 1.

Radygin, A. D. 1996. On Some Perspectives of 'Loans-for-Shares' Privatization. In *Russian Economy: Trends and Perspectives*. Monthly Bulletin. Moscow: Institute for the Economy in Transition.

Razumova, T., and S. Roshin. 2001. Economic Analysis of Second Employment Causes. *Voprosy ekonomiki*, no. 9.

RF Ministry of Labor and Social Development. 2002. *Social Indicators of Population's Income and Living Standard (as of April 20, 2002)*. Moscow: Department of Population Income and Living Standard.

Savchenko P., M. Fedorova, and E. Shelkova. 2000. The Living Standard and Quality of Life: Notions, Indicators, and Present State in Russia. *Russian Economic Journal* 7: 68.

10

Privatization's Effects on Social Welfare in Ukraine: The SigmaBleyzer Experience

MICHAEL BLEYZER, EDILBERTO SEGURA, NEAL SIGDA, DIANA SMACHTINA, and VICTOR GEKKER

When Ukraine declared independence in August 1991, it became Europe's second-largest country in terms of land mass and its fourth largest in population, with 50 million people. Owing to its rich agricultural soil, Ukraine is the breadbasket of the former Soviet Union, providing must of its agricultural needs. The country is noted for its mineral resources, particularly iron ore and coal. It has an adequate infrastructure and a well-educated, skilled labor force, with a significant foundation in engineering and science. These resources have made it possible for Ukraine to supply much of the former Soviet Union's heavy industry.

Economic Challenge: An Overview

Despite such favorable conditions, Ukraine has, since independence, faced one of the most difficult economic challenges in Eastern Europe, including an eight-year recession. From 1991 to 1999, GDP declined every year, with a cumulative decline of about 60 percent. This recession was protracted because of the country's unfavorable conditions immediately following independence, including major structural weaknesses and an economy highly dependent on other former Soviet Republics. The Soviet Union's

Michael Bleyzer is the founder of SigmaBleyzer and The Bleyzer Foundation. Edilberto Segura is the chief economist of SigmaBleyzer and chairman of the advisory board of The Bleyzer Foundation. Neal Sigda and Diana Smachtina are directors of SigmaBleyzer Research. Victor Gekker is the director of The Bleyzer Foundation.

collapse cut these production and trade relations. In addition, Ukraine's military industries—25 percent of all its companies produced military goods—were left without markets after the Cold War ended.

Because of negligible energy costs during the Soviet era, many industrial processes were energy intensive. For example, in the early 1990s, Ukraine consumed six times more oil per unit of GDP than did Western Europe. Energy imports remain important; in 2002, oil and gas imports represented 40 percent of merchandise imports and 20 percent of GDP. These energy-intensive firms suffered greatly after independence, when energy costs increased 5 to 10 times.

Although the 1991 decline in GDP was amplified by unfavorable initial conditions, the piecemeal, uneven implementation of economic reforms—caused by lack of political consensus and opposition from parliamentary groups and others with vested interests—helped to prolong the recession that followed. In fact, the structural weaknesses that had characterized Ukraine during the Soviet era called for major corporate restructuring after independence. Unfortunately, during 1991–95, little was done. The government followed what it termed a preservation strategy—that is, it attempted to maintain the status quo by paying state-owned enterprises (SOEs) large, direct subsidies. Relying on government subsidies for their existence, SOEs had little incentive to restructure or privatize, and remained largely inefficient. These government subsidies led to large budget deficits, their monetary financing, and hyperinflation. During 1992–93, with total fiscal expenditures at about 65 percent of GDP, the fiscal budget deficit reached 25 percent and 16 percent of GDP, respectively. Monetary financing of these deficits led to high annual rates of inflation, which peaked at 2,609 percent annual average for 1992, over 1,000 percent in 1993, and remained above 100 percent per year in 1994 and 1995.

In 1994, Leonid Kuchma was elected president on the basis of a reform agenda. During 1996–98, economic reforms progressed in many areas. For example, prices and international trade were liberalized, small and mass privatization programs were advanced significantly, the National Bank of Ukraine (NBU) was strengthened, and monetary policy was implemented wisely. In addition, a new currency, hryvnia or UAH, was successfully introduced in September 1996; inflation was reduced to 10 percent by mid-1998, and the exchange rate was maintained within a narrow range (averaging about 1.9 UAH per dollar from 1995 to mid-1998). Ukraine accepted International Monetary Fund (IMF) obligations under Article VIII (which requires foreign exchange convertibility for current account payments); moreover, a new constitution was approved in 1996, which guaranteed private-property and market-based principles for the country's economy.

However, the fiscal budget deficit was not brought under control, remaining at about 6 percent of GDP from 1996 to mid-1998. During 1991–98, fiscal budgets were prepared unrealistically, with overestimated revenues and excessive expenditures. In addition, the tax base was reduced by innumerable privileges and exemptions. Through the end of 1997, these fiscal budget deficits were financed by foreign borrowings. External debt increased from $4.4 billion in 1994 to $11.5 billion in 1998. Domestic government, short-term obligations (Treasury bills) increased to UAH 10 billion ($5.2 billion equivalent) over the same period. Although the absolute size of foreign debt was not excessive, this debt was of short maturity. Therefore, the level of annual debt-service payments was high, reaching $3.2 billion in 1998, which heavily pressured government finances.

The Asian crisis, large repayments on foreign debt, and delays in implementing fiscal and structural adjustments in Ukraine changed investor perceptions of the country. Furthermore, structural reforms had not reached the critical mass needed to revive confidence, investment, and growth on a sustainable basis. In mid-1998, the Russian financial crisis accelerated capital outflows from Ukraine. Foreign reserves declined from $2.3 billion at the beginning of the year to about $1.0 billion by mid-year. With international reserves declining rapidly, the NBU was forced to stop selling foreign exchange in September 1998. Results of the financial crisis were far-reaching, including depreciation of the Hryvnia from about 1.9 UAH: US$1 in December 1997 to 3.4 UAH: US$1 by the end of 1998.

Despite the severity of the 1998 financial crisis, Ukraine dealt with it successfully without resorting to printing money. The country was able to negotiate the voluntary restructuring of its public debt. Most importantly, from September 1998 on, fiscal budget accounts were kept close to balance. The deficit for 1998 was contained at 2.1 percent of GDP (compared to 6.8 percent in 1997). In subsequent years, Ukraine has been able to maintain fiscal discipline, with fiscal deficits below 2 percent of GDP. Control of large fiscal deficits has been a significant achievement since, historically, they were the major source of the country's economic imbalance.

In addition to its broadly satisfactory fiscal and monetary policies, the Ukrainian government implemented important economic reforms in 2000–02. These included

- progress in privatizing large SOEs (six energy-distribution companies were privatized successfully in 2001);

- land reform in early 2000 that transferred ownership to individual farmers and initiated the issuance of certificates and titles;

- elimination of unwarranted government interventions in the agricultural market and its commercialization;

- elimination of barter in utilities, with cash collections in the energy sector increasing from about 12 percent of sales in 1999 to 85 percent in early 2001;

- significant reduction of barter in international trade;

- simplification of business registration requirements;

- reduction in the average number of government-agency inspections of businesses from about 70 per year in 1990 to about 30 currently;

- introduction of European import certification standards, with mutual recognition of certifications;

- improvements in aligning customs procedures to European standards;

- approval of the Laws on Banks and Banking Services;

- approval of the Criminal Code;

- approval of the Budget Code, which sets clear, transparent formulae for transfer of funds to local governments;

- introduction of personalized accounts in the pension system; and

- successful external-debt restructuring, including the Paris Club and gas debts with Russia and Turkmenistan.

Control of the fiscal deficit and implementation of these economic reforms have had a major beneficial effect on the economy, with positive GDP growth of 5.9 percent in 2000, 9.1 percent in 2001, and 4.1 percent in 2002. Furthermore, since the beginning of 2000, the country has had positive foreign trade and current account balances. The foreign exchange rate has been stable, at about 5.4 UAH: US$1 since early 2000. Foreign reserves increased from $1 billion in early 2000 to $4.3 billion in January 2003. The size of external public debt declined significantly, now representing only 25 percent of GDP (appendix 10B).

Despite these advances, significant improvements are still needed to sustain long-term growth. Revived level of investment in the economy is particularly needed. Given the high level of unused capacity, economic growth has been based on better use of existing investments. However, beyond 2002, growth based on improved use of existing capacity will be limited since existing plants are reaching full use capacity. Thus, continued growth in the future requires significant additional investment, particularly foreign investment, since domestic savings are low.

Level of foreign investment has, however, remained low. A recent study conducted by International Private Capital Task Force (IPCTF), under chairmanship of the SigmaBleyzer Corporation, outlined specific policy measures with which to attract more foreign investment to Ukraine. The study recommended nine policy measures, whose effects were estimated from statistical analyses carried out in a sample of 50 developing countries. Listed according to their estimated effect on the flow of foreign direct investment (FDI), these nine areas, in order of priority:

1. liberalize and deregulate business activities,

2. provide a stable and predictable legal environment,

3. enhance governance and reform public administration,

4. remove international capital and foreign-trade restrictions,

5. facilitate financing of businesses by the financial sector,

6. reduce corruption,

7. minimize political risk,

8. improve country promotion and image, and

9. rationalize investment incentives.

The study showed that the first three policy areas were statistically significant in the sample. Surveys carried out in Ukraine showed that these three areas were the most important investment drivers in the country, while the other six were important in attracting significant investment. Based on this study, the Ukrainian government developed an action plan in all nine areas. Successful implementation of the plan would make privatization of the remaining large SOEs more plausible.

Historical Review

Privatization in Ukraine, which began in 1992, aimed at transforming the country from a centrally planned to a market-based economy, increasing the private-sector share of industry and finding strategic investors to accelerate development of industries and companies. The privatization process, which has continued to evolve, is characterized by three distinct phases. During the first stage, 1992–94, the process advanced at a modest pace. During the second stage, 1995–98, the pace accelerated, with nearly 70 percent of all privatizations implemented. Some 80 percent of the industrial sector is now privatized. The current third stage, 1999–present, centers on privatizing the largest remaining SOEs, mainly in electricity distribution, telecommunications, and metallurgy, as well as fertilizers and petrochemicals.

First Stage: 1992–94

During 1992–94, the main form of privatization was the leasing of entire property complexes by company employees, with full ownership transferred at the end of the leasing period. Privatized enterprises were mainly companies in the food and light industrial sectors. In many of them, directors averse to losing control took advantage of this form of privatization. While the formal majority of leaseholders and shareholders were employees, top managers effectively controlled the firms.

This form of privatization did not guarantee efficient ownership or management. Traditionally, SOEs were merely production units, without any sales, marketing, or financial functions. Most managers, therefore, were not equipped for their new role. Only those enterprises able to compete in a market economy did better. The social effect of this stage of privatization—namely employment, salaries, and social welfare—depended primarily on management's ability to operate in this new business environment. The destiny of these companies and their employees, as well as these companies' effect on GDP growth and welfare improvement, depended on management's ability to maneuver current emerging-market conditions.

Still, many companies taken over and controlled by their managers succeeded. The financial results of these companies were usually positive, despite the economic crisis. Financially, privatized companies performed better than enterprises that remained in government hands. However, the reason could have been that, during this period, companies taken over by their managers were the most economically attractive before privatization.

Conversely, like other experiences in the region, few companies with broad employee ownership succeeded. Many businesses privatized in this way did not survive for long. In most cases, a wealthier group of managers took them over, generally forcing many people out of work.[1] Despite the few employee-operated success stories, such as Mariupol Illicha Steel or the Kharkiv Biscuit Factory, most ended in asset stripping or bankruptcy.

The effects of this "lease-with-an-option-to-buy" stage of privatization on Ukraine's sociopolitical situation were controversial since, by this time, the economy faced a systemwide crisis. Employees of privatized enterprises could keep their jobs, but ownership became concentrated in the hands of a few privileged, former managers. This stage resulted in the partial or complete privatization of more than 11,000 Ukrainian companies (table 10.1). It also established a legislative base on which all future privatizations would be organized. The government passed laws on privatization of small, medium, and large state companies.

Second Stage: 1995–98

During the second stage, 70,526 enterprises were privatized, representing about 70 percent of all privatizations since 1991. About 60 percent or 42,000 second-stage privatizations were small enterprises, many of which were engaged in trading activities. They were sold mainly to the firm's employees and managers. The remaining 28,000 enterprises were medium- and large-scale companies, which were sold to both employees and the public through the mass privatization program initiated and completed during this period.

1. Few statistics from this time support such conclusions; rather, they are based on the observations of this chapter's authors, all of whom were working in Ukraine during this period.

Table 10.1 Ukraine: Number of companies privatized, by size, 1992–2002

Year	Small	Medium or large	Total
1992	32	11	43
1993	2,434	1,253	3,687
1994	5,338	2,010	7,348
1995	10,320	4,562	14,882
1996	17,480	8,803	26,283
1997	8,554	7,308	15,862
1998	6,080	7,419	13,499
1999	4,518	3,660	8,178
2000	5,137	1,737	6,874
2001	5,321	929	6,250
2002	674	100	774
Total	65,888	37,792	103,680

Source: State Property Fund of Ukraine.

Begun in 1995, the mass privatization program gave all Ukrainian citizens the right to obtain privatization certificates or vouchers, a special type of security that could be exchanged for shares of state companies sold in special privatization-certificate auctions conducted by the National Certificate Auctions Network.[2] Another type of security, known as the compensatory certificate, was issued to cover losses incurred by depositors in the State Savings Bank under the Soviet Union or during the 1991–95 period of hyperinflation.

The voucher and certificate auctions worked as follows: 150 to 250 companies were put up for sale each month. By the end of this stage, their number had grown to more than 500 per month. The owner of a voucher could apply to purchase shares of any company that was auctioned. The size of each applicant's stake was then determined by the total number of applicants for that company (none were refused). At the completion of the auction, the new shareholder received documents certifying all shareholder rights. Between 1994 and 2000, 7,272 enterprises were privatized through voucher auctions. Table 10.2 shows the total number of certificate auctions made during this period with many enterprises offering shares for sale several times). Of the nearly 21,000 transactions that occurred, more than 8,000 represented small- and medium-sized state companies. By the end of this stage, enough companies had been privatized to enable the stock market to reach a critical mass. At this time, individuals and companies began over-the-counter trading of shares.

The mass privatization program had unanticipated side effects. For example, Ukrainian citizens could not purchase vouchers in large enough quantities to influence the management of their companies as the legislative base

---

2. The Economist Intelligence Unit, *Country Economic News*, February 1, 2002.

Table 10.2   Ukraine: Number of certificate auctions, by stake percentage, 1994–2000

Year	0–5	5–25	25–50	50–75	75–100	Total
1994	8	62	85	37	15	207
1995	83	455	487	231	9	1,295
1996	591	3,073	1,572	257	20	5,513
1997	945	4,335	1,569	178	25	7,052
1998	1,549	3,963	898	59	3	6,472
1999	41	144	27	0	0	212
2000	85	147	9	0	0	241
Total	3,302	12,179	4,647	762	102	20,992
Percent of total	15.7	58.0	22.1	3.6	0.5	100

Source: SigmaBleyzer.

did not—and still does not—provide for cumulative voting or other forms of protecting minority shareholder rights. Shareholders have significantly fewer mechanisms than in the West to protect their various rights. Furthermore, many Ukrainian citizens sold their certificates before the auctions. In fact, during the early and mid-1990s, high inflation rates and destruction of savings led to increased poverty. Since people needed ready cash for buying food and paying for housing, many decided it was more beneficial to sell their privatization certificates to companies and investors that purchased them for 2–8 Hryvnias (approximately US$1 to US$4 at that time), less than their par value of UAH 10. Having acquired a significant number of certificates, these investors participated directly in competitions and auctions. Similar to the Russian experience, only a handful of Ukrainians became real owners. Their ability to influence company management and operations occurred, in many cases, at the expense of unprotected minority shareholders. Thus, while the mass privatization program may have succeeded in transferring many enterprises to the general public and creating incentives for companies to improve operations, it failed to create sound corporate governance in most enterprises, which led to the abuse of minority-shareholder rights.

Third Stage: 1999 to Present

After 1998, the remaining enterprises to be privatized consisted of firms in strategic and monopolistic sectors, including electricity distribution (known as *"oblenergos"*), metallurgy, telecommunications, and petrochemicals. Unlike stages one and two, the third stage has emphasized strategic investment and raising of privatization revenue for the state. During these larger cash privatizations, large stakes in medium and large companies were usually privatized through tenders or the stock exchange. The government set criteria that potential investors had to meet if they wanted to purchase company shares. This process of privatization has been slow, with only a handful of large companies privatized to date. While six *oblenergos* were privatized in 2001, controversies surrounding the process led to stagnation.

Results of Privatization

Over the past decade (1992–2002), more than 100,000 of Ukraine's SOEs were privatized (table 10.1). Of these, about 25,000 were central and 55,000 were municipal enterprises. In 2002 alone, these companies employed 3.5 million Ukrainians or 24.2 percent of the country's workforce. More than 10,000 open joint-stock companies were created, and 8,500 enterprises in the agricultural sector were reformed.

Despite the significant economic decline that occurred in the process of transition, privatization in Ukraine has nonetheless contributed positively to creating a market-based economy. Currently, the share of nonstate companies in total production is about 85 percent; they account for 60 percent of the country's total volume of industrial output. Industries that have achieved the greatest success include food, light industry, pulp and paper, and woodworking, where the process of privatization has been virtually completed. In these sectors, growth rates are several times higher than in industry overall. For example, during 2001, when GDP grew by 9.1 percent, the fastest-growing processing industries were wood and wood processing (which grew by 28 percent), machine building (18.8 percent), pulp and paper (18.2 percent), food (18.2 percent), and textiles/apparel (14 percent). In 2002, with GDP growth of 4.1 percent, these industries grew by about 8 percent. In certain industries, such as food, most privatized companies have enjoyed relatively strong financial growth.

In addition to better financial results, the general perception is that the management of these privatized companies has improved since privatization.

Social Effects of Privatization

As noted above, collapse of the former Soviet Union, disruption of pre-1990 economic ties, and lack of economic competitiveness of the SOEs led to a sharp deterioration of Ukrainian companies' financial situation. This, in turn, greatly reduced production volume, which resulted in massive layoffs during 1991–95. It also led to the accumulation of large wage arrears, since many retained workers were paid only partially. Furthermore, many SOE employees worked only on paper—that is, their management requested that they not attend work, and they were not compensated. They remained expectant that they might be recalled to work at some future time, which rarely happened (appendix 10A).

Table 10.3   Ukraine: Selected employment statistics, 1995–2000

Statistic	1995	1996	1997	1998	1999	2000
Ukrainian population, at year end (millions)	51.3	50.9	50.5	50.1	49.7	49.3
Number employed (millions)	23.7	23.2	22.6	22.3	21.8	21.6
Unemployment rate (percent)						
Officially registered unemployment to employed population	0.5	1.3	2.3	3.7	4.3	4.2
Application per vacant position (number of people)	2	11	20	30	24	17
Wage arrears (millions of dollars)	n.a.	2,286.8	2,770.8	2,587.7	1,526.2	905.91

n.a. = not available

Source: State Statistics Committee of Ukraine.

High unemployment levels in industry—as much as 30 percent in 1995, according to unofficial estimates—and significant wage arrears forced workers to master new professions, which often required lower-level skills (e.g., doctors and engineers became taxi drivers or salespeople). The phenomenon of hidden employment in the shadow economy appeared at this time, although it already existed in some form before the breakup of the Soviet Union. During 1992–95, the shadow economy doubled to an estimated 10 million employees. Table 10.3 provides more recent data on wage arrears and official unemployment, which we believe seriously underestimate the reality of the situation.

The major reduction in employment that occurred during the 1990s was not caused by privatization. Rather, it was a remnant from the Soviet era—that is, highly inefficient, industrial enterprises—energy, raw materials, and human resources—producing for a declining military demand and unable to compete in a market economy. In fact, studies show that, during the Soviet era, many SOEs created no value (they had negative rates of returns if outputs and inputs were valued at international prices). After independence in 1991, most Ukrainian enterprises were either idle or ran at 10 to 15 percent capacity.

Under these circumstances, a short-term positive outcome of privatization—and thereby the country's transition to a market economy—did not increase employment dramatically; nonetheless, in those firms that successfully restructured, salary levels and productivity improved and wage arrears were reduced. Switching to modern management methods at privatized companies resulted in improved efficiency. Interested owners (investors) stimulated and improved companies' operations, which was reflected in increased employee productivity, better use of labor, and higher average monthly salaries compared to state companies. Tables 10.4 and 10.5 provide comparisons for 2000 and 2001, respectively.

Table 10.4   Ukraine: Average monthly wages in selected industries, 2000 (US dollars)

Sector	Average	State	Nonstate
Coke production and oil refining	87.06	41.02	88.70
Electricity, gas, and water production	69.24	64.83	71.61
Food industry and processing of agricultural products	49.08	41.74	49.74
Light industry	28.84	20.46	29.08
Machine building	40.40	38.70	40.88
Metallurgy and metalworking	74.92	62.46	77.09
Mining	74.12	69.28	82.77

Source: State Property Fund of Ukraine.

Table 10.5   Ukraine: Relationship between form of ownership and average salary, 2001 (percent)

Sector	State	Nonstate
Chemicals and plastics	105	98
Coke production and oil refining	47	102
Electricity, gas, and water production	96	106
Energy materials production	92	126
Food industry and processing of agricultural products	85	101
Light industry	71	101
Machinery	96	101
Metallurgy and metalworking	83	103
Mining	93	112
Nonenergy materials production	98	101
Other nonmetal mineral products	127	98
Other production sectors	101	100
Processing industry	95	101
Wood processing, pulp, and paper	119	97

Note: Average salary is 100 percent.

Source: State Property Fund of Ukraine.

As tables 10.4 and 10.5 show, in nearly every industry, most privatized companies have higher salary levels than nonprivatized ones. In the metallurgy industry, a sector in which no new enterprises were created over the past decade, privatization caused a significant increase in average monthly salaries. These increases were, in some cases, more than 100 percent higher than preprivatization levels (e.g., in 2001, the average monthly salary at Zaporizhstal was $182, compared to $75 in 1998, before privatization). In 2001, the salaries of employees at privatized metallurgical companies were more than 20 percent higher than those of employees at comparable government-owned companies. In the mining and energy-materials production sectors, salaries at privatized companies were as much as 20 percent higher than those of nonprivatized ones in 2000 and up to 35 percent higher in 2001. In general, nonstate companies have significantly outperformed state companies in terms of both productivity and resolution of wage arrears. Lower level of arrears is a significant factor in employees' ability to support their families and general well-being. Wage arrears have long been a problem in the public sector—for example, many teachers and miners must wait several months to receive their salaries. In table 10.6, this differential is even more apparent. For example, in the mining industry, the average arrears in the private sector are more than two times less than in the public sector. In only two industries—metallurgy and light industry—is a difference in this trend not significantly different. This may result from those sectors' small sample of state companies remaining to be privatized.

A margin analysis of sales and costs of Ukrainian companies provides a similar view of the economic efficiency of state ownership versus fully privatized companies. In 2001, fully privatized enterprises showed better profitability than SOEs (table 10.7). Moreover, fully privatized companies paid higher taxes than SOEs, which potentially benefited the citizens of Ukraine.

Conclusions[3]

The first stage of privatization in Ukraine was particularly difficult. Even though most companies were sold to employees, their backing came from a small circle of wealthy managers. Certain companies privatized with such consolidated ownership control did well. Conversely, few companies with broad employee ownership succeeded; many businesses privatized in this way did not improve until wealthier managers or backers took over, generally forcing many people out of work.

During the second stage, Ukrainian mass privatization attempted to implement a social-equality model. All citizens—from the very young to the elderly—had an opportunity to purchase state-run companies through a system of auctions. However, as the legislative and normative base of privatization lacked depth, not all levels of the population had equal opportunity to participate.

Because of hyperinflation, income instability, and the general economic contraction that Ukraine experienced through 1999, many privatized companies were sold for relatively small amounts. Through this process

---

3. These conclusions represent the view of the authors and all staff of The Bleyzer Foundation and SigmaBleyzer Corporation. These views may be regarded as biased since SigmaBleyzer has been an active participant in the privatization process. The authors are certain, however, that this interpretation is shared by many other economic observers and private-sector actors.

Table 10.6 Ukraine: Labor data, showing form of ownership by sector, 2001

Sector/form of ownership	Companies (number)	Employees on payroll (number)	Labor productivity (one thousand UAH per person)	Average wage arrears (number of months)
Chemical and petrochemical industry				
Total	2,785	217,482	57.12	1.28
State	70	57,075	51.87	1.80
Nonstate	2,715	160,407	58.99	1.10
Electricity, gas, and water production				
Total	1,731	537,810	49.80	1.01
State	1,071	255,611	46.44	1.19
Nonstate	660	282,199	52.83	0.87
Energy materials production				
Total	432	439,363	34.06	3.01
State	258	372,006	26.65	3.30
Nonstate	174	67,357	74.96	1.92
Food industry and processing of agricultural products				
Total	8,586	54,872	56.80	0.96
State	278	42,199	37.73	1.05
Nonstate	8,308	500,673	58.41	0.95
Light industry				
Total	4,287	254,620	11.99	1.33
State	129	4,355	16.14	1.10
Nonstate	4,158	250,265	11.91	1.33
Machinery				
Total	10,039	976,189	22.55	1.84
State	372	196,438	16.64	2.60
Nonstate	9,667	779,751	24.04	1.65
Metallurgy and metalworking				
Total	2,733	456,308	81.01	0.95
State	80	69,591	86.77	0.90
Nonstate	2,653	386,717	79.97	0.96
Mining				
Total	990	592,863	36.64	2.47
State	325	412,874	27.44	3.05
Nonstate	665	179,989	57.75	1.34
Nonenergy materials production				
Total	558	153,500	44.02	0.87
State	67	40,868	34.56	0.96
Nonstate	491	112,632	47.46	0.84
Processing industry				
Total	42,704	2,951,964	42.92	1.26
State	1,932	405,513	36.49	1.70
Nonstate	40,772	2,546,451	43.94	1.19

Source: State Statistics Committee.

Table 10.7 Ukraine: Margin analysis, 2001 (percent of net sales)

Ownership type (100 percent)	Net sales (percent)	Cost of goods sold	Gross income/ loss	Operating income	Other expenses/ income	Pretax income	Extraordinary revenues/ costs	Taxes	Net income/ loss
State	100	88.7	11.3	3.9	0.9	4.8	1.2	−0.9	5.2
Privatized	100	77.6	22.4	12.9	−1.3	11.7	0.0	−3.9	7.8

Source: State Statistics Committee.

there arose powerful industrial groups and other regional players—the so-called oligarchs—who began to control significant segments of the Ukrainian economy.

Throughout the entire process, owners were not as numerous as had been hoped. On the other hand, companies with concentrated ownership were more likely to restructure and turn their businesses around. This, of course, resulted in greater social improvements and individual benefits. Therefore, in many industries, concentrated ownership has largely accounted for short-term improvements in firm performance. We hope that this will eventually lead to improved social welfare.

Our overall assessment of the Ukrainian privatization model during the second stage is mixed. On the positive side, 70,000 SOEs were privatized during 1995–98, which helped to create a private-sector, market-oriented economy. On the negative side, the process was not transparent. Percentages of large companies were often sold at excessively discounted prices. Moreover, purchasers rarely had the company's best interests at heart; rather, they were more interested in stripping assets or damaging competitors, and new owners did not always understand the businesses they had purchased.

In addition, the process was protracted. Such countries as Hungary and the Czech Republic, which privatized faster, were clearly at an advantage. Ukraine took more than a decade to reach a level that other countries achieved in less than half the time. This resulted in a time delay between the act and results of privatization. Only in the past few years have companies begun to show positive results, which have contributed to three years of positive GDP growth: 5.9 percent in 2000, 9.1 percent in 2001, and 5.2 percent in 2002 (appendix 10B). The attempt to equitably distribute state property through vouchers failed to achieve the anticipated results, and the method was costly in terms of promoting efficiency and growth.

It is still too early to evaluate results of the third stage of privatization. The Ukrainian government has focused more on helping the fiscal budget by making money from privatization and less on transforming the economic environment through privatization. While the government needs additional revenues to improve its citizens' quality of life, we are of the opinion that this goal could have been reached quicker by creating healthier and more profitable privatized businesses, thereby bringing in more tax revenue, rather than having attempted to maximize privatization proceeds in an environment unfriendly to investors. This accelerated privatization approach would have resulted in higher economic growth, additional jobs, and a significantly improved economic situation for Ukrainian citizens.

Despite the above problems, we believe that privatization was an important factor in improving the welfare of the Ukrainian people. Quality of life for employees at privately owned companies improved. Salaries at these companies increased and were more likely to be paid on time, an important characteristic considering the high levels of inflation during those periods. In addition, privatized companies paid higher taxes, thereby enabling the government to use larger revenues to provide Ukrainians badly needed services.

A View from the Private Sector: SigmaBleyzer

SigmaBleyzer, a leading investment bank in southeastern Europe, has operated in Ukraine for more than a decade. The company participated in all stages of privatization and postprivatization; at one time, its portfolio included more than 85 companies representative of most industrial sectors across all regions of Ukraine. Today, the firm manages three funds, working with a portfolio of more than 60 companies. Portfolio diversification and consolidation have resulted from an in-depth analysis of the Ukrainian economy at both the macro and micro levels.[4]

The first years of transition in Ukraine were characterized by a sharp decline in production volume. Most Ukrainian enterprises were either idle or running at 10 to 15 percent of capacity-use levels. Official statistics did not reflect levels of unemployment since many people registered as employed were, in reality, on indefinite leave without pay. However, this situation led indirectly to the positive effect of privatization. Since efficient management of joint-stock companies had not yet evolved, the most active workers on leave-without-pay created their own small businesses, often remaining officially employed by privatized companies. Most of these employees never returned to the parent firm.

Deterioration of official employment, which continues in certain government-owned companies today, was not directly caused by privatization. As mentioned above, it was a remnant of Soviet-era inefficiencies, when production was oriented mainly to the military-industrial complex. At the time of transition, companies suddenly had to change their focus to new customers (primarily consumers), and most had no experience in doing so. Most were inefficient in production and energy consumption, had to recreate supply chains, and suffered severe disruptions in trade. These combined factors put tremendous pressure on companies trying to transition to a market economy.

---

4. Using its financial expertise and international contacts network, SigmaBleyzer has helped implement Western management practices, attracted venture capital, advised on restructuring, assisted the transition to International Accounting Standards (IAS), implemented modern information systems, developed strong marketing and sales capabilities, and bought and sold shares in its target companies in Ukraine. In 2001, it created The Bleyzer Foundation, an international nongovernmental organization (NGO) that promotes private-sector development and best practices in developing government policies in Ukraine and other transition countries. A prime objective is to create capital-friendly business environments and assist in promoting improved quality of life for the people of Ukraine and the region.

Several cases in the portfolio of Ukrainian Growth Funds (UGF) highlight how privatization has helped both companies and social welfare. These cases, discussed below, are the

- Sevastopol Shipyard (SSY Company),

- Poltava Confectionery, and

- Berdyansk Agricultural Machinery and Melitopol Tractor Hydro Units Plants.

Sevastopol Shipyard

The SSY was significantly transformed by privatization. Established in 1783, the SSY was originally charged with building and repairing naval vessels on the Black Sea. Located in the port city of Sevastopol on the Crimean peninsula, SSY enjoys a favorable climate and protected bays that allow it to work year round. For most of its history, the Shipyard catered mainly to the military, producing and repairing military vessels. Today, SSY has shifted its focus to commercial orders.

SigmaBleyzer acquired relative control (and the largest stake) of SSY in 1998, when it increased its previous holdings to 47.4 percent. It acquired an additional 2.8 percent the following year, bringing its total to 50.2 percent. During this time, military ship-repair contracts could not be relied on since both Russia and Ukraine lacked sufficient resources to pay for such repairs. Before privatization, SSY had tried and failed to attract a significant number of commercial customers to its docks. The company was in crisis and desperately needed restructuring.

Before 1998, the Ukrainian government—majority owner and manager of SSY—had split the company into 39 companies. This action was not based on analysis; each department was simply established as a separate company. This resulted in companies within SSY misallocating and misusing resources, paying extra value-added tax (VAT) payments, and causing general chaos. In addition, the company had not developed a Western-style marketing function.

SSY also had organizational problems. For example, when a ship enters a repair yard, the industry norm is to assign a single foreman as the company representative to oversee all aspects of the repair. This person acts as a focal point for the customer. At SSY, several representatives of the 39 subcompanies vied for control to ensure their individual parts were completed, without caring about the overall product or customer. Not surprisingly, delays in job delivery were frequent, causing customers to develop a negative opinion of the company; as a result, sales plummeted. At the end of 1997, the last full year under government control, SSY posted revenues and net income of $12.7 million and −$0.8 million, respectively.

Table 10.8   Ukraine: Key data for Sevastopol Shipyard, 1996–2001

Item	1996	1997	1998	1999	2000	2001
Net sales (millions of dollars)	9.40	12.70	12.81	11.28	14.62	18.06
Net income (millions of dollars)	−1.50	−0.80	0.80	0.76	0.52	1.70
Port cargo loaded (tons)	n.a.	176	146	263	705	790
Ships repaired	n.a.	7	8	25	44	47

n.a. = not available

Source: Sevastopol Shipyard Company.

After privatization, a project team was assembled to lead the company out of crisis. Western experts were brought in to make key recommendations on how to improve and restructure the company. These included Libis Engineering, Ltd.; Naval Architects & Marine Consultants; Pricewaterhouse-Coopers; Thunderbird Corporate Consulting; Barrents Group (United States Agency for International Development program); and Citizen Development Corps. Such expertise was often relatively inexpensive—sometimes free under grants from bilateral institutions—and easy to find; yet, government managers had made no attempt to do so. In addition, a team of SigmaBleyzer restructuring experts was assigned to live and work in Sevastopol.

Working with external experts, a plan was developed to divide the company into five profit centers. New controls were put into place to gain a handle on the business. A strategic decision was made to focus on ship repair and the port and to abandon floating cranes (because of high capital outlays and low demand). A full market analysis of the region was carried out, and a professional marketing department was created. Modern systems to control work progress were installed. The company began to focus on customer needs—pricing, delivery time, quality, and services—which it had previously ignored.

Best practices of Western shipyards were adopted for use at SSY. Examples included attracting agents, visiting owners, conducting exit interviews with ship owners, establishing an estimate department, and facilitating yard visits with potential clients. Small investments were targeted, most of which came from internal funds.

All of these changes, which the government had been unable to achieve over the previous five years, occurred within two years. As a result, by 2001, revenues had increased 43 percent, net income increased to $0.8 million, port volumes increased 349 percent, the number of repaired ships grew to 44 (523 percent), and debts (salary, payments to the government, and social insurance) decreased from $7.91 million to $1.44 million (tables 10.8 and 10.9). Without these changes, the company would most likely have gone bankrupt.

These changes not only improved the overall condition of the company; they also helped city employees and residents. The city and central government received nearly $6.5 million in back payments, and profit tax

Table 10.9 Ukraine: Selected comparison data for Sevastopol Shipyard, 1997 and 2001

Year	Average monthly salary (dollars)	Net revenue per employee (dollars)	Number of employees	VAT payment (thousands of dollars)	Profit tax (thousands of dollars)
1997	48	1,728	7,352	1,592	497
2001	96	5,424	3,330	1,319	861

VAT = value-added tax

Source: Sevastopol Shipyard Company.

payments increased by about 75 percent. The VAT would have increased were it not for company restructuring and special laws freeing SSY from part of the burden. From 1997 to 2001, average salaries doubled (from $48 to $96). This salary of $96 was more than 50 percent higher than the average for the city of Sevastopol and Ukraine overall (State Statistics Committee).

As table 10.9 shows, from 1997 to 2001, the number of workers decreased by more than half (from 7,352 to 3,330). To reiterate, the causes were structural problems that originated during the Soviet era. Furthermore, in 1997, many official employees neither reported to work nor received salaries. Those who did go to work on a daily basis and received a steady salary numbered 2,880 in 1980, when SigmaBleyzer took over the company. As of 2001, this number had increased to more than 3,330, reflecting the company's improved performance and competitiveness (appendix 10A).

Finally, local officials have made a 180-degree change in attitude toward the benefits of private ownership. When SigmaBleyzer initially took control of the Shipyard, city officials were both aggressive and aloof. They believed that SigmaBleyzer should immediately create more jobs and supply more investment. However, as the Shipyard began to function more profitably, they saw that investments were beginning to flow more regularly (from profits) and that the demand for employment also rose to meet company needs (figure 10.1).

Today, SSY has a good working relationship with regional officials, who have come to appreciate the large tax base, employment base, and revenue that the company can generate for local businesses. In Sevastopol, more than 350 small- and medium-sized businesses employ workers and pay taxes, in part because SSY is successful—that is, these companies' existence and success are directly tied to SSY's success and improvement. They provide products or services that the Shipyard uses to meet its clients' needs. These include ship-design studios, architectural firms, machinery shops, cargo movers, parts suppliers, marine companies, agents, subcontractors, and other businesses that depend on the company's continued success. Although employees of these businesses may no longer work for SSY directly, they

Figure 10.1   Ukraine: Key data from Sevastopol Shipyard, 1997 and 2001

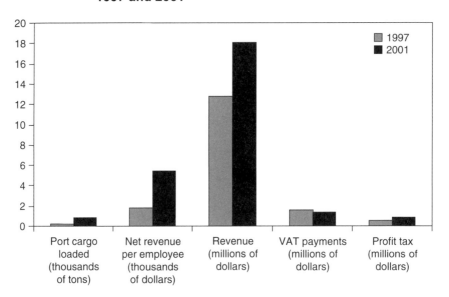

VAT = value-added tax
Sources: Sevastopol Shipyard Company and SigmaBleyzer.

are gainfully employed by healthy, tax-paying enterprises that create value by working with SSY.

The financial results of these other small businesses are not known; however, it is clear that they rely heavily on demand from SSY. Increased port activities—to approximately 800,000 tons of cargo in 2001—has generated significant revenues for customs authorities and railroad movers (figure 10.1). The English-language summer camp created at the SSY resort attracts more than 800 children and 1,200 other guests per year, bringing more spending to the region. This generates a greater tax base for the city, more employed citizens, fewer expenditures on social services, increased revenue from public transportation, and an overall increase in consumer spending.

Could this turnaround have occurred under government control? We do not believe so. First, the government did not understand SSY's problems or how to correct them. In fact, their remedy nearly destroyed the business. Second, the government lacked the contacts and inclination to involve Western expertise, a crucial element in the turnaround. Third, if restructuring had been government led, it would have become highly political and not optimal for SSY. Fourth, SSY lacked a marketing function, a crucial bit of know-how that previous government owners had failed to understand or acquire.

Table 10.10 Ukraine: Annual results for Poltava Confectionery, 1996–2001

Item	1996	1997	1998	1999	2000	2001
Net sales (millions of dollars)	7.16	9.84	11.14	13.35	15.35	20.36
Net income (millions of dollars)	1.03	1.28	1.09	1.18	1.23	1.37
Production output (tons)	4,921	7,110	9,160	15,970	19,540	21,820

Source: Poltava Confectionery.

Table 10.11 Ukraine: Selected comparison data for Poltava Confectionery, 1997 and 2001

Year	Average monthly salary (dollars)	Net revenue per employee (dollars)	Number of employees	VAT payments (thousands of dollars)	Profit tax (thousands of dollars)
1997	60	13,526	987	1,555	560
2001	84	14,330	1,421	2,735	665

VAT = value-added tax
Source: Poltava Confectionery.

Poltava Confectionery

Privatization of controlling stake in Poltava Confectionery—producer of chocolates, biscuits, caramel, and other candies—was a key event in the company's life. State-owned until 1996, Poltava showed continuing declines, producing only 4,921 tons of confectionery products that year (it had produced about 20,000 tons in 1990). In 1996, managers acquired control of the company. SigmaBleyzer bought a controlling majority three years later. Since then, growth has been phenomenal (tables 10.10 and 10.11).

Through improved performance, Poltava Confectionery has improved the welfare of Poltava's citizens. More people are employed, tax payments have increased, and salaries have risen. According to management, Poltava Confectionery was one of the city's top five taxpayers in 2001. This would not have been possible without increased revenues and profitability at the Confectionery (figure 10.2).

At the end of 2002, the company completed a $4 million investment project in a new confectionery facility that should produce an additional 60,000 tons of confectionery products. All construction was done locally, which supported several construction, electrical, and other local companies, as well as suppliers of parts and construction materials. More importantly, Poltava plans a threefold increase in sales over the next few years, which will produce more jobs, higher wages, and increased tax payments. While these wage and tax increases have reduced the ratio of net income to sales, they have resulted in general improvement of the community.

Figure 10.2 Ukraine: Poltava Confectionery results, 1996–2001

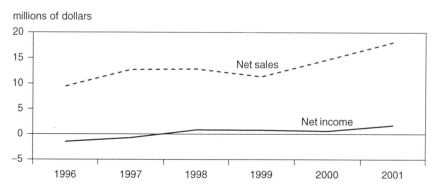

Source: Poltava Confectionery.

Berdyansk Agricultural Machinery and Melitopol Tractor Hydro Units Plants

In 1998–99, SigmaBleyzer bought controlling stakes in Berdyansk Agricultural Machinery and Melitopol Tractor Hydro Units Plants. This led to both plants' economic turnaround and 1999–2001 restructuring, the main changes of which are described below.

Berdyansk produces agricultural machinery, including grain and grain/legume reapers; tractor-mounted mowers, bailers, and cultivators as well as some 200 spare parts for agricultural machinery (particularly harvesters). When privatized, the company was operating at only 30 percent capacity due to lack of demand. Historically, about 80 percent of Berdyansk's sales were exports to Russia and Kazakhstan; however, this trade was disrupted after the breakup of the Soviet Union, leaving the company headed for bankruptcy. The reconstruction plan included concrete measures for tapping into new markets, recovering sales to Russia and Kazakhstan, and reducing unit-material consumption, labor costs, and power consumption. Berdyansk also undertook major restructuring of its facilities to improve production efficiency. All useful equipment—particularly welding and assembly—was relocated from many sites (which were scrapped) to only one. In addition, the company outsourced certain uneconomical activities, such as its foundry. While the company still faces difficulties, it is experiencing a turnaround, with increased sales of 11 percent (in US dollars) over the last two years.

The Melitopol Tractor Hydro Units Plant was once the former Soviet Union's largest producer of hydraulic parts for tractors and other farm equipment; its production included hydraulic distributors, cylinders, and steering units; shock absorbers; clutches; differential blocking sensors; electro-hydraulic distributors; and pressure-sensitive valves and hoses. Plant

Table 10.12 Ukraine: Net sales of two companies in the UGF portfolio in selected years (thousands of dollars)

Company	1999	2000	2002
Berdyansk Reapers	3,635	3,417	3,798
Melitopol Tractor Hydro Units Plant	2,865	3,128	3,624

UGF = Ukrainian Growth Funds

Source: Company financials.

customers included 200 assembly plants and more than 200 machinery-repair shops. Since the breakup of the Soviet Union, many of these companies have been working at a small fraction of their previous output levels, greatly reducing the potential size of Melitopol's market. Before privatization, lack of demand resulted in the company cutting its workforce from 10,000 to 2,200. The rehabilitation plan included an aggressive program to find customers both within and outside Ukraine. As a result, exports are now principally directed toward Russia, Italy, France and the United States. In addition, various cost-reduction programs were introduced to lower operating costs. During the first stage, the plant focused on the manufacturing of spare parts to serve the large stock of older tractors in countries of the former Soviet Union. It also reduced costs by scrapping unneeded equipment and concentrating production facilities in a few areas. Consequently, since 1999, Melitopol has been able to increase annual sales (in US dollars) by 8 percent (table 10.12).

At the time of privatization, Berdyansk and Melitopol were significantly indebted (table 10.13), had decreasing sales and production volumes, were having difficulty finding customers, and appeared headed for bankruptcy. However, as table 10.12 shows, by 2002, both companies had rebounded; the 2002 figures show how quickly the companies improved after the restructuring plans were implemented.

Reduction in Government Debt and Back Wages

SigmaBleyzer companies have been able to pay off or significantly reduce their debts to the government and wage arrears to employees (table 10.13).

From 1997 to 2001, SigmaBleyzer companies had a 94 percent drop in unpaid debts to the government and an 80 percent drop in unpaid wages to employees. Clearly, the improved situation with wage arrears has been a key reason for employees shifting from the public to the private sector. The wage-arrears problem in Ukraine has been documented for some time. As shown in table 10.6, the backlog has generally been higher in the public, rather than private, sector. Thus, the private sector has done a better job at improving the welfare of its employees than has the state.

Table 10.13   Ukraine: Debts of UGF portfolio companies, 1997 and 2001 (thousands of dollars)

Company name	Government debts		Wage arrears	
	1997	2001	1997	2001
Central Ore Mining	8,654	881	2,152	755
Chimik	54	9	21	5
Conditioner	678	523	207	187
Dneporazot	2,020	1,533	5	373
Kharkiv Machine-Building Plant (Svitlo Shakhtarya)	1,018	63	432	62
Khartsyzsk Pipe Works	6,214	241	4,176	1,109
Kherson Combines	192	847	870	1,017
Kyiv Refrigarator #2	16	18	59	33
Makiivka Pipe Rolling Plant	408	80	179	337
Marganets Repair	1,107	6	505	17
Mariupol Illicha Steel	9,551	1,809	3,625	4,224
Markokhim	5,135	615	145	102
Melitopol Compressor Plant (data for 2000)	910	468	583	69
Melitopol Tractor Hydro Units Plant	865	10	527	152
Nikopol Pipe	208	61	226	11
Northern Ore Mining	295,650	876	52,417	1,232
Ordzhonikidze Ore Mining (data for 2000)	5,788	801	2,654	408
Pershotravnevy Agricultural Machinery Plant (Berdyansk Reapers)	1,387	177	864	132
Poltava Confectionary	86	50	42	123
Poninka Paper Combine	408	258	179	235
Rosava Tires	17,008	7,903	1,105	79
Sevastopol Shipyard	1,952	375	3,880	728
Slavyansk High Voltage Insulators	933	20	557	29
Zaporizhstal	4,055	3,372	3,074	1,995
Zaporizhya Meat Processing	43	15	51	35
Zhydachiv Pulp and Paper Combine	320	54	469	178
Total	366,657	23,066	81,001	15,628

UGF = Ukrainian Growth Funds

Source: Company financials and SigmaBleyzer.

Repayment of wage arrears by private companies has been an important social and psychological issue of the postprivatization period. As the most acute social consequence of the financial crisis, wage arrears created a psychologically tense atmosphere. This often created a negative attitude toward the privatization process, even though wage arrears in SOEs were equal to or greater than those in most privatized firms. While poorly regarded by the public, the postprivatization concentration of equity and subsequent formation of corporate management ensured the appearance of efficient owners and management bodies controlled by joint-stock companies.

As table 10.3 shows, wage arrears increased until 1997, and then fell in 1998, with major declines in 1999 and 2000. From 1997 to 2000, wage arrears fell by more than 50 percent to less than $1 billion (State Statistics Committee). This decrease is significant since most concentrated private owners took control only in 1997–99. Therefore, results in the reduction of wage arrears appear to have directly followed these privatization events.

This result was clearly part of the government's strategy as well. In most third-stage privatizations, the government generally stipulated two aspects of the transaction: (1) purchase price and (2) debt payments. Naturally, buyers pay less for the company, knowing that they must then pay off inherited debt. A good example is the Okean Shipyard, which was privatized in 2000. Before privatization, the company had suddenly increased long-term debts to $8.7 million (these had fluctuated within a range of only $0.6 to 0.8 million during 1995–97). When Damen Shipyards purchased a 78 percent stake in 2000—at that time, SigmaBleyzer already owned nearly 9 percent—it paid approximately $4.8 million. However, according to the agreement, it paid an additional UAH 8 million ($1.5 million) for unpaid salaries and debts to the government. This provided immediate support to both public services and the local community, which would never have occurred without privatization.

Conclusion

Privatization has played a key role in improving the welfare of Ukraine's people. Wages have increased, debts have been reduced, communities now receive more money from successful companies, and more small- and medium-sized companies have sprung up to support larger privatized companies. Overall, privatized companies have enjoyed growing support from most regional or city leaders as taxable income has increased and more people have become employed.

The first two stages of privatization were not carried out transparently enough, and too much wealth was concentrated in too few owners. We believe these events limited the full positive effect that privatization could have brought. However, the most recent phase of privatization has been better at providing a more transparent form of transaction. Such a trend must continue.

The pace of remaining privatizations must be significantly accelerated. Objections by government officials are based on their assertion that they cannot receive fair prices in the current environment. Our response is that it is up to the marketplace to determine fair prices; waiting may result in even lower, not higher, prices. The best way for the Ukrainian government to maximize returns from privatization is to do all it can to improve the country's business and investment environment.

Appendix 10A
Data Challenges

The former Soviet Union poses a significant challenge to evaluating the validity of data on a company level, especially when comparing companies across time periods. The planned economy under the Soviet government was the prime driver for building companies, allocating their expenses, creating a supply chain, and stimulating demand. When this system broke down, many companies could not sustain the business on their own and failed. Others looked to the government to continue supporting them, either directly or indirectly. A few began to survive on their own.

Current data of privatized companies is somewhat more reliable, certainly more so than a decade, or even two years, ago. However, older data is subject to significant doubt, as the case of the Sevastopol Shipyard (SSY) illustrates. In 1990, SSY had 15,700 workers, with sales of $30.2 million; by 2001, it had 3,609 workers, with revenues of $18.1 million.

The authors believe that these numbers do not reflect a workforce reduction of more than 75 percent. First, these numbers include so-called phantom workers—that is, official statistics did not reflect the level of unemployment since many registered as employed were on indefinite leave without pay. Thus, they stayed on the company's list as employed, while finding work elsewhere. Second, since everyone under the Soviet system was required to work, companies were not set up to use their employees efficiently, and many workers performed useless tasks. As spending was rationalized, it was clear that many employees were not needed or performed work that another employee could have easily added to his or her workload. This also explains why production per employee often increased radically. This phenomenon was typical of most companies before privatization, especially during the Soviet era.

Third, many employees supported government-funded municipal services, such as public housing, schools, and hospitals. Following transition and collapse of the old system, company sales could no longer support such expensive public works; thus, they were forced to transfer these services back to local governments (this was true of both state and privatized firms). Finally, certain services were spun off or sold off, including company resorts and other businesses outside the company's core competencies.

Net sales revenue from 1990 is also suspect since it was under a command economy, with only internal clients provided by the government (thus, the comparison is not particularly helpful). With loss of government orders, revenues and income at most companies declined significantly. The disruption of supply chains forced companies to become more competitive, something for which they were unprepared and often failed to achieve.

Experience shows that other numbers have either been inflated or reduced in order to make the company look better or worse, depending on need.

Today, many companies do everything possible to reduce net income to $0 in order to avoid taxes, and the law still provides latitude for doing so. This practice should diminish as the government continues to institute Generally Accepted Accounting Principles (GAAP) and IAS rules.

Therefore, all of these numbers should be viewed somewhat skeptically. At the same time, while the numbers may differ, trends still point to the same conclusions. Anecdotal evidence in our portfolio companies indicates that most companies improved their situations dramatically after privatization.

Appendix 10B
Key Economic Data for Ukraine, 1996–2002

Statistic	1996	1997	1998	1999	2000	2001	2002
GDP							
Real GDP (percent)	−10.0	−3.1	−1.9	−0.4	5.9	9.1	5.2
GDP (UAH billion)	82.0	93.0	103.0	130.0	170.0	202.0	221.0
GDP/capita (US dollars)	870.0	856.0	828.0	612.0	555.0	775.0	859.0
Savings (percent GDP)	20.0	19.0	18.0	22.0	20.0	20.0	22.0
Investments (percent GDP)	23.1	21.5	20.7	17.4	18.6	20.4	18.9
Industrial growth rate (percent)	−5.1	−0.3	−1.0	4.0	12.4	14.2	7.0
Public finances (percent GDP)							
Fiscal balance	−4.9	−6.6	−2.2	−1.5	0.6	−0.4	0.7
Revenues	37.0	30.0	28.0	25.0	29.0	27.0	28.0
Expenditures	42.0	37.0	30.0	27.0	28.0	28.0	27.0
Monetary statistics							
Consumer prices (percent YOY)	39.7	10.1	20.0	19.2	25.8	6.1	−0.6
Monetary base (percent YOY)	38.0	45.0	22.0	30.0	40.0	37.0	33.6
Money supply-M3 (percent YOY)	35.0	34.0	25.0	40.0	45.0	42.0	42.0
Exchange rate (UAH/dollar)	1.9	1.9	3.4	5.2	5.4	5.3	5.3
Balance of payments (billions of dollars)							
Goods exports	15.5	15.4	13.7	12.5	15.7	16.3	18.7
Goods and NFSE	20.3	20.4	17.6	16.2	19.5	21.1	23.4
Goods imports	19.8	19.6	16.3	12.9	14.9	15.8	18.0
Goods and NFSI	21.5	21.9	18.8	15.2	17.9	20.5	21.5
Trade balance	−4.3	−1.5	−1.2	1.8	1.5	0.6	0.7
Current account balance	−1.2	−1.3	−1.3	1.7	1.5	1.4	3.2
Direct investments	0.5	0.6	0.7	0.4	0.6	0.8	0.8
Gross reserves	1.9	2.3	0.8	1.1	1.7	3.2	4.4
Public debt (billions of dollars)							
External debt	8.8	9.6	11.5	12.5	10.3	9.8	10.2
External debt service	1.2	1.2	1.8	2.0	1.7	0.3[a]	1.4
Domestic debt	1.3	4.6	3.7	2.9	3.8	4.0	4.0

NFSE = nonfactor services exports
NFSI = nonfactor services imports
YOY = year over year

a. Direct public external-debt service.

Source: SigmaBleyzer, *Ukraine: Economic Situation and Reforms in 2001* (April).

11

China's Shareholding Reform: Effects on Enterprise Performance

GARY H. JEFFERSON, SU JIAN, JIANG YUAN,
and YU XINHUA

Over the past two decades, ownership structure of Chinese enterprises has changed dramatically. In 1980, China's industrial sector consisted almost exclusively of state-owned enterprises (SOEs) and collective-owned enterprises (COEs). Subsequently, numbers of SOEs and COEs rose; however, as table 11.1 shows, by 1995, they were outnumbered by the infusion of newly created enterprises: more than 29,000 foreign and overseas firms, a proliferation of shareholding enterprises (SHRs), and nearly 4,000 fully private companies. Some eight million individually owned enterprises with eight or fewer employees added a new dimension to China's industrial enterprise sector, unanticipated in 1980.

In 1998, China's National Bureau of Statistics (NBS) revised its formal statistical system to include broad statistical coverage for all of China's SOEs and all other industrial enterprises with more than 5 million yuan in

Gary H. Jefferson is professor of economics and chair of the Department of Economics at Brandeis University. Su Jian is assistant professor of economics at Peking University. Jiang Yuan and Yu Xinhua are researchers at China's National Bureau of Statistics. The authors appreciate the work of Nancy Birdsall and John Nellis in organizing the project that made this chapter possible. Helpful comments were provided during the conference, Distributional Consequences of Privatization, held at the Center for Global Development in Washington, February 23–24, 2003. The authors acknowledge the comments of conference discussants Bert Keidel and Minxin Pei. In addition, Guan Xiaojing, Blake LeBaron, Michael Lim, John Nellis, and Qian Jinchang provided helpful advice. Thanks also go to the Asian Development Bank and the National Science Foundation. The US Department of Energy's Biological and Environmental Research Program and the Rockefeller Center at Dartmouth College provided critical research support. Finally, special thanks are extended to China's National Bureau of Statistics, notably Ren Caifeng, Xu Jianyi, and Ma Jingkui, whose participation was instrumental to this study.

Table 11.1 Change in ownership distribution of industrial enterprises in China (number of enterprises)

Measure	Old accounting system[a]			New accounting system[b]	
	1980	1993	1997	1998	2001
Ownership type					
State	83,400	80,586	84,397	64,737	46,767
Collective	293,500	339,617	319,438	47,745	31,018
Hong Kong, Macao, and Taiwan	n.a.	11,621	3,020	15,725	18,257
Foreign	n.a.	8,434	19,861	10,717	13,166
Shareholding	n.a.	2,579	3,898	4,120	5,692
Private	n.a.	n.a.	13,188	10,667	36,218
Other domestic[c]	400	6,379	24,704	11,369	20,138
Total in the system (A)	377,300	449,216	468,506	165,080	171,256
National total	n.a.	9,911,600	7,922,900	7,974,600	n.a.
Of which: Individual enterprises	n.a.	7,971,200	5,974,700	6,033,800	n.a.
Other [including (A)]	n.a.	1,940,400	1,948,200	1,940,800	n.a.

n.a. = not available
Other = Other enterprises is derived by deducting the number of individual enterprises from the national total.
a. Includes all industrial enterprises that operate as independent accounting units at or above the township level.
b. Includes all state-owned enterprises (SOEs), plus nonstate enterprises that report annual sales in excess of 5 million yuan.
c. Computed as the difference between total in row (A) and the ownership types listed above.

Sources: NBS (1980 data in NBS, 1985, p. 305; 1993 data in NBS 1994, pp. 374, 378; 1997 data in NBS 1998 (Industry section); 1998 and 2001 data in NBS, 2003, pp. 462–463.

sales per year.[1] Table 11.1 shows that, in 2001, among the 171,256 enterprises with broad statistical coverage, approximately three-quarters operated outside the state sector.[2] The 36,000 private-sector firms, with sales in excess of 5 million yuan, exceeded the number of COEs and approached the number of surviving SOEs. In that year, the 46,767 reporting SOEs represented a precipitous decline from the number recorded four years earlier. Many SOEs had been converted into SHRs, for which the number of firms in excess of 5 million yuan had grown to 5,692 by 2001.

Indeed, since the late 1990s, conversion of former SOEs and COEs into SKTs has been China's principal mode of enterprise restructuring. Such conversion always entails a change in the firm's formal ownership classification; it generally involves corporatization, with establishment of a board of directors consisting of major shareholder representatives (i.e., legal persons [*faren*]), and frequently involves infusion of new assets from outside the state system, sometimes through initial public offerings. At least during

---

1. The scope of enterprises enjoying full coverage includes all SOEs, regardless of annual sales.

2. In the year 2000, these larger enterprises (with sales in excess of 5 million yuan) accounted for approximately 56 percent of China's total reported industrial output. See *China Statistical Yearbook* (NBS 2001, 49, 416).

the duration of this study's dataset, conversions of SOEs into shareholder firms did not necessarily lead to private majority ownership. This wide variety of shareholding conversions constitutes the focus of this chapter.

In addition to examining conventional measures—labor and capital productivity and profitability—we also consider conversion's effects on employment and wages, taxes, and two dynamic measures of enterprise performance: (1) research and development (R&D) expenditures, and (2) new product sales. A central objective of this analysis is to identify the distributive effects of shareholder reform on key stakeholders.

This study explicitly distinguishes between two channels of conversion's effects: (1) the direct effect on enterprise performance, holding constant the firm's asset mix, and (2) the induced effect, resulting from the ability of converted firms to attract new investment from outside the state sector. We document the range of effects of nonstate investment on firm performance for both formally converted and unconverted firms.

Ownership Reform: An Overview

China's enterprise reform has spanned four related processes:

- entry of many new, nonstate enterprises;

- reform of incentive structures within established public-ownership systems, such as strengthening managerial incentives through the contract responsibility system;

- change in asset structures resulting from nonstate investment in the state sector; and

- outright conversion of enterprises, usually from state or collective ownership to another formal ownership classification (we argue that this fourth process can be viewed as the outcome of the first three).

New Entry

Until the mid-1990s, the most dramatic avenue of ownership reform in Chinese industry was the entry of new firms through (1) collectives, mainly township and village enterprises (TVEs), during the 1980s;[3] (2) individually owned enterprises (*getihu*) with eight or fewer employees, whose numbers proliferated into the millions by 1994; and (3) foreign-owned enterprises

---

3. Subsequent to the conversion of commune enterprises to TVEs in the early 1980s, many townships and villages, in an effort to build on their success, established new TVEs.

(FORs), from investors in Hong Kong, Macao, and Taiwan (HKT) and foreign sources, primarily Organization for Economic Cooperation and Development (OECD) and Southeast Asian countries. Table 11.1 shows the magnitude of new entry: Relative to 1980, the number of industrial enterprises in China had, by 1994, multiplied by a factor of approximately 25. One consequence of this rapid entry of both domestic and foreign investment was intense competition in many sectors, which spurred a secular decline in profitability across all ownership types. The resulting erosion of monopoly rents in state industry motivated a search throughout Chinese industry for technical innovations and new governance mechanisms.[4]

Reform of Control Rights

The enterprise contract responsibility system, introduced in the mid-1980s, was intended to strengthen and clarify the incentives and rewards system for SOE managers and workers, without extending to ownership change. Jefferson, Zhang, and Zhao (1998) and Jefferson, Lu, and Zhao (1998) document the vertical reassignment of control rights from government supervisory agencies to enterprises and the horizontal allocation of managerial control rights among managers, workers' councils, and party secretaries within enterprises.

The restructuring of SOEs without formal ownership conversion met with limited success. McMillan and Naughton (1992) found that managers responded to expanded autonomy, including greater profit retention, by strengthening worker discipline, increasing the proportion of workers' income paid through bonuses, and raising the fraction of workers on fixed-term contracts. However, while most studies document efficiency gains in the state sector, productivity growth in state industry has generally lagged outside the state sector (Jefferson et al. 2000). One important outcome of these reforms was the emergence of a managerial class, with strong vested interest in privatization.

Changing Asset Structure

In China's enterprise sector, the association between formal ownership classification and the assets ownership structure has become increasingly fluid. For example, in this study's dataset of large- and medium-sized enterprises for 1999, 1,417 of the approximately 11,000 companies classified as SOEs reported a minority of state-owned assets. Conversely, 1,935 of the more than 11,000 so-called nonstate enterprises reported that most of their assets were state owned. These somewhat confusing patterns of asset ownership across the range of ownership classifications call into question the formal

---

4. For documentation on the rise of state-industry competition, see Naughton (1992).

classification system. The following discussion on the historical progression of China's ownership reform shows that asset restructuring often created de facto conversion, making formal conversion a mere formality.

Conversion

In the mid-1990s, the results of new entry, which fostered competition, eroded profit margins and intensified the search for technical and organizational change; strengthened managerial control, which motivated the quest for privatization; and increased accumulation of nonstate assets, which contributed to the de facto erosion of government control and created pressures for deep restructuring, including formal conversion of SOEs (Su and Jefferson 2003). At the same time, the accumulation of nonperforming loans and attention to financial stability associated with the Asian financial crisis and the Chinese leadership's quest for entry into the World Trade Organization (WTO) magnified pressures for enterprise restructuring.

In response to these systemic pressures and the leadership's search for improved efficiency and financial performance, while avoiding the ideological and political perils of extensive, overt private ownership, three restructuring policies emerged during the mid-1990s. The first was a furlough policy (*xiagang*), which, by the end of the decade, had led to the laying off of some 6 million of the 44 million SOE industrial workforce (Rawski 2002). In the late 1990s, two additional policy initiatives shifted the locus of enterprise reform to the formal conversion of both state and collective enterprise. As it diminished the role of the state sector as the locus of guaranteed employment, the government's furlough program made conversion more politically feasible.

Under the slogan "retain the large, release the small" (*juada fangxiao*), China's leadership, in principle, mandated converting all but the largest 300 or so of the nation's industrial SOEs. As part of this initiative, Premier Zhu Rongji placed China's loss-making SOEs on a strict three-year schedule, during which time they were to implement a "modern enterprise system" and convert losses to surpluses. The principal response to these mandates was rapid acceleration in the number of conversions across China's state and collective sectors.

Although the shareholding experiment was first introduced in 1993, it was not until the restructuring initiatives of 1997–98 that shareholding conversion became a broad-based initiative, involving the conversion of numerous SOEs and COEs. In 1997, the Chinese Communist Party's 15th Party Congress made the shareholding system a centerpiece of China's enterprise restructuring. While formal privatization was ruled out for ideological reasons, the shareholding experiment was widely viewed as a covert mandate for privatization (Li, Li, and Zhang 2000, 269). During 1997–2001, the number of registered SOEs declined by nearly half. According to Fan

(2002, 3), "preliminary provincial data indicate that, in some regions, more than 70 percent of small SOEs have been privatized or restructured." This SOE conversion was not limited to small-sized enterprises. Over this period, the number of large- and medium-sized SOEs declined from 14,811 to 8,675, while the number of large- and medium-sized SHRs mushroomed from 1,801 to 5,659.

Furthermore, the conversion process extended to COEs, including the township and village enterprise sector, earlier celebrated for its competitive performance (Weitzman and Xu 1994). Li and Rozelle (2000) reported a fundamental privatization of rural industry, finding that more than 50 percent of local government-owned firms had transferred their shares, either partially or completely, to the private sector. This conversion process has been extensive, even among the largest, most successful COEs. During 1998–2001, the number of large- and medium-sized COEs declined by 35 percent (from 3,613 to 2,465).

In sum, we hold that the convergence of three factors—new entry and competition, strengthened managerial control, and accumulation of nonstate assets—created the conditions for formal conversion during the late 1990s. Many local governments were anxious to rid themselves of loss-making enterprises (or to cash in on profitable ones before they turned sour), insider managers were poised to secure greater control over these enterprises, and asset structures were often already extensively diversified. Together, these three conditions were a strong motivation to complete the administrative formalities of shareholder conversion.

Literature Review and Comparative Perspective

This section reviews the growing body of research on enterprise conversion, drawing lessons from the surveys of enterprise restructuring and privatization literature, most of which had focused on the experiences of Eastern Europe and the Commonwealth of Independent States (CIS). The section also reviews literature that has centered specifically on restructuring China's enterprises.

Privatization and Restructuring

Privatization literature includes three reviews of experiences from transition and developing economies: Megginson and Netter (2001), Djankov and Murrell (2002), and Birdsall and Nellis (2002). Megginson and Netter (2001) examine privatization's effectiveness on the transition economies of Central and Eastern Europe (12 studies) and the CIS, including Russia and the former Soviet Republics (excluding the Baltic states) (six studies). They also review salient privatization episodes in OECD and nontransition developing economies. Their key conclusions are that (1) privatization improves firm-level performance; (2) concentrated private ownership, foreign ownership, and majority outside ownership are associated with significantly greater improvement than the alternatives; and (3) privatization's effect on employment is ambiguous, since employment decreases for virtually all firms in transition economies.

Djankov and Murrell (2002), drawing on more than 100 studies of enterprise restructuring in transition economies, synthesize them into composite effectiveness rankings of various privatization strategies and outcomes. Like Megginson and Netter, Djankov and Murrell find that state ownership within traditional state firms is less effective than all other ownership types. Privatization to outsiders is associated with the largest restructuring gains; furthermore, privatization to workers has no effect in Eastern Europe but is detrimental in the CIS. Privatization to outsiders is associated with 50 percent more restructuring than privatization to insider managers and workers. Investment funds, foreigners, and other blockholders produce more than 10 times as much restructuring as diffuse individual ownership. Majority state ownership within partially privatized firms is surprisingly effective, producing more restructuring than enterprise insiders and non-blockholder outsiders. Djankov and Murrell conclude that various regions—particularly Eastern Europe and CIS economies—respond differently to similar privatization strategies. For example, privatization had no significant effect on enterprise performance in Eastern Europe, whereas the same form of privatization had substantial negative effects on firms in CIS economies. Also, opening to import competition had significant opposite effects on firm performance in Eastern Europe and the CIS. Such disparate effects across regions raise the possibility that aspects of the privatization experience elsewhere in the world may have limited application in China.

Birdsall and Nellis (2002) develop the idea that, by altering the distribution of ownership costs and benefits, privatization potentially affects a broader range of stakeholders than accounted for in the conventional privatization literature. They find that privatization programs have worsened the distribution of assets and income, at least in the short run. This tendency toward less equal distribution of assets is more evident in transition economies than in Latin America. Birdsall and Nellis also distinguish distributive effects across industries. They find that privatization's adverse distributional effects (e.g., for banks, oil companies, and other natural resource producers) have been less severe for utilities (such as electricity and telecommunications)—areas in which the poor have tended to benefit from greater access.

We accessed, as relevant to China, findings on

- relative effectiveness of outsider privatization,
- relatively poor performance of insider privatization,

- effectiveness of state ownership within partially privatized firms,

- distributional effects of asset privatization, and

- ambiguous employment effects.

Chinese Enterprise Restructuring

In recent years, research has been published on the determinants and effects of privatization and ownership conversion in China. Tian (2000), for example, uses a sample of 826 corporations listed on China's stock market to study the effects of state shareholding on corporate value. Tian discovers a U-shaped relationship between the proportion of government equity and corporate value with higher values for low and high shares of government equity than for values associated with intermediate shares of government ownership. He argues that the U-shape reflects the behavior of a government that is maximizing its overall interests. In the intermediate range, governments tend to exhibit a "grabbing hand," which induces lower corporate values. As the government's equity share increases, becoming sufficiently large, the government provides "helping hands," thereby increasing overall corporate value.

Li and Rozelle (2000), focusing on a sample of 168 township enterprises (88 of which have been privatized) in Jiangsu and Zhejiang provinces, find that "transitional costs apparently reduce private firm efficiency in the year that firms are being privatized." However, they find that two or more years after privatization, private firms produce 5 to 7 percent more output with the same inputs. They further surmise that, as privatized firms complete the transition to ownership and continue adapting to China's business environment, gains could further rise. An important insight is the presence of adjustment costs in the conversion process, which may result in a lag between conversion and realized benefits.

Dong, Bowles, and Ho (2002a), in their analysis of the determinants of employee share ownership in Jiangsu and Shandong provinces, show that privatization resulted in a higher concentration of share ownership in management and other board members. While regular employees owned shares in 16 of the 39 privatized enterprises in the sample, even in these enterprises, share distribution was highly skewed toward wealthier, local male residents in managerial positions. Dong, Bowles, and Ho find that the privatization process exhibits an important political dimension in which local leaders sell dominant ownership shares to managers, subject to the leaders' revenue objectives and managers' wealth constraints. The effect of this shareholding pattern is increased earnings inequality within the enterprise and, more broadly, in China's rural society.

In their report on share ownership's effects on employee attitudes (based on the survey used above), Dong, Bowles, and Ho (2002b) indicate that, in general, employee shareholders have higher levels of job satisfaction, perceive greater degrees of participation in enterprise decision making, display stronger organizational commitment, and exhibit more positive attitudes toward the privatization process than nonshareholders in privatized firms.

Su and Jefferson (2003), investigating the determinants of ownership conversion in China's large- and medium-sized enterprises, find that the probability of ownership conversion increases with the firm's profitability, productivity, and intensity of competition faced by the firm. The probability of conversion falls with firm size, a result consistent with the government's policy of releasing smaller firms and retaining larger ones. These results indicate selection bias in the privatization process of Chinese SOEs. In evaluating the effects of ownership and ownership restructuring on firm performance, estimation procedures should recognize and account for this phenomenon.

Building on the findings of Su and Jefferson (2003) regarding competition's role in driving conversion, Li, Li, and Zhang (2000) conclude that competition requires local governments to improve the efficiency of SOEs and COEs under their jurisdiction. They also conclude that, because managers' efforts are not verifiable, local governments often respond by granting total or partial residual shares to managers. By concluding that "intense competition stimulates the rise of a private property system," they postulate a certain inevitable quality to a process in which reform and competition lead to privatization, with an emphasis on insider privatization (Li, Li, and Zhang 2000, 269). These findings are consistent with our heuristic model of Chinese enterprise conversion, in which entry and competition, as well as reform of managerial control rights, served as antecedents to the conversion movement that began in the late 1990s.

Large- and Medium-Sized Enterprises: The Dataset

The statistical system China uses to track its industrial enterprises has three concentric circles, or populations, of enterprises. The outer circle includes all enterprises in the industrial system. According to table 11.1, in 1998, this broad measure included 7.9 million enterprises. For this inclusive enterprise population, China's statistical authorities report only skeletal information—generally not more than the total number and gross industrial output.

The middle circle, consisting of less than 5 percent of China's total industrial enterprise population, includes enterprises reporting more than 5 million yuan (approximately $600,000) of annual sales; all firms classified as SOEs are included, regardless of annual sales. For these enterprises, the statistical authorities collect and report a broader set of measures, including basic ones of financial performance, such as profits and losses.

Finally, the inner circle consists of the country's some 22,000 large- and medium-sized enterprises. NBS data indicate that, in 2001, these enterprises accounted for approximately 62 percent of total sales of enterprises with annual sales exceeding 5 million yuan. These firms and the detailed annual census data that the NBS collected directly from these firms constituted the database for this study.

These large- and medium-sized enterprises, whose performance the NBS carefully tracks, are China's most successful companies—those that have grown and sustained their status at the pinnacle of the country's industrial enterprise sector—and many of its most troubled enterprises. As the focus of decades of central planning and administered allocations of subsidized capital, skilled labor, and raw materials, some of these large- and medium-sized SOEs continue to impede China's transition to an advanced market economy.

During 1995–2001, the period covered by this study's panel of data, the NBS changed its system of ownership classification. For the purpose of comparing categories of ownership and tracking ownership reform between 1995 and 2001, we use the concordance shown in appendix 11A, which aligns the 1999 system of ownership classification with the preexisting one. This aggregation of 23 detailed categories into 7 broader ones—state; collective; Hong Kong, Macao, and Taiwan; foreign; shareholding; private; and other domestic—closely tracks the classification system currently used in the *China Statistical Yearbook*.[5] Using this concordance, we have compiled a description of the changing ownership profile of China's large- and medium-sized enterprise sector (table 11.2).

Performance of Firms with Established Ownership Classifications

As shown in table 11.1, China's enterprise system currently combines a wide variety of ownership types. One approach to evaluating the implications of ownership change is to compare the performance of firms already established in an ownership classification. To determine why ownership matters in China's economy, we first compared the performance of firms that reported different ownership classifications. They included eight measures of performance: labor productivity, capital productivity, profitability, employment, wages, taxes paid, new product sales, and R&D intensity. The profitability measure represented the difference between sales revenue and the production costs of sold output. Thus, it excluded certain taxes,

---

5. Exceptions are that the concordance (1) excludes individually owned enterprises (none of which qualify as large- or medium-sized enterprises), (2) distinguishes between FORs and HKT enterprises, and (3) separates private ownership and other type of ownership. See *China Statistical Yearbook* (NBS 2000, 407).

Table 11.2 China: LME ownership distribution, 1994 and 2001

Ownership category	1994		2001	
	Number	Percent	Number	Percent
State	15,533	67.9	8,675	37.9
Collective	4,068	17.8	2,465	10.8
Hong Kong, Macao and Taiwan	967	4.2	2,271	9.9
Foreign	1,041	4.6	2,675	11.7
Shareholding	961	4.2	5,659	24.7
Private	7	0.0	984	4.3
Other domestic	293	1.3	149	0.7
Total	**22,870**	**100.0**	**22,878**	**100.0**

LME = large and medium-sized enterprise

Source: NBS (1995, 2001).

pension payments, welfare subsidies, and other costs not directly associated with production.

To identify the "pure" ownership effect, we held constant differences in the composition of asset ownership across enterprises. This approach allowed for the fact that some SOEs contain asset structures that are mostly nonstate owned, whereas significant numbers of nonstate-owned enterprises retain a majority of state-owned assets. By controlling for differences in asset ownership, we could distinguish between ownership classification and asset composition effects (table 11.3).

Ownership Classification Effect

Table 11.3 (rows COE, FOR, GAT, OTH, PRI, and SHR) demonstrates that, since SOEs are the reference intercept in the regression and because most of the estimates of the ownership classification dummies are highly statistically significant, one can infer that ownership matters for performance. The results show that SOE productivity—both labor and capital—is significantly lower than that of the other ownership types. However, with the exception of FORs and SHRs, the ratio of sales profit to sales revenue is higher for SOEs. While lower wages in SOEs may explain a tendency toward higher SOE sales profits, table 11.3 also shows that employment and taxes are frequently higher in SOEs than in other ownership classifications. The tendency for SOEs to operate in less competitive industries, such as tobacco and petroleum, may also explain their relative profit advantage, although a portion of this effect is captured by including regression dummies at the two-digit industry level.

Asset Composition Effect

In table 11.3, rows STATE and FOR/HKT control for the effect of asset composition—share of state-owned assets and combined share of FOR and

Table 11.3 China: Comparison of ownership classification and asset composition

Variable	VA/L	VA/K	Profit/sales	Employment	Wages (average)	Taxes/sales	New product sales/total sales	R&D expenditure/sales
Constant	1.086 (44.507)	1.086 (44.508)	-2.295 (130.261)	7.697 (402.711)	1.700 (130.869)	-5.214 (203.023)	-11.257 (70.368)	-18.015 (133.412)
K/L	0.580 (164.763)	-0.420 (119.419)	n.a.	n.a.	n.a.	n.a.	n.a.	n.a.
COE	0.308 (24.005)	0.308 (24.005)	-0.054 (4.983)	-0.335 (28.698)	-0.175 (22.016)	0.110 (7.030)	-1.655 (16.940)	-0.994 (12.046)
FOR	0.563 (26.914)	0.563 (26.914)	0.118 (6.741)	-1.013 (53.505)	0.507 (39.395)	-0.599 (23.211)	-3.958 (24.988)	-2.677 (20.018)
GAT	0.342 (16.404)	0.342 (16.404)	-0.038 (2.161)	-0.902 (47.689)	0.206 (16.025)	-0.659 (25.333)	-3.333 (21.047)	-1.576 (11.789)
OTH	0.315 (9.398)	0.315 (9.398)	-0.065 (2.297)	-0.422 (13.821)	0.146 (7.015)	-0.113 (2.773)	-0.838 (3.282)	-1.240 (5.749)
PRI	0.509 (19.609)	0.509 (19.609)	-0.108 (4.942)	-0.494 (20.919)	-0.129 (8.064)	0.072 (2.268)	-1.901 (9.630)	-1.569 (9.413)
SHR	0.428 (40.585)	0.428 (40.585)	0.118 (13.31)	0.017 (1.740)	0.024 (3.662)	0.261 (20.438)	0.401 (4.986)	0.217 (3.203)

	(1)	(2)	(3)	(4)	(5)	(6)	(7)	(8)
STATE Asset share	-0.046 (31.394)	-0.046 (31.394)	0.004 (3.257)	0.041 (30.673)	-0.028 (30.674)	0.009 (4.912)	0.044 (3.941)	0.080 (8.461)
FOR/HKT Asset share	0.062 (23.786)	0.062 (23.786)	-0.008 (-3.571)	0.062 (26.563)	0.041 (25.782)	-0.05 (-15.71)	0.193 (9.793)	0.022 (1.304)
IND	Yes	Yes	Yes	Yes	Yes	Yes	Yes	Yes
Time	Yes	Yes	Yes	Yes	Yes	Yes	Yes	Yes
Adjusted R-squared (observations)	0.392 (96,908)	0.298 (96,908)	0.106 (87,820)	0.261 (96,908)	0.268 (96,908)	0.240 (92,718)	0.179 (96,908)	0.099 (96,908)

COE = collective-owned enterprise
FOR = foreign-owned enterprise
FOR/HKT = foreign sources including Hong Kong, Macao, and Taiwan
GAT = Hong Kong, Macao, or Taiwan owned enterprise
IND = industry dummy
K/L = net value of fixed assets/employment
n.a. = not applicable
OTH = other
PRI = private enterprise
R&D = research and development
SHR = shareholding enterprises
STATE = state-owned assets
VA/K = value added/net value of fixed assets
VA/L = value added/total employment

HKT-owned assets—on firm performance.[6] The results showed that STATE negatively affects labor and capital productivity and wages; conversely, STATE is positively associated with profitability, employment, new products, and R&D expenditures. The FOR/HKT asset share exhibits a pattern of performance outcomes, which, with the exception of employment, new product sales, and R&D intensity, is the inverse of STATE asset shares. Enterprises rich in FOR/HKT assets exhibit high levels of labor and capital productivity and wages.

These results demonstrated the importance of distinguishing between the effects of a change in ownership classification and a change in asset composition on enterprise performance. However, this analysis may be of limited predictive value regarding the effect of change from state ownership to shareholding status on a given firm. Ambiguity intrudes for the following reasons:

- **Selection bias.** The differential quality of converted and unconverted firms may reflect selection bias—that is, the SOEs chosen for conversion may not be typical of the existing population. If converted SOEs tend to be well-above-average performers, then, following a period after the conversion, any measured quality advantage of the converted SOEs may reflect selection bias rather than the salutary consequences of conversion. In sum, it may be that conversion does not improve performance, but that good performers become converted.

- **Adjustment costs.** Following conversion, time may be required to adjust to new governance arrangements and achieve efficiency improvements associated with changes in the firm's labor force, asset composition, and product mix. In their investigation of privatization of rural collectives, Li and Rozelle (2000) find evidence of transition costs. Gains ensuing from privatization may appear only one to two years after conversion.

This study formally tests for selection bias, but can only speculate on the importance of transition costs.

Sample of Converted Enterprises

Using the balanced samples of converted and unconverted SOEs and COEs, this study tested whether the firms selected for conversion are more or less

---

6. We constructed two measures of asset shares: those for state-owned assets (STATE) and those originating from foreign sources, including Hong Kong, Macao, and Taiwan (FOR/HKT). The effect of OTH, the omitted third assets category, was represented by the constant in each of the equations. The coefficients on STATE and FOR/HKT should therefore be interpreted in relation to the magnitudes shown in the constants.

Table 11.4a   China: Converted SOEs, 1996–2001

Old	New[a]	1996	1997	1998	1999	2000	2001	Total
Total population of SOE conversions								
SOE	DSOE	12,909	13,268	11,326	9,824	8,711	6,899	62,937
SOE	DCOE	16	69	145	64	52	52	398
SOE	DSHR	87	342	546	319	517	454	2,265
SOE	DPRI	1	10	31	14	30	36	122
SOE	DFOR	11	15	21	5	5	6	63
SOE	DGAT	3	13	16	14	10	14	70
SOE	DOTH	5	28	40	23	12	10	118
Total		13,032	13,745	12,125	10,263	9,337	7,471	3,036
Conversions for which data are continuously available during 1995–2001								
SOE	DSOE	5,343	5,235	4,964	4,887	4,697	4,425	29,551
SOE	DCOE	5	17	66	26	18	30	162
SOE	DSHR	31	110	210	110	204	236	901
SOE	DPRI	0	2	8	5	10	19	44
SOE	DFOR	2	4	5	3	2	2	18
SOE	DGAT	0	3	3	6	1	4	17
SOE	DOTH	2	10	18	4	5	5	44
Total		5,383	5,381	5,274	5,041	4,937	4,721	1,186
Conversions for which data are continuously available during 1995–2001, have only one conversion, and data are plausible								
SOE	SOE	3,484	3,413	3,225	3,170	3,107	0	13,292[b]
SOE	SHR	13	48	128	69	146	0	258

COE = collective-owned enterprise
FOR = foreign-owned enterprise
GAT = Hong Kong, Macao, or Taiwan owned enterprise
OTH = other
PRI = private enterprise
SHR = shareholding enterprise
SOE = state-owned enterprise

a. Entries in this column represent the status in year t relative to $t-1$.
b. Total for 1996–99.

Source: National Bureau of Statistics large- and medium-size industrial enterprise dataset, 1995–2001.

likely in the year before conversion, $t - 1$, to have exhibited a high or low measure of any of the eight performance measures.

Before conducting this selection bias analysis, we constructed samples of both converted and unconverted enterprises to establish a control. To be included in the sample, a firm had to have reported data for the year before its conversion ($t - 1$) continuously through 2001. Within the sample, the included conversion years were $t = 1996, 1997, 1998$, and 1999. Because the proximity of 2000 to 2001 was likely to diminish the realized effect of conversion, the study excluded firms converted in 2000. It also eliminated enterprises that reported multiple conversions (i.e., those that converted from SOE or COE to SHR and then converted to another ownership type). Finally,

Table 11.4b China: Converted COEs, 1996–2001

Old	New	1996	1997	1998	1999	2000	2001	Total
Total population of COE conversions								
COE	DSOE	37	45	56	27	12	22	199
COE	DCOE	3,109	3,526	2,566	2,698	2,539	1,716	16,154
COE	DSHR	35	124	211	157	187	256	970
COE	DPRV	5	8	35	30	73	65	216
COE	DFOR	8	10	18	10	10	11	67
COE	DGAT	6	9	41	15	14	12	97
COE	DOTH	11	12	24	8	4	6	65
Total		3,211	3,734	2,951	2,945	2,839	2,088	1,614
Conversions for which data are continuously available during 1995–2001								
COE	DSOE	9	14	21	9	2	12	67
COE	DCOE	1,053	1,008	924	968	938	834	5,725
COE	DSHR	12	44	64	42	49	91	302
COE	DPRV	1	2	7	9	20	26	65
COE	DFOR	3	2	5	4	2	4	20
COE	DGAT	3	1	14	7	3	2	30
COE	DOTH	2	5	7	6	1	1	22
Total		1,083	1,076	1,042	1,045	1,015	970	506
Conversions for which data are continuously available during 1995–2001 have only one conversion, and data are plausible								
COE	COE	1,053	1,002	849	787	723	0	4,414
COE	SHR	3	20	47	23	0	0	93

Source: National Bureau of Statistics large- and medium-size industrial enterprise dataset, 1995–2001.

the study eliminated firms that reported implausible figures for key variables, such as zero or negative sales or fixed capital stock.[7]

Tables 11.4a and 11.4b profile the conversions of SOEs and COEs during 1996–2001. As table 11.4a shows, 3,036 SOEs were converted to nonstate enterprises during the period. Of these, 2,265 or 75 percent entailed conversions to SHRs. The lower panel identifies the number of enterprises that reported a single conversion, for which key data were continuously available from $t-1$ to 2001, and for which the data observations were plausible. Within the sample, 404 enterprises satisfied these criteria. Since the study did not include conversions reported in the year 2000, the effective sample size for SOE conversions was 258.[8] The 13,292 unconverted SOEs that

---

7. Appendix 11A specifies three types of SOEs, of which this study sample included two: SOEs and wholly SOEs; it did not include jointly operated SOEs, which involve hybrid ownership and already include certain SHR attributes.

8. Many converted enterprises changed their identification (ID) in the conversion process and therefore could not be tracked before and after conversion. Efforts to match pre and postconverted enterprises indicated that conversions involving changes in industry or size classifications or locations increased the likelihood of issuing a new ID. Thus, this study sample, while a fraction of the total number of converted enterprises, tend to control for industry, size, and location so that the comparative statistical analysis focused on the independent effect of conversion.

existed in 1995 (i.e., thereby constituting a total of 13,292 observations during the sample period) constituted the part of the sample that allowed one to identify the nature of selection bias and the independent effect of conversion. For the collectives, table 11.4b shows that, among the 1,614 reported conversions, 970 were from COEs to SHRs. Of these, 93 enterprises satisfied the criteria for a single conversion, continuous data, and plausible observations. The unconverted subset consisted of 4,414 COEs.

Applying logit analysis to the sample described above, we estimated the probability of firms with certain performance characteristics being converted. The major findings showed that, relative to the unconverted SOEs, the firms selected for conversion exhibit high levels of both labor and capital productivity and profitability; they also exhibit relatively low levels of employment and relatively high tax burdens (table 11.5). The COEs selected for conversion were distinguished by relatively high R&D intensity and marginally greater profitability.

Finally, the study examined the regional bias of the conversion process. Because we found that more successful firms tended to enjoy a higher probability of conversion, it was not surprising that, relative to other regions, SOEs located in China's eastern and southern provinces had a larger probability of conversion. COEs located in the eastern provinces also exhibited a higher probability of conversion; however, those in the southern provinces were among the least likely to be converted. These findings revealed the phenomenon of selection bias—that is, the tendency for SOEs with certain characteristics to participate in the conversion process. As a result of selection bias, researchers may have difficulty determining whether certain characteristics that converted enterprises exhibit (e.g., greater productivity and profitability) existed before conversion or resulted from it. The study method, described below, attempts to control for such bias.

Effects of Conversion on Enterprise Performance: Research Method

To analyze the effects of conversion on firm performance, we first identified the relevant set of performance variables, which included eight measures: labor productivity, capital productivity, profitability, employment, wages, taxes paid, new product sales, and R&D intensity. For each measure, we compared 2001 performance levels for converted, versus unconverted, enterprises, controlling for performance levels in the year before conversion ($t - 1$) (to control for selection bias).

Second, we formulated an equation used to estimate the individual contributions of six factors to each of the eight performance measures. Our formal estimation equation was:

Table 11.5   China: Characteristics of converted enterprises in $t-1$ (includes conversions for 1996–2000)

Characteristic	Conversion type	
	SOE-SHR	COE-SHR
$(VA/L)_{t-1}$	0.004 (2.916)	0.005 (1.230)
$(VA/K)_{t-1}$	0.006 (4.115)	0.003 (0.781)
$(Profit/sales)_{t-1}$	0.005 (2.764)	0.008 (1.501)
$(Employment)_{t-1}$	−0.003 (1.852)	0.004 (0.754)
$Wage_{t-1}$	−0.001 (0.228)	0.008 (1.215)
$(Taxes/sales)_{t-1}$	0.007 (5.945)	0.006 (1.633)
$(NP/sales)_{t-1}$	−0.000 (0.872)	0.001 (2.259)
$(RDE/sales)_{t-1}$	−0.000 (0.591)	0.001 (1.096)
IND	Yes	Yes
Region	Yes	Yes
Year	Yes	Yes

COE = collective-owned enterprise
IND = industry dummy
K = net value of fixed assets
L = employment
NP = new products
R&D = research and development
RDE = R&D spending
SHR = shareholding enterprise
SOE = state-owned enterprise
VA = value added

Note: Estimation results for each variable are drawn from regressions that include the single performance measure with control dummies for industry, region, and year.

$$\ln Z_{j,01} = \alpha_0 + \alpha_1 SHR_t + \alpha_2 \Delta \ln ST\_SH_{t-1\,to\,01}$$
$$+ \alpha_3 \left(\Delta \ln ST\_SH_{t-1\,to\,01} \right) * DSHR$$
$$+ \alpha_4 DSTA\_LP_{t-1\,to\,01} + \alpha_5 \ln Z_{j\,,t-1} + \varepsilon_1, \tag{11.1}$$

where $Z_{j,01}$ included the set of eight performance measures (i.e., $j = 1 \ldots 8$). The six factors that determined $Z_{j,01}$ were

- independent effect of conversion, holding the firm's asset structure fixed (i.e., $\alpha_1 SHR_t$);

- reduced share of state-owned assets, controlling for the firm's formal ownership classification (i.e., $\alpha_2 \Delta lnST\_SH_{t-1 \, to \, 01}$);

- differential effect of reductions on share of state-owned assets in converted, versus unconverted, enterprises (i.e., $\alpha_3 [\Delta lnST\_SH_{t-1 \, to \, 01}]^* DSHR$) (if $\alpha_3 < 0$, then a given reduction in the state-owned asset share of a converted enterprise would have a larger effect on the relevant performance measure than a similar reduction in the state-owned asset share for an unconverted enterprise);

- increased share of state-owned assets (i.e., $\alpha_4 DSTA\_LP_{t-1 \, to \, 01}$) (this study used a [0,1] dummy to capture its effect following conversion);

- tendency for lagging firms to revert to the mean (i.e., $\alpha_5 lnZ_{it-1}$); and

- unexplained part captured by the residual or error term (i.e., ε_{i6}).

Estimates of Conversion Equations

The study estimated equation (11.1), using the six factors described above. The results for SOEs and COEs are shown in tables 11.6a and 11.6b, respectively. The first step was to review the regression results for the SOE sample. In addition to the results shown in table 11.6a, a summary list of outcomes is grouped in the left-hand column of table 11.7.

Direct Effect of Conversion

Absent changes in asset structure, the effects of converting SOEs into shareholding enterprises included increased capital productivity, employment, new product sales, R&D intensity, and reduced wages and profitability. In terms of resulting growth or slower decline in employment, it should be noted that the conversions occurred during a period when state-sector, worker furloughs (*xiagang*) were widespread. Moreover, as table 11.5 shows, the enterprises selected for conversion exhibited relatively low levels of employment before conversion. It is possible that efforts to obtain public authorities' approval to convert SOEs into SHRs may have included negotiations and agreements with workers—key stakeholders in the conversion process—to avoid or limit layoffs. The additional finding that conversion alone tended to be associated with downward wage adjustments suggests that the quid pro quo for retaining workers was wage reduction or slower wage growth. Finally, reduction in profit associated with conversions may reflect what Li and Rozelle (2000) characterize as "transitional costs." They may also reflect the "grabbing hand" of the government (Tian 2000) or other stakeholders during the conversion process.

Table 11.6a China: All SOE conversions, 1996–99, (lnZ_{2001})

Independent variable (Z_{2001})	VA/L	VA/K	Profit/sales	Employment	Wages (average)	Taxes/sales	New products/ sales	R&D expenditure/ sales
Constant	1.512 (53.863)	−0.394 (20.430)	−1.192 (46.845)	0.094 (3.110)	0.927 (46.760)	−1.594 (37.472)	−7.639 (44.201)	−9.271 (43.165)
DSHR dummy	0.020 (0.344)	0.146 (2.224)	−0.124 (2.174)	0.073 (2.274)	−0.095 (2.456)	−0.050 (0.709)	1.476 (2.432)	1.262 (2.155)
Δ in share state assets, $t-1$ to 01	−0.039 (7.179)	−0.023 (3.923)	−0.003 (0.487)	0.011 (3.912)	−0.035 (10.070)	0.015 (2.319)	−0.200 (4.125)	−0.099 (2.117)
Δ in share state assets, $t-1$ to 01 *SHR	n.a.	n.a.	n.a.	n.a.	n.a.	n.a.	0.603 (2.092)	0.454 (1.634)
Dummy for increase in share state asset	0.049 (1.632)	0.001 (0.305)	−0.051 (1.741)	−0.010 (0.629)	−0.002 (0.093)	−0.033 (0.935)	0.133 (0.502)	0.194 (0.762)
lnZ_{t-1}	0.497 (54.591)	0.579 (57.697)	0.500 (43.423)	0.944 (234.471)	0.637 (65.329)	0.632 (71.601)	0.506 (62.506)	0.308 (31.518)
1997	−0.033 (1.488)	−0.164 (6.716)	0.040 (1.851)	0.008 (0.679)	−0.039 (2.732)	0.029 (1.103)	0.174 (0.885)	−0.520 (2.737)
1998	−0.058 (2.584)	−0.238 (9.582)	0.060 (2.709)	0.010 (0.800)	−0.048 (3.312)	0.042 (1.568)	0.483 (2.431)	−0.557 (2.894)
1999	−0.065 (2.877)	−0.221 (8.747)	0.125 (5.607)	0.078 (6.418)	−0.065 (4.421)	0.026 (0.980)	0.374 (1.870)	−0.667 (3.440)
Adjusted R-sq (observations)	0.226 (10,758)	0.263 (10,758)	0.171 (9,232)	0.837 (10,758)	0.298 (10,722)	0.329 (10,497)	0.273 (10,758)	0.087 (10,758)

n.a. = not applicable

Table 11.6b   China: All COE conversions, 1996–99 (lnZ_{2001})

Independent variable (Z_{2001})	VA/L	VA/K	Profit/sales	Employment	Wages (average)	Taxes/sales	New products/sales	R&D expenditure/ RDE/sales
Constant	1.214 (17.222)	-0.092 (2.586)	-1.152 (20.224)	-0.043 (0.475)	1.053 (28.902)	-2.490 (24.697)	-8.983 (23.453)	-11.492 (25.574)
SHR dummy	0.130 (1.554)	0.266 (2.809)	0.136 (1.788)	0.152 (3.071))	0.044 (0.935)	0.098 (0.931)	2.084 (2.645)	0.083 (0.122)
Increase in share state assets, $t-1$ to 01	-0.014 (0.859)	0.001 (0.052)	-0.024 (1.550)	0.004 (0.427	0.009 (1.013)	0.003 (0.155)	0.235 (1.553)	-0.101 (0.775)
Dummy for increase in share state asset	0.087 (0.861)	0.047 (0.411)	0.143 (1.443)	-0.055 (0.911)	-0.030 (0.522)	0.216 (1.638)	-0.458 (0.481)	0.469 (0.571)
lnZ_{t-1}	0.688 (35.679)	0.754 (33.587)	0.607 (24.625)	0.967 (71.573)	0.555 (30.434)	0.445 (21.444)	0.397 (20.672)	0.268 (12.226)
1998	0.005 (0.127)	-0.025 (0.517)	0.014 (0.348)	-0.009 (0.363)	-0.037 (1.521)	0.030 (0.548)	0.044 (0.110)	-0.112 (0.322)
1999	0.017 (0.389)	0.018 (0.369)	0.122 (3.013)	0.058 (2.277)	-0.021 (0.850)	0.012 (0.217)	0.129 (0.321)	0.118 (0.337)
Adjusted R^2 (observations)	0.369 (2,184)	0.346 (2,184)	0.235 (2,003)	0.705 (2,184)	0.303 (2,168)	0.180 (2,121)	0.169 (2,184)	0.065 (2,184)

Source:

Table 11.7 China: Summary of selection-bias conversion results, ranked by statistical significance (all are statistically significant at ≥ 90 percent level)

Variable change	Sign	SOEs	COEs
Selection bias (baseline performance relative to unconverted firms) (see tables 11.6a and 11.6b)[a]	+	VA/L* VA/K* Profit/sales* Tax/sales*	n.a.
	–	Employment***	n.a.
Direct conversion effect (assuming no change in asset structure)	+	VA/L*, VA/K* Employment** RDE/sales** NP/sales**	VA/K* Profit/sales*** Employment* NP/sales*
	–	Average wage** Profit/sales*	n.a.
Effect of a decrease in state-owned asset share	+	VA/L* VA/K* Wages* NP/sales[a] RDE/sales[a]	n.a.
	–	Employment* Taxes/sales**	n.a.
Dummy for an increase in state-owned asset share	+	—	n.a.
	–	Profit/sales***	n.a.

COE = collective-owned enterprise
n.a. = statistically significant at less than the 10 percent level
NP = new products
RDE = research and development spending
SOE = state-owned enterprise
VA/K = value added/net value of fixed assets
VA/L = value added/employment
* = statistically significant at the 1 percent level
** = statistically significant at the 5 percent level
*** = statistically significant at the 10 percent level

a. Effect consists of two estimated coefficients.

Effect of Reduced State Asset Share

Reducing the state's asset ownership share following conversion—associated significantly with rising labor and capital productivity—accounts for some of the most robust effects of the conversion process. Paradoxically, notwithstanding the rise in labor and capital productivity, profitability is relatively unaffected by declining state asset shares. The elasticities of gains in labor productivity growth and wage growth, with respect to decline in state asset shares, are of similar magnitude and may therefore cancel out each other's effect. However, the gain in capital productivity, coupled with a reduced tax burden, might be expected to translate into higher profitability. Reductions in the share of nonstate assets are also associated with a rise in both R&D intensity and new product sales, which may auger still greater productivity advantages for the converted SHRs. Increased R&D spending may help to explain the apparent decline in profitability. Comparing the induced and direct effects of conversion indicates that certain effects operate in opposite directions (e.g., employment and wages), whereas others (e.g., capital productivity, new product sales, and R&D intensity) are directly enhanced by conversion and associated reductions in state asset shares.

Reduced State Asset Shares for Converted and Unconverted Enterprises: Differential Effect

For all but two performance measures, the study samples found that the effect of reducing state asset shares exhibited no distinguishable differences between converted and unconverted enterprises. Where the study found no significant effect, the coefficient was restricted to $\alpha_3 = 0$. For the sample of converted SOEs, equivalent reductions in state asset shares had comparatively smaller effects on new product sales and R&D intensity. We accounted for these differences in calculating the total conversion effects.

Effect of Increased State Asset Share

Some enterprises experienced increases in the share of state-owned assets over the period $t - 1$ to 2001.[9] We found that such increases generally had no effect. While larger state shares were associated with higher labor productivity growth and lower profitability growth, the statistical significance of these associations was not robust.

Catch Up: Reversion to the Mean

The coefficient on the lagged performance measure (i.e., $\alpha_5 ln Z_{it-1}$) identifies the degree of catch up or convergence—the extent to which firms with unusually high or low initial performance levels tended, by 2001, to revert to the mean. For example, the profitability equation (for which $\alpha_5 = 0.500$) indicates substantial catch up—that is, firms with high profitability in $t - 1$ tended to sustain only half of their initial advantage, after controlling for conversion and asset mix. By comparison, the employment equation (for which $\alpha_5 = 0.944$) indicates little change in relative employment levels over the period $t - 1$ to 2001. The catch-up phenomenon may overturn the anticipated effects of conversion on actual performance measures. In particular, since selection bias is associated with higher levels of productivity and profitability, the catch-up phenomenon may diminish the effect of conversion on these measures.

---

9. This study sample of converted SOEs included only three such cases.

Table 11.6b reports the estimation results for the sample of COEs, whose results table 11.7 summarizes.

Direct Effects of Conversion

Converting COEs to SHRs was found to accelerate capital productivity growth and weakly improve profitability. Similar to converted SOEs, one consequence of conversion was the tendency to retain or add employment relative to the unconverted sample. Again, this outcome may have reflected the efforts of workers and local leaders to use conversion as an opportunity to stem layoffs or increase jobs. Relative to unconverted COEs, new product sales rose. Other performance measures were not significantly affected by the independent effect of conversion.

Effect of Reduced State Asset Share

For COEs, reducing the state's asset share had no highly significant effect on firm performance. This outcome is not surprising, given the state's relatively low share of ownership in COEs. As table 11.9 shows, for unconverted firms, the state's asset share fell from 7.3 to 3.2 percent; for converted firms, the share declined from 9.1 to 2.1 percent. The study found no evidence that reductions in the state's asset share exerted differential effects on converted and unconverted COEs.

Effect of Increased State Asset Share

An increase in the share of state-owned assets subsequent to conversion exhibited no effects on any of the eight performance measures.

Catch Up: Reversion to the Mean

As with SOEs, the study found a general pattern of catch up or reversion to the mean, conditional on controlling for the conversion variables. With the exception of labor, for which the study found little tendency for catch up, most variables exhibited a substantial tendency to revert to the mean.

Effect of Conversion on Asset Structure

For SOEs, the study found that reductions in state asset shares substantially affected many of the performance measures examined. It may be that formally converting an SOE to an SHR does not affect the asset composition of the firm; alternatively, conversion might substantially enhance the firm's abil-

Table 11.8 China: Change in state asset share ($\Delta lnST\_SH_{t-1\ to\ 01}$) in converted enterprises relative to unconverted ones

Variable	SOE-SHR conversions	COE-SHR conversions
Constant	−0.017	−0.075
	(15.579)	(2.255)
DSHR	−0.078	−0.052
	(9.209)	(0.317)
Adjusted R^2	0.008	0.000
(observations)	(3,851)	(961)

COE = collective-owned enterprise
DSHR = enterprise that has been converted to share-
holder ownership status
SHR = shareholding enterprise
SOE = state-owned enterprise

ity to reduce the state-owned share of its assets. This study used the follow-ing equation to test the effect of conversion on the firm's asset composition.

$$\Delta lnST\_SH_{t-1to01} = \beta_0 + \beta_1 DSHR_t + \varepsilon_2 \qquad (11.2)$$

If in equation 11.2 $\beta_1 > 0$, one could conclude that conversion speeds the reduction in the state's asset share. Table 11.8 shows that the estimate of β_1 is highly statistically significant; converted SOEs are significantly more able than unconverted SOEs to reduce their share of state-owned assets. Consistent with this result, table 11.9 shows that, for converted SOEs, the ratio of state-owned assets falls to nearly one-half of the ratio before con-version, whereas for unconverted enterprises, the decline is closer to 20 percent. The estimated coefficients for the conversion dummy (DSHR) indicate that, compared with SOEs, COEs do not enjoy an advantage rela-tive to their unconverted counterparts in achieving reductions in state-owned asset shares (table 11.8).

Reducing State Share of Assets

Do reductions in the state's share of asset ownership result from either the accumulation of new nonstate investment or conversion of state-owned assets to nonstate ownership? In converted enterprises, the quantity of state-owned assets rises from an average of 38.6 billion yuan in $t-1$ to 43.1 billion yuan in 2001. The concurrent increase in nonstate assets from 47.6 to 98.6 bil-lion yuan accounts for the decline in state-owned asset ownership in 2001 to nearly one-half (i.e., 0.520) of their share in $t-1$.

Table 11.9 China: Reduction in state asset share, $t-1$ to 2001

$\Delta lnST\_SH_{t-1\ to\ 01}$	Unconverted firms			Firms converted to SHRs		
	$t-1$	2001	Ratio 2001/$t-1$	$t-1$	2001	Ratio 2001/$t-1$
SOEs	91.6	72.5	0.792	78.1	40.6	0.520
COEs	7.3	3.2	0.438	9.1	2.1	0.231

COE = collective-owned enterprise
SHR = shareholding enterprise
SOE = state-owned enterprise

These findings show that conversion results in a substantially enhanced ability to attract nonstate investment. The associated finding that conversion tends not to reduce the volume of existing state-owned assets carries two implications: (1) conversion does not result in the transfer—either through sale or give away—of state-owned assets to nonstate interests, and (2) conversion is not associated with breakup of the SOE into parts with high-performing state assets captured by the converted enterprise and chronic nonperforming assets and debt obligations left behind as wards of the state and banking system. Examples of these arrangements—involving both stripping and creaming the best of the state-owned assets—can be found; however, they do not characterize the firms in this sample.

Endogeneity

Before summarizing these regression results, we address the issue of potential endogeneity bias in the estimates of equation 11.1. Of specific concern is the case in which nonstate investors take into account the rate of change in one performance measure to determine where to invest. Appendix 11B explains this study's approach to correcting for potential endogeneity bias; with two exceptions, the pattern of estimates for the contemporaneous and lagged values of the dependent variable, $\Delta lnST\_SH_{t-1\ to\ 01}$, are similar.[10]

Estimating Total Effect of Conversion

To estimate the total effect of conversion, the study evaluated the combined effects of two avenues of effect associated with the conversion process: (1) the direct effect (α_1) and (2) the effect of reducing the share of state-owned assets resulting from conversion [$\alpha_3(\Delta lnST\_SH_{t-1\ to\ 01})$]. Because reducing state

---

10. This set of results is not reported; results can be made available, upon request to the authors.

asset shares affects performance of the innovation variables—new products and R&D spending—differently for converted and unconverted firms, this study incorporated the differences for these two performance measures into the calculations $[\alpha_3(\Delta lnST\_SH_{t-1 \text{ to } 01})*DSHR]$. We estimated and reported the effect of an increase in share of state-owned assets because only a few firms exhibited such increases (tables 11.6a and 11.6b). However, we omitted this factor from our calculations. By computing growth rates in the performance measures from $t - 1$ to 2001, which the study presented as average annual rates, selection bias did not affect estimates.

The study first focused on the state-owned sector. Table 11.10 shows three sets of growth rates. Two rates compare overall rates of growth of the performance measures for converted and unconverted enterprises, while the third uses the above method to compute only that portion of each growth rate attributable to conversion. These are to be compared with zero (0), the comparable implicit growth rates for the unconverted SOEs. This third set of rates shows that conversion has systematic, extensive effects on the newly created SHRs. Resulting growth of labor and capital productivity, employment, and taxes in converted enterprises exceeds that of counterpart unconverted enterprises, controlling for the catch-up factor. Conversion most dramatically affects growth rates of innovation expenditure and activity (i.e., R&D spending and new product sales). Simultaneously, in comparison with the counterpart unconverted SOEs, the study observed negative profit and wage growth. Where directions of the effect of direct and induced channels differed (e.g., employment and wages), the direct effect dominated, at least within the sample period. For employment, the direct effect of increased employment associated with the conversion event dominated the attrition of workers resulting from additional nonstate investment. Likewise, the dampening direct effect of conversion on wage growth persisted, even as converted firms succeeded in attracting new nonstate investment, which worked to increase the pace of wage growth.

The lower half of table 11.10 shows this study's estimates of the total effect of conversion on performance for the sample of converted collectives. For each performance measure in which no relevant estimated coefficients (shown in table 11.6b) were significant, at least at the 10 percent level, we assumed that the relevant figure displayed in table 11.10 was not statistically significant and therefore ignored it. Study results showed that conversion increased the growth rates of capital productivity, profitability, employment, and new product sales (table 11.10).

Conclusions and Implications for Distribution and Governance

Building on the empirical results presented in this chapter, one can speculate on certain governance and control, efficiency, and distributional

Table 11.10 China: Comparison of actual and estimated growth rates

Enterprise growth rate	VA/L	VA/K	Profit/sales	Employment	Wages (average)	Taxes/sales	New product/ sales	R&D expenditure/ sales
SOE								
Actual growth, t – 1 to 2001								
Converted	0.026	-0.028	-0.092	-0.054	0.047	-0.036	0.021	0.377
Unconverted	0.042	-0.025	-0.050	-0.067	0.058	0.007	-0.264	0.202
Estimated growth (resulting from conversion)	0.012[a]	0.041[a]	-0.032[a]	0.020[a]	-0.020[a]	0.007[a]	-0.268[a]	0.197[a]
COE								
Actual growth, t – 1 to 2001								
Converted	0.054	0.032	-0.037	-0.021	0.049	0.007	-0.217	0.081
Unconverted	0.043	-0.022	-0.071	-0.065	0.053	0.001	-0.278	0.153
Estimated growth (resulting from conversion)	0.033	0.067[a]	0.035[a]	0.035[a]	0.011	0.025	0.511[a]	0.025

COE = collective-owned enterprise
R&D = research and development
SOE = state-owned enterprise
VA/K = value added/net value of fixed assets
VA/L = value added/employment

a. At least one coefficient relevant to the total conversion effect is statistically significant at the 10 percent level or greater.

issues associated with China's shareholding experiment. With regard to its effects on corporate governance and control, Albert Keidel observed: "... control rather than ownership in China is clearly the most important issue. Because the ownership classification very often doesn't give you a clue about who really controls the enterprise ... the Party can govern who is the manager; [it] governs a lot of the goals of the enterprise in terms of its ancillary social investments ... even [for a] privately-owned enterprise. ..."[11] While we lacked data on pre and postconversion managerial control rights, the most robust of the documented performance changes strongly suggest that conversion has led to a reorientation of corporate goals and behavior. Extensive reallocation of effort and resources toward innovation—both R&D and new product development and sales—suggests two forms of change: (1) an emphasis on deep restructuring that entails process and product innovation, and (2) an extension of the time horizon of the firm's owners and management.

Distributive Implications

In addition to changes bearing on long-term efficiency, the conversion of Chinese SOEs to SHRs has distributive implications. In examining the normative or public-policy implications of these distribution effects, we conclude (table 11.10) the following:

- Conversion increases the growth rate of employment and slows wage growth. As table 11.10 shows, the rate of change of these variables is of equal and opposite magnitude. Thus, we surmise that, in the near-to-medium term, the tenure of incumbent workers is extended by conversion, while growth of their compensation is curtailed. Over the long term, the accumulation of nonstate investment and decline in the state's asset share tend to reverse the directions of change in employment and wages.

- Conversion has an insignificant effect on labor's income share. The share of the wage bill (product of employment and wage) in total sales revenue shows no change as a result of either the direct effect of conversion or the subsequent decline in state asset share. Therefore, in China, to date, conversion does not appear to have affected appreciably the income distribution between labor and capital.

---

11. Albert Keidel is senior associate at the Carnegie Endowment for International Peace (CEIP). A transcript of Keidel's comments on an earlier draft of this chapter was presented at the conference on Distributional Consequences of Privatization, Center for Global Development, DC, February 23–24, 2003. Minxin Pei, senior associate and director of the China Program at CEIP, also raised the issue of implications of enterprise restructuring in China for governance.

- Following conversion, at least among the SHRs within this study sample, the state and the public retain the assets that had existed in the pre-converted SOEs. Decline in state asset shares results not from the dissolution of state assets either by sale or stripping—rather, it results from converted enterprises' ability to attract new investment.

- Although we lack data on the assets managers own, we anticipate that, because managers tend to serve as key players in the process of converting Chinese SOEs to SHRs and because nonstate stakeholders' asset ownership has increased significantly, managers will capture a portion of the new assets that enter the firm. We have no reason to believe that the findings of Li, Li, and Zhang (2000) and Dong, Bowles, and Ho (2002b) are not applicable to this study's sample—that is, as the principal instigators of ownership reform, which results, on average, in a doubling of nonstate assets within the firm, managers of converted enterprises increase their net wealth.

- Evidence in support of deep restructuring—expansion of R&D and new product development, as well as short- and medium-term efficiency gains resulting from conversion—suggests that those who maintain an employment or financial interest in the firm stand to gain over time.

- Beyond the immediate stakeholders of the firm, China's consumer sector benefits from resources drawn into R&D and innovation. During the past 10 to 15 years, a striking range of consumer goods and improvements in medical technologies and education sectors, including increased access to computer and telecommunications equipment, have become widely available in China. Thus, conversion appears to contribute to product quality and variety.

- As a result of the concentration of SOEs in China's northeastern and eastern regions and the somewhat higher probability of their conversion in these regions, stakeholders residing in coastal provinces are more likely to benefit from China's shareholding experiment than those in other regions. By comparison, in northern and southwestern provinces—China's two poorest regions—SOEs are scattered, and their probability of conversion is somewhat less. Thus, such biases may cause China's shareholding experiment to contribute to growing regional inequality.

Public-Policy Implications

Two key normative aspects of the distributive findings outlined above are

- the role of growing inequality in China's economy, and
- appropriate public-policy measures to deal with the growing inequality.

The implications of the distributive effect of enterprise restructuring differ across countries and regions. In Latin America, for example, privatization that exacerbates an already skewed distribution of income should be—and, for the most part, is—viewed critically. In China, by contrast, restructuring that creates skewed asset ownership may be a more defensible phenomenon. The reasoning is that, before China's economic reforms, accumulation of personal wealth was generally banned; thus, it is inevitable that introducing elements of a market economy would lead to greater inequality of wages and assets. In short, increasing inequity may be a painful, but necessary, price that must be paid to transit to a more dynamic economic system. Independent of the conversion of China's domestic SOEs, introducing foreign investment and the entry of private enterprise would also lead to skewing.

This background leads to two observations. First, the original SOE stakeholders may perceive that conversion leads to more unequal distribution of assets. From a broader perspective, by increasing China's emergent managerial and entrepreneurial class, SOE conversion creates a source of innovation in the country's economy—factors in scarce supply before ownership reform. By helping to enlarge China's entrepreneurial and investment class, and possibly competing away some of the monopoly rents captured by emergent entrepreneurs and investors, the shareholding experiment, arguably, is creating more, not less, equality.

The second issue centers on ideal income distribution.[12] Most analysts and many ordinary Chinese citizens would agree that, during the period of central planning and socialist ownership, opportunities for personal investment in human, financial, and physical capital and prospects of a competitive return on such investment were too limited. China's income and asset distribution was far too uniform. SOE conversion is one avenue to redress this inefficiency. While growth of inequality may be a necessary and desirable aspect of China's economic transition, a key issue is whether reallocation and accumulation of income and assets are being accomplished through an appropriately transparent and fair process. While anecdotal evidence suggests that aspects of the conversion process are not transparent and equitable, we infer, at least from this limited study sample, that assets the state retained at the beginning of the process remain intact. In contrast to many documented instances in Eastern and Central Europe and the former Soviet Union, this study sample does not reveal widespread evidence of asset stripping.

What is the appropriate policy response to the finding that enterprise conversion contributes to inequality—assuming that the shareholding conversion process in China is generally lawful and legitimate? Public control

---

12. Forbes (2000), for example, found that, on average, countries grow faster if their Gini coefficient is lower; over time, however, individual countries that lower their Gini coefficients face slower growth of overall living standards.

over corporate governance is but one of many instruments available to governments in their pursuit of equity. Others include taxation, education, economic freedom (e.g., mobility), and international trade policies. Across China, provincial and local governments are attempting to construct effective unemployment, pension, and other social insurance systems—at least in urban areas where SOEs are being converted. Compared with established systems in other industrialized economies, these institutional arrangements remain rudimentary; however, by facilitating the transfer of workers across firms, they may serve as a more effective avenue of remunerative employment than the relatively uncompetitive jobs sustained through government impediments to enterprise conversion and restructuring.

China remains in the early stages of movement toward private control of corporate activity; thus, it is still too soon to draw conclusions about shareholding reform's effects on wealth and income distribution across Chinese society. As shown above, the various channels through which conversion affects enterprise performance and distribution of rewards often operate in countervailing directions. Through 2001, for example, the shareholding experiment reduced layoffs and simultaneously slowed wage growth. However, the longer-term, induced effect suggests a reversal that reflects privatization outcomes in other countries. This study observed a robust shift in resources toward innovation and investment following conversion; however, it is premature to anticipate these changes' sustainability or measure their precise effect.

Finally, China's shareholding experiment is contributing to the emergence of an increasingly broad-based managerial and professional class. The extent to which this emergent class uses these assets effectively to create new employment and more broadly disperse wealth remains unclear. Overall, China's shareholding experiment is apparently creating a more vibrant enterprise system, providing opportunities for nonstate investment, innovation, and new product development. In the immediate aftermath of conversion, labor's employment and income shares remain undiminished. The largest distributive effect is likely an enlargement of China's managerial and entrepreneurial class, centered mainly in the country's coastal regions.

References

Birdsall, Nancy, and John Nellis. 2002. *Winners and Losers: Assessing the Distributional Impact of Privatization.* Working Paper 6. Washington: Center for Global Development.

Djankov, Simeon, and Peter Murrell. 2002. Enterprise Restructuring in Transition: A Quantitative Survey. *Journal of Economic Literature* 40, no. 3: 739–92.

Dong, Xiao-yuan, Paul Bowles, and Samuel P. S. Ho. 2002a. The Determinants of Employee Ownership in China's Privatized Rural Industry: Evidence from Jiangsu and Shandong. *Journal of Comparative Economics* 30: 415–37.

Dong, Xiao-yuan, Paul Bowles, and Samuel P. S. Ho. 2002b. Share Ownership and Employee Attitudes: Some Evidence from China's Postprivatization Rural Industry. *Journal of Comparative Economics* 30, no. 4: 812–35.

Fan, Gang. 2002. Progress in Ownership Changes and Hidden Risks in China's Transition. *Transition Newsletter* 133 (May-June): 1–5.

Forbes, Kristen J. 2000. A Reassessment of the Relationship Between Inequality and Growth. *American Economic Review* 90, no. 4: 868–87.

Jefferson, Gary H., Mai Lu, and John Z. Q. Zhao. 1998. Reforming Property Rights in Chinese Industry. In *Enterprise Reform in China: Ownership, Transition, and Performance*, ed. G. Jefferson and I. Singh. New York: Oxford University Press.

Jefferson, Gary H., Ping Zhang, and John. Z. Q. Zhao. 1998. Structure, Authority, and Incentives in Chinese Industry. In *Enterprise Reform in China: Ownership, Transition, and Performance*, ed. G. Jefferson and I. Singh. New York: Oxford University Press.

Jefferson, Gary H., Thomas G. Rawski, Li Wang, and Yuxin Zheng. 2000. Ownership, Productivity Change, and Financial Performance in Chinese Industry. *Journal of Comparative Economics* 28, no. 4: 786–813.

Li, Hongbin, and Scott Rozelle. 2000. Savings or Stripping Rural Industry: An Analysis of Privatization and Efficiency in China. *Agricultural Economics* 23, no. 3: 241–52.

Li, Shaomin, Shuhe Li, and Weiying Zhang. 2000. The Road to Capitalism: Competition and Institutional Change in China. *Journal of Comparative Economics* 28: 269–92.

McMillan, John, and Barry Naughton. 1992. How To Reform a Planned Economy: Lessons from China. *Oxford Review of Economics and Politics* 8, no. 1: 130–43.

Megginson, William L., and Jeffrey M. Netter. 2001. From State to Market: A Survey of Empirical Studies on Privatization. *Journal of Economic Literature* 39, no. 2: 321–89.

Naughton, Barry. 1992. Implications of the State Monopoly over Industry and Its Relaxation. *Modern China* 18, no. 1: 14–41.

Rawski, Thomas G. 2002. Recent Developments in China's Labor Market. Report prepared for the International Policy Group, International Labor Office, Geneva.

Tian, George Lihu. 2000. *State Shareholding and Corporate Performance: A Study of a Unique Chinese Enterprise Data Set*. Working paper. London Business School.

Su, Jian, and Gary H. Jefferson. 2003. The Determinants of Decentralized Privatization: Theory and Evidence from China. Graduate School of Economics and Finance, Brandeis University. Photocopy.

Weitzman, Martin, and Chenggang Xu. 1994. Chinese Township and Village Enterprises as Vaguely Defined Cooperatives. *Journal of Comparative Economics* 18, no. 2: 121–45.

Appendix 11A
Concordance of Ownership Classifications, 1994 and 1999

| Ownership category | Code (year) | |
	1994	1999
State		
State-owned enterprises	11	110
State-owned, jointly operated enterprises	12	141
Wholly state-owned companies	n.a.	151
Collective		
Collective-owned enterprises	21	120
Shareholding cooperatives	n.a.	130
Collective, jointly operated enterprises	22	142
Hong Kong, Macao, and Taiwan		
Overseas joint ventures	81	210
Overseas cooperatives	82	220
Overseas, wholly owned enterprises	83	230
Overseas shareholding limited companies	n.a.	240
Foreign		
Foreign joint ventures	71	310
Foreign cooperatives	72	320
Foreign, wholly owned enterprises	73	330
Foreign shareholding limited companies	n.a.	340
Shareholding		
Limited liability company	62	159
Shareholding limited companies	61	160
Private		
Private, wholly owned enterprises	31	171
Private cooperative enterprises	32	172
Private limited-liability companies	33	173
Private shareholding companies		174
Other domestic		
State-collective, jointly operated enterprises	51	143
State-private, jointly operated enterprises	52	n.a.
Collective-private, jointly operated enterprises	53	n.a.
State-collective-private, jointly operated enterprises	54	n.a.
Other jointly operated enterprises	n.a.	149
Other enterprises	90	190

n.a. = not applicable

Source: National Bureau of Statistics large and medium-size industrial enterprise dataset, 1995–2001.

Appendix 11B
The Endogeneity Issue

One insufficiently investigated issue in this chapter is endogeneity. Looking at equation (11.), one might anticipate that, in deciding whether to invest, a potential nonstate investor considers the rate of change in one or more of the performance measures—i.e., dependent variables. To illustrate, if investment is attracted to firms that enjoy the most robust growth of profitability, then the rate of nonstate investment and the dependent variable, $\Delta lnST\_SH_{t-1\,to\,01}$, will be correlated for two reasons. First, nonstate investment may be raising profitability, the effect that coefficient α_2 is intended to capture. Second, such investment will further strengthen the link between investment and profitability. This reverse causality from profit growth to reduction in state asset share will cause econometric estimates of the magnitude of α_2 to be biased upward. The estimation procedure attributes more importance than it should to the effect of nonstate investment—i.e., reductions in state-asset share.

In principle, one of two approaches to address the problem of simultaneity bias can be used. The first is to create an instrumental variable for $\Delta lnST\_SH_{t-1\,to\,01}$, which this study attempted without success.[13] The second is to create a lag structure between the dependent and independent variables. Again, illustrating this remedy for the case of investment and profitability, this second approach is justified if one expects investment to act on profitability with a lag, but does not expect profitability to affect past values of investment (which it might if investors correctly anticipated patterns of profitability). Under the condition of unidirectionality of causality, from current investment to future profitability, a lag structure should mitigate any tendency toward endogeneity of the investment decision and bias in estimates.

To correct for potential endogeneity, this study lagged the asset ownership variable by one year and reestimated the eight performance equations. With two exceptions, the pattern of estimates for the contemporaneous and lagged values of the dependent variable, $\Delta lnST\_SH_{t-1\,to\,01}$, are similar. Notable changes appear in the capital productivity equation, in which the estimate on the lagged asset variable becomes statistically insignificant. At the same time, compared with the estimate shown in table 11.6a, the coefficient on the lagged asset variable in the profit equation becomes statistically significant. The remaining estimates retain levels of statistical significance comparable to those reported using the original contemporaneous time structure. That estimates of the coefficient on lagged values of $\Delta lnST\_SH_{t-1\,to\,01}$ in the capital

---

13. The authors attempted a variety of instrumental variables, for $\Delta lnZ_{j,t-1\,to\,01}$; however, none reported an adjusted R-square in excess of 0.06.

productivity equation turn insignificant suggest that investment behavior may be particularly sensitive to capital productivity.

While high growth of profitability would attract a high rate of investment, the absence of any evidence of endogeneity in the contemporaneous estimates may result from the measure of profit the study used, which was not observed profit. Rather, it was sales profit, the difference between sales revenue and production cost of goods sold, which omits overhead, pension obligations, income taxes, and other indirect costs.

12

Assessing Privatization in Sri Lanka: Distribution and Governance

MALATHY KNIGHT-JOHN
and P. P. A. WASANTHA ATHUKORALA

In Sri Lanka, privatization is ideologically allied to the liberalization process that jumpstarted the economy in 1977. It was only a decade later, however, that privatization became a state policy, and after 1989 that the sale of public enterprises began to gather momentum. This slow start to privatization is largely attributed to the continued use of state-owned enterprises (SOEs) as vehicles of employment and political patronage (Knight-John 1995).

The 1977–89 period, characterized by macroeconomic instability and political violence, was not conducive to rigorous reform efforts. During the first wave of privatization (1989–94), the government divested 43 commercial enterprises (typified as relatively less complex), raising about rupees (Rs.) 11.6 billion.[1] The second wave of privatization (1995–present), which has witnessed the divestiture and restructuring of several public utilities and major ventures in the services sector, amounts to Rs.46.2 billion.

More recently, the need for structural reforms, including privatization, has been accentuated by the country's dismal economic performance, stemming from a series of adverse external shocks, domestic political uncertainties, and entrenched structural rigidities. In 2001, the economy recorded a negative real growth rate of 1.5 percent—the first economic contraction since

Malathy Knight-John is a research fellow at the Institute of Policy Studies in Colombo, Sri Lanka. P.P.A. Wasantha Athukorala is a lecturer in the department of economics at the University of Peradeniya, Sri Lanka. The authors gratefully acknowledge Saman Kelegama and other colleagues at the Institute of Policy Studies for their valuable comments on earlier drafts of this chapter.

1. In this chapter, the term *divestiture* refers to both a partial and total sale of state assets to private parties (the one exception is the Public Enterprise Reform Commission [PERC], which classifies six licenses to import and market finished lubricants as divestiture).

independence in 1948—and the public debt to GDP ratio reached 103.2 percent (Central Bank of Sri Lanka 2001a). While a Stand-By Arrangement (SBA) with the International Monetary Fund (IMF), signed in April 2001, eased some of the burden, in terms of external reserve losses, only strong policy commitment and intensive structural reforms can provide long-term economic relief.[2]

In the current context of economic crisis, privatization's distributional effects require policy prioritization. As the World Bank (2002) emphasized, the burden of macroeconomic crises falls disproportionately on the poor. In an environment of slow or negative growth, high inflation, and high unemployment, such issues as who reaps the benefits of privatization and how the government uses the proceeds from privatization become increasingly pertinent. These distributional questions are especially important given that most of the remaining transactions and those completed during the second wave are in the services and plantations[3] sectors, where price, access, and labor issues are particularly significant. Moreover, given the ongoing political conflict, ignoring equity considerations will have severe adverse economic, social, and political effects on the country.[4]

This chapter documents and analyzes Sri Lanka's privatization program of 1989–2002 from a distributional perspective. It aims to identify the program's winners and losers, consider the government's role in devising the form of privatization and mitigating adverse distributional effects, and to better grasp the political economy forces that structure, condition, and ultimately shape the outcome of the privatization process. The chapter is structured according to the conceptual framework outlined in Birdsall and Nellis (2002).

Study Methods and Limitations

Research for this study was conducted mainly through interviews with key stakeholders from eight selected companies and policymakers from such agencies as the Ministry of Finance, PERC, and the Colombo Stock Exchange and (CSE).[5] Secondary data from the Central Bank, World Bank, and CSE, as well as academic publications by local privatization experts, complemented the interview data. The set of companies selected for the study does not represent a random sample; their choice was governed by

---

2. Under the SBA, the government agreed to deepening the privatization process.

3. Sri Lanka's plantation sector has a large resident labor population.

4. Even if privatization is not the cause of the poor's economic and social problems, the perception that it causes or exacerbates inequitable income distribution could create political opposition to the privatization process, irrespective of its costs or benefits to society.

5. Appendix 12A briefly describes each target company, and appendix 12B contains the study questionnaire.

data availability and the need to ensure a suitable mix between entities in the manufacturing, services/utilities and plantation sectors in the first and second waves of privatization.

The paucity and incompleteness of existing data present the biggest obstacle to a rigorous analysis of privatization's distributional effects in Sri Lanka. A notable feature, with likely adverse consequences for public policy, is the general unwillingness of players in privatization transactions to divulge information on the process. Thus, lacking sufficient data, much of the study is necessarily based on anecdotal information.

Moreover, vital bits of information—for example, the link between utility privatization and the poor—could not be fully evaluated because of lack of datasets on relevant household-level observations. The latest available household survey is based on 1996–97 data and the two utilities selected for this study: Colombo Gas Company Ltd. (CGCL) and Sri Lanka Telecom (SLT) (privatized in 1995 and 1997, respectively). As such, the study could only use household-level data related to the gas sector.

Socioeconomic Profile

Sri Lanka is a lower-middle-income country, with a per capita GDP of $872, as of 2002.[6] Since independence, GDP growth has averaged 4 to 5 percent, with the civil war depressing growth by an estimated 2 percent per year since 1983.[7] Arunatilake, Jayasuriya, and Kelegama (2001) estimate the economic cost of the war from 1983–96 at about 168 percent of 1996 GDP, equivalent to $20.6 billion.

In mid-2002, Sri Lanka's population totaled approximately 19 million— with about 80 percent residing in rural areas—and a growth rate of about 1.5 percent. In 2001, labor-force participation was 48.3 percent, and the unemployment rate was 7.8 percent. Approximately 32 to 35 percent of the labor force was employed in the agriculture sector. Given the country's social upheavals, it is particularly disturbing that most of the unemployed are youth: for those 14-to-18 years of age, the unemployment rate is about 36 percent; and for those 19-to-25 years of age, the rate is about 30 percent. Among educated youth, unemployment is approximately 24 percent.

Compared with other countries at a similar level of development, Sri Lanka has a relatively advanced social development status. Life expectancy is 73 years, infant mortality is 15 per 1,000 live births, maternal mortality rate is 23 per 100,000, and adult literacy is 93 percent. Even so, approximately 22 percent of Sri Lankans live below the poverty line.

---

6. The information in this section draws largely from Central Bank of Sri Lanka (2001a) and the Government of Sri Lanka's Draft Poverty Reduction Strategy from April 2002.

7. During the 1990s, per capita GDP growth averaged about 5 percent per year.

Over the last two decades, income equality has improved relatively, though not substantially. During this period, the Gini coefficient, an indicator of income distribution, declined marginally for income receivers (from 0.52 in 1981–82 to 0.48 in 1996–97). A comparison of the two surveys suggests that absolute poverty decreased marginally between 1990–91 and 1996–97 (from 20 to 19 percent, according to the lower poverty line, and from 33 to 31 percent, according to the higher poverty line). Because of unreliable data, it is not possible to determine how the poverty level changed during the late 1990s. However, the incidence of consumption poverty (head count index) varies significantly across provincial boundaries; the Uva, northwestern, and north central provinces have significantly higher levels of poverty than do the other provinces. According to the higher poverty line, Uva province recorded the highest incidence (55 percent), while the Western province had the lowest (23 percent). A breakdown of incidence of poverty by sector indicates that rural and estate (plantation) sectors have a relatively higher level of vulnerability. The evidence shows that chronic and transitory poverty combined affects about 25 percent of the urban population and 41 to 45 percent of those in the rural and estate sectors, respectively.

The poor also have limited access to basic services—for example, people living in remote areas lack access to markets, information, and basic infrastructure facilities (e.g., good roads, rail, and port systems; well-functioning bus transportation systems; telecommunications networks; and information technology). While basic education and health facilities are widely available, the quality of services available to the poor is vastly inferior to that available to better-off, urban households.

Evolution of Privatization Program

When liberalization began in 1977, the state sector played a significant role in all spheres of the country's economic activities, reflecting the highly interventionist policies adopted from the mid-1950s to the late 1970s.[8] During this period, the government set up new public enterprises, nationalized several private entities, and created state monopolies. The state secured public support for these policies by emphasizing such populist goals as employment creation, price controls on essential goods and services, distributional equity and regional development in SOE operations.

According to Kelegama (1997a), as a percentage of GDP, the SOE sector grew from about 5.7 percent in 1961 to 12.2 percent in 1974, and to more

---

8. In 1965–70, a brief, unsuccessful attempt at liberalization was undertaken, in collaboration with international financial institutions.

than 15 percent in 1977. By 1977, the public sector accounted for about one-third of investment and 40 percent of formal-sector employment. Even after 1977, the state sector continued to expand as a result of the large donor-funded infrastructure projects implemented and the political economy factors that restricted the government's ability to carry out intensive public-sector reforms.

Many of these public enterprises became loss-making entities, plagued with problems of overstaffing, mismanagement and corruption, inefficient procurement systems, and excessive government intervention and politicization. Budgetary transfers to SOEs, averaging about 10 percent of GDP in the mid-1980s, were highly unsustainable. Although budget speeches of the then government mentioned privatization, the final push came only after the World Bank highlighted the urgent need to address the massive burden that the state sector imposed on the budget. In 1987, privatization was announced as a state policy, with the primary objectives of alleviating fiscal burden and improving enterprise efficiency through private-sector norms.[9]

Privatization's other stated objectives were encouraging development of an entrepreneurial middle-class, broad-basing share ownership, and activating the capital market. Popular support was sought by dubbing the process "peoplization," meaning handing back the people's assets from the bureaucrats to the people. A presidential decree stated that workers should not lose their jobs as a result of privatization. During the second wave of privatization after 1994, such objectives as "enhancing investment, employment, and quality of service in the privatized sectors"[10] were added to the government's stated expectations from the privatization program. In practice, however, fiscal imperatives—both reducing expenditure on SOEs and raising revenue from the sale of state assets—have influenced and shaped both phases of privatization.[11]

The modalities for privatization varied somewhat. The most widely used approach was the 51:30:10 formula, whereby a major shareholding of about 51 to 60 percent of an SOE was sold to a corporate investor on the basis of open tenders and competitive bidding; 30 percent of equity was offered on par to the public; and 10 percent was given free of charge to employees based on their length of service. The rationale for the strategy was that corporate investors were given majority share ownership as an incentive to transfer technology and invest productive capital in the enterprises; the

---

9. Knight-John (1995) documents details of the few random privatization transactions initiated between 1977 and 1989.

10. Quoted from policy statement by Sri Lankan President Chandrika Bandaranaike Kumaratunga, January 1995.

11. Jayasuriya and Knight-John (2002) argue that penetration of rent-seeking activities under weak regulatory conditions, such as those in Sri Lanka, can dilute long-term fiscal benefits through efficiency gains.

public share offering aimed at boosting a shallow capital market and widening share ownership, while the employee share ownership plan (ESOP) was put in place to win the support of trade unions, a group traditionally opposed to privatization.

This standard formula deviated somewhat in the case of particular enterprises: employee buy-outs (Buhari Hotel); gifting of 50 percent of shares to workers in the bus transportation sector; sale of assets of public corporations with the state assuming the liabilities (Ceylon Plywood Corporation); negotiated sale of shares (Thulhiriya Textile Mills to a South Korean company, Kabool); and management contracts (plantation sector).

The five-year management contracts earlier used in the plantation sector were a disincentive to longer-term capital investment in this industry. Thus, in 1995, steps were taken to divest 51 percent of shares of profit-making plantation companies, with the initial offer for purchase made to the management company. Fifty-one percent of loss-making companies were later sold on an all-or-nothing basis on the CSE. More recently in October 2002, a 39 percent stake of six bus companies was to be sold on an all-or-nothing basis on the CSE, with seven other companies in the pipeline for sale. Plans were also underway to forge a management agreement with the successful investor in the transaction. However, difficulties in determining these bus companies' current shareholding structure have delayed this transaction.

During the first wave of privatization, four principles determined which assets were chosen to sell:

- The SOE had the potential to be turned around with an infusion of private-sector capital and technology;

- The stock market had the capacity to absorb the privatized enterprise;

- The enterprise was not involved in an essential economic activity; and

- The enterprise provided little revenue to, or required substantial transfers from, the government.

According to Crowe and de Soysa (1995), the SOEs chosen for divestiture at that time received few public transfers.

By the time the second wave began, the privatization program had graduated to a stage where it could undertake reforms in sectors involved in core economic activities, such as utilities and plantations. According to the PERC and Central Bank reports, 86 SOEs were privatized from December 1989 to September 2002 in the manufacturing, trade, agriculture, plantations, petroleum, financial, utility, and services sectors. However, according to the Central Bank of Sri Lanka (2001a), more than 70 public enterprises still operate in these various sectors of the economy, with cumulative losses in 2000 estimated at about 2 percent of GDP.

Institutional, Legal, and Regulatory Framework

Following the 1987 announcement of privatization as state policy, several measures were undertaken to set up the necessary legal, institutional, and regulatory structures for reform. Two pieces of legislation—Conversion of Government Owned Business Undertakings into Public Corporations Act No. 22 and Conversion of Public Corporations or Government Owned Business Undertakings into Public Companies Act No. 23—were enacted in 1987 to facilitate commercialization of SOEs.

The Public Enterprise Rehabilitation Act, passed in 1996, primarily protected the interests of workers in failed privatized enterprises and limited industrial disputes and social unrest. Under this Act, seven entities were revested with the government, at a cost of nearly Rs.1 billion to the Treasury.[12] However, this Act was operational for only six months, because the private-sector chambers of commerce began voicing concerns about renationalization, and the government did not want to send the wrong signals to the investor community.

Several successive institutions—Presidential Commission on Privatization (later renamed Presidential Committee on Peoplization), Public Investment Management Board, and Commercialization of Public Enterprises Division (COPED), Ministry of Finance—were developed in 1987–95 to facilitate the privatization process. The new Plantation Restructuring Unit handled privatization of the plantation sector, and a special unit in the Ministry of Industries oversaw privatization of industrial enterprises.

These changes in the institutional framework and diversification of responsibility for the privatization program to various institutions were caused largely by the political climate at the time. With the president facing impeachment proceedings, coalition management was the primary objective of political leadership. Given the need for coalition building, support of the line ministries was vital, and it was not politically feasible to restrict management of the privatization program to one umbrella institution. The involvement of these various line ministries, with their ministers' respective political agendas, led to a systemic politicization of the privatization process.

Politicization of the implementation network raised questions about COPED's transparency, with allegations of closed-door deals by those opposed to the sale of public assets. To a certain extent, transparency was sacrificed for speed of execution, with policymakers preferring a relatively rapid sale of assets. External donor pressure and the government's desire to prove its commitment drove the need for fast-paced privatization.

In its election campaign, the administration that assumed power in 1994 highlighted the alleged corruption associated with the privatization

---

12. Three of these enterprises were later reprivatized.

program of its predecessor as a major issue. In 1996, PERC was set up under an Act of Parliament to undertake sole responsibility for the privatization program, with the stated intention of effecting privatization in a structured and transparent environment.

Transparency and access to information with regard to the privatization program improved with establishment of the new institution. Publication of annual reports and other materials, frequent press notices, and the posting of pertinent transaction details on a PERC Web site have, to some extent, increased the public's awareness of the privatization process. However, allegations of questionable deals still prevail.

Several regulatory bodies linked to the program aim to ensure that privatization will bring about both allocative efficiency and distributional equity. However, weak regulatory governance is a major obstacle to realization of positive distributional effects.

Sri Lanka lacks a comprehensive, effective competition policy framework, a prerequisite for an economy moving toward greater private-sector activity. Until early 2003, the Fair Trade Commission, set up in 1987, handled issues related to monopolies, mergers and acquisitions, and anti-competitive behavior. The Department of Internal Trade (DIT), established in 1979, dealt with consumer protection matters. The institutional separation of these complementary functions proved extremely inefficient, and the government eventually integrated the two bodies into the Consumer Affairs Authority (CAA).

However, the process of instituting a competition policy framework faces many challenges, with no assurance that the new authority is equipped to handle the increased private-sector activity. At the time of this writing, the new authority was to be stripped of its powers to consider monopolies and mergers and would function solely as a consumer protection agency. Although reports of a separate Monopolies and Mergers Commission abound in the press, no such body has been created. While it is conceivable and justifiable that the government may want to abolish the perception of a restrictive regulatory regime in order to attract investment and facilitate efficiency-enhancing mergers, the current gap in the competition policy framework is a recipe for disaster.

Currently, sectoral regulation exists more in name than reality, in the cases of bus transport (National Transport Commission) and telecommunications (Telecommunications Regulatory Authority) services.[13] Links between competition policy/consumer protection authorities and these sectoral regulators, essential for ensuring that competition and distributional goals are met, are rare. The financial sector has relatively more effective

---

13. For details on Sri Lanka's telecommunications regulation, see Jayasuriya and Knight-John (2002). Establishment of a multisector regulatory framework encompassing the water, power, and energy sectors is in the final stages of implementation.

regulation, handled by the Bank and Non-Bank Supervision Division of the Central Bank, the Securities and Exchange Commission (SEC), and the Insurance Board, set up in 2001 to supervise the insurance industry.

Lessons from Earlier Studies

To date, no studies have looked at the distributional effects of Sri Lanka's privatization using formal empirical methods, such as cost-benefit analyses or construction of elaborate counterfactual models. For lack of data, this study, as well as earlier ones, has been forced to use a second-best approach of the case study.

Kelegama (1995) conducted a seminal study on Sri Lanka's privatization and equity, which traces the distributional consequences of the privatization process from inception until 1993, the period characterized as the first wave. This chapter looks, inter alia, at the distributional implications of the divestiture modalities, pricing and valuation of entities for sale, privatization's employment effects, use of sales proceeds, and privatization's social effects (e.g., regional effects and ramifications of removing state subsidies).

The study found that the government underpriced shares of the entities sold on the stock exchange in order to promote share ownership in a larger proportion of the population, minimize new investors' financial risk, and avoid overburdening the domestic capital market. Although the sales were a success—nearly all share issues were oversubscribed—most of these shares were bought by the relatively wealthy. Substantial, persistent underpricing of SOEs came at a high cost to the state, given that the share price of many privatized entities rose considerably immediately after divesture.

Along with the government's deliberate effort to keep share prices low, SOE sale prices were affected by Valuation Department capacity problems and the rapid pace of the divestiture program (as the structural adjustment recommendations of the World Bank and IMF insisted). Another political economy consideration for the low sale prices was the quest to attract foreign capital, with associated technological know-how.[14]

Kelegama (1995) reviewed the ESOP's distributional effect on workers in the entities being privatized. The policy decision to distribute free shares to these employees had three objectives: (1) give workers greater incentive for dedicated work through the sharing of profits, (2) safeguard employee rights by giving them a voice in decision making, and (3) making trade unions more receptive to privatization. The study argues, however, that only the last objective was realized, and to a limited extent because many workers tended to dispose quickly of their shares to meet personal financial commitments.

---

14. Plantation-sector privatization is a classic case of underpricing, where the market clearing price for a 20 percent stake of the profitmaking entities offered on the stock exchange was also the price set for the 51 percent majority stake.

Kelegama (1995) also notes that privatized entities are located predominately in urban areas and the more developed provinces and districts. This reality creates the possibility of worker discontent, given the asymmetric and more privileged position of workers in privatized enterprises—with share ownership, wage increases, and long-term dividend payments (some workers did retain their shares)—compared with those in other entities. Kelegama posits that the goal of public benefit—theoretically the driving force of SOEs—became secondary to that of revenue maximization. Divestiture proceeds, for example, were used primarily to address the fiscal deficit resulting from high levels of debt servicing and defense expenditure; investment of these monies in infrastructure or social welfare projects was, at best, marginal. In addition, removal of state subsidies and resulting price increases associated with the privatization program negatively affected the general public (most clearly seen in the bus transportation case).

A more recent study on privatization's effects on Sri Lanka's employment—specifically, the labor retrenchment experience—is that of Kelegama and Salih (1998). The study focuses on three key issues: voluntary versus involuntary retrenchment, using a compensation package as a safety net, and pre versus postprivatization retrenchment. The findings show that the adverse selection problem tends to undermine voluntary retirement packages; fixed compensation packages prove superior to flexible ones, given rent-seeking trade union behavior and downwardly rigid compensation packages; and preprivatization retrenchment may be suboptimal since it fails to account for more efficient postprivatization restructuring options.

Kelegama (1997b) offers interesting insight into the privatization process's political economy:

> The Sri Lankan experience shows that the acts of divestiture defy enunciations of underlying rationale or orderly policy. As in the case of nationalization, privatization consisting of a series of political actions which are guided by diverse, sometimes conflicting factors, implemented by different governments and people, discerning some order out of an essentially disorderly situation could be an academic exercise of little interest to the doers. Even if some enunciation of broad policy could be made, political expediency would compel the practitioners to choose the most feasible path of action, and yet be consistent, given the inevitably broad general character of the policy statement. (92)

Expanding on this argument, one could speculate that, in choosing the most feasible path of action in the face of the political-economy constraints linked to privatization—for example, instituting a rapid divestiture program in an uncertain political milieu when investor interest is minimal—maintaining transparency may not be a priority for implementers, giving rise to allegations of questionable transactions, such as those highlighted in Kelegama (1997b). In the early years, the perception of shady deals was only enhanced by lack of an effective regulatory framework to support the privatization program, reflecting the prevalent thinking at the time that regulatory intervention would restrict flexibility of the privatization exercise.

**Table 12.1   Gross and net privatization proceeds
as a percent of GDP, selected years**

Year	Gross proceeds (Rs. million)	Gross proceeds (percent of GDP)	Net proceeds (percent of GDP)
1990	588.3	0.2	0.10
1992	4,423.5	1.1	0.55
1993	4,918.6	0.9	0.45
1995	3,124.6	0.5	0.25
1996	4,542.0	0.6	0.30
1997	22,396.0	2.5	1.25
1998	4,516.0	0.4	0.20
2001	8,601.0	0.6	0.30

Sources: Central Bank and PERC annual reports and COPED data.

Evaluating Privatization's Distributional Effects

The principal questions this chapter addresses involve privatization's fiscal
and investment effects and their link to distributional concerns.

Macroeconomic Effects

During 1989–2002, Sri Lanka's gross proceeds amounted to more than Rs.57
billion. An official figure for net proceeds over this period is unavailable,
given that government expenses incurred before privatization for administration, sale, and enterprise restructuring have not been systematically documented. However, we attempt to estimate them, based on IMF estimates,
which found, in a sample set of 18 countries, net proceeds averaged about
half of gross proceeds (IMF 2000) (table 12.1).

Proceeds from the first wave of privatization were not used methodically
for budgetary management or to retire public debt. Kelegama (1997a) estimated that privatization during this period would contribute to an average reduction in the budget deficit of only about 0.6 percent per year.
Privatization proceeds went into a fungible consolidated fund, where they
were bundled with other sources of fiscal revenue. These monies were used
mostly to finance current expenditures. According to the Central Bank of Sri
Lanka (2001a), social expenditures throughout the privatization period have
remained at about 1 percent of GDP. In terms of distribution, additional privatization proceeds have not been used for social investment projects.

The situation improved after 1995, when privatization proceeds were
used more systematically for debt reduction. In the much-cited, Sri Lankan
Telecommunications (SLT) case, the government used a substantial portion
of the proceeds to retire part of its public debt, thereby lowering the stock
of debt, as a percentage of GDP, from 93 percent (1996) to 86 percent (1997).
The hope was to reduce interest costs, which posed a major impediment to
private-sector activity.

Figure 12.1 Divestiture proceeds and debt burden, selected years
(as percent of GDP)

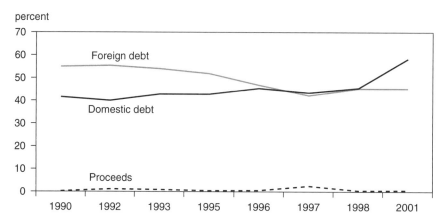

Source: Central Bank annual reports.

Central Bank annual reports show that, as a percentage of GDP, public debt decreased from 1995 to 1997, reflecting, at least in part, the use of privatization proceeds to retire debt. The subsequent increase from 1998 to 2000 reflects the decline in privatization proceeds during those years.[15] The exceptionally high level of public debt in 2001 stemmed mainly from the increased rupee value of foreign debt, brought about by depreciation of the exchange rate during the year, an oil price hike, and increased military hardware purchases in 2000. The emerging story is that the fiscal crisis (and any negative distributional fallout from it) would probably have been worse without privatization.

The divestiture program was undertaken within the context of a civil war, which has taken a tremendous toll on state resources, and in a macroeconomic milieu where public debt exceeded 100 percent of GDP. Total proceeds from privatization, for example, would cover only one year's defense expenditure, on average. The July 2001 terrorist attack on Sri Lanka's international airport illustrates how small a proportion divestiture proceeds are within the country's political context. In that attack, the government incurred losses of about Rs.28.8 billion (nearly six times the Rs.5 billion the country earned from privatizing the national airline industry). Figure 12.1, which maps privatization proceeds against Sri Lanka's foreign and domestic debt, further illustrates this point.

Table 12.2 and figure 12.2 show that the sales receipts from privatization have, for most of the companies studied, totaled more than the net change in revenue flows to the government before and after privatization.

---

15. As a percentage of GDP, privatization proceeds were negligible in 1999 and 2000.

Table 12.2 Sales receipts and average revenue flows to the government before and after privatization (net present value)[a]

Company	Before privatization (Rs. million)	Number of years	After privatization (Rs. million)	Number of years	Change (Rs. million)	Sales price (Rs. million)
Sri Lanka Telecom (SLT)	2,806.4	4	1,116.8	4	−1,689.60	8,920.0
Sri Lankan Airlines (SLAL)	305.9	4	−206.5	4	−512.40	3,031.6
National Development Bank (NDB)	341.9	3	172.1	8	−169.10	2,705.1
Caltex Lanka Ltd. (CLL)	106.9	3	113.8	7	6.68	968.3
Lanka Ceramics Ltd. (LCL)	56.6	4	12.1	6	−44.50	203.6
Lanka Salt Ltd. (LSL)	11.7	6	1.7	5	−10.00	238.4

a. The discount rate used, 11.1 percent, is the average value of the Commercial Bank weighted average deposit rate for the last 10 years.
Sources: Company annual reports (various years) and Ministry of Finance (1990).

The privatization program has attracted increased domestic and foreign investment (both direct and portfolio) to key sectors of the economy. Total cumulative investment of seven of the eight companies selected for this study, as a percentage of the country's total private-sector investment, varied from 1.7 to 3.7 over the 1992–2000 period.[16] Its maximum value was recorded in 1997 at 4.5, while its minimum value was in 1992 at 1.7. Emerging stories from individual companies indicate that investment in these entities increased after privatization. For example, since 1999, capital investments of nearly Rs.11 billion went into the plantation sector, averaging about Rs.550 million per company. Over the past five years, SLT has invested more than Rs.40 billion in developing a state-of-the-art communications infrastructure; during 1996–2001, capital investment in the Colombo Gas Company, Ltd. (CGCL) (Shell) averaged about Rs.7 billion (including investment on a storage terminal).

A World Bank commissioned study on infrastructure privatization in 2000–01 indicated that capital investments, measured in terms of capital expenditure to sales and capital expenditure to assets, have fallen with privatization—indicative, perhaps, of a rationalization of capital expenditure (table 12.3).

---

16. Investment information for Colombo Gas Company Ltd. was not available at the time of writing.

Figure 12.2   Change in privatization revenue flows to government
(net present value)

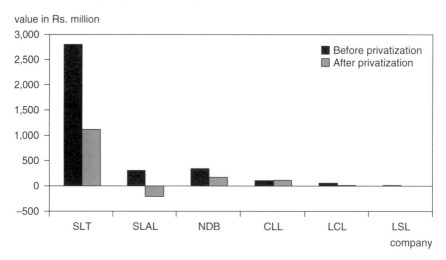

value in Rs. million

The companies in this sample show mixed results in dividends per share and in profitability profiles after privatization, as illustrated in tables 12.4 and 12.5. Although detailed annual information on the CGCL was unavailable, the World Bank (2001a) indicates that profitability, measured as a return on investment and a return on sales, showed a mean increase of 0.021 after privatization.

No evidence confirms whether the increased investments, where they have occurred, have had positive distributional spillovers. While one could argue that increased investment, particularly in the utilities and services sectors, could be beneficial from an equity perspective (if it led to increased network coverage and service availability), the extent to which this happens depends on key factors, ranging from ownership structures to efficacy of regulatory institutions. For example, Jayasuriya and Knight-John (2002) show that SLT privatization could have had better results (in terms of overall industry competition, prices, and access) if it had not had a monopoly on international telephony and had the regulatory regime been more effective.

One positive result of the privatization program, from a distributional perspective, is the boosting of the CSE, reflected to a certain extent in the market capitalization figures in table 12.6. As Kelegama (1995) argues, foreign investment has tended to drive the share market, with foreign buyers taking up large quantities at relatively high prices, creating an opportunity for smaller investors to make quick money from the bourse. In recent years,

Table 12.3   Capital investment in selected privatized companies

Company	Preprivatization (mean)	Postprivatization (mean)	Change (mean)
Sri Lanka Telecom Ltd.			
Capital expenditure to sales	0.670	0.980	0.310
Capital expenditure to assets	1.420	1.050	−0.370
Colombo Gas Company Ltd.			
Capital expenditure to sales	0.386	0.051	−0.335
Capital expenditure to assets	0.180	0.060	−0.120
Sri Lankan Airlines			
Capital expenditure to sales	0.386	0.089	−0.297
Capital expenditure to assets	0.179	0.059	−0.120

Source: World Bank (2001a).

Table 12.4   Dividend per share, selected companies, 1991–2000 (rupees)

Year	National Development Bank (NDB)	Caltex Lanka, Ltd. (CLL)	Bogawantalawa Plantations, Ltd. (BPL)	Sri Lanka Telecom (SLT)
1991	0.6	n.a.	n.a.	n.a.
1992	3.0	n.a.	n.a.	n.a.
1993	3.5	n.a.	n.a.	n.a.
1994	4.0	n.a.	n.a.	n.a.
1995	4.5	6.00	n.a.	n.a.
1996	5.5	4.00	0.75	n.a.
1997	6.5	4.15	1.00	2.32
1998	6.5	7.60	0.00	1.22
1999	4.5	7.60	0.50	0.70
2000	4.5	7.60	1.50	0.12

n.a. = not available

Source: Company annual reports.

however, civil war and other domestic, political, and economic uncertainties have dampened this positive effect on the stock market.

Ownership Concerns

The distributional effects of sales methods involve such issues as who obtained shares and why, whether share prices reflected the entities' actual value, what measures the government took to ensure that a wide spectrum of stakeholders benefited from privatization, and whether the sales process was transparent.

Table 12.5   After-tax profit for selected companies, 1991–2000
             (Rs. million)

Year	BPL	CLL	LCL	LSL	NDB	SLAL	SLT
1991	n.a.	n.a.	n.a.	n.a.	n.a.	201.06	n.a.
1992	n.a.	n.a.	n.a.	n.a.	289.4	218.36	3,205
1993	−67.51	49.46	211.71	n.a.	544.2	127.61	2,531
1994	1.06	73.01	264.48	n.a.	678.3	188.6	3,861
1995	59.67	142.51	268.22	n.a.	616.0	650.05	1,176
1996	113.69	134.83	160.54	18.44	619.2	118.53	1,242
1997	258.21	265.19	210.13	0.45	727.3	449.51	2,390
1998	−2.28	544.40	218.68	5.37	818.9	2,361.36	2,201
1999	108.93	654.53	73.85	8.07	744.7	2,518.63	1,269
2000	168.83	559.00	175.82	8.89	555.8	−750.41	221

n.a. = not available

Sources: Company annual reports.

With regard to the eight companies selected for this study, the government retained a portion of shares in five of them, with a majority shareholding in SLT and Sri Lankan Airlines (SLAL) (table 12.7). Its stated reason for share retention was to protect national interests in what were considered strategic economic sectors. An equally important reason might have been its hope that these shares could later be sold at a premium after the new private owner had driven up the firms' value. In any event, the government postponed, until November 2002, divestiture of an additional tranche of 12 percent of shares (bringing its SLT stake below 51 percent) because of dismal international and domestic financial market conditions and decline in telecom share prices in the international market.

Like many other countries, Sri Lanka has not realized the expected increase in financial gain from secondary sales, as illustrated in two recent transactions: National Insurance Corporation (NIC) privatization and SLT initial public offering (IPO). In the case of NIC, a 51 percent stake was divested in 2001; further privatization was left for a later date, in the hope that the new owner would increase investment in the entity and drive up the share value. However, during the second stage of privatization, the original private investor, who had increased bargaining power because of few takers for the shares, bought a 39 percent stake for a lower per-share price than that originally paid. Similarly, the 2002 SLT IPO saw a 12 percent stake sold for Rs.3,250 million, while a 35 percent stake fetched Rs.13, 380 million in 1997. From both a revenue generation and equity perspective, one might argue that the sale of all shares in the first round would more likely maximize proceeds (and thus increase available resources for assisting distribution). Another reason for retaining shares for later sale in the form of an IPO was to reserve equity for sale to local investors. Thus, the approach had a distributional objective.

Table 12.6 Market capitalization, selected years

Year	Total (Rs. billion)	Total privatized companies (Rs. billion)	Total privatized companies as percent of total	Selected companies	Selected companies as percent of total
1990	36.8	1.1	3.0	n.a.	n.a.
1992	66.2	2.8	4.2	0.7	1.1
1994	143.2	4.4	3.1	0.5	0.3
1996	104.2	7.3	6.9	1.0	0.9
1997	129.4	8.6	6.6	1.1	0.8
1998	116.7	9.4	8.1	1.3	1.1
1999	112.8	9.6	8.5	1.3	1.2
2000	98.2	28.0[a]	28.5	19.5[a]	19.8

n.a. = not available

a. The SLT debenture issue in March 2000 accounts for relatively high market capitalization.

Sources: Central Bank of Sri Lanka (2001a) and CSE data.

Nonetheless, we believe the government generally gave fiscal concerns precedence over distributional ones. For example, in the SLT privatization, Nippon Telegraph and Telephone Corporation (NTT) received a five-year monopoly to provide international telephony. In the case of CGCL privatization, the contract specified that Shell Overseas International BV/Royal Dutch (Shell) would be the only company to undertake liquefied petroleum gas (LPG) business for a five-year exclusive period. The justifications for exclusivity periods range from attempting to attract Fortune-500 companies as owners, to needing the new owners to make a firm investment commitment (particularly important for infrastructure firms, where underinvestment had produced problems of service quantity and quality), to having to make a political choice between increased prices (particularly in the case of utilities) and time-bound exclusivity.

The reasons for awarding exclusivity periods to investors in the utility sector may be economically valid—it was indeed necessary to find a solution for lack of investment capital in these sectors. However, lack of strong, effective regulatory mechanisms resulted in the abuse of this mechanism. Jayasuriya and Knight-John (2002) argue SLT is not only granted the monopoly in international telephony; it also dominates competitive portions of the market, which has had an unfavorable spillover effect on consumers and competitors. Weak, unenforced regulation is illustrated by SLT's refusal to acknowledge the Telecom Regulatory Commission's (TRC) decision on interconnection and its repeated blocking of competitors' calls.

Deciding to hand over management control to a strategic, often foreign, investor was based on the reasonable premise that a single core investor would show greater commitment to increasing profitability and efficiency and would also be more likely to introduce new technology and better management practices in the privatized entities. However, frequent allegations of nontransparent tender procedures undermined public confidence in privatization, as it was generally believed that those given the opportunity to

Table 12.7 Method of sale for selected companies

Company	Privatization modality (percent)	Stock-market listing status
BPL	• 51 (strategic investor with management control) • 39 (public share issue) • 10 (ESOP)	Listed
CGCL	• 39 (retained by government) • 51 (on tender to strategic investor) • 10 (ESOP) • Management control to strategic investor for 5 years	Not listed
CLL	• 51 (on tender to strategic investor) • 39 (public share issue) • 10 (ESOP)	Listed
LCL	• 32.67 (retained by government) • 15 (sale of majority shareholding on an all-or-nothing basis) • 42.33 (public share issue) • 10 (ESOP)	Listed
LSL	• 90 (on tender to Employees Trust Fund Board) • 10 (ESOP)	Not listed
NDB	• 26.3 (retained by government) • 20.9 (sale of majority shareholding on an all-or-nothing basis) • 34.4 (public share issue) • 8.4 (international placement and on CSE) • 10 (ESOP)	Listed
SLAL	• 51 (retained by government) • 40 (on tender to strategic investor) • 9 (ESOP) • Management control to strategic investor for 10 years	Not listed
SLT	• 61.5 (retained by government) • 35 (on tender to strategic investor) • 3.5 (ESOP) • Management control to strategic investor for 5 years	Only debenture issue listed

CSE = Colombo Stock Exchange
ESOP = employee share ownership plan

Note: This initial composition of shareholdings could have changed over time with the subsequent resale of shares, such as the case of SLT, where some employees chose to sell their shares to NTT, thereby lowering employees' share to 3.3 percent and raising NTT's to 35.2 percent.

Sources: COPED, CSE, and PERC data.

purchase enterprises were the politically well-connected. Thus, belief was widespread that more competitive bidders might have been locked out, with potentially beneficial distributional opportunities lost in the process.

Two examples of questionable deals, repeatedly cited in the media and public fora, are the Kotagala Plantation divestiture and the Prima flour-milling operation. These transactions spanned the regimes of successive governments from 1977 onward (Kelegama 1995). The Kotagala transaction controversy related to the winning party's connection to the law firm retained by PERC to act on its behalf, raising the suspicion that the selected buyer might have been privy to information unavailable to other investors.

Prima stands out as an imposed monopoly, whereby successive governments enhanced the concessions handed out by their predecessors, calling into question the government's capacity to treat important private firms with neutrality. According to Prima's 1977 agreement with the government, the company was to set up a flour-milling operation and was given a 20-year lease, starting the date the mill became operational. This was the country's first build-own-transfer (BOT) project. In 1986, the agreement period was extended five years; due to an import ban on wheat until 2005, a monopoly ensued, requiring the government to obtain Prima's concurrence to import flour, even in emergency situations.

The company also had the benefit of a tax holiday during this entire period. According to PERC's 2000 annual report, even the personal effects of Prima's expatriate employees were exempt from income tax for a five-year period. The controversy surrounding Prima's monopoly rights grew more complex when the company was discovered to have been engaged in anticompetitive business practices in the chicken feed market. Although the administration that came into power in 1994 had spoken disparagingly of Prima's monopoly rights of operation, this period witnessed the conversion of the BOT project into a build-own-operate (BOO) project and the below-market sale of mill assets.

Lack of openness in the sales process has created antiprivatization ripples among the general public, particularly when strategic investors have been foreign nationals. Table 12.8 illustrates a more positive view of wider share ownership. Accordingly, the percentage of nonresident enterprise ownership is not significant, indicating that remittances abroad are unlikely to be high, as opposed to such foreign strategic investors as NTT, Emirates Airlines, and Shell.

Figures 12.3 and 12.4 show how value added has been distributed among the stakeholders in the National Development Bank (NDB) and Bogawantalawa Plantations, Ltd. (BPL).[17] In the case of NDB, employee remuneration and shareholder dividends have improved in relative terms; for BPL, employee remuneration has declined over the selected time period.

Although an accurate picture of shareholder income and regional breakdown is not attainable, given that private companies do not make this information public, standard investment behavior among the Sri Lankan public suggests that relatively poor, semi-urban, and rural investors have not been

---

17. Value added is calculated as total turnover minus bought materials and service fees (including management fees).

Table 12.8   Total shareholders, showing resident and nonresident ownership, for selected listed companies, 1995 and 2000

Year	Total number of shareholders	Resident ownership (percent)	Nonresident ownership (percent)
1995	1,409	98.2	1.7
2000	33,990	97.3	2.6

Note: Selected listed companies are BPL, CLL, LCL, and NDB.

Sources: Company annual reports.

drawn into the stock market. Clearly, low-income groups have little disposable income to invest, and traditional forms of Sri Lankan investment continue (e.g., house and property, and gold and jewelry) (Kelegama 1995).

While unit trusts, which aimed to bring small investors into the stock market, were introduced as early as the 1990s—with initiation of the privatization program—they have not been popular, perhaps because of poor marketing, especially in suburban and rural localities and among lower-income groups. Thus, it is not surprising that those who have benefited from the sale of shares under the privatization program are overwhelmingly urban residents and wealthier segments of Sri Lankan society.

A particularly controversial issue is the alleged underpricing of enterprises sold. Among the privatization program's stated objectives was pricing shares affordably for a large segment of the population and minimizing the financial risks of first-time (presumably small) investors. Kelegama (1995) views the subsequent rise in privatized entities' share prices as evidence of shares having been sold below their true value at the time of divestiture. Underpricing is a plausible explanation for the dramatic rise in share price on the day of privatization; however, in many cases, increased share price came several months after privatization, making it difficult to determine whether the cause was underpricing or improved performance under new ownership and management. To the extent that underpricing was the cause, government and taxpayers lost out at the expense of new owners; moreover, the larger the loss, the greater the negative distributional effect. The second wave of privatization, by contrast, has witnessed the adoption of a more professional procedure, whereby a business valuation is implemented parallel to the government valuation.

Whatever the position with regard to divestiture pricing, persistent and widespread allegations of state asset undervaluation have had a harmful effect on the public's perception of privatization. One example was the media's outcry over what was perceived as gross undervaluation of national assets in the SLAL privatization. Press critics, in particular, objected to the

Figure 12.3 NBD distribution of value added, 1995 and 2001 (percent)

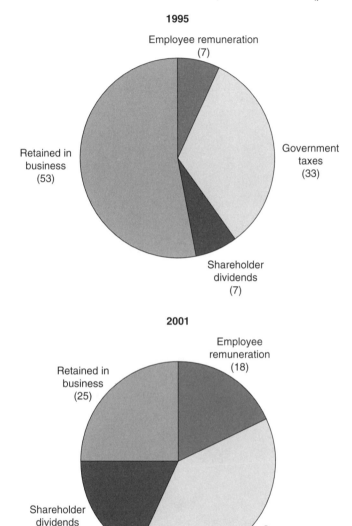

Source: Company annual reports.

government's allowing the purchaser, Emirates Airlines, to pay US$45 million (of the total US$70 million sales price) upfront, with the balance to be paid over the ensuing 30 months.

The government's efforts to democratize share ownership through ESOPs have had mixed results. The most positive outcome is that trade unions

Figure 12.4 BPL distribution of value added, 1995 and 1999 (percent)

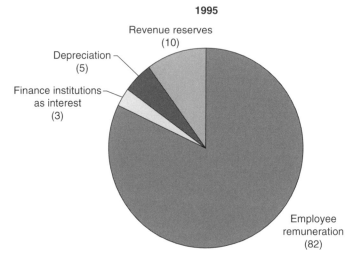

1995

Revenue reserves (10)

Depreciation (5)

Finance institutions as interest (3)

Employee remuneration (82)

Note: Government taxes and shareholders dividend equal zero percent.

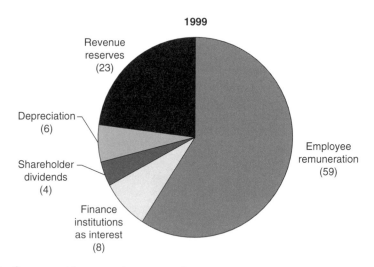

1999

Revenue reserves (23)

Depreciation (6)

Shareholder dividends (4)

Finance institutions as interest (8)

Employee remuneration (59)

Note: Government taxes equal zero percent.

Source: Company annual reports.

are appeased and somewhat more receptive to privatization. However, employees at higher management levels, with more knowledge about how to make and use share-market investments, have benefited most. Attempts to create a share-owning culture among employees of the privatized enterprises have been diluted by employees' tendency to sell their shares in the short term. For example, according to company annual reports, shares held by SLT and SLAL employees stood at 3.3 percent and 5.37 percent, respectively, in 2001, in contrast to initial holdings given out at the time of privatization of 3.5 percent and 9 percent, respectively.

Whether those employees who held onto shares gained or lost over time has depended on the country's overall stock market conditions and individual company performance. As table 12.9 indicates, the per-share earnings given out at the time of privatization of the companies in the sample set chosen for this study have increased over time, on average, with the exception of Lanka Ceramics, Ltd. (LCL), implying that NDB, Caltex Lanka, Ltd. (CLL), and BPL employees would have benefited from holding onto shares.[18]

Labor Force Costs and Benefits

In every country, privatization's effect on employment is highly contentious. It inevitably leads to confrontations with trade unions, a visible, vocal, and well-organized group with strong political bargaining power (as opposed to consumers who are dispersed, often silent, and unorganized). In Sri Lanka, for example, organized labor's leverage on governments contributed significantly to the overstaffing of SOEs and postponement of public-enterprise reforms.

In analyzing privatization's costs and benefits to the labor force, the principal questions are: What are privatization's direct effects on job losses or gains? How have remaining employees in the privatized entities benefited from ownership and management change? What are the distributional effects of severance packages given to retrenched workers? We also consider privatization's indirect employment effects stemming from location of privatized entities and privatization's effects on input suppliers. In Sri Lanka's current macroeconomic climate—characterized by high unemployment and a looming social crisis, with youth comprising 71 percent of the country's unemployed—employment concerns are significant.[19]

During the period before and just after privatization, the net job loss was 5,419 employees (table 12.10). According to company annual reports, gross job reduction was 6,432 employees, with only 2,533 or 39 percent compensated for their loss. Of the selected companies, BPL, CGCL, CLL, LCL, and Lanka Salt, Ltd. (LSL) reported overemployment before privatization. After privatization, CGCL reported average labor redundancy of 55 percent, while BPL reported 17 percent, and LCL 45 percent. Although SLAL did not report overemployment problems at the time of privatization, the loss of 50 percent of its aircraft fleet due to the July 2001 terrorist attack on Sri

---

18. It should be noted that, in this case, the equity effect of retaining or selling shares is closely associated with a worker's individual utility trade-off.

19. Draft Poverty Reduction Strategy, April 2002.

Table 12.9   Earnings per share for selected listed companies, 1991–2000

Year	BPL	CLL	LCL	NDB	SLT
1991	n.a.	n.a.	n.a.	4.7	n.a.
1992	n.a.	n.a.	n.a.	5.4	n.a.
1993	(135.04)	1.65	n.a.	10.1	n.a.
1994	2.13	2.43	0.97	12.6	n.a.
1995	6.88	4.75	0.17	11.5	n.a.
1996	5.68	4.49	0.27	11.5	n.a.
1997	11.21	8.84	2.24	13.5	1.32
1998	(0.07)	18.15	1.81	14.9	1.22
1999	3.25	21.82	(1.97)	13.3	0.72
2000	5.04	18.63	(2.31)	10.2	0.12

n.a. = not available

Sources: Company annual reports.

Lanka's international airport led to a downsizing of 1,016 employees in 2001 under two voluntary severance schemes.

Sri Lanka, like many countries, has practiced retrenchment before and after privatization. Guided by the 1987 Presidential Commission Report on Privatization, the government carried out retrenchment before privatization in several entities during the first wave. One of the earliest compensation packages, Bulumulla Formula (Kelegama and Salih 1998), was devised in negotiations with workers' representatives before the enterprise was sold. The rationale for downsizing before privatization was to placate labor, make the entities more attractive to private investors, and obtain a higher price for the entity. However, private owners also had the option of retrenching excess labor by implementing compensation schemes approved by the commissioner of labor. In recent years, the government has tended toward postprivatization retrenchment mainly because it can no longer afford the large compensation demanded by trade unions.[20]

Before May 1992, both voluntary and involuntary retrenchment schemes were used when the then-president pronounced that no worker should lose employment as a direct result of privatization. Following this announcement, voluntary retirement became state policy. According to Kelegama and Salih (1998), before privatization, the government gave workers at least three months to decide whether they would take voluntary retirement, compared to only two or three weeks after privatization.

---

20. According to Kelegama and Salih (1998), during 1987–97, average compensation, excluding gratuity payments, increased from 17.5 months of salary to 53 months of salary for a 40-year-old worker with 20 years of service.

**Table 12.10 Direct employment effects of privatization for
selected companies** (average employment)

Company	Year of privatization	Before privatization	After privatization	Change
SLT	1997	7,599	8,499	900
SLAL	1998	4,358	4,908	550
CGCL	1995	646	292	–354
NDB	1993	188	311	123
CLL	1994	320	275	–45
BPL	1992	20,031	16,501	–3,530
LCL	1992	4,082	2,021	–2,061
LSL	1997	1,562	560	–1,002
Total		**38,786**	**33,367**	**−5,419**

Sources: Company annual reports.

Anecdotal evidence suggests that involuntary dismissals after privatization were common. However, a mitigating factor was the Termination of Employment Act of 1971 (TEA), which applied only to the private sector, under which an employer with 15 or more workers wishing to dismiss an employee (with one or more years of service) on nondisciplinary grounds must obtain the employee's written consent or labor commissioner's approval.

Overall, employees retained in privatized entities benefited from improved pay and better working conditions because second-wave privatization agreements required investors to guarantee employment under the same terms and conditions as before privatization and because of increased productivity in several entities.[21] The companies selected for this study reported increased labor productivity after privatization (table 12.11).[22] Table 12.12 shows the average nominal wage investment increment after privatization for the eight surveyed companies.

Privatization's overall distributional effect on workers retrenched under severance schemes can be estimated only roughly, given that precise

---

21. When comparing the terms and conditions of SOE workers with private-company workers, one should consider that SOE workers are given pensions after retirement that can be accessed on a monthly basis, while private company workers have provident fund schemes, whereby the total amount can be withdrawn at one time. From a life-cycle perspective (and that of smoothing out consumption over time), the option of a one-time withdrawal may not necessarily benefit the worker.

22. Although comparative SLAL numbers were unavailable, interviews with company personnel revealed that salaries of nonexecutive staff increased 44 percent in 1999 and that salaries and other pecuniary allowances of pilots, engineers, and management staff increased substantially after privatization.

Table 12.11 Labor productivity for selected companies

Company	Before privatization	After privatization	Change
BPL (total production per employee) (kg)			
Rubber	3.2	4.9	1.7
Tea	2.1	2.7	0.6
LSL (total production per employee) (metric tons)	96.6	128.6	32.0
SLAL (load carried per employee) (ton-km)	104,855.3	122,331.7	17,476.4
SLT (exchange capacity per employee) (lines)	30.7	80.0	49.3

Sources: Company annual reports and Ministry of Finance.

information is unavailable on such variables as laid-off worker characteristics (e.g., age, sex, and skill level) and the average period of time to find a new job. Moreover, although three severance or compensation packages—Bulumulla, Leather Corporations, and Lanka Ceramics—have been used in the privatization process, several companies have also formulated individual severance schemes, making it difficult to draw conclusions on retrenched workers as a group (Kelegama 1995).

The companies selected for this study have used a range of schemes: individual (CGCL, CLL, and SLAL), Bulumulla Formula (BPL and LSL), and the Lanka Ceramics and Bulumulla Formulas together (LCL). While these schemes vary somewhat, all have adopted a compensation procedure based on number of years of service, whereby employees with longer service are more highly compensated. This approach could negatively affect distribution in situations where those retrenched are younger and have more working years ahead of them, have worked for relatively few years in an enterprise, or belong to employment categories in which job opportunities are scarce. On the other hand, surveys in many countries indicate that workers with these characteristics are likely to find replacement jobs comparatively easily. That the government has not made unemployment safety nets (e.g., retraining and assistance in developing business skills) a policy priority exacerbates the issue.

Kelegama and Salih (1998) argue that, if the majority of those who opt for compensation packages are over the age of 45 and if those who leave are—as in the case of bus transportation system privatization—white-collar workers (Knight 1993), who are more easily reemployable, then the distributional results would have differed. To reiterate, the high financial costs of retrenchment and resulting fiscal effects suggest that at least some retrenched workers would have benefited at the expense of the relatively poor and unemployed.

Table 12.12   **Privatization's effects on wages of selected companies** (percent increase after privatization, until 2001)

Company	Average nominal wage increase
BPL	50.0
CGCL	140.0
CLL	120.0
LCL	17.5
LSL	35.0
NDB	150.0
SLAL	52.0
SLT	60.0

Sources: Company annual reports.

Kelegama (1995) posits that, although privatized enterprises were located predominantly in urban areas during the first wave of privatization, the second wave might have had more favorable distributional results, given the location of several privatized entities—plantations, sugar companies, and rural seed-paddy farms—which might well have produced an increase in local and regional employment opportunities.

Privatization has not especially benefited input suppliers whose linkages with SOEs were severed after divestiture. In instances where sourcing arrangements were altered for reasons of efficiency, one might argue that the broader distributional effects of these shifts would be positive, although it might still impose costs on certain local producers. For example, Kelegama (1997b) cites the cases of the Distilleries Corporation, which shifted its purchase of sugar inputs from the local Sevanagala Sugar Corporation to cheaper South African imports, and the privatized Puttalam Cement, which stopped purchasing sacks from Colombo sack makers.

Price and Access Effects

How has privatization affected consumers in terms of affordability, access, and quality? Given that distributional issues are particularly relevant in the utilities sector, what has happened to prices after privatization and why? With regard to telecommunications- and LPG-sector privatizations, have services expanded and, if so, in which localities?

As Jayasuriya and Knight-John (2002) highlight, SLT's international tariffs fell 8 percent in 1998 and 1999. At the same time, a rate rebalancing agreement was reached with the government to substantially increase domestic tariffs during 1998–2002 in five stages: 1998 (25 percent), 1999 (25 percent), 2000 (20 percent), 2001 (15 percent), and 2002 (15 percent). The other fixed telephony operators tend to follow the tariff rates set by SLT, the market leader (with about 85 percent control of the fixed access market).

A sound economic argument underlies rate rebalancing. When state-owned, the firm set local call rates at levels below marginal cost. However, because most fixed-access customers subscribe to domestic call services and only a small proportion (the relatively wealthy) has access to international direct-dialing services, the distributional effect of rate rebalancing may not be optimal. In the telecommunications market, price issues were exacerbated by the five-year monopoly on international telephony given to SLT under the privatization agreement, which kept tariff rates in the international segment above competitive rates and stifled other subsector growth, such as Internet services, which could positively affect rural connectivity.

In the oil and gas sector, after privatization, the LPG market recorded price hikes, with the average LPG unit rising about 54 percent (from Rs.18 per kg before privatization to Rs.27.8 per kg after privatization in 1995). Unlike the period before privatization, when the state entity absorbed global price increases, Shell passed these increases on to the consumer. However, given that middle- and high-income groups account for about 92 percent of total Sri Lankan consumption (and that LPG penetration among Sri Lankan households is only about 20 percent, with 80 percent still using kerosene and firewood for cooking), the distributional effect of price increases on the relatively poor is not significant, or is perhaps even positive, depending on how the government directs the funds formerly used to subsidize LPG prices for upper-income consumers.

CGCL company representatives cite high import dependence (of nearly 90 percent of domestic LPG requirements), higher international LPG prices, and devaluation of the rupee as the main reasons for these price hikes. Cost components of the LPG tariff include the product cost (FOB), freight and insurance, terminal throughput fee, company recovery, distributor and dealer margin, and government taxes and duties. The cost of LPG is exogenous—based on the Saudi Aramco contract, which is indexed to spot prices of crude and other oil products.

Although isolating privatization's effects from other exogenous factors proves difficult without accurate data, that LPG prices decreased when another supplier entered the market in 2001–02, consequent to the ending of Shell's five-year exclusive period, suggests that lack of competition contributed to the earlier price increases. Shell representatives argue, perhaps justifiably, that its competitor can sell its product at a lower price since it purchases LPG from the Ceylon Petroleum Corporation (CPC) at subsidized rates. Whatever the case with regard to the pricing issue, opponents of

Figure 12.5   Telecommunications-sector geographic access, 1991–2000

thousands of new connections

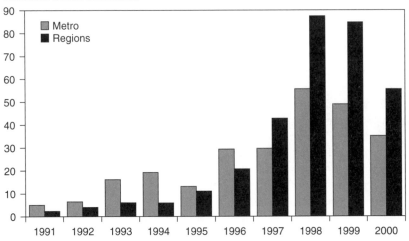

Source: Company annual reports.

the privatization process have been vociferous about Shell's price increases after privatization.

Lack of a sectoral regulator has heightened negative perceptions about gas privatization. Although the privatization agreement signed between the government and Shell stipulates that the DIT would function as the regulator, company representatives claim that their regulatory dealings during the monopoly period have been with PERC, indicating a significant inconsistency in the policy process. Whether an entity set up to facilitate privatization transactions can simultaneously carry out regulatory functions and remain effective in the dual roles is questionable.[23]

Price increases after privatization result partially from the shift from a system of hidden subsidies and administered price mechanisms to more market-determined, cost-based price structures. Moreover, the opportunity costs of lower, subsidized prices could be of poor quality, as was the case in Sri Lanka's telecom sector. In this industry, the distributional effect of rising prices has been offset, to some extent, by qualitative improvements after privatization. For example, the average waiting time for a line

---

23. The five-year monopoly recently given to Shell's competitor to purchase LPG from CPC, apparently without calling for tenders, suggests that lack of an effective regulator could have effects that go beyond the issue of Shell privatization.

has been reduced from seven years to less than one year, call completion rates are now about 46 percent (because of the increase in lines and relocation of equipment to high usage areas), fault clearance rates have improved, and the billing system has been computerized.

SLT and CGCL network expansion after privatization resulted in improved access to these services in absolute terms. Both companies' annual reports show an increase in the average number of consumers; SLT recorded an average increase of 473,000, while CGCL had an increase of 329,000. Further evidence of improved access to these services is SLT's average increase in new connections—from 30,487 before privatization to 109,972 afterward—and a 150 percent increase in the number of LPG cylinders issued between 1994 and 1999. Thus, to a certain degree, expanded service after privatization compensates price increases. Although one cannot state with certainty that privatization is responsible for the increased access, the rate of network expansion grew significantly after privatization.

One can link the average gas expenditure before and after privatization to income levels. The pattern that emerges from these calculations is that the gas expenditure of lower-income groups decreased after privatization. According to the Central Bank's annual reports, for consumers whose monthly income was less than Rs.600 in 1986–87, the average gas expenditure was Rs.0.307; for the same income level in 1996–97, its value was Rs.0. However, the average gas expenditure for middle- (Rs.600–Rs.3,000) and higher-income (more than Rs.3,000) groups increased drastically over the same period. It is evident that the average annual gas expenditure for middle- and higher-income groups increased 61 percent and 11 percent, respectively, during this period.

As figure 12.5 indicates, the growth rate of SLT's new connections in the metro areas decreased, while regional rates increased. However, given that SLT classifies all nonmetro areas, including suburban localities, as regional, these numbers do not accurately portray access in rural areas, where poorer residents are concentrated.

Moreover, Jayasuriya and Knight-John (2002) indicate that, while universal service obligations (USOs) in Sri Lanka relate primarily to rural connectivity, SLT's rural penetration rate is only 1.70, and SLT has no legally binding USOs under the privatization agreement. While data constraints make it impossible to calculate changes in the rural poor's access to telecommunications service after privatization, the low penetration rate (in absolute terms) indicates that privatization would have had only a limited, if any, effect on rural access.

Political Economy Effects

Two interrelated themes that recur in Sri Lanka are public perceptions of privatization and political economy determinants of the divestiture process.[24] Privatization's opponents have figured more prominently in public debate than have its proponents; even supporters have had reservations with regard to the process, particularly regarding such issues as the sales price of entities, exclusivity provisions, and labor retrenchment. Strong ideological feelings of national pride, combined with the general public's lack of awareness about the program and absence of procedural transparency, provide an excellent opportunity for politicizing the issues and stirring up antiprivatization sentiments among those with vested interests.

According to the survey contained in the 2001 World Bank–commissioned study (World Bank 2001b), most Sri Lankans had heard of privatization, but were pessimistic about it; more than 50 percent believed that social life and economic stability had deteriorated with privatization and over 80 percent perceived that privatization would negatively affect poverty and living standards. While only about 60 percent and 50 percent of respondents knew about telecommunications and bus privatizations, respectively, as many as 50 percent thought that the electricity sector was already privatized, which was not the case. On the other hand, more than 80 percent of respondents were aware of gas privatization—perhaps because, after divestiture, the media constantly highlighted the controversial issue of Shell gas prices.

Regarding the rationale for privatization in Sri Lanka, the perceived reasons recorded by the survey ranged from donor pressure (SLT), government escape from mismanagement and a loss-making situation (SLAL and Shell), and formulating an exercise in "peoplization" (buses). Survey respondents viewed telecom privatization as having brought about better service and access, and saw it as a fair trade-off for increased prices. They also perceived bus privatization as having improved service and access to a certain extent, but thought that lack of well-defined sectoral procedures and discipline negatively affected service quality and consumer welfare. The privatization of SLAL was thought to have been disadvantageous to the country. In general, price increases and loss of job security were viewed as the most problematic outcomes of privatization.

With regard to future privatization plans, more than 60 percent of respondents opposed the sale of ports and banks; more than 50 percent opposed sale of the insurance sector; and more than 70 percent opposed divestiture of electricity, water, and railway sectors. Clearly, this scenario is unfavorable, given that all of these sectors are included in the government's imminent privatization pipeline.

---

24. Our analysis of public attitudes toward privatization draws from a 2001 World Bank–commissioned study, whose more salient findings and claims are presented in this chapter. See World Bank (2001b).

Reactions to privatization vary among the various stakeholders involved in the process; perceptions and reactions are shaped by what one stands to gain or lose through the reform. Not surprisingly, the most enthusiastic promoters are the relatively well-off, who have the opportunity to purchase (possibly underpriced) state assets through a process tainted by lack of transparency. The promise of continued rents from handing out exclusivity provisions under many privatization agreements in the second wave has further strengthened this favored group's support.

Unsurprisingly, labor has not supported the privatization process, given the SOEs' guarantee of job security and the perception, cultivated over years of heavy government intervention in the economy, of a benefactor state. The presence of vociferous trade unions with strong bargaining power and the ability to create industrial unrest has prompted the government to introduce such measures as the ESOPs and generous retrenchment packages to placate workers, often at high financial costs to the state and taxpayers.[25]

Consumers tend to be perceived as the silent majority who may lose out from privatization, particularly because of post-sale price increases in the services and utilities sectors. To the general public, price hikes after privatization stand out as the most tangible effect of ownership change and as proof of a negative effect. Although direct lobbying by consumers has been minimal in the absence of organized consumer groups, the media—a strong critic of the country's privatization process—has often taken up their case. However, either the users or the taxpayers (or a combination of the two) must pay for utility services. While antiprivatization complaints are often couched in terms of privatization's negative effects on the people as a whole, certain pricing regimes before privatization—LPG, for example—subsidized consumption of a small group of upper-income citizens at the expense of the overall society.

Despite negative media coverage, particularly during the second wave (which coincided with the free press becoming a reality in Sri Lanka), there is little commitment toward making the process more transparent or genuinely addressing equity concerns. The government's apparent willingness to sustain monopolies and impose regulatory restrictions hindering competition after privatization, as in the cases of SLT and Shell, perhaps suggest that the enormous prospects for rent extraction have not been lost on politicians and their favored supporters.

Nonetheless, one must consider the procedural political economy factors that have contributed to handing out exclusivity provisions and the underpricing of entities to be privatized. While such deals cannot be considered optimal, numerous harsh realities and difficult trade-offs confront government authorities in the reform and negotiation processes. Both Shell and telecom transactions, for example, were negotiated at a time when

---

25. In the case of the SLT divestiture, a unique and successful (in terms of worker cooperation) procedure was followed, whereby PERC informed workers' families about privatization's benefits directly.

terrorist attacks were rampant in the country. The dilapidated national airline had only three potential bidders, only one of which ran an airline. Government sales policy made it mandatory for all new owners of all privatized companies to provide ESOPs and retain all workers, at least for a time. These factors—imposed by the poor state of assets being sold and political and economic conditions outside the control of selling agents— limited the freedom to negotiate optimal sales.

Moreover, multinational companies often drove a hard bargain with developing country governments facing severe budget constraints and in dire need of foreign investment (partly to meet revenue generation goals imposed by international financial institutions [IFIs]). In return for commitments to invest, they demanded various exclusivities, barriers to entry, and pricing regimes that allowed them a substantial return on their investment. A case in point is the SLT privatization. The investor, NTT, laid out a range of choices for the government, whereby granting a three-year monopoly entailed an immediate and substantial price hike, while a five-year monopoly allowed for a more gradual tariff increase.

A closer look at the history of weak regulation that has paralleled the privatization process leads us to conclude that (1) the government deliberately decided to adopt a hands-off policy in order to attract private investment; (2) weak regulation allowed for rent-seeking behavior; and (3) the pace of privatization required by the IMF and World Bank did not allow for a proper sequence of events, whereby an effective regulatory framework would precede divestiture.

What is conspicuous over time is the privatization program's lack of ownership, with political leadership either reluctant to make tough decisions because of other political priorities (e.g., the need for coalition building), sending conflicting signals, or reversing or making ad hoc changes in the process entered into by a predecessor government. Such conditions provide fertile ground for vested interests intent on slowing, ending, or hijacking the privatization process or engaging in rent-seeking activities that deflect privatization's beneficial effects. To date, the most raucous opponents of the process have largely come from political parties outside the government. Despite all the opposition and negative press, the program has not provoked widespread social opposition, perhaps because those who stand to lose the most are the ones least able to voice their protests. Therefore, the question is: How long will it take for the process to backfire and for widespread social turbulence to make reform no longer possible?

Conclusion

What emerges from this analysis of Sri Lanka's divestiture program is that successive governments have not done enough to maximize distributional gains or minimize distributional losses that result from privatization. Overall, the relatively poor have had little or no access to privatization's gains, while the well-connected (both local and foreign), who usually fall into higher-income groups, have benefited from increased rent-seeking opportunities under a nontransparent divestiture process. The sincerity of the government's commitment to distributional ends appears questionable, as fiscal objectives and maximization of sales revenues through perpetuating monopolies under privatization agreements take priority over equitable asset distribution. Moreover, as the examples in this chapter illustrate, the government has displayed little genuine concern with regard to the lack of effective regulation after privatization and the prevalence of poor regulatory governance, which has facilitated rent-seeking activities in privatized entities.

Clearly, it is time to rethink and reorient privatization in Sri Lanka. If the process continues moving along the same path, the concept of privatization (as opposed to the way in which privatization has been implemented in the country) will be blamed for the socioeconomic problems of the poor. This outcome would be unfortunate, given that the alternative to privatization—return to a state-controlled system, with SOEs' high levels of inefficiency and rent-seeking opportunities—would not offer an improvement.

The issue, then, is how to make privatization work in an institutionally weak setting that lacks competition polices. More basically, how willing is the government to reorient the process, and what are the political incentives to do so. Until now, the political incentives to make the privatization process more equitable have been absent, and politicians have put distributional concerns on the back burner. However, the country's worsening macroeconomic condition and unstable sociopolitical climate suggest that the day of reckoning may not be far off.

References

Arunatilake, N., S. Jayasuriya, and S. Kelegama. 2001. The Economic Cost of the War in Sri Lanka. *World Development* 29, no. 9: 1483–1500.

Birdsall, Nancy, and John Nellis. 2002. Winners and Losers: Assessing the Distributional Impact of Privatization. *World Development* 31, no. 10: 1617–769.

Central Bank of Sri Lanka. 1990. *Report on Consumer Finances and Socio Economic Survey Sri Lanka 1986/1987.* Colombo: Central Bank.

Central Bank of Sri Lanka. 1998. *Economic Progress of Independent Sri Lanka, 1948–1998.* Colombo: Central Bank.

Central Bank of Sri Lanka. 2001a. *Annual Report.* Colombo: Central Bank.

Central Bank of Sri Lanka. 2001b. *Economic and Social Statistics of Sri Lanka.* Colombo: Central Bank.

Crowe, P., and A. de Soysa. 1995. *Impact of Privatization in Sri Lanka.* Washington: US Agency for International Development.

IMF (International Monetary Fund). 2000. *Fiscal and Macroeconomic Impact of Privatization.* Washington: International Monetary Fund.

Jayasuriya, S., and M. Knight-John. 2002. *Sri Lanka's Telecommunications Industry: From Privatization to Anti-Competition?* Working Paper Series 14. Manchester: Centre on Regulation and Competition, University of Manchester.

Kelegama, S. 1995. The Impact of Privatization on Distributional Equity. In *Distributional Aspects of Privatization in Developing Countries,* ed. V. V. Ramanadham. London: Routledge.

Kelegama, S. 1997a. "Privatization and the Public Exchequer: Some Observations from the Sri Lankan Experience." *Asia Pacific Development Journal* 4, no. 1: 14–25.

Kelegama, S. 1997b. Privatization: An Overview of the Process and Issues. In *Dilemmas of Development: Fifty Years of Economic Change in Sri Lanka,* ed. W. D. Lakshman. Colombo: Sri Lanka Association of Economists.

Kelegama, S., and R. Salih. 1998. Labour Retrenchment in a Privatization Programme: The Sri Lankan Experience. *Sri Lanka Journal of Social Sciences* 21, nos. 1–2: 1–36.

Knight, M. 1993. Privatization and Sri Lanka's Bus Transport Policy. Paper presented at the National Conference on Law and Economy, Law & Society Trust, Colombo (July).

Knight-John, M. 1995. Privatization in a Developing Country: The Sri Lankan Experience. Paper presented at the Asian Productivity Organization Symposium on Privatization, Bangkok (July).

LCL (Lanka Ceramics, Ltd.). Various years. *Annual Report.* Colombo: Lanka Ceramics, Ltd.

LSL (Lanka Salt, Ltd.). Various years. *Annual Report.* Colombo: Lanka Salt, Ltd.

Ministry of Finance. 1994. *A Handbook on Public Enterprises in Sri Lanka (1988–1993).* Colombo: Department of Public Enterprises, Ministry of Finance.

SGLL (Shell Gas Lanka, Ltd.). Various years. *Annual Report.* Colombo: Shell Gas Lanka, Ltd.

World Bank. 2001a. *Impact Study of Infrastructure Privatization in Sri Lanka.* Washington: World Bank.

World Bank. 2001b. Communications for Privatization in Sri Lanka: Audit Report and Draft Strategy. World Bank, Washington. Photocopy.

World Bank. 2002. *World Development Report.* Washington: World Bank.

Appendix 12A
Company Descriptions

Sri Lanka Telecom. In August 1997, Sri Lanka Telecom (SLT) was privatized, with sale of a 35 percent stake in the company and a five-year period of management control to Nippon Telegraph and Telephone Corporation (NTT).

Sri Lankan Airlines. Sri Lankan Airlines (SLAL), formerly known as Air Lanka, was privatized in 1998. The strategic investor, Emirates International Airlines, was given a 10-year period of management control. SLAL is not a listed company.

Colombo Gas Company. Colombo Gas Company, Ltd. (CGCL), renamed Shell Gas Lanka, Ltd. (SGLL) after its privatization in 1995, provides liquified petroleum gas (LPG) to the country's domestic and industrial customers. The company is not listed. SGLL is the strategic investor and was given management control for five years.

Lanka Ceramics. Sri Lanka's ceramics industry has tremendous growth potential, given this industry's high level of expertise, abundant artistic talent, and 80 percent local availability of required raw materials. In 1992, Lanka Ceramics, Ltd. (LCL) was privatized, and was listed on the Colombo Stock Exchange the following year.

National Development Bank. In 1979, Sri Lanka's National Development Bank (NDB) was incorporated through an Act of Parliament, and was privatized and listed in 1993. The NDB aims primarily to promote economic development through the financing of medium- and long-term projects.

Bogawantalawa Plantations. Creation of regional plantation companies and privatization of their management in 1992 through competitive bidding was the first step in the privatization process. The strategic investor is Metropolitan Management Services. Bogawantalawa Plantations, Ltd. (BPL) is a listed company.

Caltex Lanka. Caltex Lanka, Ltd. (CLL) was formerly Ceylon Petroleum Corporation, the lubricating oil blending plant. In 1992, it was incorporated as a public company, and in July 1994, 51 percent of the company was sold to Caltex Trading and Transportation Corporation. CLL is a listed company.

Lanka Salt. In 1990, Lanka Salt, Ltd. (LSL) was incorporated under Public Companies Act No. 23 of 1987. The Employees Trust Fund Board bought 90 percent of LSL, and it was privatized in 1997. LSL is not a listed company.

Appendix 12B
Questionnaire for Data Collection

1. Income distribution:

   - What are Sri Lanka's income distribution trends?

   - What happened to the Gini coefficient over the last decade?

2. What state transfers and subsidies enabled SOEs to meet their debt obligations in 1990, 1994, and 2001?

3. Ownership issues:

   - What were domestic and foreign share ownership as a percentage of total privatized industries?

   - What was the percentage value of shareholders, based on regional and ethnic aspects?

   - Who bought more shares and benefited most: higher- or lower-income groups?

   - Did those who bought shares borrow from state banks or at market rates?

   - How open was access to shares?

   - What was the number of shareholders in each industry and total number of shareholders in the country?

   - Did resale of shares lead to consolidation of shares in the hands of a few?

4. Access issues:

   - What was the rate of access in selected industries several years before privatization and after privatization (what was the percentage of households with access)?

   - How has the rate of access changed after privatization of the firm?

   - How many consumers with informal connections were connected to the formal network after privatization?

5. What has happened to the quality of goods and services after privatization?

6. What happened to consumers' expenditure on utilities after privatization? Has it increased or decreased over time? What has been the effect on consumer welfare?

7. Firm efficiency and profitability data

8. Employee issues:

- How many workers were employed in the relevant sector before and after privatization?

- How has the real wage and job security changed after privatization, and what has the effect been on social security entitlements?

- What was the degree of overemployment (specific numbers)?

- How many employees were let go, and how many resigned voluntarily after the firm was privatized?

- Were they compensated? What was the firm's compensation procedure?

- Were new employees recruited?

- What steps has the company taken on behalf of employee welfare?

- Would employees have gained if they had held on to shares?

- What is the minimum wage? Labor productivity trends?

9. Divestiture pricing:

- What were stock market indices/valuations?

- Were shares underpriced?

10. Fiscal issues:

- How has the dividend yield changed over time?

- What were the taxation effects of divestiture?

- How much did the government earn each year through the privatization program? Did the program help to reduce the budget deficit? How did it affect the government's tax policy?

- What were the government gross receipts from these companies before privatization? Differentiate gross and net proceeds.

- Were the SOEs sold the more lucrative ones?

- What is the government cost of subsidized prices?

- Did the government acquire anything other than money in return for the sale of assets?

About the Contributors

P. P. A. **Wasantha Athukorala** is a lecturer in the department of economics at the University of Peradeniya, Sri Lanka. She is also a researcher at the International Center for Ethnic Studies in Sri Lanka. She worked as a research assistant at the Institute of Policy Studies and as a lecturer in management and development at the Centre for Continuing Education and Extension. She holds a BA in economics and an MPhil in agricultural economics from the University of Peradeniya, Sri Lanka.

Gover Barja is the director of the master's program in public policy at the Bolivian Catholic University in La Paz. He has researched and written on Bolivia's experience with reform of infrastructure industries for the World Institute for Development Economics Research (WIDER), the Economic Commission for Latin America and the Caribbean (ECLAC), and the Center for Global Development (CGD), and on macroeconomic performance for the Inter-American Development Bank and the Global Development Network. He is also a consultant with the Bolivian Regulatory System and the World Bank. He received his PhD in economics and MS in statistics from Utah State University.

Michael Bleyzer is the founder of SigmaBleyzer and the developer of its business model. His career took him to Russia, Uzbekistan, and Turkmenistan, before he came to the United States in 1978. He then embarked on a career in finance and management and held senior positions at Exxon and Ernst & Young. He serves on the board of the Houston Holocaust Museum and is a member of the Thunderbird School of International Management's Global Council. He graduated from the

Kharkov Institute of Radioelectronics with an MS in digital electronics and quantum physics.

Huberto M. Ennis is a senior economist at the research department of the Federal Reserve Bank of Richmond. He has written several articles on industrial organization, macroeconomics, and optimal government policy. He regularly visits the National University of La Plata in Argentina as a visiting professor and the Central Bank of Argentina. He obtained a BA in economics from the National University of La Plata, MA in public policy from the Torcuato Di Tella Institute in Argentina, and PhD in economics from Cornell University in 2000.

Antonio Estache has been an economist with the World Bank since 1983. He has advised governments in Africa, Asia, and Latin America on public-sector pricing, tax reform, infrastructure privatization, and regulation. He is also a research fellow at the European Center for Advanced Research in Economics and Statistics (ECARES) in Brussels, Belgium. He has published over 60 articles in economic journals and is author or coauthor of eight books on infrastructure. He holds a PhD in economics from the Université Libre de Bruxelles.

Victor Gekker is the director of The Bleyzer Foundation. He joined SigmaBleyzer, USA-Ukraine Investment Bank in May 1996. He acted as the head of the information and analytical department and was the member of SigmaBleyzer's Board of Directors. He participated in the formation of the portfolio of the family of Ukrainian Growth Funds (UGF), international private funds. He graduated from the Kharkiv Polytechnical Institute (energy machine–building faculty) in 1960. After graduation, he worked for 33 years in Kharkiv Research and Development Institute on the problems of thermal and nuclear power development.

Svetlana Pavlovna Glinkina is the deputy director for research at the Institute for International Economic and Political Studies, Russian Academy of Sciences. Her research interests embrace the theory and practice of system transformations, private-sector formation in post-socialist countries' economy, current tendencies in the development of shadow economy, and organized crime. She has authored more than 170 publications, including two monographs. Her works have been published in the Russia, the United States, the United Kingdom, Hungary, Germany, Croatia, Estonia, and Finland. She has worked with a number of different research organizations including the Research Committee at the International Council of Social Sciences (France) and the International Center for Studying Transnational Organized Crime and Corruption (American University, Washington). She is also a professor in the Russian-German High School of Management at the Moscow School of Economics.

Gary H. Jefferson is professor of economics and chair of the Department of Economics at Brandeis University. His research interests include China's economy, innovation and technology transfer, institutional reform, and energy conservation. His work on China is supported by the National Science Foundation and the Department of Energy. He has consulted extensively with the World Bank and has taught at the Chinese University of Hong Kong and Wuhan University in China. His publications include *Enterprise Reform in China: Ownership, Transition, and Performance* (Oxford University Press, 1998). He holds degrees from Dartmouth College, the London School of Economics, and Yale University (PhD in economics).

Su Jian is an assistant professor of economics at Peking University. From 1995 to 2000, he was an assistant professor at Beijing University. Having worked in a big state-owned enterprise (SOE) of China as an engineer for five years (1987–92), he is very familiar with the inner workings of SOEs. He is currently studying the ownership restructuring and privatization of Chinese SOEs. His working papers include *The Determinants of Decentralized Privatization: Theory and Evidence from China and Globalization and Privatization: Evidence from China*. He holds a PhD from the Graduate School of International Economics and Finance, Brandeis University.

Malathy Knight-John is a research fellow and head of public enterprise reform, competition policy, and regulation research at the Institute of Policy Studies, Colombo, Sri Lanka. She has written extensively in these areas both locally and internationally and has also contributed directly to national economic policy by producing policy briefs and serving on various committees appointed by the government. She is currently reading for a PhD at the Institute of Development Policy and Management (IDPM), University of Manchester, focusing on the topic, *The Political Economy of Telecommunications Reform and Regulation in Developing Countries: The Case of Sri Lanka*.

Roberto Macedo is professor of economics at the University of São Paulo, Brazil, and Presbyterian Mackenzie University, also in São Paulo. He was a research associate at the Foundation Institute of Economic Research and a lecturer at the Foundation Armando Álvares Penteado. From 1991 to 1992, he served in the Brazilian federal government as secretary for economic policy and as president of the National Institute for Applied Economic Research and was also part of the economic team led by Minister Marcilio Marques Moreira. He holds a BA from the University of São Paulo, Brazil, and an MA and PhD in economics from Harvard University.

David McKenzie spent four years as an assistant professor of economics at Stanford University and is now an economist in the Development Research Group of the World Bank. He is also a junior fellow of the Bureau for

Research and Economic Analysis of Development (BREAD). He is an expert in the application and development of econometric methods for household data in developing countries. His empirical research has focused on the mechanisms households in Mexico and Argentina use to cope with risk and shocks; the distributional consequences of privatization in Latin America; the development impacts of international migration from Mexico to the United States; and on the evidence for production nonconvexities among Mexican microenterprises. He obtained his PhD in economics from Yale University in 2001.

Dilip Mookherjee has been a professor of economics at Boston University since 1995 and director of the Institute for Economic Development since 1998. He taught at Stanford University and the Indian Statistical Institute, New Delhi. He studied economics at Presidency College, Calcutta; the Delhi School of Economics; and the London School of Economics. He served on an academic advisory panel at the International Monetary Fund and as a consultant to the Chelliah Tax Reforms Committee of the Government of India. His research interests include land reform, decentralization, governance, corruption and poverty in developing countries, and contract and organization theory. He recently coedited *Understanding Poverty* (Oxford University Press, forthcoming) and *Decentralization and Local Governance in Developing Countries: A Comparative Perspective* (MIT Press, forthcoming). He is coauthor of *Incentives and Institutional Reform in Tax Enforcement* and author of *The Crisis in Government Accountability* (both published by Oxford University Press).

Alberto Pascó-Font is a Peruvian economist working in regulatory economic issues as well as in promotion of private investment and public transport infrastructure. He was the director of Group of Analysis for Development, a prestigious Peruvian economic and social research center; executive president of Ositran, the regulatory agency in charge of supervising private investment in infrastructure; and executive director of Proinversion, the agency responsible for promoting private investment through privatizations and concessions. He is currently a member of Comite Especial de Promocion de la Inversion Privada en Infraestructura, the committee responsible for granting concession in public infrastructure. He holds a PhD in economics from the University of Pennsylvania.

Santiago Pinto joined the department of economics at West Virginia University in August 2002. He has also been a faculty research associate of the Regional Research Institute at West Virginia University since 2003. He teaches undergraduate and graduate courses in microeconomics, urban economics, and mathematical economics. He has focused his research in the areas of public economics, state and local public finance, urban economics, and applied microeconomics. He works on issues related to household mobility, tax competition, local labor markets, assistance to poor households, and equality of opportunity and access to specific goods and services. He has published his research in academic journals such as the *Journal of Urban Economics* and the *Journal of Public Economics*. He holds a PhD in economics from the University of Illinois at Urbana-Champaign in 2001.

Luis A. Rivas is chief economic advisor at the Ministry of Finance and the Central Bank of Nicaragua. At the time of this writing, he was a visiting professor at the department of economics in Vanderbilt University.

Samuel Freije Rodríguez is the director of the Institute for Public Policy and Development Studies and associate professor in the department of economics at Universidad de las Américas, Puebla. He has been a consultant for the Inter-American Development Bank, the Organization for Economic Cooperation and Development (OECD), the International Finance Corporation (IFC), and the United Nations Development Program (UNDP), as well as for the Mexican Social Development Secretary (SEDESOL). He has published articles and chapters in books on labor markets and income distribution in Latin American countries. He holds a PhD in labor economics from the New York State School of Industrial and Labor Relations at Cornell University.

Enrique Schroth is assistant professor at the finance department of the business school of the University of Lausanne, Switzerland, where he has taught game theory and corporate finance since 2002. He is also a research fellow with the International Center for Financial Asset Management and Engineering in Geneva. He specializes in industrial organization, corporate finance, and microeconometrics and studies financial innovation and the market structure of the banking industry. His research has been published in the *Review of Financial Studies and Economia*. He holds a PhD in economics from New York University.

Edilberto Segura is chief economist at SigmaBleyzer , director of SigmaBleyzer's Kiev office, and chairman of the advisory board of The Bleyzer Foundation. He is also a professor of economics at the Kiev School of Economics of the National Kiev-Mohila University in Ukraine. For several years, he was a fellow and visiting professor at the Said Business School of the University of Oxford in the United Kingdom, where he lectured on emerging capital markets. Before joining SigmaBleyzer in 1998, he worked at the World Bank for 27 years, where he became a division chief, country director, and technical director. He was also a chief of the World Bank's office in Kiev from 1996 to 1998. He holds PhD and MA degrees from Columbia University in New York, an MBA degree from Stanford University in California, and an industrial engineering degree from Peru. He also attended the advanced management program at Harvard University.

Neal Sigda spent most of his time in the former Soviet Union as a freelance consultant in Kaliningrad and as director of finance for a joint venture in St. Petersburg (1994–97). He joined SigmaBleyzer in 1999 as a financial analyst and is now a director of SigmaBleyzer Research. Over the past four years, he has recommended companies in which to invest, provided valuations of target companies, consulted for large Ukrainian companies, and helped restructure UGF portfolio companies. During that time his responsibilities have grown to managing the portfolio and interacting directly with investors. He holds a BA from Cornell University and an MA in international management from Thunderbird, the American Graduate School of International Management (with specialization in finance)

Diana Smachtina, a director of SigmaBleyzer Research, has been working for SigmaBleyzer since its inception in 1993. She is well known in Ukraine as the leading specialist in issues of privatization and stock market development. She was one of the organizers and is a permanent member of the governing council of the Ukrainian stock market. For more than 15 years, she has given lectures on economy and management. She is certified in privatization, asset management of investment funds, and stock brokerage. She has developed creative approaches to modern education. In 1995, under her supervision and with SigmaBleyzer's direct participation, the Ukrainian Association of Investment Business published a directory titled *Investment Business: Professionally from Professionals*. Her interviews in the mass media and appearances at conferences constantly attract attention due to her deep understanding of the problems of privatization and corporate culture in Ukraine.

Máximo Torero is a research fellow in the markets, trade, and institutions division of the International Food Policy Research Institute. His research primarily focuses on poverty, inequality, the importance of geography and (private/public) assets in relation to poverty, and policies aimed at poverty alleviation. He has gained a unique expertise in the information and communication technology sector. His activities in this sector can be divided into three categories: regulation of telephony services; estimation of demand for telecommunications services; and access and use of available information and telecommunications technologies in urban and rural areas. He has collaborated closely with regulatory agencies to develop models on the functioning of the telecommunications industry that support the agency's regulation efforts and simulate demand (residential and commercial) for telecommunication services in order to evaluate the impact of different rate schedules. He holds a PhD in economics from the University of California, Los Angeles.

Miguel Urquiola is an assistant professor of economics and international affairs at Columbia University. His research focuses on educational issues in developing countries and the United States. He worked at the economics department at Cornell University, the World Bank's research department, the Bolivian government, and the Bolivian Catholic University's MBA and public policy programs. He received a BA from Swarthmore College and a PhD in economics from the University of California at Berkeley.

Yu Xinhua is the senior statistician at the department of industrial and transportation statistics in China's National Bureau of Statistics. She holds a BA in economics from Renmin (People's) University in Beijing

Jiang Yuan is deputy director and senior statistician in the Department of Industry and Transportation Statistics in China's National Bureau of Statistics. He holds a BA in engineering from Beijing Industry University.

Index

Aguas de Tunari, 48, 149–51
Andina. *See* Bolivia: Empresa Ferroviaria Andina (Andina)
Arequipa, 33
Argentina, 3
  access to services, 42–45, 43*t*
  Aguas Argentinas, S.A., 186
  Buenos Aires, 42, 48–49, 64, 67, 180, 183–88
  consumption effects, 188, 192–93, 194*t*, 195, 214
    change in consumer surplus, 195–201, 200*t*, 201*t*, 202*t*, 203*t*, 204*t*, 216–17
    household budget shares, 188–89
    price evolution, 189–92, 191*f*, 192*f*, 193*f*, 199*t*
  data sources and limitations, 41–42, 74–75, 187–88
  Distribución Troncal (STEEDT), 184
  Edelap, 185
  Edenor, 184–85
  Edesur, 184–85
  electricity sector, 184–87
  employment effects, 204–207, 207*t*, 214
    qualitative changes, 207–209, 208*t*
  employment layoffs, 64–66, 77
  Empresa Nacional de Telecomunicaciones (ENTEL), 182–83
  Ente Nacional de Obras Hídricas de Saneamiento, 185
  Ente Nacional Regulador del Gas (ENARGAS), 187
  fiscal effects, 72, 77, 211–13, 214
  inequality and poverty, 60–63, 61*t*, 202–204, 205*t*, 206*t*, 212*t*
  employment level, 210–11
    measurement of, 84
    relative wages, 211, 213*t*
  infrastructure sector, budget shares, 55*t*
  labor reallocation, 71
  macroeconomic issues, 180–81, 181*t*
  Mercado Eléctrico Mayorista (MEM), 184
  National Communication Commission (CNC), 183
  natural gas, 186–87
  perceptions of economic reforms, 81*t*
  price changes, 45–49, 46*t*, 47*t*, 214
    measurement of, 51–58
  privatization process, 37, 38*t*, 181–82, 182*t*
    rules governing, 179
  proceeds from privatization, 72
  Public Sector Reform Law (No. 23696), 179
  regulation, 183, 199
  SEGBA, 184–85
  Sistema de Transporte de Energía Eléctrica de Alta Tensión (STEEAT), 184
  social public expenditure, 213, 213*n*
  telecommunications sector, 47, 55*t*, 58*t*, 182–84, 188–89, 190, 214, 292
  Transener, 184
  wage rates, 68–69, 211, 213*t*
  water and sewerage, 185–86
  welfare effects of access and price changes, 58–59, 58*t*, 82–83, 214
  Yacimientos Petrofíleros Fiscales (YPF), 186–87
Armenia, 15
Asian economies, 3, 27–28
asset stripping, 10, 141, 170, 330, 382

Banco do Brasil, 257
Banzer-Quiroga administration, 168–69
Barrents Group, 342
Bechtel Enterprises, 33*n*, 48*n*, 149–51. *See also*
    Aguas de Tunari
Belgorod, 320*n*
Bolivia, 3, 127–28
    access definitions and utilities expenditure, 177
    access to services, 42–45, 43*t*, 45*t*, 144–45, 146*t*,
        147*t*, 148
    Aguas de Tunari, 48, 149–51
    asset transfers, 124
    Banzer-Quiroga administration, 168–69
    Bechtel Enterprises, 33n, 48*n*, 149–51 (*See also*
        Aguas de Tunari)
    Bonosol, 73, 135–36, 170
    capacity and output increases, 124
    capitalization
        preconditions for, 126–27
        versus privatization, 123, 123*n*, 174–75
        promise of, 164–65
    Capitalization Law, 166
    capitalized firms, return on equity, 124
    Chaco, 129, 139, 141, 172
    Cochabamba water concession, 125, 133, 149–50
    Compañía Boliviana de Energía Eléctrica
        (COBEE), 128, 141, 149
    Compañía Eléctrica Sucre (CESSA), 128, 138
    Cooperativa Rural Eléctrica (CRE), 128, 138, 141
    corruption, 167
    data sources and limitations, 41–42, 74–75
    Electricity Law, 128
    electricity sector, 39, 48*f*, 127–28, 133–34, 139,
        141, 144–45, 147*t*, 149, 151–61
    ELECTROPAZ, 128, 138, 141, 142*t*
    employment layoffs, 66–67, 77
    Empresa de Luz y Fuerza Eléctrica Cochabamba
        (ELFEC), 128, 138, 141, 142*t*
    Empresa Ferroviaria Andina (Andina), 129, 132,
        139, 141, 172
    Empresa Nacional de Electricidad (ENDE),
        127–28, 137*t*, 139, 140*t*, 141, 167
    Empresa Nacional de Telecomunicaciones
        (ENTEL), 39, 66, 131, 151, 153, 167
        internal efficiency, 141
        profitability, 139–40
        rates, 148–49
    ENTEL-Movil, 131, 138, 151, 153
    Estenssoro administration, 164
    firm performance, 140*t*, 142*t*–43*t*
        employment and productivity, 136, 138, 139
        investment, 136, 137*t*
    fiscal effects, 72–73, 77, 139, 141, 144
    foreign direct investment (FDI), 163–64, 169
    Guaracachi, 128
    household surveys, 176
    Hydrocarbons Law, 129
    hydrocarbons sector, 128–31
        companies, 129–30
        natural gas exports, 129–30, 169, 171–72
        tariffs, 130–31

infrastructure sector, 55*t*, 127
Lloyd Aéreo Boliviano (LAB), 139, 141, 167, 170
Lozada, Sanchez de administration, 165, 170
macroeconomic issues, 162–64
Maxus, 129
National Interconnected System (NIS), 127–28
Nuevatel-Viva, 131
ownership effects, 134–36, 135*t*
Pension Law, 171
perceptions of economic reforms, 75–76, 81*t*,
    124–26, 169–73
poverty and inequality, 60–63, 61*t*, 161–62, 162*t*
    measurement of, 84
price changes, 45–49, 46*t*, 48*t*, 49*t*, 148–52, 150*t*
    measurement of, 51–58
privatization process, 37, 38*t*, 39, 126–27
    conflicts, 166–68
    electricity sector, 127–28
    organized labor and, 168
    proceeds from privatization, 72–73
regulation, 124–28, 163, 169, 173–74
    hydrocarbons sector, 130
    telecommunications sector, 131–34
service quality, 49–51, 52*t*, 124, 127, 152
Servicios Eléctricos de Potosí (SEPSA), 128, 138,
    142*t*
Sistema de Regulación Sectorial (SIRESE), 127,
    127*n*, 133–34
structural reform, 173
taxes, payment of, 124, 172
telecommunications sector, 55*t*, 127, 131–32,
    138, 151, 152*t*
Transportadora de Electricidad, 128
transportation sector, 132
Transredes, 129–30, 139, 141, 167, 172
utility services, access to, 124
Valle Hermoso, 128
wage rates, 69
water and sewerage, 132–33
"water war," 125, 133, 149–51
welfare effects of price and access changes, 57*t*,
    59, 161
    measurement of, 82–83, 154–58, 159*t*, 160*t*
Yacimientos Petrolíferos Fiscales Bolivianos
    (YPFB), 128–30, 139, 141, 165, 167, 172–73
Zamora administration, 165
Brazil, 1, 3
    assets, 258–59
        ownership of, 261–62
        public offerings, 259, 263*t*
    Banco do Brasil, 257
    Cardoso administration, 253, 261, 263, 270
    Companhia Vale do Rio do Doce (CVRD), 27,
        259, 261–62
    company efficiency, 254–55
    cooking gas, 272–73
    costs of living, 264*t*, 265*t*
    Economic Dominance Intervention
        Contribution (CIDE), 275–76
    electricity sector, 257–58, 269–72

macroeconomic costs, 255
National Program of "Desestatization" (NPD), 254
National Savings Bank (CEF), 259
National Social and Economic Development Bank (BNDES), 253, 254, 258n
perceptions of economic reforms, 81t, 254–57
Petrobrás, 129, 130, 259, 261–62, 275–77
cooking gas, 272–73
monopolies, 257, 265
poverty and inequality, 258–59, 264–65
pricing, 262–65
privatization process, 254
legal framework, 260–61
regulation, 265
Tax on the Turnover of Goods and Services (ICMS), 275–76
telecommunications sector, 11–12, 253, 254, 256, 257n, 263, 266
telephone, electricity, cooking gas (TEG) services, 273–75, 274f, 275f
taxes on, 275–76, 276t
telephone services, 265–69, 266t, 267t
National Telecommunications Agency (ANATEL), 266, 268
price indexes and, 267–68
Viação Aérea São Paulo S/A (VASP), 141, 170
Workers' Party, 258, 261, 262
Workers' Tenure Guarantee Fund (FGTS), 259, 262, 262n, 263t, 277
Buenos Aires, 42, 48–49, 64, 67, 180, 183–88

capitalization versus privatization, 123, 123n, 174–75
Central Bank of Nicaragua, 87, 96
CEPRIs. See Peru: Special Privatization Committees (CEPRIs)
CESSA. See Bolivia: Compañía Eléctrica Sucre (CESSA)
CGCL. See Sri Lanka: Colombo Gas Company, Ltd. (CGCL) (Shell)
Chelyabinsk, 320n
Chile, 129, 171, 224t, 290
Bolivia and, 171n
perceptions of economic reforms, 81t, 255, 284
telecommunications sector, 240, 245n, 245t, 247
China, 3, 27
Asian financial crisis and, 357
asset composition, 363–64, 364t
adjustment costs, 365
selection bias, 365
China Statistical Yearbook, 362
collective-owned enterprises (COEs), 353–54, 357–58, 361–78
Communist Party, 357, 379
conversion
asset structure, 375–76
direct, 369t, 370, 374–75
endogeneity, 354t, 376–77, 386–87
effects on enterprise performance, 369–75

equations, estimates of, 354t, 370, 371t, 372t, 373t
preconditions for, 357–58
reversion to the mean, 374, 375
state asset share changes, 370, 373–74, 375, 376
total effect, 377, 378t, 379
converted enterprises, 365–67, 367t, 368t, 369t
R&D intensity, 367
regional bias, 367
corporatization, 354–55
data sources and limitations, 354t, 361
distributive effects, 354t, 380–81
endogeneity, 354t, 376–77, 386–87
foreign-owned enterprises (FORs), 355–56, 362n, 363–68, 365n
furlough policy, 357
Hong Kong, 354t, 356, 362
literature, review of
on enterprise restructuring, 360–61
on privatization, 358–60
Macao, 354t, 356, 362, 367t, 385t
National Bureau of Statistics (NBS), 353, 362
ownership
classification effect, 363, 364t
classifications, concordance of, 385
distribution changes, 354t
profiles, 363t
reform preconditions, 355–58
research and development (R&D), 369t, 381
expenditures, 355, 365
as performance measure, 362, 367, 373–74
Rongji, Zhu administration, 357
shareholding enterprises, 366, 366n, 370, 373, 374–76, 377, 380
changes in ownership of, 353–54, 358
ownership classification effect, 363, 364t
state-owned enterprises (SOEs), 353–58, 361–63, 365–67, 367t
conversions, 371t–72t, 373t
regional concentrations of, 380–82
Taiwan, 354t, 356, 362, 367t, 385t
township enterprises, 360
World Trade Organization (WTO) and, 357
COBEE. See Bolivia: Compañía Boliviana de Energía Eléctrica (COBEE)
Cochabamba, 44, 45t, 46t, 48, 48f, 49f, 57t, 59, 61t. See Also Bolivia: Cochabamba water concession
Commonwealth of Independent States (CIS), 358, 359
COPED. See Sri Lanka: Commercialization of Public Enterprises Division (COPED)
Corani, 128
CORNAP. See Nicaragua: Corporación Nicaragüense del Sector Público (CORNAP)
corruption, 3, 10, 94n
Bolivia, 167
Russia, 3, 5, 8, 303, 320–21
Sri Lanka, 393, 395
transition economies, 6–7, 27–28

CPT. *See* Peru: Peruvian Telephone Company (CPT)
Cuba, 5, 6*f*
Czech Republic, 20, 25, 320*n*, 339

divestiture, 256, 421
  Bolivia, 128
  Brazil, 256
  Latin America, 25
  Nicaragua, 88–89, 89*t*, 90*t*, 95, 95*t*
  Sri Lanka, 389, 389*n*, 394, 397–98, 400*f*, 403, 403–407, 408
  transition and Asian economies, 27

East Asia, 3
Eastern Europe, 9, 27, 34, 317, 358–59
Ecuador, 33
El Alto, 42, 44
electricity sector
  in Argentina, 184–87
  in Bolivia, 39, 48*f*, 127–28, 133–34, 139, 141, 144–45, 147*t*, 149, 151–61
  in Brazil, 257–58, 269–72
  in Nicaragua, 91–92, 110*t*, 111*t*, 112*t*, 115*t*, 116*t*, 119*t*
  in Peru, 8–9, 9*f*
  in United Kingdom, 10, 11*f*, 21
Emirate Airlines, 408
ENDE. *See* Bolivia: Empresa Nacional de Electricidad (ENDE)
Engel curves, 197*f*
ENITEL. *See* Nicaragua: Empresa Nicaragüense de Telefonía (ENITEL)
ENTEL. *See* Bolivia: Empresa Nacional de Telecomunicaciones (ENTEL); under Peru: telecommunications sector
enterprise performance, effects of conversion on, 368–75
ENTRENSA. *See* Nicaragua: Empresa Nicaragüense de Transmisión de Energía, S.A. (ENTRENSA)

foreign direct investment (FDI), 163–65, 173–74, 286–87, 286*n*
FORs. *See* China: foreign-owned enterprises (FORs)
Foster, Greer, and Thorbecke poverty index, 60, 161, 203, 203*n*, 210

Gini coefficients, 180, 202–203, 210, 211*t*, 213*t*, 315, 317, 392
government revenue, privatization and, 12–13

Heckman's selection correction, 54, 114*t*, 155, 157*t*, 199, 200, 200*t*
household consumption, 14, 87, 188, 278, 289. *See also* specific regions and countries
household income, 14, 41, 41*n*, 60, 97, 237*t*, 266. *See also* specific regions and countries

India, 3
International Monetary Fund (IMF), 94
  Sri Lanka and, 390, 397, 420
Ivory Coast, 12

Kazakhstan, 20

La Paz, 44, 45*t*, 46*t*, 48, 48*f*, 49*f*, 57*t*, 59, 61*t*
  water concession, 42, 44
Latin America, 2, 3, 27–28, 123 *See also* specific countries
  data sources and limitations, 36–37
  employment layoffs, 63–64
  infrastructure sectors, 292–93
    affordability versus access, 287–89
    foreign direct investment (FDI) and, 286–87
    initial conditions, 284–86, 293
    literature, review of, 282–83
    macroeconomic context, 293
    policy gaps, 281–82
    politics and, 282, 293
    poor people, needs of, 287–89
    private-sector participation, 286–87
    regulation, importance of, 282, 291–92
    safety nets, 289–90, 293
    taxation, 281, 291
    utility subsidies, 290
  perceptions of economic reforms, 26–27, 81*t*
  regulation, 282, 291–92
  telecommunications sectors, 290
  wage rates, 68–71
Latinbarometer, 2*n*, 80, 255
Libis Engineering, Ltd., 342
Lima, 33, 239*n*
Lloyd Aéreo Boliviano (LAB), 139, 141, 167, 170

Malaysia, 1
Mexico, 3, 12, 129, 246*n*
  access to services, 22, 42–45, 43*t*, 50–51, 51*t*
  data sources and limitations, 35–37, 41–42, 46, 74–75
  employment layoffs, 64, 67–68, 77
  fiscal effects, 73, 77
  infrastructure sector, 54–55, 55*t*, 283
  labor reallocation, 71
  perceptions of economic reforms, 81*t*
  poverty and inequality, measurement of, 84
  price changes, 45–49, 46*t*, 50*t*
    measurement of, 51–58
  privatization process, 37–40, 38*t*
  proceeds from privatization, 73
  salary levels, 21
  Salinas administration, 39
  service quality, 49–51, 51*t*, 52*t*
  telecommunications sector, 55*t*
  wage rates, 69
  welfare changes, measurement of, 82–83
Middle East, 3
Moldova, 13, 20
Mongolia, 20
Moscow, 320*n*
Mozambique, 12

Naval Architects & Marine Consultants, 342
Nicaragua, 3, 35
  access to services, 42–45, 43t
  Central Bank of Nicaragua, 87
  compared with other Latin American countries,
    118–19
  concessions, 92–93
  Corporación Nicaragüense del Sector Público
    (CORNAP), 41, 86, 93, 94–95, 95t, 96, 119
  divestment, 88–89, 89t, 90t
  data sources and limitations, 36–37, 41–42,
    74–75, 86–87, 93
  Eastern European transition economies and,
    85–86
  electricity sector, 91–92, 110t, 111t, 112t, 115t,
    116t, 119t
  employment and wage inequality, 96–97
  employment layoffs, 77
  Empresa Nicaragüense de Acueductos y
    Alcantarillados (ENACAL), 92–93, 96
  Empresa Nicaragüense de Telefonía (ENITEL),
    90–91, 90n, 96, 97t
  Empresa Nicaragüense de Transmisión de
    Energía, S.A. (ENTRENSA), 91
  ENEL, 96, 97t
  fiscal effects, 35–36, 73, 77, 93–96, 119
  future research, 120
  Household Income and Expenditure Survey,
    86–87
  immigration pressures, 86
  infrastructure sector, budget shares, 55t
  Instituto Nicaragüense de Energía (INE), 91–92
  International Monetary Fund (IMF) adjustment
    program, 94
  labor markets, 119
  labor reallocation, 71
  Living Standard Measurement Surveys, 86–87
  Nicaraguan Instituto de Estadísticas Censos, 87
  perceptions of economic reforms, 81t
  poverty and inequality, 60–63, 62t, 119, 120t
    measurement of, 84, 86–87
  price changes, 45–49, 46t
    measurement of, 51–58
  privatization process, 38t, 40–41, 87–89
    wage levels and earnings inequality, 35
  proceeds from privatization, 73, 93–95, 94t, 97t
  service quality, 49–51, 51t, 52t
  socialism, 86
  tax revenues, 95–96
  telecommunications sector, 55t, 90–91, 107,
    107n, 120
  Telecomunicaciones y Correos de Nicaragua
    (TELCOR), 90–91
  variance decomposition, first-order assessment,
    97–101, 100t
  wages, 69–71, 98t, 103t, 104t, 105t, 106t
    attributes and market values, 101–107
  welfare changes, measurement of, 82–83
  welfare effects of access and price changes,
    54–55, 56t
Nippon Telegraph and Telephone (NTT), 403, 420
Nizhny Novgorod, 320n
Novgorod, 320n

oligarchs, 298, 303–6, 321
Organization for Economic Cooperation and
    Development (OECD), 28, 356, 358–59
Oruro, 128, 130
OSIPTEL. See Peru: Supervisory Agency for
    Private Investment in Telecommunications
    (OSIPTEL)

Paraguay, 33
PERC. See Sri Lanka: Public Enterprise Reform
    Commission (PERC)
perceptions of economic reforms, 1–2, 2n, 22, 24,
    24–28
  in Bolivia, 75–76, 124–26, 169–73
  in Brazil, 254–57
  in Chile, 255, 284
  in Latin America, 81t
  in Russia, 319–21
  in Sri Lanka, 405–408, 417–20
Peru, 3, 220
  electricity sector, 8–9, 9f
  perceptions of economic reforms, 81t
  telecommunications sector, 219–51
Petrobrás, 129, 130, 259, 261–62, 275–77
  cooking gas, 272–73
  monopolies, 257, 265
Poland, 25
PricewaterhouseCoopers, 342
privatization
  access to services, 15–17, 22–23
  asset distribution, 14
  versus capitalization, 123, 123n
  competition, 1, 3n, 13, 15, 16, 45–46
  desirability of, 13–14
  distributional effects, 2–3, 14–17, 18, 22–23, 78
  efficiency versus equity, 1n, 4–12, 4f, 4n, 5n, 9f,
    11f, 28
    Brazil, telecommunications sector, 10–11, 11f
    competitive markets and, 4f
    Peru, electricity sector, 8–10, 9f
    Soviet Union and Russia, 9f
    United Kingdom, electricity sector, 10, 11f, 18
    United States and Cuba, 6f
  employment effects, 21–22, 78
  fiscal effects, 17, 23–24, 72–73, 78
  framework for the study of, 4–12
  government budgets and, 12–13
  inequality and poverty, 2–3, 3n, 61t, 62t
    measurement of, 60–63
  initial effects, 19f
  investment policies and, 8, 10–12, 16, 22
  Latin America, 26–27
  main features of, 38t
  overall economic record, 12–14
  ownership change, 1n, 18–20
  perceptions of, 1–2, 2n, 20, 22, 25, 33–34, 75–76

privatization—*continued*
  performance improvements, 12–14
  preconditions for, 8
  prices and access, 15–17, 22–23
  production frontier, 5–6, 13
  regulation, 10, 12, 16, 28, 45–46
  returns on assets, 15
  service quality, 12–14, 152
  wealth and income distributions, effects on,
    24–25
  welfare effects, 1, 34
    measurement of, 216–17
  worker effects, evaluating, 63–71

Rio de Janeiro, 33
Rongji, Zhu, 357
Russia, 3, 8, 298–300, 302–303, 318*t*, 328
  adaptation strategies, 319–21
  agro-industrial sector, 306
  barter economy, 319*n*
  Belgorod, 320*n*
  capital flight, 322
  Chelyabinsk, 320*n*
  Committee for Property Management, 300
  cooperatives, 307*n*
  corruption, 1, 3, 8, 303, 320–21
  economic reforms, perceptions of, 4, 27
  efficiency and equity, 11*f*
  employment patterns, 306–307, 308*f*, 309*f*, 321*t*
    secondary employment, 312–14, 313*t*
    surplus employment, 309–12, 312*t*
    unemployment, 307–309, 312
    wage arrears, 308, 310
    wage rates, 314, 317, 318*t*, 319
    workers' benefits, 310–11, 315*t*, 319
  Evenk Autonomous Region, 320
  financial crisis (1998), 306
  financial services sector, 306
  income distribution
    employment and, 322*f*
    ownership and, 321, 322*f*
  inequality, 315, 316*t*, 317, 319
  inequities, 19, 20
  Labor Code, 314, 317
  loans-for-shares schemes, 304–306
  Moscow, 320*n*
  Nizhny Novgorod, 320*n*
  Norilsk Nickel, 304
  North Ossetian-Alaniya Republic, 320
  Novgorod, 320*n*
  oligarchs, 303–306, 321
  perceptions of economic reforms, 319–21
  population patterns, 319–21, 319*n*, 320*n*
  privatization process, 297, 298, 303–306
    company managers and, 301–303, 305
    "insiders," 299–303
    money privatization, 303–306
    voucher phase, 8, 22*n*, 298–99
  regulation, 302, 317
  Russian Economic Barometer, 302
  Sberbank, 306

shadow economy, 321
Sibneft, 305
small- and medium-sized businesses, 320*n*
social stratification, 320, 320*n*
State Committee for Property Management, 304
State Employment Service, 308
State Privatization of State-Owned and
  Municipal Enterprises, 310–11
Ulyanovsk, 320*n*
workers' motivation and behavior, 300–301
Yukos, 304–305

Santa Cruz, 44, 45*t*, 46*t*, 48, 48*f*, 49*f*, 57*t*, 59, 61*t*
Saudi Aramco, 416
Shell Overseas International, 403, 416
SigmaBleyzer, 325, 340, 340*n*, 343, 345, 347, 348
SLAL. *See* Sri Lanka: Sri Lankan Airlines (SLAL)
SLT. *See* Sri Lanka: Sri Lanka Telecom (SLT)
South Asia, 5
Soviet Union, 10, 11*f*
Sri Lanka, 5
  Bogawantalawa Plantations, Ltd. (BPL), 423
  build-own-operate (BOO) projects, 405
  build-own-transfer (BOT) projects, 405
  Bulumulla Leather Corporations, 413
  Ceylon Petroleum Corporation (CPC), 416
  Colombo Gas Company, Ltd. (CGCL) (Shell),
    391, 411, 413, 415–16, 423
    capital investment in, 401
    liquefied petroleum gas (LPG) monopoly,
      403–404
  Colombo Stock Exchange (CSE), 390, 402
  Commercialization of Public Enterprises
    Division (COPED), Ministry of Finance, 395
  company descriptions, 423–24
  company performance, 401, 404*t*, 405*t*
  competition policies, 421
  competitive policy framework, lack of, 396
  Consumer Affairs Authority (CAA), 396
  Conversion of Government Owned Business
    Undertakings into Public Corporations (Act
    No. 22), 395
  Conversion of Public Corporations or
    Government Owned Business Undertakings
    into Public Companies (Act No. 23), 395
  corruption in, 393, 395
  data sources and limitations, 390–91
  Department of Internal Trade (DIT), 396
  distributional effects, 398
  distributional shifts, 421
  distribution of value added, 406, 409*f*, 410*f*
  divestiture, 389*n*, 397–98
    debt burden and, 400, 400*f*, 401*f*, 402*f*
  economic and political instability, 389–90
  Emirate Airlines, 408
  employee share ownership plans (ESOPs),
    393–94, 397, 408, 411*t*, 420
  enterprise ownership, 402–403, 407*t*, 408*t*
  enterprise performance, 408
  exclusivity periods, 403–404

Fair Trade Commission, 396
fiscal versus distributional concerns, 403–404, 421
infrastructure sectors, 403*t*
institutional, legal and regulatory framework, 394–96
International Monetary Fund (IMF) and, 390, 397, 420
interviews, 390–91, 425
job loss, 411
Kotagala Plantation, 404–405
labor force costs and benefits, 409–15, 412*t*, 413*t*, 414*t*
　urban versus rural, 414
labor retrenchment, 398, 411–13
Lanka Caltex, Ltd. (LCL), 423
Lanka Ceramics, Ltd. (LCL), 413, 423
Lanka Salt, Ltd. (LSL), 424
liquefied petroleum gas (LPG), 403–404
literature, review of, 397–98
macroeconomic effects, 399, 399*t*
market capitalization, 406*t*
Monopolies and Mergers Commission, 396
National Development Bank (NDB), 423
National Insurance Corporation (NIC), 403
Nippon Telegraph and Telephone (NTT), 403, 420
north central province, 392
northwestern province, 392
ownership concerns, 402–408
perceptions of economic reforms, 405–408, 417–20
Plantation Restructuring Unit, 395
plantation sector, 401
political economy effects, 420–21
political environment, 395
Presidential Commission on Privatization, 395
Presidential Commission Report on Privatization, 411–12
price and access changes, 415–17
pricing of enterprises, 406–408
Prima, 404–405
privatization process, 392–94, 407*t*
　asset selection, 394
　goals, 393
　management contracts and, 394
　trade unions and, 393
provincial differences, 392
public benefits versus revenue maximization, 398
Public Companies Act (No. 23), 395, 424
Public Enterprise Reform Commission (PERC), 389*n*, 390, 395–96, 405, 416
Public Enterprise Rehabilitation Act, 395
Public Investment Management Board, 395
questionnaire for data collection, 425–26
regulation, 396, 404, 420, 420–21
revenue from enterprise sales, 403
Saudi Aramco contract, 416
sectoral regulation, 396

services and plantations sectors, 390
Shell Overseas International, 416
socioeconomic profile, 391–92
Sri Lankan Airlines (SLAL), 402–403, 408, 423
Sri Lanka Telecom (SLT), 391, 399, 401–406, 408, 415–20, 423
telecommunications sector, 392, 396, 399, 415, 417–18
Telecom Regulatory Commission (TRC), 404
Termination of Employment Act of 1971 (TEA), 412
unemployment, 391
unit trusts, 406
Valuation Department, 397
World Bank and, 390, 393, 397, 420
SSY. *See* Ukraine: Sevastopol Shipyard (SSY) Company
state-owned enterprises (SOEs), 3, 37, 38*t*, 39–40, 65–66, 72, 76. *See also* specific regions and countries
Stiglitz, Joseph, 1

TdP. *See* Peru: Telefónica del Perú (TdP)
TELCOR. *See* Nicaragua: Telecomunicaciones y Correos de Nicaragua (TELCOR)
telecommunications sector
　in Argentina, 47, 55*t*, 58*t*, 182–84, 188–89, 190, 214, 292
　in Bolivia, 55*t*, 127, 131–34, 138, 151, 152*t*
　in Brazil, 10–11, 253, 254, 256, 257*n*, 263, 266
　in Chile, 240, 245*n*, 245*t*, 247
　in Mexico, 55*t*
　in Nicaragua, 55*t*, 90–91, 107, 107*n*, 120
　in Peru, 219–51
　in Sri Lanka, 392, 396, 399, 415, 417–18
　in Ukraine, 359
Thunderbird Corporate Consulting, 342
Total Exploration, 129
transition economies, 3, 27–28
TRC. *See* Sri Lanka: Telecom Regulatory Commission (TRC)
Turkmenistan, 328

Ukraine, 3, 325, 331, 339
　asset stripping, 330
　auctions, 331, 332*t*
　Berdyansk Agricultural Machinery and Melitopol Tractor Hydro Units Plants, 345–47, 348*t*
　Bleyzer Foundation, 340*n*
　Budget Code, 328
　Citizen Development Corps, 342
　compensatory certificates, 331
　Criminal Code, 328
　Damen Shipyards, 348
　data sources and limitations, 350–51
　economic reform challenges
　　Asian crisis, 327
　　budget deficits, 326
　　currency depreciation, 327

Ukraine—*continued*
    energy use, 326
    external debt, 326–27
    preservation strategy, 326
    recession, 325–26
    Russian crisis, 327
    tax base, 326–27
  economic reform program, 327–28
  foreign direct investment (FDI), 328–29
  government subsidies, 326
  key economic data, 352*t*
  Kharkiv Biscuit Factory, 330
  Kuchma, Leonid, 326
  labor productivity, 334–35, 335*t*, 336*t*
  Laws on Banks and Banking Services, 328
  Mariupol Illicha Steel, 330
  market-based economy, 333
  National Bank of Ukraine, 326
  National Certificate Auctions Network, 331
  Okean Shipyard, 348
  oligarchy, 337, 339
  Paris Club, 328
  Poltava Confectionery, 345, 345*t*, 346*tt*
  privatization process
    first stage, 329–30, 331*t*
    "lease-with-an-option-to-buy," 330
    second stage, 330–32, 332*t*
    shareholder rights, 332
    third stage, 332–33
  profitability, 335, 338*t*
  Sevastopol Shipyard (SSY) Company, 341–44
    efficiency, 343–44, 344*t*
    inefficiencies, 341
    military customers, 341
    reforms, 342, 342*t*, 343*t*, 344
    wages and employment, 342–43, 343*t*

SigmaBleyzer, 328, 336*n*, 340, 340*n*, 343, 345, 347, 348
  social effects, 333–35
  taxation, 335, 339
  telecommunications sector, 359
  Ukrainian Growth Funds, 341, 349*t*
  unemployment, 334, 334*t*
  wage arrears, 333, 334*t*, 337*t*, 347–48, 349*t*, 350–51
  wage levels and earnings, 335
  welfare gains, 348
Ulyanovsk, 320*n*
United Kingdom (UK), 10, 11*f*, 19, 25
United States (US), 5, 6*f*

variance decomposition, first-order assessment of (Nicaragua), 97–101
Vietnam, 3
voucher programs, 8, 20, 21–22, 22*n*
  Russia, 298–300, 302–303
  Ukraine, 331, 339

Washington Consensus, 1
water and sewerage
  Argentina, 185–86
  Bolivia, 125, 132–33, 149–50
welfare, approximations of mean decile change, 216–17
World Bank, 37
  Living Standards Measurement Study, 87
  Sri Lanka and, 390, 393, 397, 420
World Trade Organization (WTO), 357

YPFB. *See* Bolivia: Yacimientos Petrolíferos Fiscales Bolivianos (YPFB)

Past Publications from the
Center for Global Development

The United States as a Debtor Nation
William Cline
September 2005   ISBN 0-88132-399-3

The Hardest Job in the World:
Five Crucial Tasks for the New President
of the World Bank
Nancy Birdsall et al.
June 2005   ISBN 1-933286-04-0

Does Foreign Direct Investment
Promote Development?
Theodore H. Moran, Edward M. Graham,
and Magnus Blomström, eds.
April 2005   ISBN 0-88132-381-0

Making Markets for Vaccines:
Ideas to Action
Owen Barder, Michael Kremer,
and Ruth Levine
April 2005   ISBN 1-933286-02-4

Overcoming Stagnation
in Aid-Dependent Countries
Nicolas van de Walle
March 2005   ISBN 1-933286-01-6

A Better Globalization: Legitimacy,
Governance, and Reform
Kemal Dervis, assisted by Ceren Özer
March 2005   ISBN 0-8157-1763-6

Millions Saved: Proven Successes
in Global Health
Ruth Levine and the What Works
Working Group, with Molly Kinder
November 2004   ISBN 0-88132-372-1

Financing Development:
The Power of Regionalism
Nancy Birdsall and Liliana Rojas Suarez
September 2004   ISBN 0-88132-353-5

On the Brink, Weak States
and US National Security
Jeremy M. Weinstein, John Edward
Porter, and Stuart E. Eizenstat
June 2004

Trade Policy and Global Poverty
William Cline
June 2004   ISBN 0-88132-365-9

From Social Assistance to Social
Development: Targeted Education
Subsidies in Developing Countries
Samuel Morley and David Coady
September 2003   ISBN 0-88132-357-8

The Other War: Global Poverty
and the Millennium Challenge
Account
Lael Brainard, Carol Graham,
Nigel Purvis, Steven Radelet,
and Gayle Smith
June 2003   Paper, ISBN 0-8157-1115-8
           Cloth, ISBN 0-8157-1114-x

Challenging Foreign Aid:
A Policymaker's Guide to the
Millennium Challenge Account
Steven Radelet
May 2003   ISBN 0-88132-354-3

Delivering on Debt Relief: From IMF
Gold to a New Aid Architecture
Nancy Birdsall and John Williamson,
assisted by Brian Deese
April 2002   ISBN 0-88132-331-4